COMPUTER GRAPHICS USING JAVA™ 2D AND 3D

Hong Zhang
Y. Daniel Liang

Armstrong Atlantic State University

PEARSON
Prentice
Hall

Upper Saddle River, NJ 07458

Library of Congress Cataloging-in-Publication Data

Zhang, Hong.
    Computer graphics using Java 2 and 3D / Hong Zhang, Y. Daniel Liang
        p. cm.
    Includes index.
    ISBN 0-13-035118-0
    1. Java (Computer program language) 2. Computer graphics. I. Liang, Y. Daniel. II.

Title

QA76.73.J38Z43 2006
005.13'3—dc22   2006049804

Vice President and Editorial Director, ECS: *Marcia J. Horton*
Executive Editor: *Tracy Dunkelberger*
Associate Editor: *Carole Snyder*
Editorial Assistant: *Christianna Lee*
Executive Managing Editor: *Vince O'Brien*
Managing Editor: *Camille Trentacoste*
Production Editor: *Donna Crilly*
Director of Creative Services: *Paul Belfanti*
Creative Director: *Juan Lopez*
Art Director and Cover Manager: *John Christiana*
Interior Design: *JMC Design*
Cover Design: *Kiwi Design*
Managing Editor, AV Management and Production: *Patricia Burns*
Art Editor: *Xiaohong Zhu*
Director, Image Resource Center: *Melinda Reo*
Manager, Rights and Permissions: *Zina Arabia*
Manager, Visual Research: *Beth Brenzel*
Manager, Cover Visual Research and Permissions: *Karen Sanatar*
Manufacturing Manager, ESM: *Alexis Heydt-Long*
Manufacturing Buyer: *Lisa McDowell*
Executive Marketing Manager: *Robin O'Brien*
Marketing Assistant: *Mack Patterson*

Cover Image: *Albert J Copley / Photodisc Green / Getty Images, Inc.*
Chapter Opener Image: *Philip Colmentz / Brand X Pictures*

© 2007 Pearson Education, Inc.
Pearson Prentice Hall
Pearson Education, Inc.
Upper Saddle River, NJ 07458

Pearson Prentice Hall™ is a trademark of Pearson Education, Inc.
All other trademarks or product names are the property of their respective owners.

The author and publisher of this book have used their best efforts in preparing this book. These efforts include the development, research, and testing of the theories and programs to determine their effectiveness. The author and publisher make no warranty of any kind, expressed or implied, with regard to these programs or the documentation contained in this book. The author and publisher shall not be liable in any event for incidental or consequential damages in connection with, or arising out of, the furnishing, performance, or use of these programs.

Printed in the United States of America

10 9 8 7 6 5 4 3 2 1

ISBN 0-13-0351180-0

Pearson Education Ltd., *London*
Pearson Education Australia Pty. Ltd., *Sydney*
Pearson Education Singapore, Pte. Ltd.
Pearson Education North Asia Ltd., *Hong Kong*
Pearson Education Canada, Inc., *Toronto*
Pearson Educación de Mexico, S.A. de C.V.
Pearson Education—Japan, *Tokyo*
Pearson Education Malaysia, Pte. Ltd.
Pearson Education, Inc., *Upper Saddle River, New Jersey*

To My Parents, Xuemei Sun and Zhongyi Zhang
—HZ

To Samantha, Michael, and Michelle
—YDL

CONTENTS

PREFACE

On March 3, 2001, the first Oscar of the new millennium was awarded to three computer scientists, Rob Cook, Loren Carpenter, and Ed Catmull, "for their significant advancements to the field of motion picture rendering as exemplified in Pixar's 'RenderMan.'" This incredible event symbolizes the emergence of computer graphics and its applications, once an esoteric research subject, as an essential part of the digital community. The rapid development of computer hardware, graphical applications, and network technologies has made computer graphics indispensable in mainstream computing.

Modeling and rendering virtual graphics objects with digital computers are the main objectives of computer graphics. The topics involved in this process span a wide range of disciplines from mathematics and computer science to psychology and arts. From the big model of the universe to the small details of rasterizing a graphical primitive, sophisticated and ingenious methods, algorithms, and paradigms have been developed to address the problems of modeling and rendering in computer graphics. A thorough treatment of this subject, therefore, would require a broad and deep coverage of many related areas. A traditional computer graphics course, due to its complexity and mathematical sophistication, is usually beyond the scope of a standard undergraduate computer science curriculum.

However, we believe that the new technological developments and the availability of well-designed and easy-to-use graphics programming packages have made an elementary graphics course feasible. This development is analogous to the evolution of programming languages. Programming used to be a very tedious task when only low-level languages such as machine instructions were available. The development of high-level languages freed programmers from the low-level technical details. Programs at the more abstract levels are much more manageable and logical. The performance loss due to the abstraction has become negligible with the improvement of hardware and compiler technologies. Most programmers today may never need to program in machine or assembly languages. Computer graphics programming is going through a similar process. High-level, portable systems are rapidly replacing the tedious low-level approaches in many aspects of computer graphics. The rapid development of hardware technologies is also erasing the performance gap.

high-level approach

The primary focus of this book is the fundamental concepts of computer graphics and applications of Java 2D and Java 3D to graphics programming. Rather than studying the technical details of low-level implementations, we will emphasize the techniques of developing practical applications using existing graphics packages. This approach enables us to provide an introductory computer graphics text that is accessible to undergraduate computer science and engineering students and most computer professionals.

Java 2D and Java 3D are the ideal graphics packages for such a purpose. They are high-level comprehensive graphics packages that offer a much-needed layer of abstraction. They are also platform independent and provide state-of-the-art graphics programming capabilities.

why Java?

Java 2D and Java 3D are parts of the Java platform. Java is a relatively new programming language, yet it has quickly gained popularity because of its unique characteristics and features, such as platform independence, simplicity, and object-oriented programming support. Java 2D and Java 3D provide powerful, natural, and object-oriented interfaces for graphics modeling and rendering.

Java 2D and 3D

This book is intended for students and computer professionals who want to learn basic computer graphics concepts and techniques and to get started in programming with Java 2D and Java 3D. However, it is not just another tutorial on Java 2D or Java 3D. Its purpose is to introduce the fundamentals of computer graphics to the readers, and the powerful Java packages serve as useful and convenient tools to achieve the goal.

audience

prerequisite

The prerequisite of this book is a basic knowledge of programming with Java, including GUI programming (AWT and Swing). Appendix B, "GUI Programming with AWT and Swing," illustrates the differences in programming with AWT and Swing components. Basic mathematical courses in geometry and linear algebra will be helpful but are not required. Appendix A, "Mathematical Background for Computer Graphics," provides a brief review of some relevant mathematical concepts.

Companion Website

The companion website at **www.cs.armstrong.edu/liang/graphics** contains the following resources:

- Answers to review questions
- Solutions to even-numbered programming exercises
- Source code for the examples in the book
- Resource links
- Errata

Instructor Resource Website

The Instructor Resource website accessible from **www.prenhall.com/liang** or www.cs.armstrong.edu/liang/graphics contains the following resources:

- Microsoft PowerPoint slides with interactive buttons to view full-color, syntax-highlighted source code and to run programs without leaving the slides.
- Sample exams.
- Solutions to all the exercises. Students will have access to the solutions of even-numbered exercises in the book's companion website.

Some readers have requested the materials from the Instructor Resource Website. Please understand that these are for instructors only. Such requests will not be answered.

Acknowledgments

The computer science department at Armstrong Atlantic State University is a great place to work. We thank Ray Greenlaw and our colleagues at Armstrong Atlantic State University for their support of this book.

Our thanks to anonymous reviewers and our students for their critics, comments, and suggestions, which have greatly improved this book.

It is a great pleasure and privilege to work with the legendary computer science team at Prentice Hall. We thank Marcia Horton, Tracy Dunkelburger, Robin O'Brien, Christianna Lee, Jennifer Cappello, Barrie Reinhold, Mack Patterson, Vince O'Brien, Camille Trentacoste, Donna Crilly, Xiaohong Zhu, and their colleagues for organizing, managing, and promoting this project, and Robert Lentz for copy editing.

Hong Zhang (hong@armstrong.edu)
Y. Daniel Liang (liang@armstrong.edu)
www.cs.armstrong.edu/liang/graphics

CHAPTER 1

OVERVIEW OF COMPUTER GRAPHICS

Objectives

- To understand the basic objectives and scope of computer graphics.

- To identify computer graphics applications.

- To understand the basic structures of 2D and 3D graphics systems.

- To understand evolution of graphics programming environments.

- To identify common graphics APIs.

- To understand the roles of Java language and the Java 2D and Java 3D packages.

- To identify fields related to computer graphics.

1.1 Introduction

Computer graphics studies the theory and techniques of modeling, processing, and rendering of graphical objects in computers. The basic objective of computer graphics is to build a virtual world of graphics objects and to render a scene of the virtual model from a specific view onto a graphic device, as shown in Figure 1.1.

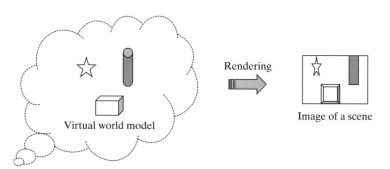

FIGURE 1.1   Main tasks of computer graphics: modeling a virtual world and rendering a scene.

A graphics system typically consists of two major components: a modeler and a renderer. The *modeler* is responsible for the construction of the virtual world models and the *renderer* performs the rendering of a scene. A "retained-mode" system maintains a persistent model of graphics objects and the modeler's function is explicit. An "immediate-mode" system renders the objects immediately and the model is more transient. This view of the modeling–rendering paradigm is convenient for studying graphics systems, even if the separation may not be clear in some systems.

Typically the graphics objects to be modeled are in either a 2D or a 3D space. This common space to host all the graphics objects is often called the *world space*. A rendered scene of the world space, the main output of a graphics system, is typically in a 2D form. Consequently the techniques involved in 2D and 3D graphics are considerably different. Because 3D graphics problems are significantly more complex, 2D and 3D graphics are often treated as separate topics.

The graphics objects to be modeled in a world space are usually geometric entities such as lines and surfaces, but they also include other special objects such as lights, texts and images. The graphics objects may possess many characteristics and properties such as color, transparency and texture.

Various mathematical representations are used to model geometric objects. Straight-line segments and simple polygon meshes provide simple and compact representations. Only the vertices of the structures need to be stored and they are easy to implement. More sophisticated representations include spline curves and surfaces. They are versatile and require only the storage of relatively few control points.

Geometric transformations are applied to the objects to achieve the proper placement of the objects in the virtual space. Transformations of this type are called *object transformations*. Transformations are also used for the viewing; these are known as *viewing transformations*. A useful family of the geometric transforms is the *affine transforms*, which include the most common types such as translations, rotations, scalings and reflections. A more general set of transforms, the *projective transformations*, are useful for 3D viewing.

A *view* is used to see the model in the virtual world from a specific perspective. A *2D viewing* process is relatively simple. The viewing transformation is usually indistinguishable from the object transformation. Rendering features such as composition rules and clipping

modeler
renderer

world space

object transformations
viewing transformations
affine transforms

projective transformations
view
2D viewing

paths may be applied. A *3D view* is much more complicated. Like eyes or cameras, 3D viewing involves a projection process that maps 3D objects to a 2D plane. Many parameters such as the projection, view position, orientation, and field of view could affect the 3D rendering.

3D viewing

In order to achieve a realistic rendering of the virtual world, numerous rendering issues need to be addressed. Relative locations of the objects need to be correctly reflected in the rendered images. For example, an object may be hidden behind another object, and the hidden portion should not be shown in the image. Light sources of various characteristics should be considered. The properties of the materials of the objects will affect the appearance. Many of the methods for solving the problems have significant computational demands.

The capabilities and characteristics of *hardware devices* have great impact on graphics systems. The most common output devices for displaying the results of the graphics rendering are video monitors and printers. Other output devices include plotters and holographic projectors. For input devices, mice, joysticks and tablets with pens are widely available. There are also more sophisticated input devices and sensors such as six-degree-of-freedom trackers.

hardware devices

Animation is also an important part of computer graphics. Instead of still images, animation produces dynamic graphics contents and rendering. In applications such as movie-scene rendering and gaming, animation plays a crucial role. Another dynamic aspect of computer graphics is *interaction*. In response to user inputs, the graphics model may change accordingly. The fundamental principle of GUI (graphical user interface) is based on the user interactions with graphics systems. Another example of extensive application of interaction is video games.

animation

interaction

Computer graphics has a wide range of applications. The popularity of GUI environments has made graphics an integral part of ordinary user programs. CAD (computer-aided design) and other engineering applications depend heavily on graphics systems. Data visualization and other scientific applications also make extensive use of graphics. With the rapid development of new computer-based instrumentation such CT (computer tomography), PET (positron emission tomography), and MRI (magnetic resonance imaging), medical systems have increasingly employed computer graphics technologies. Computer graphics is also a crucial ingredient in video games and other entertainment applications.

Traditionally computer graphics has to deal with implementation details, using the low-level algorithms to convert primitives such as lines to pixels, to determine the surfaces hidden from the view, to calculate the color values of points on a surface, and so on. These algorithms and methods have made the subject technically difficult and complex. In this book we shall rely on the Java 2D and Java 3D packages to avoid dealing with most of the low-level details directly. This will enable us to focus on the big picture of modeling and rendering problems in graphics, rather than the tedious implementation details.

1.2 Evolution of Computer Graphics Programming

Graphics programming has appeared in almost every level of computer architecture. Generally it is moving from low-level, platform-dependent methods toward abstract, high-level, and portable environments.

Figure 1.2 gives examples of graphics programming environments at various levels of computer architecture. The subsections that follow discuss the characteristics of graphics programming at the different levels.

Platform independent (Java 2D and Java 3D)
Graphics standard (GKS, PHIGS, OpenGL)
OS (WIN32, X, Mac OS)
Hardware (direct register/video buffer programming)

Figure 1.2 Graphics programming at different levels.

1.2.1 Hardware Level

Computer graphics programs depend on output devices with graphical capabilities. The most common display devices for computer graphics are CRT (cathode ray tube) monitors and LCD (liquid crystal display) panels. These are 2D raster devices that provide a display surface consisting of a rectangular array of discrete dots. A display device of this kind is usually driven by a dedicated graphics board with its own processor and memory.

Lower-level graphics applications often program the graphics hardware directly. In the popular environment of personal computers running MS-DOS, for example, most graphics applications directly access the display memory. Even though BIOS and DOS provide certain primitive support for graphics functions, they are considered too slow for graphics-intensive programs. Such programs are typically written in assembly language and manipulate the hardware registers and video buffers in a highly machine-dependent way.

Listing 1.1 gives an assembly program that demonstrates low-level graphics programming. It uses Microsoft Macro Assembler and can be executed on any IBM PC compatible machine with a VGA graphics card. It draws a circle by directly writing to the memory locations of the video buffer. An ideal circle centered at the origin has the equation:

$$x^2 + y^2 = R^2$$

A computer monitor only displays discrete pixels. Therefore a set of pixels approximating the curve must be computed. Only one-eighth of the circle needs to be calculated; other portions can be obtained through symmetry. As illustrated in Figure 1.3, the algorithm generates a series of pixels close to the curve. Consider the top right arc of the circle. Starting from the top pixel $(x = 0, y = R)$, the algorithm attempts to obtain the next pixel to the right of the current one. There are only two possible directions of movement: "east" or "southeast." Between the two pixels, the one closer to the curve is selected. The two cases can be decided by testing the midpoint $(x + 1, y - 0.5)$. If the midpoint is inside the circle, the "east" pixel should be chosen; if it is outside, the "southeast" pixel is the closer one. The equation of the circle is used to perform the test. By using certain difference variables, the actual operations of the test can be further simplified to only integer additions.

Listing 1.1 Circle.asm

```
 1 .model small,stdcall
 2 .stack 100h
 3 .386
 4
 5 .data
 6 saveMode BYTE ?    ; saved video mode
 7 xc WORD ?          ; center x
 8 yc WORD ?          ; center y
 9 x SWORD ?          ; x coordinate
10 y SWORD ?          ; y coordinate
11 dE SWORD ?         ; east delta
12 dSE SWORD ?        ; southeast delta
13 w WORD 320         ; screen width
14
15 .code
16 main PROC
17    mov ax,@data
18    mov ds,ax
19
20    ;Set Video Mode 320X200
21    mov   ah,0Fh    ; get current video mode
22    int   10h
23    mov   saveMode,al      ; save mode
24
```

```
25    mov ah,0          ; set new video mode
26    mov al,13h        ; mode 13h
27    int 10h
28
29    push 0A000h       ; video segment address
30    pop es            ; ES = A000h (video segment)
31
32    ;Set Background
33    mov dx,3c8h       ; video palette port (3C8h)
34    mov al,0          ; set palette index
35    out dx,al
36
37    ;Set screen background color to dark blue
38    mov dx,3c9h       ; port address 3C9h
39    mov al,0          ; red
40    out dx,al
41    mov al,0          ; green
42    out dx,al
43    mov al,32         ; blue (32/63)
44    out dx,al
45
46    ; Draw Circle
47    ; Change color at index 1 to yellow (63,63,0)
48    mov dx,3c8h       ; video palette port (3C8h)
49    mov al,1          ; set palette index 1
50    out dx,al
51
52    mov dx,3c9h       ; port address 3C9h
53    mov al,63         ; red
54    out dx,al
55    mov al,63         ; green
56    out dx,al
57    mov al,0          ; blue
58    out dx,al
59
60    mov xc,160        ; center of screen
61    mov yc,100
62
63    ; Calculate coordinates
64    mov x, 0
65    mov y, 50         ; radius 50
66    mov bx, -49       ; 1-radius
67    mov dE, 3
68    mov dSE, -95
69
70    DRAW:
71    call Draw_Pixels       ; Draw 8 pixels
72
73    cmp bx, 0         ; decide E or SE
74    jns MVSE
75
76    add bx, dE        ; move east
77    add dE, 2
78    add dSE, 2
79    inc x
80    jmp NXT
81    MVSE:
82    add bx, dSE       ; move southeast
83    add dE, 2
84    add dSE, 4
85    inc x
```

```
86    dec y
87  NXT:
88    mov cx, x          ; continue if x < y
89    cmp cx, y
90    jb DRAW
91
92    ; Restore Video Mode
93    mov ah,10h      ; wait for keystroke
94    int 16h
95    mov ah,0        ; reset video mode
96    mov al,saveMode        ; to saved mode
97    int 10h
98
99    .EXIT
100 main ENDP
101
102 ; Draw 8 pixels symmetrical about the center
103 Draw_Pixels PROC
104   ; Calculate the video buffer offset of the pixel.
105   mov ax, yc
106   add ax, y
107   mul w
108   add ax, xc
109   add ax, x
110   mov di, ax
111   mov BYTE PTR es:[di],1; store color index
112   ; Horizontal symmetrical pixel
113   sub di, x
114   sub di, x
115   mov BYTE PTR es:[di],1; store color index
116   ; Vertical symmetrical pixel
117   mov ax, yc
118   sub ax, y
119   mul w
120   add ax, xc
121   add ax, x
122   mov di, ax
123   mov BYTE PTR es:[di],1; store color index
124   ; Horizontal pixel
125   sub di, x
126   sub di, x
127   mov BYTE PTR es:[di],1; store color index
128   ; Switch x, y to get other 4 pixels
129   mov ax, yc
130   add ax, x
131   mul w
132   add ax, xc
133   add ax, y
134   mov di, ax
135   mov BYTE PTR es:[di],1; store color index
136   sub di, y
137   sub di, y
138   mov BYTE PTR es:[di],1; store color index
139   mov ax, yc
140   sub ax, x
141   mul w
142   add ax, xc
143   add ax, y
144   mov di, ax
145   mov BYTE PTR es:[di],1; store color index
```

```
146    sub di, y
147    sub di, y
148    mov BYTE PTR es:[di],1; store color index
149
150    ret
151  Draw_Pixels ENDP
152
153  END main
```

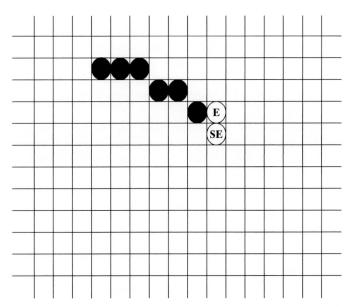

FIGURE 1.3 Determination of the pixels on a circle. From the current pixel, the next pixel will be either to the "east" or to the "southeast."

The program first saves the current video mode and switches to mode 13h by using the BIOS interrupt 10h (line 27). The video mode 13h is an easy-to-use graphics mode with 320 by 200 pixels and 256 colors. Each pixel color is represented by a byte value in the video buffer starting from the segment address A000h. Each byte value is a color index to represent a color given in a color table. Because the aspect ratio of this mode does not match that of a standard monitor, the display may appear to be stretched vertically and the circle may actually appear as an ellipse.

The background color of the screen is set to a dark blue by writing to the register at port address 3c9h (lines 38–44). The color to the circle is set to yellow (lines 48–58).

The circle is centered at the middle of the screen and has a radius 50. The variables (xc, yc) define the center. A loop starting at the label DRAW (line 70) is set to calculate and draw the pixels approximating the circle. The variables (x, y) represent current pixel coordinates. The variables dE and dSE represent differences used for deciding the next move. The loop calls the procedure Draw_Pixels to draw the current pixel and seven other pixels in the symmetrical positions. It decides the movement for the next pixel and updates the variables. The loop terminates when the calculation of one-eighth of the circle is completed.

The Draw_Pixels procedure (line 103) draws eight pixels corresponding to the current calculation. It writes a color index to the memory locations corresponding to the pixels. A calculation of the proper offset in the video buffer is necessary because the memory addresses of the pixels are organized linearly:

$$offset = 320 * x + y$$

The video buffer starts from the segment address A000h, which is placed in the register ES. To draw a pixel, the pixel offset is calculated and placed in DI. The color index (the yellow color index 1 in this case) is directly written to the memory address.

After the circle is drawn, the program waits for a keystroke from the user, using an interrupt 16h. Upon receiving the keystroke, it will then restore the video mode and terminate.

1.2.2 Operating-System Level Support

The low-level graphics infrastructures provide basic facilities for programming the displays. However, directly programming video buffers and hardware registers is not an effective approach for general graphics applications. As illustrated in the previous section, programming at the hardware level requires intimate knowledge of the devices. It is tedious even for simple tasks. Programs written at this level are not portable, even for different devices in the same platform.

High-level programming interfaces are needed to ease the burden of graphics programming. Because of the inherent complexities in graphics problems, it is certainly desirable to provide a layer of abstraction for application programming. One natural place to add the abstraction is the operating system.

GUI

With the development and widespread application of graphical user interface (*GUI*) in modern computer systems, graphics support in operating systems has become common and extensive. Graphics *APIs* (application programming interfaces) provided at the operating-system level offer a uniform interface for graphics programming within the same platform. Typically hardware differences are accommodated by using device-specific software drivers. A software driver implements a standard interface with the operating system for a particular device. Application programs only need to call standard graphics functions provided by the operating system and do not have to deal with hardware specifics.

API

WIN32

WIN32 is the API for 32-bit Windows operating systems such as Windows 9x/ME/NT/2000/XP. The code example in Listing 1.2 shows a WIN32 program that draws a circle (Figure 1.4). This example is a simple Windows program written in the C language. The program creates a standard window and calls WIN32 API directly to draw a circle in the client area of the main program window. The circle is centered in the window and the size is adjusted automatically if the window is resized.

Listing I.2 `WinCircle.c`

```
 1 #include <windows.h>
 2 #include <string.h>
 3
 4 LRESULT CALLBACK
 5 MainWndProc (HWND hwnd, UINT nMsg, WPARAM wParam, LPARAM lParam) {
 6   HDC hdc;               /* Device context used for drawing */
 7   PAINTSTRUCT ps;        /* Paint structure used during drawing */
 8   RECT rc;               /* Client area rectangle */
 9   int cx;                /* Center x-coordinate */
10   int cy;                /* Center y-coordinate */
11   int r;                 /* Radius of circle */
12
13     /* Message processing.*/
14     switch (nMsg) {
15
```

```
16      case WM_DESTROY:
17        /* The window is being destroyed, close the application */
18        PostQuitMessage (0);
19        return 0;
20
21      case WM_PAINT:
22        /* The window needs to be redrawn. */
23        hdc = BeginPaint (hwnd, &ps);
24        GetClientRect (hwnd, &rc);
25        /* Calculate center and radius */
26        cx = (rc.left + rc.right)/2;
27        cy = (rc.top + rc.bottom)/2;
28        if (rc.bottom - rc.top < rc.right - rc.left)
29          r = (rc.bottom - rc.top) / 2 - 20;
30        else
31          r = (rc.right - rc.left) / 2 - 20;
32
33        Ellipse(hdc, cx-r, cy-r, cx+r, cy+r);
34
35        EndPaint (hwnd, &ps);
36        return 0;
37
38      }
39
40      return DefWindowProc (hwnd, nMsg, wParam, lParam);
41  }
42
43  int WINAPI
44  WinMain (HINSTANCE hInst, HINSTANCE hPrev, LPSTR lpCmd, int nShow) {
45      HWND hwndMain;                          /* Main window handle */
46      MSG msg;                                /* Win32 message structure */
47      WNDCLASSEX wndclass;                    /* Window class structure */
48      char* szMainWndClass = "WinCircle";/* The window class name */
49
50      /* Create a window class */
51      /* Initialize the entire structure to zero */
52      memset (&wndclass, 0, sizeof(WNDCLASSEX));
53
54      /* The class Name */
55      wndclass.lpszClassName = szMainWndClass;
56
57      /* The size of the structure. */
58      wndclass.cbSize = sizeof(WNDCLASSEX);
59
60      /* All windows of this class redraw when resized. */
61      wndclass.style = CS_HREDRAW | CS_VREDRAW;
62
63      /* All windows of this class use the MainWndProc window function. */
64      wndclass.lpfnWndProc = MainWndProc;
65
66      /* This class is used with the current program instance. */
67      wndclass.hInstance = hInst;
68
69      /* Use standard application icon and arrow cursor */
70      wndclass.hIcon = LoadIcon (NULL, IDI_APPLICATION);
71      wndclass.hIconSm = LoadIcon (NULL, IDI_APPLICATION);
72      wndclass.hCursor = LoadCursor (NULL, IDC_ARROW);
73
```

```
74    /* Color the background white */
75    wndclass.hbrBackground = (HBRUSH) GetStockObject (WHITE_BRUSH);
76
77    /* Register the window class */
78    RegisterClassEx (&wndclass);
79
80    /* Create a window using the window class */
81    hwndMain = CreateWindow (
82      szMainWndClass,              /* Class name */
83      "Circle",                    /* Caption */
84      WS_OVERLAPPEDWINDOW,         /* Style */
85      CW_USEDEFAULT,               /* Initial x (use default) */
86      CW_USEDEFAULT,               /* Initial y (use default) */
87      CW_USEDEFAULT,               /* Initial x size (use default) */
88      CW_USEDEFAULT,               /* Initial y size (use default) */
89      NULL,                        /* No parent window */
90      NULL,                        /* No menu */
91      hInst,                       /* This program instance */
92      NULL                         /* Creation parameters */
93      );
94
95    /* Display the window */
96    ShowWindow (hwndMain, nShow);
97    UpdateWindow (hwndMain);
98
99    /* The message loop */
100   while (GetMessage (&msg, NULL, 0, 0)) {
101     TranslateMessage (&msg);
102     DispatchMessage (&msg);
103   }
104   return msg.wParam;
105 }
```

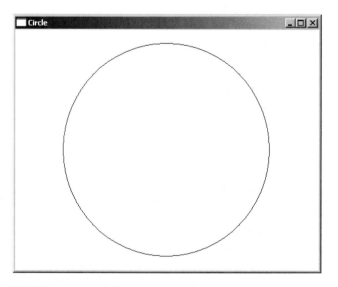

FIGURE 1.4 A WIN32 program in C displaying a circle.

This is a typical C program for WIN32 API. The `WinMain` function (line 44) is the entry point of the program. In the method a window class named "WinCircle" is created with a set of commonly used options. The window class is then registered with Windows. A window is created based on the registered window class. The window is displayed and updated.

As in most GUI environments, Windows programming follows an event-driven model. Messages are sent to a window and the message handler of the window performs certain actions in response to a message. The loop near the end of `WinMain` function is a standard message loop which is set up to dispatch the messages received.

The function `MainWndProc` (line 5) is the window procedure responsible for handling the message events of the window. It is a callback function specified in the definition of the window class. In this example, it handles two types of messages: `WM_DESTROY`, which is usually sent when the user tries to close the window, and `WM_PAINT`, which is sent when the system attempts to repaint the window. If a `WM_DESTROY` message is received, the handler terminates the program by posting a quit message. When a `WM_PAINT` message is received, the handler draws a circle in the window. The drawing is done through a device context obtained by a call to the `BeginPaint` function. The `Ellipse` function (line 33) draws a circle when the width and the height are the same. The `EndPaint` function ends the drawing. The center and radius of the circle are calculated based on the size of the window client area, which is obtained by calling the function `GetClientRect`.

1.2.3 GKS and PHIGS

Graphics programming based on operating-system APIs is a major step forward from hardware-level approaches in terms of device independency and convenience. However, graphics programs that rely on operating-system functions are certainly not portable across platforms. Microsoft Windows and Mac OS, for example, are both operating systems with graphical user interfaces (GUI). However, their APIs are different and incompatible at the level of system calls.

It is easy to see the advantages of a standard interface for graphics programming. A graphics programming standard will provide a layer of abstraction necessary for device and platform independence. In the short history of computer graphics, several graphics standards have risen to the prominence. Graphics Kernel System (*GKS*) is the first international standard for computer graphics. GKS (ISO 7942 1985) is a standard for 2D graphics. It specifies basic graphics functions independent of computer platforms. Several levels are defined to accommodate different capabilities of the hardware systems. A specific implementation of GKS in a programming language will certainly require a syntax definition appropriate for the language. A *language binding* is used to define the specific format of GKS in the programming language. The most common language binding for GKS is FORTRAN. Other language bindings such as Pascal and C are also available.

GKS — *GKS-3D* (ISO 8805 1988) is an extension of GKS to support 3D graphics. GKS and GKS-3D APIs are designed mainly for drawing individual objects with certain attributes. They are useful for static unstructured graphics primitives, but they do not directly support more complex graphics models.

PHIGS (Programmer's Hierarchical Interactive Graphics System, ISO 9592 1991) is a graphics standard similar to GKS. PHIGS and PHIGS+ include the capabilities of GKS, even though they are not strict supersets of GKS. They have additional functionalities for hierarchical organizations of graphics primitives and dynamic editing.

Listing 1.3 demonstrates GKS programming in the FORTRAN binding. The simple FORTRAN program draws a red circle using a GKS polyline primitive (Figure 1.5). The

Margin notes: GKS; language binding; GKS-3D; PHIGS

points on the circle are calculated with high-level trigonometric functions provided by FORTRAN.

$$x = x_0 + r \cos \theta$$

$$y = y_0 + r \sin \theta$$

Listing 1.3 `circle.f`

```
1          PROGRAM CIRCLE
2 C
3 C  Define error file, Fortran unit number, and workstation type,
4 C  and workstation ID.
5 C
6          PARAMETER (IERRF=6, LUNIT=2, IWTYPE=1, IWKID=1)
7          PARAMETER (ID=121)
8          DIMENSION XP(ID),YP(ID)
9 C
10 C  Open GKS, open and activate a workstation.
11 C
12          CALL GOPKS (IERRF,IDUM)
13          CALL GOPWK (IWKID,LUNIT,IWTYPE)
14          CALL GACWK (IWKID)
15 C
16 C  Define colors.
17 C
18          CALL GSCR(IWKID,0, 1.0, 1.0, 1.0)
19          CALL GSCR(IWKID,1, 1.0, 0.0, 0.0)
20 C
21 C  Draw a circle.
22 C
23          X0 = .5
24          Y0 = .5
25          R  = .3
26          JL = 120
27          RADINC = 2.*3.1415926/REAL(JL)
28          DO 10 J=1,JL+1
29          X = X0+R*COS(REAL(J)*RADINC)
30          Y = Y0+R*SIN(REAL(J)*RADINC)
31          XP(J) = X
32          YP(J) = Y
33       10 CONTINUE
34          CALL GSPLI(1)
35          CALL GSPLCI(1)
36          CALL GPL(JL+1,XP,YP)
37 C
38 C  Deactivate and close the workstation, close GKS.
39 C
40          CALL GDAWK (IWKID)
41          CALL GCLWK (IWKID)
42          CALL GCLKS
43 C
44          STOP
45          END
```

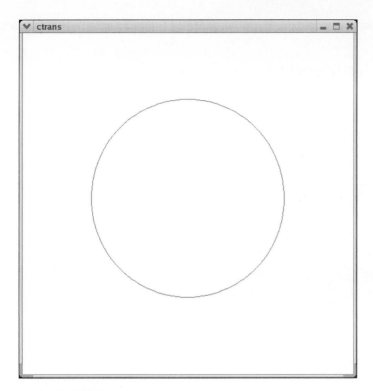

FIGURE 1.5 A simple GKS program displaying a circle.

The GKS routines usually have a "G" prefix in their names. The calls to GOPKS, GOPWK and GACWK (lines 12–14) set up the GKS environment. The GSCR calls define color indices. The circle is defined as a polyline of 120 points, which are calculated directly using COS and SIN functions. An extra point is added to close the curve. The GPL call (line 36) draws the polyline.

The program is compiled under the Linux operating system using the NCAR graphics package.

1.2.4 OpenGL

OpenGL is a popular 2D/3D graphics API derived from GL (Graphics Library) of Silicon Graphics Inc. GL is the graphics programming interface used on SGI's successful graphics workstations. OpenGL is designed to be an open and vendor-neutral industry standard. It is available virtually on all computer platforms. In fact, many hardware vendors offer OpenGL interfaces for their graphics cards and devices. With over 200 functions, OpenGL provides a much more powerful graphics API than the earlier standards such as GKS.

OpenGL is a relatively low-level API with a procedural-oriented interface. Different language bindings for OpenGL are possible, as for GKS. There is an official FORTRAN binding and currently there is a Java binding under development. However, the deep root of OpenGL in the C language is still apparent. The C binding is the most popular one.

OpenGL consists of two libraries: *GL* and *GLU* (OpenGL Utility Library). The GL library contains the core functions for basic graphics features, and the GLU library contains higher-level utility functions built on top of GL functions. OpenGL itself does not have functions for constructing a user interface. A simple portable package called *GLUT* (OpenGL Utility Toolkit) can be used with OpenGL to construct a complete graphics program.

Listing 1.4 is a simple OpenGL example that draws a circle (Figure 1.6). The program uses GLUT to construct the user interface and uses GL and GLU functions to construct the display.

OpenGL

GL
GLU

GLUT

The function names from the GL, GLU, and GLUT libraries usually have their library names as prefixes.

Listing 1.4 OpenGLCircle.c

```
1 #include <GL/glut.h>
2 #include <math.h>
3
4 void display(void) {
5     int i;
6     int n = 80;
7     float a = 2*3.1415926535/n;
8     float x;
9     float y;
10
11     glClear(GL_COLOR_BUFFER_BIT);
12     glColor3f(1.0,0,0);
13
14     glBegin(GL_LINE_LOOP);
15     for (i = 0; i < n; i++) {
16         x = cos(i*a);
17         y = sin(i*a);
18         glVertex2f(x, y);
19     }
20     glEnd();
21     glFlush();
22 }
23
24 int main(int argc, char** argv) {
25     glutInit(&argc, argv);
26     glutCreateWindow("Circle");
27     glutDisplayFunc(display);
28     glMatrixMode(GL_PROJECTION);
29     glLoadIdentity();
30     gluOrtho2D(-1.2, 1.2, -1.2, 1.2);
31     glClearColor(1.0, 1.0, 1.0, 0.0);
32     glutMainLoop();
33 }
```

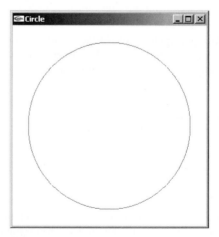

FIGURE 1.6 An OpenGL circle program.

The `main` function calls several GLUT functions to set up the display window, the display function, and the message loop. The `glutInit` function (line 25) initializes GLUT. The `glutCreateWindow` function creates a window. The `glutDisplayFunc` function sets the display function, which is a callback function for graphics drawing. The `glutMainloop` function (line 32) starts the event loop.

The projection matrix of the display is set to a 2D orthogonal projection using several GL functions and the GLU function `gluOrtho2D`.

The function `display` (line 4) is defined as the display function for this program. It draws a circle by using a sequence of vertices in the mode GL_LINE_LOOP. The vertices are calculated with a parametric equation for the circle and set with the function `glVertex2f`.

Of course OpenGL, as a 3D API, is capable of much more than drawing a circle. Another simple OpenGL example is given in Listing 1.5. It displays a spinning 3D sphere (Figure 1.7).

Listing 1.5 `OpenGLSphere.c`

```
1 #include <GL/glut.h>
2
3 GLUquadricObj* sphere;
4
5 void display(void) {
6     glClear(GL_COLOR_BUFFER_BIT);
7     glMatrixMode(GL_MODELVIEW);
8     glRotatef(0.2, 0.0, 0.0, 1.0);
9     gluSphere(sphere, 1.8, 24, 24);
10    glutSwapBuffers();
11 }
12
13 void idle(void) {
14     glutPostRedisplay();
15 }
16
17 int main(int argc, char** argv) {
18     glutInit(&argc, argv);
19     glutInitDisplayMode(GLUT_DOUBLE | GLUT_RGB);
20     glutCreateWindow("Spinning Sphere");
21     glutDisplayFunc(display);
22     glMatrixMode(GL_PROJECTION);
23     glLoadIdentity();
24     glOrtho(-2.0, 2.0, -2.0, 2.0, -2.0, 2.0);
25     glClearColor(1.0, 1.0, 1.0, 0.0);
26     glColor3f(1.0, 0.5, 0.5);
27     sphere = gluNewQuadric();
28     gluQuadricDrawStyle(sphere, GLU_LINE);
29     glutIdleFunc(idle);
30     glEnable(GL_CULL_FACE);
31     glCullFace(GL_BACK);
32     glMatrixMode(GL_MODELVIEW);
33     glLoadIdentity();
34     gluLookAt(1.0, 1.0, 1.0, 0.0, 0.0, 0.0, 0.0, 1.0, 0.0);
35     glutMainLoop();
36 }
```

Figure 1.7 An OpenGL program displaying a 3D spinning sphere.

Double buffering is applied in this example through the function `glutInitDisplayMode` (line 19). The projection matrix of the display is set to an orthogonal projection using GL functions. The function call `gluLookAt` (line 34) defines the view to have the eye positioned at (1, 1, 1) looking at (0, 0, 0). A sphere object is created with GLU functions.

In this case, in addition to the display callback, an idle callback is also defined to drive the animation. The idle function (line 13) calls `glutPostRedisplay` to request a call to the display function. In the display function, the model view matrix is rotated by a small angle. The sphere is then redrawn on the hidden buffer. Finally the two buffers are swapped to show the new drawing.

1.2.5 Java

OpenGL provides a standard and efficient rendering interface to graphics hardware. However, with the rapid development of computer hardware and software technology, it can be argued that an even higher level abstraction of graphics programming is now feasible. OpenGL offers a C-like procedural abstraction. It is not designed to directly accommodate the graphics modeling in an object-oriented programming paradigm. A high-level OOP-based graphics API (potentially built on top of OpenGL) may offer great benefits to application programmers.

Java 2D and Java 3D are newer graphics APIs associated with the Java programming language. They are high-level object-oriented APIs with high portability. Java 2D and Java 3D will be the APIs used in this book. Java 3D is typically implemented on top of other lower-level APIs such as OpenGL. Figure 1.8 shows a typical graphics-system layout.

An overview of the Java language and its graphics facilities is given in the next three sections.

Graphics application	
Java APIs	Java 3D
Java VM	OpenGL
OS	
Display driver	
Graphics card	
Display	

Figure 1.8 Graphics-system layers.

1.3 Java Programming Language

Java is a full-featured, general-purpose programming language that is capable of developing robust mission-critical applications. In recent years, Java has gained enormous popularity and has quickly become the programming language of choice for a wide range of applications.

Today, it is used not only for Web programming, but also for developing standalone applications across platforms on servers, desktops, and mobile devices.

A Java program is compiled to a standard, platform-independent format called "byte code." The compiled byte code can be executed without any change on any machine with a *Java Virtual Machine*. This platform independence makes Java the ideal language for delivering applications over the Internet.

Java Virtual Machine

Java is designed from the ground up to support object-oriented programming (OOP). A Java program consists entirely of class definitions. Object instantiations and interactions constitute the main actions of a Java program.

The Java language also maintains the simplicity, elegance, and efficiency of its predecessor, the C programming language. At the same time, Java avoids many of the pitfalls and deficiencies of C and C++.

While the language itself is very simple, the Java platform offers a comprehensive set of APIs (application programming interfaces). The Java APIs cover a wide range of tasks and applications: file I/O, graphics, multimedia, database, network, security, and so on.

Java contains two nearly parallel sets of facilities for GUI programming: *AWT* and *Swing*. The early versions of Java offered limited graphics support. Only minimal graphics features were included in JDK 1.x. Graphical user interface (GUI) support and graphics drawing features were provided in the Abstract Window Toolkit (AWT) package. GUI components in AWT are heavyweight—they are mapped to native components of the operating system. Besides a simple set of features to create GUI elements, AWT offers capabilities to control certain rendering attributes such as drawing color and to draw simple graphics primitives such as lines, rectangles, and ovals. There is also some support for images. However, these features are severely limited. For example, there is no way to control the width of drawing lines. Because of the limitations, early Java versions certainly did not provide adequate support for modern computer graphics programming. The Swing package is a completely redesigned GUI programming API included in the Java 2 platform. Most Swing components are lightweight—they are not implemented as native components. The graphics support in Java 2 is also greatly enhanced. The Java 2D package provides comprehensive 2D graphics features. Listing 1.6 shows a simple Java GUI program using AWT only. A Swing example will be given in the next section.

AWT
Swing

The program in Listing 1.6 is a simple Java GUI application using only the drawing facilities provided by AWT without more advanced features from Java 2D. It draws a circle in a frame (Figure 1.9). If the user clicks on the frame, the circle will move to a new location with the center at the mouse pointer. A menu is added to the frame with an item "Exit," which will terminate the program when selected.

Listing 1.6 `AWTDemo.java`

```
1 package chapter1;
2
3 import java.awt.*;
4 import java.awt.event.*;
5
6 public class AWTDemo extends Frame implements ActionListener{
7   int x = 100;
8   int y = 100;
9
10  public static void main(String[] args) {
11    Frame frame = new AWTDemo();
12    frame.setSize(640, 480);
13    frame.setVisible(true);
14  }
15
16  public AWTDemo() {
17    setTitle("AWT Demo");
18    // create menu
19    MenuBar mb = new MenuBar();
```

```
20      setMenuBar(mb);
21      Menu menu = new Menu("File");
22      mb.add(menu);
23      MenuItem mi = new MenuItem("Exit");
24      mi.addActionListener(this);
25      menu.add(mi);
26      // end program when window is closed
27      WindowListener l = new WindowAdapter() {
28        public void windowClosing(WindowEvent ev) {
29          System.exit(0);
30        }
31      };
32      this.addWindowListener(l);
33      // mouse event handler
34      MouseListener mouseListener = new MouseAdapter() {
35        public void mouseClicked(MouseEvent ev) {
36          x = ev.getX();
37          y = ev.getY();
38          repaint();
39        }
40      };
41      addMouseListener(mouseListener);
42    }
43
44    public void paint(Graphics g) {
45      g.drawOval(x-50, y-50, 100, 100);
46    }
47
48    public void actionPerformed(ActionEvent ev) {
49      String command = ev.getActionCommand();
50      if ("Exit".equals(command)) {
51        System.exit(0);
52      }
53    }
54 }
```

Figure 1.9 A simple Java GUI program with AWT.

This program is a GUI application using AWT. It has a main window with a menu and a circle. The menu contains only one item, "Exit," which closes the window when selected. The graphical drawing responds to a mouse click by redrawing the figure at the mouse location.

The AWTDemo class is defined to be a subclass of Frame (line 6). It defines the main program window. The menu in the frame is created with objects of the classes MenuBar, Menu, and MenuItem (lines 19–25). The AWTDemo class implements the Action Listener interface to process the ActionEvent generated by menu selections. The actionPerformed method defined in the interface is the handler for the events. When the "Exit" menu item is selected, the program exits by calling the method System. exit(0).

Two other event handlers are defined in the constructor of the AWTDemo class. A WindowListener is defined as an anonymous inner class from WindowAdapter (lines 27–32). It overrides the windowClosing method to terminate the program upon receiving the closing event for the window. The other listener is a MouseListener, derived from the MouseAdapter class (lines 34–41). The mouseClicked method is overridden to handle the mouse-click events. In the mouseClicked method, the mouse location is saved to the variables x and y, and a call to the repaint method is made to refresh the drawing and to move the figure to the new location.

The method paint (line 44) draws a circle of radius 50 with the method drawOval in the Graphics object. The center of the circle is determined by the variables x and y.

The main method creates and displays an instance of AWTDemo. The frame is set to the size 640 by 480.

One graphics programming option for Java is OpenGL. There are several projects to develop Java language bindings for OpenGL. *JOGL* is an implementation of JSR 231: Java language   JOGL
bindings for OpenGL. JOGL provides the classes GL and GLU to encapsulate the functions in GL and GLU. The two components GLCanvas and GLJPanel provide the drawing surfaces for the OpenGL calls. The GLCanvas is a heavyweight component that will use the hardware acceleration. The GLJPanel is a lightweight component implemented in memory. No hardware acceleration is available to GLJPanel. A typical procedure for programming JOGL is outlined below.

1. Create a GLCanvas or GLJPanel object through the GLDrawableFactory class.

2. Add a GLEvent listener to the canvas object.

3. Implement the listener by implementing the four methods: init, display, reshape, and displayChanged.

Listing 1.7 is the JOGL equivalent of Listing 1.4.

Listing 1.7 JOGLDemo.java

```
1 package chapter1;
2
3 import java.awt.*;
4 import java.awt.event.*;
5 import javax.swing.*;
6 import net.java.games.jogl.*;
7
8 public class JOGLDemo {
9
10    public static void main(String[] args) {
11       Frame frame = new Frame("JOGL Demo");
12       GLCapabilities cap = new GLCapabilities();
```

```
13    GLCanvas canvas =
14    GLDrawableFactory.getFactory().createGLCanvas(cap);
15    canvas.setSize(300, 300);
16    canvas.addGLEventListener(new Renderer());
17    frame.add(canvas);
18    frame.pack();
19    frame.addWindowListener(new WindowAdapter() {
20      public void windowClosing(WindowEvent e) {
21        System.exit(0);
22      }
23    });
24    frame.show();
25  }
26
27  static class Renderer implements GLEventListener {
28    private GL gl;
29    private GLU glu;
30    private GLDrawable gldrawable;
31
32    public void init(GLDrawable drawable) {
33      gl = drawable.getGL();
34      glu = drawable.getGLU();
35      this.gldrawable = drawable;
36      gl.glMatrixMode(GL.GL_PROJECTION);
37      gl.glLoadIdentity();
38      glu.gluOrtho2D(-1.2, 1.2, -1.2, 1.2);
39      gl.glClearColor(1.0f, 1.0f, 1.0f, 0.0f);
40    }
41
42    public void display(GLDrawable drawable) {
43      int i;
44      int n = 80;
45      float a = (float)(2*3.1415926535/n);
46      float x;
47      float y;
48
49      gl.glClear(GL.GL_COLOR_BUFFER_BIT);
50      gl.glColor3f(1.0f,0,0);
51      gl.glBegin(GL.GL_LINE_LOOP);
52      for (i = 0; i < n; i++) {
53        x = (float)Math.cos(i*a);
54        y = (float)Math.sin(i*a);
55        gl.glVertex2f(x, y);
56      }
57      gl.glEnd();
58      gl.glFlush();
59    }
60
61    public void reshape(GLDrawable drawable, int x, int y, int width,
62      int height) {}
63    public void displayChanged(GLDrawable drawable,
64      boolean modeChanged, boolean deviceChanged) {}
65  }
66 }
```

JOGL, as a language binding for OpenGL, has the same advantages and shortcomings as OpenGL. It is an efficient renderer, but it does not offer a full-fledged modeler with Java's OOP features.

1.4 Java 2D

The Java 2 platform brings significant improvements in graphics capabilities with the introduction of Swing and Java 2D and 3D APIs. The well-designed APIs offer comprehensive support for many tasks of computer graphics. Together with the unique advantages of the Java programming language, they have made the combination of Java with Java 2D and Java 3D a very attractive option for graphics programming and learning computer graphics.

The graphics support in early versions of Java is very primitive and limited. Java 2D provides a rather complete set of functionalities to manipulate and render 2D graphics. Specifically the enhancements include:

- A separate class hierarchy for geometric objects is defined in Java 2D.

- The rendering process is much more refined.

- Completely new image-processing features are introduced.

- Color models, fonts, printing, and other graphics-related supports are also greatly improved.

The `Graphics2D` class, a subclass of the `Graphics` class, is the rendering engine for Java 2D. It provides methods to render geometric shapes, images, and texts. The rendering process can be controlled by selecting transformation, paint, line properties, composition, clipping path, and other properties.

The *Swing* components and Java 2D included in the Java 2 platform are more advanced than the graphics facilities in earlier Java platforms. The Java 2D examples in this book will use the Swing classes and avoid the old AWT components whenever possible.

Swing

Listing 1.8 is a simple demonstration of Java 2D graphics features. It uses certain advanced capabilities of Java 2D such as transparency, gradient paint, transformation, and font glyphs that are not available in AWT. (See Figure 1.10.)

Listing 1.8 `Demo2D.java`

```
 1 package chapter1;
 2
 3 import java.awt.*;
 4 import java.awt.event.*;
 5 import javax.swing.*;
 6 import java.awt.font.*;
 7 import java.awt.geom.*;
 8
 9 public class Demo2D extends JApplet {
10   public static void main(String s[]) {
11     JFrame frame = new JFrame();
12     frame.setTitle("Java 2D Demo");
13     frame.setDefaultCloseOperation(JFrame.EXIT_ON_CLOSE);
14     JApplet applet = new Demo2D();
15     applet.init();
16     frame.getContentPane().add(applet);
17     frame.pack();
18     frame.setVisible(true);
19   }
20
21   public void init() {
22     JPanel panel = new Panel2D();
23     getContentPane().add(panel);
24   }
25 }
26
27 class Panel2D extends JPanel{
```

```
28    public Panel2D() {
29      setPreferredSize(new Dimension(500, 400));
30      setBackground(Color.white);
31    }
32
33    public void paintComponent(Graphics g) {
34      super.paintComponent(g);
35      Graphics2D g2 = (Graphics2D)g;
36      // draw an ellipse
37      Shape ellipse = new Ellipse2D.Double(150, 100, 200, 200);
38      GradientPaint paint =
39      new GradientPaint(100,100, Color.white, 400, 400, Color.gray);
40      g2.setPaint(paint);
41      g2.fill(ellipse);
42      // set transparency
43      AlphaComposite ac =
44      AlphaComposite.getInstance(AlphaComposite.SRC_OVER, 0.4f);
45      g2.setComposite(ac);
46      g2.setColor(Color.blue);
47      // draw transparent text
48      Font font = new Font("Serif", Font.BOLD, 120);
49      g2.setFont(font);
50      g2.drawString("Java", 120, 200);
51      // get outline of text glyph
52      FontRenderContext frc = g2.getFontRenderContext();
53      GlyphVector gv = font.createGlyphVector(frc, "2D");
54      Shape glyph = gv.getOutline(150,300);
55      // draw rotated glyph
56      g2.rotate(Math.PI/6, 200, 300);
57      g2.fill(glyph);
58    }
59 }
```

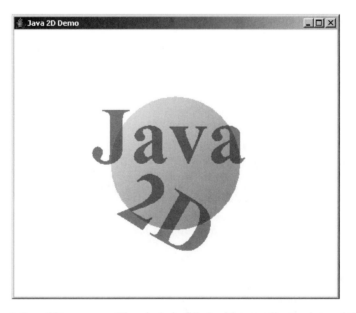

FIGURE 1.10 A Java 2D program. The circle is filled with a gradient paint and the text is semitransparent.

The class names of Swing components typically have a prefix "J." The class Panel2D (line 27) extends the JPanel class and overrides the paintComponent method (line 33). The Graphics parameter in the method is cast to Graphics2D to take advantage of the extended functionality in Java 2D. A circle is drawn with a gradient paint that changes its color based on locations. The composite rule is then set to achieve a degree of transparency. The font glyphs for text string "2D" are retrieved and the outlines are used as geometric shapes. The shape for the string "2D" is rotated 30 degrees ($\pi/6$). The details of Java 2D programming are introduced in the later chapters.

A Java program can often be written as both an applet and an application. This program is an example of such "dual-purpose" programs. The Demo2D class is a subclass of JApplet (line 9) and can be executed as an applet. However, it also contains a main method (line 10) so it can also be executed as an application. The main method creates an instance of JFrame and adds an instance of Demo2D to the frame. It simulates the execution of the applet by calling the init method. The results from the application and the applet are almost identical. Most examples in this book will use this format.

Java 2D is a standard part of the core Java 2 platform. Any Java 2 Standard Edition (J2SE) Software Development Kit (SDK) or Java Runtime Environment (JRE) installation automatically includes Java 2D. This example can be compiled under such an SDK without additional packages.

1.5 Java 3D

Java 3D is an optional package of the Java platform. It can be obtained from the site: http://www.javasoft.com/java3d. Java 3D provides an incredibly comprehensive framework for 3D graphics, including such advanced features as animation, 3D interaction, and sophisticated viewing. Yet it still provides a relatively simple and intuitive programming interface.

The Java 3D programming paradigm is very different from that of Java 2D. It closely follows the modeling–rendering paradigm. An abstract model known as the *scene graph* is used to organize and retain the visual objects and behaviors in the virtual scene. The scene graph contains the complete information of the virtual graphics world. The Java 3D rendering engine renders the scene graph automatically.

scene graph

Java 3D renders a scene on a Canvas3D object. Canvas3D is a heavyweight component that does not work well with the new Swing components. For this reason, the Java 3D examples in this book will use AWT objects.

 Note
The reason that Java 3D still does not have a lightweight canvas is to take advantage of hardware acceleration. With heavyweight components, the hardware graphics acceleration provided through the native platform support is automatically used. It is possible to mix heavyweight and lightweight components, but care must be taken to avoid some undesirable effects. See Appendix B for more details.

Listing 1.9 is a simple Java 3D application. It displays a rotating globe and a 3D text string "Java 3D" in front of the globe as shown in Figure 1.11.

Listing 1.9 Demo3D.java

```
1 package chapter1;
2
3 import javax.vecmath.*;
4 import java.awt.*;
5 import java.applet.*;
6 import java.awt.event.*;
7 import java.net.URL;
8 import javax.media.j3d.*;
9 import com.sun.j3d.utils.universe.*;
10 import com.sun.j3d.utils.geometry.*;
11 import com.sun.j3d.utils.image.*;
12 import com.sun.j3d.utils.applet.MainFrame;
13 public class Demo3D extends Applet {
14   public static void main(String[] args) {
```

```
15        new MainFrame(new Demo3D(), 480, 480);
16    }
17
18    private SimpleUniverse su;
19
20    public void init() {
21      GraphicsConfiguration gc =
22      SimpleUniverse.getPreferredConfiguration();
23      Canvas3D cv = new Canvas3D(gc);
24      setLayout(new BorderLayout());
25      add(cv);
26      BranchGroup bg = createSceneGraph();
27      bg.compile();
28      su = new SimpleUniverse(cv);
29      su.getViewingPlatform().setNominalViewingTransform();
30      su.addBranchGraph(bg);
31    }
32
33    public void destroy() {
34      su.cleanup();
35    }
36
37    private BranchGroup createSceneGraph() {
38      BranchGroup root = new BranchGroup();
39      TransformGroup spin = new TransformGroup();
40      spin.setCapability(TransformGroup.ALLOW_TRANSFORM_WRITE);
41      root.addChild(spin);
42      // 3d text
43      Appearance ap = new Appearance();
44      ap.setMaterial(new Material());
45      Font3D font = new Font3D(new Font("Helvetica", Font.PLAIN, 1),
46      new FontExtrusion());
47      Text3D text = new Text3D(font, "Java 3D");
48      Shape3D shape = new Shape3D(text, ap);
49      // transform for text
50      Transform3D tr = new Transform3D();
51      tr.setScale(0.2);
52      tr.setTranslation(new Vector3d(-0.35,-0.15,0.75));
53      TransformGroup tg = new TransformGroup(tr);
54      root.addChild(tg);
55      tg.addChild(shape);
56      // globe
57      ap = createAppearance();
58      spin.addChild(new Sphere(0.7f,
59      Primitive.GENERATE_TEXTURE_COORDS, 50, ap));
60      // rotation
61      Alpha alpha = new Alpha(-1, 6000);
62      RotationInterpolator rotator =
63      new RotationInterpolator(alpha, spin);
64      BoundingSphere bounds = new BoundingSphere();
65      rotator.setSchedulingBounds(bounds);
66      spin.addChild(rotator);
67      // background and lights
68      Background background = new Background(1.0f, 1.0f, 1.0f);
69      background.setApplicationBounds(bounds);
70      root.addChild(background);
71      AmbientLight light =
72      new AmbientLight(true, new Color3f(Color.red));
73      light.setInfluencingBounds(bounds);
74      root.addChild(light);
```

```
75      PointLight ptlight = new PointLight(new Color3f(Color.white),
76      new Point3f(3f,3f,3f), new Point3f(1f,0f,0f));
77      ptlight.setInfluencingBounds(bounds);
78      root.addChild(ptlight);
79      return root;
80    }
81
82    private Appearance createAppearance(){
83      Appearance ap = new Appearance();
84      URL filename =
85      getClass().getClassLoader().getResource("images/earth.jpg");
86      TextureLoader loader = new TextureLoader(filename, this);
87      ImageComponent2D image = loader.getImage();
88      Texture2D texture =
89      new Texture2D(Texture.BASE_LEVEL, Texture.RGBA,
90      image.getWidth(), image.getHeight());
91      texture.setImage(0, image);
92      texture.setEnable(true);
93      texture.setMagFilter(Texture.BASE_LEVEL_LINEAR);
94      texture.setMinFilter(Texture.BASE_LEVEL_LINEAR);
95      ap.setTexture(texture);
96      return ap;
97    }
98 }
```

FIGURE 1.11   A Java 3D program that displays a rotating globe and a 3D text string.

This is a typical Java 3D application. The main task of the program is centered on the construction of a conceptual data structure called scene graph. The visual effects of the program are achieved by creating a scene graph and placing the appropriate graphics elements into it. The scene graph for the program is shown in Figure 1.12. It is a treelike structure containing objects such as the sphere, the 3D text, appearance, transforms, background, lights, and so on.

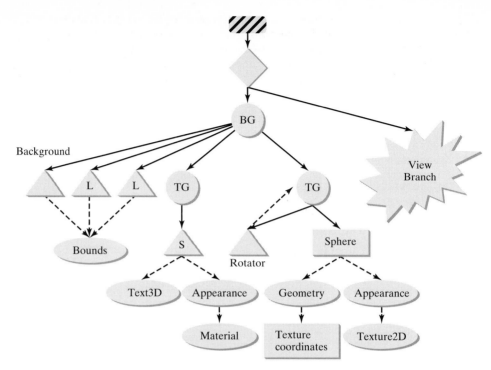

FIGURE 1.12 The scene graph of the Java 3D program.

The rendering of the scene is done automatically by the Java 3D engine. The results are shown in Figure 1.11. The concepts and techniques of programming Java 3D with scene graphs will be introduced in the later chapters.

The program is also constructed as a dual-purpose applet/application. The class Demo3D is defined as a subclass of Applet. A main method also exists in Demo3D to run the class as an application. The utility class MainFrame (line 16) included in Java 3D provides the necessary functionality to run an applet in a frame.

1.6 Related Fields

Computer graphics, image processing, and computer vision are all computer-related fields that deal with graphical objects. They are different in their objectives and techniques. However, close relationships exist among them, and the lines between them have been increasingly blurred.

image processing

Image processing is concerned with techniques of processing digital raster images. It typically deals with problems such as image enhancement, noise reduction, image compression, and edge detection. Image processing takes an existing image as input and performs appropriate actions. Computer graphics, on the other hand, generates synthetic images from a virtual world.

Image processing is closely related to computer graphics. The results of graphics rendering are usually images. Raster images are used extensively in computer graphics as graphics primitives. They are also used as textures to enhance graphics rendering. Listing 1.9 shows a globe that is constructed as a sphere with an earth image mapped on its surface. Examples of basic image-processing techniques will be given in Chapter 4.

computer vision

Computer vision attempts to derive an understanding from images of the real world. In a way a computer vision system is the inverse of a computer graphics system. Its main goal is to reconstruct a virtual world from real-world images. Therefore, computer vision and computer graphics are complementary to each other. They provide different perspectives to a common system.

The theory and practice of computer graphics depend heavily on certain important mathematical concepts. Closely related mathematics areas include analytic geometry and linear algebra. *Analytic geometry* provides a numerical representation for graphical objects. Linear *algebra* studies the operations and transformations of vector spaces, which are important in many fundamental problems of computer graphics. Relevant mathematical topics will be introduced in the chapters associated with the graphics problems. Appendix A provides a summary of graphics-related mathematical background.

analytic geometry
linear algebra

1.7 Resources

A classical reference for computer graphics is:

- J. Foley, A. van Dam, S. Feiner, and J. Hughs, *Computer Graphics, Principles and Practices*, 2d ed., Reading, MA: Addison-Wesley, 1990.

  Many current computer graphics textbooks use OpenGL:

- E. Angel, *Interactive Computer Graphics, A Top-Down Approach with OpenGL*, 2d ed., Reading, MA: Addison-Wesley, 2000.

- D. Hearn and M. P. Baker, *Computer Graphics with OpenGL*, 3d ed., Upper Saddle River, NJ: Prentice Hall, 2003.

- F. S. Hill, *Computer Graphics Using OpenGL*, 2d ed., Upper Saddle River, NJ: Prentice Hall, 2001.

  GKS and other ISO standards are available at the ISO site:

  http://www.iso.ch

  The NCAR Graphics package contains an implementation of GKS and is available at:

  http://ngwww.ucar.edu/ng4.4/

  The classical OpenGL books include:

- OpenGL Architecture Review Board, *OpenGL Programming Guide*, 4th ed., Reading, MA: Addison-Wesley, 2004.

- OpenGL Architecture Review Board, *OpenGL Reference Manual*, 4th ed., Reading, MA: Addison-Wesley, 2004.

  Many websites for OpenGL are available. The official OpenGL site contains useful information and links:

  http://opengl.org

  The website for the JOGL project is:

  http://jogl.dev.java.net

  You may find tutorials, documentations, software downloads, and other useful information at the official Java developer site:

  http://java.sun.com

  A useful reference book on Java 3D is the API specification:

- H. Sowizral, K. Rushforth, and M. Deering, *The Java 3D API Specification*, 2d ed., Reading, MA: Addison-Wesley, 2000.

Web resources for Java 3D include:

http://java.sun.com/products/java-media/3D/index.jsp

http://j3d.org

https://java3d.dev.java.net/

KEY CLASSES AND METHODS

- **`javax.swing.JFrame`** A Swing class for the main window of an application.
- **`javax.swing.JFrame.setDefaultCloseOperation(int)`** A method to set the operation in response to the window close event.
- **`java.lang.System.exit(int)`** A method to end the program.
- **`java.awt.Frame`** An AWT class for the main window of an application.
- **`javax.swing.JPanel`** A Swing component that can be used as a container or a base class for a custom drawing canvas.
- **`javax.awt.Graphics`** A class for all graphics drawing facilities in AWT.
- **`javax.awt.event.MouseListener`** An interface for listening and handling mouse events.
- **`javax.awt.event.MouseListener.mouseClicked(MouseEvent)`** The method to implement the handler for mouse clicking.

KEY TERMS

modeling The process of constructing a graphics model.
rendering The process of constructing an image of a scene from a graphics model.
virtual world A graphics model constructed in a computer.
API Application Programmer's Interface. A standardized software interface to specify the usage of functionalities provided by a software package.
GKS Graphics Kernel System. A standard graphics API.
PHIGS Programmer's Hierarchical Interactive Graphics System. A graphics API.
OpenGL A popular graphics API derived from Silicon Graphics' GL (Graphics Library). It has a programming interface typically associated with the C language.
JOGL A Java language binding for OpenGL.
image processing A field of electrical engineering and computer science to study the computer processing of digital images.
computer vision A computer and engineering field to study the perception and reconstruction of a scene from captured images.
AWT Abstract Window Toolkit. A Java graphics package existing since the early versions of Java API.
Swing A new enhanced Java graphics package.
OOP Object-oriented programming. A software engineering paradigm that views a program as a system of interrelated objects.

CHAPTER SUMMARY

- This chapter provides an overview of computer graphics, its basic structures, its applications, its relationships with other fields, and the graphics supports in the Java platform.

■ The fundamental objectives of computer graphics include the construction of a virtual world of graphics objects and the rendering of a scene from the virtual world. Modeling and rendering are the two major topics of computer graphics.

■ The characteristics of problems involved in 2D and 3D graphics systems may be quite different. Usually 2D and 3D graphics systems have different structures and they may be implemented as separate packages. This is the case in the Java platform. Java 2D and Java 3D are separate packages with different programming models.

■ The graphics programming environment has been evolving from low-level hardware-specific methods to high-level object-oriented paradigms. To reduce platform dependency and to achieve high levels of abstraction, many graphics APIs have been developed. Examples of the standard graphics packages include GKS, PHIGS, OpenGL, Java 2D, and Java 3D.

■ Unlike early Java versions, the Java 2 platform offers extensive graphics support. The Java 2D and Java 3D packages are high-level, full-featured graphics systems. This book will use Java 2D and Java 3D as the main tools to introduce graphics programming.

■ Computer graphics, as a computer discipline, is different from image processing and computer vision. But it maintains close ties to these fields, which also deal with visual images.

REVIEW QUESTIONS

1.1 List three applications that use 2D computer graphics.

1.2 Name a nongame application that uses 3D computer graphics.

1.3 Search the Internet to assemble a list of movies that have applied computer graphics.

1.4 Identify the fields (computer graphics, image processing, and computer vision) that are applicable to the following applications:

  a. Locate small bright spots in a mammogram image.

  b. Construct a 3D model of a building from a set of its pictures.

  c. Display a simulation of the solar system with the sun and nine planets in motion.

  d. Recognize the brain region in a MRI scan and display a 3D model of the brain.

  e. Use computers to generate the scene of a car collision.

  f. Make a computer identification of a person from a photograph.

1.5 Search the Internet to find an example program that uses GKS.

1.6 Search the Internet to find an example program that uses PHIGS.

1.7 Compare OpenGL and Java 3D. List the advantages of each API.

1.8 Discuss the advantages and disadvantages of including graphics support in a standard language platform such as Java.

1.9 List the major GUI components of AWT and find their approximate equivalents in Swing.

1.10 Read the documentation of Java 3D and list the Java packages in Java 3D.

PROGRAMMING EXERCISES

1.1   Write a console-based Java program that fills a double array with 100 random values and prints their mean and standard deviation.

1.2   Write a Java AWT program that draws a circle in the middle of the window.

1.3   Write a Java Swing program that draws a circle in the middle of the window.

1.4   Write a Java GUI program that responds to a mouse click by drawing a filled circle at the mouse location.

1.5   Edit, compile, and run the Java 2D program in Listing 1.8 on your local machine.

1.6   Edit, compile, and run the Java 3D program in Listing 1.9 on your local machine.

CHAPTER 2

2D GRAPHICS: BASICS

Objectives

■ To understand the architecture and operations of a 2D graphics system.

■ To understand 2D coordinate systems and equations of graphs.

■ To be able to identify the various coordinate spaces in a rendering pipeline.

■ To understand Java 2D program structure and the `Graphics2D` object.

■ To graph equations with Java programs.

■ To use basic 2D geometric primitives.

■ To construct custom shapes using the `GeneralPath` class.

■ To construct geometric shapes through constructive area geometry.

2.1 Introduction

This chapter introduces basic concepts of 2D computer graphics systems and the Java 2D package. A 2D graphics system models the virtual world with a two-dimensional space. Compared to 3D graphics, 2D graphics is simpler in both modeling and rendering. 2D objects are easier to create and manipulate. The 2D rendering usually does not involve any complicated projections such as those in 3D graphics. Even though a 2D model cannot completely capture the full nature of a 3D space, 2D computer graphics is widely applied because of its simplicity and efficiency. It is an essential ingredient of modern GUI-based programs.

The key concepts related to 2D graphics include the rendering pipeline, the object space, the world space, the device space, coordinate systems, graphics primitives, geometric transformations, colors, clipping, composition rules, and other topics. Java 2D provides comprehensive support for 2D graphics. This chapter covers the basic structures of Java 2D programs and the geometric-object models. Additional topics for 2D graphics and Java 2D programming will be discussed in the next two chapters.

2.2 2D Rendering Process

In 2D graphics, the virtual world space and the viewing space are both two dimensional. The rendering involves composing various objects through some relatively straightforward transformations. Often the 2D world space is not even needed in order to explicitly model the relationships among the graphics objects. However, to achieve the clarity of system structures and to keep the analogy with 3D graphics, the notion of a virtual world space will be retained.

object space
world space

Conceptually, a graphics object can be defined in its own *object space* and then placed in the 2D *world space* by an object transformation. A 2D rendering takes a snapshot of the world and produces an image representing a particular view in a device space.

Figure 2.1 shows a typical procedure for 2D graphics rendering.

FIGURE 2.1   A 2D graphics object is processed in a pipeline of transformation and viewing.

The essential components of a 2D graphics system include the 2D object model to be rendered, the geometric transformations applied to the objects, and the rendering engine that creates a particular view of the virtual world on a display device. The basic steps for rendering graphics in a simple 2D graphics program can be outlined as follows:

1. Construct the 2D objects.

2. Apply transformations to the objects.

3. Apply color and other rendering properties.

4. Render the scene on a graphics device.

The graphics objects in the model are two dimensional. Besides geometric objects constructed from basic primitives such as lines, polygons, and ellipses, the model may also include objects such as texts and images.

The transformations involved in 2D graphics are usually affine transforms. The object transformations change the shapes and locations of the visual objects to which the transforms are applied. The viewing transformations do not change the virtual world model, but they change the views of the entire scene on the world space. For example, in a virtual model with a circle and a triangle, a translation applied to the circle as an object transformation will move only the circle without changing the triangle. A translation as a viewing transformation, on the other hand, will move the entire view.

In addition to the geometry, many other attributes will affect the rendering of a scene. Colors, transparency, textures, and line styles are examples of such attributes. A 2D graphics system will render a scene based on the geometry information, transformation, and a graphics context involving other attributes.

2.3 2D Geometry and Coordinate Systems

The fundamental components of a graphics model are geometric objects. In order to represent geometry precisely and efficiently in computers, *coordinate systems* are employed. The most commonly used 2D coordinate system employs rectangular (Cartesian) coordinates, as illustrated in Figure 2.2.

coordinate system

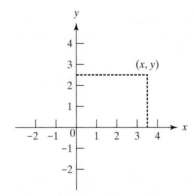

FIGURE 2.2   The 2D coordinate system with the *x*-axis and *y*-axis.

Two perpendicular axes are placed in the plane. Each axis is labeled with the set of real numbers. The horizontal axis is customarily called the *x*-axis and the vertical axis the *y*-axis. The intersection of the axes is identified with the number 0 on both axes and is called the origin. Each point on the plane is associated with a pair of real numbers (x, y) known as the *x*-coordinate and the *y*-coordinate. The coordinates measure the horizontal and vertical position of the point relative to the axes.

A 2D geometric object is a set of points in the plane. The number of points in the set that constitutes the geometric object is usually infinite. To effectively represent such an object, an equation is used to define the relation that the *x*- and *y*-coordinates of a point in the object must satisfy.

For example, a *line* (see Figure 2.3) can be represented by a polynomial equation of degree 1 (a linear equation):

line

$$Ax + By + C = 0$$

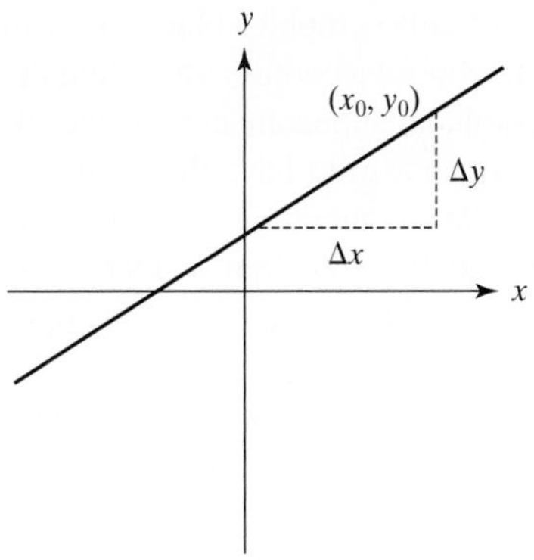

FIGURE 2.3   A line can be represented by a linear equation.

circle

A *circle* centered at the origin with radius R is represented by the equation:

$$x^2 + y^2 = R^2$$

ellipse

More generally, an *ellipse* centered at (x_0, y_0) has the standard equation:

$$\frac{(x - x_0)^2}{a^2} + \frac{(y - y_0)^2}{b^2} = 1$$

parametric equation

Another common type of equation to represent a curve is the *parametric equation*. Instead of an equation relating x and y, a third variable, t, is introduced. Both x and y are expressed as functions of t.

$$x = f(t)$$
$$y = g(t)$$

An advantage of parametric equations is that they provide explicit functional forms for evaluating the coordinates. The ellipse shown in Figure 2.4 can also be expressed using the parametric equation:

$$x = x_0 + a \cos t$$
$$y = y_0 + b \sin t$$

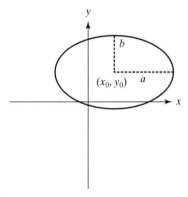

Figure 2.4　An ellipse can be represented by a quadratic equation.

space
object space
world space
device space

The collection of all points or coordinates is also known as a *space*. Three types of spaces are typically involved in a graphics system: *object space*, *world space*, and *device space*. Each space is usually characterized by its own coordinate system. Geometric objects in one space can be mapped to another by transformations.

modeling coordinate system

An object coordinate system, also known as *local* or *modeling coordinate system*, is associated with the definition of a particular graphics object or primitive. In constructing such an object, it is usually convenient to choose a coordinate system that is natural to the object without concerning its final destination and appearance in the world space. For example, when we define a circle primitive, we may choose to have the origin of the coordinate system at the center of the circle and simply define a unit circle (a circle of radius 1). The circle can later be

translation

placed anywhere in the world space through a transformation called *translation*. Its radius can be changed to any value by scaling. It can even be transformed to an ellipse by using a nonuniform scaling.

world coordinate system
user coordinate system

The *world coordinate system,* or *user coordinate system*, defines a common reference space for all the objects in a graphics model. It represents the virtual world shared by the modeling and rendering subsystems. Geometric objects are placed into this space through object transforms. The rendering system takes a snapshot of the space and produces a rendered image on an output device.

The *device coordinate system* represents the display space of an output device such as a screen or a printer. Figure 2.5 shows a typical example of such a coordinate system. The origin is located at the upper left corner, and the positive direction of the *y*-axis is pointing downward. The coordinate values are usually integers only. This choice is obviously different from the usual mathematical representation, but it is more natural for most computer display devices.

device coordinate system

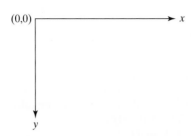

FIGURE 2.5   Java 2D's coordinate system originates from origin (0, 0) with the *x*-axis increasing rightward and the *y*-axis increasing downward.

By default, Java 2D's world coordinates coincide with the device coordinates. With the available transformation facilities in a graphics system, it is easy to define a different world space that may be more appropriate for a particular application.

2.4 The Graphics2D Class

In Java 2D, the rendering engine is accessed through the class Graphics2D. In early versions of Java, graphics drawings are obtained through the class java.awt.Graphics. The Graphics class contains basic methods for rendering graphics primitives and controlling the rendering modes. Java 2D uses the more extensive Graphics2D class for its graphics rendering. Graphics2D extends the Graphics class to maintain compatibility with the early AWT rendering in GUI components.

Graphics2D

Graphics

Graphics and Graphics2D classes are abstract, because their implementations will necessarily be platform dependent. Consequently, you cannot directly instantiate the Graphics2D class. There are two ways to retrieve a Graphics2D object. It can be obtained as the parameter in the paintComponent method or by calling the getGraphics method. The standard approach to draw graphics in a JComponent object is to override the paint-Component method:

```
void paintComponent(Graphics g)
```

The parameter g is declared to be Graphics, but it is also a Graphics2D object. It can be cast to a Graphics2D object. The paintComponent method is called automatically by Java Virtual Machine whenever the display needs to be redrawn, such as when the window is restored after it is minimized. Therefore the drawing made in the method will appear to be persistent.

Java does not explicitly provide a "retained-mode" modeling facility for 2D graphics. The custom code in the paintComponent method may be regarded implicitly as a model for the graphics system.

Another way to obtain a reference to a Graphics2D object is to call the method get-Graphics in the class Component.

```
Graphics getGraphics()
```

Again the `Graphics` object returned from the method can be cast to a `Graphics2D`, and it can be used to perform graphics rendering. However, usually the drawings obtained this way will not be persistent.

In AWT, the `Graphics` class provides the methods to control all aspects of rendering. It contains methods to set colors and fonts, to translate the coordinates, to set XOR mode, and to draw primitives such as lines and ovals directly. Some of the methods in `Graphics` are listed below.

Graphics methods

```
void setColor(Color c)
void setFont(Font f)
void setXORMode(Color c)
void setPaintMode()
void translate(int x, int y)
void drawLine(int x1, int y1, int x2, int y2)
void drawRect(int x1, int y1, int width, int height)
void drawOval(int x1, int y1, int width, int height)
void drawArc(int x1, int y1, int width,
    int height, int start, int arc)
void drawRoundRect(int x1, int y1,
    int width, int height, int arcW, int arcH)
void drawPolygon(int[] xPoints, int[] yPoints, int nPoints)
void fillRect(int x1, int y1, int width, int height)
void fillOval(int x1, int y1, int width, int height)
void fillArc(int x1, int y1, int width,
    int height, int start, int arc)
void fillRoundRect(int x1, int y1, int width,
    int height, int arcW, int arcH)
void fillPolygon(int[] xPoints, int[] yPoints, int nPoints)
void drawString(String str, int x, int y)
```

There is no clear separation between the modeler and the renderer in AWT. For example, a single method `drawOval` is responsible for both defining (modeling) an ellipse and drawing (rendering) the ellipse.

Java 2D, on the other hand, is required to handle much more sophisticated graphics objects. Therefore, instead of bundling all rendering functions into a single class, the modeling and transformation features are implemented with additional classes separated from the `Graphics2D` class. `Graphics2D` provides some generic methods such as `draw(Shape)` and `fill(Shape)` to render separately defined objects. The objects to be drawn are implemented as `Shape` objects. Similarly, the transformations can be constructed with the `AffineTransform` class. `Graphics2D` provides the method `setTransform(AffineTransform)` to set the current transformation to the separately defined transformation object. A partial list of `Graphics2D` methods is given below.

Graphics2D methods

```
void draw(Shape s)
void fill(Shape s)
void setTransform(AffineTransform Tx)
void transform(AffineTransform Tx)
void setPaint(Paint p)
void setStroke(Stroke s)
void clip(Shape s)
void setComposite(Composite c)
void addRenderingHints(Map hints)
```

The separation of modeling and rendering is more apparent in `Graphics2D`. For example, to draw an ellipse you will create an instance of `Ellipse2D` (which implements the `Shape` interface) and call the `draw` method to render it.

A typical Java 2D graphics program uses the JPanel class as the drawing canvas. By overriding the paintComponent method, custom painting is achieved. The associated Graphics2D object can be configured for proper settings such as colors, paints, strokes, and transformations. A graphical object is constructed as an instance of a class implementing the Shape interface. It can be rendered through the Graphics2D object.

Listing 2.1 shows a simple Java 2D program. It illustrates the basic structure of a Java 2D program and the use of the Graphics2D class. The program displays a transformed circle and a text string with a blue color, as shown in Figure 2.6.

Listing 2.1 Hello2D.java

```
1 package chapter2;
2
3 import java.awt.*;
4 import java.awt.event.*;
5 import javax.swing.*;
6 import java.awt.geom.*;
7
8 public class Hello2D extends JApplet {
9   public static void main(String s[]) {
10     JFrame frame = new JFrame();
11     frame.setTitle("Hello 2D");
12     frame.setDefaultCloseOperation(JFrame.EXIT_ON_CLOSE);
13     JApplet applet = new Hello2D();
14     applet.init();
15     frame.getContentPane().add(applet);
16     frame.pack();
17     frame.setVisible(true);
18   }
19
20   public void init() {
21     JPanel panel = new Hello2DPanel();
22     getContentPane().add(panel);
23   }
24 }
25
26 class Hello2DPanel extends JPanel {
27   public Hello2DPanel() {
28     setPreferredSize(new Dimension(640, 480));
29   }
30
31   public void paintComponent(Graphics g) {
32     super.paintComponent(g);
33     Graphics2D g2 = (Graphics2D)g;
34     g2.setColor(Color.blue);
35     Ellipse2D e = new Ellipse2D.Double(-100, -50, 200, 100);
36     AffineTransform tr = new AffineTransform();
37     tr.rotate(Math.PI / 6.0);
38     Shape shape = tr.createTransformedShape(e);
39     g2.translate(300,200);
40     g2.scale(2,2);
41     g2.draw(shape);
42     g2.drawString("Hello 2D", 0, 0);
43   }
44 }
```

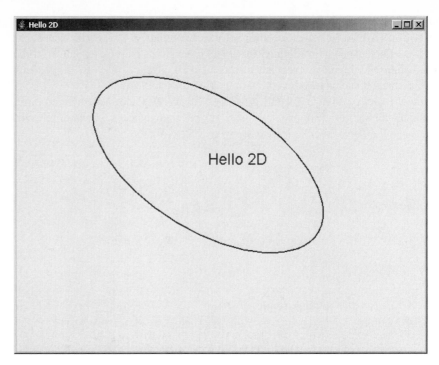

FIGURE 2.6   A simple Java 2D application draws a rotated ellipse and a text string.

The program is written to run as both an applet and an application. The Hello2D class extends JApplet. A main method is also included that creates a JFrame window and adds an instance of Hello2D to the window. The applet contains an instance of the Hello2DPanel. The Hello2DPanel class extends the JPanel class and overrides the paintComponent method to draw the graphics display.

The main graphics functions are carried out inside the paintComponent method (line 31). The paintComponent method of the superclass is invoked first to handle the necessary cleanup operations. The Graphics object g is cast into a Graphics2D object g2 to use the Java 2D features (line 33). The parameter g is declared as Graphics, but it is actually a Graphics2D object in all versions of Java that include Java 2D. The drawing color is then set to blue by calling the method setColor() in the Graphics object. More sophisticated drawing attributes that exist in the Graphics2D class will be introduced later in this chapter.

An ellipse is created using the Ellipse2D.Double class (line 35). A rotation of $\pi/6$ is constructed as an AffineTransfrom object. The rotation is an object transformation applied only to the ellipse. The transformed shape is obtained by calling the createTransformedShape method of the AffineTransform object.

The viewing transformation consists of a translation by (300, 200) and a scaling of factor 2. The transformation is achieved by directly calling the methods translate and scale in the Graphics2D object.

Using the draw method the rotated ellipse is drawn to the screen (line 41). A string "Hello 2D" is drawn with the method drawString in the Graphics2D object.

2.5 Graphing Equations

Mathematical equations are important in modeling graphics objects. Conversely, graphical plots offer a useful tool for studying mathematical functions and equations. Plotting an equation is a simple graphics application.

A simple way to graph an equation is to generate a sequence of coordinates satisfying the equation and then plot the points. For a function of the form $y = f(x)$, it is straightforward to choose a set of x-coordinates and calculate the corresponding y-coordinates. An equation of the

function

implicit form $F(x, y) = 0$ is more difficult to calculate, because, given a value of the x- (or y-) coordinate, it would in general require solving an equation to find the other coordinate. Certain equations can be expressed in the parametric form that is convenient for calculations.

A sample run of the program is shown in Figure 2.7.

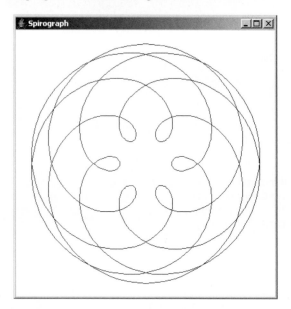

FIGURE 2.7   A spirograph plot using a parametric equation.

Listing 2.2 plots a spirograph based on a parametric equation. Consider a circle rolling on another circle. The curve formed by a pen attached to the rolling circle is called an *epicycloid* or *spirograph*. Using the angle of rolling as the parameter, a parametric equation can be derived:

$$x = (r_1 + r_2) \cos t - p \cos((r_1 + r_2)t/r_2)$$
$$y = (r_1 + r_2) \sin t - p \sin((r_1 + r_2)t/r_2)$$

The radii of the fixed circle and the rolling circle are denoted by r1 and r2. The offset of the pen position relative to the center of the rolling circle is p. A variety of curves can be generated by changing the values of r1, r2, and p.

Listing 2.2 `Spirograph.java`

```
1 package chapter2;
2
3 import java.awt.*;
4 import java.awt.event.*;
5 import javax.swing.*;
6 import java.awt.geom.*;
7
8 public class Spirograph extends JApplet {
9   public static void main(String s[]) {
10     JFrame frame = new JFrame();
11     frame.setTitle("Spirograph");
12     frame.setDefaultCloseOperation(JFrame.EXIT_ON_CLOSE);
13     JApplet applet = new Spirograph();
14     applet.init();
15     frame.getContentPane().add(applet);
16     frame.pack();
17     frame.setVisible(true);
18   }
19
```

```
20    public void init() {
21       JPanel panel = new SpiroPanel();
22       getContentPane().add(panel);
23    }
24 }
25
26 class SpiroPanel extends JPanel{
27    int nPoints = 1000;
28    double r1 = 60;
29    double r2 = 50;
30    double p = 70;
31
32    public SpiroPanel() {
33       setPreferredSize(new Dimension(400, 400));
34       setBackground(Color.white);
35    }
36
37    public void paintComponent(Graphics g) {
38       super.paintComponent(g);
39       Graphics2D g2 = (Graphics2D)g;
40       g2.translate(200,200);
41       int x1 = (int)(r1 + r2 - p);
42       int y1 = 0;
43       int x2;
44       int y2;
45       for (int i = 0; i < nPoints; i++) {
46          double t = i * Math.PI / 90;
47          x2 = (int)((r1+r2)*Math.cos(t)-p*Math.cos((r1+r2)*t/r2));
48          y2 = (int)((r1+r2)*Math.sin(t)-p*Math.sin((r1+r2)*t/r2));
49          g2.drawLine(x1, y1, x2, y2);
50          x1 = x2;
51          y1 = y2;
52       }
53    }
54 }
```

The SpiroPanel class is defined as a subclass of JPanel. The plotting is performed inside the paintComponent method (line 37). The variable nPoints defines the number of points to evaluate. The variables for the parametric equation are set to the values:

```
r1 = 60
r2 = 50
p = 70
```

The parameter t is initialized to 0 and incremented by $\pi/90$ for each point. The x- and y-coordinates are calculated based on the parametric equation. A line segment is drawn between two adjacent points.

2.6 Geometric Models

2D graphics objects that constitute a virtual world model may include geometric shapes, text objects, and images. More detailed discussions on fonts, texts, and images will be presented later in Chapters 3 and 4. This section will focus on the geometric objects.

2.6.1 Shapes

In Java 2D, a geometric object can be rendered by Graphics2D if it implements the Shape interface. Graphics2D contains draw(Shape s) and fill(Shape s) methods that draws the outline of the shape or fills the interior of the shape. Java 2D provides facilities to construct basic shapes and to combine them to form more complex shapes. The Shape class hierarchy is shown in Figure 2.8.

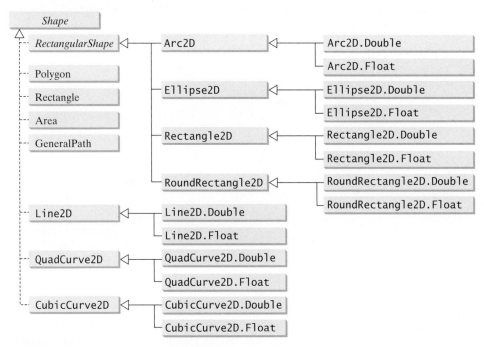

FIGURE 2.8 Java 2D defines various shapes.

The classes Line2D, QuadCurve2D, CubicCurve2D, Rectangle2D, RoundRectangle2D, Arc2D, and Ellipse2D are abstract classes. Each has two concrete *inner subclasses* named *X.Double* and *X.Float* that represent the coordinates using double or float data types, respectively. For example, Line2D.Double and Line2D.Float are subclasses of Line2D and they are also inner classes of Line2D. The two inner subclasses both represent lines, but they differ in their data types for coordinate representation. To create a Line2D object with double data type, you may use the following constructor: — inner subclasses

```
Line2D line = new Line2D.Double(x1, y1, x2, y2);
```

QuadCurve2D represents a *quadratic curve*, which is mathematically defined as a quadratic polynomial and specified by three control points. The first and last control points are the endpoints of the curve. The middle control point usually is not on the curve but instead defines the trend of the quadratic curve, as shown in Figure 2.9. A QuadCurve2D object may be created using a constructor as shown below. The coordinates of the three control points are specified with the six parameters. — quadratic curve

```
QuadCurve2D quad = new QuadCurve2D.Double(x1, y1, x2, y2, x3, y3);
```

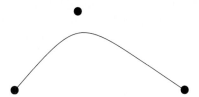

FIGURE 2.9 A quadratic curve is specified by three control points.

cubic Bézier curve

CubicCurve2D represents a *cubic Bézier curve*, which is defined as a cubic polynomial and specified by four control points. As in the quadratic curves, the first and last control points are the endpoints of the curve. The middle two control points define the shape of the curve but are not necessarily on the curve, as shown in Figure 2.10. An example of constructing a CubicCurve2D object is given below.

```
CubicCurve2D cubic = new CubicCurve2D.Float(x1,y1,x2,y2,x3,y3,x4,y4);
```

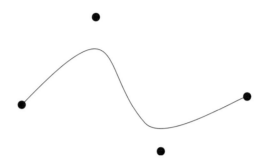

FIGURE 2.10   A cubic Bézier curve is specified by four control points.

rectangle

The Rectangle2D class defines *rectangles* with horizontal and vertical sides. The Rectangle class defined in JDK 1.1 has been integrated into Java 2D. Rectangle is now a subclass of Rectangle2D. Rectangle uses integer coordinates. Rectangle2D.Double and Rectangle2D.Float, the other subclasses of Rectangle2D, use double and float, respectively, to represent coordinates. The following code fragment creates three Rectangle2D objects with different data type. The upper left corner of the rectangles is (20, 30) and the dimension is (100, 80).

```
Rectangle2D ri = new Rectangle(20,30,100,80);
Rectangle2D rd = new Rectangle2D.Double(20.0,30.0,100.0,80.0);
Rectangle2D rf = new Rectangle2D.Float(20f,30f,100f,80f);
```

round rectangle

RoundRectangle2D defines rectangles with *round corners*. The constructor for a RoundRectangle2D object may contain two more parameters that specify the width and height of the arch. For example, the arch in the following round rectangle has dimension 5 by 5:

```
RoundRectangle2D rrect = new RoundRectangle2D.Double(20,30,100,80,5,5);
```

ellipse

Ellipse2D represents a full *ellipse*. The parametric equation of the ellipse centered at the origin can be written as

$$x = a \cos \theta$$
$$y = b \sin \theta$$

The parameter θ varies from 0 to 2π or 0 to 360 degrees. The location and size of an Ellipse2D object are specified using its bounding rectangle. An Ellipse2D object with float data type can be created with the following constructor. The upper left corner of the bounding rectangle is (20, 30) and the dimension is (100, 80).

```
Ellipse2D ellipse = new Ellipse2D.Float(20f, 30f, 100f, 80f);
```

Arc2D defines an elliptic *arc*. The underlying ellipse is defined in the same way as arc Ellipse2D and can be represented with the same parametric equation. The portion of the arc is specified by a range on the parameter θ. Arc2D defines three ways to close an arc: OPEN, CHORD, and PIE. For example, the following code constructs an arc with the parameter ranging from $\theta = 30$ degrees to $\theta = 75$ degrees, and the arc is closed with a pie shape.

```
Arc2D arc = new Arc2D.Float(20f, 30f, 100f, 80f, 30f, 45f, Arc2D.PIE);
```

Note

The angle θ is specified in degrees instead of radians. The parameter θ in general does not correspond to the radial angle of a given point. For example, when $\theta = 45$ degrees, the line from the center to the point on the ellipse corresponds to the diagonal of the bounding rectangle, as shown in Figure 2.11. Clearly the angle of the line is not 45 degrees, unless the ellipse is a circle.

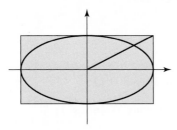

FIGURE 2.11 The geometric angle of the radial line for a point on the ellipse is not necessarily equal to the parameter value.

The classes Rectangle2D, RoundRectangle2D, Ellipse2D, and Arc2D provide only for the construction of objects that have their bounding rectangles parallel to the *x*- and *y*-axes. However, this is not a severe limitation, because the general "rotated" versions of these objects can be obtained easily with proper transformations. A detailed discussion of transformations will be given in the next chapter.

The Polygon class, similar to the Rectangle class, comes from the old AWT, and it polygon supports only integer coordinates. To construct a Polygon object you may use the following constructor:

```
Polygon(int[] xcoords, int[] ycoords, int npoints);
```

The two integer arrays define the vertices of the polygon. The first point and last point are joined to form a closed path.

2.6.2 Example

Listing 2.3 is an interactive drawing program. It allows a user to draw various geometric shapes in Java 2D, including rectangles, round rectangles, ellipses, arcs, lines, quadratic curves, cubic curves, and polygons (Figure 2.12). A menu is used to select drawing shapes, and the user draws a particular shape on the screen by dragging the mouse. The drawings are persistent—that is, they will not disappear when the window is repainted.

Listing 2.3 DrawShapes.java

```
1 package chapter2;
2
3 import java.awt.*;
4 import java.awt.geom.*;
5 import java.awt.event.*;
6 import java.util.*;
7 import javax.swing.*;
8
9 public class DrawShapes extends JApplet implements ActionListener {
10   public static void main(String s[]) {
11     JFrame frame = new JFrame();
12     frame.setTitle("Drawing Geometric Shapes");
13     frame.setDefaultCloseOperation(JFrame.EXIT_ON_CLOSE);
14     JApplet applet = new DrawShapes();
15     applet.init();
16     frame.getContentPane().add(applet);
17     frame.pack();
18     frame.setVisible(true);
19   }
20
21   JavaDraw2DPanel panel = null;
22
23   public void init() {
24     JMenuBar mb = new JMenuBar();
25     setJMenuBar(mb);
26     JMenu menu = new JMenu("Objects");
27     mb.add(menu);
28     JMenuItem mi = new JMenuItem("Rectangle");
29     mi.addActionListener(this);
30     menu.add(mi);
31     mi = new JMenuItem("RoundRectangle");
32     mi.addActionListener(this);
33     menu.add(mi);
34     mi = new JMenuItem("Ellipse");
35     mi.addActionListener(this);
36     menu.add(mi);
37     mi = new JMenuItem("Arc");
38     mi.addActionListener(this);
39     menu.add(mi);
40     mi = new JMenuItem("Line");
41     mi.addActionListener(this);
42     menu.add(mi);
43     mi = new JMenuItem("QuadCurve");
44     mi.addActionListener(this);
45     menu.add(mi);
46     mi = new JMenuItem("CubicCurve");
47     mi.addActionListener(this);
48     menu.add(mi);
49     mi = new JMenuItem("Polygon");
50     mi.addActionListener(this);
51     menu.add(mi);
52     panel = new JavaDraw2DPanel();
53     getContentPane().add(panel);
54   }
55
56   public void actionPerformed(ActionEvent ev) {
57     String command = ev.getActionCommand();
58     if ("Rectangle".equals(command)) {
59       panel.shapeType = panel.RECTANGLE;
```

```
60        } else if ("RoundRectangle".equals(command)) {
61          panel.shapeType = panel.ROUNDRECTANGLE2D;
62        } else if ("Ellipse".equals(command)) {
63          panel.shapeType = panel.ELLIPSE2D;
64        } else if ("Arc".equals(command)) {
65          panel.shapeType = panel.ARC2D;
66        } else if ("Line".equals(command)) {
67          panel.shapeType = panel.LINE2D;
68        } else if ("QuadCurve".equals(command)) {
69          panel.shapeType = panel.QUADCURVE2D;
70        } else if ("CubicCurve".equals(command)) {
71          panel.shapeType = panel.CUBICCURVE2D;
72        } else if ("Polygon".equals(command)) {
73          panel.shapeType = panel.POLYGON;
74        }
75      }
76 }
77
78 class JavaDraw2DPanel extends JPanel
79    implements MouseListener, MouseMotionListener {
80    private Vector shapes = new Vector();
81    static final int RECTANGLE = 0;
82    static final int ROUNDRECTANGLE2D = 1;
83    static final int ELLIPSE2D = 2;
84    static final int ARC2D = 3;
85    static final int LINE2D = 4;
86    static final int QUADCURVE2D = 5;
87    static final int CUBICCURVE2D = 6;
88    static final int POLYGON = 7;
89    static final int GENERAL = 8;
90    static final int AREA = 9;
91
92    int shapeType = RECTANGLE;
93    // vector of input points
94    Vector points = new Vector();
95    int pointIndex = 0;
96    Shape partialShape = null;
97    Point p = null;
98
99    public JavaDraw2DPanel() {
100       super();
101       setBackground(Color.white);
102       setPreferredSize(new Dimension(640, 480));
103       addMouseListener(this);
104       addMouseMotionListener(this);
105    }
106
107    public void paintComponent(Graphics g) {
108       super.paintComponent(g);
109       Graphics2D g2 = (Graphics2D)g;
110       for (int i = 0; i < shapes.size(); i++) {
111         Shape s = (Shape)shapes.get(i);
112         g2.draw(s);
113       }
114    }
115    public void mouseClicked(MouseEvent ev) {
116    }
117
118    public void mouseEntered(MouseEvent ev) {
119    }
120
```

```
121    public void mouseExited(MouseEvent ev) {
122    }
123
124    public void mousePressed(MouseEvent ev) {
125      points.add(ev.getPoint());
126      pointIndex++;
127      p = null;
128    }
129
130    public void mouseReleased(MouseEvent ev) {
131      Graphics g = getGraphics();
132      Point p1 = (Point)(points.get(pointIndex-1));
133      p = ev.getPoint();
134      Shape s = null;
135      switch (shapeType) {
136        case RECTANGLE:
137          s = new Rectangle(p1.x, p1.y, p.x-p1.x, p.y-p1.y);
138          break;
139        case ROUNDRECTANGLE2D:
140          s = new RoundRectangle2D.Float(p1.x, p1.y,
141          p.x-p1.x, p.y-p1.y, 10, 10);
142          break;
143        case ELLIPSE2D:
144          s = new Ellipse2D.Float(p1.x, p1.y, p.x-p1.x, p.y-p1.y);
145          break;
146        case ARC2D:
147          s = new Arc2D.Float(p1.x, p1.y, p.x-p1.x,
148          p.y-p1.y, 30, 120, Arc2D.OPEN);
149          break;
150        case LINE2D:
151          s = new Line2D.Float(p1.x, p1.y, p.x, p.y);
152          break;
153        case QUADCURVE2D:
154          if (pointIndex > 1) {
155            Point p2 = (Point)points.get(0);
156            s = new QuadCurve2D.Float(p2.x, p2.y, p1.x, p1.y, p.x, p.y);
157          }
158          break;
159        case CUBICCURVE2D:
160          if (pointIndex > 2) {
161            Point p2 = (Point)points.get(pointIndex-2);
162            Point p3 = (Point)points.get(pointIndex-3);
163            s = new CubicCurve2D.Float(p3.x, p3.y, p2.x, p2.y,
164            p1.x, p1.y, p.x, p.y);
165          }
166          break;
167        case POLYGON:
168          if (ev.isShiftDown()) {
169            s = new Polygon();
170            for (int i = 0; i < pointIndex; i++)
171              ((Polygon)s).addPoint(((Point)points.get(i)).x,
172              ((Point)points.get(i)).y);
173            ((Polygon)s).addPoint(p.x, p.y);
174          }
175
176      }
177      if (s != null) {
178        shapes.add(s);
179        points.clear();
180        pointIndex = 0;
```

```
181        p = null;
182        repaint();
183      }
184    }
185
186    public void mouseMoved(MouseEvent ev) {
187    }
188
189    public void mouseDragged(MouseEvent ev) {
190      Graphics2D g = (Graphics2D)getGraphics();
191      g.setXORMode(Color.white);
192      Point p1 = (Point)points.get(pointIndex-1);
193      switch (shapeType) {
194        case RECTANGLE:
195          if (p != null) g.drawRect(p1.x, p1.y, p.x-p1.x, p.y-p1.y);
196          p = ev.getPoint();
197          g.drawRect(p1.x, p1.y, p.x-p1.x, p.y-p1.y);
198          break;
199        case ROUNDRECTANGLE2D:
200          if (p != null) g.drawRoundRect(p1.x, p1.y,
201          p.x-p1.x, p.y-p1.y,10,10);
202          p = ev.getPoint();
203          g.drawRoundRect(p1.x, p1.y, p.x-p1.x, p.y-p1.y,10,10);
204          break;
205        case ELLIPSE2D:
206          if (p != null) g.drawOval(p1.x, p1.y, p.x-p1.x, p.y-p1.y);
207          p = ev.getPoint();
208          g.drawOval(p1.x, p1.y, p.x-p1.x, p.y-p1.y);
209          break;
210        case ARC2D:
211          if (p != null) g.drawArc(p1.x, p1.y, p.x-p1.x, p.y-p1.y, 30, 120);
212          p = ev.getPoint();
213          g.drawArc(p1.x, p1.y, p.x-p1.x, p.y-p1.y, 30, 120);
214          break;
215        case LINE2D:
216        case POLYGON:
217          if (p != null) g.drawLine(p1.x, p1.y, p.x, p.y);
218          p = ev.getPoint();
219          g.drawLine(p1.x, p1.y, p.x, p.y);
220          break;
221        case QUADCURVE2D:
222          if (pointIndex == 1) {
223            if (p != null) g.drawLine(p1.x, p1.y, p.x, p.y);
224            p = ev.getPoint();
225            g.drawLine(p1.x, p1.y, p.x, p.y);
226          } else {
227            Point p2 = (Point)points.get(pointIndex-2);
228            if (p != null) g.draw(partialShape);
229            p = ev.getPoint();
230            partialShape = new QuadCurve2D.Float(p2.x, p2.y,
231            p1.x, p1.y, p.x, p.y);
232            g.draw(partialShape);
233          }
234          break;
235        case CUBICCURVE2D:
236          if (pointIndex == 1) {
237            if (p != null) g.drawLine(p1.x, p1.y, p.x, p.y);
238            p = ev.getPoint();
239            g.drawLine(p1.x, p1.y, p.x, p.y);
240          } else if (pointIndex == 2) {
```

```
241              Point p2 = (Point)points.get(pointIndex-2);
242              if (p != null) g.draw(partialShape);
243              p = ev.getPoint();
244              partialShape = new QuadCurve2D.Float(p2.x, p2.y,
245              p1.x, p1.y, p.x, p.y);
246              g.draw(partialShape);
247          } else {
248              Point p2 = (Point)points.get(pointIndex-2);
249              Point p3 = (Point)points.get(pointIndex-3);
250              if (p != null) g.draw(partialShape);
251              p = ev.getPoint();
252              partialShape = new CubicCurve2D.Float(p3.x, p3.y,
253              p2.x, p2.y, p1.x, p1.y, p.x, p.y);
254              g.draw(partialShape);
255          }
256        break;
257      }
258    }
259 }
```

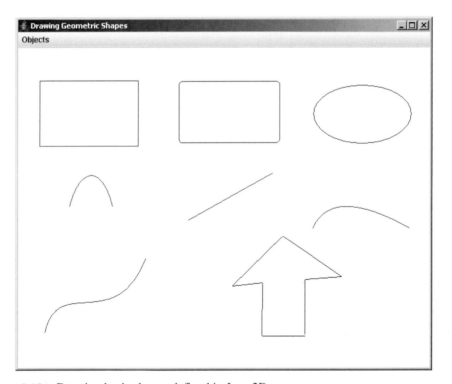

Figure 2.12   Drawing basic shapes defined in Java 2D.

This is a simple drawing program that does not have all the supporting features, such as file I/O, but does have the essential functionality of a typical drawing package. It allows users to draw an arbitrary number of basic shapes with the mouse operations.

The DrawShapes class defines an applet with a menu. The type of shape to be drawn is selected from the menu. The JavaDraw2DPanel, a subclass of JPanel, implements the actual drawing logic. The variable panel holds an instance of the JavaDraw2DPanel (line 52). The menu selection is handled in the DrawShapes class. The action event handler sets the selected shape to the shapeType variable in panel.

The `JavaDraw2DPanel` class contains a vector `shapes` that holds all the shapes drawn by the user. When the drawing of a particular figure is completed, it is added to the vector. Because the `Vector` class defines a dynamic data structure, the number of shapes is virtually unlimited. The `paintComponent` method is surprisingly simple. It traverses the vector and calls the `draw` method on each shape regardless of the types of shapes (lines 110–112). This elegant approach is made possible by the powerful polymorphism support of Java and the `Graphics2D` class.

The `JavaDraw2DPanel` class handles the mouse events to implement the drawing functions. The details of drawing a shape depend on the type of the shape. Rectangles, rounded rectangles, ellipses, arcs, and lines are defined by their bounding rectangles. They are drawn by dragging the mouse from one corner of the bounding rectangle to the opposite. Quadratic curves are defined by three control points, and they are drawn by dragging the mouse twice to define two line segments. Cubic curves are defined by four control points and are constructed with three mouse drags. The polygons may have arbitrary numbers of points and are constructed by dragging the mouse repeatedly and terminating with a double click.

During the construction of a shape, "rubber-banding" is implemented to provide a visual clue. As the user drags the mouse, the shape corresponding to the current mouse location is displayed and updated continuously. This is done inside the mouse event handlers and through the use of XOR drawing mode. When the mouse button is pressed, the current mouse location is saved to the vector `points` (line 125). When the mouse is dragged, a `Graphics2D` object is retrieved (line 190) and its XOR mode is set by calling the `setXORMode` method (line 191). A temporary shape is drawn based on the shape type and current points. This temporary shape is erased by subsequent calls and replaced with new a temporary shape, thus creating a dynamic "rubber-banding" effect. In the XOR mode, drawing the same figure a second time will erase the first drawing. When the mouse is released (line 130), a new point is created. If enough points are present for the current shape type, a new complete shape is constructed and added to the `shapes` vector. If the number of points is not enough for the shape, a partial shape is defined.

2.7 Constructive Area Geometry

One way to create more complex shapes is to combine several existing shapes. This is known as constructive area geometry. The class `Area` is designed to perform constructive area geometry. Four operations are supported: union, intersection, difference, and symmetric difference. These set-theoretic operations are performed on the regions of two areas, resulting in a new area. The union of two sets consists of all points that belong to either set. The intersection of two sets consists of points that belong to both sets. The difference of two sets consists of points that belong to the first set but not the second set. The symmetric difference of two sets consists of the points that belong to exactly one of the two sets. An `Area` object can be constructed from any `Shape` object using the following constructor:

```
Area(Shape s)
```

The four operations can be performed using the following methods of an `Area` object: `Area` methods

```
void add(Area a)
void intersect(Area a)
void subtract(Area a)
void exclusiveOr(Area a)
```

The results of the operations are placed in the current `Area` object. The second `Area` object passed as a parameter to the methods will not be altered by the operations.

Listing 2.4 shows a program demonstrating the effects of four operations of constructive area geometry. Two shapes are combined using the four operations to obtain four new shapes (Figure 2.13).

Listing 2.4 AreaGeometry.java

```
1 package chapter2;
2
3 import java.awt.*;
4 import java.awt.event.*;
5 import javax.swing.*;
6 import java.awt.geom.*;
7
8 public class AreaGeometry extends JApplet {
9   public static void main(String s[]) {
10     JFrame frame = new JFrame();
11     frame.setTitle("Constructive Area Geometry");
12     frame.setDefaultCloseOperation(JFrame.EXIT_ON_CLOSE);
13     JApplet applet = new AreaGeometry();
14     applet.init();
15     frame.getContentPane().add(applet);
16     frame.pack();
17     frame.setVisible(true);
18   }
19
20   public void init() {
21     JPanel panel = new AreaPanel();
22     getContentPane().add(panel);
23   }
24 }
25
26 class AreaPanel extends JPanel {
27   public AreaPanel() {
28     setPreferredSize(new Dimension(760, 400));
29   }
30
31   public void paintComponent(Graphics g) {
32     Graphics2D g2 = (Graphics2D)g;
33     Shape s1 = new Ellipse2D.Double(0, 0, 100, 100);
34     Shape s2 = new Ellipse2D.Double(60, 0, 100, 100);
35     Area a1;
36     Area a2 = new Area(s2);
37     g2.translate(20, 50);
38     g2.draw(s1);
39     g2.draw(s2);
40     g2.translate(0,200);
41     a1 = new Area(s1);
42     a1.add(a2);
43     g2.fill(a1);
44     g2.translate(180,0);
45     a1 = new Area(s1);
46     a1.intersect(a2);
47     g2.fill(a1);
48     g2.translate(180,0);
49     a1 = new Area(s1);
50     a1.subtract(a2);
51     g2.fill(a1);
52     g2.translate(180,0);
53     a1 = new Area(s1);
54     a1.exclusiveOr(a2);
55     g2.fill(a1);
56   }
57 }
```

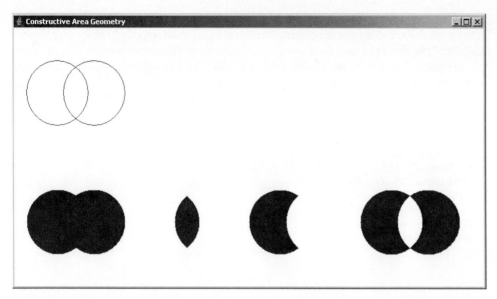

FIGURE 2.13   Top row: Two shape objects. Bottom row: The results of four area operations: add, `intersect`, `subtract`, `exclusiveOr`.

Two overlapping circles `s1` and `s2` are used as the original shapes, and they are drawn on the top of the screen. `Area` objects `a1` and `a2` are created from the shapes (lines 35–36). Each of the four operations is applied to `a1` and `a2` by calling the methods `add`, `intersect`, `subtract`, and `exclusiveOr`. The resulting areas are displayed as filled shapes in the bottom row (lines 42–55). Because the `Area` class implements the `Shape` interface, the `Area` objects can be passed directly to the `fill` method of the `Graphics2D` object.

2.8 General Path

The `Graphics2D` engine internally uses five basic types of curve segments or operations to render the borders of any shape. The `Shape` interface provides methods to retrieve a `PathIterator` that is an interface describing the path of the shape border using the five types of segments. `PathIterator` defines the five segment constants:

```
SEG_MOVETO
SEG_LINETO
SEG_QUADTO
SEG_CUBICTO
SEG_CLOSE
```

A powerful way to construct custom shapes is to use the `GeneralPath` class, which directly supports the path construction with the five basic curve segments known to `Graphics2D`. The following methods in the `GeneralPath` class perform the segment constructions corresponding to the five segment types:

```
void moveTo(float x, float y);
void lineTo(float x, float y);
void quadTo(float x1, float y1, float x2, float y2);
void curveTo(float x1, float y1, float x2,
float y2, float x3, float y3);
void closePath();
```

`GeneralPath` methods

The process of the path construction can be viewed as drawing with a "pen." At any moment, the pen has a "current location." The `moveTo` method moves the pen to the new location (*x*, *y*) without drawing anything. The `lineTo` method draws a line from the current location to the point (x, y), and the pen takes the new point as its current location. The quadTo method draws a quadratic curve from the current location to ($x2$, $y2$) using ($x1$, $y1$) as the middle control point. The curveTo method draws a cubic curve from the current point to ($x3$, $y3$) using ($x1$, $y1$) and ($x2$, $y2$) as its two middle control points. The closePath method draws a line back to the point defined by the last moveTo method.

For example, the following code segment constructs the shape shown in Figure 2.14.

```
GeneralPath path = new GeneralPath();
path.moveTo(-2f, 0f);
path.quadTo(0f, 2f, 2f, 0f);
path.quadTo(0f, -2f, -2f, 0f);
path.moveTo(-1f, 0.5f);
path.lineTo(-1f, -0.5f);
path.lineTo(1f, 0.5f);
path.lineTo(1f, -0.5f);
path.closePath();
```

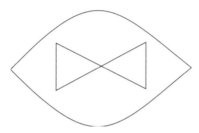

FIGURE 2.14   A shape defined by a GeneralPath object.

The path defines the boundary or outline of a shape. To completely define the shape, however, we must specify what constitutes the interior or the exterior of the shape. This information is needed, for example, in drawing a filled figure of the shape. Because multiple regions with complicated relationships may be formed from the path, the interior region problem is not always trivial. The *winding rules* define the conditions in which a region is considered inside the shape. Two winding rules are defined by PathIterator:

winding rules

```
WIND_EVEN_ODD
WIND_NON_ZERO
```

To determine whether a particular region formed by the path is in the interior, draw a line through the region and consider the number of crossings with the path from the outside to reach the region. With the *even–odd rule*, the region is in the interior if the number of crossings is odd and exterior if the number is even. Essentially the path is considered as the boundary separating the interior from the exterior, and consequently the designation of interior and exterior alternates every time the line crosses the path.

even–odd rule

With the *nonzero rule*, the direction of the path crossing is taken into consideration, and the crossing number can be positive or negative. If the line crosses the path from left to right as you view it in the direction of the path, the crossing number is increased by 1, otherwise it is decreased by 1. The region is interior if the signed crossing number is not zero. The nonzero rule essentially defines the left side of the path, when you move along the path, as the interior and the right side as the exterior.

nonzero rule

For example, Figure 2.15 shows a path that consists of two squares. With the even–odd rule, the inner square region is considered "outside" because the crossing number is even. With the nonzero rule, if the path is oriented as shown, the inner square is considered "inside" because the crossing number is not zero.

FIGURE 2.15   Even–odd rule and nonzero rule for interior definition.

Another example is given in Figure 2.16. With the even–odd rule, both triangles in the region are considered to be in the exterior. They are holes in the curved region. With the nonzero rule, however, only one triangle is considered a hole. The triangle on the right is considered to be inside, because the orientation of its path is in the same direction as the outer path and the crossing numbers do not cancel out as a line goes through them.

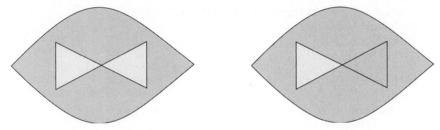

FIGURE 2.16   Left: Even–odd rule. Right: Nonzero rule.

The program in Listing 2.5 shows the construction of shapes using the GeneralPath and the effects of the winding rules. Two shapes are created, and they are displayed in three different styles: path only, even–odd rule, and nonzero rule (Figure 2.17).

Listing 2.5 CustomPath.java

```
1 package chapter2;
2
3 import java.awt.*;
4 import java.awt.event.*;
5 import javax.swing.*;
6 import java.awt.geom.*;
7
8 public class CustomPath extends JApplet {
9   public static void main(String s[]) {
10     JFrame frame = new JFrame();
11     frame.setTitle("GeneralPath and Winding Rules");
12     frame.setDefaultCloseOperation(JFrame.EXIT_ON_CLOSE);
13     JApplet applet = new CustomPath();
14     applet.init();
15     frame.getContentPane().add(applet);
16     frame.pack();
17     frame.setVisible(true);
18   }
19
20   public void init() {
21     JPanel panel = new PathPanel();
22     getContentPane().add(panel);
23   }
24 }
25
```

```
26 class PathPanel extends JPanel {
27   public PathPanel() {
28     setPreferredSize(new Dimension(640, 480));
29   }
30
31   public void paintComponent(Graphics g) {
32     super.paintComponent(g);
33     Graphics2D g2 = (Graphics2D)g;
34     GeneralPath path = new GeneralPath(GeneralPath.WIND_EVEN_ODD);
35     float x0 = 1.0f;
36     float y0 = 0.0f;
37     float x1 = (float)Math.cos(2*Math.PI/5.0);
38     float y1 = (float)Math.sin(2*Math.PI/5.0);
39     float x2 = (float)Math.cos(4*Math.PI/5.0);
40     float y2 = (float)Math.sin(4*Math.PI/5.0);
41     float x3 = (float)Math.cos(6*Math.PI/5.0);
42     float y3 = (float)Math.sin(6*Math.PI/5.0);
43     float x4 = (float)Math.cos(8*Math.PI/5.0);
44     float y4 = (float)Math.sin(8*Math.PI/5.0);
45     path.moveTo(x2,y2);
46     path.lineTo(x0,y0);
47     path.lineTo(x3,y3);
48     path.lineTo(x1,y1);
49     path.lineTo(x4,y4);
50     path.closePath();
51     AffineTransform tr = new AffineTransform();
52     tr.setToScale(100,100);
53     g2.translate(120,120);
54     path = (GeneralPath)tr.createTransformedShape(path);
55     g2.draw(path);
56     g2.translate(200,0);
57     g2.fill(path);
58     path.setWindingRule(GeneralPath.WIND_NON_ZERO);
59     g2.translate(200,0);
60     g2.fill(path);
61
62     path.reset();
63     path.moveTo(x0, y0);
64     path.lineTo(x1, y1);
65     path.lineTo(x2, y2);
66     path.lineTo(x3, y3);
67     path.lineTo(x4, y4);
68     path.closePath();
69     path.moveTo(x0, y0);
70     path.quadTo(x4, y4, x1, y1);
71     path.quadTo(x2, y2, x3, y3);
72     path.closePath();
73     path.moveTo(x4,y4);
74     path.curveTo(x1,y1,x3,y3,x2,y2);
75     path.curveTo(x1,y1,x3,y3,x4,y4);
76     path = (GeneralPath)tr.createTransformedShape(path);
77     g2.translate(-400,220);
78     g2.draw(path);
79     path.setWindingRule(GeneralPath.WIND_EVEN_ODD);
80     g2.translate(200,0);
81     g2.fill(path);
82     path.setWindingRule(GeneralPath.WIND_NON_ZERO);
83     g2.translate(200,0);
84     g2.fill(path);
85   }
86 }
```

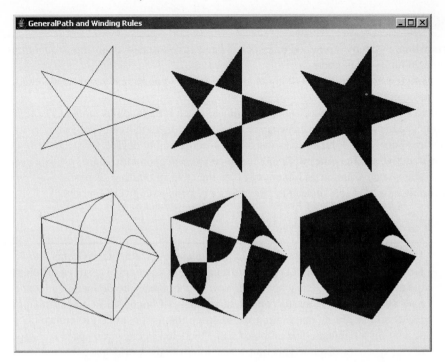

FIGURE 2.17   General paths and regions formed with the even–odd rule and the nonzero rule.

Two shapes are constructed with the `GeneralPath` class. The star is formed entirely by line segments. The vertices of the star are calculated by dividing a circle into five equally spaced parts (lines 35–44). The method `reset` clears the path in a `GeneralPath` object (line 62). The other shape is a pentagon with several segments of lines, quadratic curves, and cubic curves. Three versions of each shape are displayed in three columns. First the `draw` method is called to draw the outline path of the shape (lines 55, 78). Then the winding rule of the shape is set to even–odd and the `fill` method is called to display the shape with filled interior (lines 57, 81). Finally the winding rule is changed to nonzero and the shape is displayed with a filled interior again in the third column (lines 60, 84). It is clear that the nonzero winding rule will often yield more interior regions than the even–odd rule.

KEY CLASSES AND METHODS

- **`javax.swing.JComponent.paintComponent(Graphics)`** A method usually overridden to perform custom painting for the component.
- **`java.awt.Graphics2D`** A class providing an interface to the Java 2D rendering engine.
- **`java.awt.Graphics2D.draw(Shape)`** A method to draw the outlines of a shape.
- **`java.awt.Graphics2D.fill(Shape)`** A method to fill the interiors of a shape.
- **`java.awt.Shape`** An interface for 2D geometric shapes.
- **`java.awt.geom.GeneralPath`** A class to define a general 2D contour using all segment types in the `Shape` interface.
- **`java.awt.geom.Area`** A class for constructive area geometry.

KEY TERMS

coordinate system A method to associate geometric points with algebraic quantities of ordered tuples of numbers.

parametric equation A set of equations that express coordinate variables as functions of parameters.

world space A common reference coordinate space for a graphics model.

object space A local coordinate space associated with an individual object.

device space A coordinate space used by a specific output device.

constructive area geometry A method to create new geometric shapes by using set operations such as union and intersection on the areas of existing shapes.

winding rule A rule to determine the interior regions with given contours.

CHAPTER SUMMARY

■ In this chapter we discuss the basic principles of 2D graphics systems and Java 2D programming. A typical 2D graphics rendering pipeline involves three different coordinate spaces. In an object space, various visual objects are defined in a local coordinate system convenient for object modeling. Through object transformations the object spaces are mapped into a world space that is a common reference coordinate system for all objects. The graphics scene modeled in the world space is mapped to a device space for display. This transformation from the world space to the device space is known as the *viewing transformation*.

■ A 2D curve can often be represented as an equation. Parametric equations are convenient for graphics applications.

■ The geometric model of a visual object is constructed from primitive elements and constructive operations. Java 2D provides a rich family of graphics primitives, including line, rectangle, rounded rectangle, ellipse, arc, quadratic curve, and cubic curve. The Shape interface provides a general framework for the geometric descriptions.

■ Constructive area geometry is a technique to create new shapes based on operations on existing areas. Java 2D supports four set-theoretical operations for constructive area geometry.

■ Five basic operations are recognized in the Shape interface to define a path with different segments. The GeneralPath class provides direct access to the five segment types. Two winding rules are available to determine the interior of a region.

REVIEW QUESTIONS

2.1 What are the differences between object transformations and viewing transformations?

2.2 Plot the following points in a 2D coordinate system:

(1,3), (−2,1.5), (0,−2), (0,0)

2.3 Find the coordinates of the vertices of the triangle in Figure 2.18.

2.4 Write the Java code to construct an ellipse of width 80 and height 100 centered at (100, 300).

2.5 Find the actual angle spanned by the following arc:

```
new Arc2D.Float(0, 0, 100, 200, 0, 45);
```

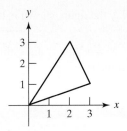

FIGURE 2.18   A triangle for Question 2.3.

2.6   Use the `GeneralPath` class to construct a shape of regular octagon.

2.7   Determine the interior of the shape in Figure 2.19 using the even–odd rule.

2.8   Determine the interior of the shape in Figure 2.19 using the nonzero rule.

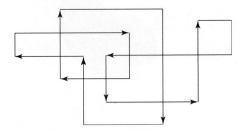

FIGURE 2.19   Define shape interior from the path.

PROGRAMMING EXERCISES

2.1   Write a Java program to plot the following parametric equation:

$$x = t^2$$
$$y = t^3$$

2.2   Write a Java program to plot the following parametric equation:

$$x = 20t \cos t$$
$$y = 20t \sin t$$
$$0 \le t \le 8\pi$$

2.3   Write a Java program to display a square centered at the origin and rotated by 45°.

2.4   Write a Java program to draw an 8 × 8 chessboard.

2.5   Write a Java program to display the accompanying filled shape (Figure 2.20) using constructive area geometry.

FIGURE 2.20   A moon shape.

2.6 Write a program to display the figure shown in the preceding problem using a general path.

2.7 Write a Java program to draw a Ying-Yang symbol as shown in Figure 2.21. (*Hint*: Use constructive area geometry.)

FIGURE 2.21 A Ying-Yang symbol.

CHAPTER 3

2D GRAPHICS: RENDERING DETAILS

Objectives

- To understand color spaces.

- To use the Java `Color` class.

- To be able to use different types of paints in drawing visual objects.

- To apply stroke types.

- To construct affine transforms including translation, rotation, scaling, shearing, and reflection.

- To understand object transformations and viewing transformations.

- To combine basic transformations to form more complex ones.

- To identify the compositing rules.

- To use clipping path.

- To apply fonts and font metrics.

- To understand glyph, ligature, and derived font.

3.1 Introduction

This chapter introduces several important attributes associated with 2D graphics rendering and their implementation in Java 2D. Besides the geometry that defines the structure of the graphics objects, many other attributes and operations contribute significantly to the appearance of rendered images. Colors, stroke types, transformations, compositing rules, clipping paths, and rendering hints are some of the factors affecting the outcome of rendering.

Colors and paints are highly visible attributes. Colors are usually represented in numerical forms called color spaces. Java defines the class `Color` to represents colors as objects. A generalization of color is the concept of paint that can represent complex color patterns. Java 2D uses the `Paint` interface to unify different paints. The classes `Color`, `GradientPaint`, and `TexturePaint` all implement the `Paint` interface and can be used by a `Graphics2D` object.

stroke *Strokes* define the details of painting pens such as the width, end style, join style, and dash type. Similar to `Paint`, `Graphics2D` allows the selection of a `Stroke` object as one of its rendering attributes. The concrete class `BasicStroke` implements the `Stroke` interface and provides common stroke settings.

transformation *Transformations* are crucial parts of computer graphics. Transformations can be used to modify geometric objects and to change the views. Affine transforms are the common family of transformations in computer graphics. Transforms such as translation, rotation, scaling, reflection, and shearing are all examples of affine transforms.

Related to colors, transparency and more general compositing rules for overlapping objects are
Porter–Duff rules interesting rendering attributes. A general set of compositing rules known as *Porter–Duff rules* are often applied in 2D graphics. The recent versions of Java 2D fully support Porter–Duff rules.

clip path *Clip path* is another rendering attribute. It defines a region in which the rendered objects will actually be visible.

text *Texts* are special graphics objects that have very compact representations. The actual geometric shapes of texts are predefined by fonts. Java 2D provides extensive support for fonts. In addition to the standard application of drawing texts with various settings of fonts, advanced features such as retrieving the outline of a character are also available.

3.2 Colors and Paints

3.2.1 Color Space

Colors are important attributes in graphics systems. The color of light is associated with the wavelength or frequency of the light. Usually light has a spectrum of frequencies whose exact description will be complex. In practical terms, only colors visible and distinguishable to
color space human eyes need to be defined in graphics systems. A system called *color space* is often used to define visible colors with numerical values. Several different color spaces exist to specify colors in a precise and quantitative way. The general approach is to select a small number of fixed primary colors such as (red, green, blue) and represent an arbitrary color as a combination of the primary colors:

$$c = r \cdot p_r + g \cdot p_g + b \cdot p_b$$

The coefficients (r, g, b) represent the components of the color c in red, green, and blue. They provide a convenient numerical specification for colors.

CIEXYZ The *CIEXYZ* is a color standard that uses three primary colors, X, Y, and Z, instead of red, green, and blue. Any visible color can be represented as a positive combination of X, Y, and Z. However, it is usually difficult to directly implement CIEXYZ in physical devices.

RGB Most monitors use *RGB* (red, green, blue) color spaces and printers typically use *CMYK*
CMYK (cyan, magenta, yellow, black) spaces. The combinations of the primary colors are used to represent different colors. These systems are natural to the devices, but they are usually device dependent and they cannot represent all visible colors with positive coefficients.

sRGB (standard RGB) is an absolute device-independent color space. It uses the same type
of red, green, and blue components as other RGB systems, but it standardizes the color definitions so that they are independent of any specific device.

3.2.2 Color

When the geometry of a shape is constructed, it can be rendered with the `fill(Shape)` or
`draw(Shape)` methods in `Graphics2D`. To set the color for rendering the object, the following method of the `Graphics` class may be used:

```
void setColor(Color c)
```

A `Color` object defines a color. The `Color` class by default uses the sRGB color space, a
proposed standard color space. A color contains Red, Green, Blue and Alpha components.
The Alpha component defines the transparency of the color. The `Color` class defines the following constant color values:

```
black
blue
cyan
darkGray
gray
green
lightGray
magenta
orange
pink
red
white
yellow
```

 Note

These names do not follow the Java naming convention, which specifies that constants should
be in all capital letters. Since JDK 1.4, you can also use the new constants: `BLACK`, `BLUE`, `CYAN`,
`DARK_GRAY`, `GREEN`, `LIGHT_GRAY`, `MAGENTA`, `ORANGE`, `PINK`, `RED`, `WHITE`, and `YELLOW`.

Other colors can be easily constructed using one of many constructors of the `Color` class.
You may directly specify the RGB values using the following constructors:

```
Color(int r, int g, int b);
Color(int rgb);
Color(float r, float g, float b);
```

The first version specifies the three-color components using `int` values in the range 0–255.
The second version is similar, but the three values are packed into a single `int` value. The
third version uses `float` values in the range 0.0–1.0 to define the color components.

Besides RGB values, an alpha value related to the transparency of the color can be specified. The following constructors allow alpha value specification:

```
Color(int r, int g, int b, int a);
Color(int rgba, boolean hasAlpha);
Color(float r, float g, float b, float a);
```

Another constructor of the `Color` class allows the specification of a color space.

```
Color(ColorSpace colorSpace, float[] components, float alpha);
```

The following code fragment draws three squares of different colors:

```
public void paintComponent(Graphics g) {
  g.setColor(Color.red);
```

```
      g.draw(new Rectangle(0, 0, 100, 100));
      g.setColor(new Color(0, 255, 128));
      g.draw(new Rectangle(100, 0, 100, 100));
      g.setColor(new Color(0.5f, 0.0f, 1.0f));
      g.draw(new Rectangle(200, 0, 100, 100));
  }
```

Listing 3.1 illustrates the combinations of primary colors and the usage of colors in Java 2D rendering. The program displays three overlapping circles representing red, green, and blue. Seven different regions represent various combinations of the three primary components. Three sliders on the right of the window control the values of the red, green, and blue components (Figure 3.1).

Listing 3.1 TestColors.java

```
 1 package chapter3;
 2
 3 import java.awt.*;
 4 import java.awt.event.*;
 5 import javax.swing.*;
 6 import javax.swing.event.*;
 7 import java.awt.geom.*;
 8
 9 public class TestColors extends JApplet {
10   public static void main(String s[]) {
11     JFrame frame = new JFrame();
12     frame.setTitle("Colors");
13     frame.setDefaultCloseOperation(JFrame.EXIT_ON_CLOSE);
14     JApplet applet = new TestColors();
15     applet.init();
16     frame.getContentPane().add(applet);
17     frame.pack();
18     frame.setVisible(true);
19   }
20
21   ColorPanel panel;
22   public void init() {
23     panel = new ColorPanel();
24     Container cp = getContentPane();
25     cp.setLayout(new BorderLayout());
26     cp.add(panel, BorderLayout.CENTER);
27     JPanel p = new JPanel();
28     cp.add(p,BorderLayout.EAST);
29     p.setLayout(new GridLayout(1,3,30,10));
30     JSlider slider = new JSlider(JSlider.VERTICAL,0,255,100);
31     p.add(slider);
32     slider.addChangeListener(new ChangeListener() {
33       public void stateChanged(ChangeEvent ev) {
34         panel.red = ((JSlider)(ev.getSource())).getValue();
35         panel.repaint();
36       }
37     });
38     slider = new JSlider(JSlider.VERTICAL,0,255,100);
39     p.add(slider);
40     slider.addChangeListener(new ChangeListener() {
41       public void stateChanged(ChangeEvent ev) {
42         panel.green = ((JSlider)(ev.getSource())).getValue();
43         panel.repaint();
44       }
45     });
```

```
46        slider = new JSlider(JSlider.VERTICAL,0,255,100);
47        p.add(slider);
48        slider.addChangeListener(new ChangeListener() {
49          public void stateChanged(ChangeEvent ev) {
50            panel.blue = ((JSlider)(ev.getSource())).getValue();
51            panel.repaint();
52          }
53        });
54      }
55  }
56
57  class ColorPanel extends JPanel{
58    int red = 100;
59    int green = 100;
60    int blue = 100;
61
62    public ColorPanel() {
63      setPreferredSize(new Dimension(500, 500));
64      setBackground(Color.white);
65    }
66
67    public void paintComponent(Graphics g) {
68      super.paintComponent(g);
69      Graphics2D g2 = (Graphics2D)g;
70      Shape rc = new Ellipse2D.Double(100, 113, 200, 200);
71      Shape gc = new Ellipse2D.Double(50, 200, 200, 200);
72      Shape bc = new Ellipse2D.Double(150, 200, 200, 200);
73      Area ra = new Area(rc);
74      Area ga = new Area(gc);
75      Area ba = new Area(bc);
76      Area rga = new Area(rc);
77      rga.intersect(ga);
78      Area gba = new Area(gc);
79      gba.intersect(ba);
80      Area bra = new Area(bc);
81      bra.intersect(ra);
82      Area rgba = new Area(rga);
83      rgba.intersect(ba);
84      ra.subtract(rga);
85      ra.subtract(bra);
86      ga.subtract(rga);
87      ga.subtract(gba);
88      ba.subtract(bra);
89      ba.subtract(gba);
90      // fill the color regions
91      g2.setColor(new Color(red,0,0));
92      g2.fill(ra);
93      g2.setColor(new Color(0,green,0));
94      g2.fill(ga);
95      g2.setColor(new Color(0,0,blue));
96      g2.fill(ba);
97      g2.setColor(new Color(red,green,0));
98      g2.fill(rga);
99      g2.setColor(new Color(0,green,blue));
100     g2.fill(gba);
101     g2.setColor(new Color(red,0,blue));
102     g2.fill(bra);
103     g2.setColor(new Color(red,green,blue));
104     g2.fill(rgba);
105     // draw three circles
```

```
106     g2.setColor(Color.black);
107     g2.draw(rc);
108     g2.draw(gc);
109     g2.draw(bc);
110  }
111 }
```

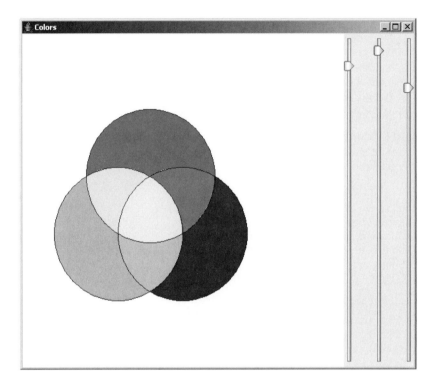

FIGURE 3.1 Colors formed by combinations of red, green, and blue.

The ColorPanel class has three int fields red, green, and blue to represent the primary color components. In the paintComponent method (line 67), the seven regions of the picture are formed from three circles using constructive area geometry. Each region is filled with a combination of primary colors covering the region. For example, the region covered by the red circle is filled with the red component. The region covered by the red and blue circles is filled with the color composed of red and blue components. The center region covered by all three circles is colored with all three components. The three circles are drawn in black.

Three vertical JSlider objects are placed on the right side of the window. They are used to control the values of the fields red, green, and blue in the ColorPanel. The values of the slides have the range 0 to 255. When a slider is changed, the corresponding ChangeListener implementation will change the color variable and repaint the panel (lines 30–53).

3.2.3 Paint

The setColor(Color c) method belongs to the older Graphics class. It sets only a solid color for rendering. The Graphics2D class of Java 2D contains a much more powerful setPaint(Paint p) method to control the rendering colors. Paint is a generalization of color. The Paint interface is implemented by the Color class and also implemented by other classes (see Figure 3.2) that can represent more attributes than simple solid colors.

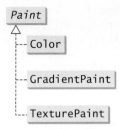

FIGURE 3.2   Paint class hierarchy.

The GradientPaint class defines a type of paint with varying colors. A *gradient paint* is specified by two points and two colors. As the location moves from the first point to the second, the paint color changes gradually from the first color to the second. A gradient paint can be cyclic or acyclic. A cyclic gradient paint repeats the same pattern periodically. To create an acyclic gradient paint, the following constructors can be used:

gradient paint

```
GradientPaint(float x1, float y1, Color c1, float x2, float y2, Color c2);
GradientPaint(Point2D p1, Color c1, Point2D p2, Color c2);
```

In either version, two points are specified with their associated colors. The colors for points between the two given points will change gradually from one specified color to the other color. Cyclic gradient paints can be created with the following constructors.

```
GradientPaint(float x1, float y1, Color c1, float x2, float y2, Color c2,
   boolean cycl);
GradientPaint(Point2D p1, Color c1, Point2D p2, Color c2, boolean cycl);
```

Setting the last parameter to true will construct a cyclic gradient paint.

The TexturePaint class allows an object to be filled with a *texture pattern*. An image and an anchor rectangle are used to define a texture paint. When painting with the texture, the image is repeatedly applied to the tiled rectangular regions. A TexturePaint object is created with the following constructor:

texture paint

```
TexturePaint(BufferImage image, Rectangle2D anchor);
```

The image defines the texture for painting. The anchor rectangle specifies the positioning of the image in the user space.

Listing 3.2 demonstrates the effects of graphics drawing with gradient and texture paints. A sample run of the program is shown in Figure 3.3.

Listing 3.2 `TestPaints.java`

```
 1 package chapter3;
 2
 3 import java.awt.*;
 4 import java.awt.event.*;
 5 import java.awt.image.*;
 6 import javax.swing.*;
 7 import java.awt.font.*;
 8 import java.awt.geom.*;
 9 import java.io.*;
10 import java.net.URL;
11 import javax.imageio.*;
12
13 public class TestPaints extends JApplet {
14    public static void main(String s[]) {
15       JFrame frame = new JFrame();
```

```
16        frame.setTitle("Gradient and Texture Paints");
17        frame.setDefaultCloseOperation(JFrame.EXIT_ON_CLOSE);
18        JApplet applet = new TestPaints();
19        applet.init();
20        frame.getContentPane().add(applet);
21        frame.pack();
22        frame.setVisible(true);
23      }
24
25      public void init() {
26        JPanel panel = new PaintPanel();
27        getContentPane().add(panel);
28      }
29   }
30
31  class PaintPanel extends JPanel{
32     private BufferedImage image;
33
34     public PaintPanel() {
35       setPreferredSize(new Dimension(500, 500));
36       setBackground(Color.white);
37       URL url = getClass().getClassLoader().getResource
38         ("images/earth.jpg");
39       try {
40         image = ImageIO.read(url);
41       } catch (IOException ex) {
42         ex.printStackTrace();
43       }
44     }
45
46     public void paintComponent(Graphics g) {
47       super.paintComponent(g);
48       Graphics2D g2 = (Graphics2D)g;
49       GradientPaint gp = new GradientPaint(100,50,
50         Color.white, 150, 50, Color.gray, true);
51       g2.setPaint(gp);
52       g2.fillRect(100, 40, 300, 20);
53       TexturePaint tp = new TexturePaint(image,
54         new Rectangle2D.Double(100, 100, image.getWidth(),
55           image.getHeight()));
56       g2.setPaint(tp);
57       Shape ellipse = new Ellipse2D.Double(100, 100, 300, 200);
58       g2.fill(ellipse);
59       GradientPaint paint = new GradientPaint(100, 300, Color.white,
60         400, 400, Color.black);
61       g2.setPaint(paint);
62       Font font = new Font("Serif", Font.BOLD, 144);
63       g2.setFont(font);
64       g2.drawString("Java", 100, 400);
65     }
66   }
```

This program draws three visual objects in the paintComponent method (line 46). Three different types of paints are used to draw the figures. The top rectangle is drawn with a cyclic gradient paint created by the following constructor:

```
new GradientPaint(100,50, Color.white, 150, 50, Color.gray, true);
```

The gradient paint specifies a gradual change of colors from the white at the point (100, 50) to the gray at the point (150, 50). The pattern is cyclically repeated. Because the two points have the same y-coordinates, you will see a vertical pattern.

FIGURE 3.3   Shapes drawn with cyclic gradient paint, texture paint, and acyclic gradient paint.

The ellipse is filled with a texture paint defined by an image.

```
new TexturePaint(image, new Rectangle2D.Double(100, 100, image.getWidth(),
   image.getHeight()));
```

The image is a `BufferedImage` object loaded from a file using the `read` method of the `ImageIO` class.

The text string is drawn with an acyclic gradient paint:

```
new GradientPaint(100,300, Color.white, 400, 400, Color.black);
```

The gradient paint changes the color from white to black as the location moves from (100, 300) to (400, 400). The paint is acyclic, and the color pattern does not repeat.

3.3 Strokes

A line rendered in computer graphics is not an ideal line with zero width. To be practically realizable, lines must have specific shapes. The attributes that define the fine details of such shapes are called *strokes*. A stroke may include attributes such as the width of lines, the dash style of lines, the cap shape at the ends of lines, and the style at the joins of lines.

Java 2D includes the interface `Stroke` to represent strokes. A concrete implementation of the `Stroke` interface is the class `BasicStroke`. `BasicStroke` provides settings for width, end style, join style, and dash. The constructors of `BasicStroke` are listed below.

BasicStroke constructors

```
BasicStroke()
BasicStroke(float width)
BasicStroke(float width, int cap, int join)
BasicStroke(float width, int cap, int join, float miterlimit)
BasicStroke(float width, int cap, int join, float miterlimit,
   float[] dash, float dashphase)
```

The parameter width defines the width of the drawing pen. The parameter cap sets the end cap style and can take values:

```
CAP_BUTT
CAP_ROUND
CAP_SQUARE
```

The parameter join defines the join style with values:

```
JOIN_BEVEL
JOIN_MITER
JOIN_ROUND
```

The miterlimit sets a limit for JOIN_MITER to prevent a very long join when the angle between the two lines is small.

The dash array defines a dash pattern by specifying the lengths of the ON/OFF segments. The dashphase defines the starting point in the dash pattern.

Graphics2D has the following method to set the current stroke:

void setStroke(Stroke s)

Listing 3.3 demonstrates the effects of graphics drawing with different stroke settings. Three end styles, three join styles, and a dash array with two different dash phase values are illustrated. A sample run of the program is shown in Figure 3.4.

Listing 3.3 TestStrokes.java

```
 1 package chapter3;
 2
 3 import java.awt.*;
 4 import java.awt.event.*;
 5 import javax.swing.*;
 6 import java.awt.geom.*;
 7
 8 public class TestStrokes extends JApplet {
 9   public static void main(String s[]) {
10     JFrame frame = new JFrame();
11     frame.setTitle("Different Strokes");
12     frame.setDefaultCloseOperation(JFrame.EXIT_ON_CLOSE);
13     JApplet applet = new TestStrokes();
14     applet.init();
15     frame.getContentPane().add(applet);
16     frame.pack();
17     frame.setVisible(true);
18   }
19
20   public void init() {
21     JPanel panel = new StrokePanel();
22     getContentPane().add(panel);
23   }
24 }
25
26 class StrokePanel extends JPanel {
27   public StrokePanel() {
28     setPreferredSize(new Dimension(700, 400));
```

```
29      setBackground(Color.white);
30    }
31
32    public void paintComponent(Graphics g) {
33      super.paintComponent(g);
34      Graphics2D g2 = (Graphics2D)g;
35      GeneralPath path = new GeneralPath(GeneralPath.WIND_EVEN_ODD);
36      path.moveTo(0,120);
37      path.lineTo(80,0);
38      path.lineTo(160,120);
39      Stroke stroke = new BasicStroke(20, BasicStroke.CAP_BUTT,
40        BasicStroke.JOIN_BEVEL);
41      g2.setStroke(stroke);
42      g2.translate(50,50);
43      g2.draw(path);
44      g2.drawString("JOIN_BEVEL",100,0);
45      g2.drawString("CAP_BUTT", 40, 120);
46      stroke = new BasicStroke(20, BasicStroke.CAP_ROUND,
47        BasicStroke.JOIN_MITER);
48      g2.setStroke(stroke);
49      g2.translate(200,0);
50      g2.draw(path);
51      g2.drawString("JOIN_MITER",100,0);
52      g2.drawString("CAP_ROUND", 40, 120);
53      stroke = new BasicStroke(20, BasicStroke.CAP_SQUARE,
54        BasicStroke.JOIN_ROUND);
55      g2.setStroke(stroke);
56      g2.translate(200,0);
57      g2.draw(path);
58      g2.drawString("JOIN_ROUND",100,0);
59      g2.drawString("CAP_SQUARE", 40, 120);
60      float[] dashArray = {60,20,20,40};
61      float dashPhase = 0;
62      stroke = new BasicStroke(10, BasicStroke.CAP_BUTT,
63        BasicStroke.JOIN_BEVEL, 0, dashArray, dashPhase);
64      g2.setStroke(stroke);
65      g2.translate(-400,200);
66      g2.drawLine(100, 50, 550, 50);
67      g2.drawString("dash=60 20 20 40", 250, 10);
68      g2.drawString("phase=0", 0, 50);
69      dashPhase = 20;
70      stroke = new BasicStroke(10, BasicStroke.CAP_BUTT,
71        BasicStroke.JOIN_BEVEL, 0, dashArray, dashPhase);
72      g2.setStroke(stroke);
73      g2.translate(0,50);
74      g2.drawLine(100, 50, 550, 50);
75      g2.drawString("phase=20", 0, 50);
76    }
77 }
```

A GeneralPath is constructed with two joining line segments (lines 34–37). The path is drawn three times on the top row. Three BasicStroke instances with different end styles and join styles are applied to the drawings. The width is set to 20 in order to show the details of stroke styles.

The bottom two rows display dashed lines. The dash array is defined to be {60, 20, 20, 40} (line 59), and the width is 10 for both strokes, but the dash phase values are 0 and 20, respectively. The shifting of the dash pattern due to nonzero dash phase is clearly visible.

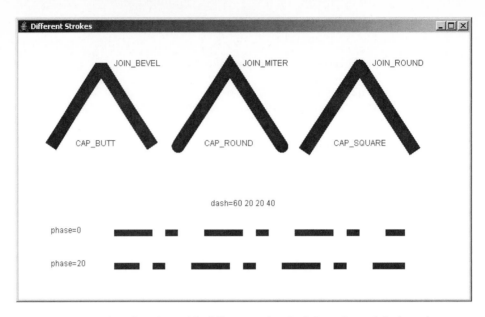

FIGURE 3.4   Examples of strokes with different end style, join style, and dash settings.

3.4 Affine Transformation

Geometric objects go through a transformation stage before being rendered. A general family of geometric transforms commonly used in computer graphics is called *affine transforms*. An affine transform preserves the parallel lines. The affine transforms that also preserve distances are called *isometries, Euclidean motions,* or *rigid motions*. The common affine transforms include:

isometry

- Translation

- Rotation

- Reflection

- Scaling

- Shearing

translation

A *translation* moves all points of the object by a fixed amount (see Figure 3.5). It is specified by the amounts of movements in the *x*- and *y*-directions. A translation is an isometry, since it does not change lengths and angles. Figure 3.5 shows a translation of $(3, -1)$. The object is moved 3 units to the right and 1 unit up.

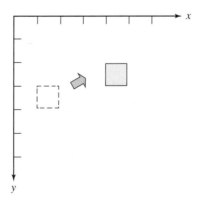

FIGURE 3.5   A translation of $(3, -1)$.

A *rotation* rotates the object about a point by an angle (see Figure 3.6). It is determined by   rotation
the point and the angle. A rotation is also an isometry, though it changes the orientation of the
shape. Figure 3.6 shows a rotation of 45 degrees about the origin.

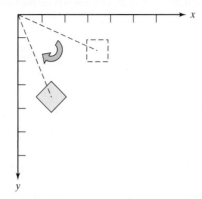

FIGURE 3.6   A rotation about the origin.

A *reflection* maps the object to its mirror image about a line (see Figure 3.7). It is deter-   reflection
mined by the line. A reflection is an isometry, though it changes the orientation of an angle.
Figure 3.7 shows a reflection about the 45 degree line between the *x*- and *y*-axes.

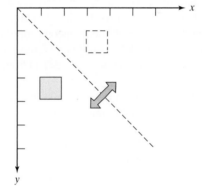

FIGURE 3.7   A reflection about the diagonal line.

A *scaling* resizes the object by certain fixed factors in the *x*- and *y*-directions (see Figure 3.8).   scaling
A scaling is not an isometry, because it will change distances and angles. However, it preserves
parallelism. Figure 3.8 shows a scaling by the factors (1.5, 2).

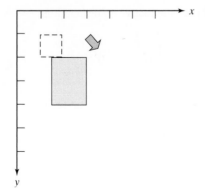

FIGURE 3.8   A scaling by factors (1.5, 2).

shearing

A *shearing* about a line shifts a point by an amount proportional to the signed distance to the line (see Figure 3.9). The movements of the points are parallel to the line. Points on the line are not moved. Points on the opposite sides of the line are moved in the opposite directions. A shearing is not an isometry, but it still preserves parallelism. Figure 3.9 shows a shearing by the factor 1.0 along the horizontal line $y = 2$.

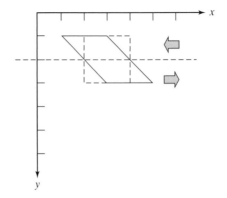

FIGURE 3.9   A shearing by factor 1 along the dashed horizontal line.

matrix

Mathematically a 2D affine transformation can be represented as a 3×3 *matrix*. An affine transform requires a 3×3 instead of a 2×2 matrix, because transforms such as translations are not linear in a 2D space. Using the concept of homogeneous coordinates, it is possible to treat all affine transforms in a linear framework by adding one dimension to the vector representation of the points. A more detailed discussion on matrices and homogeneous coordinates can be found in Appendix A.

For basic transforms, it is usually easy to find the transformation matrices directly. A rotation of an angle θ about the origin is represented as the matrix:

$$\begin{bmatrix} \cos\theta & \sin\theta & 0 \\ -\sin\theta & \cos\theta & 0 \\ 0 & 0 & 1 \end{bmatrix}$$

A translation by the amount (a, b) has the matrix:

$$\begin{bmatrix} 1 & 0 & a \\ 0 & 1 & b \\ 0 & 0 & 1 \end{bmatrix}$$

A scaling by the factors (α, β) has the matrix representation:

$$\begin{bmatrix} \alpha & 0 & 0 \\ 0 & \beta & 0 \\ 0 & 0 & 1 \end{bmatrix}$$

A reflection about the line $y = kx$ is represented by the matrix:

$$\begin{bmatrix} \dfrac{2}{1 + k^2} - 1 & \dfrac{2k}{1 + k^2} & 0 \\ \dfrac{2k}{1 + k^2} & \dfrac{2k^2}{1 + k^2} - 1 & 0 \\ 0 & 0 & 1 \end{bmatrix}$$

A shear along the *x*-axis by the factor *s* is given by the matrix:

$$\begin{bmatrix} 1 & s & 0 \\ 0 & 1 & 0 \\ 0 & 0 & 1 \end{bmatrix}$$

Java 2D uses the `AffineTransform` class to define an affine transform. It offers convenient methods to set up most of the basic affine transforms defined above. The following methods of `AffineTransform` directly set these named transforms,

```
void setToIdentity()
void setToRotation(double theta)
void setToRotation(double theta, double x, double y)
void setToScale(double sx, double sy)
void setToShear(double shx, double shy)
void setToTranslation(double tx, double ty)
```

One transform missing from this list of methods is the reflection. However, you may define a reflection by setting its matrix. The following matrix defines a reflection about the *y*-axis:

$$\begin{bmatrix} -1 & 0 & 0 \\ 0 & 1 & 0 \\ 0 & 0 & 1 \end{bmatrix}$$

The `AffineTransform` class has constructors and methods to directly set the first two rows of the transformation matrix.

```
AffineTransform(double m00, double m10, double m01,
   double m11, double m02, double m12)
AffineTransform(float m00, float m10, float m01,
   float m11, float m02, float m12)
AffineTransform(double[] flatmatrix)
AffineTransform(float[] flatmatrix)
void setTransform(double m00, double m10, double m01,
   double m11, double m02, double m12)
```

Because the last row of an affine transformation matrix is always (0 0 1), it is omitted in the parameter list. The reflection matrix defined above may be set by the following method:

```
transform.setTransform(-1, 0, 0, 1, 0, 0);
```

Because the `AffineTransform` class allows a scaling with negative factors, the reflection can also be defined as a special kind of scaling:

```
transform.setToScale(-1, 1);
```

An `AffineTransform` object can be used for both *object transformations* and viewing transformations. The following methods of the `AffineTransform` class apply the transform to geometric objects:

object transformations

```
Shape createTransformedShape(Shape shape)
void transform(double[] src, int srcOff, double[] dst,
   int dstOff, int numPts)
void transform(double[] src, int srcOff, float[] dst,
   int dstOff, int numPts)
void transform(float[] src, int srcOff, double[] dst,
   int dstOff, int numPts)
void transform(float[] src, int srcOff, float[] dst,
   int dstOff, int numPts)
Point2D transform(Point2D src, Point2D dst)
```

```
Point2D transform(Point2D[] src, int srcOff, Point2D[] dst,
  int dstOff, int numPts)
void deltaTransform(double[] src, int srcOff, double[] dst,
  int dstOff, int numPts)
Point2D deltaTransform(Point2D src, Point2D dst)
```

The createTransformedShape method transforms an entire shape. The transform methods perform the transformation on a set of points. The deltaTransform methods perform the transformation on a set of vectors.

A viewing transformation can be realized with the transformation in the Graphics2D object. The Graphics2D class has the following methods to manipulate its transformation:

```
void setTransform(AffineTransform tx)
void transform(AffineTransform tx)
```

The method setTransform replaces the current transformation with the given AffineTransform object. The method transform concatenates the current transformation with the given AffineTransform object on the right.

Listing 3.4 illustrates the effects of affine transforms through an interactive approach. A user is allowed to perform the transformations on a graphics object using the mouse. The affine transforms are selected with a menu that includes translation, rotation, scaling, shearing, and reflection. A sample run of the program is shown in Figure 3.10.

Listing 3.4 Transformations.java

```
1 package chapter3;
2
3 import java.awt.*;
4 import java.awt.geom.*;
5 import java.awt.event.*;
6 import java.util.*;
7 import javax.swing.*;
8
9 public class Transformations extends JApplet implements
10     ActionListener {
11   public static void main(String s[]) {
12     JFrame frame = new JFrame();
13     frame.setTitle("Affine Transforms");
14     frame.setDefaultCloseOperation(JFrame.EXIT_ON_CLOSE);
15     JApplet applet = new Transformations();
16     applet.init();
17     frame.getContentPane().add(applet);
18     frame.pack();
19     frame.setVisible(true);
20   }
21
22   TransformPanel panel = null;
23
24   public void init() {
25     JMenuBar mb = new JMenuBar();
26     setJMenuBar(mb);
27     JMenu menu = new JMenu("Transforms");
28     mb.add(menu);
29     JMenuItem mi = new JMenuItem("Translation");
30     mi.addActionListener(this);
31     menu.add(mi);
32     mi = new JMenuItem("Rotation");
33     mi.addActionListener(this);
34     menu.add(mi);
```

```
35      mi = new JMenuItem("Scaling");
36      mi.addActionListener(this);
37      menu.add(mi);
38      mi = new JMenuItem("Shearing");
39      mi.addActionListener(this);
40      menu.add(mi);
41      mi = new JMenuItem("Reflection");
42      mi.addActionListener(this);
43      menu.add(mi);
44
45      panel = new TransformPanel();
46      getContentPane().add(panel);
47    }
48
49    public void actionPerformed(ActionEvent ev) {
50      String command = ev.getActionCommand();
51      if ("Translation".equals(command)) {
52        panel.transformType = panel.TRANSLATION;
53      } else if ("Rotation".equals(command)) {
54        panel.transformType = panel.ROTATION;
55      } else if ("Scaling".equals(command)) {
56        panel.transformType = panel.SCALING;
57      } else if ("Shearing".equals(command)) {
58        panel.transformType = panel.SHEARING;
59      } else if ("Reflection".equals(command)) {
60        panel.transformType = panel.REFLECTION;
61      }
62    }
63 }
64
65 class TransformPanel extends Jpanel
66      implements MouseListener, MouseMotionListener {
67    static final int NONE = 0;
68    static final int TRANSLATION = 1;
69    static final int ROTATION = 2;
70    static final int SCALING = 3;
71    static final int SHEARING = 4;
72    static final int REFLECTION = 5;
73
74    int transformType = NONE;
75    Shape drawShape = null;
76    Shape tempShape = null;
77    Point p = null;
78    int x0 = 400;
79    int y0 = 300;
80
81    public TransformPanel() {
82      super();
83      setPreferredSize(new Dimension(800, 600));
84      setBackground(Color.white);
85      drawShape = new Rectangle(-50, -50, 100, 100);
86      addMouseListener(this);
87      addMouseMotionListener(this);
88    }
89
90    public void paintComponent(Graphics g) {
91      super.paintComponent(g);
92      Graphics2D g2 = (Graphics2D)g;
93      g2.translate(x0, y0);
94      g2.drawLine(-200, 0, 200, 0);
```

```
95      g2.drawLine(0, -200, 0, 200);
96      g2.draw(drawShape);
97    }
98
99    public void mouseClicked(MouseEvent ev) {
100   }
101
102   public void mouseEntered(MouseEvent ev) {
103   }
104
105   public void mouseExited(MouseEvent ev) {
106   }
107
108   public void mousePressed(MouseEvent ev) {
109     p = ev.getPoint();
110   }
111
112   public void mouseReleased(MouseEvent ev) {
113     Graphics g = getGraphics();
114     Point p1 = ev.getPoint();
115     AffineTransform tr = new AffineTransform();
116     switch (transformType) {
117       case TRANSLATION:
118         tr.setToTranslation(p1.x-p.x, p1.y-p.y);
119         break;
120       case ROTATION:
121         double a = Math.atan2(p1.y-y0, p1.x-x0) - Math.atan2
122           (p.y-y0, p.x-x0);
123         tr.setToRotation(a);
124         break;
125       case SCALING:
126         double sx = Math.abs((double)(p1.x-x0)/(p.x-x0));
127         double sy = Math.abs((double)(p1.y-y0)/(p.y-y0));
128         tr.setToScale(sx, sy);
129         break;
130       case SHEARING:
131         double shx = ((double)(p1.x-x0)/(p.x-x0))-1;
132         double shy = ((double)(p1.y-y0)/(p.y-y0))-1;
133         tr.setToShear(shx, shy);
134         break;
135       case REFLECTION:
136         tr.setTransform(-1, 0, 0, 1, 0, 0);
137         break;
138     }
139     drawShape = tr.createTransformedShape(drawShape);
140     repaint();
141   }
142
143   public void mouseMoved(MouseEvent ev) {
144   }
145
146   public void mouseDragged(MouseEvent ev) {
147     Point p1 = ev.getPoint();
148     AffineTransform tr = new AffineTransform();
149     switch (transformType) {
150       case TRANSLATION:
151         tr.setToTranslation(p1.x-p.x, p1.y-p.y);
152         break;
153       case ROTATION:
154         double a = Math.atan2(p1.y-y0, p1.x-x0) - Math.atan2
155           (p.y-y0, p.x-x0);
```

```
156            tr.setToRotation(a);
157            break;
158          case SCALING:
159            double sx = Math.abs((double)(p1.x-x0)/(p.x-x0));
160            double sy = Math.abs((double)(p1.y-y0)/(p.y-y0));
161            tr.setToScale(sx, sy);
162            break;
163          case SHEARING:
164            double shx = ((double)(p1.x-x0)/(p.x-x0))-1;
165            double shy = ((double)(p1.y-y0)/(p.y-y0))-1;
166            tr.setToShear(shx, shy);
167            break;
168          case REFLECTION:
169            tr.setTransform(-1, 0, 0, 1, 0, 0);
170            break;
171          }
172          Graphics2D g = (Graphics2D)getGraphics();
173          g.setXORMode(Color.white);
174          g.translate(x0, y0);
175          if (tempShape != null)
176            g.draw(tempShape);
177          tempShape = tr.createTransformedShape(drawShape);
178          g.draw(tempShape);
179        }
180 }
```

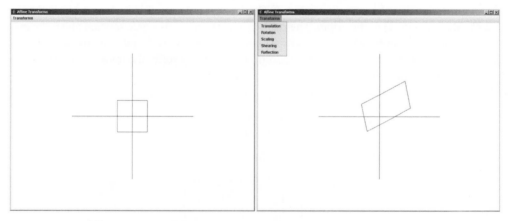

FIGURE 3.10   Affine transforms applied to a rectangle.

The program initially displays a set of axes for the coordinate system and a rectangle. A menu is defined to select an affine transformation from a list including translation, rotation, scaling, shearing, and reflection (lines 25–43). To perform a selected transformation, drag the mouse in the desired direction. The amount of mouse movement is used to determine the corresponding transformation on the object.

Two classes are defined in this program, Transformations and TransformPanel. The Transformations class is a subclass of JApplet and contains the menu for selecting the current affine transform. The class is also the action event handler to handle the menu selection actions and to set the appropriate values for the transformType variable in TransformPanel.

The TransformPanel class is a subclass of JPanel and it handles the mouse events. When a transform is requested, an AffineTransform object is set to the value determined by the selected transform type and the mouse movements. The transform is then applied to the shape as an object transformation using the method createTransformedShape (line 139).

The shape is initially a rectangle, but the transformations on the shape are accumulative, and the newly transformed shape becomes the current shape. The transformations do not affect other objects such as the axes, because they are object transformations applied locally to the shape only.

The rubber-banding technique is also used to provide visual clues while the user is dragging the mouse. The method is the same as that in Listing 2.3. The XOR drawing mode is applied to draw and erase the temporary shapes.

3.5 Compositions of Transformations

Transformations can be combined to form new transformations. For example, you may apply a translation followed by a rotation and followed by another translation. Any *composition* of affine transforms is still an affine transform. Any composition of rigid motions is still a rigid motion. Conversely, a transform may be decomposed into a series of (usually simpler) transforms.

The transformation matrix of a composite transform is the product of matrices of the individual transforms. For example, if M_1, M_2, M_3 are the matrices for the affine transforms T_1, T_2, T_3, respectively, then the matrix for the composition $T_1 \circ T_2 \circ T_3$ is $M_1 M_2 M_3$. Note that the operation of transformation composition is *noncommutative*, so the order of applying the transforms is significant. In our notation, the transforms in a composite transform are applied from right to left. For example, when the composite transform $T_1 \circ T_2 \circ T_3$ is applied to a point p, the order of the transforms is T_3, T_2, T_1:

$$(T_1 \circ T_2 \circ T_3)(p) = T_1(T_2(T_3(p)))$$

Composite transforms are useful in constructing complex transforms from simpler ones. If you need a rotation about the point (3, 4) by 30 degrees, you may first perform a translation to move the point (3, 4) to the origin. Then you may perform a 30-degree rotation about the origin. Finally you can translate the origin back to the point (3, 4). Combining the three transforms, you will obtain the required transform. In the matrix form, the translation that moves (3, 4) to the origin is given by:

$$\begin{bmatrix} 1 & 0 & -3 \\ 0 & 1 & -4 \\ 0 & 0 & 1 \end{bmatrix}$$

The rotation of 30 degrees about the origin is

$$\begin{bmatrix} \sqrt{3}/2 & -1/2 & 0 \\ 1/2 & \sqrt{3}/2 & 0 \\ 0 & 0 & 1 \end{bmatrix}$$

The second translation is

$$\begin{bmatrix} 1 & 0 & 3 \\ 0 & 1 & 4 \\ 0 & 0 & 1 \end{bmatrix}$$

Combing three transforms, the final rotation has the transformation matrix:

$$\begin{bmatrix} 1 & 0 & 3 \\ 0 & 1 & 4 \\ 0 & 0 & 1 \end{bmatrix} \begin{bmatrix} \sqrt{3}/2 & -1/2 & 0 \\ 1/2 & \sqrt{3}/2 & 0 \\ 0 & 0 & 1 \end{bmatrix} \begin{bmatrix} 1 & 0 & -3 \\ 0 & 1 & -4 \\ 0 & 0 & 1 \end{bmatrix}$$

In Java 2D, the AffineTransform class provides the following methods to support composite transforms:

```
void rotate(double theta)
void rotate(double theta, double x, double y)
```

```
void scale(double sx, double sy)
void shear(double shx, double shy)
void translate(double tx, double ty)
```

Unlike the setTo* methods introduced in the previous section, these methods do not clear the existing transforms in the current objects, but combine the current transforms with the newly specified transforms. The new transforms are appended to the right of the current ones. Instead of the simple transformations listed above, it is also possible to combine the current transform with another AffineTransform object:

```
void concatenate(AffineTransform tx)
void preConcatenate(AffineTransform tx)
```

The first method concatenates the other transform to the right of the current. The second concatenates the other transform to the left of the current.

Note that the order of transform composition is from left to right, and the methods above (except for preConcatenate) concatenate the transform from the right. If you create a composite transform by calling the above methods, the transforms are applied in the opposite order of your calling sequence. For example, consider the following code:

```
AffineTransform transform = new AffineTransform();
transform.rotate(Math.PI/3);
transform.scale(2, 0.3);
transform.translate(100, 200);
```

The first transform to be applied is the translation and the last transform is the rotation.

Listing 3.5 illustrates the use of transform composition. To rotate an ellipse about its center that is not located at the origin, you may first translate the object to the origin. Then rotate around the origin. Finally, translate the center of the rotated ellipse to its original point. (See Figure 3.11.)

Listing 3.5 Composition.java

```
1 package chapter3;
2
3 import javax.swing.*;
4 import java.awt.*;
5 import java.awt.geom.*;
6
7 public class Composition extends JApplet {
8   public static void main(String s[]) {
9     JFrame frame = new JFrame();
10     frame.setTitle("Transformation Composition");
11     frame.setDefaultCloseOperation(JFrame.EXIT_ON_CLOSE);
12     JApplet applet = new Composition();
13     applet.init();
14     frame.getContentPane().add(applet);
15     frame.pack();
16     frame.setVisible(true);
17   }
18
19   public void init() {
20     JPanel panel = new CompositionPanel();
21     getContentPane().add(panel);
22   }
23 }
24
25 class CompositionPanel extends JPanel {
26   public CompositionPanel() {
```

```
27      setPreferredSize(new Dimension(640, 480));
28      this.setBackground(Color.white);
29    }
30
31    public void paintComponent(Graphics g) {
32      super.paintComponent(g);
33      Graphics2D g2 = (Graphics2D)g;
34      g2.translate(100,100);
35      Shape e = new Ellipse2D.Double(300, 200, 200, 100);
36      g2.setColor(new Color(160,160,160));
37      g2.fill(e);
38      AffineTransform transform = new AffineTransform();
39      transform.translate(-400,-250);
40      e = transform.createTransformedShape(e);
41      g2.setColor(new Color(220,220,220));
42      g2.fill(e);
43      g2.setColor(Color.black);
44      g2.drawLine(0, 0, 150, 0);
45      g2.drawLine(0, 0, 0, 150);
46      transform.setToRotation(Math.PI / 6.0);
47      e = transform.createTransformedShape(e);
48      g2.setColor(new Color(100,100,100));
49      g2.draw(e);
50      transform.setToTranslation(400, 250);
51      e = transform.createTransformedShape(e);
52      g2.setColor(new Color(0,0,0));
53      g2.draw(e);
54    }
55  }
```

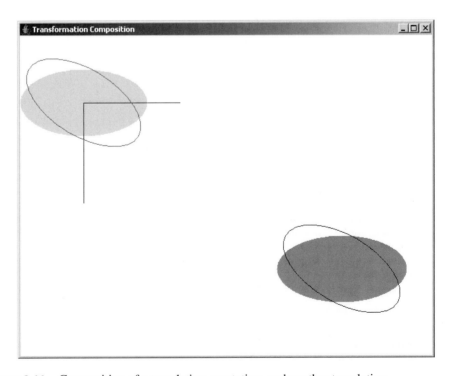

FIGURE 3.11 Composition of a translation, a rotation, and another translation.

The program shows a shape at different stages of a composite transformation. The shape is an ellipse originally constructed with a bounding rectangle (300, 200, 200, 100), so its center is located at (400, 250) (line 35). The objective is to rotate the ellipse by 30 degrees around the center (400, 250). To achieve this transformation, a composition of three transformations is used. First a translation of $(-400, -250)$ will move the ellipse so that it is centered at the origin. Then a rotation of 30 degrees about the origin is applied. The ellipse is rotated and still centered at the origin. Finally a translation of (400, 250) moves the ellipse back so that its center is again at (400, 250). The composition of the three transforms is the desired transformation.

To show all parts of the figures, a viewing transformation is used to move the origin of the world space from the upper left corner of the screen to (100, 100) (line 34). The x- and y-axes are drawn to show the new origin. The ellipse at each stage of the transformation is displayed with different gray levels. The rotated ellipses are not filled.

3.6 Transparency and Compositing Rules

Compositing rules determine the results of rendering overlapped objects. Various visual effects such as different degrees of transparency can be obtained by choosing compositing rules.

To establish the compositing rules, the concept of an *α-channel* is needed. The α-channel can be viewed as a part of color properties that specifies the transparency. An α-value is a number between 0.0 and 1.0, with 0.0 representing complete transparency and 1.0 complete opaqueness. α-channel

Given the source and destination pixel color and α-values, the *Porter–Duff* rules define the resulting color and α-values as linear combinations of the source and destination values: Porter–Duff rules

$$\alpha \cdot C = F_s \cdot \alpha_s \cdot C_s + F_d \cdot \alpha_d \cdot C_d$$
$$\alpha = F_s \cdot \alpha_s + F_d \cdot \alpha_d$$

Often the color components may have their α-values premultiplied to speed up the computation. The different choices of the two coefficients F_s and F_d in the equation define the different compositing rules. There are twelve Porter–Duff rules, having the coefficients shown in Table 3.1.

The Porter–Duff rules can be derived systematically from a *probabilistic model*. The α-value of a color can be interpreted as the probability that the color will be shown, or more concretely as the portion of the pixel area covered by the specified color. To combine the source and destination colors with their respective α-values, four different cases need to be considered: source color occurs only, destination color occurs only, both colors occur, and neither color occurs. Figure 3.12 illustrates the four events, which occur with probabilities $\alpha_s(1 - \alpha_d)$, $\alpha_d(1 - \alpha_s)$, $\alpha_s\alpha_d$, and $(1 - \alpha_s)(1 - \alpha_d)$, respectively. A compositing rule simply decides whether to retain a color when the color occurs. In the source-color-only event, a rule can choose to retain the source color or to omit it. In the destination-color-only event, the destination color can be selected or omitted. In the both-colors event, a rule can choose the source color, the destination color, or no color. In the neither-color event, a rule can only select no color. Therefore, the total number of rules based on this model is $2 \times 2 \times 3 \times 1 = 12$.   probabilistic model

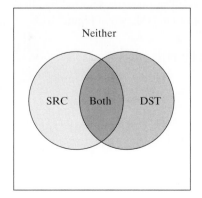

FIGURE 3.12   Four different events of color occurrence in the probabilistic model of compositing.

For example, the SrcOver rule chooses the source color in the event of source color only and the event of both colors. It chooses the destination color in the destination-color-only event. It must choose no color in the neither-color event. Consequently the probability of source color occurring in the combined color is $\alpha_s(1 - \alpha_d) + \alpha_s\alpha_d = \alpha_s$, and the probability of destination color is $\alpha_d(1 - \alpha_s)$. This leads to the selection of the coefficients $F_s = 1, F_d = (1 - \alpha_s)$, as shown in Table 3.1.

TABLE 3.1

Porter–Duff Rule	F_s	F_d
Clear	0	0
SrcOver	1	$1 - \alpha_s$
DstOver	$1 - \alpha_d$	1
SrcIn	α_d	0
DstIn	0	α_s
SrcOut	$1 - \alpha_d$	0
DstOut	0	$1 - \alpha_s$
Src	1	0
Dst	0	1
SrcAtop	α_d	$1 - \alpha_s$
DstAtop	$1 - \alpha_d$	α_s
Xor	$1 - \alpha_d$	$1 - \alpha_s$

Early versions of Java 2D supports the first eight rules in Table 3.1. Starting with J2SDK 1.4, all twelve rules are supported. The AlphaComposite class encapsulates the rules. An instance of AlphaComposite for a rule can be obtained by a static field of AlphaComposite with the name shown in Table 3.1. To apply a compositing rule to a Graphics2D object, simply call the setComposite method. For example, the following statement sets the compositing rule to SrcIn:

```
Graphics2D g2 = (Graphics2D)g;
g2.setComposite(AlphaComposite.SrcIn);
```

Listing 3.6 illustrates the application of the AlphaComposite class to implement Porter–Duff rules. This example shows several visual objects rendered with the twelve different Porter–Duff compositing rules. The rules are selected by clicking the mouse on the display panel. A sample run of the program is shown in Figure 3.13.

Listing 3.6 Compositing.java

```
1 package chapter3;
2
3 import java.awt.*;
4 import java.awt.event.*;
5 import java.awt.image.*;
6 import javax.swing.*;
7 import java.awt.font.*;
8 import java.awt.geom.*;
9 import java.io.*;
10 import java.net.URL;
```

```
11 import javax.imageio.*;
12
13 public class Compositing extends JApplet {
14   public static void main(String s[]) {
15     JFrame frame = new JFrame();
16     frame.setTitle("Compositing Rules");
17     frame.setDefaultCloseOperation(JFrame.EXIT_ON_CLOSE);
18     JApplet applet = new Compositing();
19     applet.init();
20     frame.getContentPane().add(applet);
21     frame.pack();
22     frame.setVisible(true);
23   }
24
25   public void init() {
26     JPanel panel = new CompositePanel();
27     getContentPane().add(panel);
28   }
29 }
30
31 class CompositePanel extends JPanel implements MouseListener {
32   BufferedImage image;
33   int[] rules = {AlphaComposite.CLEAR, AlphaComposite.SRC_OVER,
34     AlphaComposite.DST_OVER, AlphaComposite.SRC_IN,
35     AlphaComposite.DST_IN, AlphaComposite.SRC_OUT,
36     AlphaComposite.DST_OUT, AlphaComposite.SRC,
37     AlphaComposite.DST, AlphaComposite.SRC_ATOP,
38     AlphaComposite.DST_ATOP, AlphaComposite.XOR};
39   int ruleIndex = 0;
40
41   public CompositePanel() {
42     setPreferredSize(new Dimension(500, 400));
43     setBackground(Color.white);
44     URL url =
45       getClass().getClassLoader().getResource("images/earth.jpg");
46     try {
47       image = ImageIO.read(url);
48     } catch (IOException ex) {
49       ex.printStackTrace();
50     }
51     addMouseListener(this);
52   }
53
54   public void paintComponent(Graphics g) {
55     super.paintComponent(g);
56     Graphics2D g2 = (Graphics2D)g;
57     g2.drawImage(image, 100, 100, this);
58     AlphaComposite ac =
59       AlphaComposite.getInstance(rules[ruleIndex], 0.4f);
60     g2.setComposite(ac);
61     Shape ellipse = new Ellipse2D.Double(50, 50, 120, 120);
62     g2.setColor(Color.red);
63     g2.fill(ellipse);
64     g2.setColor(Color.orange);
65     Font font = new Font("Serif", Font.BOLD, 144);
66     g2.setFont(font);
67     g2.drawString("Java", 90, 240);
68   }
69
70   public void mouseClicked(MouseEvent e) {
```

```
71      ruleIndex++;
72      ruleIndex %= 12;
73      repaint();
74    }
75    public void mousePressed(MouseEvent e) {
76    }
77    public void mouseReleased(MouseEvent e) {
78    }
79    public void mouseEntered(MouseEvent e) {
80    }
81    public void mouseExited(MouseEvent e) {
82    }
83 }
```

FIGURE 3.13 Overlapping objects rendered with the SRC_OVER rule, one of the twelve compositing rules demonstrated in this example.

This program demonstrates the twelve Porter–Duff compositing rules. The class `Compositing` extends the `JPanel` class and implements the `MouseListener` interface.

The list of compositing rules is placed in an `int` array using the constants defined in the `AlphaComposite` class (line 33). The variable `ruleIndex` points to the current compositing rule. The `mouseClicked` method rotates the compositing rules by incrementing the `ruleIndex` modulo 12 (lines 71–72). A `repaint` method is called to refresh the display with the new compositing rule. Therefore, every time the panel is clicked, the panel switches to a different compositing rule.

In the constructor of `CompositePanel` an image is loaded from a disk file (line 41). In the `paintComponent` method (line 54), the image is drawn first. The composite rule is then set to the current compositing rule with an α-value of 0.4, using the static method `getInstance` of the `AlphaComposite` class. A red circle is drawn, and the string "Java" is also drawn with a white color.

The on-screen drawing surface does not maintain an α-channel itself, and the α-value of any pixel is always implicitly assumed to be 1.0. Consequently, as soon as an object is painted to the screen, the destination α becomes 1.0. Because of this behavior, some of the compositing rules do not produce interesting results. For example, the rules `DstOver`,

DstOut, DstATop, and Xor will always ignore the source, since the destination α is 1. One way to show more interesting effects is to draw on an off-screen image with an α-channel.

3.7 Clipping

A clipping path defines a region in which the objects will actually be visible. Graphics2D maintains a current clipping region. When an object is drawn, it is clipped against the clipping path. Portions of the object falling outside the clipping path will not be drawn. Any Shape object can be used for clipping. The following code segment sets an ellipse as the clipping shape and draws an image. Only the portion of the image which lies inside the ellipse will be visible.

```
Graphics2D g2 = (Graphics2D)g;
Shape ellipse = new Ellipse2D.Double(0, 0, 300,200);
g2.setClip(ellipse);
g2.drawImage(image, 0, 0, this);
```

Another method of Graphics2D that can change the clip region is:

```
void clip(Shape path)
```

This method will clip the current clipping region further with the specified shape.

Listing 3.7 demonstrates the use of clipping path. Another example will be given in the next section. In this simple example, a special shape is created and used as the clip path for a Graphics2D object. The subsequent drawings are clipped by the shape. A sample run of the program is shown in Figure 3.14.

Listing 3.7 TestClip.java

```
1 package chapter3;
2
3 import java.awt.*;
4 import javax.swing.*;
5 import java.awt.geom.*;
6
7 public class TestClip extends JApplet {
8   public static void main(String s[]) {
9     JFrame frame = new JFrame();
10     frame.setTitle("Clip Path");
11     frame.setDefaultCloseOperation(JFrame.EXIT_ON_CLOSE);
12     JApplet applet = new TestClip();
13     applet.init();
14     frame.getContentPane().add(applet);
15     frame.pack();
16     frame.setVisible(true);
17   }
18
19   public void init() {
20     JPanel panel = new ClipPanel();
21     getContentPane().add(panel);
22   }
23 }
24
25 class ClipPanel extends JPanel {
26   public ClipPanel() {
27     setPreferredSize(new Dimension(500, 500));
```

```
28      setBackground(Color.white);
29  }
30
31  public void paintComponent(Graphics g) {
32    super.paintComponent(g);
33    Graphics2D g2 = (Graphics2D)g;
34    GeneralPath path = new GeneralPath(GeneralPath.WIND_EVEN_ODD);
35    path.moveTo(100,200);
36    path.quadTo(250, 50, 400, 200);
37    path.lineTo(400,400);
38    path.quadTo(250,250,100,400);
39    path.closePath();
40    g2.clip(path);
41    g2.setColor(new Color(200,200,200));
42    g2.fill(path);
43    g2.setColor(Color.black);
44    g2.setFont(new Font("Serif", Font.BOLD, 60));
45    g2.drawString("Clip Path Demo",80,200);
46    g2.drawOval(50, 250, 400, 100);
47  }
48 }
```

FIGURE 3.14 The gray area is enclosed by the clip path. Graphical drawings are clipped by the clip path.

The program has a structure similar to that in the previous examples. An applet with a main method is created to form an application as well as an applet. The ClipPanel class extends JPanel to form the drawing canvas of the program.

In the paintComponent method (line 31), a GeneralPath object with two line segments and two quad curves is constructed. The closed path is set as the current clip path of the Graphics2D object by calling the method clip. The path is used again with the fill method to show the clip area in a light gray shade. Two graphics objects are drawn: a text string "Clip

Path Demo" and an ellipse. The effect of clipping is obvious. Only the portions of the objects lying inside the clip path are visible.

3.8 Text and Font

In computer graphics, text represents a special type of geometric objects. A text string can be compactly represented by a sequence of characters with standard coding schemes, such as ASCII and Unicode. The actual rendering shapes of the characters are determined by predefined fonts. The geometry describing the shape of a character is known as a *glyph*. A font is a collection of glyphs for an entire alphabet.

glyph

 Note

The relation between characters and glyphs is not always one to one. Sometimes one glyph may correspond to several characters, as in the case of a *ligature*. A ligature occurs in some fonts when certain two-character sequences are rendered in a combined fashion. A common ligature is "fi" in some fonts, as shown in Figure 3.15.

ligature

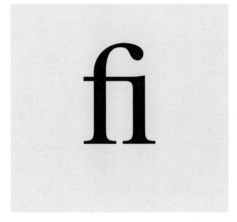

Figure 3.15   A common ligature.

Java 2D offers a rich set of font and text-manipulation features. The most common high-level usages of texts involve creating a `Font` object and calling the methods `setFont` and `drawString` in `Graphics2D`.

A `Font` object can be created with the following constructor:

```
Font(String name, int style, int size)
```

The `name` parameter specifies the font face name or the logical name of a font. A font is identified by the font face name (also called font name), such as "Times New Roman." The fonts available in an environment are platform dependent. Java also supports *logical fonts* to improve portability. A logical font is mapped to a physical font on a particular system. For example, the logical font "SansSerif" is mapped to "Arial" in a Windows system. Five logical font families are always supported in Java.

logical font

```
Serif
SansSerif
Monospaced
Dialog
DialogInput
```

font style

The `style` parameter is a mask to select *font styles*. Three bit masks are defined in `Font`, and they may be combined with the bitwise OR "|" operator:

```
PLAIN
ITALIC
BOLD
```

The `size` parameter specifies the point size of the font.
A `Font` object can be selected in a `Graphics2D` object with the method:

```
void setFont(Font font)
```

The font will take effect for subsequent calls to methods for drawing texts:

```
void drawString(String s, int x, int y)
void drawString(String s, float x, float y)
```

derived fonts

In addition to applying existing fonts in the system, it is also possible to derive new fonts from existing ones by modifying certain attributes. The following methods in the `Font` class generate *derived fonts*:

```
Font deriveFont(int style)
Font deriveFont(float size)
Font deriveFont(int style, float size)
Font deriveFont(AffineTransform tx)
Font deriveFont(int style, AffineTransform tx)
Font deriveFont(Map attributes)
```

font metrics

The point size of a font provides only a crude indication of the size of the text drawn. The actual size of the rendered text usually depends on the characters in the string. In tasks such as centering the text, it may be useful to know the actual geometric size of the text. *Font metrics* are measurements of rendered texts with a specific font. The following methods of `Font` provide font metric information:

```
Rectangle2D getStringBounds(String str, FontRenderContext frc)
LineMetrics getLineMetrics(String str, FontRenderContext frc)
```

Because the precise metrics also depend on the options of rendering, the above methods use a `FontRenderContext` object to obtain the additional information. The `FontRenderContext` object can be obtained through a method in `Graphics2D`:

```
FontRenderContext getFontRenderContext()
```

baseline
ascent
descent
leading

The `getStringBounds` method returns a bounding rectangle for the string. The `getLineMetrics` method returns a `LineMetrics` object that contains more detailed line metric data. The *baseline* is the reference line of a font. The *ascent* is the amount that the font extends above the baseline. The *descent* is the amount extending below the baseline. The *leading* is the extra space between the two lines. The following methods of `LineMetrics` retrieve the metrics:

```
float getAscent()
float getDescent()
float getLeading()
```

Listing 3.8 demonstrates font-related features. The derived fonts and font metrics are demonstrated in this example. Three lines of text are displayed. The first line is drawn with a derived font that is slanted to the left. The second line shows the bounding rectangle together with the text. The third line displays the baseline, ascent, descent, and leading for the text. A sample run of the program is shown in Figure 3.16.

Listing 3.8 `FontFun.java`

```java
1 package chapter3;
2
3 import java.awt.*;
4 import javax.swing.*;
5 import java.awt.geom.*;
6 import java.awt.font.*;
7
8 public class FontFun extends JApplet {
9   public static void main(String s[]) {
10     JFrame frame = new JFrame();
11     frame.setTitle("Fonts");
12     frame.setDefaultCloseOperation(JFrame.EXIT_ON_CLOSE);
13     JApplet applet = new FontFun();
14     applet.init();
15     frame.getContentPane().add(applet);
16     frame.pack();
17     frame.setVisible(true);
18   }
19
20   public void init() {
21     JPanel panel = new FontPanel();
22     getContentPane().add(panel);
23   }
24 }
25
26 class FontPanel extends JPanel {
27   public FontPanel() {
28     setPreferredSize(new Dimension(640, 480));
29     setBackground(Color.white);
30   }
31
32   public void paintComponent(Graphics g) {
33     super.paintComponent(g);
34     Graphics2D g2 = (Graphics2D)g;
35     Font font = new Font("Serif", Font.BOLD, 36);
36     AffineTransform tx = new AffineTransform();
37     tx.shear(0.5, 0);
38     g2.setFont(font.deriveFont(tx));
39     g2.drawString("Derived font", 100, 100);
40
41     g2.setFont(font);
42     FontRenderContext frc = g2.getFontRenderContext();
43     String str = "String bounds";
44     Rectangle2D bounds = font.getStringBounds(str, frc);
45     g2.translate(100, 200);
46     g2.draw(bounds);
47     g2.drawString(str, 0, 0);
48
49     str = "Baseline, ascent, descent, leading";
50     g2.translate(0,100);
51     int w = (int)font.getStringBounds(str, frc).getWidth();
52     LineMetrics lm = font.getLineMetrics(str, frc);
53     g2.drawLine(0, 0, w, 0);
54     int y = -(int)lm.getAscent();
55     g2.drawLine(0, y, w, y);
56     y = (int)lm.getDescent();
57     g2.drawLine(0, y, w, y);
58     y = (int)(lm.getDescent()+lm.getLeading());
```

```
59      g2.drawLine(0, y, w, y);
60
61      g2.drawString(str,0,0);
62   }
63 }
```

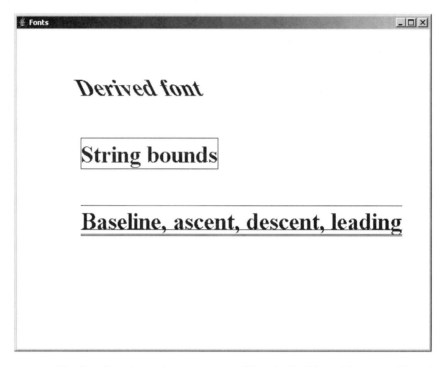

FIGURE 3.16 The first line shows the text drawn with a derived font. The second line draws the bounding rectangle. The third line shows the baseline and the amounts of ascent, descent, and leading.

Three lines of text are drawn in the paintComponent method of the FontPanel class (line 32). An AffineTransform object is created to perform a horizontal shear. A new font is derived from a 36-point bold Serif font with the transformation. The derived font is slanted to the left because of the shear transform. The text string "Derived font" is drawn using the derived font.

A FontRenderContext object is obtained from the Graphics2D object (line 42). It is used in the method getStringBounds of the Font object to retrieve the bounding rectangle for the string "String bounds." The string is drawn together with the bounding rectangle.

The third line of text is the string "Baseline, ascent, descent, leading." The baseline of the text is drawn based on the width of the text. The LineMetrics object for the string is retrieved through the method getLineMetrics (line 52). The values for ascent, descent, and leading are obtained from the object, and the lines corresponding to the values are drawn relative to the baseline.

glyphs Java 2D also provides advanced functions for font-related operations. In particular, *glyphs* of characters in a font can be retrieved as Shape objects. This enables sophisticated processing and application of the glyphs to achieve varieties of visual effects. The class Font represents a font. The class GlyphVector encapsulates the geometric description of a sequence of glyphs. To obtain a `GlyphVector` object for a string corresponding to a font, use the following method of `Font`:

```
GlyphVector createGlyphVector(FontRenderContext frc, String str)
```

The `FontRenderContext` object defines certain measurements necessary to render a font. It can be obtained from a `Graphics2D` object by calling the method `getFontRenderContext`. Once the `GlyphVector` object is created, the `Shape` object corresponding to the glyphs can be obtained by the following methods of `GlyphVector`:

```
Shape getOutline()
Shape getOutline(float x, float y)
```

The *x*- and *y*-parameters specify the starting location for rendering the glyphs. The returned `Shape` object corresponding to the glyphs can be processed and rendered like other `Shape` objects. Listing 3.9 illustrates the use of glyphs as a clipping shape. The program shows the technique of retrieving the glyphs of a text string as a `Shape` and use it as a clip path. A sample run of the program is shown in Figure 3.17.

Listing 3.9 `GlyphClip.java`

```java
1 package chapter3;
2
3 import java.awt.*;
4 import java.awt.event.*;
5 import javax.swing.*;
6 import java.awt.font.*;
7 import java.awt.geom.*;
8
9 public class GlyphClip extends JApplet {
10    public static void main(String s[]) {
11       JFrame frame = new JFrame();
12       frame.setTitle("Glyph and Clip");
13       frame.setDefaultCloseOperation(JFrame.EXIT_ON_CLOSE);
14       JApplet applet = new GlyphClip();
15       applet.init();
16       frame.getContentPane().add(applet);
17       frame.pack();
18       frame.setVisible(true);
19    }
20
21    public void init() {
22       JPanel panel = new GlyphPanel();
23       getContentPane().add(panel);
24    }
25 }
26
27 class GlyphPanel extends JPanel {
28    public GlyphPanel() {
29       setPreferredSize(new Dimension(500, 400));
30       setBackground(Color.white);
31    }
32    public void paintComponent(Graphics g) {
33       super.paintComponent(g);
34       Graphics2D g2 = (Graphics2D)g;
35       Font font = new Font("Serif", Font.BOLD, 144);
36       FontRenderContext frc = g2.getFontRenderContext();
37       GlyphVector gv = font.createGlyphVector(frc, "Java");
38       Shape glyph = gv.getOutline(100,200);
39       g2.setClip(glyph);
```

```
40     g2.setColor(Color.red);
41     for (int i = 0; i < 2000; i++) {
42       Shape shape = new Ellipse2D.Double(Math.random()*500,
43         Math.random()*400, 30, 20);
44       g2.draw(shape);
45     }
46   }
47 }
```

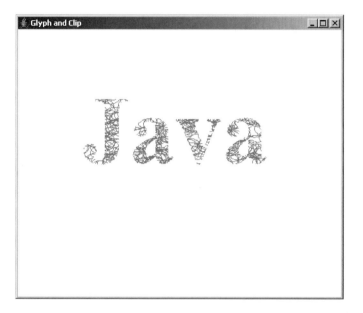

FIGURE 3.17   Two thousand random ellipses drawn on a clipping shape defined by the glyphs of the string "Java."

The program displays the special figure in a subclass of JPanel. The paintComponent method is overridden to perform the drawing. A bold, 144-point "Serif" font object is created. A FontRenderContext object is obtained through the Graphics2D object.

The glyphs from the string "Java" are obtained from the font and font render context and they are kept in a GlyphVector variable (line 37). The glyph vector is converted to a Shape object through the getOutline methods (line 38). The shape is then set to the clipping path of the rendering by calling the method setClip of the Graphics2D object.

Two thousand ellipses with random locations are drawn on the panel (lines 41–44). Only the portions inside the glyphs are visible. The text string is never explicitly drawn, but the drawing inside the clipping region clearly highlights the outline of the glyphs.

KEY CLASSES AND METHODS

- **java.awt.Color** A class encapsulating colors.
- **java.awt.Paint** An interface for Color, GradientPaint, and TexturePaint classes.
- **java.awt.GradientPaint** A class for gradient paint.
- **java.awt.TexturePaint** A class for texture paint.
- **java.awt.Stroke** An interface for stroke definitions.
- **java.awt.BasicStroke** An implementation of common strokes.
- **java.awt.geom.AffineTransform** A class encapsulating 2D affine transformations.
- **javax.awt.AlphaComposite** A class for alpha compositing rules.

- `java.awt.Graphics2D.setClip(Shape)` A method to set the current clipping path.
- `java.awt.Graphics2D.setComposite(AlphaComposite)` A method to set the current compositing rule.
- `java.awt.Font` A class encapsulating a font.
- `java.awt.font.LineMetrics` A class for font metrics.
- `java.awt.font.GlyphVector` A class encapsulating a series of glyphs for a text string.

KEY TERMS

color space A system to specify colors with numerical values.

affine transformation A transform that preserves parallelism.

transform composition A combining of two or more transforms to form a new one.

Porter–Duff rules A method to create new geometric shapes by using set operations such as union and intersection on the areas of existing shapes.

clip path A shape defining a region to constrain rendering.

font A design of the shapes for a set of characters.

font metrics Measurements of the rendered text such as ascent, descent, and leading.

glyph A geometric description of a text string in a specific font.

ligature A special combination of multiple characters forming one glyph.

CHAPTER SUMMARY

- In this chapter we discuss several important aspects of 2D graphics rendering and their implementations in Java 2D. Main topics covered include colors, strokes, transformations, clip paths, compositing rules, and fonts.

- Colors and, more generally, paints are attributes that can be applied to visual objects when they are rendered. Java 2D provides three types of paints using the classes `Color`, `GradientPaint`, and `TexturePaint`.

- Strokes define the details of line styles. Java 2D contains the `Stroke` interface for general stroke definitions and a specific implementation `BasicStroke` for commonly used stroke attributes such as line width, end cap style, and join style.

- Affine transformations are a large set of transformations commonly used for object transformations and viewing transformations. An affine transform preserves parallelism. Basic affine transforms include translation, rotation, scaling, shearing, and reflection. Java 2D provides comprehensive supports for affine transformation. The class `AffineTransform` defines an affine transform and contains many constructors and methods to specify the transform. The method `createTransformedShape` provides a way to perform the object transformations. An `AffineTransform` object can also be used by a `Graphics2D` object to set the viewing transformation. Transformations can be combined to form more complex ones.

- The Porter–Duff rules define the compositing operations with an α-channel. The twelve compositing rules specify various ways that colors from the source and the destination may be combined. Interesting visual effects such as transparency can be achieved by using appropriate compositing rules.

- Clipping is a rendering facility that can produce complex visual effects. In Java 2D, a clipping path for a Graphics2D object can be set to any Shape object.

- Text strings are useful visual objects. A font defines the glyphs of all the characters. Besides the usual rendering of texts with the drawString method, glyphs for a text string can be retrieved as a Shape object that can be directly manipulated as other Shape objects.

Review Questions

3.1   What is the wavelength range of visible color?

3.2   In an RGB system, if each of the red, green, and blue components is represented by a byte, how many different colors can be formed?

3.3   Construct a Color object equivalent to the following using float parameters:

```
new Color(255, 0, 128);
```

3.4   Construct a Color object equivalent to the following using int parameters:

```
new Color(0f, 0.5f, 0.125f);
```

3.5   Construct a cyclic gradient paint that varies from the color red at the point $(0, 0)$ to the color blue at the point $(100, 100)$.

3.6   Construct an acyclic gradient paint that varies from the color yellow at the point $(100, 0)$ to the color green at the point $(800, 600)$.

3.7   What is the transformation matrix of the rotation of 45 degrees about the origin?

3.8   Construct an AffineTransform object for a general reflection about a line through the origin.

3.9   Is it possible to transform an ellipse to a circle using affine transformations? Rigid motions?

3.10   Is it possible to transform a trapezoid to a square using affine transformations? Rigid motions?

3.11   What is the inverse of the rotation of angle $\pi/3$ about the origin?

3.12   Find an affine transform that maps x-axis to y-axis and y-axis to x-axis.

3.13   Find the transformation matrix for the rotation θ of angle about the point (a, b).

3.14   Find the transformation matrix for the reflection about the line $y = 2x$.

3.15   Find the transformation matrix for the reflection about the line $y = 2x - 1$.

3.16   Find the transformation matrix for the shear along the y-axis with the factor 0.5.

3.17   Find the transformation matrix for the composition of a rotation of $\pi/3$ about the origin and a reflection about the line $y = 2x$.

3.18   If the RGB and α-values of a source pixel are 0.5, 0.0, 0.8, and 0.4, and the values for the destination pixel are 0.2, 1.0, 0.5, and 0.6, find the RGB and α-values of the composite using the SrcOver rule.

3.19   Repeat the previous problem using the DstOver rule.

3.20   Repeat the previous problem using the Src rule.

3.21   Repeat the previous problem using the Dst rule.

3.22   Repeat the previous problem using the SrcOut rule.

3.23   Repeat the previous problem using the DstOut rule.

3.24 If the destination color has an α-value 1.0, which compositing rules will not be affected by the source color?

3.25 Write a code segment that draws the outline of a text string in the `paintComponent` method.

PROGRAMMING EXERCISES

3.1 Write a Java program to draw a series of rectangles filled with colors defined by the constants in the `Color` class.

3.2 Write a Java program to draw the shape in Figure 3.18 filled with green color.

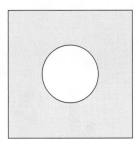

FIGURE 3.18   A filled shape.

3.3 Write a Java program to display the shape in Figure 3.18 using a gradient paint with colors varying vertically from black to white.

3.4 Write a Java program to display the shape in Figure 3.18 using a texture paint.

3.5 Swing contains the class `JColorChooser` that allows interactive color selections through a dialog box. Modify the program in Exercise 3.2 to allow the selection of drawing colors using the `JColorChooser` class.

3.6 Draw a pentagon with a stroke of width 20 and a round join style.

3.7 Apply an `AffineTransform` to a `Rectangle2D` object to create a shape of a square centered at the origin and rotated by 45 degrees. Display the shape.

3.8 Write a Java program to display the mirror image of the string "Hello 2D." (*Hint*: Use a reflection.)

3.9 Write a Java program that performs a reflection about the line $y = 2x$. Draw an original rectangle of size 100 by 50 at (0, 100). Apply the reflection to the rectangle and draw the transformed shape in a different color.

3.10 Write a Java program to draw a circular text around the point (300, 300) as shown in Figure 3.19. (*Hint*: Use the `drawString` method for each character and apply a rotation repeatedly.)

3.11 Write a Java program that performs a scaling of factor 3 along the line $y = x$. Draw an original square of size 100 centered at (0, 0). Apply the scaling to the square and draw the transformed shape in a different color. (*Hint*: Decompose the transform into a standard scaling and two rotations.)

3.12 Use the shape in Figure 3.18 as the clip path and draw the text string "Java 2D" with a large font.

FIGURE 3.19   A circular text.

3.13   Write a program to load an image and display only an elliptic region of the image. Use a clipping path to achieve this effect.

3.14   Derive a font by a rotation of 45 degrees and draw a string with the font.

3.15   Use the glyph shapes and area geometry to display the outline of the superimposed glyphs of the characters "N" and "Y."

CHAPTER 4

2D GRAPHICS: ADVANCED TOPICS (OPTIONAL)

Objectives

- To understand B-spline curves.
- To construct custom shape primitives.
- To apply basic image-processing techniques.
- To create fractal images.
- To create 2D animation.
- To perform graphics printing.

4.1 Introduction

In the preceding chapters we discussed basic concepts and techniques of 2D computer graphics systems and the Java 2D package. In this chapter we discuss more advanced topics of 2D graphics and several features not directly available in Java 2D.

Spline curves are important modeling tools for computer graphics. A B-spline curve is a smooth curve defined by a sequence of control points. Java 2D does not offer direct support for drawing spline curves. However, a B-spline curve can be converted to a series of Bézier curves. This technique is introduced in this chapter.

Java 2D offers a set of common graphics primitives through a class hierarchy implementing the `Shape` interface. You may also implement your own primitives. This chapter will introduce a technique to implement a custom `Shape` class so it can be passed to a `Graphics2D` object for rendering just like the built-in classes.

Even though image processing is a separate subject, it is closely related to computer graphics. Images are useful objects in computer graphics, as you have seen from the example of texture paints. The image-handling features of Java 2D will be introduced in this chapter. Java 2D offers an image model much improved over the previous AWT model. Images can be conveniently loaded, processed, and saved through the support of Java APIs. It is also possible to create an image from scratch. Fractal images will be used to illustrate image creation in Java.

Animation creates an images series of a dynamic scene. It adds a new dimension of time to the graphics system. Java's multithreading capability provides crucial support for implementing animation in a Java 2D program. Several examples of animation including cellular automata will be introduced.

Printing is a part of many graphics applications. Java 2D offers convenient printing support that is highly consistent with the drawing on screen. We will discuss the implementation of graphics printing in Java.

4.2 Spline Curves

A *spline curve* consists of a sequence of smoothly joined polynomial curves. A type of spline curves widely used in CAD and other computer graphics applications is the *B-spline curves*. In particular, the *cubic B-spline curves* are the most commonly used B-spline curves in computer graphics.

general Bézier curve

The mathematical definitions of Bézier curves can be given in parametric equations. A *general Bézier curve* of degree n with control points $p_0, p_1, \ldots, p_n$ is given by

$$s(t) = \sum_{i=0}^{n} p_i B_{n,i}(t)$$

Bernstein basis

where $B_{n,i}(t)$ is known as the Bernstein polynomials or *Bernstein basis*.

$$B_{n,i}(t) = \binom{n}{i} t^i (1 - t)^{n-i}$$

The quadratic curves and cubic curves supported in Java 2D are special cases of Bézier curves with degrees $n = 2$ and $n = 3$, respectively. Their equations may be expressed as follows:

$$s_2(t) = (1 - t)^2 p_0 + 2t(1 - t)p_1 + t^2 p_2$$

$$s_3(t) = (1 - t)^3 p_0 + 3t(1 - t)^2 p_1 + 3t^2(1 - t)p_2 + t^3 p_3$$

A *B-spline curve* is defined by a sequence of control points. Like a Bézier curve, the B-spline curve follows the general directions of the control points, but it need not always interpolate the points. A general B-spline curve of degree k is defined by $n + 1$ control points $p_0, p_1, \ldots, p_n$ and a sequence of $n + k + 2$ parameter values known as the knots: $t_0 \leq t_1 \leq \cdots \leq t_{n+k+1}$. The parametric equation of the B-spline curve can be expressed as:

B-spline curve

$$p(t) = \sum_{i=0}^{n} p_i N_{k,i}(t)$$

The curve is defined only over the interval $[t_3, t_{n+k-2})$. The functions $N_{k,i}(t)$ are called the *normalized B-spline blending functions* and may be defined recursively:

normalized B-spline blending function

$$N_{0,i}(t) = \begin{cases} 1, & t \in [t_i, t_{i+1}) \\ 0, & \text{otherwise} \end{cases}$$

$$N_{k,i}(t) = \frac{t - t_i}{t_{i+k} - t_i} N_{k-1,i}(t) + \frac{t_{i+k+1} - t}{t_{i+k+1} - t_{i+1}} N_{k-1,i+1}(t)$$

The B-spline curves are versatile modeling tools. The smoothness and continuity of a curve can be controlled by the knots. When the differences between adjacent knot values are a constant: $t_{i+1} - t_i = c$, the curve is called a *uniform B-spline*. In general, the curve is a nonuniform B-spline. The B-spline formulation can also be applied to homogeneous coordinates with the same blending functions for the w components. When the control points are represented in homogeneous coordinates, the curve is known as a *rational B-spline curve*. The most general family of B-spline curves is therefore called the NURBS (nonuniform rational B-spline).

uniform B-spline

rational B-spline curve

In this section, we consider only a special type of cubic B-spline curves that are direct extensions of cubic Bézier curves. The knots are chosen to be uniformly distributed, except that the first four and the last four knots are set to be equal:

$$t_0 = t_1 = t_2 = t_3$$
$$t_{i+1} - t_i = 1, \qquad i = 3, 4, \ldots, n$$
$$t_{n+1} = t_{n+2} = t_{n+3} = t_{n+4}$$

The duplicated knots will cause the first and the last control points to be interpolated by the curve, similar to a Bézier curve. In fact, if $n = 3$, a cubic B-spline of this type is exactly a regular cubic Bézier curve:

$$N_{0,0}(t) = N_{0,1}(t) = N_{0,2}(t) = 0, \qquad N_{0,3}(t) = \chi_{0,1},$$
$$N_{0,4}(t) = N_{0,5}(t) = N_{0,6}(t) = 0$$

$$N_{1,0}(t) = N_{1,1}(t) = 0, \qquad N_{1,2}(t) = (1 - t)\chi_{0,1}, \qquad N_{1,3}(t) = t\chi_{0,1},$$
$$N_{1,4}(t) = N_{1,5}(t) = 0$$

$$N_{2,0}(t) = 0, \qquad N_{2,1}(t) = (1 - t)^2 \chi_{0,1}, \qquad N_{2,2}(t) = 2t(1 - t)\,\chi_{0,1},$$
$$N_{2,3}(t) = t^2 \chi_{0,1}, \qquad N_{2,4}(t) = 0$$

$$N_{3,0}(t) = (1 - t)^3 \chi_{0,1}, \qquad N_{3,1}(t) = 3t(1 - t)^2 \chi_{0,1}, \qquad N_{3,2}(t) = 3t^2(1 - t)\,\chi_{0,1},$$
$$N_{3,3}(t) = t^3 \chi_{0,1}$$

$\chi_{0,1}$ denotes the characteristic function of the interval $[0,1)$. The parametric equation of the B-spline is:

$$p(t) = (1-t)^3 p_0 + 3t(1-t)^2 p_1 + 3t^2(1-t)p_2 + t^3 p_3, \qquad t \in [0, 1)$$

This is exactly the equation for a cubic Bézier curve. When $n > 3$, the B-spline has more than one polynomial segment and more control points than a Bézier curve.

Java 2D does not directly support B-spline curves. However, a cubic B-spline curve may be converted to a series of cubic Bézier curves that can be rendered with the cubic Bézier curve support of Java 2D. Let $p_0, p_1, \ldots, p_n$ be the control points of a B-spline. Each segment of the B-spline can be converted to a cubic Bézier curve. Let the control points of a Bézier curve be b_0, b_1, b_2, b_3. Then, except for the first and the last segment, the conversion is given by the following formula:

$$b_{-1} = (p_{i-1} + 2p_i)/3$$

$$b_1 = (2p_i + p_{i+1})/3$$

$$b_0 = (b_{-1} + b_1)/2$$

$$b_2 = (p_i + 2p_{i+1})/3$$

$$b_4 = (2p_{i+1} + p_{i+2})/3$$

$$b_3 = (b_2 + b_4)/2$$

The first and the last segments are handled differently, because the first and last control points are the endpoints of the curve. The conversion of the first segment is given by the following formula:

$$b_0 = p_0$$

$$b_1 = p_1$$

$$b_2 = (p_1 + p_2)/2$$

$$b_4 = (2p_2 + p_3)/3$$

$$b_3 = (b_2 + b_4)/2$$

The last segment uses the following formula:

$$b_{-1} = (2p_{n-2} + p_{n-3})/3$$

$$b_1 = (p_{n-1} + p_{n-2})/2$$

$$b_0 = (b_{-1} + b_1)/2$$

$$b_2 = p_{n-1}$$

$$b_3 = p_n$$

Listing 4.1 illustrates the conversion and rendering of a B-spline curve. In this example a B-spline curve is converted to a series of cubic Bézier curves which is represented with a `GeneralPath`. A simple drawing program is implemented to allow the user to input control points with a mouse. The B-spline and its control points are displayed. A sample run of the program is shown in Figure 4.1.

Listing 4.1 `BSpline.java`

```
 1 package chapter4;
 2
 3 import java.awt.*;
 4 import java.awt.geom.*;
 5 import java.awt.event.*;
 6 import java.util.*;
 7 import javax.swing.*;
 8
 9 public class BSpline extends JApplet {
10   public static void main(String s[]) {
11     JFrame frame = new JFrame();
12     frame.setTitle("B-Spline");
13     frame.setDefaultCloseOperation(JFrame.EXIT_ON_CLOSE);
14     JApplet applet = new BSpline();
15     applet.init();
16     frame.getContentPane().add(applet);
17     frame.pack();
18     frame.setVisible(true);
19   }
20
21   public void init() {
22     JPanel panel = new BSplinePanel();
23     getContentPane().add(panel);
24   }
25 }
26
27 class BSplinePanel extends Jpanel
28     implements MouseListener, MouseMotionListener {
29   Vector points = null;
30   boolean completed = true;
31
32   public BSplinePanel() {
33     setPreferredSize(new Dimension(640, 480));
34     setBackground(Color.white);
35     addMouseListener(this);
36     addMouseMotionListener(this);
37     points = new Vector();
38   }
39
40   public void paintComponent(Graphics g) {
41     super.paintComponent(g);
42     Graphics2D g2 = (Graphics2D)g;
43     Point p0 = null;
44     Point p1 = null;
45     Point p2 = null;
46     Point p3 = null;
47     float x1, y1, x2, y2, x3, y3, x4, y4;
48     Iterator it = points.iterator();
49     if (it.hasNext()) {
50       p1 = (Point)(it.next());
51     }
52     while (it.hasNext()) {
53       p2 = (Point)(it.next());
54       g2.drawLine(p1.x, p1.y, p2.x, p2.y);
55       p1 = p2;
56     }
57
58     GeneralPath spline = new GeneralPath();
```

```
59        int n = points.size();
60        if (n == 0) return;
61        p1 = (Point)points.get(0);
62        spline.moveTo(p1.x, p1.y);
63        g2.drawRect(p1.x-3, p1.y-3, 6, 6);
64        p1 = (Point)points.get(1);
65        p2 = (Point)points.get(2);
66        p3 = (Point)points.get(3);
67        x1 = p1.x;
68        y1 = p1.y;
69        x2 = (p1.x + p2.x)/2.0f;
70        y2 = (p1.y + p2.y)/2.0f;
71        x4 = (2.0f*p2.x+p3.x)/3.0f;
72        y4 = (2.0f*p2.y+p3.y)/3.0f;
73        x3 = (x2+x4)/2.0f;
74        y3 = (y2+y4)/2.0f;
75        spline.curveTo(x1, y1, x2, y2, x3, y3);
76        g2.drawRect((int)x1-3, (int)y1-3, 6, 6);
77        g2.drawRect((int)x2-3, (int)y2-3, 6, 6);
78        g2.drawRect((int)x3-3, (int)y3-3, 6, 6);
79        for (int i = 2; i < n - 4; i++) {
80          p1 = p2;
81          p2 = p3;
82          p3 = (Point)points.get(i+2);
83          x1 = x4;
84          y1 = y4;
85          x2 = (p1.x+2.0f*p2.x)/3.0f;
86          y2 = (p1.y+2.0f*p2.y)/3.0f;
87          x4 = (2.0f*p2.x+p3.x)/3.0f;
88          y4 = (2.0f*p2.y+p3.y)/3.0f;
89          x3 = (x2+x4)/2.0f;
90          y3 = (y2+y4)/2.0f;
91          spline.curveTo(x1,y1,x2,y2,x3,y3);
92          g2.drawRect((int)x1-3, (int)y1-3, 6, 6);
93          g2.drawRect((int)x2-3, (int)y2-3, 6, 6);
94          g2.drawRect((int)x3-3, (int)y3-3, 6, 6);
95        }
96        p1 = p2;
97        p2 = p3;
98        p3 = (Point)points.get(n-2);
99        x1 = x4;
100       y1 = y4;
101       x2 = (p1.x+2.0f*p2.x)/3.0f;
102       y2 = (p1.y+2.0f*p2.y)/3.0f;
103       x4 = (p2.x+p3.x)/2.0f;
104       y4 = (p2.y+p3.y)/2.0f;
105       x3 = (x2+x4)/2.0f;
106       y3 = (y2+y4)/2.0f;
107       spline.curveTo(x1,y1,x2,y2,x3,y3);
108       g2.drawRect((int)x1-3, (int)y1-3, 6, 6);
109       g2.drawRect((int)x2-3, (int)y2-3, 6, 6);
110       g2.drawRect((int)x3-3, (int)y3-3, 6, 6);
111       p2 = p3;
112       p3 = (Point)points.get(n-1);
113       x1 = x4;
114       y1 = y4;
115       x2 = p2.x;
116       y2 = p2.y;
117       x3 = p3.x;
118       y3 = p3.y;
```

```
119      spline.curveTo(x1,y1,x2,y2,x3,y3);
120      g2.drawRect((int)x1-3, (int)y1-3, 6, 6);
121      g2.drawRect((int)x2-3, (int)y2-3, 6, 6);
122      g2.drawRect((int)x3-3, (int)y3-3, 6, 6);
123      g2.draw(spline);
124    }
125    public void mouseClicked(MouseEvent ev) {
126    }
127
128    public void mouseEntered(MouseEvent ev) {
129    }
130
131    public void mouseExited(MouseEvent ev) {
132    }
133
134    public void mousePressed(MouseEvent ev) {
135      Graphics g = getGraphics();
136      if (completed) {
137        points.clear();
138        completed = false;
139      }
140      if (ev.getClickCount() == 1) {
141        Point p =ev.getPoint();
142        points.add(p);
143        g.fillOval(p.x-3, p.y-3, 6, 6);
144      }
145    }
146
147    public void mouseReleased(MouseEvent ev) {
148      if (ev.getClickCount() > 1) {
149        completed = true;
150        repaint();
151      }
152    }
153
154    public void mouseMoved(MouseEvent ev) {
155    }
156
157    public void mouseDragged(MouseEvent ev) {
158    }
159 }
```

Note

The B-spline curve conversion shown above is only for the simple type of B-spline discussed in this section. More general types of B-splines with nonuniform *knots* can also be converted to Bézier curves.

The class `BSplinePanel` extends the `JPanel` class and provides a panel for drawing a B-spline curve. A vector `points` (line 29) is defined to hold the input control points of the B-spline curve. Mouse events are processed to enter the control points. A single mouse click defines one control point, and the point is shown as a small filled circle. A double click defines the last control point of the curve and completes the control-point entry. For simplicity only one B-spline curve is defined at any moment. After all control points are entered, the B-spline curve is drawn by the `paintComponent` method.

The conversion from the B-spline curve to Bézier curves is performed in the `paint-Component` method. The conversion uses the formulas introduced in this section. A `General-Path` object is used to hold the converted sequence of Bézier curves (line 58). The path is

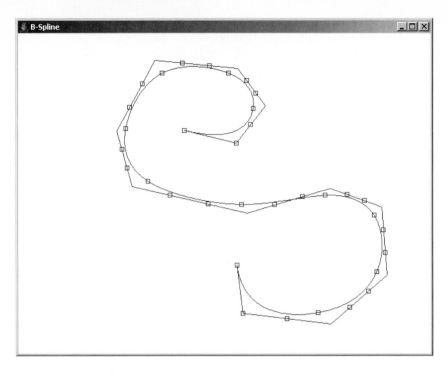

FIGURE 4.1 A B-spline curve rendered with a series of Bézier curves. The polygon represents the control points of the B-spline curve, and the small squares indicate the locations of control points of the Bézier curves.

drawn after all curve segments are converted. The control polygon formed by the control points is shown as a series of line segments (line 54). The small squares in the display show the Bézier control points after the conversion.

4.3 Custom Primitives

As seen from the previous chapters, geometric primitives defined as classes in the Shape family can be transformed and rendered in a uniform fashion. It is also possible to define your own primitives that behave just like the built-in classes. The key is the Shape interface that has ten abstract methods.

Shape methods

```
public boolean contains(Rectangle2D rect)
public boolean contains(Point2D point)
public boolean contains(double x, double y)
public boolean contains(double x, double y, double w, double h)
public Rectangle getBounds()
public Rectangle2D getBounds2D()
public PathIterator getPathIterator(AffineTransform at)
public PathIterator getPathIterator(AffineTransform at, double flatness)
public boolean intersects(Rectangle2D rect)
public boolean intersects(double x, double y, double w, double h)
```

The contains methods test whether the given point or rectangle is entirely contained in the shape. The intersects methods test for intersections. The getBounds and getBounds2D methods return the bounding rectangle of the shape. The getPathIterator method returns a PathIterator object that describes the path using the basic drawing segments.

Extending the class GeneralPath may appear to be an easy way to implement a custom primitive, because GeneralPath provides an implementation for all the Shape methods and it allows all the basic drawing functions for a path. Unfortunately, this approach is not possible,

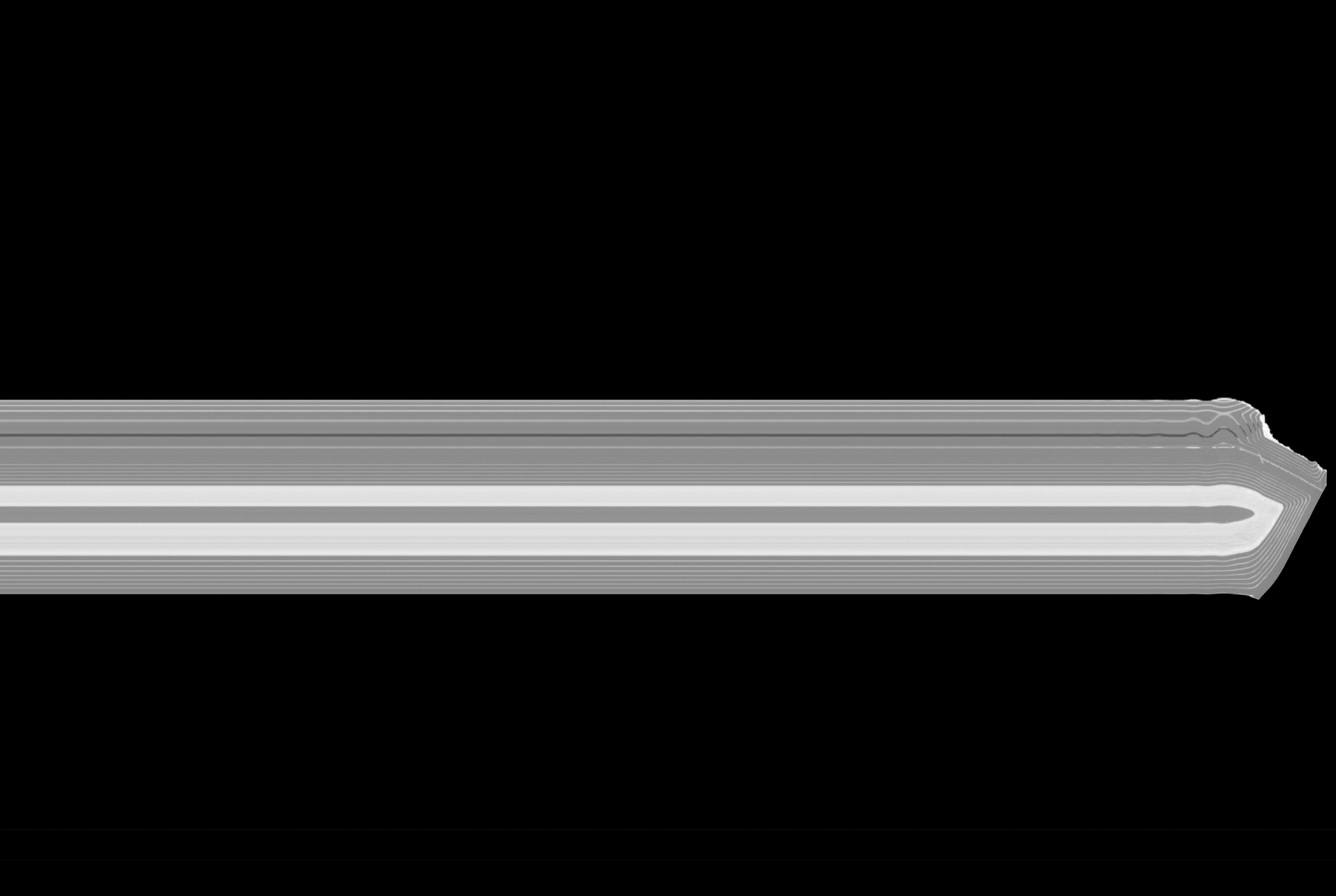

```
119       spline.curveTo(x1,y1,x2,y2,x3,y3);
120       g2.drawRect((int)x1-3, (int)y1-3, 6, 6);
121       g2.drawRect((int)x2-3, (int)y2-3, 6, 6);
122       g2.drawRect((int)x3-3, (int)y3-3, 6, 6);
123       g2.draw(spline);
124     }
125     public void mouseClicked(MouseEvent ev) {
126     }
127
128     public void mouseEntered(MouseEvent ev) {
129     }
130
131     public void mouseExited(MouseEvent ev) {
132     }
133
134     public void mousePressed(MouseEvent ev) {
135       Graphics g = getGraphics();
136       if (completed) {
137         points.clear();
138         completed = false;
139       }
140       if (ev.getClickCount() == 1) {
141         Point p =ev.getPoint();
142         points.add(p);
143         g.fillOval(p.x-3, p.y-3, 6, 6);
144       }
145     }
146
147     public void mouseReleased(MouseEvent ev) {
148       if (ev.getClickCount() > 1) {
149         completed = true;
150         repaint();
151       }
152     }
153
154     public void mouseMoved(MouseEvent ev) {
155     }
156
157     public void mouseDragged(MouseEvent ev) {
158     }
159 }
```

> **Note**
> The B-spline curve conversion shown above is only for the simple type of B-spline discussed in
> this section. More general types of B-splines with nonuniform *knots* can also be converted to
> Bézier curves.

The class BSplinePanel extends the JPanel class and provides a panel for drawing a
B-spline curve. A vector points (line 29) is defined to hold the input control points of the
B-spline curve. Mouse events are processed to enter the control points. A single mouse click
defines one control point, and the point is shown as a small filled circle. A double click
defines the last control point of the curve and completes the control-point entry. For simplicity
only one B-spline curve is defined at any moment. After all control points are entered, the
B-spline curve is drawn by the paintComponent method.

The conversion from the B-spline curve to Bézier curves is performed in the paint-
Component method. The conversion uses the formulas introduced in this section. A General-
Path object is used to hold the converted sequence of Bézier curves (line 58). The path is

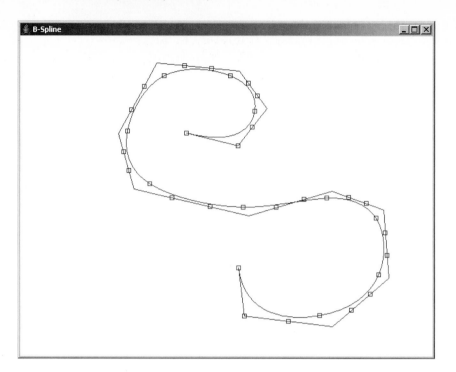

FIGURE 4.1 A B-spline curve rendered with a series of Bézier curves. The polygon represents the control points of the B-spline curve, and the small squares indicate the locations of control points of the Bézier curves.

drawn after all curve segments are converted. The control polygon formed by the control points is shown as a series of line segments (line 54). The small squares in the display show the Bézier control points after the conversion.

4.3 Custom Primitives

As seen from the previous chapters, geometric primitives defined as classes in the Shape family can be transformed and rendered in a uniform fashion. It is also possible to define your own primitives that behave just like the built-in classes. The key is the Shape interface that has ten abstract methods.

Shape methods

```
public boolean contains(Rectangle2D rect)
public boolean contains(Point2D point)
public boolean contains(double x, double y)
public boolean contains(double x, double y, double w, double h)
public Rectangle getBounds()
public Rectangle2D getBounds2D()
public PathIterator getPathIterator(AffineTransform at)
public PathIterator getPathIterator(AffineTransform at, double flatness)
public boolean intersects(Rectangle2D rect)
public boolean intersects(double x, double y, double w, double h)
```

The contains methods test whether the given point or rectangle is entirely contained in the shape. The intersects methods test for intersections. The getBounds and getBounds2D methods return the bounding rectangle of the shape. The getPathIterator method returns a PathIterator object that describes the path using the basic drawing segments.

Extending the class GeneralPath may appear to be an easy way to implement a custom primitive, because GeneralPath provides an implementation for all the Shape methods and it allows all the basic drawing functions for a path. Unfortunately, this approach is not possible, because GeneralPath is declared as a final class, so further extension is not allowed. You may still take advantage of the GeneralPath implementation by wrapping it in your class. The required methods declared in the Shape interface can be implemented simply by invoking the corresponding methods in GeneralPath. Listing 4.2 illustrates this approach. This example shows the construction of a custom Shape by wrapping a GeneralPath object. A heart shape is constructed with two cubic curves (Figure 4.2).

Listing 4.2 Heart.java

```
1 package chapter4;
2
3 import java.awt.*;
4 import java.awt.geom.*;
5 import javax.swing.*;
6
7 public class Heart implements Shape {
8    GeneralPath path;
9
10   public Heart(float x, float y, float w, float h) {
11     path = new GeneralPath();
12     float x0 = x + 0.5f*w;
13     float y0 = y + 0.3f*h;
14     float x1 = x + 0.1f*w;
15     float y1 = y + 0f * h;
16     float x2 = x + 0f * w;
17     float y2 = y + 0.6f * h;
18     float x3 = x + 0.5f * w;
19     float y3 = y + 0.9f * h;
20     float x4 = x + 1f * w;
21     float y4 = y + 0.6f * h;
22     float x5 = x + 0.9f * w;
23     float y5 = y + 0f * h;
24     path.moveTo(x0, y0);
25     path.curveTo(x1, y1, x2, y2, x3, y3);
26     path.curveTo(x4, y4, x5, y5, x0, y0);
27   }
28
29   public boolean contains(Rectangle2D rect) {
30     return path.contains(rect);
31   }
32
33   public boolean contains(Point2D point) {
34     return path.contains(point);
35   }
36
37   public boolean contains(double x, double y) {
38     return path.contains(x, y);
39   }
40
41   public boolean contains(double x, double y, double w, double h) {
42     return path.contains(x, y, w, h);
43   }
44
45   public Rectangle getBounds() {
46     return path.getBounds();
47   }
48
49   public Rectangle2D getBounds2D() {
50     return path.getBounds2D();
51   }
```

```
52
53   public PathIterator getPathIterator(AffineTransform at) {
54     return path.getPathIterator(at);
55   }
56
57   public PathIterator getPathIterator(AffineTransform at,
58   double flatness) {
59     return path.getPathIterator(at, flatness);
60   }
61
62   public boolean intersects(Rectangle2D rect) {
63     return path.intersects(rect);
64   }
65
66   public boolean intersects(double x, double y, double w, double h) {
67     return path.intersects(x, y, w, h);
68   }
69 }
```

Figure 4.2 A heart-shape primitive constructed with a GeneralPath object using two symmetric cubic curves.

The class Heart implements the Shape interface so it can be used like other geometric primitives in the Shape family. A GeneralPath object is created and stored in the variable path (line 8). The ten required methods in Shape are implemented by calling the corresponding methods in path.

The Heart class defines a constructor that specifies a bounding rectangle for the shape. In the constructor (line 10), the GeneralPath object is constructed and the path of the heart shape is defined. Two symmetric cubic curves define the left and right sides of the heart. The control points are calculated and the curves are constructed with the curveTo method of the GeneralPath class. The closed path forms a region that can be filled.

In Listing 4.3, an applet `TestHeart` with a `main` method is included to test the `Heart` primitive. An anonymous subclass of `JPanel` is created and added to the applet. The panel overrides the `paintComponent` method to paint a `Heart` object filled with the color red.

Listing 4.3 `TestHeart.java`

```
1 package chapter4;
2
3 import java.awt.*;
4 import java.awt.event.*;
5 import javax.swing.*;
6 import java.awt.geom.*;
7
8 public class TestHeart extends JApplet {
9   public static void main(String s[]) {
10     JFrame frame = new JFrame();
11     frame.setTitle("Heart");
12     frame.setDefaultCloseOperation(JFrame.EXIT_ON_CLOSE);
13     JApplet applet = new TestHeart();
14     applet.init();
15     frame.getContentPane().add(applet);
16     frame.pack();
17     frame.setVisible(true);
18   }
19
20   public void init() {
21     JPanel panel = new JPanel() {
22       public void paintComponent(Graphics g) {
23         super.paintComponent(g);
24         Heart h = new Heart(0,0,500,500);
25         g.setColor(Color.red);
26         ((Graphics2D)g).fill(h);
27       }
28     };
29     panel.setBackground(Color.white);
30     panel.setPreferredSize(new Dimension(500,500));
31     getContentPane().add(panel);
32   }
33 }
```

4.4 Image Processing

A digital image is a raster representation of a 2D picture and is defined by an array of point values called *pixels*. Each pixel value represents the color, gray level, and other attributes of the corresponding point. Even though image processing is a separate specialized subject, it does have a close connection with computer graphics. Images are useful objects in graphics rendering. The output of graphics rendering is typically an image. Java 2D offers powerful image-processing facilities.

In AWT, an image is represented by the `Image` class. AWT uses a "*push*" *model* for images. The data for the image is not necessarily available when the `Image` is created. An object implementing the `ImageProducer` interface is a producer, and an object implementing the `ImageConsumer` is a consumer. A producer acts as the source of the image, and a consumer receives the data from a producer. Between a producer and a consumer, there can also be a chain of filters that implement both `ImageProducer` and `ImageConsumer`. A producer pushes the data to the consumer in an asynchronous fashion. The consumer cannot request data. The data transfer process can be monitored by an instance of `ImageObserver`. This

push model

model is designed with the idea of loading images over a network. However, the "push" model is not very convenient for image processing.

immediate model

Java 2D introduces a new "*immediate*" model. The new image class `BufferedImage` is used to represent an image with an immediately available data store. A `BufferedImage` contains a `Raster` and a `ColorModel`. A `Raster` represents pixel values in numerical forms and a `ColorModel` specifies the mapping between the numerical values in the `Raster` and the actual colors.

> ### Note
> Java Advanced Image (JAI) is an optional package that offers even more advanced and comprehensive image-processing capabilities. JAI is not covered in this book.

A typical image-processing cycle is illustrated in Figure 4.3.

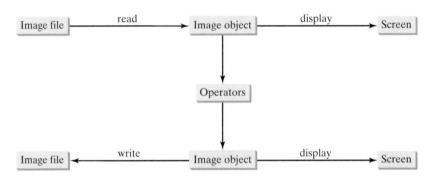

FIGURE 4.3   An image-processing system.

The source image is usually given as a file in one of many image-file formats. An image object is created in the Java program to represent an image. The external image file needs to be read into the image object. The image may be displayed in a device such as a screen or a printer. The next step is to process the image through one or more image-processing operators. The result is another image object. The processed image can be displayed and written to an external image file.

A Java 2D image processing program usually uses `BufferedImage` to represent images. A `BufferedImage` object can be created using one of its constructors. For example, the following statement creates a blank buffered image:

```
BufferedImage bi = new BufferedImage(300, 400, BufferedImage.
    TYPE_INT_RGB);
```

To draw on a `BufferedImage`, we need to obtain a `Graphics2D` object:

```
Graphics2D g2 = (Graphics2D)(bi.createGraphics());
```

With the `Graphics2D` object `g2` you may perform all types of graphics renderings on the `BufferedImage`, just like drawing to the screen.

In J2SDK versions prior to 1.4, standard Java 2D does not directly support loading a `BufferedImage` from external files or network sources. To load an image from a file to an `Image` object, we can use the old AWT facilities, as follows:

```
Image image = Toolkit.getDefaultToolkit().getImage(imageFileName);
```

In an applet, instead of using the `Toolkit` object, an image can be loaded from a network URL using the `getImage(url)` method of the `Applet` class.

In the push model, the images are loaded asynchronously. The above call will return immediately without waiting for the image loading to complete. If we want to be sure that the image is fully loaded, we may use a `MediaTracker` object to force the loading and wait for its completion.

```
MediaTracker tracker = new MediaTracker(new Component() {});
tracker.addImage(image, 0);
try {
    tracker.waitForID(0);
} catch (InterruptedException ex) {
}
```

The constructor of `MediaTracker` requires a parameter of class `Component`. Because `Component` is an abstract class, it is not possible to create a generic instance of `Component`. Instead, the above code uses an instance of an anonymous subclass `new Component() {}` as the parameter.

The above procedure only reads an external image to an `Image` object `image`. To convert the externally loaded `Image` to a `BufferedImage`, you may use the `Graphics2D` object `g2` associated with the `BufferedImage` object `bi`. The `drawImage` method of `g2` allows the drawing of the `image` into `bi`.

```
g2.drawImage(image, 0, 0, new Component() {});
```

If the size of `bi` is the same as that of `image`, the effect of the above method call is a conversion from an `Image` object to a `BufferedImage` object. The last parameter of the `drawImage` method is an `ImageObserver`. Because the class `Component` implements the `ImageObserver` interface, the anonymous subclass can be used as a generic parameter. You may also use `null` for the image observer. If this code is in a GUI application, then a GUI component such a `JPanel` object is usually used as the image observer. The purpose of the `ImageObserver` object is to support asynchronous loading of images in the original AWT push model. The default implementation for `ImageObserver` in `Component` is to repaint the component so that the image can be drawn incrementally as the image data arrives.

J2SDK 1.4 includes the new ImageIO API that offers support for direct reading and writing of `BufferedImage`. To read an image from a file, you can simply call the following static method:

```
BufferedImage bi = ImageIO.read(file);
```

Once we have a `BufferedImage` object properly set up, we may apply image-processing operations to it. Java 2D contains a set of classes for image operations. These classes implement the `BufferedImageOp` interface, as shown in Figure 4.4.

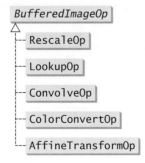

FIGURE 4.4 `BufferedImageOp` is a common interface for buffered image operations.

`RescaleOp` performs pixel-by-pixel rescaling of the pixel values by a linear function. A pixel value is multiplied by a scaling factor and then an offset is added. If $f(x, y)$ and $g(x, y)$ represent the pixel values of the images before and after the processing, then the rescale operation can be written as

$$g(x, y) = af(x, y) + b$$

`ColorConvertOp` performs pixel-by-pixel conversions of colors. The operation can be specified with color spaces.

`LookupOp` performs pixel-by-pixel conversions of pixel values based on lookup tables. The operator can be expressed as

$$g(x, y) = T(f(x, y))$$

`AffineTransformOp` performs affine transforms on the image. The operator does not change the value of a pixel, but it moves the pixel to a different location. The `AffineTransform` object is used to set the transform. The formula for affine transform operator is

$$g(x, y) = f(A(x, y))$$

`ConvolveOp` defines convolution operators. A convolution is a linear transformation. If an image is represented mathematically by a function $f(x, y)$, the convolution can be expressed as

$$g(x, y) = \iint K(x - u, y - v)f(u, v) \, du \, dv$$

where K is a fixed function known as the *kernel*. The property of the convolution is determined by the kernel. By choosing appropriate kernels, you may achieve various effects on the images, such as smoothing, sharpening, and edge detection.

For digital images, the integrals become summations.

$$g(x, y) = \sum_i \sum_j K(x - i, y - j)f(i, j)$$

The indices i, j run through the entire image. To improve the efficiency, the kernel is often chosen to have a finite support; that is, K is 0 except for a neighborhood of the origin. For example, $K(i, j)$ may have only nine nonzero values when $-1 \le i, j \le 1$. In this case, the above convolution formula becomes

$$g(x, y) = \sum_{i=x-1}^{x+1} \sum_{j=y-1}^{y+1} K(x - i, y - j)f(i, j)$$

At each point, only the nine pixels around the point need to be considered for the calculation.

In Java 2D, to apply an operator to a `BufferedImage`, simply call the `filter` method of the operator object.

```
dst = op.filter(src, null);
```

A `BufferedImage` can be displayed using the `drawImage` method of the `Graphics` object. For example,

```
public void paintComponent(Graphics g) {
    super.paintComponent(g);
    g.drawImage(bi, 0, 0, this);
}
```

This code segment may be inside a component such as `JPanel`. The `drawImage` call paints the `BufferedImage` starting at the location $(0, 0)$.

Prior to J2SDK 1.4, Java 2D does not contain direct support for exporting a `BufferedImage` to an external file or encoding the image in a standard image file format. The new `ImageIO` class offers the static `write` method to store the image to an external file:

```
ImageIO.write(bi, "png", file);
```

The first parameter is the BufferedImage object to be saved. The second parameter is a string specifying the file format. The third object is a File object representing the external file to write.

Listing 4.4 shows a complete image-processing program with I/O, processing, and display. A user may load an image from a disk file, perform several common image-processing operations, and save the processed image to a disk file. A sample run of the program is shown in Figure 4.5.

Listing 4.4 `ImageProcessing.java`

```
 1 package chapter4;
 2
 3 import java.awt.*;
 4 import java.awt.event.*;
 5 import java.awt.image.*;
 6 import java.awt.color.*;
 7 import java.awt.geom.*;
 8 import java.io.*;
 9 import javax.swing.*;
10 import javax.imageio.*;
11
12 public class ImageProcessing extends JFrame implements
13   ActionListener {
14   public static void main(String[] args) {
15     JFrame frame = new ImageProcessing();
16     frame.setDefaultCloseOperation(JFrame.EXIT_ON_CLOSE);
17     frame.pack();
18     frame.setVisible(true);
19   }
20
21   ImagePanel imageSrc, imageDst;
22   JFileChooser fc = new JFileChooser();
23
24   public ImageProcessing() {
25     JMenuBar mb = new JMenuBar();
26     setJMenuBar(mb);
27
28     JMenu menu = new JMenu("File");
29     JMenuItem mi = new JMenuItem("Open image");
30     mi.addActionListener(this);
31     menu.add(mi);
32     mi = new JMenuItem("Open image (awt)");
33     mi.addActionListener(this);
34     menu.add(mi);
35     mi = new JMenuItem("Save image");
36     mi.addActionListener(this);
37     menu.add(mi);
38     menu.addSeparator();
39     mi = new JMenuItem("Exit");
40     mi.addActionListener(this);
41     menu.add(mi);
42     mb.add(menu);
43
44     menu = new JMenu("Process");
45     mi = new JMenuItem("Copy");
46     mi.addActionListener(this);
47     menu.add(mi);
48     mi = new JMenuItem("Smooth");
49     mi.addActionListener(this);
50     menu.add(mi);
51     mi = new JMenuItem("Sharpen");
52     mi.addActionListener(this);
53     menu.add(mi);
```

```
54        mi = new JMenuItem("Edge");
55        mi.addActionListener(this);
56        menu.add(mi);
57        mi = new JMenuItem("Rescale");
58        mi.addActionListener(this);
59        menu.add(mi);
60        mi = new JMenuItem("Rotate");
61        mi.addActionListener(this);
62        menu.add(mi);
63        mi = new JMenuItem("Gray scale");
64        mi.addActionListener(this);
65        menu.add(mi);
66        mb.add(menu);
67
68        Container cp = this.getContentPane();
69        cp.setLayout(new FlowLayout());
70        imageSrc = new ImagePanel();
71        imageDst = new ImagePanel();
72        cp.add(imageSrc);
73        cp.add(imageDst);
74      }
75
76      public void actionPerformed(ActionEvent ev) {
77        String cmd = ev.getActionCommand();
78        if ("Open image".equals(cmd)) {
79          int retval = fc.showOpenDialog(this);
80          if (retval == JFileChooser.APPROVE_OPTION) {
81            try {
82              BufferedImage bi = ImageIO.read(fc.getSelectedFile());
83              imageSrc.setImage(bi);
84              pack();
85            } catch (IOException ex) {
86              ex.printStackTrace();
87            }
88          }
89        } else if ("Open image (awt)".equals(cmd)) {
90          int retval = fc.showOpenDialog(this);
91          if (retval == JFileChooser.APPROVE_OPTION) {
92            Toolkit tk = Toolkit.getDefaultToolkit();
93            Image img = tk.getImage(fc.getSelectedFile().getPath());
94            MediaTracker tracker = new MediaTracker(new Component() {});
95            tracker.addImage(img, 0);
96            try {
97              tracker.waitForID(0);
98            } catch (InterruptedException ex) {}
99            BufferedImage bi = new BufferedImage(img.getWidth(this),
100             img.getHeight(this), BufferedImage.TYPE_INT_RGB);
101            bi.getGraphics().drawImage(img, 0, 0, this);
102            imageSrc.setImage(bi);
103          }
104        } else if ("Save image".equals(cmd)) {
105          int retval = fc.showSaveDialog(this);
106          if (retval == JFileChooser.APPROVE_OPTION) {
107            try{
108              ImageIO.write(imageDst.getImage(), "png",
109                fc.getSelectedFile());
110            } catch (IOException ex) {
111              ex.printStackTrace();
112            }
113          }
```

```
114      } else if ("Exit".equals(cmd)) {
115        System.exit(0);
116      } else if ("Copy".equals(cmd)) {
117        imageSrc.setImage(imageDst.getImage());
118      } else {
119        process(cmd);
120      }
121    }
122
123    void process(String opName) {
124      BufferedImageOp op = null;
125      if (opName.equals("Smooth")) {
126        float[] data = new float[9];
127        for (int i = 0; i < 9; i++) data[i] = 1.0f/9.0f;
128        Kernel ker = new Kernel(3,3,data);
129        op = new ConvolveOp(ker);
130      } else if (opName.equals("Sharpen")) {
131        float[] data = {0f, -1f, 0f, -1f, 5f, -1f, 0f, -1f, 0f};
132        Kernel ker = new Kernel(3,3,data);
133        op = new ConvolveOp(ker);
134      } else if (opName.equals("Edge")) {
135        float[] data = {0f, -1f, 0f, -1f, 4f, -1f, 0f, -1f, 0f};
136        Kernel ker = new Kernel(3,3,data);
137        op = new ConvolveOp(ker);
138      } else if (opName.equals("Rescale")) {
139        op = new RescaleOp(1.5f, 0.0f, null);
140      } else if (opName.equals("Gray scale")) {
141        op = new ColorConvertOp(ColorSpace.getInstance
142          (ColorSpace.CS_GRAY), null);
143      } else if (opName.equals("Rotate")) {
144        AffineTransform xform = new AffineTransform();
145        xform.setToRotation(Math.PI/6);
146        op = new AffineTransformOp(xform, AffineTransformOp.
147          TYPE_BILINEAR);
148      }
149      BufferedImage bi = op.filter(imageSrc.getImage(), null);
150      imageDst.setImage(bi);
151      pack();
152    }
153 }
154
155 class ImagePanel extends JPanel {
156    BufferedImage image = null;
157
158    public ImagePanel() {
159      image = null;
160      setPreferredSize(new Dimension(256, 256));
161    }
162
163    public ImagePanel(BufferedImage bi) {
164      image = bi;
165    }
166
167    public void paintComponent(Graphics g) {
168      Graphics2D g2 = (Graphics2D)g;
169      if (image != null)
170        g2.drawImage(image, 0, 0, this);
171      else
172        g2.drawRect(0, 0, getWidth()-1, getHeight()-1);
173    }
```

```
174
175    public BufferedImage getImage() {
176       return image;
177    }
178
179    public void setImage(BufferedImage bi) {
180       image = bi;
181       setPreferredSize(new Dimension(bi.getWidth(), bi.getHeight()));
182       invalidate();
183       repaint();
184    }
185 }
```

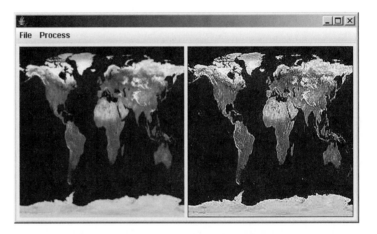

FIGURE 4.5   Image sharpening is one of the operations supported by this image-processing example program.

This program is an example of image-processing systems. It provides basic functions of image I/O, operations, and displays. The main frame of the program contains two menus. The "File" menu has items to open an image file, to open an image file using AWT facilities, to save an image to a file, and to exit the program. The "Process" menu contains items to select various image-processing operations. The content pane of the frame contains two `ImagePanel` objects, the source image on the left and the processed image on the right.

The `ImagePanel` class extends the `JPanel` class and it displays a `BufferedImage`. An image can be passed to the `ImagePanel` by a constructor or by the method `setImage`.

The program implements two different ways to load image files. One method uses the static method `read` of the `ImageIO` class to load an image file directly to a `BufferedImage` object (line 82). The other uses AWT image loading and a `BufferedImage` is obtained by drawing the image (lines 92–101). A `JFileChooser` object is used to allow the user to select an image file to open.

Several operations are implemented to perform common image-processing tasks including: smooth, sharpen, edge detection, rescale, rotation, and grayscale. The smooth operator is a convolution defined by the following 3×3 kernel:

$$\begin{bmatrix} 1/9 & 1/9 & 1/9 \\ 1/9 & 1/9 & 1/9 \\ 1/9 & 1/9 & 1/9 \end{bmatrix}$$

The sharpen operator is defined with the kernel

$$\begin{bmatrix} 0 & -1 & 0 \\ -1 & 5 & -1 \\ 0 & -1 & 0 \end{bmatrix}$$

The edge-detection operator has the kernel

$$\begin{bmatrix} 0 & -1 & 0 \\ -1 & 4 & -1 \\ 0 & -1 & 0 \end{bmatrix}$$

The rescale operation uses the `RescaleOp` class. It is designed to brighten the image.

The rotation operation uses the `AffineTransformOp` class. A rotation of $\pi/6$ is defined by an `AffineTransform` object and applied to the `AffineTransformOp` object.

The grayscale operation uses the `ColorConvertOp` class to convert the source image to a grayscale image.

The copy operation simply copies the processed image back to the source image so that additional processing can be applied.

The processed image can be saved to a disk file in PNG format. A `JFileChooser` is used to select a file to write. The ImageIO static method `save` is used to save an image.

4.5 Creating Fractal Images

In the last section, we discussed how to create, load, save, process, and display a `BufferedImage`. It is also possible to perform low-level operations and directly manipulate the pixels in a `BufferedImage`.

The `Raster` class encapsulates the pixel data of the `BufferedImage`. The `WritableRaster` is a subclass of `Raster` that is writable. To obtain a `WritableRaster` object from a `BufferedImage`, you may use the `getRaster` method:

Raster

```
BufferedImage bi = new BufferedImage(640, 480, BufferedImage.TYPE_ARGB);
WritableRaster raster = bi.getRaster();
```

The `Raster` class provides a number of methods to get pixel data, and `WritableRaster` adds methods to set pixel data.

```
int[] getPixel(int x, int y, int[] data);
float[] getPixel(int x, int y, float[] data);
double[] getPixel(int x, int y, double[] data);
int[] getPixels(int x, int y, int w, int h, int[] data);
float[] getPixels(int x, int y, int w, int h, float[] data);
double[] getPixels(int x, int y, int w, int h, double[] data);
void setPixel(int x, int y, int[] data);
void setPixel(int x, int y, float[] data);
void setPixel(int x, int y, double[] data);
void setPixels(int x, int y, int w, int h, int[] data);
void setPixels(int x, int y, int w, int h, float[] data);
void setPixels(int x, int y, int w, int h, double[] data);
```

The parameters x, y specify the location of the pixel and w, h define the dimension of a rectangle of pixels. The *data* array holds the pixel data. The size of the array depends on the type of the image. For example, if the `BufferedImage` is TYPE_INT_RGB, then the data array for each pixel has three elements containing the RGB values.

Mandelbrot set

Through the `WritableRaster` object, the contents of an image can be created at the pixel level. This method of pixel-by-pixel image generation may be illustrated by the example of building a fractal image. A fractal is a self-similar geometric structure. Fractals often exhibit a great deal of complexity, even though they might be generated by some rather simple procedures. The *Mandelbrot set* is a well-known example of fractals. It is defined on the complex plane. A complex number has the form

$$x + iy$$

where x and y are real numbers and i satisfies the equation $i^2 = -1$. The addition and multiplication of two complex numbers $z_1 = x_1 + iy_1$ and $z_2 = x_2 + iy_2$ are defined as:

$$z_1 + z_2 = (x_1 + x_2) + i(y_1 + y_2)$$

$$z_1 z_2 = (x_1 x_2 - y_1 y_2) + i(x_1 y_2 + y_1 x_2)$$

The absolute value of a complex number is $|x + iy| = \sqrt{x^2 + y^2}$. A complex number can be interpreted as a point on a 2D plane by identifying the (x, y) values as the coordinates of the point. The absolute value of the complex number corresponds to the distance of the point to the origin.

To define the Mandelbrot set, we consider the iteration on the complex plane:

$$z_{n+1} = z_n^2 + c$$

c is a complex number, and the starting point of iteration is $z_0 = 0$. For a given c the iteration will produce a sequence of complex numbers: $z_0, z_1, \ldots, z_n, \ldots$. It can be shown that the sequence either tends to infinity or stays bounded. The Mandelbrot set is defined to be the set of points c such that the iteration sequence is bounded. The Mandelbrot set is surprisingly complex. It contains recursively self-similar substructures. It is known that the Mandelbrot set is contained in the circle of radius 2 centered at the origin, and if at any step of the iteration the point goes outside the circle, the sequence will escape to infinity and the corresponding c does not belong to the Mandelbrot set.

Listing 4.5 illustrates a way to build an image based on the Mandelbrot set. This example creates an image approximating the Mandelbrot set. The iteration process is carried out for each pixel and the number of iterations is color coded to create the image. A sample run of the program is shown in Figure 4.6

Listing 4.5 `Mandelbrot.java`

```
1 package chapter4;
2
3 import javax.swing.*;
4 import java.awt.*;
5 import java.awt.image.*;
6
7 public class Mandelbrot extends JApplet {
8   public static void main(String s[]) {
9     JFrame frame = new JFrame();
10    frame.setTitle("Mandelbrot set");
11    frame.setDefaultCloseOperation(JFrame.EXIT_ON_CLOSE);
12    JApplet applet = new Mandelbrot();
13    applet.init();
14    frame.getContentPane().add(applet);
15    frame.pack();
```

```
16      frame.setVisible(true);
17    }
18
19    public void init() {
20      JPanel panel = new MandelbrotPanel();
21      getContentPane().add(panel);
22    }
23 }
24
25 class MandelbrotPanel extends JPanel{
26    BufferedImage bi;
27
28    public MandelbrotPanel() {
29      int w = 500;
30      int h = 500;
31      setPreferredSize(new Dimension(w, h));
32      setBackground(Color.white);
33      bi = new BufferedImage(w, h, BufferedImage.TYPE_INT_RGB);
34      WritableRaster raster = bi.getRaster();
35      int[] rgb = new int[3];
36      float xmin = -2;
37      float ymin = -2;
38      float xscale = 4f/w;
39      float yscale = 4f/h;
40      for (int i = 0; i < h; i++) {
41        for (int j = 0; j < w; j++) {
42          float cr = xmin + j * xscale;
43          float ci = ymin + i * yscale;
44          int count = iterCount(cr, ci);
45          rgb[0] = (count & 0x07) << 5;
46          rgb[1] = ((count >> 3) & 0x07) << 5;
47          rgb[2] = ((count >> 6) & 0x07) << 5;
48          raster.setPixel(j, i, rgb);
49        }
50      }
51    }
52
53    private int iterCount(float cr, float ci) {
54      int max = 512;
55      float zr = 0;
56      float zi = 0;
57      float lengthsq = 0;
58      int count = 0;
59      while ((lengthsq < 4.0) && (count < max)) {
60        float temp = zr * zr - zi * zi + cr;
61        zi = 2 * zr * zi + ci;
62        zr = temp;
63        lengthsq = zr * zr + zi * zi;
64        count++;
65      }
66      return max-count;
67    }
68
69    public void paintComponent(Graphics g) {
70      super.paintComponent(g);
71      g.drawImage(bi, 0, 0, this);
72    }
73 }
```

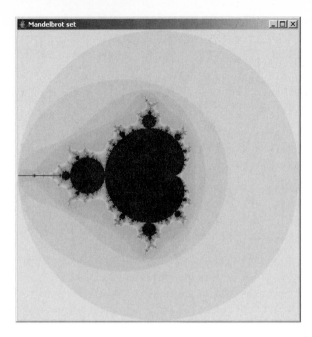

FIGURE 4.6 The Mandelbrot set colored with the number of iterations.

This program creates an image depicting the Mandelbrot set in the complex plane over the square:

$$-2 \leq x, y \leq 2$$

A BufferedImage is created with the size 500×500 and with the integer RGB pixel type. A WritableRaster object is obtained from the image (line 34). The pixels of the image are set through the raster. The pixel indices are mapped to the coordinates on the complex plane by linear functions.

The iterations are carried out by the method iterCount. A complex number is represented by two float variables. The iteration terminates if the value goes outside the circle $|z_n| > 2$ (or, equivalently, $|z_n|^2 > 4$). The maximum number of iterations for each pixel is limited to 512, so the iteration count is in the range [1, 512]. The complement of the counter *max-count* is used to color a pixel. It has the range [0, 511]. The 9-bit counter value is divided into three 3-bit RGB components.

The paintComponent method draws the completed image to MandelbrotPanel, a subclass of JPanel. Because of the large number of calculations required in generating the Mandelbrot image, it may take a while for the image to appear in the window.

4.6 Animation

Animation introduces dynamic changes to graphics contents and often creates a visual effect of motion. An animation produces a series of rendered images (frames) that depicts the changes in a scene. When the frames are displayed consecutively at certain rate (for example, 60 frames per second), we may perceive continuous motion in the scene rather than discrete images. Animation adds a dimension of time to the graphics model. Each rendered frame at a specific time instance is essentially a regular still image. However, the content of the frames may change over time. Higher *frame rates* represent smoother animations, but the frame rate of an animation is limited by the capability of the rendering system.

frame rate

Implementing animation in Java usually requires additional threads to handle the time-related changes. Because an animation typically runs indefinitely, placing all animation code in the event dispatch thread will make the GUI program not responsive. However, when using Swing components to display graphics animation, you need to avoid direct manipulation of the Swing components from the thread other than the event dispatch thread, because Swing components are not *thread safe*. For example, in the animation thread, you should not call getGraphics() method and use the Graphics object to do graphics painting. There are several methods of Swing components that are safe to call from other threads:

thread safe

```java
public void repaint()
public void revalidate()
```

Therefore, a proper way to create an animation on Swing components is to separate the rendering from the model changes. The rendering code is placed in the paintComponent method of the Swing component only. The animation logic is placed in the separate thread without actual rendering. When the data for a frame is ready, the method repaint() is called to trigger the rendering. An outline of a typical multithread animation is shown below.

```java
public void paintComponent(Graphics g) {
    <* render a frame *>
}

public void run() {
  while(true) {
    <* update frame data *>
    repaint();
    try {
      Thread.sleep(sleepTime);
    } catch (InterruptedException ex) {}
  }
}
```

The paintComponent method contains all the rendering code to generate a frame. The run method of the Runnable interface or the Thread class is overridden to perform the animation. It typically contains an infinite loop to continuously generate the frames. A frame is rendered by calling the repaint method. Between two frames, the thread typically goes to sleep for a specific period of time. The sleep method of Thread specifies a sleep time in milliseconds.

Runnable interface
Thread class

Listing 4.6 creates a simple scene of simulated rain. Numerous vertical line segments are moving downward. The locations and the lengths of the lines are random. A sample run of the program is shown in Figure 4.7.

Listing 4.6 `Rain.java`

```java
1 package chapter4;
2
3 import java.awt.*;
4 import java.awt.geom.*;
5 import java.awt.event.*;
6 import java.util.*;
7 import javax.swing.*;
8
9 public class Rain extends JApplet {
10    public static void main(String s[]) {
11       JFrame frame = new JFrame();
12       frame.setTitle("Rain");
13       frame.setDefaultCloseOperation(JFrame.EXIT_ON_CLOSE);
```

```
14      JApplet applet = new Rain();
15      applet.init();
16      frame.getContentPane().add(applet);
17      frame.pack();
18      frame.setVisible(true);
19    }
20
21    public void init() {
22      JPanel panel = new RainPanel();
23      getContentPane().add(panel);
24    }
25 }
26
27 class RainPanel extends JPanel implements Runnable{
28    Point2D.Double[] pts = new Point2D.Double[1200];
29
30    public RainPanel() {
31      setPreferredSize(new Dimension(640, 480));
32      setBackground(Color.gray);
33      for (int i = 0; i < pts.length; i++) {
34        pts[i] = new Point2D.Double(Math.random(), Math.random());
35      }
36      Thread thread = new Thread(this);
37      thread.start();
38    }
39
40    public void paintComponent(Graphics g) {
41      super.paintComponent(g);
42      g.setColor(Color.white);
43      for (int i = 0; i < pts.length; i++) {
44        int x = (int)(640*pts[i].x);
45        int y = (int)(480*pts[i].y);
46        int h = (int)(25*Math.random());
47        g.drawLine(x, y, x, y+h);
48      }
49    }
50
51    public void run() {
52      while(true) {
53        for (int i = 0; i < pts.length; i++) {
54          double x = pts[i].getX();
55          double y = pts[i].getY();
56          y += 0.1*Math.random();
57          if (y > 1) {
58            y = 0.3*Math.random();
59            x = Math.random();
60          }
61          pts[i].setLocation(x, y);
62        }
63        repaint();
64        try {
65          Thread.sleep(100);
66        } catch (InterruptedException ex) {}
67      }
68    }
69 }
```

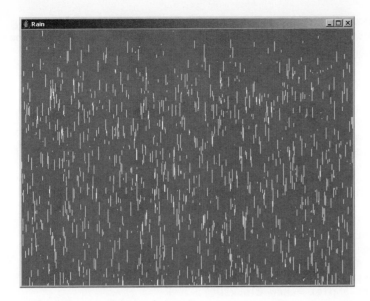

FIGURE 4.7   A rainy animation.

The class `RainPanel` extends `JPanel` and implements `Runnable` interface. An array `pts` of `Point2D.Double` is used to store the locations of the lines (line 28). They are initialized to random values.

The `paintComponent` method draws the vertical lines based on the values in the `pts` array (scaled to component size) and random lengths.

A new thread is created in the constructor of `Rain` to execute the code provided by the `run` method in the same class. The `run` method (line 51) contains an infinite loop that updates line locations in the `pts` array. Each point is increased by a random amount in the *y*-coordinate, so the line drops down. When a line reaches the bottom, the point is reset to a random location in the top region. After the array is updated, the `repaint` method is called to redraw the panel. The thread then goes to sleep for 100 milliseconds.

An instance of `RainPanel` is placed in the applet `Rain`. A standard main method is included to run the animation as an application.

An alternative to creating your own thread is to use the `Timer` class provided by Swing. A `Timer` object periodically generates an action event at a predefined rate. The events will trigger the listeners, which may perform the rendering of a frame. To set up a `Timer` object, you may specify its period and listeners in its constructor and call its `start()` method:

Timer

```
Timer timer = new Timer(period, listener);
timer.start();
```

The `ActionListener` object should implement the rendering in its `actionPerformed` method:

```
public void actionPerformed(ActionEvent event) {
  <* do frame rendering *>
}
```

The `Timer` class provides a more convenient approach for animation than explicit creation of threads. Because the `actionPerformed` method is invoked in the event dispatch thread, it is safe to perform rendering on Swing components in the method.

Listing 4.7 demonstrates the application of the `Timer` class. A real-time analog clock is displayed as shown in Figure 4.8. The time of the clock is from the system time. The clock is updated continuously to achieve the visual effect of clock movements.

Listing 4.7 `Clock2D.java`

```
1 package chapter4;
2
3 import java.awt.*;
4 import java.awt.geom.*;
5 import java.awt.event.*;
6 import java.util.Calendar;
7 import javax.swing.*;
8
9 public class Clock2D extends JApplet {
10   public static void main(String s[]) {
11     JFrame frame = new JFrame();
12     frame.setTitle("Clock");
13     frame.setDefaultCloseOperation(JFrame.EXIT_ON_CLOSE);
14     JApplet applet = new Clock2D();
15     applet.init();
16     frame.getContentPane().add(applet);
17     frame.pack();
18     frame.setVisible(true);
19   }
20
21   public void init() {
22     JPanel panel = new ClockPanel();
23     getContentPane().add(panel);
24   }
25 }
26
27 class ClockPanel extends JPanel implements ActionListener{
28   AffineTransform rotH = new AffineTransform();
29   AffineTransform rotM = new AffineTransform();
30   AffineTransform rotS = new AffineTransform();
31
32   public ClockPanel() {
33     setPreferredSize(new Dimension(640, 480));
34     setBackground(Color.white);
35     Timer timer = new Timer(500, this);
36     timer.start();
37   }
38
39   public void paintComponent(Graphics g) {
40     super.paintComponent(g);
41     Graphics2D g2 = (Graphics2D)g;
42     g2.translate(320,240);
43     // clock face
44     Paint paint = new GradientPaint
45     (-150,-150,Color.white,150,150,Color.gray);
46     g2.setPaint(paint);
47     g2.fillOval(-190, -190, 380, 380);
48     g2.setColor(Color.gray);
49     g2.drawString("Java 2D", -20, 80);
50     Stroke stroke = new BasicStroke(3);
51     g2.setStroke(stroke);
52     g2.drawOval(-190, -190, 380, 380);
53     for (int i = 0; i < 12; i++) {
54       g2.rotate(2*Math.PI/12);
```

```
55        g2.fill3DRect(-3, -180, 6, 30, true);
56     }
57     // clock hands
58     Shape hour = new Line2D.Double(0, 0, 0, -80);
59     hour = rotH.createTransformedShape(hour);
60     Shape minute = new Line2D.Double(0, 0, 0, -120);
61     minute = rotM.createTransformedShape(minute);
62     Shape second = new Line2D.Double(0, 0, 0, -120);
63     second = rotS.createTransformedShape(second);
64     g2.setColor(Color.black);
65     g2.setStroke(new BasicStroke(5,
66     BasicStroke.CAP_ROUND, BasicStroke.JOIN_ROUND));
67     g2.draw(hour);
68     g2.draw(minute);
69     g2.setStroke(new BasicStroke(2));
70     g2.draw(second);
71   }
72
73   public void actionPerformed(ActionEvent e) {
74     int hour = Calendar.getInstance().get(Calendar.HOUR);
75     int min = Calendar.getInstance().get(Calendar.MINUTE);
76     int sec = Calendar.getInstance().get(Calendar.SECOND);
77     rotH.setToRotation(Math.PI * (hour+min/60.0)/6.0);
78     rotM.setToRotation(Math.PI * min /30.0);
79     rotS.setToRotation(Math.PI * sec /30.0);
80     repaint();
81   }
82 }
```

FIGURE 4.8   A real-time analog clock.

The class `ClockPanel` extends `JPanel` and implements `ActionListener` interface. Three `AffineTransform` fields define the rotations for the hour, minute, and second hands (lines 28–30).

The `paintComponent` method paints the clock face and the three hands. The face consists of a circle filled with a gradient paint and drawn with a gray color, twelve tick marks created with filled 3D rectangles, and a text string "Java 2D." The hour, minute, and second hands are drawn as lines. Their positions are determined by the rotation fields that specify the correct angles for the current time. The rotations are applied to the corresponding hands that start from the 12 o'clock position.

A `Timer` object is created and started in the constructor of `ClockPanel`. It uses the `ClockPanel` object as the listener and sets a period of 500 ms (line 35). Responding to the action events generated by the `Timer`, the `actionPerformed` method (line 73) implements the animation functions. It uses the `Calendar` class to get the current system time and sets appropriate angles for the three rotations. After the rotations are updated, a `repaint` method call is made to update the display.

cellular automaton

A *cellular automaton* is a simple iterative system on a grid that evolves based on a fixed set of rules. Many cellular automata generate surprisingly complex patterns. A 2D cellular automaton is defined on a 2D grid. Each cell has two states: black and white (also called live and dead). A cell has eight neighbors. In some systems, only four neighbors are considered. The iteration of the system proceeds by assigning the next state of each cell based on the previous configuration. Each cell follows the same set of rules, and the new state depends only upon the current states of the same cell and its neighbors. For example, Figure 4.9 shows one iteration step with the rule: "A cell is black if exactly one of its neighbors in the current configuration is black."

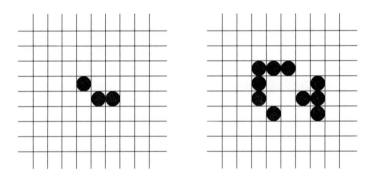

FIGURE 4.9   One step in the evolution of a cellular automaton.

Game of Life

A well-known example of cellular automata is Conway's *Game of Life*, as illustrated in Listing 4.8. A sample run of the program is shown in Figure 4.10.

The Game of Life is a 2D cellular automaton. The rules are quite simple:

1. (birth). A dead cell becomes live if it has exactly three live neighbors.

2. (survival). A live cell remains live if it has two or three live neighbors.

3. (death). Otherwise, a cell dies.

Listing 4.8 `Life.java`

```
1 package chapter4;
2
3 import java.awt.*;
4 import java.awt.event.*;
5 import javax.swing.*;
6 import java.awt.geom.*;
7
8 public class Life extends JApplet {
```

```
 9    public static void main(String s[]) {
10      JFrame frame = new JFrame();
11      frame.setTitle("Game of Life");
12      frame.setDefaultCloseOperation(JFrame.EXIT_ON_CLOSE);
13      JApplet applet = new Life();
14      applet.init();
15      frame.getContentPane().add(applet);
16      frame.pack();
17      frame.setVisible(true);
18    }
19
20    public void init() {
21      JPanel panel = new LifePanel();
22      getContentPane().add(panel);
23    }
24 }
25
26 class LifePanel extends JPanel implements ActionListener{
27    int n = 30;
28    boolean[][] cells1;
29    boolean[][] cells2;
30
31    public LifePanel() {
32      setPreferredSize(new Dimension(400, 400));
33      setBackground(Color.white);
34      cells1 = new boolean[n][n];
35      cells2 = new boolean[n][n];
36      for (int i = 0; i < n; i++) {
37        for (int j = 0; j < n; j++) {
38          cells1[i][j] = Math.random() < 0.1;
39          cells2[i][j] = false;
40        }
41      }
42      Timer timer = new Timer(1000, this);
43      timer.start();
44    }
45
46    public void paintComponent(Graphics g) {
47      super.paintComponent(g);
48      Graphics2D g2 = (Graphics2D)g;
49
50      g2.setColor(Color.lightGray);
51      int p = 0;
52      int c = 16;
53      int len = c*n;
54      for (int i = 0; i <= n; i++) {
55        g2.drawLine(0, p, len, p);
56        g2.drawLine(p, 0, p, len);
57        p += c;
58      }
59      g2.setColor(Color.black);
60      for (int i = 0; i < n; i++) {
61        for (int j = 0; j < n; j++) {
62          if (cells1[i][j]) {
63            int x = i*c;
64            int y = j*c;
65            g2.fillOval(x, y, c, c);
66          }
67        }
68      }
```

```
69    }
70
71    public void actionPerformed(ActionEvent e) {
72      boolean[][] cells = cells1;
73      for (int i = 0; i < n; i++) {
74        for (int j = 0; j < n; j++) {
75          cells2[i][j] = cells[i][j];
76          int nb = neighbors(cells, i, j);
77          if (nb == 3)
78            cells2[i][j] = true;
79          if (nb < 2 || nb > 3)
80            cells2[i][j] = false;
81        }
82      }
83
84      cells1 = cells2;
85      cells2 = cells;
86      repaint();
87    }
88
89    private int neighbors(boolean[][] cells, int x, int y) {
90      int x1 = (x>0)?x-1:x;
91      int x2 = (x<n-1)?x+1:x;
92      int y1 = (y>0)?y-1:y;
93      int y2 = (y<n-1)?y+1:y;
94      int count = 0;
95      for (int i = x1; i <= x2; i++) {
96        for (int j = y1; j <= y2; j++) {
97          count += (cells[i][j])?1:0;
98        }
99      }
100     if (cells[x][y]) count--;
101     return count;
102   }
103 }
```

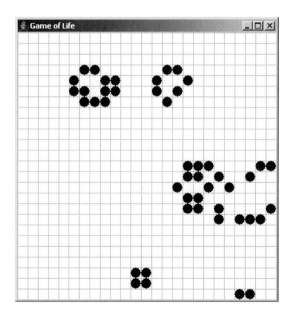

FIGURE 4.10 Game of Life.

The program creates an *n*-by-*n* board to display the game. A 2D array of `boolean` is used to hold the states of the cells. The initial configuration is set randomly, with the probability of live cells being 0.1.

A timer of 1000 milliseconds is used to animate the progress of the game (line 42). The `LifePanel` object is the action listener for the timer. Every time the event is fired, one step of the game is performed. In order to avoid repeated creation of arrays, only two arrays for the cell configurations are used (lines 28–29). `cells1` references the array for the currently displayed cells. `cells2` is for the next configuration. After the computation for a board update is completed, the two arrays are swapped.

4.7 Printing

Printing is a common task in computer applications. The rendering problems involved in printing graphics are essentially the same as those in drawing on the screen. However, printing does present some special problems such as pagination. Java API provides convenient facilities for printing.

The `PrinterJob` class can be used to manage a printing process. The following static method returns an instance of `PrinterJob`:

`PrinterJob`

```
static PrinterJob getPrinterJob();
```

At the beginning of a print job the user is usually presented with a printer selection dialog box. You may do that by simply invoking the method of `PrinterJob`:

```
boolean printDialog();
```

The method returns `true` if the user chooses to proceed with the printing. You may initiate the printing by calling the following method:

```
void print() throws PrinterException;
```

The actual graphics contents of printing are defined using the `Printable` interface. An object implementing `Printable` is selected to a `PrinterJob` through the method:

`Printable`

```
void setPrintable(Printable painter);
```

The `Printable` interface provides a callback structure to define the custom drawing of the printing job. The interface contains the following method for custom implementation:

```
int print(Graphics g, PageFormat pf, int pageIndex);
```

The implementation of this method is very similar to that of `paintComponent`. The code can often be shared between the two methods. The `Graphics` parameter, which can be cast to a `Graphics2D` object, provides access to the 2D rendering engine. All the drawing, transformation, and other features are available to printing.

The `pageIndex` parameter provides the page number of the page currently being rendered. It starts with 0. The implementation of the method should return either the value `NO_SUCH_PAGE` if the page should not be printed or the value `PAGE_EXISTS` if the page is rendered.

The `PageFormat` object contains information about the printer's page settings. The following are some of the methods in `PageFormat`:

`PageFormat`

```
int getOrientation();
double getWidth();
double getHeight();
double getImageableX();
```

```
double getImageableY();
double getImageableWidth();
double getImageableHeight();
```

The last four methods retrieve the rectangle of the printable area of the page.

Listing 4.9 demonstrates the usage of these classes in implementing printing functionalities in Java applications. The program displays a window containing a panel with the text "Welcome!" and a button labeled "Print." If the button is clicked, a printer selection dialog box is displayed. When a printer is chosen, the same text string will be printed on two pages, as shown in Figure 4.11. The rendered image is cut against the printable area, but the fragments are properly aligned across the pages.

Listing 4.9 `Printing.java`

```java
1 package chapter4;
2
3 import java.awt.*;
4 import java.awt.geom.*;
5 import java.awt.event.*;
6 import java.awt.print.*;
7 import javax.swing.*;
8
9 public class PrintGraphics extends JFrame implements ActionListener {
10    public static void main(String[] args) {
11       JFrame frame = new PrintGraphics();
12       frame.setTitle("Printing");
13       frame.setDefaultCloseOperation(JFrame.EXIT_ON_CLOSE);
14       frame.pack();
15       frame.setVisible(true);
16    }
17
18    PrinterJob pj;
19    PrintPanel painter;
20
21    public void actionPerformed(ActionEvent e) {
22       if (pj.printDialog()) {
23          try {
24             pj.print();
25          } catch (PrinterException ex) {
26             ex.printStackTrace();
27          }
28       }
29    }
30
31    public PrintGraphics() {
32       Container cp = this.getContentPane();
33       cp.setLayout(new BorderLayout());
34       JButton button = new JButton("Print");
35       cp.add(button, BorderLayout.SOUTH);
36       button.addActionListener(this);
37       painter = new PrintPanel();
38       cp.add(painter, BorderLayout.CENTER);
39       pj = PrinterJob.getPrinterJob();
40       pj.setPrintable(painter);
41    }
42 }
43
```

```
44 class PrintPanel extends JPanel implements Printable {
45   public PrintPanel() {
46     setPreferredSize(new Dimension(800, 400));
47     setBackground(Color.white);
48   }
49
50   public int print(Graphics g, PageFormat pf, int pageIndex) {
51     switch (pageIndex) {
52       case 0:
53         draw(g);
54         break;
55       case 1:
56         g.translate(-(int)pf.getImageableWidth(), 0);
57         draw(g);
58         break;
59       default:
60         return NO_SUCH_PAGE;
61     }
62     return PAGE_EXISTS;
63   }
64
65   public void paintComponent(Graphics g) {
66     super.paintComponent(g);
67     draw(g);
68   }
69
70   private void draw(Graphics g) {
71     g.setFont(new Font("Serif", Font.BOLD, 144));
72     g.drawString("Welcome!",  200, 300);
73   }
74 }
```

FIGURE 4.11   Printing over multiple pages.

The class `PrintPanel` extends `JPanel` and implements the `Printable` interface. An instance of `PrintPanel` is added to the main frame of the program. It is also used for printing. The panel paints the string "Welcome!" using a 144-point font. A private method `draw` is defined to perform the drawing (line 70). Both `paintComponent` and `print` methods call the `draw` method.

The `print` method has additional logic to handle the page split. The first page (`pageIndex = 0`) is printed without change. In the second page, a translation is performed to move the page so that it covers the area to the right of the first page. To determine the precise offset, we use the `PageFormat` object to retrieve the width of the printable area (line 56).

KEY CLASSES AND METHODS

- **`javax.awt.geom.GeneralPath.curveTo(...)`** A method to construct a cubic curve segment.
- **`javax.awt.image.BufferedImage`** A class encapsulating an image.
- **`javax.awt.image.BufferedImageOp`** An interface for image-processing operators.
- **`java.swing.Timer`** A class generating action events in a periodic fashion.
- **`java.lang.Runnable`** An interface to define code executable as a separate thread.
- **`java.lang.Thread`** A class encapsulating a thread of execution of a program.
- **`java.lang.Thread.sleep(long ms)`** A method to place the thread to sleep for a specified time period.
- **`java.util.Calendar`** A class encapsulating a calendar for date and time.
- **`java.awt.image.Raster`** A class encapsulating image data.
- **`java.awt.image.WritableRaster`** A class encapsulating writable image data.
- **`java.awt.print.PrinterJob`** A class for printing management.
- **`java.awt.print.Printable`** An interface to define print contents.

KEY TERMS

B-spline curve A curve defined as a parametric equation of piecewise polynomials blending with a sequence of control points.
Bézier curve A curve defined as a parametric equation of polynomials blending with control points.
NURBS Nonuniform rational B-spline.
image processing Computer manipulation of digital images to enhance or extract information.
convolution A type of linear operations often used in signal and image processing.
kernel A function to define a convolution.
complex numbers An extension of real numbers.
complex plane The set of complex numbers interpreted as points on a plane.
frame rate The speed of an animation measured in frames per second (fps).
thread A line of execution in a running program. In a multithreading environment a single program may have several threads running simultaneously.
cellular automata A dynamic system on a grid of cells, evolving based a simple set of rules that specify the next state of a cell using the previous states of itself and its neighbors.

CHAPTER SUMMARY

- In this chapter we present several advanced techniques in 2D computer graphics.

- B-spline curves are important tools in modeling 2D geometry. A B-spline curve can be converted to a sequence of Bézier curves, which may then be rendered directly by the

Graphics2D object. The control points of each Bézier curve are linear combinations of the control points of the B-spline curve.

- Java 2D provides a basic set of graphics primitives. We discussed how to build custom primitives by implementing the Shape interface. Even though it is not possible to extend the GeneralPath class, you may still include it in your own class to take advantage of its implementation.

- A brief introduction to image processing is given in this chapter. Java 2D provides supports for image reading, writing, rendering, and processing. The BufferedImage class is the main representation for images in Java 2D. Image-processing operators implementing the BufferedImageOp interface provides convenient ways to process BufferedImage objects.

- Images can also be created and manipulated in a program at the pixel level. Raster and WritableRaster classes offer access to the pixel data in a BufferedImage. An example in constructing an image for the Mandelbrot set is given.

- Animation is an important part of computer graphics. Implementing a 2D animation in Java usually requires multiple threads to separate the continuous rendering from the regular user interface handling. The Thread class and the Runnable interface provide essential multithreading support. The Timer class of the Swing package provides a convenient utility to trigger the periodic frame rendering.

- Printing in Java fits the general rendering scheme of Java 2D quite well. The same Graphics2D class provides the rendering engine. The Printable interface allows for the necessary callback structure for defining the graphics output. The PrinterJob class facilitates the special tasks in printing.

REVIEW QUESTIONS

4.1   Given a cubic B-spline curve as defined in this chapter with n control points, how many Bézier curves will be generated from the conversion?

4.2   Another kind of B-spline curve does not impose special restrictions of the endpoints of the curves. The first and the last segments are treated in the same way as other segments. It uses the same formula for the conversion to Bézier curves on every segment. Consequently, the first and the last control points are not necessarily interpolated by the curve. Find the conversion formula for this type of B-spline curve.

4.3   If you apply a smoothing operator to an image followed by a sharpening operator, will you recover the original image?

4.4   Perform five iterations in the Mandelbrot set definition for $c = i$.

4.5   Perform five iterations in the Mandelbrot set definition for $c = 1$.

4.6   If it takes 0.01 second to complete a frame rendering, and the thread sleeps for 50 milliseconds for each frame, calculate the frame rate.

4.7   How many different rules are there for cellular automata with four neighbors?

PROGRAMMING EXERCISES

4.1   Implement the type of B-spline curve defined in Review Question 4.2.

4.2   Add the Heart primitive to the program in Listing 2.3 so it can be selected and drawn like other shapes.

4.3 Write a `Triangle` class that implements the `Shape` interface. Provide a constructor to define the three vertices of the triangle.

4.4 Implement a regular *n*-gon primitive. Define the class to implement the `Shape` interface and provide a constructor to specify the number of sides *n*.

4.5 Add an invert operation to the program in Listing 4.4. The color of every pixel is turned to its opposite color; that is, a color with components *r, g, b* is changed to $1 - r, 1 - g, 1 - b$.

4.6 Write a Java program with a text field, a button, and a text area as shown in Figure 4.12. A user may enter a string in the text field. When the button "Print" is clicked, the text area will display the pattern of the string formed with the character '*'.

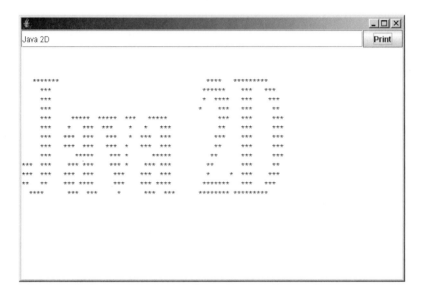

FIGURE 4.12 ASCII art.

4.7 Modify the program in Listing 4.5 to allow a general rectangular region of the complex plane to be viewed in the image. The user may select the rectangle by dragging the mouse.

4.8 The Julia set uses the same type of iterations as in the Mandelbrot set. The constant *c* is always fixed. The starting point of the iteration is not necessarily 0. A point is in the Julia set if the sequence generated by the iteration starting at the point is bounded. Write a Java program to display the Julia set when $c = -0.672 + 0.435i$.

4.9 Modify the program in Listing 3.6 so that the drawing with compositing rules is done on an off-screen image that supports the α-channel. The image is drawn to the screen after the drawing is completed.

4.10 Write a program to display a running fan with four blades.

4.11 Write a Java 2D program that animates a ball bouncing inside a rectangle, as illustrated in Figure 4.13. The ball initially moves on a randomly chosen line. When the ball hits a side of the rectangle, it bounces back in another random direction.

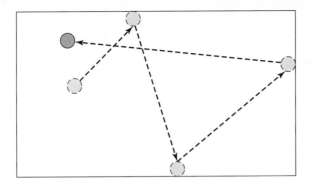

FIGURE 4.13   A bouncing ball.

4.12   Write a Java program simulating an analog stopwatch. Use mouse clicking to operate the stopwatch which cycles through three states: Start–Stop–Reset.

4.13   Implement a cellular automaton with the following rules based on the four-neighbors of a cell:

1. A white cell becomes black if the number of its black neighbors is not 1;

2. A black cell stays black if the number of its black neighbors is either 1 or 3;

3. Otherwise, the cell becomes white.

Starting from a single black cell at the center of the board, the amazing pattern shown in Figure 4.14 will emerge. Use a `Timer` object to animate the process, and allow the user to stop the animation by a mouse click.

FIGURE 4.14   A pattern generated by a simple cellular automaton.

4.14   Write a Java program to print an analog clock showing the current time.

4.15   Add a "Print" menu item to the drawing program in Listing 2.3. When selected, it will initiate a printing of the current drawing.

CHAPTER 5

BASIC 3D GRAPHICS

Objectives

- To describe the 3D rendering process.

- To present an overview of Java 3D programs.

- To define the Java 3D scene graph.

- To classify components of a scene graph.

- To apply background nodes.

- To understand and apply bounds.

- To make changes in live scene graphs.

5.1 Introduction

Our perception of the physical world is clearly three dimensional. However, the visual images that we see through our eyes are two dimensional. A special type of mapping called *perspective projections* is the underlying mechanism to capture a 3D scene to a 2D image. The basic objective of 3D computer graphics is to simulate this process in computers.

3D computer graphics studies the modeling and rendering of a 3D world. The geometric objects in the 3D space may have dimension 0 (points), dimension 1 (curves), dimension 2 (surfaces), or dimension 3 (solids). The objects may have different kinds of material properties. There may exist light sources of various characteristics illuminating the scene in the virtual space. The virtual cameras that capture the scenes of the virtual world may be placed at different locations in the space and have different characteristics. A 3D computer graphics system needs to address many problems in representing the graphics objects and their properties, facilitating transformations, organizing all the components, and rendering the scene.

scene graph

Java 3D is an object-oriented API for 3D computer graphics. The entire graphics model of a Java 3D program is organized in a structure called the *scene graph*. Each node of the scene graph is an object of a class representing one of many graphics entities. The scene graph provides a systematic model for the Java 3D rendering engine to automatically render a scene constructed by a Java 3D program.

In this chapter, we will introduce the basic concepts of a 3D graphics system. In particular you will learn the overall architecture of Java 3D, the concept of a Java 3D scene graph, and an overview of different categories of scene-graph components. You will be able to construct Java 3D scene graphs and write simple Java 3D programs.

5.2 3D Rendering Process

Rendering a 3D scene to produce an image (typically 2D) is an inherently complex process. Unlike 2D graphics, a rendered image of a 3D object is significantly different from its original 3D version. To directly model the object based on its rendered image would not be feasible. Therefore, a 3D graphics system invariably involves the construction of a virtual world in which various graphics objects and light sources are defined. Rather than constructing the scene "on the fly," as often seen in the 2D cases, a persistent "retained" model of the virtual world separated from the rendering engine is often needed. The scene is then viewed in a structured way within the virtual world, and the rendering engine produces the image of the view. A simple illustration of 3D graphics concepts is shown in Figure 5.1.

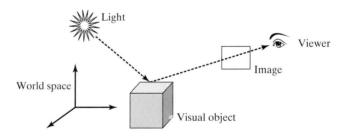

FIGURE 5.1 3D graphics model and view.

The rendering process of a static graphics scene is similar to that of a real camera taking a picture. The virtual world contains visual objects that reflect light from various light sources. The camera is located at a specific point in the virtual world and projects the visible portions of the virtual world along a specific direction onto a 2D plane. The graphics objects as well as the views may be dynamic. Consequently, the scene and the rendered images may continuously change over time. There may be interactions between the virtual world and the real physical world. User and sensor inputs may affect the virtual models.

In order to implement or use such a 3D graphics system, we have to consider many problems related to the modeling of the virtual world and the rendering of a scene—for example,

■ Geometry of the graphics objects.

■ Location and position of the objects.

■ Geometric transformations applied to objects and views.

■ Material properties and texture of the objects.

■ Lights and their characteristics.

■ Type of projections in a view.

■ View position, field of view, and other properties.

■ Illumination and shading models.

■ Dynamic behaviors of various components.

■ Reactions to the user inputs

Geometric descriptions of the graphics objects are the most fundamental aspect of building a virtual world in a 3D graphics system. Basic building blocks for 3D graphics objects include points, lines, surfaces, and solids. Simple polygon meshes are commonly used to approximate complex objects. A 3D graphics system usually offers convenient facilities to generate certain high-level geometries such 3D texts and geometric primitives (for example, spheres, cones, and boxes). More advanced modeling tools include spline curves and surfaces.

Transformation is an important tool in a graphics system. Geometric transforms are used to place the geometric objects in the virtual world space and to change their shapes, sizes, and positions when necessary. *3D affine transforms* are the commonly used family of transforms in the virtual world space. Another family known as *projective transforms* is more general. Projective transforms are important parts of a 3D viewing process.

3D affine transform

projective transform

Besides its geometry, a graphics object also has appearance properties that determine how the object is rendered. These properties may include colors, textures, and material properties for more sophisticated shading. The lighting, illumination, or shading policy controls the way that colors and light intensities on objects are calculated. The choice of illumination model also influences the outcome of rendering. Certain geometric information such as the surface normals is closely related to the appearance in some illumination models. The *normal at a point of the surface* is the direction perpendicular (vertical) to the tangent plane at the point. In the Phong illumination model that considers specular reflection, for example, the light intensity at the point is associated with the angle between the direction of the view and the direction of the light reflection. The reflection vector is determined by the direction of the light and the surface normal. The details of illumination and shading models will be introduced in Chapter 9.

The 3D viewing process typically involves a projective transformation that maps a 3D scene to a 2D plane. A view can have many parameters to control its characteristics. The projection may be parallel or perspective. For a particular view, the visible volume of the virtual world is usually finite, and this volume is known as the *view frustum*. Simply applying a mathematical transformation of projection may not be enough for the rendering. For example, the relative positions among the objects may also be important to the rendering process. A portion of an object may be hidden by another object. These problems need to be properly addressed to achieve acceptable visual results.

view frustum

Of course, the 3D rendering is not limited to a static scene. The virtual world can change over time. The viewing system may be associated with a dynamic device such as a head-mounted display. The dynamic effects of the rendering process may include animation and interaction. *Interaction* is an alteration of the scene resulting from user feedbacks. *Animation* is a change designed internally in the virtual world. The distinction between the two types of dynamics is often blurred. The dynamic behaviors may be originated from the changes in the graphics objects in the virtual world or from the changes of the viewer. The viewers (cameras or eyes) may themselves be objects located in the virtual world and may dynamically change their positions, directions, and other properties.

Java 3D API provides a comprehensive implementation of the basic graphics algorithms, enabling us to concentrate on the main concepts and problems in graphics instead of tedious details of lower-level implementations. This book uses the Java 3D package as the tool to study and implement 3D graphics systems and applications.

5.3 Java 3D API Overview

Java 3D provides a high-level API for modeling and rendering 3D graphics scenes. The Java 3D rendering engine automatically renders a scene with all the structures and properties specified by the programmer. Programming with Java 3D API, therefore, will require only the specifications of the desired graphics scene and the associated properties, and will not need to implement the highly complex and tedious low-level rendering process.

Java 3D takes advantage of the object-oriented programming features of the Java programming language. Almost all elements involved in the graphics rendering (such as geometry, transformation, light, and animation) are implemented as Java classes. Such objects are created simply by instantiating the corresponding classes.

scene graph

In order to organize all the objects involved in rendering a scene, Java 3D uses a special structure called a *scene graph*. This, with its superstructure objects, node objects, and node components, defines the entire virtual graphics world to be rendered. The Java 3D rendering engine will traverse the scene graph to continuously perform the actual rendering. The scene graph defines geometries, appearances, transformations, lights, and views in a 3D scene. It may also include animations, interactions, and sounds.

5.3.1 A Simple Example

Listing 5.1 shows a simple Java 3D applet and application. It demonstrates the basic structure of a Java 3D program. The program displays a solid 3D text "Hello 3D" illuminated by a point light (Figure 5.2).

Listing 5.1 Hello3D.java

```
 1 package chapter5;
 2
 3 import java.awt.*;
 4 import java.applet.*;
 5 import java.awt.event.*;
 6 import javax.media.j3d.*;
 7 import javax.vecmath.*;
 8 import com.sun.j3d.utils.universe.*;
 9 import com.sun.j3d.utils.geometry.*;
10 import com.sun.j3d.utils.applet.MainFrame;
11
12 public class Hello3D extends Applet {
13   public static void main(String s[]) {
14     new MainFrame(new Hello3D(), 640, 480);
15   }
16
17   public void init() {
18     GraphicsConfiguration gc =
19     SimpleUniverse.getPreferredConfiguration();
20     Canvas3D cv = new Canvas3D(gc);
21     setLayout(new BorderLayout());
22     add(cv, BorderLayout.CENTER);
23     BranchGroup bg = createSceneGraph();
```

```
24    bg.compile();
25    SimpleUniverse su = new SimpleUniverse(cv);
26    su.getViewingPlatform().setNominalViewingTransform();
27    su.addBranchGraph(bg);
28  }
29
30  private BranchGroup createSceneGraph() {
31    BranchGroup root = new BranchGroup();
32    // object
33    Appearance ap = new Appearance();
34    ap.setMaterial(new Material());
35    Font3D font = new Font3D(new Font("SansSerif", Font.PLAIN, 1),
36                            new FontExtrusion());
37    Text3D text = new Text3D(font, "Hello 3D");
38    Shape3D shape = new Shape3D(text, ap);
39    // transformation
40    Transform3D tr = new Transform3D();
41    tr.setScale(0.5);
42    tr.setTranslation(new Vector3f(-0.95f, -0.2f, 0f));
43    TransformGroup tg = new TransformGroup(tr);
44    root.addChild(tg);
45    tg.addChild(shape);
46    // light
47    PointLight light = new PointLight(new Color3f(Color.white),
48                                      new Point3f(1f,1f,1f),
49                                      new Point3f(1f,0.1f,0f));
50    BoundingSphere bounds = new BoundingSphere();
51    light.setInfluencingBounds(bounds);
52    root.addChild(light);
53    return root;
54  }
55 }
```

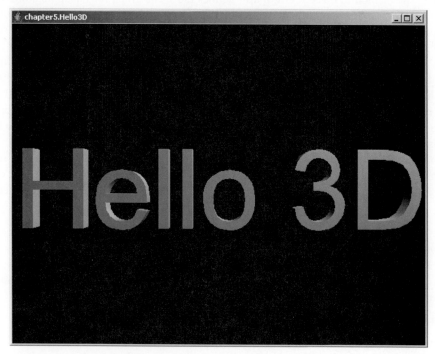

FIGURE 5.2   A simple Java 3D program displays a 3D text string.

This example is a complete Java 3D program. It shows a frame containing a 3D text string "Hello 3D." You can see the depths of the characters and the illumination of the characters originated from a light. The background of the scene is black.

Besides the AWT packages, the program imports the following packages from Java 3D API:

```
javax.media.j3d
javax.vecmath
com.sun.j3d.utils.universe
com.sun.j3d.utils.geometry
```

`javax.media.j3d` is the main package of Java 3D. `javax.vecmath` contains classes for vectors, matrices, and other mathematical objects that are useful for Java 3D. The other two packages contain many convenient utility classes for building primitives, views, and other objects in Java 3D, even though the `com.sun.j3d.*` packages are not considered in the core of Java 3D.

The visual components used in the program `Hello3D` are the old-style AWT components instead of the Swing components. For example, an `Applet` object is used instead of `JApplet`. This is because the GUI component `Canvas3D` used for Java 3D rendering is a heavyweight component. Even though it is possible to place heavyweight components into a Swing component `JFrame`, doing so may cause some irregularities in the display. For example, the menu may not be shown properly.

An applet derived from the `Applet` class can be implemented as an application as well by adding the applet to a `Frame` instance in a `main` method, similar to the Swing implementation. Because the `Frame` class does not have the `setDefaultCloseOperation` method, the window-closing operation for the frame needs to be implemented by handling the `WindowEvent`. The class `com.sun.j3d.utils.applet.MainFrame` provides an implementation for running an applet as an application (line 14). `Hello3D` and most subsequent examples will use this convenient utility class to create the dual-purpose program.

A `Canvas3D` object is created to display the 3D rendering (line 20). `Canvas3D` is a subclass of the AWT component `Canvas` and therefore the `Canvas3D` object can be added to this `Frame`. The method `createSceneGraph` defines the scene graph for the application. It returns a `BranchGroup` object that can be attached to a `SimpleUniverse` object. The utility class `SimpleUniverse` provides a basic framework for Java 3D rendering. Once the scene graph branch is attached to the `SimpleUniverse` object, the rendering will begin.

In the `createSceneGraph` method (line 30), first a `BranchGroup` object is created to act as the root. The visual object to be displayed is a 3D text string represented by a `Text3D` object. It is constructed with a 3D font and an appearance. A transformation is then defined with the `Transform3D` class. It performs a scaling and a translation. The transformation is applied to the `Text3D` object. A light is constructed and placed in the scene. The influence of the light is limited to a region defined by a `BoundingSphere` object.

To fully understand the Java 3D program, it is necessary first to understand Java 3D scene graphs. The details of Java 3D scene graphs will be introduced in the next sections, and the complete analysis of the scene graph contained in this example will be given later in the chapter.

5.3.2 Install Java 3D

To compile and execute a Java 3D program, you need a Java software development environment and the Java 3D package. Java 3D is an optional package of the Java 2 platform. A standard Java installation does not automatically include it. You may download the Java 3D package at the site:

download Java 3D

http://java.sun.com/products/java-media/3D/

Java 3D is available for various platforms including Solaris, Windows, Linux, and Mac OS. After installing the Java 3D package on top of a Java 2 software development kit, you will be able to compile and run a Java 3D program such as the one in Listing 5.1.

A Java 3D distribution includes native code and Java libraries. The Java classes are packaged in four jar files:

```
j3dcore.jar
j3dutils.jar
j3daudio.jar
vecmath.jar
```

In a Windows installation, the jar files are typically placed in the directory:

```
<j2sdk directory>/jre/lib/ext
```

The native code is implemented in three dynamic link libraries: J3D.dll, j3daudio.dll, and J3DUtils.dll under the directory:

```
<j2sdk directory>/jre/bin
```

You may also build Java 3D programs in IDEs such as JBuilder and Netbeans. Additional configurations may be required to use the Java 3D packages. In JBuilder, you need to create a new library to include the four jar files above, using the Tools menu item Configure Libraries. After the library is created, you may set the Project properties to use the library. In Netbeans (Sun ONE Studio, Forte), you will be able to compile and run Java 3D applications as soon as the Java 3D package is installed to the J2SDK associated with the Netbeans installation. However, to take advantage of the context-sensitive code-completion feature of the IDE, you may need to update the parser database for the jar files. This can be done by mounting the four jar files and selecting "Update Parser Database" on each. This step is not necessary for newer versions of Netbeans.

A Java 3D application can be executed in a Java Runtime Environment (JRE) with the Java 3D package installed. A Java 3D program may also be built as an applet. To view a Java 3D applet in a browser, you need to install a Java plug-in associated with a JRE for Java 2 environment and install the Java 3D package on top of the JRE.

Java 3D is usually built on top of other low-level graphics API such as OpenGL. For example, there are two Java 3D distributions for the Windows environment: one for OpenGL and the other DirectX. Rendering 3D graphics is usually a computationally intensive task. To achieve better performance, Java 3D will attempt to take advantage of the acceleration features offered by the graphics hardware. Because of the large variety of different graphics boards, software drivers, and vendors, you may encounter some compatibility problems when using Java 3D on certain platforms. The following suggestions may help you resolve some of the problems:

- Update your video driver to the latest stable version.

- Use the most recent release of Java 3D.

- Set the depth buffer in the OpenGL options of your graphics card to 24 bits or higher.

- Turn off hardware acceleration of the graphics card.

- Join the Java 3D interest group: java3d-interest@java.sun.com

5.4 Java 3D Scene Graphs

In order to organize various elements in the 3D rendering effectively, Java 3D uses the concept of scene graph to build a virtual universe that includes everything relevant to a 3D rendering. A scene graph is an abstract mathematical model for the organization of a scene. It is not a picture or an image of the scene. The scene graph can be conceptually drawn as a diagram, but its actual implementation is done in the program through object instantiation and method invocation. The scene graph enables programmers to specify complex graphics structures and actions in a uniform manner. It also enables the Java 3D rendering engine to process the scene systematically and efficiently.

A scene graph is a treelike data structure known as *DAG* (*directed acyclic graph*). A directed graph consists of a set of vertices (or nodes) connected with directed edges (or links). Figure 5.3 shows a directed graph with 6 vertices and 8 edges. A (directed) path in a directed graph is a vertex-edge sequence that moves along the edges of the graph. For example, in Figure 5.3, b-c-f-e is a path. A cycle in a directed graph is a closed path—that is, a path having the same initial and terminal vertex. For example, in Figure 5.3, a-c-f-e-a is a cycle. A DAG is a directed graph without any cycles. Therefore Figure 5.3 is not a DAG. However, if the edge e-a is removed, then it becomes a DAG.

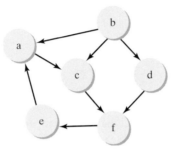

FIGURE 5.3 A directed graph.

tree

A (directed) *tree* is a special type of DAG. A tree is constructed starting from one vertex known as the *root* of the tree. There can be a number of edges originated from the root leading to other distinct vertices called the *children* of the root. Each child can then have a number of edges leading to its children in the same fashion. This process can iterate an arbitrary number of steps to produce a tree. Figure 5.4 shows an example of a tree. The vertex a is the root of the tree. In a tree, a vertex may have any number of children (including 0), but it cannot have more than one parent. A vertex that has no child is called a *leaf*. A nonleaf vertex is called an *internal node*. In Figure 5.4, the nodes e, h, c, g are leaves and the nodes a, b, d, f are internal nodes.

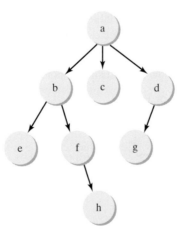

FIGURE 5.4 A directed tree.

The nodes of a scene graph represent objects of the various classes related to graphics functions. The links between nodes represent the logical relationships between them. In an actual Java 3D program, the nodes are created by instantiation of the classes defined in the Java 3D API, or the classes derived from the API classes and interfaces. The links are created by calling the appropriate methods or constructor in the classes. Figure 5.5 shows a very simple Java 3D scene graph.

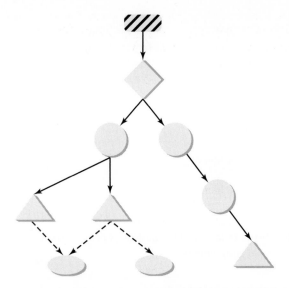

FIGURE 5.5 A scene graph as a DAG.

Different types of nodes and links are represented by different symbols in the diagram drawing of a scene graph. Figure 5.6 shows the symbols conventionally used for scene graph nodes and edges.

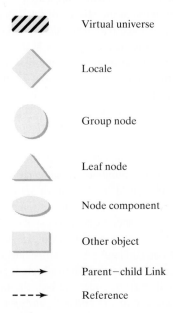

Virtual universe

Locale

Group node

Leaf node

Node component

Other object

Parent−child Link

Reference

FIGURE 5.6 Legend of scene graphs.

A scene graph has three major parts. On the top is the superstructure, which consists of objects from VirtualUniverse and Locale classes. The main body of the scene graph is a tree of objects belonging to the Node class. The third part is a set of NodeComponent objects. The leaf nodes in the tree structure can reference the node component objects. One NodeComponent object may be referenced by several Leaf objects. Therefore, the overall structure of a scene graph is not a tree but only a DAG.

The main class hierarchy for the scene graph elements is shown in Figure 5.7. The VirtualUniverse and Locale are classes for the superstructure and they are not derived

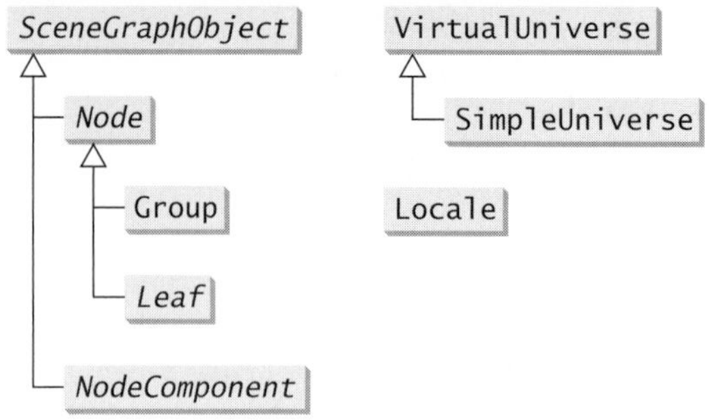

FIGURE 5.7 Scene-graph class hierarchy.

from the `SceneGraphObject` abstract class. The tree nodes in a scene graph are defined by the subclasses of the abstract class `Node`. The `NodeComponent` abstract class serves as the base class for various node components.

5.5 The Superstructure

VirtualUniverse

The `VirtualUniverse` and `Locale` objects are the superstructure objects of scene graphs. A Java 3D program typically has only one `VirtualUniverse` object. The `VirtualUniverse` is designed to potentially represent the entire space that is of interest to any Java 3D program. In order to accommodate the size and precision of a "universe," `VirtualUniverse` uses three high-resolution 256-bit fixed-point numbers to represent its coordinates. A high-resolution fixed-point number has its binary point at the middle of the 256 bits, so it has 128 bits for the integer part and 128 bits for the fractional part. The number 1.0 represents the unit of 1 meter. Numbers of this type can provide a distance measure as high as 2^{127} meters with a resolution of 2^{-128} meters. This should be adequate to measure any real objects in the universe. For example, the distance from the Earth to the Sun is only about 2^{37} meters and the radius of a proton is believed to be about 2^{-50} meters.

The class `HiResCoord` is defined to represent such a high-resolution coordinate. It contains three 256-bit high-resolution fixed-point numbers to represent the x-, y-, z-coordinates of a location.

Locale

While the `VirtualUniverse` is capable of modeling essentially the entire universe known to us through the `HiResCoord` numbers, it is clearly very inefficient to represent all coordinates using `HiResCoord` objects. Therefore, Java 3D uses the `Locale` class to represent smaller local spaces and to achieve much greater efficiency. A `Locale` object defines a local coordinate system anchored at a specific location specified by `HiResCoord` in the virtual universe. Within a specific locale, the coordinates of the points are represented by usual floating-point numbers. A `VirtualUniverse` contains one or more `Locale` objects. A `Locale` may have branch graphs attached to it. When a branch graph is attached to a `Locale`, the Java 3D rendering engine will start to render the branch, and the graph becomes live. A `Locale` object is always attached to one `VirtualUniverse` object. This association is established with constructors of `Locale`.

```
Locale(VirtualUniverse vu)
Locale(VirtualUniverse vu, HiResCoord location)
Locale(VirtualUniverse vu, int[] x, int[] y, int[] z)
```

The location of a `Locale` object in the universe can be specified using a `HiResCoord` object or three `int` arrays specifying the high-resolution numbers. The default location is (0, 0, 0). The following statements will create a superstructure for a scene graph:

```
VirtualUniverse universe = new VirtualUniverse();
Locale locale = new Locale(universe);
```

Branches of a scene graph rooted at `BranchGroup` objects can be attached to a `Locale` object by using the following method in `Locale`:

```
void addBranchGraph(BranchGroup branch)
```

The branches can be edited with the following methods:

```
void replaceBranchGraph(BranchGroup oldBranch, BranchGroup newBranch)
void removeBranchGraph(BranchGroup branch)
```

The following methods return the number of branches and all the branches in a `Locale`:

```
int numBranchGraphs()
Enumeration getAllBranchGraphs()
```

The class `SimpleUniverse` is a utility class derived from `VirtualUniverse`. It includes a `Locale` object and a set of objects to define a standard view. A `SimpleUniverse` object can be combined with the visual content branch to quickly form a complete scene graph. The world coordinate system in Java 3D is a right-handed rectangular system. The default view position is located on the z-axis looking toward the negative z-axis. From the viewer's perspective, the x-axis is pointing to the right and the y-axis up.

5.6 The Nodes

The `Node` objects are the nodes in the main tree structure of a scene graph. There are two main categories of nodes: the `Group` nodes and the `Leaf` nodes. The `Group` nodes are internal nodes of the tree representing certain relations and operations for the child nodes. The `Leaf` nodes are leaves of the tree representing certain graphics entities. The leaf nodes in a scene graph usually reference some `NodeComponent` object to define its attributes and properties. The node components may be shared among different leaf nodes.

5.6.1 The Group Nodes

Group nodes are the internal nodes in a scene graph. The main group-node class hierarchy is given in Figure 5.8. Group nodes are the main building blocks of the scene-graph tree structures. They may have children. A child of a group node can be a leaf node or another group node. Because of the tree structure imposed on the `Node` objects in a scene graph, two group nodes cannot share the same child-node object. A child node has only one parent, and there is a unique path from the root to a leaf node.

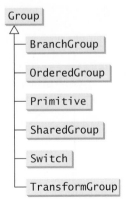

FIGURE 5.8 The Group-node classes.

A `Group` node maintains a list of children. To add a child node to a `Group` node, you may call the following methods:

```
void addChild(Node child)
void insertChild(Node child, int index)
```

A child can be accessed through an index.

```
Node getChild(int index)
void setChild(Node child, int index)
```

The methods to retrieve information about children include

```
int numChildren()
int indexOfChild(Node child)
```

Other methods related to children of a `Group` node include

```
Enumeration getAllChildren()
void removeChild(Node child)
void removeChild(int index)
void removeAllChildren()
```

BranchGroup   A `BranchGroup` node is the root of a branch of a scene graph. It is the only type of node that can be attached to a `Locale` object. Therefore, there must be at least one `BranchGroup` node in a scene graph. A `BranchGroup` node does not perform any special operations other than bringing its children together.

OrderedGroup   An `OrderedGroup` node specifies an order of rendering on its children. The Java 3D rendering engine renders a scene by traversing the scene graph from the root to all the leaf nodes. Normally at a particular node the order of visiting the children is not specified. Java 3D may choose to render the children in any order. The `OrderedGroup` node provides a way to enforce a specific ordering on traversing the children. The children of an `OrderedGroup` node are guaranteed to be rendered in the order of their indices. For example, the following code constructs a portion of a scene graph in which the three shapes will be guaranteed to render in the order `shape1`, `shape2`, `shape3`. The corresponding scene graph is shown in Figure 5.9.

```
Shape3D shape1 = new Shape3D();
Shape3D shape2 = new Shape3D();
Shape3D shape3 = new Shape3D();
OrderedGroup group = new OrderedGroup();
group.addChild(shape1);
group.addChild(shape2);
group.addChild(shape3);
```

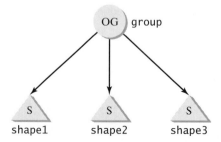

FIGURE 5.9   An `OrderedGroup` node and its children.

A `Primitive` node represents a complete geometric primitive such as a sphere. It is a util- `Primitive`
ity class in the package `com.sun.j3d.utils.geometry`. Primitives will be discussed in
Chapter 6, "Graphics Contents."

A `SharedGroup` node is the root of a branch graph that can be shared by several `Link` leaf `SharedGroup`
nodes. It is not uncommon that certain branches of a scene graph are identical. But the common
branch cannot be shared among group nodes, because of the requirement of tree structure. In
this case, you may define the common branch using a `SharedGroup` object as the root. This
branch can then be shared by several `Link` leaf nodes through references, instead of the parent–child relations. Consider the simple example in Figure 5.10. In the scene graph on the left,
two branches have the same structure and attributes. To share the common branch, a
`SharedGroup` node is added as the root of the shared branch. Two `Link` nodes referencing the
shared branch are introduced to replace the original common branches. The result is the scene
graph on the right. Note that this structure does not violate the requirement for a tree, because
the `SharedGroup` node is not a child of the `Link` nodes.

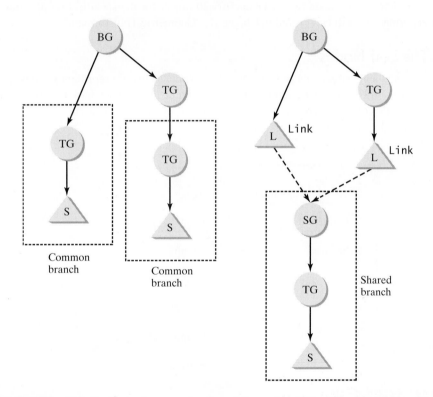

FIGURE 5.10   Identical branches may be shared through a `SharedGroup` node and `Link`
leaf nodes.

A `Switch` node acts as a switch to select a particular set of children of the node for ren- `Switch`
dering. In the list children of a `Switch` node, you may turn on the rendering of a specific
child, none of the children, all of the children, or a set of children using the following method:

    void setWhichChild(**int** whichChild)

The parameter `whichChild` may be a nonnegative integer specifying the index of a child, or
one of the predefined constants: CHILD_NONE, CHILD_ALL, CHILD_MASK. If the constant
CHILD_MASK is used, then the set of selected children is defined by a mask. The mask may be
set with the following method:

    void setChildMask(BitSet mask)

For example, the following code segment selects the **shape1** and **shape3** for rendering:

```
Shape3D shape1 = new Shape3D();
Shape3D shape2 = new Shape3D();
Shape3D shape3 = new Shape3D();
Switch group = new Switch();
group.addChild(shape1);
group.addChild(shape2);
group.addChild(shape3);
BitSet mask = new BitSet();
mask.set(0);
mask.set(2);
group.setChildMask(mask);
group.setWhichChild(Switch.CHILD_MASK);
```

TransformGroup

A TransformGroup node represents a geometric transform that applies to all of its children. A TransformGroup node uses a Transform3D object for the specification of a transform. Transformations will be covered in Chapter 7, "Geometric Transformation."

5.6.2 The Leaf Nodes

The Leaf class is an abstract subclass of Node. Leaf nodes generally represent various geometric objects, sounds, and other graphics objects in a scene graph. They have no child node, but they usually do contain references to node component objects. The class hierarchy of leaf nodes is given in Figure 5.11.

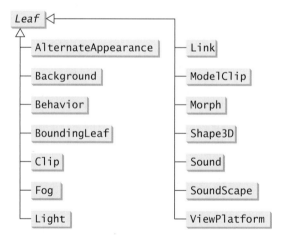

FIGURE 5.11 Leaf-node class.

Shape3D

A Shape3D leaf node represents a graphics object to be rendered. It holds the references to node components that describe the geometry and appearance of the object. The details about the Shape3D and its subclasses can be found in Chapter 6.

Behavior

The Behavior class encapsulates the actions that can be defined in a scene graph to achieve dynamic effects. It is the foundation for animation and interaction. The details of animation and interaction are covered in Chapters 10 and 11.

Morph

A Morph node is similar to Shape3D, but it facilitates the blending of multiple geometries. A Morph node can be used with a Behavior object to achieve morphing effects on an object.

Light

A Light leaf node defines a light that illuminates the scene when lighting is enabled. Lighting models are discussed in Chapter 9, "Lighting and Texturing."

Fog

The Fog node provides a special rendering effect of blending object colors with another color. The degree of blending is related to the distance to the viewer. This creates an effect of fading or fog. The details about Fog class will be presented in Chapter 9.

A `ViewPlatform` node represents the positioning of a view in the scene graphs. It is a part of the sophisticated Java 3D viewing system and is associated with a `View` object. Views are discussed in Chapter 8, "Views."

ViewPlatform

The `Background` node defines a background for a scene. The usage of `Background` is discussed later in this chapter.

Background

The `BoundingLeaf` node defines a bound that limits the influences of certain nodes such as backgrounds, lights, and behaviors. The concept of bounds will be covered later in this chapter.

BoundingLeaf

`Clip` and `ModelClip` nodes define planes that clip the view. A `Clip` node specifies the far clip plane. Anything beyond the plane is clipped and excluded from rendering. A `ModelClip` node specifies six planes to clip the view.

Clip, ModelClip

The `Link` node is used to reference a `SharedGroup` node of a shared branch in a scene graph, as introduced before.

Link

An `AlternateAppearance` node overrides the appearance of visual objects. `Shape3D` and `Morph` nodes will have their appearance overridden by an `AlternateAppearance` node if they are in the influence bound of the node and they allow the appearance to be overridden.

AlternateAppearance

`Sound` and `SoundScape` nodes represent audio objects. Java 3D allows incorporation of sounds in a scene graph. This is a useful feature for applications such as video games.

Sound, SoundScape

5.7 The Node Components

Group nodes and leaf nodes define the structure of a scene, but usually the attributes of the nodes are defined separately by other objects. Most of the attribute objects belong to the `NodeComponent` class. The `NodeComponent` objects define certain attributes such as geometries, colors, textures, and materials. The `NodeComponent` objects themselves are not nodes in the main tree structure of a scene graph, but they are usually referenced by leaf nodes in the scene graph. The class hierarchy of `NodeComponent` is shown in Figure 5.12.

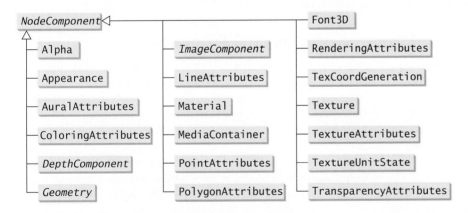

FIGURE 5.12   The NodeComponent classes.

The `Geometry` class (and its subclasses) defines the geometry of a graphics object. A `Shape3D` leaf node depends on `Geometry` objects to define its geometric attributes.

Geometry

The `Appearance` class controls the appearances of the rendered objects by holding references to other attribute objects. An `Appearance` object defines the complete rendering states of a `Shape3D` node. It holds other attribute objects including `ColoringAttributes`, `TransparencyAttributes`, `Material`, `PointAttributes`, `LineAttributes`, `PolygonAttributes`, `RenderingAttributes`, `Texture`, `TextureAttributes`, and `TexCoordGeneration`. Geometry and Appearance are discussed in Chapter 6.

Appearance

The `ColoringAttributes` class defines the color and shading model for rendering a visual object.

The `TransparencyAttributes` class sets the transparency properties including transparency mode, blend function, and blend value.

The `Material` class defines more sophisticated material properties than does `ColoringAttributes`. `Material` objects are used in lighting and illumination models. Detailed discussions of material attributes and their effects can be found in Chapter 9.

`RenderingAttributes` specify certain rendering-related parameters such as depth buffer and alpha test.

`PointAttributes`, `LineAttributes`, and `PolygonAttributes` objects define attributes related to the rendering of points, lines, and polygons. The point attributes include the point size and antialiasing setting. The line attributes include line width, line pattern, and antialiasing. The polygon attributes include polygon rendering related property settings such as polygon drawing mode, culling, backface normal flip, and offset.

The classes `Texture`, `TextureAttributes`, `TextureUnitState` are related to a rendering technique known as texture mapping. Texture mapping allows images to be used in rendering details of visual objects. The `ImageComponent` class encapsulates the images for the mapping. An `ImageComponent` object can also be used to set the background of a scene. The `TexCoordGeneration` class facilitates automatic generations of texture coordinates that are important parts of texture mapping. The details of texture mapping are presented in Chapters 9 and 12.

The `AuralAttributes` class defines certain parameters related to audio rendering. The `MediaContainer` class is used to define sound data. Examples of using sounds in Java 3D can be found in Chapter 12.

An `Alpha` object converts time values to floating-point numbers between 0 and 1 (alpha-values). It acts as a signal or waveform generator that can trigger certain actions. `Alpha` objects are useful in animations. Animations are covered in Chapter 11, "Animation."

The `DepthComponent` class encapsulates the concept of a depth buffer (also known as a z-buffer)—that is, a 2D array to store the depth values (z-values).

The `Font3D` class defines a solid 3D font. A `Font3D` object is based on an AWT `Font` object that defines the 2D glyphs of the font and a `FontExtrusion` object that defines the extrusion path in the third dimension.

5.8 The Structure of a Java 3D Program

In a simplistic view, to write a Java 3D program is essentially to assemble a scene graph. Of course it is necessary to create the usual user interface elements and other features relevant to an application, but the 3D modeling and rendering of the graphics program mainly consists of the construction of the scene graph. The scene graph is a complete specification of all the graphics objects and their attributes in the system and it is also linked to AWT components for displaying rendered images.

A Java 3D program needs to create a `Canvas3D` object. `Canvas3D` is a subclass of `java.awt.Canvas`, so its instances can be placed in AWT containers in the same way as any other AWT components. A `Canvas3D` object serves as the panel to display a rendered scene of the virtual world.

The Java 3D program should build a complete and correct scene graph using the objects of the classes provided or derived from the API. A `VirtualUniverse` object and a `Locale` object are needed for the superstructure of the scene graph.

A viewing branch of the scene graph is needed to set up a view of the scene. Typically it contains objects of `BranchGroup`, `TransformGroup`, `ViewPlatform`, `View`, `PhysicalBody`, and `PhysicalEnvironment`. The viewing branch is attached to the `Locale` and is linked to the `Canvas3D` object to deliver the rendered view.

At least one other branch of the scene graph should be constructed for the graphics contents of the virtual world. This content branch should have a `BranchGroup` node as its root, so that it can be attached to the `Locale`. Other nodes can be added to build the virtual world. `Shape3D`, `Light`, and other nodes can be used to create graphics objects. A `Shape3D` node can establish its geometry and appearance by referencing appropriate `Geometry` and `Appearance` objects. `TransformGroup` nodes can be used to apply necessary transformations to the child nodes.

To simplify the process of scene graph creation, Java 3D provides a convenient utility class `SimpleUniverse`. `SimpleUniverse` creates a `VirtualUniverse`, a `Locale`, and objects for a standard view. The `SimpleUniverse` is adequate for setting up the superstructures and views in most Java 3D applications using an ordinary video monitor display.

SimpleUniverse

With a basic understanding of Java 3D scene graphs, we can now examine the structure of the program in Listing 5.1. The scene graph corresponding to the Java 3D application in Listing 5.1 is shown in Figure 5.13.

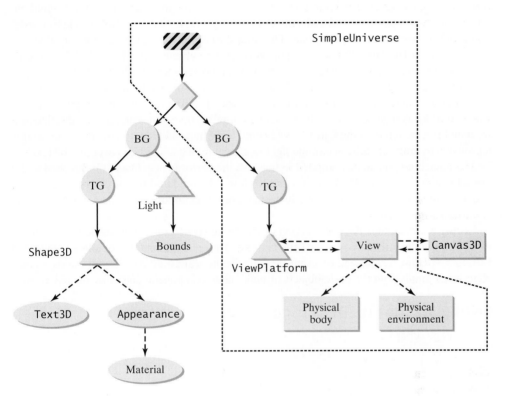

FIGURE 5.13   The scene graph for Listing 5.1.

The `SimpleUniverse` object contains objects of classes `VirtualUniverse`, `Locale`, `BranchGroup`, `TransformGroup`, `ViewPlatform`, `View`, `PhysicalBody`, and `PhysicalEnvironment`. The branch outside `SimpleUniverse` is a content branch that defines graphics objects in the virtual world. To attach the branch graph to the `Locale` object, use the method `attachBranchGraph()` in `SimpleUniverse`.

The `View` object inside `SimpleUniverse` is associated with a `Canvas3D` object that is an AWT component. The `Canvas3D` object is created separately, and it can be placed in an AWT container to display the rendered view. The `View` object in the `SimpleUniverse` defines a set of default parameters. A partial list of the parameters is given below.

Projection policy	PERSPECTIVE_PROJECTION
Field of view	$\pi/4$
Front clip distance	0.1
Back clip distance	10.0

The `PhysicalBody` and `PhysicalEnvironment` objects are also created with default values appropriate for the normal screen views. The viewing branch of the scene graph inside `SimpleUniverse` consists of a `BranchGroup` node, a `TransformGroup` node, and a `ViewPlatform` leaf. The BG object is the required node to attach the viewing branch the `Locale`. The TG node defines a transform for the `ViewPlatform`. The default view has the view plane pass through the origin. This is not convenient if some objects in the scene are also near the origin. One way to avoid the problem is to move the view back along the *z*-axis by changing the view transform. This procedure is done by the `setNominalViewingTransform` method in `ViewingPlatform` class. The following line from Listing 5.1 retrieves the `ViewingPlatform` from the `SimpleUniverse` and calls this method to move the view:

```
su.getViewingPlatform().setNominalViewingTransform();
```

The content branch in this program contains a `BranchGroup` node BG as the root. The left child of BG is a `TransformGroup` node TG that performs an affine transform on its children. The transform is a scaling of 0.5 and a translation by $(-0.95, -0.2, 0)$. There is one leaf node, a `Shape3D` object, under the TG node. The `Shape3D` object references a geometry that is a `Text3D` object. The `Text3D` node component is set to represent text "Hello 3D." The appearance is set to reference a `Material` object with default parameters. With the `Material` object set, the lighting mode is enabled. The 3D text is illuminated by a light defined in the scene.

A light leaf node is another child of the BG node. The light is defined as a point light of white color located at (3, 3, 3) with an attenuation of (1, 0, 0). For computational efficiency, we may limit the range of the light. There is only one `Shape3D` object in the program, so it is reasonable to limit the influence of the light to a local region enough to cover the 3D text.

The branch graph can be compiled to improve the performance. Once it is attached to the `Locale`, it becomes "live." A *live scene graph* will be rendered by the Java 3D rendering engine automatically. The objects in a live scene graph can no longer be edited unless specific permissions are given.

live scene graph

Listing 5.2 illustrates the construction of the entire scene-graph with scene-graph objects without using the utility class `SimpleUniverse`. This example is functionally equivalent to Listing 5.1. However, instead of using the `SimpleUniverse` utility class, it builds a complete scene graph from the basic objects of node, node component, and other related classes.

Listing 5.2 `Hello3DfullGraph.java`

```
1 package chapter5;
2
3 import java.awt.*;
4 import java.awt.event.*;
5 import javax.media.j3d.*;
6 import javax.vecmath.*;
7 import com.sun.j3d.utils.universe.*;
8 import com.sun.j3d.utils.geometry.*;
9 import java.applet.*;
10 import com.sun.j3d.utils.applet.MainFrame;
11
12 public class Hello3DFullGraph extends Applet {
13   public static void main(String[] args) {
14     new MainFrame(new Hello3DFullGraph(), 640, 480);
15   }
16
17   public void init() {
18     // create canvas
19     GraphicsConfiguration gc =
20     SimpleUniverse.getPreferredConfiguration();
21     Canvas3D cv = new Canvas3D(gc);
22     setLayout(new BorderLayout());
23     add(cv, BorderLayout.CENTER);
24
25     // create superstructure
26     VirtualUniverse vu = new VirtualUniverse();
27     Locale loc = new Locale(vu);
```

```java
28
29      // create view branch
30      BranchGroup bgView = createViewBranch(cv);
31      bgView.compile();
32      loc.addBranchGraph(bgView);
33
34      // create content branch
35      BranchGroup bg = createContentBranch();
36      bg.compile();
37      loc.addBranchGraph(bg);
38    }
39
40    private BranchGroup createViewBranch(Canvas3D cv) {
41      View view = new View();
42      view.setProjectionPolicy(View.PERSPECTIVE_PROJECTION);
43      ViewPlatform vp = new ViewPlatform();
44      view.addCanvas3D(cv);
45      view.attachViewPlatform(vp);
46      view.setPhysicalBody(new PhysicalBody());
47      view.setPhysicalEnvironment(new PhysicalEnvironment());
48      Transform3D trans = new Transform3D();
49      Point3d eye = new Point3d(0, 0, 1/Math.tan(Math.PI/8));
50      Point3d center = new Point3d(0, 0, 0);
51      Vector3d vup = new Vector3d(0, 1, 0);
52      trans.lookAt(eye, center, vup);
53      trans.invert();
54      TransformGroup tg = new TransformGroup(trans);
55      tg.addChild(vp);
56      BranchGroup bgView = new BranchGroup();
57      bgView.addChild(tg);
58      return bgView;
59    }
60
61    private BranchGroup createContentBranch() {
62      BranchGroup root = new BranchGroup();
63      // object
64      Appearance ap = new Appearance();
65      ap.setMaterial(new Material());
66      Font3D font = new Font3D(new Font("SansSerif", Font.PLAIN, 1),
67                              new FontExtrusion());
68      Text3D text = new Text3D(font, "Hello 3D");
69      Shape3D shape = new Shape3D(text, ap);
70      // transformation
71      Transform3D tr = new Transform3D();
72      tr.setScale(0.5);
73      tr.setTranslation(new Vector3f(-0.95f, -0.2f, 0f));
74      TransformGroup tg = new TransformGroup(tr);
75      root.addChild(tg);
76      tg.addChild(shape);
77      // light
78      PointLight light = new PointLight(new Color3f(Color.white),
79                                        new Point3f(1f,1f,1f),
80                                        new Point3f(1f,0.1f,0f));
81      BoundingSphere bounds = new BoundingSphere();
82      light.setInfluencingBounds(bounds);
83      root.addChild(light);
84      return root;
85    }
86  }
```

This example is essentially equivalent to Listing 5.1. Its scene graph is the same as that of Listing 5.1, as shown in Figure 5.13. The difference is that the superstructure and view branch are created explicitly without using the SimpleUniverse class.

The superstructure objects of VirtualUniverse and Locale are created with default settings (lines 26–27). The Locale object is anchored at the default location (0, 0, 0). The content branch is identical to that in Listing 5.1. The view branch is new, and its construction is done in the method createViewBranch (line 40). As shown in Figure 5.13, the view branch consists of objects of BranchGroup, TransformGroup, View, ViewPlatform, PhysicalBody, and PhysicalEnvironment.

The TransformGroup uses a Transform3D object to represent the transform. The transform is constructed using the methods lookAt and invert (lines 52–53). lookAt sets up a transform based on the eye position, view direction and view up direction. The inverse of this transform is used for setting the view transform group. The transformation settings used in this example are the same as those in SimpleUniverse with the setNominalViewing Transform call. Consequently the display of this example is identical to that of Listing 5.1, as shown in Figure 5.2.

5.9 Backgrounds and Bounds

The default background in a scene is black. If you do not place any visual object or light in the scene graph, you will see a black canvas. The background can be changed by using the Background leaf nodes. A Background leaf may define a solid background color or a background image. It may even define a background geometry. A background will be rendered behind all other visual objects. The constructors of Background are listed below.

```
Background()
Background(Color3f color)
Background(float r, float g, float b)
Background(ImageComponent2D image)
Background(BranchGroup geometry)
```

Listing 5.3 shows an application using a Background node. This program is similar to Listing 5.1. Instead of the default black color, the background color of the rendered scene is white.

Listing 5.3 Hello3Dbackground.java

```
1 package chapter5;
2
3 import java.awt.*;
4 import java.applet.*;
5 import java.awt.event.*;
6 import javax.media.j3d.*;
7 import javax.vecmath.*;
8 import com.sun.j3d.utils.universe.*;
9 import com.sun.j3d.utils.geometry.*;
10 import com.sun.j3d.utils.applet.MainFrame;
11
12 public class Hello3DBackground extends Applet {
13   public static void main(String[] args) {
14     new MainFrame(new Hello3DBackground(), 640, 480);
15   }
16
17   public void init() {
18     GraphicsConfiguration gc =
19     SimpleUniverse.getPreferredConfiguration();
20     Canvas3D cv = new Canvas3D(gc);
21     setLayout(new BorderLayout());
22     add(cv, BorderLayout.CENTER);
```

```
23      BranchGroup bg = createSceneGraph();
24      bg.compile();
25      SimpleUniverse su = new SimpleUniverse(cv);
26      su.getViewingPlatform().setNominalViewingTransform();
27      su.addBranchGraph(bg);
28   }
29
30   private BranchGroup createSceneGraph() {
31      BranchGroup root = new BranchGroup();
32      // object
33      Appearance ap = new Appearance();
34      ap.setMaterial(new Material());
35      Font3D font = new Font3D(new Font("SansSerif", Font.PLAIN, 1),
36      new FontExtrusion());
37      Text3D text = new Text3D(font, "Hello 3D");
38      Shape3D shape = new Shape3D(text, ap);
39      // transformation
40      Transform3D tr = new Transform3D();
41      tr.setScale(0.5);
42      tr.setTranslation(new Vector3f(-0.95f, -0.2f, 0f));
43      TransformGroup tg = new TransformGroup(tr);
44      root.addChild(tg);
45      tg.addChild(shape);
46      // light
47      PointLight light = new PointLight(new Color3f(Color.white),
48      new Point3f(1f,1f,1f),
49      new Point3f(1f,0.1f,0f));
50      BoundingSphere bounds = new BoundingSphere();
51      light.setInfluencingBounds(bounds);
52      root.addChild(light);
53      // background
54      Background background = new Background(1.0f, 1.0f, 1.0f);
55      background.setApplicationBounds(bounds);
56      root.addChild(background);
57      return root;
58   }
59 }
```

This example is similar to Listing 5.1. The visible difference is that the background of the scene is changed to white, as shown in Figure 5.14.

The new scene graph is given in Figure 5.15. A `Background` leaf node is added to the content branch of the scene graph (lines 54–56). The background is created with a constructor that specifies color RGB values:

```
Background background = new Background(1.0f, 1.0f, 1.0f);
background.setApplicationBounds(bounds);
root.addChild(background);
```

The application bound of the background is a `BoundingSphere` object shared with the light.

Environmental nodes such as `Background` and `Light` may potentially influence the entire universe. To achieve a reasonable rendering efficiency it is necessary to limit the influence. The *bounds* for environmental nodes can be set in two different ways: through the `Bounds` objects or the `BoundingLeaf` leaf nodes. `Bounds` objects are node components and `BoundingLeaf` objects are leaf nodes of a scene graph. The main difference between the two approaches is the coordinates of the bounds. A node that sets a bound by directly referencing a `Bounds` object will have the bound positioned relative to the node. A `BoundingLeaf` node has its own position defined for the bound. A node referencing the `BoundingLeaf` will acquire a bound positioned according to the `BoundingLeaf`.

FIGURE 5.14 A simple Java 3D program with a white background.

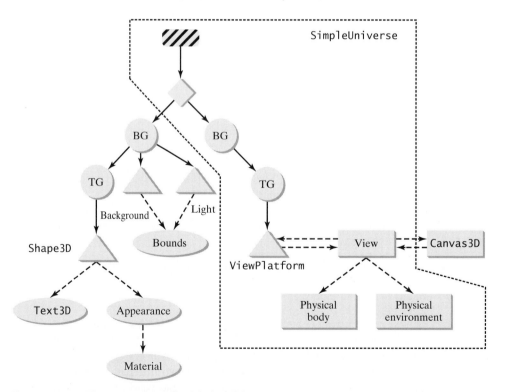

FIGURE 5.15 The scene graph for Listing 5.3.

The Bounds classes are shown in Figure 5.16. The abstract class Bounds has three subclasses BoundingBox, BoundingSphere, and BoundingPolytope to represent different types of bounding volumes.

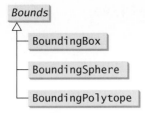

FIGURE 5.16 The Bounds class hierarchy.

The `BoundingBox` class defines a bound as a rectangular box with edges parallel to the axes. The `BoundingSphere` class defines a sphere as the bounding volume. The `BoundingPolytope` class defines a bounding volume of a general polytope.

The following statements create three bounds of different types:

```
Point3d lower = new Point3d(0,0,0); // lower corner of box
Point3d upper = new Point3d(1.0,0.5,1.5); // upper corner of box
BoundingBox box = new BoundingBox(lower, upper); // a bounding box
BoundingSphere sphere = new BoundingSphere(lower, 2);
                           // a bounding sphere
BoundingPolytope polytope = new BoundingPolytope(); // a polytope
```

A `BoundingLeaf` object is leaf node in the tree of a scene graph and has a specific location in the locale of the scene. A `BoundingLeaf` object uses a `Bounds` object to define its bounding region. This bounding region is positioned according to the position of the `BoundingLeaf` node. If several nodes located at different places in the virtual world need to reference a common bounding region, it is easier to use a `BoundingLeaf` node.

Consider an example of setting the influence bound of a light. The two different approaches are illustrated below.

```
// set bounds directly
BoundingSphere bounds = new BoundingSphere(); // a bounding sphere
light.setInfluencingBounds(bounds);
// set bounds by referencing a BoundingLeaf
BoundingSphere bounds = new BoundingSphere(); // a bounding sphere
BoundingLeaf leaf = new BoundingLeaf(bounds);
root.addChild(leaf); // add to scene graph
light.setInfluencingBoundingLeaf(leaf);
```

In the first case, a unit `BoundingSphere` is created and the influencing bound of a light is set directly to the bound. The sphere will be centered at the origin in the coordinate space of the light.

In the second case, a similar `BoundingSphere` is created, but it is referenced by a `BoundingLeaf` node. The influencing bound of the light is set to the `BoundingLeaf` node. The bounding sphere will be centered at the origin in the local coordinate system of the leaf node, which may be different from the local coordinate system of the light. The distinction between `Bounds` and `BoundingLeaf` will be more apparent if several lights under different transformation paths in the scene graph reference the same `Bounds` or `BoundingLeaf` objects. With direct `Bounds` references, their actual influencing bounds defined by the object are different. With a `BoundLeaf`, the actual bounds defined will be the same.

Listing 5.4 demonstrates the effects of `Bounds` objects on a light. A scene with an image background, three spheres and a light is created and rendered as shown in Figure 5.17. The spheres are lit by the light when they are within the influencing bounds of the light. When a user clicks the mouse on the panel, the influencing bound of the light is changed to the next of the three bounds. The first click will reduce the bounds, avoiding the left sphere. The second click reduces the bounds further to include only the right sphere. The third click will return to the original bounds.

Listing 5.4 TestBounds.java

```java
1 package chapter5;
2
3 import java.awt.*;
4 import java.awt.event.*;
5 import javax.media.j3d.*;
6 import javax.vecmath.*;
7 import com.sun.j3d.utils.universe.*;
8 import com.sun.j3d.utils.geometry.*;
9 import java.awt.image.*;
10 import java.io.*;
11 import java.net.URL;
12 import javax.imageio.*;
13 import java.applet.*;
14 import com.sun.j3d.utils.applet.MainFrame;
15
16 public class TestBounds extends Applet {
17   public static void main(String[] args) {
18     new MainFrame(new TestBounds(), 640, 480);
19   }
20
21   Light light = null;
22   Bounds[] bounds = new Bounds[3];
23   int bIndex = 0;
24
25   public void init() {
26     // create canvas
27     GraphicsConfiguration gc =
28     SimpleUniverse.getPreferredConfiguration();
29     Canvas3D cv = new Canvas3D(gc);
30     setLayout(new BorderLayout());
31     add(cv, BorderLayout.CENTER);
32     cv.addMouseListener(new MouseAdapter() {
33       // change background color and image on mouse click
34       public void mouseClicked(MouseEvent ev) {
35         bIndex = (bIndex+1) % 3;
36         System.out.println(bIndex);
37         light.setInfluencingBounds(bounds[bIndex]);
38       }
39     });
40     BranchGroup bg = createSceneGraph();
41     bg.compile();
42     SimpleUniverse su = new SimpleUniverse(cv);
43     su.getViewingPlatform().setNominalViewingTransform();
44     su.addBranchGraph(bg);
45   }
46
47   private BranchGroup createSceneGraph() {
48     BranchGroup root = new BranchGroup();
49     // first sphere
50     Sphere sphere = new Sphere();
51     Transform3D tr = new Transform3D();
52     tr.setScale(0.1);
53     TransformGroup tg = new TransformGroup(tr);
54     root.addChild(tg);
55     tg.addChild(sphere);
56     // second sphere
57     sphere = new Sphere();
58     tr.setTranslation(new Vector3f(-0.4f, 0f, 0f));
```

```
59      tg = new TransformGroup(tr);
60      root.addChild(tg);
61      tg.addChild(sphere);
62      // third sphere
63      sphere = new Sphere();
64      tr.setTranslation(new Vector3f(-0.8f, 0f, 0f));
65      tg = new TransformGroup(tr);
66      root.addChild(tg);
67      tg.addChild(sphere);
68      // light
69      light = new PointLight(new Color3f(Color.white),
70      new Point3f(1f,1f,1f),
71      new Point3f(1f,0f,0f));
72      light.setCapability(Light.ALLOW_INFLUENCING_BOUNDS_WRITE);
73      // bounds
74      bounds[0] = new BoundingSphere(new Point3d(0,0,0), 1);
75      bounds[1] = new BoundingSphere(new Point3d(0,0,0), 0.6);
76      bounds[2] = new BoundingSphere(new Point3d(0,0,0), 0.2);
77      light.setInfluencingBounds(bounds[0]);
78      root.addChild(light);
79      // background
80      URL url = getClass().getClassLoader().getResource
81        ("images/bg.jpg");
82      BufferedImage bi = null;
83      try {
84        bi = ImageIO.read(url);
85      } catch (IOException ex) {
86        ex.printStackTrace();
87      }
88      ImageComponent2D image =
89      new ImageComponent2D(ImageComponent2D.FORMAT_RGB, bi);
90      Background background = new Background(image);
91      background.setApplicationBounds(bounds[0]);
92      root.addChild(background);
93      return root;
94    }
95 }
```

FIGURE 5.17   The effects of influencing bounds. Left: The light has influencing bounds including all three spheres. Center: The light has influencing bounds including only two spheres. Right: The influencing bounds of the light are further reduced to cover only one sphere.

The abbreviated scene graph is shown in Figure 5.18. Three Sphere objects are added to the scene graph. Each sphere is attached to a TransformGroup node to scale it down in size and to translate the sphere to a different location. The amounts of translations for the three spheres are different so they do not overlap (lines 49–67).

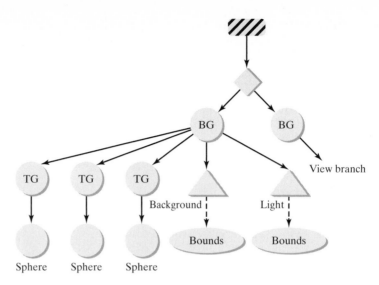

FIGURE 5.18 The scene graph for Listing 5.4.

A light is placed at (1, 1, 1) to illuminate the spheres. The light has influencing bounds that determines whether an object is lit by the light. Three different BoundingSphere objects of radii 1, 0.6, and 0.2 are created and stored in the bounds array (lines 74–76). An integer field bIndex is an index to keep track of the current bounds. Initially bounds[0] is used by the light, and it is large enough to include all three spheres.

A MouseListener is added to the Canvas3D object to handle the mouse events. In an event of a mouse click, the current bounds index is changed:

```
bIndex = (bIndex + 1) % 3;
light.setInfluencingBounds(bounds[bIndex]);
```

Therefore, the elements in the bounds array are selected in a cyclic way in response to mouse clicks. When bounds[1] is selected, the left sphere is outside the influencing bounds of the light, and it becomes black. When bounds[2] is selected, only the right sphere remains in the bounds, and the other two spheres are black.

The background is defined using a Background leaf node. The background is set to an image loaded from an image file. The Background node also needs a Bounds object to limit its application. In this example the BoundingSphere object in bounds[0] is also used by the background node for its application bounds:

```
background.setApplicationBounds(bounds[0]);
```

5.10 Compiling Scene Graphs and Capability Bits

compiling

A scene graph rooted at a BranchGroup node can be compiled before it is attached to a Locale and becomes live. The BranchGroup class contains a method compile for *compiling* the scene graph. Compiling a scene graph converts it to an internal representation that will be more efficient for the Java 3D rendering engine to use in rendering the scene. Compiling the scene graph also gives Java 3D an opportunity to perform certain optimizations that can speed up the rendering. The optimizations are not defined by the Java 3D specification and may be implementation dependent.

capability bits

You may change a scene graph after it is live, but to do so you have to explicitly get permission for every operation attempted on a live scene-graph object. The permissions are expressed in the form of *capability bits* that exist in the node and node-component objects.

Each individual operation in an individual object has an independent capability bit. By default, all capability bits are turned off to improve the rendering performance. In order to make a dynamic change on any aspect of a live scene graph, you need to turn on the corresponding capability bit in advance. The capability bits must be set before the scene graph is compiled with the method call `compile`. If an operation is performed without the appropriate capability bit being set, a runtime exception will be thrown.

The capability bits can be set with the following method of the `SceneGraphObject` class,

```
public final void setCapability(int bit);
```

The capability bits are defined as constants in individual classes. If multiple capability bits need to be set, you have to make several calls to the `setCapability` method. Each call can set only one bit. It is not allowed to combine multiple capability bits into one and to make only one call. For example, to allow the change of color in a `ColoringAttributes` object, you need to set the corresponding capability bit:

```
coloring.setCapability(ColorAttributes.ALLOW_COLOR_WRITE);
```

To read the color when the scene graph is live, you need to give the read permission:

```
coloring.setCapability(ColorAttributes.ALLOW_COLOR_READ);
```

To be able to read and write the color, you need to set the two bits:

```
coloring.setCapability(ColorAttributes.ALLOW_COLOR_READ);
coloring.setCapability(ColorAttributes.ALLOW_COLOR_WRITE);
```

If you need to modify the geometry of a Shape3D node, you must set the capability bit:

```
shape.setCapability(Shape3D.ALLOW_GEOMETRY_WRITE);
```

Listing 5.5 shows the use of capability bits and the modification of the background in a live scene graph. This program demonstrates the process of changing the attributes of a live scene graph. The background image and color in the scene are changed in response to mouse clicks. (See Figure 5.19.)

Listing 5.5 `ChangeBackground.java`

```java
 1 package chapter5;
 2
 3 import java.awt.*;
 4 import java.awt.event.*;
 5 import javax.media.j3d.*;
 6 import javax.vecmath.*;
 7 import com.sun.j3d.utils.universe.*;
 8 import com.sun.j3d.utils.geometry.*;
 9 import java.awt.image.*;
10 import java.io.*;
11 import java.net.URL;
12 import javax.imageio.*;
13 import java.applet.*;
14 import com.sun.j3d.utils.applet.MainFrame;
15
16 public class ChangeBackground extends Applet {
17   public static void main(String[] args) {
18     new MainFrame(new ChangeBackground(), 640, 480);
19   }
20
21   Background background = null;
```

```
22    ImageComponent2D image = null;
23
24    public void init() {
25      GraphicsConfiguration gc =
26      SimpleUniverse.getPreferredConfiguration();
27      Canvas3D cv = new Canvas3D(gc);
28      setLayout(new BorderLayout());
29      add(cv, BorderLayout.CENTER);
30      cv.addMouseListener(new MouseAdapter() {
31        // change background color and image on mouse click
32        public void mouseClicked(MouseEvent ev) {
33          if (background.getImage() == null)
34            background.setImage(image);
35          else {
36            background.setImage(null);
37            float r = (float)Math.random();
38            float g = (float)Math.random();
39            float b = (float)Math.random();
40            background.setColor(r, g, b);
41          }
42        }
43      });
44      BranchGroup bg = createSceneGraph();
45      bg.compile();
46      SimpleUniverse su = new SimpleUniverse(cv);
47      su.getViewingPlatform().setNominalViewingTransform();
48      su.addBranchGraph(bg);
49    }
50
51    private BranchGroup createSceneGraph() {
52      BranchGroup root = new BranchGroup();
53      // object
54      Appearance ap = new Appearance();
55      ap.setMaterial(new Material());
56      Font3D font = new Font3D(new Font("SansSerif", Font.PLAIN, 1),
57      new FontExtrusion());
58      Text3D text = new Text3D(font, "Hello 3D");
59      Shape3D shape = new Shape3D(text, ap);
60      // transformation
61      Transform3D tr = new Transform3D();
62      tr.setScale(0.5);
63      tr.setTranslation(new Vector3f(-0.95f, -0.2f, 0f));
64      TransformGroup tg = new TransformGroup(tr);
65      root.addChild(tg);
66      tg.addChild(shape);
67      // light
68      PointLight light = new PointLight(new Color3f(Color.white),
69      new Point3f(1f,1f,1f),
70      new Point3f(1f,0.1f,0f));
71      BoundingSphere bounds = new BoundingSphere();
72      light.setInfluencingBounds(bounds);
73      root.addChild(light);
74      // background
75      background = new Background(1.0f, 1.0f, 1.0f);
76      background.setApplicationBounds(bounds);
77      // load image
78      URL url = getClass().getClassLoader().
79      getResource("images/bg.jpg");
80      BufferedImage bi = null;
```

```
81     try {
82       bi = ImageIO.read(url);
83     } catch (IOException ex) {
84       ex.printStackTrace();
85     }
86     image = new ImageComponent2D(ImageComponent2D.FORMAT_RGB, bi);
87     // set capability bit to allow color and image change
88     background.setCapability(Background.ALLOW_COLOR_WRITE);
89     background.setCapability(Background.ALLOW_IMAGE_READ);
90     background.setCapability(Background.ALLOW_IMAGE_WRITE);
91     root.addChild(background);
92     return root;
93   }
94 }
```

FIGURE 5.19 The background toggles between a sky image and a random solid color.

This example is similar to Listing 5.2. They have the identical scene graph. Two kinds of backgrounds are applied in this example: an image and a solid color.

An image is read from a file "bg.jpg" to a `BufferedImage` object and is then passed to an `ImageComponent2D` object (lines 77–84). The `Background` node has the following capability bits set to allow live changes of its color and image and to read its image (lines 88–90):

```
ALLOW_COLOR_WRITE
ALLOW_IMAGE_READ
ALLOW_IMAGE_WRITE
```

In the constructor, the `Canvas3D` object is set to listen to mouse events. In the mouse-click handler, `mouseClicked`, the background is checked for the existence of a background image. If there is no image in the background, the loaded image is assigned to the background. If there is already an image in the background, the image of the background is set to null and the color of the background is changed to a random color. Therefore, successive clicking of the canvas will toggle the background between the image and a random solid color.

KEY CLASSES AND METHODS

- ■ `com.sun.j3d.util.applet.MainFrame` A utility class to display an applet in a frame.
- ■ `javax.media.j3d.VirtualUniverse` A class encapsulating a coordinate space of the entire virtual universe.

- **javax.media.j3d.Locale** A class defining a coordinate space with float data type anchored in the virtual universe.
- **javax.media.j3d.HiResCoord** A fixed-point data type to represent high-resolution coordinates of the virtual universe.
- **com.sun.j3d.util.universe.SimpleUniverse** A convenience class with a default implementation of the virtual universe, a locale, and a view branch of the scene graph.
- **javax.media.j3d.SceneGraphObject** An abstract class served as the root class for all scene-graph elements.
- **javax.media.j3d.Node** A class for nodes in a scene graph.
- **javax.media.j3d.NodeComponent** A class for node components in a scene graph.
- **javax.media.j3d.Group** A class for group nodes in a scene graph.
- **javax.media.j3d.Leaf** A class for leaf nodes in a scene graph.
- **javax.media.j3d.SceneGraphObject.setCapability(int)** A method to allow certain manipulations of the object in a live scene graph.
- **javax.media.j3d.Group.addChild(Node)** A method to add child nodes in a scene graph.
- **javax.media.j3d.BranchGroup** A special type of group nodes that can be attached to a locale.
- **javax.media.j3d.BranchGroup.compile()** A method to compile the scene graph to improve the performance.
- **javax.media.j3d.Background** A leaf node defining the background color, image, and geometry of a scene.
- **javax.media.j3d.Bounds** A node-component class encapsulating a spatial volume that is used by environmental nodes to limit their scope of activation.
- **javax.media.j3d.BoundingLeaf** A leaf class encapsulating a spatial volume that is used by environmental nodes to limit their scope of activation.
- **javax.media.j3d.BoundingBox** A class encapsulating box-shaped bounds.
- **javax.media.j3d.BoundingSphere** A class encapsulating spherical bounds.
- **javax.media.j3d.BoundingPolytope** A class encapsulating polytope bounds.

KEY TERMS

geometry A structural definition of a visual object.
appearance A collection of rendering attributes of a visual object.
DAG (directed acyclic graph) A directed graph with no directed cycles.
scene graph A DAG specifying the graph scene to be rendered.
tree A graph formed by recursively adding distinct child nodes.
leaf node A node in a tree that has no children.
internal node A node in a tree that has children.
primitive A basic visual object that may be used to build a model.
capability bit A flag in SceneGraphObject that gives permission to performing a specific operation in a live scene graph.

CHAPTER SUMMARY

- In this chapter, we discuss the fundamental concepts of 3D computer graphics and the basic architecture of the Java 3D system.

- In a 3D graphics system, a virtual world is built to model a 3D graphics scene. The model is viewed from a particular perspective to produce a rendering of the scene.

■ The Java 3D API is built on the key concept of scene graphs. A scene graph incorporates all the graphics descriptions and attributes of a scene to be rendered into a single data structure.

■ The rules for constructing the scene graphs and their building blocks are introduced. A scene graph is a DAG, with nodes being objects from classes of superstructures, nodes, and node components.

■ The overall structure of a Java 3D program is presented. By using a scene graph and its related objects, we can build a 3D graphics model and let Java 3D render the scene automatically.

■ The background of a scene can be changed using the `Background` leaf node. Environmental nodes such as `Light` and `Background` need to set bounds to limit their influence in rendering. `Bounds` and `BoundingLeaf` objects are two ways of setting bounds.

■ A branch graph can be compiled to improve rendering efficiency. A component of a live scene graph can be modified only if appropriate capability bits are set.

REVIEW QUESTIONS

5.1   If a tree has 15 nodes, how many links does it have?

5.2   Is the following graph (Figure 5.20) a tree? Is it a DAG? If it is a tree, identify its root, leaves, and internal nodes.

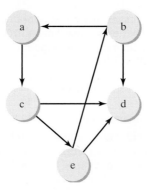

FIGURE 5.20   A graph for Problem 5.2.

5.3   Is the following graph (Figure 5.21) a tree? Is it a DAG? If it is a tree, identify its root, leaves, and internal nodes.

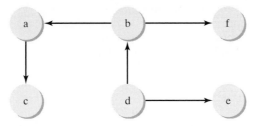

FIGURE 5.21   A graph for Problem 5.3.

5.4 Is the following graph (Figure 5.22) a tree? Is it a DAG? If it is a tree, identify its root, leaves, and internal nodes.

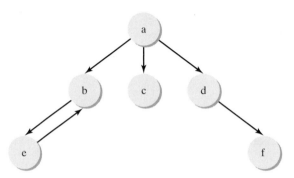

FIGURE 5.22 A graph for Problem 5.4.

5.5 Draw a scene graph corresponding to the following Java 3D code segment:

```
BranchGroup root = new BranchGroup();
TransformGroup trans = new TransformGroup();
root.addChild(trans);
Shape3D shape1 = new Shape3D();
Shape3D shape2 = new Shape3D();
Shape3D shape3 = new Shape3D();
trans.addChild(shape1);
trans.addChild(shape2);
root.addChild(shape3);
```

5.6 Draw a scene graph corresponding to the following Java 3D code segment:

```
BranchGroup root = new BranchGroup();
TransformGroup trans1 = new TransformGroup();
TransformGroup trans2 = new TransformGroup();
root.addChild(trans1);
root.addChild(trans2);
Light light = new PointLight();
trans1.addChild(light);
Switch switch = new Switch();
Trans2.addChild(switch);
Shape3D shape1 = new Shape3D();
Shape3D shape2 = new Shape3D();
switch.addChild(shape1);
switch.addChild(shape2);
Appearance appear = new Appearance();
shape1.setAppearance(appear);
shape2.setAppearance(appear);
```

5.7 Write a Java 3D code segment corresponding to the scene graph branch shown in Figure 5.23.

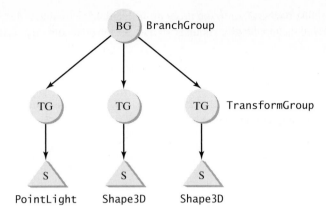

FIGURE 5.23 Scene graph for Problem 5.7.

5.8 Write a Java 3D code segment corresponding to the scene graph branch shown in Figure 5.24.

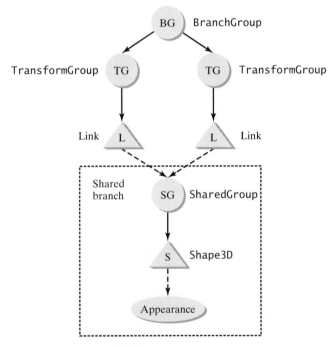

FIGURE 5.24 Scene graph for Problem 5.8.

PROGRAMMING EXERCISES

5.1 The ColorCube class is a subclass of Shape3D and can be used as a leaf node to represent a cube with colored faces. Write a Java 3D application that displays a ColorCube object using the SimpleUniverse class.

5.2 Write a Java 3D program to display a ColorCube as in Exercise 5.1 without using the SimpleUniverse class. Draw a complete scene-graph diagram for the program.

5.3 Add a blue background to the program in Exercise 5.1 using a `Background` leaf node. Set the application bounds of the background directly with a bounding sphere.

5.4 Write a Java 3D program similar to Exercise 5.3, but use a `BoundingLeaf` node to set the application bounds to a bounding box.

5.5 Write a Java 3D program similar to Listing 5.4, but use a `BoundingLeaf` node for the influencing bounds of the light.

Chapter 6

Graphics Contents

Objectives

- To understand geometry and appearance, the basic attributes of visual objects.

- To describe the representations of points and vectors.

- To apply the `GeometryArray` family of classes for constructing geometry.

- To apply the `GeometryInfo` class for constructing geometry.

- To use geometric primitives.

- To use texts and fonts as geometric objects.

- To use the `Appearance` class and the associated node-component classes.

6.1 Introduction

The fundamental graphics building blocks in a 3D graphics model are the visual shape objects. They constitute the visible objects in a rendered scene. A shape object is defined by its geometry and its appearance. The geometry provides a mathematical description of the object's shape, size, and other structural properties. The appearance defines the object's color, texture, material properties, and other attributes.

primitive

The geometry of a visual object may be constructed from a set of simple objects such as triangles. More complex but useful objects such as cubes and spheres may be prebuilt as reusable objects known as *primitives*. Primitives provide a level of abstraction that will simplify the construction of many complex objects. Text objects based on fonts provide another source of geometry objects. Both 2D and 3D text objects are useful elements of a 3D graphics scene.

Java 3D provides the leaf node class `Shape3D` to represent shape objects. The geometry and appearance of a `Shape3D` node are defined by referencing the `Geometry` and `Appearance` objects. The `Geometry` class has a number of subclasses to help define various types of geometries in different ways. The `Appearance` class holds references to various other attribute objects to define different aspects of the appearance. Commonly used primitives such as boxes, spheres, cylinders, and cones are also provided by Java 3D. Java 3D offers supports to use 2D and 3D texts as geometric objects.

In this chapter, we will introduce the construction of visual objects using geometry and appearance specifications. Java 3D's facilities for the low-level construction of geometries are examined. The high-level constructs of primitives and text objects are also presented. We will discuss the basic structure and usage of Java 3D appearance attributes in this chapter. The attributes that are related to more advanced rendering options such as lighting and texturing will be covered in greater detail in later chapters.

6.2 Points and Vectors

point
vector
vector space

The modeling of geometry begins with the modeling of a *point*. To precisely represent points in computers, the algebraic concept of *vectors* and *vector spaces* is commonly used. An *n*-dimensional vector is an *n*-tuple of numbers:

$$(x_1, x_2, \ldots, x_n)$$

homogeneous coordinates

The collection of all the *n*-dimensional vectors forms an *n*-dimensional space R^n. In a 3D space, a point can be represented by a 3D vector (x, y, z). Using *homogeneous coordinates*, a point is associated with a 4D vector (x, y, z, w).

There is also a geometric concept of vectors that represents quantities with directions. Examples of such vectors include the direction of a line, force, velocity, and acceleration. A geometric vector is also represented as an *n*-tuple. Algebraically there is no distinction between a geometric point and a geometric vector. The difference exists only in the interpretations of general mathematical quantities.

In 3D graphics, geometry construction and transformation depend heavily on the mathematical notion of vectors. Java provides an extensive set of classes for representing points, vectors, and matrices in the package `javax.vecmath`. Java 3D classes frequently use the vector math classes, and the `javax.vecmath` package is included in the distribution of Java 3D.

The package `javax.vecmath` contains many variations of vector and matrix classes. A partial list of the vector classes is given below in Figure 6.1.

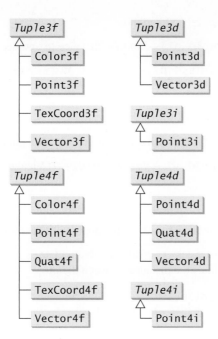

FIGURE 6.1   Vector math classes.

The suffixes in the class names indicate the dimensions and the data types of the components. The data type suffixes are listed below:

```
f: float
d: double
i: int
b: byte
```

For example, "4d" represents a four-dimensional tuple of **double** values. The stems of the class names indicate the categories of their usage.

- ▓ `Tuple*` classes: the abstract base classes for the tuples.
- ▓ `Color*` classes: color representations.
- ▓ `Point*` classes: geometric points.
- ▓ `Vector*` classes: geometric vectors.
- ▓ `TexCoord*` classes: texture-mapping coordinates.
- ▓ `Quat*` classes: quaternions.

Besides the data representation, the vector classes contain methods for standard operations related to their categories. For example, the `Tuple4f` class includes methods:

- ▓ **void** `add(Tuple4f t1)`—Add another tuple.
- ▓ **void** `sub(Tuple4f t1)`—Subtract another tuple.
- ▓ **void** `scale(`**float** `k)`—Scale the tuple.
- ▓ **void** `negate()`—Negate all components of the tuple.

`Point3d` class adds distance-related methods:

- ▪ **void** `distance(Point3d p1)`—Find the distance to another point.
- ▪ **void** `distanceL1(Point3d p1)`—Find the L^1 distance to another point.
- ▪ **void** `distanceLinf(Point3d p1)`—Find the L^∞ distance to another point.

`Vector3d` class includes methods for vector operations:

- ▪ **double** `dot(Vector3d v1)`—Find the dot product with another vector.
- ▪ **double** `cross(Vector3d v1, Vector3d v2)`—Calculate the cross product of the two vectors.
- ▪ **double** `length()`—Find the length of the vector.
- ▪ **double** `angle(Vector3d v1)`—Find the angle with another vector.

The vector math objects are easy to create and manipulate. The following example creates two `Point3d` objects and finds the distance between them:

```
Point3d p1 = new Point3d(1.0, 2.3, 0.0);
Point3d p2 = new Point3d(0.0, -0.5, 1.2);
double dist = p1.distance(p2);
```

To find the angle between two vectors, you can call the `angle` method:

```
Vector3f v1 = new Vector3f(1.0, 2.3, 0.0);
Vector3f v2 = new Vector3f(0.0, -0.5, 1.2);
double angle = v1.angle(v2);
```

6.3 Geometry

The basic geometric shapes of 3D objects are typically modeled as points, lines, and surfaces. Points and lines (including curves) are relatively simple to define because they are usually straightforward extensions of the corresponding 2D models. The surface models present some real challenges. 3D solid objects can usually be modeled as surfaces. Mathematically a surface can often be represented by an *implicit equation* on the coordinates:

implicit equation

$$F(x, y, z) = 0$$

parametric equation

Alternatively, a *parametric equation* with two parameters is usually more convenient for graphics applications:

$$x = f(u, v)$$
$$y = g(u, v)$$
$$z = h(u, v)$$

Because of the obvious complexity involved in representing an arbitrary 3D surface, it is often necessary to use a collection of simpler surfaces as an approximation. A commonly used representation is a mesh of simple polygons, such as triangles and quadrilaterals. Another versatile and powerful representation tool for surfaces is the polynomial and spline surfaces. Figure 6.2 shows an example of *polygon meshes* representing a surface.

polygon meshes

Java 3D offers direct support for arrays of points, lines, and triangles or quadrilaterals as the basic tools for geometry construction. It also offers support for high-level geometries such as primitives and 3D text.

In a Java 3D scene graph, a visual object is usually represented by a `Shape3D` leaf node. The `Shape3D` object references a `Geometry` object that defines the shape and other geometric

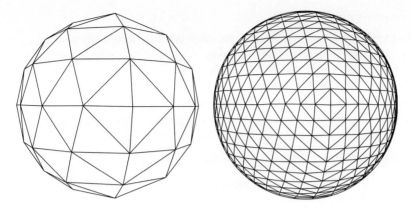

FIGURE 6.2 A sphere represented by triangle meshes of different resolutions.

characteristics of the visual object. The Shape3D node also references Appearance objects to define its appearance in rendering. A typical scene-graph Shape3D node configuration is shown in Figure 6.3.

The Geometry class is an abstract class with a large number of descendants. Figure 6.4 shows the class hierarchy of the Geometry classes.

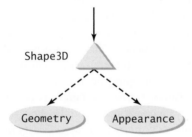

FIGURE 6.3 A typical scene-graph shape node.

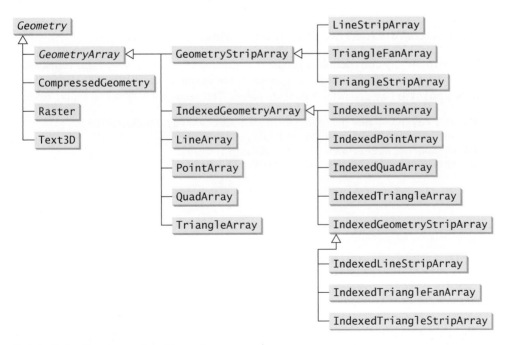

FIGURE 6.4 Geometry class hierarchy.

6.3.1 GeometryArray

The GeometryArray family of classes provides facilities to directly construct geometries with arrays of simple polygons, lines, or points. A GeometryArray defines the vertices and specifies the structural relationships among the vertices.

In a GeometryArray object, the definitions for vertices always include their coordinates, but they may also include other types of data components such as surface normals and colors. The presence of a particular type of vertex data component is indicated by a corresponding bit mask.

COORDINATES – the coordinates of vertices.

NORMALS – the surface normals of vertices.

COLOR_3 – the colors of vertices without α-channel.

COLOR_4 – the colors of vertices with α-channel.

TEXTURE_COORDINATE_2 – the 2D texture coordinates.

TEXTURE_COORDINATE_3 – the 3D texture coordinates.

TEXTURE_COORDINATE_4 – the 4D texture coordinates.

These masks can be combined using bitwise OR operator "|". The masks can be set in the constructors of GeometryArray classes. The data components, if present, are assigned to each vertex. Color specifications at the vertices may be used to determine the colors of the visual objects under given shading models. The surface normals are necessary to calculate light reflections in illuminated models. Texture coordinates define the coordinates in texture space. Lighting models and texture mapping are discussed in Chapter 9.

Typically an object in the GeometryArray family is created by calling an appropriate constructor with the specified data components and the array sizes. Then the vertex data are set through method calls. GeometryArray provides a variety of different methods to set the coordinates and other data. For example, a coordinate can be set individually or an array of coordinates can be set in one method:

```
void setCoordinate(int index, Point3f coord)
void setCoordinates(int startIndex, Point3f[] coords)
```

PointArray

The PointArray class defines a geometry consisting of a set of points. Each vertex specification corresponds to a point in the geometry. For example, the following code fragment defines a PointArray geometry with three points. The geometry is shown in Figure 6.5.

```
PointArray pa = new PointArray(3, GeometryArray.COORDINATES);
pa.setCoordinate(0, new Point3f(0f, 0f, 0f));
pa.setCoordinate(1, new Point3f(1f, 0f, 0f));
pa.setCoordinate(2, new Point3f(0f, 1f, 0f));
```

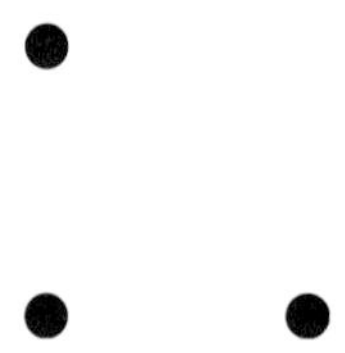

FIGURE 6.5 A PointArray geometry.

LineArray

The LineArray class defines a geometry of line segments. Every two vertices specified sequentially correspond to a line segment in the geometry:

```
LineArray la = new LineArray(6, GeometryArray.COORDINATES);
Point3f[] coords = new Point3f[6];
coords[0] = new Point3f(0f, 0f, 0f);
coords[1] = new Point3f(1f, 1f, 0f);
coords[2] = new Point3f(1f, 0f, 0f);
coords[3] = new Point3f(2f, 1f, 0f);
coords[4] = new Point3f(2f, 1f, 0f);
coords[5] = new Point3f(3f, 0f, 0f);
la.setCoordinates(0, coords);
```

The line geometry defined above is illustrated in Figure 6.6.

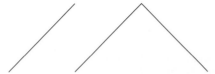

FIGURE 6.6   A `LineArray` geometry.

The `TriangleArray` class defines a surface consisting of triangle patches. Every three ver-   `TriangleArray`
tices define a triangle. The following code fragment defines a geometry object of two triangles:

```
TriangleArray ta = new TriangleArray(6, GeometryArray.COORDINATES);
Point3f[] coords = new Point3f[6];
coords[0] = new Point3f(0f, 0f, 0f);
coords[1] = new Point3f(1f, 1f, 0f);
coords[2] = new Point3f(1f, 0f, 0f);
coords[3] = new Point3f(1f, 0f, 0f);
coords[4] = new Point3f(2f, 1f, 0f);
coords[5] = new Point3f(3f, 0f, 0f);
ta.setCoordinates(0, coords);
```

The geometry defined in the `TriangleArray` is shown in Figure 6.7.

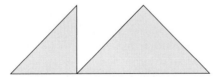

FIGURE 6.7   A `TriangleArray` geometry.

The geometry of a cone may be defined as a series of triangles using a `TriangleArray`:

```
int n = 60; // number of triangle patches
TriangleArray ta = new TriangleArray(3*n, GeometryArray.COORDINATES);
Point3f apex = new Point3f(0, 0, 1);
Point3f p1 = new Point3f(1, 0, 0);
int count = 0;
for (int ii = 1; ii <= n; ii++) {
  float x = (float)Math.cos(ii*2*Math.PI/n);
  float y = (float)Math.sin(ii*2*Math.PI/n);
  Point3f p2 = new Point3f(x, y, 0);
  ta.setCoordinate(count++, apex);
  ta.setCoordinate(count++, p1);
  ta.setCoordinate(count++, p2);
  p1 = p2;
}
```

The circular base of the cone is divided into *n* segments. The two points of each segment and the apex form a triangle. Because the `TriangleArray` requires explicit specification of each vertex in each triangle, we need to define $3n$ coordinates, even though there are only $n + 1$ distinct points.

The `QuadArray` class defines a surface of quadrilateral patches. Every four sequential vertices define a quadrilateral. The four vertices are required to be on a plane. The following `QuadArray` object consists of two squares not on the same plane, but the vertices of each square are on the same plane. (See Figure 6.8.)

```
QuadArray qa = new QuadArray(8, GeometryArray.COORDINATES);
Point3f[] coords = new Point3f[8];
coords[0] = new Point3f(0f, 0f, 0f);
coords[1] = new Point3f(1f, 0f, 0f);
coords[2] = new Point3f(1f, 1f, 0f);
coords[3] = new Point3f(0f, 1f, 0f);
coords[4] = new Point3f(1f, 1f, 0f);
coords[5] = new Point3f(0f, 1f, 0f);
coords[6] = new Point3f(0f, 1f, 1f);
coords[7] = new Point3f(1f, 1f, 1f);
qa.setCoordinates(0, coords);
```

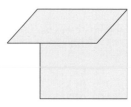

FIGURE 6.8 A QuadArray geometry.

Note that even though there are only six distinct points in this geometry, we still need to define eight vertices for the `QuadArray` object, because it is necessary to specify each quadrangle with four vertices.

Besides coordinates, other attributes of the vertices such as normals and colors may be set in a similar fashion. For example, the following `TriangleArray` object contains color definitions for vertices as well as coordinates:

```
TriangleArray ta = new TriangleArray(6,
  GeometryArray.COORDINATES | GeometryArray.COLOR_3);
Point3f[] coords = new Point3f[6];
coords[0] = new Point3f(0f, 0f, 0f);
coords[1] = new Point3f(1f, 1f, 0f);
coords[2] = new Point3f(1f, 0f, 0f);
coords[3] = new Point3f(1f, 0f, 0f);
coords[4] = new Point3f(2f, 1f, 0f);
coords[5] = new Point3f(3f, 0f, 0f);
ta.setCoordinates(0, coords);
Color3f[] colors = new Color3f[6];
colors[0] = new Color3f(1f, 0f, 0f);
colors[1] = new Color3f(0f, 1f, 0f);
colors[2] = new Color3f(0f, 0f, 1f);
colors[3] = new Color3f(1f, 1f, 0f);
colors[4] = new Color3f(0f, 1f, 1f);
colors[5] = new Color3f(1f, 0f, 1f);
ta.setColors(0, colors);
```

Surface normals can also be specified for the vertices in a geometry array. The following QuadArray object contains normal specifications:

```
QuadArray qa = new QuadArray(8,
  GeometryArray.COORDINATES | GeometryArray.NORMALS);
Point3f[] coords = new Point3f[8];
coords[0] = new Point3f(0f, 0f, 0f);
coords[1] = new Point3f(1f, 0f, 0f);
coords[2] = new Point3f(1f, 1f, 0f);
coords[3] = new Point3f(0f, 1f, 0f);
coords[4] = new Point3f(1f, 1f, 0f);
coords[5] = new Point3f(0f, 1f, 0f);
coords[6] = new Point3f(0f, 1f, 1f);
coords[7] = new Point3f(1f, 1f, 1f);
qa.setCoordinates(0, coords);
Vector3f[] normals = new Vector3f[8];
normals[0] = new Vector3f(0f, 0f, 1f);
normals[1] = new Vector3f(0f, 0f, 1f);
normals[2] = new Vector3f(0f, 0f, 1f);
normals[3] = new Vector3f(0f, 0f, 1f);
normals[4] = new Vector3f(0f, 1f, 0f);
normals[5] = new Vector3f(0f, 1f, 0f);
normals[6] = new Vector3f(0f, 1f, 0f);
normals[7] = new Vector3f(0f, 1f, 0f);
qa.setNormals(0, normals);
```

6.3.2 GeometryStripArray

Often a vertex in an array is shared by several different polygons. Using TriangleArray or QuadArray would add the shared vertices multiple times. Two approaches can improve the efficiency. The GeometryStripArray class uses the idea of strips to allow the sharing of adjacent vertices. To define separate strips, the number of vertices in each strip can be specified with an array of integers:

```
void setStripVertexCounts(int[] stripVertexCounts);
```

The length of the array is the number of strips. The number in each array entry represents the number of vertices in a strip.

GeometryStripArray has three subclasses. The LineStripArray defines a strip as a polyline. A sequence of points is used to specify the strip without duplicating the internal points. For example, the following code defines the same geometry as shown in Figure 6.6 with a LineStripArray object:

LineStripArray

```
int[] stripVertexCounts = {2, 3};
LineStripArray lsa = new LineStripArray(5, GeometryArray.COORDINATES,
  stripVertexCounts);
Point3f[] coords = new Point3f[5];
coords[0] = new Point3f(0f, 0f, 0f);
coords[1] = new Point3f(1f, 1f, 0f);
coords[2] = new Point3f(1f, 0f, 0f);
coords[3] = new Point3f(2f, 1f, 0f);
coords[4] = new Point3f(3f, 0f, 0f);
lsa.setCoordinates(0, coords);
```

The TriangleStripArray class defines strips of triangles. In each strip every three consecutive vertices define a triangle. Figure 6.9 illustrates the geometry constructed from a TriangleStripArray object.

TriangleStripArray

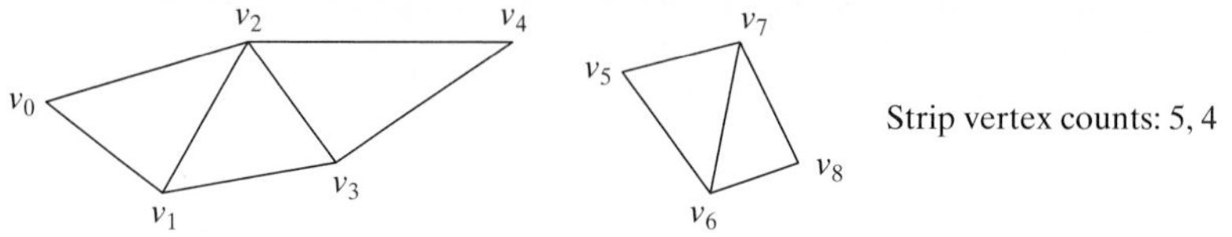

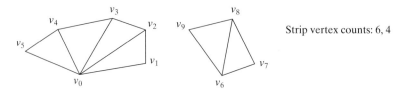

FIGURE 6.9 A `TriangleStripArray`.

TriangleFanArray

The `TriangleFanArray` class offers an alternative way to define strips of triangles. In each strip the first vertex with every two consecutive vertices form a triangle. Figure 6.10 illustrates this approach.

FIGURE 6.10 A `TriangleFanArray`.

The geometry of a cone may be defined very naturally as a `TriangleFanArray`:

```
int n = 60; // number of triangle patches
int[] stripVertexCounts = {n+2}; // 1 strip
TriangleFanArray tfa = new TriangleFanArray
  (n+2, GeometryArray.COORDINATES, stripVertexCounts);
Point3f apex = new Point3f(0, 0, 1);
tfa.setCoordinate(0, apex);
for (int ii = 0; ii <= n; ii++) {
  float x = (float)Math.cos(ii*2*Math.PI/n);
  float y = (float)Math.sin(ii*2*Math.PI/n);
  Point3f p = new Point3f(x, y, 0);
  ta.setCoordinate(ii+1, p);
}
```

The n triangle patches are defined by only $n + 2$ points in a single strip.

6.3.3 IndexedGeometryArray

IndexedGeometryArray

Another approach to avoid duplicated vertices is to use `IndexedGeometryArray`. Instead of defining a polygon by specifying the vertices directly, an `IndexedGeometryArray` object specifies the indices of the vertices in an array of points. Consequently a vertex needs to be defined only once, but it may be referenced several times through its index. For example, the following `IndexedQuadArray` object defines a geometry of two squares, as shown in Figure 6.8. It uses only six vertices instead of eight as needed by the `GeometryArray`. Each quadrangle is specified with four indices corresponding to the corner vertices.

```
IndexedQuadArray iqa = new IndexedQuadArray
  (6, GeometryArray.COORDINATES, 8);
Point3f[] coords = new Point3f[6];
coords[0] = new Point3f(0f, 0f, 0f);
coords[1] = new Point3f(1f, 0f, 0f);
coords[2] = new Point3f(1f, 1f, 0f);
coords[3] = new Point3f(0f, 1f, 0f);
coords[4] = new Point3f(0f, 1f, 1f);
coords[5] = new Point3f(1f, 1f, 1f);
```

```
iqa.setCoordinates(0, coords);
int[] indices = {0, 1, 2, 3, 2, 3, 4, 5};
iga.setCoordinateIndices(0, indices);
```

Other attributes such as normals and colors can be indexed in a similar way.

There is also an `IndexedGeometryStripArray` class with its subclasses `Indexed LineStripArray`, `IndexedTriangleStripArray`, and `IndexedTriangleFanArray`. These classes add indices to the strip arrays and combine the features of strip arrays and indexed arrays. To define separate strips, a `stripIndexCounts` array can be specified in the constructor or with the following method:

```
void setStripIndexCounts(int[] stripIndexCounts)
```

The following code shows an example of constructing an `IndexedTriangleStripArray` object:

```
int[] stripIndexCounts = {4, 4};
IndexedTriangleStripArray itsa = new IndexedTriangleStripArray(7,
  GeometryArray.COORDINATES, 8, stripIndexCounts);
Point3f[] coords = new Point3f[7];
coords[0] = new Point3f(0f, 0f, 0f);
coords[1] = new Point3f(0f, 1f, 0f);
coords[2] = new Point3f(1f, 1f, 0f);
coords[3] = new Point3f(2f, 1f, 0f);
coords[4] = new Point3f(-1f, 0f, 0f);
coords[5] = new Point3f(-1f, -1f, 0f);
coords[6] = new Point3f(-2f, -1f, 0f);
itsa.setCoordinates(0, coords);
int[] indices = {0, 1, 2, 3, 0, 4, 5, 6};
itsa.setCoordinateIndices(0, indices);
```

The resulting geometry is shown in Figure 6.11.

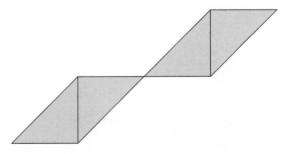

FIGURE 6.11 An `IndexedTriangleStripArray` geometry.

Listing 6.1 constructs a regular tetrahedron using the `IndexedTriangleArray` class. The tetrahedron is one of the five regular polyhedrons known as the *Platonic solids*. This example defines a tetrahedron as a subclass of `IndexedTriangleArray`. A tetrahedron is a solid consisting of four faces of congruent equilateral triangles. A test program in Listing 6.2 displays an instance of the tetrahedron rotating in space to view it from different angles.

Listing 6.1 `Tetrahedron.java`

```
1 package chapter6;
2
3 import javax.vecmath.*;
4 import javax.media.j3d.*;
```

```
 5
 6 public class Tetrahedron extends IndexedTriangleArray {
 7   public Tetrahedron() {
 8     super(4, TriangleArray.COORDINATES | TriangleArray.NORMALS, 12);
 9     setCoordinate(0, new Point3f(1f,1f,1f));
10     setCoordinate(1, new Point3f(1f,-1,-1f));
11     setCoordinate(2, new Point3f(-1f,1f,-1f));
12     setCoordinate(3, new Point3f(-1f,-1f,1f));
13     int[] coords = {0,1,2,0,3,1,1,3,2,2,3,0};
14     float n = (float)(1.0/Math.sqrt(3));
15     setNormal(0, new Vector3f(n,n,-n));
16     setNormal(1, new Vector3f(n,-n,n));
17     setNormal(2, new Vector3f(-n,-n,-n));
18     setNormal(3, new Vector3f(-n,n,n));
19     int[] norms = {0,0,0,1,1,1,2,2,2,3,3,3};
20     setCoordinateIndices(0, coords);
21     setNormalIndices(0, norms);
22   }
23 }
```

Listing 6.2 `TestTetrahedron.java`

```
 1 package chapter6;
 2
 3 import javax.vecmath.*;
 4 import java.awt.*;
 5 import java.awt.event.*;
 6 import javax.media.j3d.*;
 7 import com.sun.j3d.utils.universe.*;
 8 import com.sun.j3d.utils.geometry.*;
 9 import java.applet.*;
10 import com.sun.j3d.utils.applet.MainFrame;
11
12 public class TestTetrahedron extends Applet {
13   public static void main(String[] args) {
14     new MainFrame(new TestTetrahedron(), 640, 480);
15   }
16
17   public void init() {
18     // create canvas
19     GraphicsConfiguration gc =
20     SimpleUniverse.getPreferredConfiguration();
21     Canvas3D cv = new Canvas3D(gc);
22     setLayout(new BorderLayout());
23     add(cv, BorderLayout.CENTER);
24     BranchGroup bg = createSceneGraph();
25     bg.compile();
26     SimpleUniverse su = new SimpleUniverse(cv);
27     su.getViewingPlatform().setNominalViewingTransform();
28     su.addBranchGraph(bg);
29   }
30
31   private BranchGroup createSceneGraph() {
32     BranchGroup root = new BranchGroup();
33     TransformGroup spin = new TransformGroup();
34     spin.setCapability(TransformGroup.ALLOW_TRANSFORM_WRITE);
35     root.addChild(spin);
36     // object
37     Appearance ap = new Appearance();
38     ap.setMaterial(new Material());
```

```
39      Shape3D shape = new Shape3D(new Tetrahedron(), ap);
40      // rotating object
41      Transform3D tr = new Transform3D();
42      tr.setScale(0.25);
43      TransformGroup tg = new TransformGroup(tr);
44      spin.addChild(tg);
45      tg.addChild(shape);
46      Alpha alpha = new Alpha(-1, 4000);
47      RotationInterpolator rotator =
48      new RotationInterpolator(alpha, spin);
49      BoundingSphere bounds = new BoundingSphere();
50      rotator.setSchedulingBounds(bounds);
51      spin.addChild(rotator);
52      // light and background
53      Background background = new Background(1.0f, 1.0f, 1.0f);
54      background.setApplicationBounds(bounds);
55      root.addChild(background);
56      AmbientLight light = new AmbientLight
57        (true, new Color3f(Color.red));
58      light.setInfluencingBounds(bounds);
59      root.addChild(light);
60      PointLight ptlight = new PointLight(new Color3f(Color.green),
61        new Point3f(3f,3f,3f), new Point3f(1f,0f,0f));
62      ptlight.setInfluencingBounds(bounds);
63      root.addChild(ptlight);
64      PointLight ptlight2 = new PointLight(new Color3f(Color.orange),
65        new Point3f(-2f,2f,2f), new Point3f(1f,0f,0f));
66      ptlight2.setInfluencingBounds(bounds);
67      root.addChild(ptlight2);
68      return root;
69    }
70 }
```

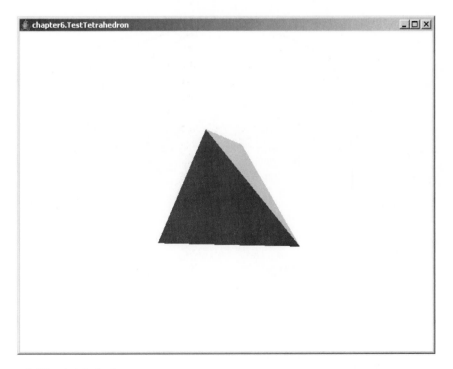

FIGURE 6.12   A tetrahedron.

Two classes are defined in this example: Tetrahedron and TestTetrahedron. The Tetrahedron class extends the IndexedTriangleArray class (line 6) so it can be used as a geometry node component for a Shape3D node in a scene graph. The vertices of the tetrahedron have the coordinates

$$(1, 1, 1), (1, -1, -1), (-1, 1, -1), (-1, -1, 1)$$

Four triangle faces are specified by an array of 12 indexes pointing to the corresponding vertices:

$$0, 1, 2, \quad 0, 3, 1, \quad 1, 3, 2, \quad 2, 3, 0$$

Four normals for the four faces are specified as four vectors in the directions:

$$(1, 1, -1), (1, -1, 1), (-1, -1, -1), (-1, 1, 1)$$

The vectors are divided by $\sqrt{3}$ to obtain unit normal vectors. Each vertex of a face is specified as a normal corresponding to the normal of the face.

The TestTetrahedron class is a typical Java 3D applet/application program that is used to test the Tetrahedron class. It creates an instance of Tetrahedron and associates it with a Shape3D node. The scene graph of the Java 3D program is given in Figure 6.13.

A Shape3D object represents the tetrahedron in the scene graph (line 39). It references the Tetrahedron object as its geometry and an Appearance object. The Appearance object references a Material object to apply lighting.

The Shape3D node is attached to a TransformGroup node to apply a scaling to the tetrahedron. The TransformGroup is attached to another TransformGroup node, which is controlled by a Behavior object called RotationInterpolator to perform the rotation.

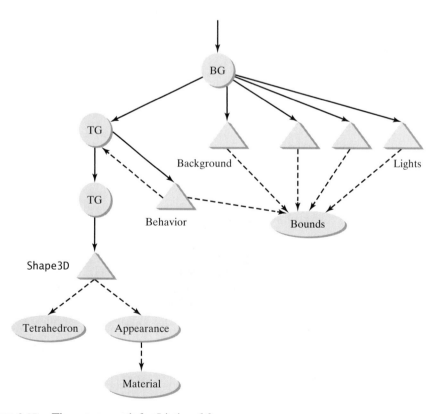

Figure 6.13 The scene graph for Listing 6.2.

A background node is defined to create a white background. Three different lights are defined to illuminate the scene. The behavior, the background, and the light nodes all share the same Bounds object, which is a sphere of radius 1.0.

6.3.4 Normals

Surface normals are important geometric attributes for sophisticated rendering modes such as lighting. The *normal* of a plane is a vector that is perpendicular to the plane (Figure 6.14). The normal of a surface at a point is the normal of the surface's tangent plane at the point.

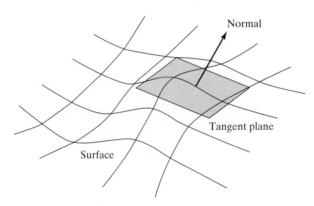

FIGURE 6.14   The surface normal is perpendicular to the tangent plane.

Because the *cross product* of two vectors is perpendicular to both vectors, it can often be used to calculate normals. For example, given three distinct points P_0, P_1, P_2 in a plane, we can form two vectors in the plane: $v_1 = P_1 - P_0$, $v_2 = P_2 - P_0$ (Figure 6.15). The cross product $v_1 \times v_2$ is the normal of the plane.

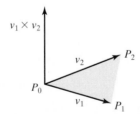

FIGURE 6.15   Calculating the normal with the cross product.

Usually the surface normals are represented with unit vectors (vectors of length 1). Any nonzero vector v can be rescaled to a unit vector: $v/\|v\|$. This is known as the *normalization*.

The Vector3f and Vector3d classes have the cross method to calculate the cross product of two three-dimensional vectors. The normalize methods of the classes perform the normalization on the vectors. For example, the following code snippet calculates the normal of the plane determined by three points:

```
Point3f p0 = new Point3f(1,1,1);
Point3f p1 = new Point3f(1,-1,-1);
Point3f p2 = new Point3f(-1,1,-1);
p1.sub(p0);
p2.sub(p0);
```

```
Vector3f v1 = new Vector3f(p1);
Vector3f v2 = new Vector3f(p2);
Vector3f normal = new Vector3f();
normal.cross(v1, v2);
normal.normalize();
```

For a geometry formed with planar faces, such as the tetrahedron, the normal for each face can be calculated separately using the method illustrated above. For a smooth surface approximated by a polygon mesh, the normal at a vertex should be calculated from the original surface rather than a polygon. Consider the case that a surface is represented by a parametric equation:

$$x = f(u, v)$$

$$y = g(u, v)$$

$$z = h(u, v)$$

Two vectors in the tangent plane can be obtained from the derivatives:

$$(dx/du, dy/du, dz/du) = (f_u, g_u, h_u)$$

$$(dx/dv, dy/dv, dz/dv) = (f_v, g_v, h_v)$$

The surface normal at a point can be found by taking their cross product:

$$n = (f_u, g_u, h_u) \times (f_v, g_v, h_v)$$

For example, an elliptic paraboloid has the following parametric equation:

$$x = u \cos v$$

$$y = u \sin v$$

$$z = u^2$$

The partial derivatives are given by:

$$(\cos v, \sin v, 2u)$$

$$(-u \sin v, u \cos v, 0)$$

Therefore the surface normal at a point defined by (u, v) is:

$$(\cos v, \sin v, 2u) \times (-u \sin v, u \cos v, 0) = (-2u^2 \cos v, 2u^2 \sin v, u)$$

The mathematical background related to surfaces and normals is discussed in Appendix A.

6.4 GeometryInfo

6.4.1 Using the GeometryInfo Class

An alternative to GeometryArray classes for generating geometry is the GeometryInfo class. This class does not have the methods to partially set the vertex data, but it allows the definitions of more general polygon faces. Using the utility classes NormalGenerator and Stripifier, it is also possible to automatically generate surface normals and stripify the geometry on GeometryInfo objects.

One constructor of GeometryInfo takes a GeometryArray parameter. It provides a conversion from a GeometryArray object to a GeometryInfo object:

public GeometryInfo(GeometryArray ga)

Another constructor of GeometryInfo creates an empty GeometryInfo object with a given primitiveType:

public GeometryInfo(int primitiveType)

The primitiveType is one of:

primitive type

```
TRIANGLE_ARRAY
TRIANGLE_FAN_ARRAY
TRIANGLE_STRIP_ARRAY
QUAD_ARRAY
POLYGON_ARRAY
```

The triangle and quad arrays are interpreted the same way as the corresponding GeometryArray classes. To set vertex data, an entire array of data values must be supplied. For example,

void setCoordinates(Point3f[] coords)

Indexed representation can be achieved by simply setting an index array:

```
void setCoordinateIndices(int[] indices)
void setNormalIndices(int[] indices)
void setColorIndices(int[] indices)
void setTextureCoordinateIndices(int[] indices)
```

Similar to the GeometryArray classes, a stripCounts array is used to define separate strips for GeometryInfo objects with TRIANGLE_FAN_ARRAY and TRIANGLE_STRIP_ARRAY flags.

A polygon array with the POLYGON_ARRAY flag can be used to define complex polygons with more than four sides and with holes. A polygon consists of one or more contours. The first contour defines the outer boundary of the polygon and subsequent contours define the holes in the polygon.

The stripCounts array for a POLYGON_ARRAY specifies the number of vertices of each contour. The contourCounts array specifies the number of contours for each polygon. For example, Figure 6.16 shows the strip counts and contour counts for the given polygon array.

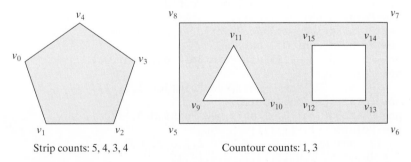

Strip counts: 5, 4, 3, 4   Countour counts: 1, 3

FIGURE 6.16   Constructing geometry using the GeometryInfo class.

Internally the GeometryInfo class will convert polygons in a POLYGON_ARRAY primitive to triangles. This triangulation is done automatically using the class Triangulator.

The surface normals of a GeometryInfo object can be generated automatically using the class NormalGenerator. The surface normals are necessary for rendering the objects by considering illumination from light sources. The automatic normal generation can help you avoid some tedious calculations. The NormalGenerator class has a method to generate normals for a GeometryInfo object:

NormalGenerator

```
public void generateNormals(GeometryInfo gi);
```

To generate normals for a GeometryInfo object gi, you may create an instance of NormalGenerator and call the generateNormals method:

```
NormalGenerator ng = new NormalGenerator();
ng.generateNormals(gi);
```

The other helper class Stripifier helps you change the geometry in a GeometryInfo object to triangle strips. The usage of Stripifier is similar to that of NormalGenerator:

```
Stripifier st = new Stripifier();
st.stripify(gi);
```

Listing 6.3 uses GeometryInfo class to define a dodecahedron, another Platonic solid. This example demonstrates the use of GeometryInfo class. Listing 6.4 shows a test program for the dodecahedron.

Listing 6.3 Dodecahedron.java

```
 1 package chapter6;
 2
 3 import javax.vecmath.*;
 4 import java.awt.*;
 5 import java.awt.event.*;
 6 import javax.media.j3d.*;
 7 import com.sun.j3d.utils.geometry.*;
 8
 9 public class Dodecahedron extends Shape3D{
10   public Dodecahedron() {
11     GeometryInfo gi = new GeometryInfo(GeometryInfo.POLYGON_ARRAY);
12     double phi = 0.5*(Math.sqrt(5)+1);
13     Point3d[] vertices = {new Point3d(1,1,1),
14     new Point3d(0,1/phi,phi),
15     new Point3d(phi,0,1/phi),new Point3d(1/phi,phi,0),
16     new Point3d(-1,1,1),
17     new Point3d(0,-1/phi,phi),new Point3d(1,-1,1),
18     new Point3d(phi,0,-1/phi),
19     new Point3d(1,1,-1),new Point3d(-1/phi,phi,0),
20     new Point3d(-phi,0,1/phi),
21     new Point3d(-1,-1,1),new Point3d(1/phi,-phi,0),
22     new Point3d(1,-1,-1),
23     new Point3d(0,1/phi,-phi),new Point3d(-1,1,-1),
24     new Point3d(-1/phi,-phi,0),
25     new Point3d(-phi,0,-1/phi),new Point3d(0,-1/phi,-phi),
26     new Point3d(-1,-1,-1)};
27     int[] indices = {0,1,5,6,2, 0,2,7,8,3, 0,3,9,4,1,
28     1,4,10,11,5, 2,6,12,13,7, 3,8,14,15,9,
29     5,11,16,12,6, 7,13,18,14,8, 9,15,17,10,4,
30     19,16,11,10,17, 19,17,15,14,18, 19,18,13,12,16};
31     gi.setCoordinates(vertices);
32     gi.setCoordinateIndices(indices);
33     int[] stripCounts = {5,5,5,5,5,5,5,5,5,5,5,5};
34     gi.setStripCounts(stripCounts);
35     NormalGenerator ng = new NormalGenerator();
36     ng.generateNormals(gi);
37     this.setGeometry(gi.getGeometryArray());
38   }
39 }
```

Listing 6.4 `TestDodecahedron.java`

```java
 1 package chapter6;
 2
 3 import javax.vecmath.*;
 4 import java.awt.*;
 5 import java.awt.event.*;
 6 import javax.media.j3d.*;
 7 import com.sun.j3d.utils.universe.*;
 8 import com.sun.j3d.utils.geometry.*;
 9 import java.applet.*;
10 import com.sun.j3d.utils.applet.MainFrame;
11
12 public class TestDodecahedron extends Applet {
13   public static void main(String[] args) {
14     new MainFrame(new TestDodecahedron(), 640, 480);
15   }
16
17   public void init() {
18     GraphicsConfiguration gc =
19     SimpleUniverse.getPreferredConfiguration();
20     Canvas3D cv = new Canvas3D(gc);
21     setLayout(new BorderLayout());
22     add(cv, BorderLayout.CENTER);
23     BranchGroup bg = createSceneGraph();
24     bg.compile();
25     SimpleUniverse su = new SimpleUniverse(cv);
26     su.getViewingPlatform().setNominalViewingTransform();
27     su.addBranchGraph(bg);
28   }
29
30   private BranchGroup createSceneGraph() {
31     BranchGroup root = new BranchGroup();
32     TransformGroup spin = new TransformGroup();
33     spin.setCapability(TransformGroup.ALLOW_TRANSFORM_WRITE);
34     root.addChild(spin);
35
36     // object
37     Appearance ap = new Appearance();
38     ap.setMaterial(new Material());
39     Shape3D shape = new Dodecahedron();
40     shape.setAppearance(ap);
41
42     Transform3D tr = new Transform3D();
43     tr.setScale(0.25);
44     TransformGroup tg = new TransformGroup(tr);
45     spin.addChild(tg);
46     tg.addChild(shape);
47
48     Alpha alpha = new Alpha(-1, 4000);
49     RotationInterpolator rotator =
50     new RotationInterpolator(alpha, spin);
51     BoundingSphere bounds = new BoundingSphere();
52     rotator.setSchedulingBounds(bounds);
53     spin.addChild(rotator);
54
55     // background and light
56     Background background = new Background(1.0f, 1.0f, 1.0f);
57     background.setApplicationBounds(bounds);
58     root.addChild(background);
```

```
59    AmbientLight light = new AmbientLight
60      (true, new Color3f(Color.red));
61    light.setInfluencingBounds(bounds);
62    root.addChild(light);
63    PointLight ptlight = new PointLight(new Color3f(Color.green),
64      new Point3f(3f,3f,3f), new Point3f(1f,0f,0f));
65    ptlight.setInfluencingBounds(bounds);
66    root.addChild(ptlight);
67    PointLight ptlight2 = new PointLight(new Color3f(Color.orange),
68      new Point3f(-2f,2f,2f), new Point3f(1f,0f,0f));
69    ptlight2.setInfluencingBounds(bounds);
70    root.addChild(ptlight2);
71    return root;
72  }
73 }
```

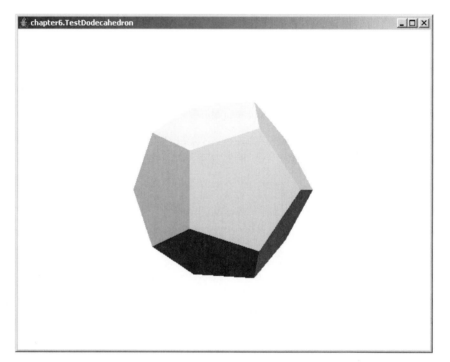

FIGURE 6.17   A dodecahedron.

The Dodecahedron class is defined as a subclass of Shape3D. The dodecahedron has 20 vertices and 12 pentagon faces. A GeometryInfo object is created to define the faces and to automatically generate the normals. Vertex coordinates are set directly in the array vertices. The 20 vertices have the following coordinates:

$$(1, 1, 1),$$
$$(0, 1/\phi, \phi), (\phi, 0, 1/\phi), (1/\phi, \phi, 0),$$
$$(-1, 1, 1), (0, -1/\phi, \phi), (1, -1, 1),$$
$$(\phi, 0, -1/\phi), (1, 1, -1), (-1/\phi, \phi, 0),$$
$$(-\phi, 0, 1/\phi), (-1, -1, 1), (1/\phi, -\phi, 0),$$
$$(1, -1, -1), (0, 1/\phi, -\phi), (-1, 1, -1),$$
$$(-1/\phi, -\phi, 0), (-\phi, 0, -1/\phi), (0, -1/\phi, -\phi),$$
$$(-1, -1, -1)$$

where $\phi = \left(\sqrt{5} + 1\right)/2$. The 12 faces are defined with indices to the vertices:

$$(0, 1, 5, 6, 2), (0, 2, 7, 8, 3), (0, 3, 9, 4, 1),$$

$$(1, 4, 10, 11, 5), (2, 6, 12, 13, 7), (3, 8, 14, 15, 9),$$

$$(5, 11, 16, 12, 6), (7, 13, 18, 14, 8), (9, 15, 17, 10, 4),$$

$$(19, 16, 11, 10, 17), (19, 17, 15, 14, 18), (19, 18, 13, 12, 16)$$

The `stripCount` array (line 33) defines the number of polygons and the number of vertices in each polygon face:

$$5, 5, 5, 5, 5, 5, 5, 5, 5, 5, 5, 5$$

A `NormalGenerator` object is created and applied on the `GeometryInfo` object to generate the normals for the faces (lines 35–36). Finally the geometry constructed in the `GeometryInfo` object is retrieved to be used as the geometry of the current `Shape3D` object.

The test program `TestDodecahedron` is nearly identical to the test program in Listing 6.2. The only significant difference is that the `Dodecahedron` object is added directly to the scene graph as a leaf node, because it is a `Shape3D` object.

6.4.2 Creating Polygon Meshes

A general curved surface typically requires an array of many small polygon patches to obtain a good approximation. For a surface defined by a parametric equation,

$$x = f(u, v)$$

$$y = g(u, v)$$

$$z = h(u, v)$$

with the two parameters varying in the rectangle $a \leq u \leq b, c \leq v \leq d$, we can usually divide the parameter range into an $m \times n$ grid to form the *patches*. The vertices of the grid are defined by the points:

patch

$$u_i = a + i(b - a)/m, \qquad i = 0, 1, 2, \ldots, m$$

$$v_j = c + j(d - c)/n, \qquad j = 0, 1, 2, \ldots, n$$

A *quadrilateral patch* is defined by four vertices with parameter values:

quadrilateral patch

$$(u_i, v_j), (u_{i+1}, v_j), (u_{i+1}, v_{j+1}), (u_i, v_{j+1})$$

It may be further divided into two triangles:

$$(u_i, v_j), (u_{i+1}, v_j), (u_{i+1}, v_{j+1}) \quad \text{and} \quad (u_i, v_j), (u_{i+1}, v_{j+1}), (u_i, v_{j+1})$$

Because of the obvious overlapping of vertices among the adjacent polygons, indexed arrays are often used to improve the efficiency.

Note that the methods for setting vertex coordinates in the `GeometryInfo` and `Geometry-Array` classes do not accept two-dimensional arrays. Consequently, the vertices in the grid must be specified in a linear fashion.

Listing 6.5 illustrates the procedure of generating an approximation to a surface with an array of polygons. It uses a `GeometryInfo` class to generate the geometry for a data set sampled from a two-variable function.

Data visualization is an important application of computer graphics. As the dimension of a dataset increases, the comprehension of the data becomes more difficult. 3D graphical data plotting may greatly enhance the representation of data sets. This example shows a 3D surface plot of a function of two variables:

$$y = 2 \cos(x^2) \sin(z^2)/e^{0.25(x^2+z^2)} - 1$$

Even though the data set used in this example is generated from a fixed function, the method can be easily adapted to plot data from other sources. The plot is rotated continuously about a vertical axis. (See Figure 6.18.)

Listing 6.5 `ViewData.java`

```java
1 package chapter6;
2
3 import javax.vecmath.*;
4 import java.awt.*;
5 import java.awt.event.*;
6 import javax.media.j3d.*;
7 import com.sun.j3d.utils.universe.*;
8 import com.sun.j3d.utils.geometry.*;
9 import java.applet.*;
10 import com.sun.j3d.utils.applet.MainFrame;
11
12 public class ViewData extends Applet {
13   public static void main(String[] args) {
14     new MainFrame(new ViewData(), 640, 480);
15   }
16
17   public void init() {
18     // create canvas
19     GraphicsConfiguration gc =
20     SimpleUniverse.getPreferredConfiguration();
21     Canvas3D cv = new Canvas3D(gc);
22     setLayout(new BorderLayout());
23     add(cv, BorderLayout.CENTER);
24     BranchGroup bg = createSceneGraph();
25     bg.compile();
26     SimpleUniverse su = new SimpleUniverse(cv);
27     su.getViewingPlatform().setNominalViewingTransform();
28     su.addBranchGraph(bg);
29   }
30
31   private BranchGroup createSceneGraph() {
32     BranchGroup root = new BranchGroup();
33     TransformGroup spin = new TransformGroup();
34     spin.setCapability(TransformGroup.ALLOW_TRANSFORM_WRITE);
35     root.addChild(spin);
36
37     // object
38     Appearance ap = new Appearance();
39     ap.setMaterial(new Material());
40     Shape3D shape = new Shape3D(createGeometry(), ap);
41
42     Transform3D tr = new Transform3D();
43     tr.setScale(0.2);
44     TransformGroup tg = new TransformGroup(tr);
45     spin.addChild(tg);
46     tg.addChild(shape);
47
48     Alpha alpha = new Alpha(-1, 12000);
49     RotationInterpolator rotator = new RotationInterpolator
50       (alpha, spin);
```

```
51      BoundingSphere bounds = new BoundingSphere();
52      rotator.setSchedulingBounds(bounds);
53      spin.addChild(rotator);
54
55      // background and light
56      Background background = new Background(1.0f, 1.0f, 1.0f);
57      background.setApplicationBounds(bounds);
58      root.addChild(background);
59      AmbientLight light = new AmbientLight
60        (true, new Color3f(Color.red));
61      light.setInfluencingBounds(bounds);
62      root.addChild(light);
63      PointLight ptlight = new PointLight(new Color3f(Color.green),
64        new Point3f(3f,3f,3f), new Point3f(1f,0f,0f));
65      ptlight.setInfluencingBounds(bounds);
66      root.addChild(ptlight);
67      return root;
68    }
69
70    private Geometry createGeometry() {
71      int m = 40;
72      int n = 40;
73      Point3f[] pts = new Point3f[m*n];
74      int idx = 0;
75      for (int i = 0; i < m; i++) {
76        for (int j = 0; j < n; j++) {
77          float x = (i - m/2)*0.2f;
78          float z = (j - n/2)*0.2f;
79          float y = 2f * (float)(Math.cos(x*x) * Math.sin(z*z))/
80                    ((float)Math.exp(0.25*(x*x+z*z)))-1.0f;
81          pts[idx++] = new Point3f(x, y, z);
82        }
83      }
84
85      int[] coords = new int[2*n*(m-1)];
86      idx = 0;
87      for (int i = 1; i < m; i++) {
88        for (int j = 0; j < n; j++) {
89          coords[idx++] = i*n + j;
90          coords[idx++] = (i-1)*n + j;
91        }
92      }
93
94      int[] stripCounts = new int[m-1];
95      for (int i = 0; i < m-1; i++) stripCounts[i] = 2*n;
96
97      GeometryInfo gi = new GeometryInfo
98        (GeometryInfo.TRIANGLE_STRIP_ARRAY);
99      gi.setCoordinates(pts);
100     gi.setCoordinateIndices(coords);
101     gi.setStripCounts(stripCounts);
102
103     NormalGenerator ng = new NormalGenerator();
104     ng.generateNormals(gi);
105
106     return gi.getGeometryArray();
107   }
108 }
```

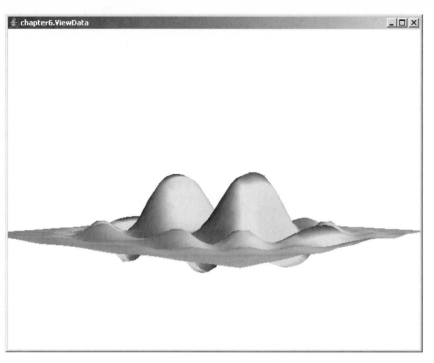

FIGURE 6.18   A 3D plot of a two-variable function.

We use the data points sampled from the function to construct the geometry. A rectangular grid of $m \times n$ values in the xz-plane is created to evaluate the function. The function values give the y-coordinates of the points. The resulting points are stored in a one-dimensional array `pts` (line 73). The surface formed by this grid of points is defined as strips of triangles. Every two adjacent rows of points define one strip of triangles.

The geometry of the surface is created using a `GeometryInfo` object with the primitive data type `TRIANGLE_STRIP_ARRAY` (line 98). The `GeometryInfo` object is indexed. The array `pts` specifies the vertex coordinates. The actual triangle strips are defined by a separate array of indices `coords` and an array of strip counts `stripCounts`. The `coords` array defines the triangle strips with the indices to the vertex array. Because the grid has m values in the x-direction, there are $m - 1$ strips. Each strip is defined by $2n$ points in two rows. Therefore, the array `coords` contains $2n(m - 1)$ indices. The indices are specified alternately from the two rows. For example, the first strip has indices

$$n, 0, n + 1, n + 2, 2, \ldots$$

The second strip has indices

$$2n, n, 2n + 1, 2n + 2, n + 2, \ldots$$

Of course all indices are stored in the single array `coords`. To break the one-dimensional index array into separate strips, the `stripCounts` array is applied to specify $m - 1$ strips with $2n$ indices in each strip.

To generate the surface normals the utility class `NormalGenerator` is used. The resulting geometry is used by a `Shape3D` object to define the surface.

The scene graph of this example is similar to that of Listing 6.2. Only two lights are used in this program.

6.5 Primitives

For convenience, Java 3D offers utility classes for commonly used geometric primitives. The abstract class `Primitive` is a subclass of `Group` and encapsulates predefined geometry attributes. They can be used as high-level components in a scene graph without setting complex geometry, using separate low-level structures such as `GeometryArray` or `GeometryInfo` objects.

Figure 6.19 shows the class hierarchy of the primitives defined in the package `com.sun.j3d.utils.geometry`. The appearance of a primitive can be set through the following methods:

```
void setAppearance()
void setAppearance(Appearance appearance)
void setAppearance(int subpart, Appearance appearance)
```

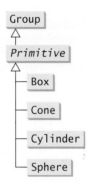

FIGURE 6.19   Primitive classes.

The sizes of the primitives can be set with some of their constructors. For example,

```
Box(float xdim, float ydim, float zdim, Appearance appearance)
Cone(float radius, float height)
Cylinder(float radius, float height)
Sphere(float radius)
```

The `Primitive` class is a subclass of `Group`. Therefore a primitive object can be added directly to a scene graph as a node.

Listing 6.6 demonstrates the applications of primitives. This program displays instances of the four basic primitives provided by Java 3D utility packages. (See Figure 6.20.)

Listing 6.6 `TestPrimitives.java`

```
 1 package chapter6;
 2
 3 import javax.vecmath.*;
 4 import java.awt.*;
 5 import java.awt.event.*;
 6 import javax.media.j3d.*;
 7 import com.sun.j3d.utils.universe.*;
 8 import com.sun.j3d.utils.geometry.*;
 9 import java.applet.*;
10 import com.sun.j3d.utils.applet.MainFrame;
11
12 public class TestPrimitives extends Applet {
13   public static void main(String[] args) {
```

```
14        new MainFrame(new TestPrimitives(), 640, 480);
15     }
16
17     public void init() {
18       // create canvas
19       GraphicsConfiguration gc =
20       SimpleUniverse.getPreferredConfiguration();
21       Canvas3D cv = new Canvas3D(gc);
22       setLayout(new BorderLayout());
23       add(cv, BorderLayout.CENTER);
24       BranchGroup bg = createSceneGraph();
25       bg.compile();
26       SimpleUniverse su = new SimpleUniverse(cv);
27       su.getViewingPlatform().setNominalViewingTransform();
28       su.addBranchGraph(bg);
29     }
30
31     private BranchGroup createSceneGraph() {
32       BranchGroup root = new BranchGroup();
33       TransformGroup spin = new TransformGroup();
34       spin.setCapability(TransformGroup.ALLOW_TRANSFORM_WRITE);
35       root.addChild(spin);
36
37       // primitives
38       Appearance ap = new Appearance();
39       ap.setMaterial(new Material());
40       Box box = new Box(1.2f, 0.3f, 0.8f, ap);
41       Sphere sphere = new Sphere();
42       Cylinder cylinder = new Cylinder();
43       Cone cone = new Cone();
44
45       Transform3D tr = new Transform3D();
46       tr.setScale(0.2);
47       TransformGroup tg = new TransformGroup(tr);
48       spin.addChild(tg);
49       tg.addChild(box);
50       tr.setIdentity();
51       tr.setTranslation(new Vector3f(0f,1.5f,0f));
52       TransformGroup tgSphere = new TransformGroup(tr);
53       tg.addChild(tgSphere);
54       tgSphere.addChild(sphere);
55       tr.setTranslation(new Vector3f(-1f,-1.5f,0f));
56       TransformGroup tgCylinder = new TransformGroup(tr);
57       tg.addChild(tgCylinder);
58       tgCylinder.addChild(cylinder);
59       tr.setTranslation(new Vector3f(1f,-1.5f,0f));
60       TransformGroup tgCone = new TransformGroup(tr);
61       tg.addChild(tgCone);
62       tgCone.addChild(cone);
63
64       Alpha alpha = new Alpha(-1, 4000);
65       RotationInterpolator rotator =
66       new RotationInterpolator(alpha, spin);
67       BoundingSphere bounds = new BoundingSphere();
68       rotator.setSchedulingBounds(bounds);
69       spin.addChild(rotator);
70
71       // background and light
72       Background background = new Background(1.0f, 1.0f, 1.0f);
```

```
73      background.setApplicationBounds(bounds);
74      root.addChild(background);
75      AmbientLight light =
76      new AmbientLight(true, new Color3f(Color.red));
77      light.setInfluencingBounds(bounds);
78      root.addChild(light);
79      PointLight ptlight = new PointLight(new Color3f(Color.green),
80        new Point3f(3f,3f,3f), new Point3f(1f,0f,0f));
81      ptlight.setInfluencingBounds(bounds);
82      root.addChild(ptlight);
83      PointLight ptlight2 = new PointLight(new Color3f(Color.orange),
84        new Point3f(-2f,2f,2f), new Point3f(1f,0f,0f));
85      ptlight2.setInfluencingBounds(bounds);
86      root.addChild(ptlight2);
87      return root;
88    }
89 }
```

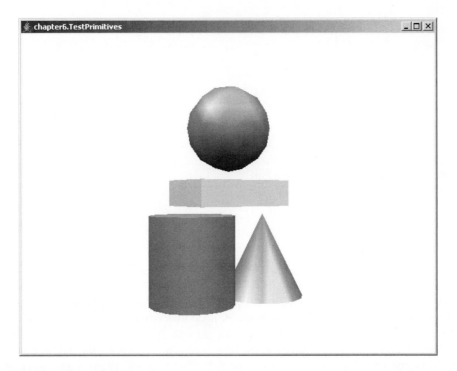

FIGURE 6.20 Four primitives.

Four instances of the primitives—a box, a sphere, a cylinder, and a cone—are created and placed in the scene graph as shown in Figure 6.21. The transformation nodes on top of the three primitive nodes help separate the objects in the virtual world. The details of applying transformation nodes will be presented in Chapter 7.

The default constructors are used for creating the Cone, Sphere, and Cylinder objects. The objects will have the surface normals generated and set up for lighting. The Box object is created with a constructor specifying its *x*-, *y*-, *z*-dimensions and its appearance (lines 40–43).

All four objects are attached to a TransformGroup which performs a scaling. Once again, the entire scene is rotated by a RotationInterpolator object through a TransformGroup node. The background and light configuration are similar to those in previous examples.

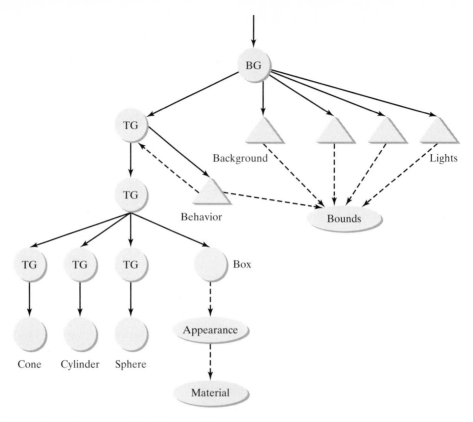

FIGURE 6.21 Scene graph for Listing 6.4.

6.6 Fonts and Texts

Fonts provide a rich source for geometry. The glyphs of text strings are complex geometric shapes predefined in the fonts.

Text3D
Text2D

Java 3D provides `Text3D` and `Text2D` classes. `Text3D` extends the `Geometry` class, so a `Text3D` object can be used by a `Shape3D` node to define its geometry. A `Text3D` object is determined by a 3D font and a string for the text. A `Font3D` object is a 3D version of a font. A `Font3D` object is constructed from a regular 2D AWT font and an extrusion defined by the `FontExtrusion` class. The following is a typical procedure to create a `Text3D` object:

- Create a `java.awt.Font` object.

- Create a `FontExtrusion` object.

- Create a `Font3D` object using the `Font` and `FontExtrusion` objects.

- Create a `Text3D` object using the `Font3D` and a `String`.

For example, the following statements create a 3D text of "Hello" using a bold Serif font of size 1 with a default extrusion:

```
Font font = new Font("Serif", Font.BOLD, 1);
FontExtrusion extrusion = new FontExtrusion();
Font3D font3d = new Font3D(font, extrusion);
Text3D text = new Text3D(font3d, "Hello");
```

Text2D is a subclass of Shape3D, so it can be used as a leaf node in a scene graph. A Text2D object is implemented as a rectangle with the text string painted as an image. The following code defines a Text2D object of the string "Hello" with a blue italic Serif font of size 16:

```
Text2D text = new Text2D("Hello", Color.blue, "Serif", 16, Font.Italic);
```

6.7 Appearance and Attributes

Besides geometry, graphics objects possess attributes that define the appearance when rendered. Different models for the graphics object's appearance exist with significant differences in rendering quality and efficiency.

Color is perhaps the most fundamental attribute. However, there are different ways to generate colors for parts of a graphics object. A simple way is to specify a solid color for each unit of the object, such as points, lines, or polygon faces.

Another approach is to assign different colors for different points by interpolations. This is known as *Gouraud shading*. Colors are specified for vertices of a polygon. At other points the colors are calculated by interpolating the color values at the vertices.

Gouraud shading

More realistic coloring schemes need to consider the influences of environment elements such as lights as well as the properties of the objects. Colors on an object may be determined by such factors as the reflective properties of the object, the geometry, the light sources, the emissive light, the ambient light, and the view position.

Texture mapping is a powerful technique to achieve sophisticated appearance. For objects with a great deal of detail it is usually more efficient to store the appearance as a raster image and place the image onto the object during rendering.

In Java 3D the Appearance node component specifies the attributes related to the rendering of the node. An Appearance object holds a set of references to attribute objects. Figure 6.22 lists the classes related to appearance.

Appearance

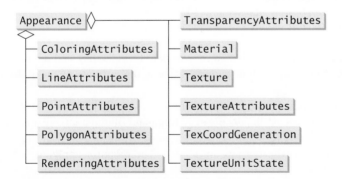

FIGURE 6.22 Appearance components.

A ColoringAttributes object defines a color to be used to color the associated geometric object when lighting is not applied and *vertex colors* are not defined. This color is ignored if vertex colors for the geometry are defined. It is also not used if lighting is enabled. ColoringAttributes also defines a *shading model*.

vertex color

shading model

- ▪ SHAD_FLAT—The flat shading assigns a fixed color to every point on a polygon or a line.

- ▪ SHAD_GOURAUD—Gouraud shading interpolates the colors at the vertices of a polygon or a line to produce a color at an interior point. The colors on a polygon are not constant. They change smoothly to give a more realistic appearance.

■ SHAD_FASTEST—This constant selects the fastest shading model for the current platform.

■ SHAD_NICEST—This constant selects the nicest shading model for the current platform.

A `PointAttributes` object defines the attributes related to rendering of points. The size of points and antialiasing can be specified with `PointAttributes` class.

A `LineAttributes` object defines the attributes related to rendering of lines. Line attributes include the line width, line pattern, and antialiasing. Line patterns are defined by the constants in the class:

```
PATTERN_SOLID
PATTERN_DASH
PATTERN_DOT
PATTERN_DASH_DOT
PATTERN_USER_DEFINED
```

A `PolygonAttributes` object defines the attributes related to rendering of polygons. The polygon drawing mode controls the way that a polygon is rendered. Three polygon modes are defined:

```
POLYGON_POINT
POLYGON_LINE
POLYGON_FILL
```

The polygon drawing mode can be set in constructors or by the method `setPolygonMode`.

transparency

The `TransparencyAttributes` node component provides a way to render the visual object with a certain degree of *transparency*. For example, the following `TransparencyAttributes` object will cause the visual object to be rendered at a transparency value of 0.6:

```
int tMode = TransparencyAttributes.BLENDED;
float tValue = 0.6f;
TransparencyAttributes ta = new TransparencyAttributes(tMode, tValue);
Appearance ap = new Appearance();
ap.setTransparencyAttributes(ta);
```

A transparency value of 1.0 indicates complete transparency and a value of 0.0 is completely opaque. Note that the transparency value is the opposite of the alpha value in color specifications.

The material settings of an appearance are related to illumination and shading of the objects. Chapter 9 will discuss the details of lighting and illumination. Texture mapping is discussed in Chapters 9 and 12.

drawing mode

The appearance attribute settings are related. The rules for applying geometric *drawing modes* are given below.

1. If the polygon drawing mode of `PolygonAttributes` is set to `POLYGON_POINT`, only the vertices of a polygon are rendered. In this mode the `PointAttributes` settings determine the point rendering characteristics.

2. If the polygon drawing mode of `PolygonAttributes` is set to `POLYGON_LINE`, the edges of a polygon are rendered. The visual objects appear in a wireframe form. In this mode the `LineAttributes` settings control the appearance of the lines.

3. If the polygon drawing mode of `PolygonAttributes` is set to `POLYGON_FILL`, the polygons are filled.

coloring

The *coloring* of the rendered object depends on the lighting model, the `ColoringAttributes` settings, and the vertex data of the geometry.

1. The lighting model is applied if the Appearance references a valid Material object and the Material object enables lighting. The following method of Material can be used to enable or disable lighting:

   void setLightingEnable(**boolean** enable)

   In this mode, colors of the object are rendered based on the interactions between light sources and visual objects.

2. If vertex colors are present and not ignored, they are used to render the polygons. The enabling of the vertex colors is controlled by a RenderingAttributes object. The following method sets this state:

   void setIgnoreVertexColors(**boolean** ignore)

   When vertex colors are used, the shading mode of the polygons is determined by the ColoringAttributes object. A flat shading assigns a single color to a polygon and a Gouraud shading interpolates the vertex colors in the interior of a polygon.

3. If lighting is not enabled and the vertex colors of the geometry are not present or ignored, the color specified by the ColoringAttributes object will be used for coloring the geometry.

Listing 6.7 is a class for tetrahedron with color specification. Listing 6.8 demonstrates the effects of various appearance attributes. A rotating tetrahedron is displayed in the main window. The appearance of the tetrahedron is controlled by Polygon Mode buttons that select rendering modes: point, line, polygon, and by Coloring Attribute buttons that select coloring options: single, flat, Gouraud, lighting. (See Figure 6.23.)

Listing 6.7 `ColorTetrahedron.java`

```
1 package chapter6;
2
3 import javax.vecmath.*;
4 import javax.media.j3d.*;
5
6 public class ColorTetrahedron extends IndexedTriangleArray{
7   public ColorTetrahedron() {
8     super(4, TriangleArray.COORDINATES | TriangleArray.NORMALS |
9         GeometryArray.COLOR_3, 12);
10    setCoordinate(0, new Point3f(1f,1f,1f));
11    setCoordinate(1, new Point3f(1f,-1,-1f));
12    setCoordinate(2, new Point3f(-1f,1f,-1f));
13    setCoordinate(3, new Point3f(-1f,-1f,1f));
14    int[] coords = {0,1,2,0,3,1,1,3,2,2,3,0};
15    float n = (float)(1.0/Math.sqrt(3));
16    setNormal(0, new Vector3f(n,n,-n));
17    setNormal(1, new Vector3f(n,-n,n));
18    setNormal(2, new Vector3f(-n,-n,-n));
19    setNormal(3, new Vector3f(-n,n,n));
20    int[] norms = {0,0,0,1,1,1,2,2,2,3,3,3};
21    setCoordinateIndices(0, coords);
22    setNormalIndices(0, norms);
23    setColor(0, new Color3f(1f, 0f, 0f));
24    setColor(1, new Color3f(0f, 1f, 0f));
25    setColor(2, new Color3f(0f, 0f, 1f));
26    setColor(3, new Color3f(1f, 1f, 1f));
27    setColorIndices(0, coords);
28  }
29 }
```

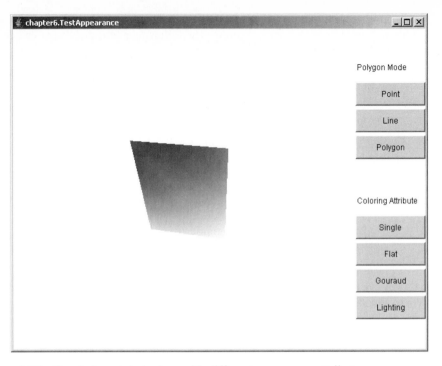

FIGURE 6.23 Rendering a tetrahedron with different appearance attributes.

Listing 6.8 TestAppearance.java

```
1 package chapter6;
2
3 import javax.vecmath.*;
4 import java.awt.*;
5 import java.awt.event.*;
6 import javax.media.j3d.*;
7 import com.sun.j3d.utils.universe.*;
8 import com.sun.j3d.utils.geometry.*;
9 import java.applet.*;
10 import com.sun.j3d.utils.applet.MainFrame;
11
12 public class TestAppearance extends Applet implements
13   ActionListener {
14   public static void main(String[] args) {
15     new MainFrame(new TestAppearance(), 640, 480);
16   }
17
18   public void init() {
19     setLayout(new BorderLayout());
20     Panel p = new Panel();
21     p.setLayout(new GridLayout(12,1,10,5));
22     add(p, BorderLayout.EAST);
23     p.add(new Panel());
24     p.add(new Label("Polygon Mode"));
25     Button button = new Button("Point");
26     p.add(button);
27     button.addActionListener(this);
28     button = new Button("Line");
29     p.add(button);
30     button.addActionListener(this);
```

```
31      button = new Button("Polygon");
32      p.add(button);
33      button.addActionListener(this);
34
35      p.add(new Panel());
36      p.add(new Label("Coloring Attribute"));
37      button = new Button("Single");
38      p.add(button);
39      button.addActionListener(this);
40      button = new Button("Flat");
41      p.add(button);
42      button.addActionListener(this);
43      button = new Button("Gouraud");
44      p.add(button);
45      button.addActionListener(this);
46      button = new Button("Lighting");
47      p.add(button);
48      button.addActionListener(this);
49
50      GraphicsConfiguration gc =
51      SimpleUniverse.getPreferredConfiguration();
52      Canvas3D cv = new Canvas3D(gc);
53      add(cv, BorderLayout.CENTER);
54      BranchGroup bg = createSceneGraph();
55      bg.compile();
56      SimpleUniverse su = new SimpleUniverse(cv);
57      su.getViewingPlatform().setNominalViewingTransform();
58      su.addBranchGraph(bg);
59    }
60
61    Appearance ap;
62    private BranchGroup createSceneGraph() {
63      BranchGroup root = new BranchGroup();
64      TransformGroup spin = new TransformGroup();
65      spin.setCapability(TransformGroup.ALLOW_TRANSFORM_WRITE);
66      root.addChild(spin);
67
68      // allow appearance change
69      ap = new Appearance();
70      ap.setCapability(Appearance.ALLOW_COLORING_ATTRIBUTES_WRITE);
71      ap.setCapability(Appearance.ALLOW_POINT_ATTRIBUTES_WRITE);
72      ap.setCapability(Appearance.ALLOW_LINE_ATTRIBUTES_WRITE);
73      ap.setCapability(Appearance.ALLOW_POLYGON_ATTRIBUTES_WRITE);
74      ap.setCapability(Appearance.ALLOW_RENDERING_ATTRIBUTES_WRITE);
75      ap.setCapability(Appearance.ALLOW_MATERIAL_WRITE);
76      Shape3D shape = new Shape3D(new ColorTetrahedron(), ap);
77
78      Transform3D tr = new Transform3D();
79      tr.setScale(0.25);
80      TransformGroup tg = new TransformGroup(tr);
81      spin.addChild(tg);
82      tg.addChild(shape);
83
84      Alpha alpha = new Alpha(-1, 4000);
85      RotationInterpolator rotator =
86      new RotationInterpolator(alpha, spin);
87      BoundingSphere bounds = new BoundingSphere();
88      rotator.setSchedulingBounds(bounds);
89      spin.addChild(rotator);
90
```

```
 91      // background and light
 92      Background background = new Background(1f, 1f, 1f);
 93      background.setApplicationBounds(bounds);
 94      root.addChild(background);
 95      AmbientLight light = new AmbientLight
 96        (true, new Color3f(Color.red));
 97      light.setInfluencingBounds(bounds);
 98      root.addChild(light);
 99      PointLight ptlight = new PointLight(new Color3f(Color.cyan),
100        new Point3f(3f,3f,3f), new Point3f(1f,0f,0f));
101      ptlight.setInfluencingBounds(bounds);
102      root.addChild(ptlight);
103      return root;
104    }
105
106    public void actionPerformed(ActionEvent actionEvent) {
107      String cmd = actionEvent.getActionCommand();
108      if ("Point".equals(cmd)) {
109        ap.setPolygonAttributes(new PolygonAttributes(
110            PolygonAttributes.POLYGON_POINT,
111            PolygonAttributes.CULL_BACK,0));
112        ap.setPointAttributes(new PointAttributes(10, false));
113      } else if ("Line".equals(cmd)) {
114        ap.setPolygonAttributes(new PolygonAttributes(
115            PolygonAttributes.POLYGON_LINE,
116            PolygonAttributes.CULL_BACK,0));
117        ap.setLineAttributes(new LineAttributes(3,
118            LineAttributes.PATTERN_DASH, false));
119      } else if ("Polygon".equals(cmd)) {
120        ap.setPolygonAttributes(new PolygonAttributes(
121            PolygonAttributes.POLYGON_FILL,
122            PolygonAttributes.CULL_BACK,0));
123      } else if ("Single".equals(cmd)) {
124        ColoringAttributes ca = new ColoringAttributes();
125        ca.setColor(0.5f, 0.5f, 0.5f);
126        ap.setColoringAttributes(ca);
127        ap.setMaterial(null);
128        RenderingAttributes ra = new RenderingAttributes();
129        ra.setIgnoreVertexColors(true);
130        ap.setRenderingAttributes(ra);
131      } else if ("Flat".equals(cmd)) {
132        ColoringAttributes ca = new ColoringAttributes();
133        ca.setShadeModel(ColoringAttributes.SHADE_FLAT);
134        ap.setColoringAttributes(ca);
135        ap.setMaterial(null);
136        RenderingAttributes ra = new RenderingAttributes();
137        ra.setIgnoreVertexColors(false);
138        ap.setRenderingAttributes(ra);
139      } else if ("Gouraud".equals(cmd)) {
140        ColoringAttributes ca = new ColoringAttributes();
141        ca.setShadeModel(ColoringAttributes.SHADE_GOURAUD);
142        ap.setColoringAttributes(ca);
143        ap.setMaterial(null);
144        RenderingAttributes ra = new RenderingAttributes();
145        ra.setIgnoreVertexColors(false);
146        ap.setRenderingAttributes(ra);
147      } else if ("Lighting".equals(cmd)) {
148        ap.setMaterial(new Material());
149        RenderingAttributes ra = new RenderingAttributes();
150        ra.setIgnoreVertexColors(true);
```

```
151        ap.setRenderingAttributes(ra);
152      }
153    }
154 }
```

The `ColorTetrahedron` class is similar to the class defined in Listing 6.1. It adds vertex colors to its definition (lines 23–26). A `ColorTetrahedron` instance is used as the geometry for a `Shape3D` leaf in the `TestAppearance` program. An `Appearance` object for the shape is created with several permission bits set:

```
ap.setCapability(Appearance.ALLOW_COLORING_ATTRIBUTES_WRITE);
ap.setCapability(Appearance.ALLOW_POINT_ATTRIBUTES_WRITE);
ap.setCapability(Appearance.ALLOW_LINE_ATTRIBUTES_WRITE);
ap.setCapability(Appearance.ALLOW_POLYGON_ATTRIBUTES_WRITE);
ap.setCapability(Appearance.ALLOW_RENDERING_ATTRIBUTES_WRITE);
ap.setCapability(Appearance.ALLOW_MATERIAL_WRITE);
```

These settings will allow dynamic changes of coloring attributes, point attributes, line attributes, polygon attributes, and material on the `Appearance` object. Note that the permission bits must be set through individual method calls. You cannot make just one call by combining the bits.

The buttons control the appearance settings (line 106). There are seven buttons in two groups for polygon modes and coloring attributes.

Point:

Only the vertices are rendered by setting the `PolygonAttributes` POLYGON_POINT. The `PointAttributes` of the `Appearance` object is set to a size of 10.

Line:

The lines of the object are rendered by setting the `PolygonAttributes` POLYGON_LINE. The `LineAttributes` of the `Appearance` object is set to a dash pattern with a width of 3.

Polygon:

The faces of the object are rendered by setting the `PolygonAttributes` POLYGON_FILL.

Single:

The object is rendered with a single gray color in a `ColoringAttributes` setting. The lighting is turned off by setting the material of the `Appearance` object to null. The vertex colors are ignored by setting a `RenderingAttributes` object.

Flat:

The object is rendered with flat colors defined in vertex data. The lighting is turned off by setting the material of the `Appearance` object to null. The flat shading mode is selected in a `ColoringAttributes` object.

Gouraud:

The object is rendered with Gouraud shading using vertex colors. The lighting is turned off by setting the material of the `Appearance` object to null. The Gouraud shading mode is selected in a `ColoringAttributes` object.

Lighting:

The object is illuminated by lights. The `Material` of the `Appearance` object is set to a new default instance. The vertex colors are ignored by setting a `RenderingAttributes` object.

The mode selection of point, line, or polygon is independent of the color selection of single, flat, Gouraud, or lighting. Consequently, even the point rendering can be illuminated with lights.

If you place a Dodecahedron object in this program, you may find that in the wireframe mode (lines only) there are extra lines rendered besides the pentagons. This is due to the automatic triangulation performed by the GeometryInfo class. The pentagons are divided into triangles.

KEY CLASSES AND METHODS

- **javax.vecmath.Point*** A family of classes encapsulating geometric points.
- **javax.vecmath.Vector*** A family of classes encapsulating geometric vectors.
- **javax.vecmath.Color*** A family of classes for color values.
- **javax.media.j3d.Shape3D** A leaf-node class encapsulating a visual object.
- **javax.media.j3d.Geometry** A node-component class defining a geometry for a Shape3D object.
- **javax.media.j3d.Appearance** A node-component class defining an appearance for a Shape3D object.
- **javax.media.j3d.GeometryArray** A family of classes for constructing geometries from vertex specifications.
- **javax.media.j3d.GeometryStripArray** A family of geometry array classes for constructing strip geometries.
- **javax.media.j3d.IndexedGeometryArray** A family of classes for constructing geometries from vertex and index specifications.
- **javax.media.j3d.IndexedGeometryStripArray** A family of classes for constructing strip geometries from vertex and index specifications.
- **javax.media.j3d.GeometryInfo** A class for constructing and manipulating geometries.
- **javax.media.j3d.Primitive** A subclass of Group for geometric primitives.
- **javax.media.j3d.ColoringAttributes** A node-component class for color and shading specifications.
- **javax.media.j3d.TransparencyAttributes** A node-component class for transparency.
- **javax.media.j3d.PointAttributes** A node-component class for point-rendering attributes including point size and antialiasing option.
- **javax.media.j3d.LineAttributes** A node-component class for line-rendering attributes such as line width, line pattern, and antialiasing.
- **javax.media.j3d.PolygonAttributes** A node-component class for polygon-rendering attributes such as rasterization mode, back-face culling, and offset.
- **javax.media.j3d.Font3D** A class encapsulating a 3D font.
- **javax.media.j3d.Text3D** A geometry class representing a 3D text string.
- **javax.media.j3d.Text2D** A subclass of Shape3D representing a 2D text string in the 3D space.
- **javax.media.j3d.FontExtrusion** A class defining an extrusion path for constructing a Font3D object from a Font object.

KEY TERMS

point A basic geometric element representing a position in a space.
vector A geometric element for a directional quantity.
polygon mesh A set of simple polygons such as triangles representing an approximation of a surface.

Platonic solids The five regular polyhedra: tetrahedron, cube, octahedron, dodecahedron, and icosahedron.

flat shading A simple coloring method that fills a polygon patch with a single color.

Gouraud shading A coloring method that assigns colors to a polygon by interpolating the colors on the vertices.

CHAPTER SUMMARY

- In this chapter we discuss the fundamentals of constructing visual objects through their geometry and appearance specifications. Geometry defines the object's shape and size, and appearance defines the rendering properties such as color, material, and texture.

- Java 3D includes a `javax.vecmath` package that defines a large number of classes for points, vectors, and matrices. They are used in other parts of Java 3D for specifying geometric properties, transformations, and other attributes.

- The `Shape3D` class represents a visual object in a scene graph. `Shape3D` references `Geometry` and `Appearance` objects to specify the geometry and appearance of the shape.

- Java 3D provides a large number of facilities for defining `Geometry`. `GeometryArray` and its subclasses define geometry by directly specifying the low-level points, lines, and simple polygons.

- `GeometryInfo` class allows more general polygons. It also facilitates the automatic generation of normals using `NormalGenerator` and automatic strip generation using `Stripifier`.

- Primitives offer high-level prebuilt geometric objects. Java 3D utility packages provide implementations of commonly used primitives including box, cone, cylinder, and sphere.

- Text can also be used as special geometric objects. `Text3D` is a subclass of `Geometry`. It defines solid 3D text objects in association with the `Font3D`, `FontExtrusion`, and Font classes. `Text2D` is a subclass of `Shape3D`. It defines 2D text objects as texture mapped rectangles.

- The appearance attributes of a shape are defined by various node components rooted at an `Appearance` object. An `Appearance` node component holds references to other components of classes such as `ColoringAttributes`, `PointAttributes`, `Line-Attributes`, `PolygonAttributes`, `TransparencyAttributes`, and `Material`.

REVIEW QUESTIONS

6.1 Construct `Point3f` objects to represent the following points:

$$(1, 2, 3), (0, 0, 0), (-1.2, 3.4, -5.6)$$

6.2 Write Java statements to calculate the three distances between the points defined in Question 6.1.

6.3   Construct `Vector3f` objects to represent the following vectors:

$$(1, 2, 3), (1, 1, 1), (-1.2, 3.4, -5.6)$$

6.4   Write Java statements to calculate the three angles between the vectors defined in Question 6.3.

6.5   Construct a `PointArray` object for the vertices of a cube centered at the origin. Its edges have length 1.0 and are parallel to the coordinate axes.

6.6   Construct a `LineArray` object for the edges of a tetrahedron.

6.7   Use a `TriangleArray` object to represent the geometry of a tetrahedron.

6.8   Use a `QuadArray` object to represent the geometry of a cube.

6.9   Construct a `LineStripArray` object for the edges of a tetrahedron.

6.10   Construct a `TriangleStripArray` object for the geometry of a tetrahedron.

6.11   Construct a `TriangleFanArray` object for the geometry of a tetrahedron.

6.12   Use an `IndexedQuadArray` object to represent the geometry of a cube.

6.13   Draw a figure corresponding to the geometry defined by the following `TriangleStripArray` object:

```java
int[] stripVertexCounts = {5, 3};
TriangleStripArray tsa = new TriangleStripArray
  (8, GeometryArray.COORDINATES, stripVertexCounts);
Point3f[] coords = new Point3f[8];
coords[0] = new Point3f(0f, 0f, 0f);
coords[1] = new Point3f(0f, 1f, 0f);
coords[2] = new Point3f(0.5f, 0.866f, 0f);
coords[3] = new Point3f(1.5f, 0.866f, 0f);
coords[4] = new Point3f(1f, 1.73f, 0f);
coords[5] = new Point3f(0f, 1f, 0f);
coords[6] = new Point3f(1.5f, 0.866f, 0f);
coords[7] = new Point3f(2f, 0f, 0f);
tsa.setCoordinates(0, coords);
```

6.14   Draw a figure corresponding to the geometry defined by the following `TriangleFanArray` object:

```java
int[] stripVertexCounts = {4, 4};
TriangleFanArray tfa = new TriangleFanArray
  (8, GeometryArray.COORDINATES, stripVertexCounts);
Point3f[] coords = new Point3f[8];
coords[0] = new Point3f(0f, 0f, 0f);
coords[1] = new Point3f(1f, 0f, 0f);
coords[2] = new Point3f(0.866f, 0.5f, 0f);
coords[3] = new Point3f(0.5f, 0.866f, 0f);
coords[4] = new Point3f(0f, 0f, 0f);
coords[5] = new Point3f(-1f, 0f, 0f);
coords[6] = new Point3f(-0.866f, -0.5f, 0f);
coords[7] = new Point3f(-0.5f, -0.866f, 0f);
tfa.setCoordinates(0, coords);
```

6.15   Draw a figure corresponding to the geometry defined by the following `IndexedTriangleStripArray` object:

```java
int[] stripIndexCounts = {5, 3};
IndexedTriangleStripArray itsa = new
  IndexedTriangleStripArray(6,
  GeometryArray.COORDINATES, 8, stripIndexCounts);
Point3f[] coords = new Point3f[6];
coords[0] = new Point3f(0f, 0f, 0f);
coords[1] = new Point3f(0f, 1f, 0f);
```

```
coords[2] = new Point3f(0.5f, 0.866f, 0f);
coords[3] = new Point3f(1.5f, 0.866f, 0f);
coords[4] = new Point3f(1f, 1.73f, 0f);
coords[5] = new Point3f(2f, 0f, 0f);
itsa.setCoordinates(0, coords);
int[] indices = {0, 1, 2, 3, 4, 1, 3, 5};
itsa.setCoordinateIndices(0, indices);
```

6.16   Use a `GeometryInfo` object to define a cube of length 1.

6.17   What are the differences between `Box` and `ColorCube` classes?

6.18   What are the differences between `Text3D` and `Text2D` besides their dimensionality?

6.19   If a geometry contains both vertex coordinate and vertex color definition, how can you use the geometry with the vertex colors ignored?

6.20   Derive an equation for the surface normals of the Möbius strip with the parametric equation:

$$x = \left(1 + v \cos \frac{u}{2}\right) \cos u$$

$$y = \left(1 + v \cos \frac{u}{2}\right) \sin u$$

$$z = v \sin \frac{u}{2}$$

$$0 \leq u \leq 2\pi, \qquad -0.3 \leq v \leq 0.3$$

PROGRAMMING EXERCISES

6.1   The octahedron is one of the five Platonic solids. It has eight faces of triangles and six vertices:

$$(0, 0, 1)$$
$$(-1, 0, 0), (0, -1, 0), (1, 0, 0), (0, 1, 0)$$
$$(0, 0, -1)$$

Implement an `Octahedron` class as a descendant of `Geometry`.

6.2   Write a test program for `Octahedron` class to display an octahedron in wireframe form.

6.3   The icosahedron is another Platonic solid with the following vertices:

$$(0, \phi, 1),$$
$$(1, 0, \phi), (-1, 0, \phi), (-\phi, 1, 0), (0, \phi, -1), (\phi, 1, 0),$$
$$(0, -\phi, 1), (-\phi, -1, 0), (-1, 0, -\phi), (1, 0, -\phi), (\phi, -1, 0),$$
$$(0, -\phi, -1)$$

where $\phi = \left(\sqrt{5} + 1\right)/2$. Implement the `Icosahedron` class as a subclass of `Shape3D` using the `GeometryInfo` class. Generate the normals for the geometry using `NormalGenerator`.

6.4   Write a test program to display the icosahedron defined in Exercise 6.3. Use lighting and rotate the object.

6.5 Create and display a 3D 4 × 4 × 4 grid using the `LineArray` class.

6.6 Use an `IndexedQuadArray` object to define a frustum with a top square of size 1 × 1, a bottom square of size 2 × 2, and height 1. Rotate the frustum in the virtual space.

6.7 Create and display a pyramid using the `GeometryInfo` class.

6.8 Replace the tetrahedron in Listing 6.8 by a dodecahedron and observe the result of triangulation from the `GeometryInfo` class in the wireframe mode.

6.9 Modify the program in Listing 5.1 to allow dynamic change of the 3D text. Implement a menu item and a dialog box to input a string from the user and display the string as a 3D text.

6.10 Write a Java 3D program similar to that in Exercise 6.9, but display the string using a `Text2D` object.

6.11 Extend the functions of the program in Listing 6.8 to include settings for different line patterns.

6.12 Implement a `ColorOctahedron` class that assigns different colors to its vertices. Write a test program to display a `ColorOctahedron` object using Gouraud shading.

6.13 Use `GeometryInfo` to create a Möbius strip defined in Review Question 6.20. Generate normals with the `NormalGenerator` class. Display the Möbius strip with lighting.

6.14 Create a Möbius strip using an `IndexedQuadArray` object. Set the normals based on the formula derived in Review Question 6.20. Display the Möbius strip with lighting.

CHAPTER 7

GEOMETRIC TRANSFORMATION

Objectives

- To describe transformations related to 3D graphics.
- To construct 3D affine transforms including translation, rotation, scaling, shearing, and reflection.
- To understand and apply transformation matrices.
- To apply transforms in scene graphs.
- To construct and apply composite transformations.
- To apply transforms in constructing geometries.

7.1 Introduction

Transformation plays a crucial role in computer graphics. Through proper geometric transforms, graphics objects can be changed in shape, size, and location to achieve their specifications. Affine transforms are used frequently in modeling the virtual world. The viewing process employs transformations in a critical way as well. A special type of transformation, the *perspective* or *orthogonal projection*, is usually used in a view to construct a mapping from a 3D space to a 2D image. Animation often involves applications of geometric transformation to achieve motions in the scene.

orthogonal projection

Java 3D provides transformation support at several levels. The matrix classes such as `Matrix4d` offer the low-level data representations of the transforms. The `Transform3D` class encapsulates the 3D transforms with facilities to set and compose transforms and to apply transforms to points and vectors. The `TransformGroup` class represents the high-level transform nodes in scene graphs.

Through the use of homogeneous coordinates, all 3D projective transformations (including affine transformations) are completely determined by 4×4 transformation matrices. The transforms with direct geometrical interpretations such as rotations and translations can be expressed in matrix forms. However, explicit matrix construction of certain transforms such as general 3D rotations may be complicated. Other representations, such as quaternion for 3D rotations, may provide more convenient intermediate forms for constructions and manipulations.

Transformations can be combined to form new transformations. The composition of simple transforms is a powerful way to construct and manage complex transforms. In Java 3D the composition can occur at the lower level of matrix or `Transform3D` objects through multiplication of the transforms. It can also occur at the higher level of a scene graph, where a chain of transform nodes creates the effect of a composite transform.

A main application of transformations is to change the geometric characteristics of objects. In a Java 3D scene graph, `TransformGroup` nodes represent transforms. A `TransformGroup` node applies the transform defined in the node to its children. The series of `TransformGroup` nodes from an object to the `Locale` will transform the object in various ways. The general tree structure of a scene graph provides great flexibility in manipulating the visual objects with transform nodes.

Another application of transformations is to aid the construction of geometries. The `Transform3D` class offers convenient methods to apply the transform to points or vectors. To construct geometries that have certain symmetric properties, we may take advantage of the transformation capabilities by generating many points of the geometries through transformations on a set of base points.

7.2 3D Affine Transformations

A transformation is a mapping from a vector space to itself or to another vector space. Certain families of transformations that preserve some geometric properties are of special significance in computer graphics. For example, projective transforms are crucial in 3D viewing. Affine transforms, a subset of projective transforms, are used extensively in modeling visual objects.

An affine transform maps lines to lines and preserves parallelism. For example, an affine transform may not map a rectangle to a rectangle, but it will always map a rectangle to a parallelogram. As in the 2D case, basic 3D affine transforms include translations, rotations, scalings, shears, and reflections. However, the 3D versions are often more complex, especially for rotations.

The affine transforms that also preserve distances are called rigid motions, Euclidean motions, or isometries. Translations, rotations, and reflections are examples of rigid motions.

7.2.1 Transformation Matrix

Affine transforms can be represented in a matrix form. If a point in a 3D space is represented by three coordinates,

$$\begin{bmatrix} x \\ y \\ z \end{bmatrix}$$

then an affine transform can be written as a matrix equation:

$$\begin{bmatrix} x' \\ y' \\ z' \end{bmatrix} = \begin{bmatrix} a_{11} & a_{12} & a_{13} \\ a_{21} & a_{22} & a_{23} \\ a_{31} & a_{32} & a_{33} \end{bmatrix} \begin{bmatrix} x \\ y \\ z \end{bmatrix} + \begin{bmatrix} b_1 \\ b_2 \\ b_3 \end{bmatrix}$$

Rotations, scalings, and shearings relative to the origin can be represented by the matrix multiplication alone. The addition of the column vector b represents a translation. Because of the required special treatment of the translation, the above transformation is not linear in the space R^3. However, using *homogeneous coordinates* to represent 3D points, all affine trans- *homogeneous coordinate* forms and projective transforms can be represented as matrix multiplications. The homogeneous coordinate of a 3D point has four components: (x, y, z, w). When w is not 0, it corresponds to a regular 3D coordinate $(x/w, y/w, z/w)$. With homogeneous coordinates, the same affine transformation given above may be represented equivalently as a linear transformation in the space R^4

$$\begin{bmatrix} x' \\ y' \\ z' \\ 1 \end{bmatrix} = \begin{bmatrix} a_{11} & a_{12} & a_{13} & b_1 \\ a_{21} & a_{22} & a_{22} & b_2 \\ a_{31} & a_{32} & a_{33} & b_3 \\ 0 & 0 & 0 & 1 \end{bmatrix} \begin{bmatrix} x \\ y \\ z \\ 1 \end{bmatrix}$$

The 4×4 *transformation matrix* in the equation above completely determines an affine *transformation matrix* transform. Operations involving the transforms can be represented as corresponding matrix operations. Combining several affine transforms produces another affine transform. The matrix of the composite transform is the product of matrices of corresponding transforms. The inverse matrix of a transform corresponds to the inverse transform. More generally, a projective transformation may be represented with a similar matrix equation:

$$\begin{bmatrix} x' \\ y' \\ z' \\ w' \end{bmatrix} = \begin{bmatrix} a_{11} & a_{12} & a_{13} & a_{14} \\ a_{21} & a_{22} & a_{22} & a_{24} \\ a_{31} & a_{32} & a_{33} & a_{34} \\ a_{41} & a_{42} & a_{43} & a_{44} \end{bmatrix} \begin{bmatrix} x \\ y \\ z \\ w \end{bmatrix}$$

An introduction to matrices and their operations can be found in Appendix A.

Java 3D offers several classes supporting transformations. Besides vector classes, `javax.vecmath` package also contains *matrix classes* representing 3×3, 4×4, and gen- *matrix classes* eral matrices: `Matrix3f`, `Matrix3d`, `Matrix4f`, `Matrix4d`, `GMatrix`. The following code fragment constructs a `Matrix4d` object:

```
double[] array = {1.0, 2.0, 3.0, 1.0,
                  0.0, 1.0, -1.0, 2.0,
                  4.0, 0.0, 0.5, -1.0,
                  0.0, 0.0, 0.0, 1.0};
Matrix4d matrix = new Matrix4d(array);
```

GMatrix class can be used to represent a matrix of arbitrary sizes with element type double. For example the following code creates a 3 × 4 matrix:

```
double[] array = {1.0, 2.0, 3.0, 1.0,
                  0.0, 1.0, -1.0, 2.0,
                  4.0, 0.0, 0.5, -1.0};
GMatrix matrix = new GMatrix(3, 4, array);
```

Basic matrix operations such as addition, multiplication, and inversion are supported. The following is a partial list of the methods in the Matrix4d class for matrix operations. Other classes contain similar methods.

- **void** add(Matrix4d m1)—Add matrix m1 to the current matrix.

- **void** sub(Matrix4d m1)—Subtract matrix m1 from the current matrix.

- **void** mul(Matrix4d m1)—Multiply matrix m1 on the current matrix.

- **void** invert()—Invert the current matrix.

- **void** add(Matrix4d m1, Matrix4d m2)—Set the current matrix to the sum of the matrices m1 and m2.

- **void** sub(Matrix4d m1, Matrix4d m2)—Set the current matrix to the difference of the matrices m1 and m2.

- **void** mul(Matrix4d m1, Matrix4d m2)—Set the current matrix to the product of the matrices m1 and m2.

- **void** invert(Matrix4d m1)—Set the current matrix to the inverse of the matrix m1.

- **void** transpose()—Transpose the current matrix.

- **void** mul(**double** scalar)—Multiply the current matrix by the number scalar.

- **double** determinant()—Return the determinant of the current matrix.

Listing 7.1 gives a class for displaying a matrix. Listing 7.2 provides an interactive user interface to view a matrix and perform certain operations on the matrix using the built-in methods of the Matrix4d class.

Listing 7.1 `MatrixPanel.java`

```
1 package chapter7;
2
3 import java.awt.*;
4 import javax.vecmath.*;
5
6 public class MatrixPanel extends Panel {
7   TextField[] fields = new TextField[16];
8
9   public MatrixPanel() {
10    setLayout(new GridLayout(4, 4));
11    for (int i = 0; i < 16; i++) {
12      fields[i] = new TextField(5);
13      if (i/4 == i%4)
14        fields[i].setText("1");
15      else
16        fields[i].setText("0");
17      add(fields[i]);
18    }
19  }
20
```

```
21    public MatrixPanel(Matrix4d m) {
22      setLayout(new GridLayout(4, 4));
23      for (int i = 0; i < 16; i++) {
24        fields[i] = new TextField(5);
25        fields[i].setText("" + m.getElement(i/4, i%4));
26        add(fields[i]);
27      }
28    }
29
30    public void set(Matrix4d m) {
31      for (int i = 0; i < 16; i++) {
32        fields[i].setText("" + m.getElement(i/4, i%4));
33      }
34    }
35
36    public void get(Matrix4d m) {
37      for (int i = 0; i < 16; i++) {
38        m.setElement(i/4, i%4, Double.parseDouble
39          (fields[i].getText()));
40      }
41    }
42  }
```

Listing 7.2 `TestMatrix.java`

```
1 package chapter7;
2
3 import java.awt.*;
4 import java.awt.event.*;
5 import javax.vecmath.*;
6 import java.applet.*;
7 import com.sun.j3d.utils.applet.MainFrame;
8
9 public class TestMatrix extends Applet implements ActionListener {
10   public static void main(String[] args) {
11     new MainFrame(new TestMatrix(), 600, 200);
12   }
13
14   MatrixPanel mp;
15   Matrix4d m = new Matrix4d();
16   TextField tf;
17
18   public void init() {
19     this.setLayout(new BorderLayout());
20
21     mp = new MatrixPanel();
22     add(mp, BorderLayout.CENTER);
23
24     Panel p = new Panel();
25     p.setLayout(new GridLayout(6,1));
26     Button button = new Button("Identity");
27     button.addActionListener(this);
28     p.add(button);
29     button = new Button("Zero");
30     button.addActionListener(this);
31     p.add(button);
32     button = new Button("Negate");
33     button.addActionListener(this);
34     p.add(button);
35     button = new Button("Transpose");
```

```
36        button.addActionListener(this);
37        p.add(button);
38        button = new Button("Invert");
39        button.addActionListener(this);
40        p.add(button);
41        button = new Button("Determinant");
42        button.addActionListener(this);
43        p.add(button);
44        this.add(p, BorderLayout.EAST);
45
46        tf = new TextField();
47        add(tf, BorderLayout.SOUTH);
48    }
49
50    public void actionPerformed(ActionEvent e) {
51        String cmd = e.getActionCommand();
52        if ("Identity".equals(cmd)) {
53          mp.get(m);
54          m.setIdentity();
55          mp.set(m);
56        } else if ("Zero".equals(cmd)) {
57          mp.get(m);
58          m.setZero();
59          mp.set(m);
60        } else if ("Negate".equals(cmd)) {
61          mp.get(m);
62          m.negate();
63          mp.set(m);
64        } else if ("Transpose".equals(cmd)) {
65          mp.get(m);
66          m.transpose();
67          mp.set(m);
68        } else if ("Invert".equals(cmd)) {
69          mp.get(m);
70          m.invert();
71          mp.set(m);
72        } else if ("Determinant".equals(cmd)) {
73          mp.get(m);
74          tf.setText("" + m.determinant());
75        }
76    }
77 }
```

The `MatrixPanel` class is a visual component to display a 4 × 4 matrix. It contains 16 text fields for the 16 elements of the matrix (line 7). It has a constructor that takes a `Matrix4d` object to initialize the display (line 21). Its default constructor initializes the display to an identity matrix (line 9). The method `set(Matrix4d m)` sets the display to the matrix given. The method `get(Matrix4d m)` retrieves the matrix from the display.

The `TestMatrix` class is the main test program. It creates a `MatrixPanel` object to represent a `Matrix4d` object (line 21) (Figure 7.1). Six buttons are placed in the EAST region of the frame to perform the corresponding matrix operations defined by methods of the `Matrix4d` class.

■ Identity – Set the matrix to the identity matrix using the `identity()` method.

■ Zero – Set the matrix to the zero matrix using the `zero()` method.

■ Negative – Set the matrix to its negative matrix using the `negate()` method.

■ Transpose – Set the matrix to its transpose using the `transpose()` method.

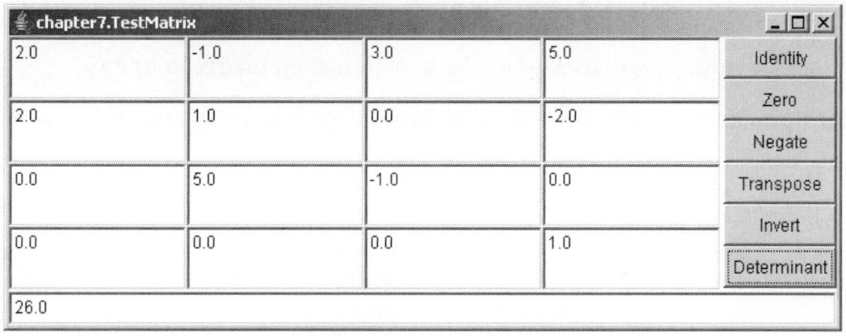

2.0	-1.0	3.0	5.0	Identity
				Zero
2.0	1.0	0.0	-2.0	Negate
				Transpose
0.0	5.0	-1.0	0.0	Invert
				Determinant
0.0	0.0	0.0	1.0	

26.0

FIGURE 7.1 A test program for matrix operations. The transformation matrix is shown in a grid of text fields. A user may edit the entries directly. Six operations on the matrix are provided. The result of the determinant is displayed in the text field at the bottom.

■ Invert – Invert the matrix and display the inverse matrix using the `invert()` method.

■ Determinant – Calculate the determinant of the matrix and display the result in the bottom text field using the `determinant()` method.

7.2.2 Transform3D

Java 3D includes the class `Transform3D` to represent a 3D affine or projective transform. In a scene graph, a `TransformGroup` node uses a `Transform3D` object to define its transformation. `Transform3D` internally maintains a 4×4 `double` matrix for the transform. To create a `Transform3D` object you may use one of many available constructors. The default constructor creates an identity matrix. You may supply a matrix object, an array, or other forms for the transformation matrix. For example, the following three `Transform3D` objects represent equivalent transforms:

`Transform3D`

```
double[] array = {1.0, 2.0, 3.0, 1.0,
                  0.0, 1.0, -1.0, 2.0,
                  4.0, 0.0, 0.5, -1.0,
                  0.0, 0.0, 0.0, 1.0};
Matrix4d matrix = new Matrix4d(array);
GMatrix gmatrix = new GMatrix(4, 4, array);
Transform3D transform1 = new Transform3D(matrix);
Transform3D transform2 = new Transform3D(gmatrix);
Transform3D transform3 = new Transform3D(array);
```

`Transform3D` contains a large number of convenience methods to set and manipulate the transform. Some of the methods that directly handle the transformation matrix are listed below.

■ **void** `set(Matrix4d m1)`—Set the transformation matrix to `m1`.

■ **void** `set(Matrix4f m1)`—Set the transformation matrix to `m1`.

■ **void** `set(GMatrix m1)`— Set the transformation matrix to `m1`.

■ **void** `set(double[] array)`—Set the transformation matrix to `array`.

■ **void** `set(float[] array)`—Set the transformation matrix to `array`.

■ **void** `get(Matrix4d m1)`—Get the transformation matrix to `m1`.

■ **void** `get(Matrix4f m1)`—Get the transformation matrix to `m1`.

■ **void** `get(GMatrix m1)`—Get the transformation matrix to `m1`.

- ▪ **void** get(**double**[] array)—Get the transformation matrix to array.

- ▪ **void** get(**float**[] array)—Get the transformation matrix to array.

The transformation can also be defined in terms of geometric specifications such as translation, scaling, rotation, and shearing.

translation matrix

A translation is represented by the *transformation matrix*

$$\begin{bmatrix} 1 & 0 & 0 & b_1 \\ 0 & 1 & 0 & b_2 \\ 0 & 0 & 1 & b_3 \\ 0 & 0 & 0 & 1 \end{bmatrix}$$

Under the translation, each point is moved by the constant amounts b_1, b_2, b_3 in x-, y-, z-directions, respectively. Clearly the shape and orientation of a geometric figure will not change under a translation. The inverse of a translation by b_1, b_2, b_3 is a translation by $-b_1, -b_2, -b_3$.

Transform3D includes the following methods to set translations:

```
void set(Vector3d trans)
void set(Vector3f trans)
void setTranslation(Vector3d trans)
void setTranslation(Vector3f trans)
```

The set methods replace the entire transform with the specified translation. The setTranslation methods modify only the translation components of the existing transform.

scaling matrix

A *scaling* by the factors s_1, s_2, s_3 in x-, y-, z-directions has the matrix representation:

$$\begin{bmatrix} s_1 & 0 & 0 & 0 \\ 0 & s_2 & 0 & 0 \\ 0 & 0 & s_3 & 0 \\ 0 & 0 & 0 & 1 \end{bmatrix}$$

If all the scaling factors are nonzero, the scaling transform is invertible. The inverse is also a scaling with factors $1/s_1, 1/s_2, 1/s_3$. A scaling is uniform if $s_1 = s_2 = s_3$.

Transform3D includes the following methods to set scales:

```
void set(double scale)
void setScale(double scale)
void setScale(Vector3d scales)
```

The set method replaces the entire transform with a scaling. The setScale methods modify only the scaling components of the existing transform.

reflection matrix

A 3D reflection is performed about a plane. A simple *reflection* about the *xy*-plane, for example, is given by the following matrix:

$$\begin{bmatrix} 1 & 0 & 0 & 0 \\ 0 & 1 & 0 & 0 \\ 0 & 0 & -1 & 0 \\ 0 & 0 & 0 & 1 \end{bmatrix}$$

A reflection is always invertible, and the inverse of a reflection is itself. More generally, a reflection about a plane through the origin with the normal vector u can be expressed as:

$$T(x) = x - \frac{2x \cdot u}{\|u\|^2} u$$

A matrix representation may be derived from this equation. An alternative way to construct such a general reflection will be considered later in this chapter.

A 3D *shear* shifts a point along a plane, and the amount of the shift depends on the distance of the point to the plane. A simple shear that changes only the x-coordinates has the following matrix: shearing matrix

$$\begin{bmatrix} 1 & 0 & sh_x & 0 \\ 0 & 1 & 0 & 0 \\ 0 & 0 & 1 & 0 \\ 0 & 0 & 0 & 1 \end{bmatrix}$$

The y- and z-coordinates are not changed by this transform. The x-coordinates are shifted according to the equation:

$$x' = x + sh_x z$$

A more general (x, y)-shear shifts both x- and y-coordinates:

$$\begin{bmatrix} 1 & 0 & sh_x & 0 \\ 0 & 1 & sh_y & 0 \\ 0 & 0 & 1 & 0 \\ 0 & 0 & 0 & 1 \end{bmatrix}$$

Shearing is invertible. The inverse of the above shear is another shear of the same type with parameters $-sh_x, -sh_y$.

7.2.3 Rotation

3D rotations are complex operations. A general 3D *rotation* has an axis of rotation that can be any line in the space. Around the axis all points are rotated by a fixed angle. A rotation of angle θ about the z-axis can be represented by the following matrix: a rotation matrix

$$\begin{bmatrix} \cos\theta & -\sin\theta & 0 & 0 \\ \sin\theta & \cos\theta & 0 & 0 \\ 0 & 0 & 1 & 0 \\ 0 & 0 & 0 & 1 \end{bmatrix}$$

Even though any rotation can be represented as a transformation matrix, it is often difficult to obtain the transformation matrix directly from a geometric specification of a general rotation. For example, it may be easy to get matrices for rotations about the x-, y-, or z-axis, but what is the matrix for the rotation of angle $\pi/3$ about the axis $(1,1,1)$? One representation of a general 3D rotation that offers a more direct connection to its geometric properties involves the use of quaternion. The *quaternion* is a number system extending the field of complex quaternion numbers. An introduction to quaternion can be found in Appendix A.

A point (x, y, z) in 3D space with a *pure quaternion* (a quaternion with real part 0): pure quaternion

$$p = xi + yj + zk$$

Let q be a fixed quaternion. A transformation in the 3D space may be defined by:

$$T_q(p) = qp\bar{q}$$

If q is a unit quaternion, then it can be shown that the transformation defined above is a rotation. In this case q can be written as

$$q = \cos\frac{\theta}{2} + u\sin\frac{\theta}{2}, \quad u = ai + bj + ck$$

The unit vector u defines the direction of the axis of rotation, and the axis goes through the origin. The angle of rotation is given by θ.

Java 3D includes the classes `Quat4f` and `Quat4d` to represent quaternions. Besides the operations inherent from `Tuple4*` classes, standard operations of quaternions such as conjugate, multiply, inverse, and normalize are supported in the quaternion classes. Because of the connection with rotations, the quaternion classes even support convenient methods to directly set a rotation quaternion based on the specified axis and angle:

void set(AxisAngle4d r)

The `Transform3D` class provides constructors and methods to directly accept quaternion parameters as rotation specifications:

```
Transform3D(Quat4d q, Vector3d translation, double scale)
Transform3D(Quat4f q, Vector3d translation, double scale)
Transform3D(Quat4f q, Vector3f translation, float scale)
void set(Quat4d q)
void set(Quat4f q)
```

Another popular way to represent a 3D rotation is to use three rotations $R_3 R_2 R_1$ of certain angles about the coordinate axes. The axis for R_2 is different from the axes of R_1 and R_3. The three angles are known as the *Euler angles*. There are different choices for the axes and different terms to describe the angles—for example, (elevation, azimuth, tilt), (roll, pitch, yaw), (precession, nutation, spin), and (heading, altitude, bank). `Transform3D` class provides a method to set the rotation based on Euler angles:

Euler angles

void setEuler(Vector3d eulerAngles)

The `Vector3d` object specifies the Euler angles about the *x*-, *y*-, *z*-axes. The angles are also known as bank, altitude, heading. However, there is no method in `Transform3D` to retrieve the *Euler angles*. You may use a `get` method to retrieve a quaternion and then convert the quaternion to Euler angles. The code in Listing 7.3 performs the conversion from a quaternion to Euler angles.

Listing 7.3 `quatToEuler`

```
1 public static Vector3d quatToEuler(Quat4d q1) {
2    double sqw = q1.w*q1.w;
3    double sqx = q1.x*q1.x;
4    double sqy = q1.y*q1.y;
5    double sqz = q1.z*q1.z;
6    double heading = Math.atan2(2.0 * (q1.x*q1.y + q1.z*q1.w),
7      (sqx - sqy - sqz + sqw));
8    double bank = Math.atan2(2.0 * (q1.y*q1.z + q1.x*q1.w),
9      (-sqx - sqy + sqz + sqw));
10   double attitude = Math.asin(-2.0 * (q1.x*q1.z - q1.y*q1.w));
11     return new Vector3d(bank, attitude, heading);
12 }
```

`Transform3D` contains methods for transformation matrix operations similar to those in the `Matrix4d` class. It also allows direct application of the transform to points or vectors. This feature facilitates construction of geometries through transformations and will be discussed later in this chapter.

Listing 7.4 demonstrates the features of the `Transform3D` class graphically. (See Figure 7.2.) Listing 7.5 gives a class for displaying a set of coordinate axes. A transformation matrix corresponding to a `Transform3D` object is displayed and can be edited by the user. The rotation, translation, and scale components of the transform are extracted and displayed separately. The user can also specify these components and apply them to the transform. The transformation may be applied to a visual object, a set of 3D coordinate axes, so its effect can be seen immediately. The program provides a tool to explore the relationship between the transformation matrices and the geometric interpretations of transforms. (See Figure 7.2.)

Listing 7.4 TestTransform.java

```java
1 package chapter7;
2
3 import javax.vecmath.*;
4 import java.awt.*;
5 import java.awt.event.*;
6 import javax.media.j3d.*;
7 import com.sun.j3d.utils.universe.*;
8 import com.sun.j3d.utils.geometry.*;
9 import java.applet.*;
10 import com.sun.j3d.utils.applet.MainFrame;
11
12 public class TestTransform extends Applet implements
13   ActionListener {
14   public static void main(String[] args) {
15     new MainFrame(new TestTransform(), 640, 300);
16   }
17
18   TransformGroup trGroup;
19   Transform3D transform = new Transform3D();
20   MatrixPanel mp = new MatrixPanel();
21   TextField rx = new TextField();
22   TextField ry = new TextField();
23   TextField rz = new TextField();
24   TextField ra = new TextField();
25   TextField tx = new TextField();
26   TextField ty = new TextField();
27   TextField tz = new TextField();
28   TextField sx = new TextField();
29   TextField sy = new TextField();
30   TextField sz = new TextField();
31
32   public void init() {
33     setLayout(new BorderLayout());
34
35     Panel eastPanel = new Panel();
36     eastPanel.setLayout(new BorderLayout());
37     eastPanel.add(mp, BorderLayout.NORTH);
38     add(eastPanel, BorderLayout.EAST);
39
40     Button button = new Button("Transform");
41     button.addActionListener(this);
42     Panel p = new Panel();
43     p.add(button);
44     eastPanel.add(p, BorderLayout.EAST);
45
46     p = new Panel();
47     p.setLayout(new GridLayout(4,5));
48     p.add(new Label("x"));
49     p.add(new Label("y"));
50     p.add(new Label("z"));
51     p.add(new Label("angle"));
52     p.add(new Label(""));
53
54     p.add(rx);
```

```
55      p.add(ry);
56      p.add(rz);
57      p.add(ra);
58      button = new Button("Rotate");
59      button.addActionListener(this);
60      p.add(button);
61
62      p.add(tx);
63      p.add(ty);
64      p.add(tz);
65      p.add(new Panel());
66      button = new Button("Translate");
67      button.addActionListener(this);
68      p.add(button);
69
70      p.add(sx);
71      p.add(sy);
72      p.add(sz);
73      p.add(new Panel());
74      button = new Button("Scale");
75      button.addActionListener(this);
76      p.add(button);
77
78      eastPanel.add(p, BorderLayout.SOUTH);
79
80      GraphicsConfiguration gc =
81        SimpleUniverse.getPreferredConfiguration();
82      Canvas3D cv = new Canvas3D(gc);
83      add(cv, BorderLayout.CENTER);
84      BranchGroup bg = createSceneGraph();
85      bg.compile();
86      SimpleUniverse su = new SimpleUniverse(cv);
87      su.getViewingPlatform().setNominalViewingTransform();
88      su.addBranchGraph(bg);
89    }
90
91    private BranchGroup createSceneGraph() {
92      BranchGroup root = new BranchGroup();
93      trGroup = new TransformGroup();
94      trGroup.setCapability(TransformGroup.ALLOW_TRANSFORM_WRITE);
95      root.addChild(trGroup);
96
97      // object
98      Appearance ap = new Appearance();
99      ap.setMaterial(new Material());
100     Group shape = new Axes();
101
102     Transform3D tr = new Transform3D();
103     tr.setScale(0.5);
104     TransformGroup tg = new TransformGroup(tr);
105     trGroup.addChild(tg);
106     tg.addChild(shape);
107
108     // background and light
109     BoundingSphere bounds = new BoundingSphere();
110     Background background = new Background(1.0f, 1.0f, 1.0f);
111     background.setApplicationBounds(bounds);
112     root.addChild(background);
113     AmbientLight light = new AmbientLight
114       (true, new Color3f(Color.red));
```

```
115       light.setInfluencingBounds(bounds);
116       root.addChild(light);
117       PointLight ptlight = new PointLight(new Color3f(Color.green),
118         new Point3f(3f,3f,3f), new Point3f(1f,0f,0f));
119       ptlight.setInfluencingBounds(bounds);
120       root.addChild(ptlight);
121       PointLight ptlight2 = new PointLight(new Color3f(Color.orange),
122         new Point3f(-2f,2f,2f), new Point3f(1f,0f,0f));
123       ptlight2.setInfluencingBounds(bounds);
124       root.addChild(ptlight2);
125       return root;
126     }
127
128     public void actionPerformed(ActionEvent e) {
129       Matrix4d m = new Matrix4d();
130       mp.get(m);
131       transform.set(m);
132       String cmd = e.getActionCommand();
133       if ("Transform".equals(cmd)) {
134         Quat4d quat = new Quat4d();
135         Vector3d translation = new Vector3d();
136         transform.get(quat, translation);
137         Vector3d scale = new Vector3d();
138         transform.getScale(scale);
139         AxisAngle4d rotation = new AxisAngle4d();
140         rotation.set(quat);
141         rx.setText("" + rotation.x);
142         ry.setText("" + rotation.y);
143         rz.setText("" + rotation.z);
144         ra.setText("" + rotation.angle);
145         tx.setText("" + translation.x);
146         ty.setText("" + translation.y);
147         tz.setText("" + translation.z);
148         sx.setText("" + scale.x);
149         sy.setText("" + scale.y);
150         sz.setText("" + scale.z);
151         trGroup.setTransform(transform);
152       } else {
153         if ("Rotate".equals(cmd)) {
154           double x = Double.parseDouble(rx.getText());
155           double y = Double.parseDouble(ry.getText());
156           double z = Double.parseDouble(rz.getText());
157           double a = Double.parseDouble(ra.getText());
158           transform.setRotation(new AxisAngle4d(x, y, z, a));
159         } else if ("Translate".equals(cmd)) {
160           double x = Double.parseDouble(tx.getText());
161           double y = Double.parseDouble(ty.getText());
162           double z = Double.parseDouble(tz.getText());
163           transform.setTranslation(new Vector3d(x, y, z));
164         } else if ("Scale".equals(cmd)) {
165           double x = Double.parseDouble(sx.getText());
166           double y = Double.parseDouble(sy.getText());
167           double z = Double.parseDouble(sz.getText());
168           transform.setScale(new Vector3d(x, y, z));
169         }
170         transform.get(m);
171         mp.set(m);
172       }
173     }
174 }
```

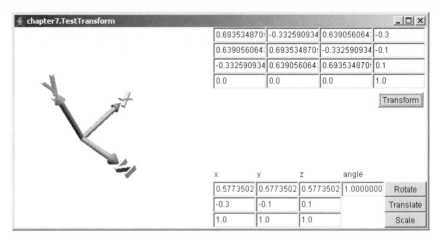

FIGURE 7.2 Visualizing the actions of transforms.

Listing 7.5 `Axes.java`

```
1 package chapter7;
2
3 import javax.vecmath.*;
4 import java.awt.*;
5 import java.awt.event.*;
6 import javax.media.j3d.*;
7 import com.sun.j3d.utils.universe.*;
8 import com.sun.j3d.utils.geometry.*;
9
10 public class Axes extends Group {
11   public Axes() {
12     Appearance ap = new Appearance();
13     ap.setMaterial(new Material());
14     Font3D font = new Font3D(new Font("SanSerif", Font.PLAIN, 1),
15                             new FontExtrusion());
16     Text3D x = new Text3D(font, "x");
17     Shape3D xShape = new Shape3D(x, ap);
18     Text3D y = new Text3D(font, "y");
19     Shape3D yShape = new Shape3D(y, ap);
20     Text3D z = new Text3D(font, "z");
21     Shape3D zShape = new Shape3D(z, ap);
22     // transform for texts
23     Transform3D tTr = new Transform3D();
24     tTr.setTranslation(new Vector3d(-0.12, 0.6, -0.04));
25     tTr.setScale(0.5);
26     // transform for arrows
27     Transform3D aTr = new Transform3D();
28     aTr.setTranslation(new Vector3d(0, 0.5, 0));
29     // x axis
30     Cylinder xAxis = new Cylinder(0.05f, 1f);
31     Transform3D xTr = new Transform3D();
32     xTr.setRotation(new AxisAngle4d(0, 0, 1, -Math.PI/2));
33     xTr.setTranslation(new Vector3d(0.5, 0, 0));
34     TransformGroup xTg = new TransformGroup(xTr);
35     xTg.addChild(xAxis);
36     this.addChild(xTg);
37     TransformGroup xTextTg = new TransformGroup(tTr);
```

```
38      xTextTg.addChild(xShape);
39      xTg.addChild(xTextTg);
40      Cone xArrow = new Cone(0.1f, 0.2f);
41      TransformGroup xArrowTg = new TransformGroup(aTr);
42      xArrowTg.addChild(xArrow);
43      xTg.addChild(xArrowTg);
44      // y axis
45      Cylinder yAxis = new Cylinder(0.05f, 1f);
46      Transform3D yTr = new Transform3D();
47      yTr.setTranslation(new Vector3d(0, 0.5, 0));
48      TransformGroup yTg = new TransformGroup(yTr);
49      yTg.addChild(yAxis);
50      this.addChild(yTg);
51      TransformGroup yTextTg = new TransformGroup(tTr);
52      yTextTg.addChild(yShape);
53      yTg.addChild(yTextTg);
54      Cone yArrow = new Cone(0.1f, 0.2f);
55      TransformGroup yArrowTg = new TransformGroup(aTr);
56      yArrowTg.addChild(yArrow);
57      yTg.addChild(yArrowTg);
58      // z axis
59      Cylinder zAxis = new Cylinder(0.05f, 1f);
60      Transform3D zTr = new Transform3D();
61      zTr.setRotation(new AxisAngle4d(1, 0, 0, Math.PI/2));
62      zTr.setTranslation(new Vector3d(0, 0, 0.5));
63      TransformGroup zTg = new TransformGroup(zTr);
64      zTg.addChild(zAxis);
65      this.addChild(zTg);
66      TransformGroup zTextTg = new TransformGroup(tTr);
67      zTextTg.addChild(zShape);
68      zTg.addChild(zTextTg);
69      Cone zArrow = new Cone(0.1f, 0.2f);
70      TransformGroup zArrowTg = new TransformGroup(aTr);
71      zArrowTg.addChild(zArrow);
72      zTg.addChild(zArrowTg);
73    }
74 }
```

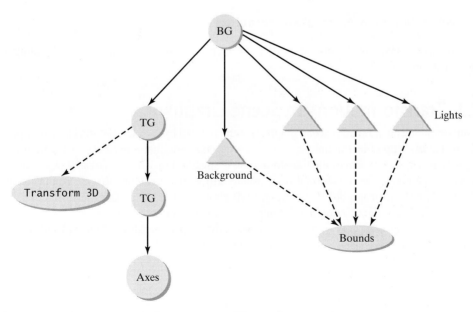

FIGURE 7.3   The scene graph for `TestTransform`.

The program `TestTransform` constructs a window to allow the user to interactively modify the transform and apply it to a scene. The Java 3D scene rendered in a `Canvas3D` is a set of 3D axes labeled with *x*, *y*, and *z*. The visual object is defined by the class `Axes`, and the detailed discussion of the `Axes` class will be given in the next section.

The `Axes` object goes through a fixed `TransformGroup` node to scale its size. The resulting branch is attached to another `TransformGroup` node that allows dynamic change of its transformation. The `Transform3D` object controls this node, and it can be set dynamically at runtime (Figure 7.3).

Similar to Listing 7.2, a `MatrixPanel` object is created to represent the transformation matrix. Three different aspects of the transformation—rotation, translation, and scale—are extracted and displayed in several `TextField` objects. The *x*-, *y*-, *z*-components are displayed separately. The rotation also includes an angle specification.

When the button "Transform" is clicked (line 133), the matrix specified in the `MatrixPanel` object is retrieved. The transform is set according to the matrix. The rotation, translation, and scale are recalculated from the transform. The rotation expressed as a quaternion and the translation as a vector can be obtained with the following method of `Transform3D`:

> **double** get(Quat4d rotation, Vector3d translation)

The above method also returns a uniform scaling factor. To obtain nonuniform scaling factors in *x*-, *y*-, and *z*-directions, the following method is used:

> **void** getScale(Vector3d scale)

The `Quat4d` object obtained from the `get` method is converted to an `AxisAngle4d` object for easy access to the axis and angle of the rotation. The rotation, translation, and scale information extracted is displayed in the text fields. The transform is also performed on the 3D scene by setting the transform of the `TransformGroup` node with the following method:

> **void** setTransform(Transform3D transform)

The actions for the buttons labeled "Rotate," "Translate," and "Scale" are opposite of those for the "Transform." When the button "Rotate" is clicked (line 153), the axis and the angle of the rotation are read from the text fields. The values are used to set the rotation of the `Transform3D` object with the method

> **void** setRotation(AxisAngle4d rotation)

Similarly, the buttons "Translate" and "Scale" apply the specified translation and scaling to the transform.

7.3 Transformations in Scene Graphs

`TransformGroup`

Transformations in a Java 3D scene graph are implemented by the class `TransformGroup`. A `TransformGroup` object defines a scene-graph group node that represents a specific transformation. The exact form of the transformation is specified by a `Transform3D` object referenced by the node. The transformation is usually affine, but it can be any type of transforms that the TransformGroup object `Transform3D` class can represent. The transformation defined by the `TransformGroup` node is applied to all of its child nodes.

The following code shows an example of setting up a transformation node using the `Matrix4d`, `Transform3D`, and `TransformGroup` objects:

```
double[] array = {1.0, 2.0, 3.0, 1.0,
                  0.0, 1.0, -1.0, 2.0,
                  4.0, 0.0, 0.5, -1.0,
                  0.0, 0.0, 0.0, 1.0};
```

```
Matrix4d matrix = new Matrix4d(array);
Transform3D transform = new Transform3D(matrix);
TransformGroup node = new TransformGroup(transform);
```

TransformGroup nodes can be used to change the shapes, sizes, and locations of geometric objects in the 3D world space. For example, the Tetrahedron class defined in the previous chapter is centered at the origin. To place an instance of Shape3D leaf node with a Tetrahedron geometry centered at $(0.5, 0, -1)$, you may create a TransformGroup node with a translation of $(0.5, 0, -1)$ and add the tetrahedron shape as its child:

```
Tetrahedron geom = new Tetrahedron();
Shape3D shape = new Shape3D();
shape.setGeometry(geom);
Transform3D tr = new Transform3D();
tr.setTranslation(new Vector3d(0.5,0,-1));
TransformGroup tg = new TransformGroup(tr);
tg.addChild(shape);
```

A TransformGroup node may be a child of another TransformGroup node. A hierarchy of TransformGroup and other nodes can be constructed to represent a complex structure of geometric models. For example, a table may be modeled as a table top with four legs. Each leg may be attached to a TransformGroup node that moves the leg to an appropriate position relative the table top. If you want to move the entire table as one object, you may then place another TransformGroup node on top of the table model.

In Listing 7.2, the Axes class constructs three perpendicular coordinate axes. Each axis consists of a cylinder for the axis line, a cone for the arrow, and a 3D text for the label. The scene graph of Axes is shown in Figure 7.4.

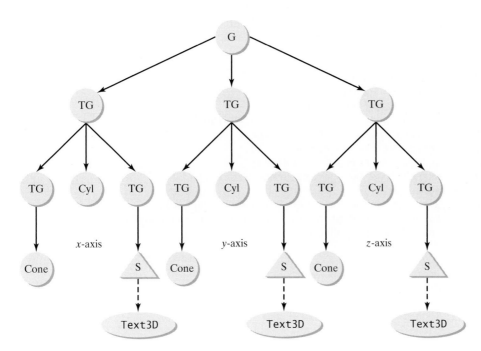

FIGURE 7.4 The scene graph for Axes class.

The `Cylinder` and `Cone` classes allow the specifications of radius and height in their constructors. However, they have fixed positions and orientations along the y-direction. Transformations are necessary to move them to the desired positions. The y-axis needs to move up by 0.5 so it will start from the origin. The x-axis and z-axis need to be rotated in addition to the translation. The arrows on the axes formed with `Cone` objects will go through similar transforms as their associated axes, but an additional translation is required to move the arrow to the top of the axis. This translation is represented as a separate `TransformGroup` node that is a child of the transform node for the axis and the parent of the arrow. Consequently, the translation is applied only to the cone-shaped arrow, and the axis transform is applied to both the axis and the translated arrow. In the similar fashion, the text label "x," "y," or "z" will first go through its own translation to appropriate positions relative to the axis. Then the same axis transform will be applied to move the label together with the axis and arrow to the final position.

Listing 7.6 demonstrates the usage of `TransformGroup` nodes and the construction of general rotations about arbitrary axes. The program illustrates the rotation of a cube around a general axis by displaying eight cubes at different stages of the rotation (Figure 7.5). The different positioning of the eight cubes is achieved by the `TransformGroup` nodes in the scene graph.

Listing 7.6 `Rotation.java`

```
1 package chapter7;
2
3 import javax.vecmath.*;
4 import java.awt.*;
5 import java.awt.event.*;
6 import javax.media.j3d.*;
7 import com.sun.j3d.utils.universe.*;
8 import com.sun.j3d.utils.geometry.*;
9 import java.applet.*;
10 import com.sun.j3d.utils.applet.MainFrame;
11
12 public class Rotation extends Applet {
13   public static void main(String[] args) {
14     new MainFrame(new Rotation(), 640, 480);
15   }
16
17   public void init() {
18     // create canvas
19     GraphicsConfiguration gc =
20       SimpleUniverse.getPreferredConfiguration();
21     Canvas3D cv = new Canvas3D(gc);
22     setLayout(new BorderLayout());
23     add(cv, BorderLayout.CENTER);
24     BranchGroup bg = createSceneGraph();
25     bg.compile();
26     SimpleUniverse su = new SimpleUniverse(cv);
27     su.getViewingPlatform().setNominalViewingTransform();
28     su.addBranchGraph(bg);
29   }
30
31   private BranchGroup createSceneGraph() {
32     BranchGroup root = new BranchGroup();
33     Background background = new Background(1.0f, 1.0f, 1.0f);
34     BoundingSphere bounds = new BoundingSphere();
35     background.setApplicationBounds(bounds);
36     root.addChild(background);
37     Shape3D shape;
38     Appearance ap = new Appearance();
```

```
39      PolygonAttributes pa = new PolygonAttributes();
40      ap.setPolygonAttributes(pa);
41      ColoringAttributes ca = new ColoringAttributes(0f, 0f, 0f,
42        ColoringAttributes.SHADE_FLAT);
43      ap.setColoringAttributes(ca);
44
45      LineArray axis = new LineArray(2, LineArray.COORDINATES);
46      axis.setCoordinate(0, new Point3d(-0.8, -0.8, -0.8));
47      axis.setCoordinate(1, new Point3d(0.5, 0.5, 0.5));
48
49      Shape3D axisG = new Shape3D(axis, ap);
50      root.addChild(axisG);
51
52      Transform3D tr = new Transform3D();
53      tr.setTranslation(new Vector3f(-0.5f, 0f, 0f));
54      tr.setScale(0.1);
55      TransformGroup tg;
56      TransformGroup rot;
57      for (int i = 0; i < 8; i++) {
58        shape = new ColorCube();
59        shape.setAppearance(ap);
60        tg = new TransformGroup(tr);
61        Transform3D trRot = new Transform3D();
62        trRot.set(new AxisAngle4d(0.5,0.5,0.5, Math.PI/4*i));
63        rot = new TransformGroup(trRot);
64        root.addChild(rot);
65        rot.addChild(tg);
66        tg.addChild(shape);
67      }
68      return root;
69   }
70 }
```

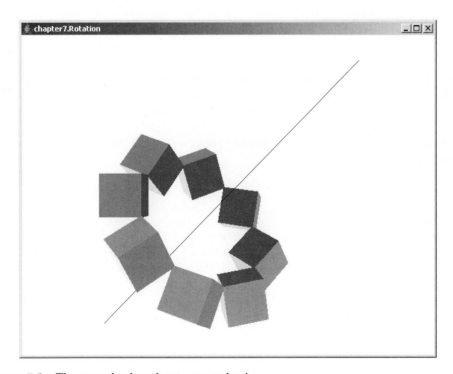

Figure 7.5   The rotated cubes about a general axis.

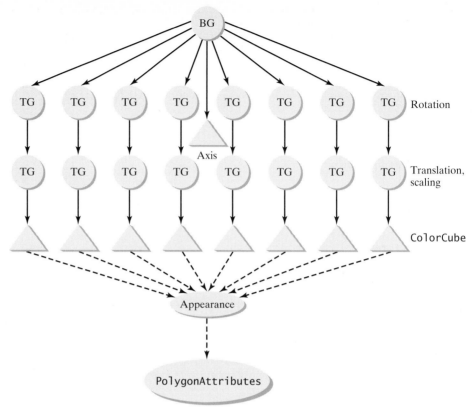

FIGURE 7.6 A partial scene graph for `Rotation` class.

The scene graph of the program is shown in Figure 7.6. Eight `ColorCube` objects are created, and they first go through an identical transformation of translation and scaling to resize and reposition. Then each transformed cube is attached to another `TransformGroup` node. These transform-group nodes are set to rotations about the same axis with different and evenly spread angles. This creates a scene with cubes at various stages of the revolution around the axis.

The axis of rotation is a line through the origin and the point (1, 1, 1). The axis is also displayed in the scene as a `LineArray` geometry. The line is defined with two points $(-0.8, -0.8, -0.8)$ and $(0.5, 0.5, 0.5)$.

The rotations are created with `AxisAngle4d` objects (line 62). The eight different angles of rotations are given by

$$\frac{2\pi}{8}i, \qquad i = 0, 1, \dots, 7$$

 Note

For clarity of presentation, the rotation transform and the initial translation/scaling are implemented as separate cascaded `TransformGroup` nodes. It would be more efficient to combine them into one node. The optimization performed by Java 3D when compiling the scene graph may in fact automatically combine transformation nodes of this type.

7.4 Composite Transforms

Two or more transformations can be combined to form a composite transformation. For example, if T_1, T_2 are two transformations, then the composite transformation is defined as

$$(T_2 T_1)(p) = (T_2(T_1(p))$$

Note that the composition of two transforms is not commutative: $T_1 T_2 \neq T_2 T_1$ in general. In our notation, composite transforms are applied from right to left. For example, $T_2 T_1$ denotes the composite transform that applies T_1 first, followed by T_2.

In matrix form, the composition of transformations corresponds to matrix multiplication. If the transformation matrices for T_1, T_2 are M_1, M_2, respectively, then the matrix for the composite transform $T_2 T_1$ is the matrix $M_2 M_1$.

The Transform3D class includes several methods for multiplying transformation matrices to form composite transforms:

- **void** mul(Transform3D t)—Multiply the transform t to the current transform on the right.

- **void** mul(Transform3D t1, Transform3D t2)—Multiply the transforms t1 by t2.

- **void** mulInverse(Transform3D t)—Multiply the inverse of the transform t to the current transform on the right.

- **void** mulInverse(Transform3D t1, Transform3D t2)—Multiply the transform t1 by the inverse of the transform t2 on the right.

- **void** mulTransposeBoth(Transform3D t1, Transform3D t2)—Multiply the transpose of the transform t1 by the transpose of the transform t2 on the right.

- **void** mulTransposeLeft(Transform3D t1, Transform3D t2)—Multiply the transpose of the transform t1 by the transform t2 on the right.

- **void** mulTransposeRight(Transform3D t1, Transform3D t2)—Multiply the transform t1 by the transpose of the transform t2 on the right.

When setting up a complex transform, it is often easier to compose the transform from some simpler transforms than to directly construct the matrix.

Suppose that we want to construct a $\pi/3$ rotation about the axis through $(1, 1, 0)$ and $(1, 2, 1)$. Because the axis does not go through the origin, we cannot directly apply the quaternion approach. However, we can first perform a translation to move the axis so that it goes through the origin, then perform the rotation about the new axis, and finally apply an inverse translation to send the axis back to its original location. Let T be the translation by $(-1, -1, 0)$. Then $T(1, 1, 0) = (0, 0, 0)$ and $T(1, 2, 1) = (0, 1, 1)$. Let R be the rotation of $\pi/3$ about the axis through the origin and $(0, 1, 1)$. Then the original rotation can be decomposed into $T^{-1}RT$.

This pattern of decomposition is very common. If a particular transformation is known in a standard position, a similar transformation in a more general position can be obtained by first transforming to the standard position, performing the given transformation in the standard form, then transforming back to the original position.

Consider another example on reflection. The reflection about the xy-plane is easy to construct, as shown earlier. A general reflection matrix will be more difficult to find. However, we may try to reduce the general problem to the simpler xy-plane reflection. Suppose that the reflection plane is a plane through the origin given by the equation:

$$ax + by + cz = 0$$

Instead of finding the transformation matrix directly, you may use a composite transform. First a rotation can be constructed to map the reflection plane to the xy-plane. Then the easy reflection about the xy-plane is performed. Finally the inverse rotation that maps the xy-plane back to the original reflection plane will complete the composite transformation. The composite transform is equivalent to the original reflection.

To obtain a rotation that maps the above reflection plane to the xy-plane, it is equivalent to map the normal vector (a, b, c) to $(0, 0, d)$, the normal vector for the xy-plane. The axis of rotation is $(b, -a, 0)$. The quaternion for the rotation has the form:

$$q = \cos(\theta/2) + \left(\frac{b}{\sqrt{a^2 + b^2}}i - \frac{a}{\sqrt{a^2 + b^2}}j \right) \sin(\theta/2)$$

The appropriate rotation angle should satisfy the condition:

$$\cos\theta = c/\sqrt{a^2 + b^2 + c^2}, \qquad 0 \le \theta < \pi$$

Denote this rotation by R, and the reflection about xy-plane by F. Then the reflection about the plane can be written as:

$$R^{-1}FR$$

Listing 7.7 illustrates the construction of reflections using this method. A plane in a general position is acting as a "mirror" for a reflection. A 3D text "Java" is rotating in the scene. Its mirror image about the plane is also displayed. The plane is shown in a semitransparent form to give an effect of mirror reflection for the transformed object (Figure 7.7).

Listing 7.7 `Mirror.java`

```
1 package chapter7;
2
3 import javax.vecmath.*;
4 import java.awt.*;
5 import java.awt.event.*;
6 import javax.media.j3d.*;
7 import com.sun.j3d.utils.universe.*;
8 import com.sun.j3d.utils.geometry.*;
9 import java.applet.*;
10 import com.sun.j3d.utils.applet.MainFrame;
11
12 public class Mirror extends Applet {
13    public static void main(String[] args) {
14      new MainFrame(new Mirror(), 640, 480);
15    }
16
17    public void init() {
18      // create canvas
19      GraphicsConfiguration gc =
20      SimpleUniverse.getPreferredConfiguration();
21      Canvas3D cv = new Canvas3D(gc);
22      setLayout(new BorderLayout());
23      add(cv, BorderLayout.CENTER);
24      BranchGroup bg = createSceneGraph();
25      bg.compile();
26      SimpleUniverse su = new SimpleUniverse(cv);
27      su.getViewingPlatform().setNominalViewingTransform();
28      su.addBranchGraph(bg);
29    }
30
31    private BranchGroup createSceneGraph() {
32      //  object
33      Appearance ap = new Appearance();
34      ap.setMaterial(new Material());
35      Font3D font = new Font3D(new Font("Serif", Font.PLAIN, 1),
36        new FontExtrusion());
37      Shape3D shape = new Shape3D(new Text3D(font, "Java"), ap);
```

```
38    // translation
39    Transform3D trans = new Transform3D();
40    trans.setTranslation(new Vector3d(-0.5,0,0));
41    TransformGroup transg = new TransformGroup(trans);
42    transg.addChild(shape);
43    // rotation
44    TransformGroup spin = new TransformGroup();
45    spin.setCapability(TransformGroup.ALLOW_TRANSFORM_WRITE);
46    spin.addChild(transg);
47    // scaling, translation
48    Transform3D tr = new Transform3D();
49    tr.setScale(0.25);
50    tr.setTranslation(new Vector3d(0.5,0,0));
51    TransformGroup tg = new TransformGroup(tr);
52    tg.addChild(spin);
53    // shared group
54    SharedGroup share = new SharedGroup();
55    share.addChild(tg);
56    // link leaf nodes to shared group
57    Link link1 = new Link(share);
58    Link link2 = new Link(share);
59    // reflection
60    Transform3D reflection = getReflection(1,1,1);
61    TransformGroup reflectionGroup = new TransformGroup(reflection);
62    reflectionGroup.addChild(link2);
63    // the mirror
64    QuadArray qa = new QuadArray(4, QuadArray.COORDINATES);
65    qa.setCoordinate(0, new Point3d(0,-0.5,0.5));
66    qa.setCoordinate(1, new Point3d(1,-0.5,-0.5));
67    qa.setCoordinate(2, new Point3d(0,0.5,-0.5));
68    qa.setCoordinate(3, new Point3d(-1,0.5,0.5));
69    ap = new Appearance();
70    ap.setTransparencyAttributes(
71      new TransparencyAttributes
72        (TransparencyAttributes.BLENDED, 0.7f));
73    Shape3D mirror = new Shape3D(qa, ap);
74    // rotator
75    Alpha alpha = new Alpha(-1, 4000);
76    RotationInterpolator rotator = new RotationInterpolator
77      (alpha, spin);
78    BoundingSphere bounds = new BoundingSphere();
79    rotator.setSchedulingBounds(bounds);
80    // background and lights
81    Background background = new Background(0.5f, 0.5f, 0.5f);
82    background.setApplicationBounds(bounds);
83    AmbientLight light = new AmbientLight
84      (true, new Color3f(Color.red));
85    light.setInfluencingBounds(bounds);
86    PointLight ptlight = new PointLight(new Color3f(Color.green),
87      new Point3f(3f,3f,3f), new Point3f(1f,0f,0f));
88    ptlight.setInfluencingBounds(bounds);
89    PointLight ptlight2 = new PointLight(new Color3f(Color.orange),
90      new Point3f(-2f,2f,2f), new Point3f(1f,0f,0f));
91    ptlight2.setInfluencingBounds(bounds);
92    // branch group
93    BranchGroup root = new BranchGroup();
94    root.addChild(link1);
95    root.addChild(reflectionGroup);
96    root.addChild(mirror);
97    root.addChild(rotator);
```

```
98      root.addChild(background);
99      root.addChild(light);
100     root.addChild(ptlight);
101     root.addChild(ptlight2);
102     return root;
103   }
104
105   static Transform3D getReflection(double a, double b, double c) {
106     Transform3D transform = new Transform3D();
107     double theta = Math.acos(c/Math.sqrt(a*a+b*b+c*c));
108     double r = Math.sqrt(a*a+b*b);
108     Transform3D rot = new Transform3D();
110     rot.set(new AxisAngle4d(b/r, -a/r, 0, theta));
111     Transform3D ref = new Transform3D();
112     ref.setScale(new Vector3d(1,1,-1));
113     transform.mulInverse(rot);
114     transform.mul(ref);
115     transform.mul(rot);
116     return transform;
117   }
118 }
```

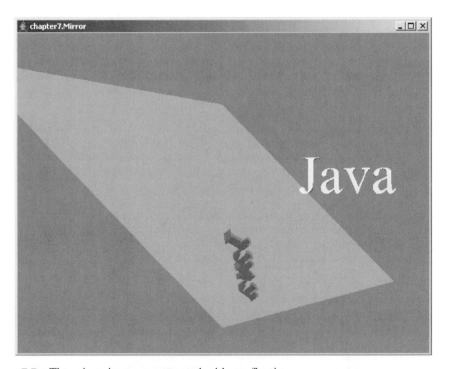

FIGURE 7.7   The mirror image constructed with a reflection.

The program constructs a "mirror" and shows a rotating object and its mirror image. The scene graph is shown in Figure 7.8.

The mirror (reflection plane) is chosen to go through the origin and have the normal vector (1, 1, 1). The mirror itself is rendered in the scene as a semitransparent rectangle using a QuadArray object (line 64).

The method getReflection (line 105) performs the calculations derived above for the reflection about the given plane. The composite transform consists of a rotation to rotate the

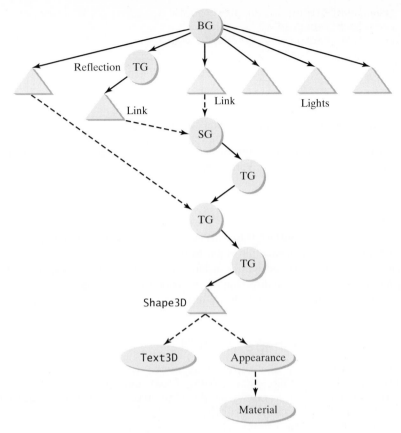

FIGURE 7.8   The scene graph for the `Mirror` class.

plane to the standard *xy*-plane, a simple reflection about the *xy*-plane, and an inverse rotation: $R^{-1}FR$. The inverse rotation is obtained by using the `mulInverse` method. The reflection and the rotation are multiplied with the `mul` method. The resulting composite transform is returned as a `Transform3D` object.

The object used for the reflection is a rotating 3D text "Java." In order to show the reflection faithfully, the visual object is placed in a `SharedGroup` branch. Both the original and the reflected object share the same branch through two `Link` leaf nodes. The link for the mirrored object goes through the reflection transform node.

7.5 Constructing Geometries with Transformations

Transformations are useful not only in transforming the completed objects, but also in constructing primitives. Geometric primitives often exhibit certain degrees of symmetry. As a result, some vertices of a primitive may be obtained by transforming other vertices. In this section, we will discuss several techniques of generating 3D geometries with affine transforms and other operations.

The `Transform3D` class provides methods for applying the transform represented by the object to points or vectors:

```
void transform(Point3d p)
void transform(Point3d p, Point3d pOut)
void transform(Point3f p)
```

transform methods

```
void transform(Point3f p, Point3f pOut)
void transform(Vector3d v)
void transform(Vector3d v, Vector3d vOut)
void transform(Vector3f v)
void transform(Vector3f v, Vector3f vOut)
void transform(Vector4d v)
void transform(Vector4d v, Vector4d vOut)
void transform(Vector4f v)
void transform(Vector4f v, Vector4f vOut)
```

The methods with one parameter transform the point or vector in place. The methods with two parameters perform the transformation on the first parameter nondestructively and save the result in the second parameter.

7.5.1 Extrusion

A simple way to create a 3D surface is to extrude (or sweep) a 2D curve through space. A 3D text created with Font3D is an example of extrusion.

Extrusion can be implemented with translations. Starting with the points on the curve, we apply a translation along the direction of extrusion to generate other points. For example, the following method takes a 2D Shape object and performs an extrusion along the z-axis.

Listing 7.8 extrudeShape Method

```
1   // Assumption: only one continuous curve in the Shape object
2   Geometry extrudeShape(Shape curve, float depth) {
3     PathIterator iter = curve.getPathIterator(new AffineTransform());
4     Vector ptsList = new Vector();
5     float[] seg = new float[6];
6     float x = 0, y = 0;
7     float x0 = 0, y0 = 0;
8     while (!iter.isDone()) {
9       int segType = iter.currentSegment(seg);
10      switch (segType) {
11        case PathIterator.SEG_MOVETO:
12          x = x0 = seg[0];
13          y = y0 = seg[1];
14          ptsList.add(new Point3f(x,y,0));
15          break;
16        case PathIterator.SEG_LINETO:
17          x = seg[0];
18          y = seg[1];
19          ptsList.add(new Point3f(x,y,0));
20          break;
21        case PathIterator.SEG_QUADTO:
22          for (int i = 1; i < 10; i++) {
23            float t = (float)i/10f;
24            float xi = (1-t)*(1-t)*x + 2*t*(1-t)*seg[0] + t*t*seg[2];
25            float yi = (1-t)*(1-t)*y + 2*t*(1-t)*seg[1] + t*t*seg[3];
26            ptsList.add(new Point3f(xi,yi,0));
27          }
28          x = seg[2];
29          y = seg[3];
30          ptsList.add(new Point3f(x,y,0));
31          break;
32        case PathIterator.SEG_CUBICTO:
33          for (int i = 1; i < 20; i++) {
34            float t = (float)i/20f;
```

```
35        float xi = (1-t)*(1-t)*(1-t)*x + 3*t*(1-t)*(1-t)*seg[0] +
36           3*t*t*(1-t)*seg[2] + t*t*t*seg[4];
37        float yi = (1-t)*(1-t)*(1-t)*y + 3*t*(1-t)*(1-t)*seg[1] +
38           3*t*t*(1-t)*seg[3] + t*t*t*seg[5];
39        ptsList.add(new Point3f(xi,yi,0));
40      }
41      x = seg[2];
42      y = seg[3];
43      ptsList.add(new Point3f(x,y,0));
44      break;
45    case PathIterator.SEG_CLOSE:
46      x = x0;
47      y = y0;
48      ptsList.add(new Point3f(x,y,0));
49      break;
50    }
51    iter.next();
52  }
53  int n = ptsList.size();
54  IndexedQuadArray qa = new IndexedQuadArray(2*n,
55     IndexedQuadArray.COORDINATES, 4*(n-1));
56  Transform3D trans = new Transform3D();
57  trans.setTranslation(new Vector3f(0,0,depth));
58  for (int i = 0; i < n; i++) {
59    Point3f pt = (Point3f)ptsList.get(i);
60    qa.setCoordinate(2*i, pt);
61    trans.transform(pt);
62    qa.setCoordinate(2*i+1, pt);
63  }
64  int quadIndex = 0;
65  for (int i = 0; i < n-1; i++) {
66      qa.setCoordinateIndex(quadIndex++, 2*i);
67      qa.setCoordinateIndex(quadIndex++, 2*i+1);
68      qa.setCoordinateIndex(quadIndex++, 2*(i+1)+1);
69      qa.setCoordinateIndex(quadIndex++, 2*(i+1));
70  }
71  GeometryInfo gi = new GeometryInfo(qa);
72  NormalGenerator ng = new NormalGenerator();
73  ng.generateNormals(gi);
74  return gi.getGeometryArray();
75 }
```

For simplicity, the method assumes that the Shape object only has one continuous curve definition. The general case can be handled in a similar manner. The parameter depth defines the depth of the extrusion.

7.5.2 Rotation

Many surfaces can be obtained through rotations. For example, a cylinder may be obtained by rotating a line, and a sphere is the result of rotating a semicircle. A *torus* can be constructed   torus by rotating a circle about an axis outside the circle. Furthermore, the circle itself can be obtained by rotating a point. Therefore, to obtain a polygon mesh for the torus, we can start from a single point. Rotating the point repeatedly with different angles generates a set of points for the circle. Rotating the circle points about a different axis generates the vertices for the torus. This procedure is illustrated in Figure 7.9.

Given a set of base points on the curve, to create a rotated surface with n strips, we may set up a rotation of the angle $2\pi/n$. By successively applying the rotation to the curve points, we

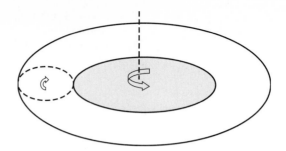

FIGURE 7.9 Construction of a torus by rotations.

will be able to generate the vertices for a quadrangle array. Listing 7.9 shows the construction of a torus via two different rotations. Listing 7.10 gives a program for displaying two tori. The vertices of the torus geometry are generated with applications of transforms. In the test program, two linked tori are shown rotating in the space.

Listing 7.9 Torus.java

```
1 package chapter7;
2
3 import javax.vecmath.*;
4 import java.awt.*;
5 import java.awt.event.*;
6 import javax.media.j3d.*;
7 import com.sun.j3d.utils.universe.*;
8 import com.sun.j3d.utils.geometry.*;
9
10 public class Torus extends Shape3D {
11   public Torus(double r1, double r2) {
12     int m = 20;
13     int n = 40;
14     Point3d[] pts = new Point3d[m];
15     pts[0] = new Point3d(r1+r2, 0, 0);
16     double theta = 2.0 * Math.PI / m;
17     double c = Math.cos(theta);
18     double s = Math.sin(theta);
19     double[] mat = {c, -s, 0, r2*(1-c),
20                     s, c, 0, -r2*s,
21                     0, 0, 1, 0,
22                     0, 0, 0, 1};
23     Transform3D rot1 = new Transform3D(mat);
24     for (int i = 1; i < m; i++) {
25       pts[i] = new Point3d();
26       rot1.transform(pts[i-1], pts[i]);
27     }
28
29     Transform3D rot2 = new Transform3D();
30     rot2.rotY(2.0*Math.PI/n);
31     IndexedQuadArray qa = new IndexedQuadArray(m*n,
32       IndexedQuadArray.COORDINATES, 4*m*n);
33     int quadIndex = 0;
34     for (int i = 0; i < n; i++) {
35       qa.setCoordinates(i*m, pts);
36       for (int j = 0; j < m; j++) {
```

```
37            rot2.transform(pts[j]);
38            int[] quadCoords = {i*m+j, ((i+1)%n)*m+j,
39              ((i+1)%n)*m+((j+1)%m), i*m+((j+1)%m)};
40            qa.setCoordinateIndices(quadIndex, quadCoords);
41            quadIndex += 4;
42          }
43        }
44        GeometryInfo gi = new GeometryInfo(qa);
45        NormalGenerator ng = new NormalGenerator();
46        ng.generateNormals(gi);
47        this.setGeometry(gi.getGeometryArray());
48      }
49  }
50
```

Listing 7.10 TestTorus.java

```
1 package chapter7;
2
3 import javax.vecmath.*;
4 import java.awt.*;
5 import java.awt.event.*;
6 import javax.media.j3d.*;
7 import com.sun.j3d.utils.universe.*;
8 import com.sun.j3d.utils.geometry.*;
9 import java.applet.*;
10 import com.sun.j3d.utils.applet.MainFrame;
11
12 public class TestTorus extends Applet {
13   public static void main(String[] args) {
14     new MainFrame(new TestTorus(), 640, 480);
15   }
16
17   public void init() {
18     // create canvas
19     GraphicsConfiguration gc =
20     SimpleUniverse.getPreferredConfiguration();
21     Canvas3D cv = new Canvas3D(gc);
22     setLayout(new BorderLayout());
23     add(cv, BorderLayout.CENTER);
24     BranchGroup bg = createSceneGraph();
25     bg.compile();
26     SimpleUniverse su = new SimpleUniverse(cv);
27     su.getViewingPlatform().setNominalViewingTransform();
28     su.addBranchGraph(bg);
29   }
30
31   private BranchGroup createSceneGraph() {
32     BranchGroup root = new BranchGroup();
33     TransformGroup spin = new TransformGroup();
34     spin.setCapability(TransformGroup.ALLOW_TRANSFORM_WRITE);
35     root.addChild(spin);
36
37     Transform3D tr = new Transform3D();
38     tr.setScale(0.8);
39     tr.setRotation(new AxisAngle4d(1, 0, 0, Math.PI/6));
40     TransformGroup tg = new TransformGroup(tr);
41     spin.addChild(tg);
42
```

```
43      // object
44      Shape3D torus1 = new Torus(0.2, 0.5);
45      Appearance ap = new Appearance();
46      ap.setMaterial(new Material());
47      torus1.setAppearance(ap);
48      tg.addChild(torus1);
49
50      Shape3D torus2 = new Torus(0.2, 0.5);
51      ap = new Appearance();
52      ap.setMaterial(new Material());
53      ap.setTransparencyAttributes(
54        new TransparencyAttributes
55          (TransparencyAttributes.BLENDED, 0.5f));
56      torus2.setAppearance(ap);
57      Transform3D tr2 = new Transform3D();
58      tr2.setRotation(new AxisAngle4d(1, 0, 0, Math.PI/2));
59      tr2.setTranslation(new Vector3d(0.5,0,0));
60      TransformGroup tg2 = new TransformGroup(tr2);
61      tg.addChild(tg2);
62      tg2.addChild(torus2);
63
64      Alpha alpha = new Alpha(-1, 8000);
65      RotationInterpolator rotator = new RotationInterpolator
66        (alpha, spin);
67      BoundingSphere bounds = new BoundingSphere();
68      rotator.setSchedulingBounds(bounds);
69      spin.addChild(rotator);
70
71      // background and lights
72      Background background = new Background(1.0f, 1.0f, 1.0f);
73      background.setApplicationBounds(bounds);
74      root.addChild(background);
75      AmbientLight light = new AmbientLight
76        (true, new Color3f(Color.blue));
77      light.setInfluencingBounds(bounds);
78      root.addChild(light);
79      PointLight ptlight = new PointLight(new Color3f(Color.white),
80        new Point3f(3f,3f,3f), new Point3f(1f,0f,0f));
81      ptlight.setInfluencingBounds(bounds);
82      root.addChild(ptlight);
83      return root;
84    }
85 }
```

The Torus class extends Shape3D. The geometry is constructed with Indexed-QuadArray. A rotation rot1 (line 23) is set to generate the points of a circle from a single point. The generated points on the circle are stored in the array pts. Another rotation rot2 (line 29) is set to generate the points on the torus from the circle points. The grid of points on the torus are generated one column at a time and are entered into the IndexedQuadArray (line 35). Then the indices for the quadrilaterals are entered (line 40). To generate normals, the IndexedQuadArray object is converted a GeometryInfo object, and NormalGenerator is used to automatically generate the surface normals for the geometry.

The TestTorus class displays two instances of Torus in different positions (Figure 7.10). They are positioned in such a way that one torus passes through the hole of the other. One of the tori is set to be semitransparent using a TransparencyAttributes object. The entire figure is rotating to allow viewing from different angles.

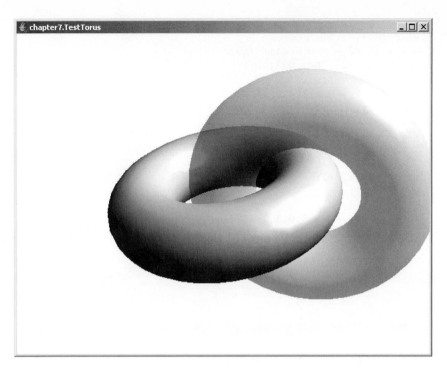

FIGURE 7.10 Two instances of Torus primitive whose vertices are generated by two sets of rotations.

7.5.3 Transformation and Shared Branch: An Example

The construction of complex visual contents often involves transformations at different levels. Listing 7.11 gives a class for displaying an arrow geometry. Listing 7.12 illustrates the combination of shared branches and transforms to reuse symmetric substructures. A 3D logo with 16 arrows and a ring around them is shown rotating about a vertical axis (Figure 7.11).

Listing 7.11 `Arrow.java`

```
1 package chapter7;
2
3 import javax.vecmath.*;
4 import javax.media.j3d.*;
5
6 public class Arrow extends IndexedTriangleArray {
7    float w = 1f;
8    float h = 0.15f;
9    float d = 0.1f;
10
11   public Arrow() {
12     super(5, TriangleArray.COORDINATES | TriangleArray.NORMALS, 12);
13     Point3f[] pts = {new Point3f(0f,0f,d),
14       new Point3f(w,0f,0f),
15       new Point3f(h,h,0f),
16       new Point3f(h,-h,0f),
17       new Point3f(0f,0f,-d)};
18     setCoordinates(0, pts);
19     int[] coords = {0,1,2,0,3,1,4,1,3,4,2,1};
20     setCoordinateIndices(0, coords);
21     Vector3f v1 = new Vector3f();
```

```
22      v1.sub(pts[1], pts[0]);
23      v1.normalize();
24      Vector3f v2 = new Vector3f();
25      v2.sub(pts[2], pts[0]);
26      v2.normalize();
27      Vector3f v = new Vector3f();
28      v.cross(v1, v2);
29      setNormal(0, v);
30      v.y = -v.y;
31      setNormal(1, v);
32      v.z = -v.z;
33      setNormal(2, v);
34      v.y = -v.y;
35      setNormal(3, v);
36      int[] norms = {0,0,0,1,1,1,2,2,2,3,3,3};
37      setNormalIndices(0, norms);
38   }
39 }
```

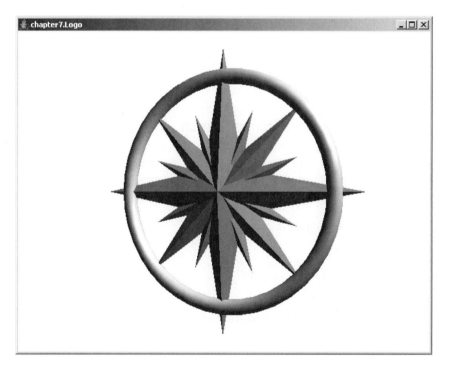

FIGURE 7.11   A 3D logo.

Listing 7.12 `Logo.java`

```
1 package chapter7;
2
3 import javax.vecmath.*;
4 import java.awt.*;
5 import java.awt.event.*;
6 import javax.media.j3d.*;
7 import com.sun.j3d.utils.universe.*;
8 import com.sun.j3d.utils.geometry.*;
```

```
 9 import java.applet.*;
10 import com.sun.j3d.utils.applet.MainFrame;
11
12 public class Logo extends Applet {
13   public static void main(String[] args) {
14     new MainFrame(new Logo(), 640, 480);
15   }
16
17   public void init() {
18     // create canvas
19     GraphicsConfiguration gc =
20       SimpleUniverse.getPreferredConfiguration();
21     Canvas3D cv = new Canvas3D(gc);
22     setLayout(new BorderLayout());
23     add(cv, BorderLayout.CENTER);
24     BranchGroup bg = createSceneGraph();
25     bg.compile();
26     SimpleUniverse su = new SimpleUniverse(cv);
27     su.getViewingPlatform().setNominalViewingTransform();
28     su.addBranchGraph(bg);
29   }
30
31   private BranchGroup createSceneGraph() {
32     BranchGroup root = new BranchGroup();
33     TransformGroup spin = new TransformGroup();
34     spin.setCapability(TransformGroup.ALLOW_TRANSFORM_WRITE);
35     root.addChild(spin);
36
37     Transform3D tr = new Transform3D();
38     tr.setScale(0.9);
39     tr.setRotation(new AxisAngle4d(1, 0, 0, Math.PI/2));
40     TransformGroup tg = new TransformGroup(tr);
41     spin.addChild(tg);
42     // torus
43     Shape3D torus = new Torus(0.04, 0.6);
44     Appearance ap = new Appearance();
45     ap.setMaterial(new Material());
46     torus.setAppearance(ap);
47     tg.addChild(torus);
48     // shared group of 4 arrows
49     SharedGroup sg = new SharedGroup();
50     Shape3D arrow;
51     Transform3D tra;
52     TransformGroup tga;
53     for (int i = 0; i < 4; i++) {
54       arrow = new Shape3D(new Arrow(), ap);
55       tra = new Transform3D();
56       tra.setRotation(new AxisAngle4d(0, 0, 1, i*Math.PI/2));
57       tga = new TransformGroup(tra);
58       sg.addChild(tga);
59       tga.addChild(arrow);
60     }
61     // four links to shared group
62     Link link = new Link();
63     link.setSharedGroup(sg);
64     tr = new Transform3D();
65     tr.setScale(0.675);
66     tg = new TransformGroup(tr);
67     tg.addChild(link);
68     spin.addChild(tg);
69
```

```
70      link = new Link();
71      link.setSharedGroup(sg);
72      tr = new Transform3D();
73      tr.setScale(0.55);
74      tr.setRotation(new AxisAngle4d(0, 0, 1, Math.PI/4));
75      tg = new TransformGroup(tr);
76      tg.addChild(link);
77      spin.addChild(tg);
78
79      link = new Link();
80      link.setSharedGroup(sg);
81      tr = new Transform3D();
82      tr.setScale(0.4);
83      tr.setRotation(new AxisAngle4d(0, 0, 1, Math.PI/8));
84      tg = new TransformGroup(tr);
85      tg.addChild(link);
86      spin.addChild(tg);
87
88      link = new Link();
89      link.setSharedGroup(sg);
90      tr = new Transform3D();
91      tr.setScale(0.4);
92      tr.setRotation(new AxisAngle4d(0, 0, 1, 3*Math.PI/8));
93      tg = new TransformGroup(tr);
94      tg.addChild(link);
95      spin.addChild(tg);
96      // rotation
97      Alpha alpha = new Alpha(-1, 8000);
98      RotationInterpolator rotator =
99      new RotationInterpolator(alpha, spin);
100     BoundingSphere bounds = new BoundingSphere();
101     rotator.setSchedulingBounds(bounds);
102     spin.addChild(rotator);
103     // background and lights
104     Background background = new Background(1.0f, 1.0f, 1.0f);
105     background.setApplicationBounds(bounds);
106     root.addChild(background);
107     AmbientLight light = new AmbientLight
108       (true, new Color3f(Color.red));
109     light.setInfluencingBounds(bounds);
110     root.addChild(light);
111     PointLight ptlight = new PointLight(new Color3f(Color.white),
112     new Point3f(2f,2f,2f), new Point3f(1f,0f,0f));
113     ptlight.setInfluencingBounds(bounds);
114     root.addChild(ptlight);
115     return root;
116   }
117 }
```

The ring is an instance of the Torus class defined in Listing 7.6. The sixteen arrows (spokes) possess a high degree of symmetries and similarities. To take advantage of the symmetries and simplify the modeling procedure, transforms and shared branches are applied.

The Arrow class defines the geometry for a single arrow primitive. It extends the class IndexedTriangleArray. Five vertices and four faces are defined for the geometry. The surface normal of a face is calculated by a cross product of the vectors of two sides. The normals of other faces are obtained from the first one by symmetries.

Four `Arrow` objects are grouped together through transforms to form a shared branch (lines 48–60). The four arrows are in the directions of 0, 90, 180, 270 degrees.

Four different `Link` objects to the `SharedGroup` node are created for the total of sixteen arrows (lines 61–95). Each link goes through a transform for appropriate rotation and scaling.

The entire assembled logo is made to rotate in the scene using a `RotationInterpolator` object, as seen in many other examples. The logo has an appearance bundle that includes a `Material` object. It is illuminated by two lights. The background of the scene is again set to white.

KEY CLASSES AND METHODS

- **`javax.vecmath.Matrix4d`** A class encapsulating a 4 × 4 `double` matrix.
- **`javax.vecmath.Matrix4f`** A class encapsulating a 4 × 4 `float` matrix.
- **`javax.media.j3d.Transform3D`** A class encapsulating a 3D transformation.
- **`javax.media.j3d.Transform3D.set(…)`** Methods to set the transformation.
- **`javax.media.j3d.Transform3D.setTranslation(…)`** Methods to set the translation component.
- **`javax.media.j3d.Transform3D.setRotation(…)`** Methods to set the rotation component.
- **`javax.media.j3d.Transform3D.setScale(…)`** Methods to set the scale component.
- **`javax.media.j3d.Transform3D.mul(…)`** Methods to multiply another transform.
- **`javax.media.j3d.Transform3D.mulInverse(…)`** Methods to multiply the inverse of another transform.
- **`javax.media.j3d.Transform3D.transform(…)`** Methods to apply the transform to points and vectors.
- **`javax.media.j3d.TransformGroup`** A group node class for transformation.
- **`javax.vecmath.Quat4d`** A class encapsulating the quaternion with `double` components.
- **`javax.vecmath.Quat4f`** A class encapsulating the quaternion with `float` components.

KEY TERMS

affine transform A geometric transform that preserves parallelism.
projective transform A geometric transform that preserves points, lines, and their incidence relations.
Euler angles A method to specify a 3D rotation with three rotations about main coordinate axes.
composite transformation A transformation as a product of several transformations.
3D transformation matrix A matrix representing a 3D projective transform.
quaternion representation A method to represent a 3D rotation with a quaternion.
3D translation A geometric transform that moves all points by a constant value.
3D rotation A geometric transform that rotates a point around a fixed axis by a constant angle.
3D scaling A geometric transform that scales the coordinates by constant factors. The scaling is uniform if the three factors in x-, y-, z-components are the same.
3D shearing A geometric transform that shifts the points parallel to a plane.
3D reflection A geometric transform that flips the points about a fixed plane.

CHAPTER SUMMARY

- In this chapter, we introduce the concepts and applications of 3D transformations, especially the family of affine transforms.

- A 3D transform is represented as a matrix. Matrix classes are provided in the package `javax.vecmath`. In Java 3D, the `Transform3D` class encapsulates the transformation matrix and the various operations related to the transform. The class includes a large number of methods for setting the transform, performing matrix operations, composing with other transforms, and transforming points and vectors.

- The `TransformGroup` nodes provide the presence of transforms in Java scene graphs. A `TransformGroup` node references a `Transform3D` object to define its transformation and applies the transformation to its child nodes.

- 3D rotations are complex transformations. Three different representations of rotations are introduced. The matrix representation is consistent with other affine transforms, but its relation to geometric parameters is often implicit. The quaternion representation for general 3D rotations is explicit and convenient because of its direct connection with the rotation axis and angle. Euler angles offer another intuitive representation for 3D rotations.

- Composition of transforms is useful especially in construction of complex transforms. A complex transform can often be decomposed into a composite transform of simpler transforms.

- Another application of transforms is in the construction of geometries. The symmetries and regularities in a geometric figure will often be associated with certain transformations. The points on such a geometry may be generated conveniently through the transformations. An extruded surface is obtained by sweeping a curve. Translations are related to extrusion. A rotated surface is generated by rotating a curve.

REVIEW QUESTIONS

7.1 Find the transformation matrix of the translation that maps the point $(3, -1, 2)$ to $(0, 5, -1)$.

7.2 Find the transformation matrix of the rotation about the y-axis by 30 degrees.

7.3 Find the transformation matrix of the reflection about the plane through the origin with the normal vector $(1, 1, 1)$.

7.4 Derive the transformation matrix of the reflection about the plane through the origin with the normal vector u as defined below:

$$T(x) = x - \frac{2x \cdot u}{\|u\|^2} u$$

7.5 Calculate the quaternion product:

$$(1 + 3i - j + k) \cdot (2i + j - 3k)$$

7.6 Let $u = (x_u, y_u, z_u)$ and $v = (x_v, y_v, z_v)$ be two orthogonal unit vectors. Find a rotation that maps u to the x-axis, v to the y-axis, and $u \times v$ to the z-axis.

7.7 An (x, y)-shear is defined by the matrix:

$$\begin{bmatrix} 1 & 0 & sh_x & 0 \\ 0 & 1 & sh_y & 0 \\ 0 & 0 & 1 & 0 \\ 0 & 0 & 0 & 1 \end{bmatrix}$$

Given the orthogonal unit vectors u and v, derive a composite transform that performs a (u, v)-shear by the factors (sh_u, sh_v).

7.8 Find the transformation matrix for the 3D rotation represented by the quaternion

$$q = w + xi + yj + zk$$

7.9 If R_x is a rotation about the x-axis of 30 degrees and R_y a rotation about the y-axis of 60 degrees, describe the composite rotation $R_y R_x$ in terms of its axis and angle.

PROGRAMMING EXERCISES

7.1 Write a Java 3D program to display two tetrahedra with a common triangle face.

7.2 Display two cones with their vertices pointing to each other.

7.3 Display a cone with its vertex pointing in the direction $(1, 1, 1)$.

7.4 Modify Listing 7.4 to include an (x, y)-shear operation. Allow the user to specify the factors (sh_x, sh_y).

7.5 Modify Listing 7.4 to include rotation specification with Euler angles.

7.6 Modify Listing 7.7 to construct the reflection matrix directly from the following formula:

$$T(x) = x - \frac{2x \cdot u}{\|u\|^2} u$$

7.7 Create and display a simple table with a square top and four cylindrical legs. Use only predefined primitives and transformations to create the visual object. Rotate the table continuously in the scene.

7.8 Create a geometry that is formed by rotating the figure in Figure 7.12 about the y-axis. Write a test program to display the object.

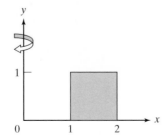

FIGURE 7.12 Rotating a square to generate a 3D object.

7.9 Implement a Shape3D class RotatedShape that represents a surface obtained by rotating a 2D Shape object about the *y*-axis. It should contain at least one constructor:

public RotatedShape(Shape curve)

You may assume that the 2D shape is a single continuous curve (with only one SEG_MOVETO). Write a test program to display a rotated surface.

CHAPTER 8

VIEWS

Objectives

- To present the concept of view in the 3D rendering process.
- To identify the parallel and perspective projections.
- To specify the viewing matrix.
- To specify the projection matrix.
- To apply the Java 3D standard view model.
- To apply the Java 3D compatibility-mode view model.
- To apply picking in a 3D scene.
- To understand head tracking in view models.
- To apply input devices, sensors, and head tracking in Java 3D.
- To use the avatar in `SimpleUniverse`.

8.1 Introduction

After a virtual world of graphics objects is constructed, it can be rendered to produce images of the world from various perspectives through a viewing process. The rendering of a scene is characterized by numerous attributes that affect different aspects of the viewing. In this chapter we focus on the geometric aspects of the rendering process. The methods for achieving realistic appearance in rendering visual objects will be discussed in later chapters.

view

The geometric configuration that defines the process of mapping a 3D virtual world scene to a 2D image is called a *view*. A view is the digital analogy of a camera. It defines the way that the virtual world and the graphics model are visualized. The views in a modern computer graphics system can be quite sophisticated and may have a large number of parameters. The viewpoint of a view is typically located in the virtual world, and it "sees" the virtual world from a specific viewing orientation and direction. A view has certain defining properties, such as the type of 3D-to-2D projections, the field of view, front and back clipping planes, view plate size, and so on. A view may resemble a static camera, or it may act like an eye of a person that can change its position and properties dynamically.

camera-based view

Most low-level graphics APIs support only a *camera-based view* model. It is typically specified with two sets of parameters: the projection properties and the camera positioning. A limitation of the static view model is the difficulty in programming the dynamic view changes. For example, the viewing device in a graphics system may be a head-mounted camera with a

head tracking

head-tracking system. The *head-tracking* information is sent back to the system, causing continuous changes in view properties. The dynamic view will be quite complex for the application program to implement and will likely be platform dependent. Java 3D provides a versatile view system that incorporates both traditional view settings and supports for dynamic view changes. The effects of physical environment changes to the view can be automatically included through separate objects without explicitly changing the basic viewing structure. Applications can use the same scene graph for a variety of display options.

picking

Another topic related to viewing is *picking*. View projection maps a 3D volume to a 2D image. Picking is a process of selecting world-space objects through the projected 2D image. It is therefore a partial inverse operation of projection. Picking facilitates interactions with a 3D scene from the rendered image. Through picking operations, for example, a user may select an object from the screen image and rotate or move the object with a mouse. Java 3D provides extensive support for picking at different levels.

8.2 Projections

The viewing of a 3D scene with a 2D image is achieved through a transformation called

projection
view plane

projection. There are two main types: *parallel projections* and *perspective projections*. In each case, a plane known as the *view plane* is placed in the virtual world. The projection maps the points in the virtual world to the plane. In order to make implementations feasible, certain restrictions on the projections will be necessary. Only a finite window (usually rectangular) on the view plane will actually be used for rendered images. This window is

view plate

called a *view plate*. It is analogous to a frame of film in an ordinary camera. Only the points in the 3D space that project to the view plate need to be calculated. The points very close to or far away from the viewer are also excluded. This results in a finite volume in the 3D space that will actually participate in the projection. This volume is known as the

view frustum
parallel projection

view frustum.

A *parallel projection* projects 3D points to a view plane through parallel lines in a fixed direction. When the lines of the projection are perpendicular to the view plane, the parallel projection is called *orthographic*. Three orthographic projections along the three axes are known as the *front-elevation*, *top-elevation*, and *side-elevation* projections. They are often used in engineering drawings. The view volume for a view with a parallel projection is a parallelogram. (See Figure 8.1.)

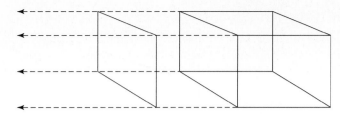

FIGURE 8.1   Parallel projection.

The formulas for parallel projections are relatively simple. Suppose that the view plane is the xy-plane and the projection is in the direction of the z-axis. Then a point (x, y, z) in the 3D space is simply mapped to the point (x, y) in the 2D view plane. The transformation is given by the matrix equation

$$\begin{bmatrix} x' \\ y' \\ z' \\ w' \end{bmatrix} = \begin{bmatrix} 1 & 0 & 0 & 0 \\ 0 & 1 & 0 & 0 \\ 0 & 0 & 0 & 0 \\ 0 & 0 & 0 & 1 \end{bmatrix} \begin{bmatrix} x \\ y \\ z \\ w \end{bmatrix}$$

In fact for purposes such as determining the hidden portions of objects, it is usually desirable to retain the information of the z-coordinates while performing the projection. Therefore, this parallel projection is essentially the identity transform:

$$\begin{bmatrix} x' \\ y' \\ z' \\ w' \end{bmatrix} = \begin{bmatrix} 1 & 0 & 0 & 0 \\ 0 & 1 & 0 & 0 \\ 0 & 0 & 1 & 0 \\ 0 & 0 & 0 & 1 \end{bmatrix} \begin{bmatrix} x \\ y \\ z \\ w \end{bmatrix}$$

In a *perspective projection*, all projection lines converge to the viewpoint (the viewer or eye position) (Figure 8.2). Objects closer to the viewer will appear larger than the distant objects. This mode resembles the projection in human eyes and regular cameras.

perspective projection

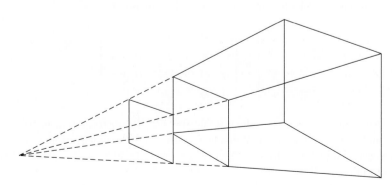

FIGURE 8.2   Perspective projection.

The mathematical formulas for perspective projection are more complex. Assume that the view plane is the xy-plane and the eye is at $(0, 0, d)$ looking down the z-axis, with the y-axis being the view up direction, as illustrated in Figure 8.3.

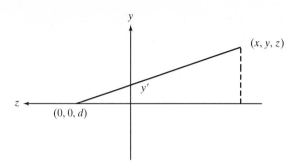

FIGURE 8.3 An example of perspective projection.

Considering the two similar triangles, we have

$$\frac{y'}{d} = \frac{y}{d + (-z)}$$

or

$$y' = \frac{y}{1 - z/d}$$

Similarly, in the x-direction

$$x' = \frac{x}{1 - z/d}$$

Therefore the transformation is not linear in the 3D space. However, it can be expressed in a linear form with homogeneous coordinates, as shown in the following equation:

$$\begin{bmatrix} x' \\ y' \\ z' \\ w' \end{bmatrix} = \begin{bmatrix} 1 & 0 & 0 & 0 \\ 0 & 1 & 0 & 0 \\ 0 & 0 & 0 & 0 \\ 0 & 0 & -1/d & 1 \end{bmatrix} \begin{bmatrix} x \\ y \\ z \\ w \end{bmatrix}$$

If the z-coordinate is to be retained, then the transformation becomes

$$\begin{bmatrix} x' \\ y' \\ z' \\ w' \end{bmatrix} = \begin{bmatrix} 1 & 0 & 0 & 0 \\ 0 & 1 & 0 & 0 \\ 0 & 0 & 1 & 0 \\ 0 & 0 & -1/d & 1 \end{bmatrix} \begin{bmatrix} x \\ y \\ z \\ w \end{bmatrix}$$

In fact, using homogeneous coordinates and the 4 × 4 transformation matrices, parallel projections and perspective projections can be treated in a uniform way. Both types of projections are projective transformations and can be represented with 4 × 4 matrices. Clearly if d approaches infinity,

$$\lim_{d \to \infty} (-1/d) = 0$$

The above matrix becomes the parallel projection matrix introduced earlier. A parallel projection can be regarded as a special case of perspective projection with the viewpoint at infinity. The viewpoint for the perspective projection has coordinates $(0, 0, d)$, or homogeneous coordinates $(0, 0, 1, 1/d)$. As $d \to \infty$, the viewpoint approaches $(0, 0, 1, 0)$, a point at infinity in homogeneous coordinates.

8.3 Specification of a View

The complete specification of a view can be divided into two parts: the view-volume definition and the view positioning. If a view is regarded as a camera, then the view volume corresponds to the characteristics of the camera itself, such as the focal length and the film size, and the view positioning corresponds to the position and aiming direction of the camera.

The definition of a view volume is often represented by a *projection matrix*. The view positioning is represented by a *viewing matrix*.

The following parameters are related to the definition of a view volume or projection matrix:

- Projection – parallel or perspective projection.

- View plate – the window for the rendered image. It is usually a rectangular region. In a real camera the view plate corresponds to the film frame.

- Field of view (fov) – the horizontal angle between the left and right plane of the frustum. The vertical field of view and the diagonal field of view can be defined similarly.

- Focal length – the distance between the view plate and the view point.

- Aspect ratio – the ratio of width over length of the view planes.

- Front clip plane – the front or near plane of the frustum.

- Back clip plane – the back or far plane of the frustum.

Not all the above parameters are independent. For example, the focal length, the horizontal field of view, and the width of the view plate are related by the formula:

$$\tan\frac{fov}{2} = \frac{width/2}{f}$$

A 35 mm camera with a standard 50 mm lens has a film size 36 mm by 24 mm, a field of view of 40 degrees, and an aspect ratio of 1.5. In a real camera, the film is placed behind the lens and the projected image is upside down, as illustrated in Figure 8.4. In computer graphics, however, the film is exactly symmetrical to the image plate. Rather than using the inverted images, it is more convenient to formulate the viewing system with the view plate in front of the eye.

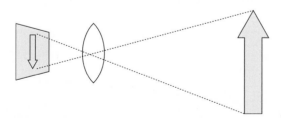

FIGURE 8.4 A real camera projection.

The *projection matrix* is defined in the eye coordinate system in which the eye is located at the origin looking at the negative direction of the z-axis with the y-axis as the up direction. The projection matrix encapsulates the view-volume settings by defining a projective transform that maps the given view volume (a frustum or box) to a standard volume, typically the cube with vertices $(\pm 1, \pm 1, \pm 1)$. For example, consider a view frustum defined by the front plane with vertices $(\pm a, \pm b, -c)$ and the back plane with vertices $(\pm a', \pm b', -d)$. In the x- and y-directions, using the arguments in Section 8.2, the projection has the form

$$x' = \frac{x/a}{-z/c}$$

$$y' = \frac{y/b}{-z/c}$$

projection matrix

In the z-direction, the transform maps the interval $[-d, -c]$ to $[-1, 1]$ and has the form

$$z' = \frac{1 + (1 + d/c)(z + c)/(d - c)}{-z/c}$$

Therefore, the projection can be expressed in the matrix form:

$$\begin{bmatrix} x' \\ y' \\ z' \\ w' \end{bmatrix} = \begin{bmatrix} 1/a & 0 & 0 & 0 \\ 0 & 1/b & 0 & 0 \\ 0 & 0 & (1 + d/c)/(d - c) & 1 + (c + d)/(d - c) \\ 0 & 0 & -1/c & 0 \end{bmatrix} \begin{bmatrix} x \\ y \\ z \\ w \end{bmatrix}$$

To completely define a camera or eye's positioning in the virtual space, it is necessary to specify the location of the camera, the direction in which the camera is pointing, and the direction that the camera considers as the "up" direction. The following parameters are usually associated with the definition of camera positioning or the *viewing matrix*:

viewing matrix

- Viewpoint, view-reference point (vrp, eye) – the camera or eye position, the 3D point where the camera is located.

- View center (look) – the center of the view plate or the point that the eye is looking at.

- View up direction (up) – the upward direction from a viewer's perspective.

- View plane – the plane of the projected image.

- View plane normal (vpn) – the normal vector of the view plane.

The viewpoint is easily specified with a 3D point. However, the viewpoint alone is not enough to completely define the camera's positioning. Clearly, at a fixed point, the camera can still point in different directions. There are several ways to define such an orientation of an object in a 3D space. For example, the pitch–roll–yaw specification is often used to describe an aircraft position.

In computer graphics, a commonly used method for defining camera orientation is to specify the view reference point, the view center, and the view up direction, as illustrated in Figure 8.5.

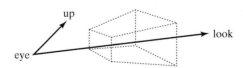

FIGURE 8.5 Viewing matrix definition with eye, look, and up.

A viewing matrix specifies the camera position by defining a transform that changes the camera from its standard position. The standard camera position (when the viewing matrix is identity) is the one defined by the eye coordinate system, typically with the eye at the origin looking down the z-axis and with the y-axis as the up direction. If the viewpoint is moved to (a, b, c) without changing its orientation, the viewing matrix will be:

$$\begin{bmatrix} 1 & 0 & 0 & -a \\ 0 & 1 & 0 & -b \\ 0 & 0 & 1 & -c \\ 0 & 0 & 0 & 1 \end{bmatrix}$$

8.4 Java 3D View Model

Java3D provides a very versatile viewing system that supports dynamic adjustments based on environmental changes as well as traditional static camera based viewing. The scene graph in Figure 8.6 illustrates a typical view setting. Attached to a `Locale` object are a content branch that defines the virtual world graphics model, and a view branch that defines a view to render the scene.

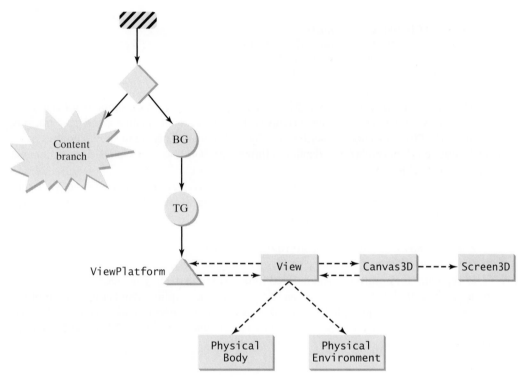

FIGURE 8.6   A typical Java 3D viewing system.

Java 3D classes that are directly related to viewing include: `ViewPlatform`, `View`, `PhysicalBody`, `PhysicalEnvironment`, `Canvas3D`, `Screen3D`.

8.4.1 Configuring a Java 3D View

A `ViewPlatform` object is a leaf node of the scene graph. It defines the presence of the view in the virtual world. Like other scene-graph nodes, the `ViewPlatform` object may go through a chain of transforms and other nodes, and it will eventually be attached to a `Locale` object. The `TransformGroup` node connected to the `ViewPlatform` defines the view-platform transformation that primarily determines the position and orientation of the view, or the viewing matrix. The viewing matrix may be affected by other factors such as the head-tracking sensor input. The `Transform3D` class has a method that helps in the construction of this transform:

void `lookAt(Point3d eye, Point3d look, Vector3d up)`

The transform is constructed to position the `ViewPlatform` so that the eye is located at the given point looking at the specified center of the view plate with the given upward direction. The inverse of the transform defined by the method can be placed in the

TransformGroup above the ViewPlatform to realize the specified positioning of the ViewPlatform.

View

The View object is the heart of the view system. It defines the main configuration of the view with properties such as the projection type and the view volume—that is, the projection matrix of the view. It can also accommodate the dynamic changes in view parameters through its connections with the PhysicalBody and PhysicalEnvironment objects. The methods of the View class for setting the view volume or projection matrix include:

```
void setFieldOfView(double fov)
void setFrontClipDistance(double d)
void setBackClipDistance(double d)
void setProjectionPolicy(int projection)
```

The PhysicalBody and PhysicalEnvironment objects provide supports for automatic calibrations with dynamic viewing systems such as head-mounted-camera and head-tracking sensors. The PhysicalBody describes the physical characteristics of the user's body or head. The PhysicalEnvironment contains information about the user's physical environment such as the tracking sensors.

The Canvas3D class is a subclass of AWT Canvas class and can be placed in an AWT container. A Canvas3D object represents the rendering surface. The following constructor is typically used to construct a Canvas3D object:

```
public Canvas3D(GraphicsConfiguration gc)
```

A separate Screen3D class is defined to describe the display devices. It is referenced by a Canvas3D object. The separation of the device description avoids duplication of the same information for multiple Canvas3D objects. The Screen3D class has no public constructor, and its instance can be retrieved by the method getScreen3D of the Canvas3D class.

8.4.2 The Compatibility Mode

compatibility mode

Java 3D also offers a compatibility view mode that supports traditional camera-based model resembling OpenGL view specification. To enable the *compatibility mode*, the following method of the View object can be used:

```
public void setCompatibilityModeEnable(boolean enabled)
```

The Transform3D class contains methods for constructing the viewing matrix and the projection matrix. The viewing matrix can be constructed using the same eye-look-up approach

```
public void lookAt(Point3d eye, Point3d look, Vector3d up)
```

The projection matrix can be constructed with one of the three different methods:

```
public void perspective(double fov, double aspect, double near,
    double far)
public void frustum(double left, double right, double bottom,
    double top, double near, double far)
public void ortho(double left, double right, double bottom,
    double top, double near, double far)
```

The coordinates in these methods are relative to the eye position or `vrp`. The `perspective` method defines a perspective projection matrix by specifying the horizontal field of view, the aspect ratio, and the near and far clip planes. Both the `frustum` method and the `ortho` method define the projection matrix by specifying the corner coordinates of the view volume. (`left`, `bottom`, `-near`) and (`left`, `bottom`, `-near`) define the lower left corner and the upper right corner of the near plane. The depth of the far plane is defined by `-far`. The `frustum` method defines a perspective projection and the `ortho` method a parallel projection.

For example, the following two calls define the same perspective projection:

```
perspective(Math.PI/2, 2, 1, 2);
frustum(-1,1, -0.5, 0.5, 1, 2);
```

The view volume has a horizontal field of view $\pi/2$ and an aspect ratio of 2.0. The near-plane distance is 1 and the far-plane distance 2. The near plane is 2×1 and the far plane 4×2. Assuming the near plane is the view plate, the projection can be written as:

$$x' = \frac{x}{-z}$$

$$y' = \frac{2y}{-z}$$

$$z' = \frac{3z + 4}{-z}$$

The projection matrix for the projection is given by:

$$\begin{bmatrix} 1 & 0 & 0 & 0 \\ 0 & 2 & 0 & 0 \\ 0 & 0 & 3 & 4 \\ 0 & 0 & -1 & 0 \end{bmatrix}$$

The appropriately constructed projection matrix and viewing matrix can be set for the view using the following methods of `View`:

```
public void setVpcToEc(Transform3D viewingMatrix)
public void setLeftProjection(Transform3D projectionMatrix)
public void setRightProjection(Transform3D projectionMatrix)
```

In the compatibility mode virtually all view parameters are set in the `View` object. On the other hand, in the standard (noncompatibility) Java 3D view mode, the final view settings may also be influenced by other objects such as `PhysicalBody` and `PhysicalEnvironment`. The above methods for directly setting the projection matrix and the viewing matrix are not valid in the noncompatibility mode.

The compatibility mode is a restricted view mode that does not have all the Java 3D view features. It is intended to be a simple mode compatible with OpenGL style calls.

Listing 8.1 displays a rotating tetrahedron using a manually constructed view in compatibility mode. It illustrates a minimal Java 3D view setting. (See Figure 8.7.)

Listing 8.1 `CompatibilityMode.java`

```
 1 package chapter8;
 2
 3 import javax.vecmath.*;
 4 import java.awt.*;
 5 import java.awt.event.*;
 6 import javax.media.j3d.*;
 7 import com.sun.j3d.utils.universe.*;
 8 import com.sun.j3d.utils.geometry.*;
 9 import chapter6.*;
10 import java.applet.*;
11 import com.sun.j3d.utils.applet.MainFrame;
12
13 public class CompatibilityMode extends Applet {
14   public static void main(String[] args) {
15     new MainFrame(new CompatibilityMode(), 640, 650);
16   }
17
18   public void init() {
19     // create canvas
20     GraphicsConfiguration gc =
21     SimpleUniverse.getPreferredConfiguration();
22     Canvas3D cv = new Canvas3D(gc);
23     setLayout(new BorderLayout());
24     add(cv, BorderLayout.CENTER);
25     VirtualUniverse universe = new VirtualUniverse();
26     Locale locale = new Locale(universe);
27     BranchGroup bg = createView(cv);
28     locale.addBranchGraph(bg);
29     bg = createContent();
30     bg.compile();
31     locale.addBranchGraph(bg);
32   }
33
34   private BranchGroup createView(Canvas3D cv) {
35     BranchGroup bg = new BranchGroup();
36     ViewPlatform platform = new ViewPlatform();
37     bg.addChild(platform);
38     View view = new View();
39     view.addCanvas3D(cv);
40     view.setCompatibilityModeEnable(true);
41     view.attachViewPlatform(platform);
42     Transform3D projection = new Transform3D();
43     projection.frustum(-0.1, 0.1, -0.1, 0.1, 0.2, 10);
44     view.setLeftProjection(projection);
45     Transform3D viewing = new Transform3D();
46     Point3d eye = new Point3d(0,0,1);
47     Point3d look = new Point3d(0,0,-1);
48     Vector3d up = new Vector3d(0,1,0);
49     viewing.lookAt(eye, look, up);
50     view.setVpcToEc(viewing);
51     PhysicalBody body = new PhysicalBody();
52     view.setPhysicalBody(body);
53     PhysicalEnvironment env = new PhysicalEnvironment();
54     view.setPhysicalEnvironment(env);
55     return bg;
56   }
57
```

```
58    private BranchGroup createContent() {
59      BranchGroup root = new BranchGroup();
60      TransformGroup spin = new TransformGroup();
61      spin.setCapability(TransformGroup.ALLOW_TRANSFORM_WRITE);
62      root.addChild(spin);
63      // object
64      Appearance ap = new Appearance();
65      ap.setMaterial(new Material());
66      Shape3D shape = new Shape3D(new Tetrahedron(), ap);
67      // rotating object
68      Transform3D tr = new Transform3D();
69      tr.setScale(0.25);
70      TransformGroup tg = new TransformGroup(tr);
71      spin.addChild(tg);
72      tg.addChild(shape);
73      Alpha alpha = new Alpha(-1, 4000);
74      RotationInterpolator rotator =
75      new RotationInterpolator(alpha, spin);
76      BoundingSphere bounds = new BoundingSphere();
77      rotator.setSchedulingBounds(bounds);
78      spin.addChild(rotator);
79      // light and background
80      Background background = new Background(1.0f, 1.0f, 1.0f);
81      background.setApplicationBounds(bounds);
82      root.addChild(background);
83      AmbientLight light =
84      new AmbientLight(true, new Color3f(Color.red));
85      light.setInfluencingBounds(bounds);
86      root.addChild(light);
87      PointLight ptlight = new PointLight(new Color3f(Color.green),
88          new Point3f(3f,3f,3f), new Point3f(1f,0f,0f));
89      ptlight.setInfluencingBounds(bounds);
90      root.addChild(ptlight);
91      PointLight ptlight2 = new PointLight(new Color3f(Color.orange),
92          new Point3f(-2f,2f,2f), new Point3f(1f,0f,0f));
93      ptlight2.setInfluencingBounds(bounds);
94      root.addChild(ptlight2);
95      return root;
96    }
97 }
```

This program creates all the components of the scene graph directly without using the utility classes. The Canvas3D, VirtualUniverse, and Locale objects are created in the constructor. The createView method (line 34) creates the view branch of the scene and the createContent method creates the content branch.

The createView method constructs the objects in the view branch: a BranchGroup, a ViewPlatform, a View, a PhysicalBody, and a PhysicalEnvironment. It enables the compatibility mode for the View object (line 40). The projection matrix is set to a perspective projection by calling the method frustum (line 43). The near clip plane is defined by the corners $(-0.1, -0.1, -0.2)$ and $(0.1, 0.1, -0.2)$. The far clip-plane distance is 10. The viewing matrix is created with the method lookAt to place the eye at $(0, 0, 1)$ looking at the point $(0, 0, -1)$ with $(0, 1, 0)$ as the up direction (line 49). Both the projection and viewing matrices are set in the View object directly with the methods setLeftProjection and setVpcToEc. Even though head tracking is not available in compatibility mode, it is still necessary to supply the PhysicalBody and PhysicalEnvironment objects to the View.

The createContent method constructs the content branch of the scene graph. It consists of a rotating tetrahedron similar to the program in Listing 6.1.

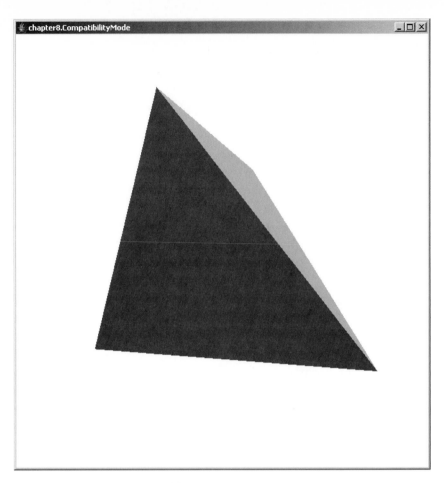

FIGURE 8.7   A view using compatibility mode.

8.4.3 View Settings in SimpleUniverse

The SimpleUniverse utility class provides a default implementation for the viewing system illustrated in Figure 8.4. The SimpleUniverse further divides the view-related components objects into two classes: the Viewer class and the ViewingPlatform class. The Viewer object consists of a View object, a ViewAvatar object, a PhysicalBody object, a Physical Environment object, and a set of Canvas3D objects. The ViewingPlatform object contains a ViewPlatform object and a MultiTransformGroup object that holds a series of TransformGroup nodes linked together. The default ViewingPlatform has one Trans formGroup node in its MultiTransformGroup object, but SimpleUniverse has constructors to specify multiple TransformGroup nodes:

```
SimpleUniverse(int numTrans)
SimpleUniverse(Canvas3D canvas, int numTrans)
```

To retrieve the View from a SimpleUniverse object, you may use the following statement:

```
View view = su.getViewer().getView();
```

To obtain the TransformGroup node above the ViewPlatform, you may make the following method calls:

```
TransformGroup tg = su.getViewingPlatform().getViewPlatformTransform();
```

To get a specific `TransformGroup` in the `MultiTransformGroup` object, use the following calls:

```
TransformGroup tg =
su.getViewingPlatform().getMultiTransformGroup().getTransformGroup(idx);
```

The default view settings in a `SimpleUniverse` object are given below:

- Compatibility mode: false

- Left projection: identity

- Right projection: identity

- vpc-to-ec transform: identity

- Field of view: $\pi/4$

- Front clip distance: 0.1

- Back clip distance: 10

The following code fragment changes the default settings in a `SimpleUniverse` object. The `ViewPlatform` is moved to $(1,1,1)$ looking at the origin. The field of view is set to 0.4π:

```
SimpleUniverse su = new SimpleUniverse(cv);
TransformGroup tg =
  su.getViewingPlatform().getMultiTransformGroup().getTransformGroup(0);
Transform3D tx = new Transform3D();
tx.lookAt(new Point3d(1,1,1), new Point3d(0,0,0), new Vector3d(0,1,0));
tx.invert();
tg.setTransform(tx);
View view = su.getViewer().getView();
view.setFieldOfView(0.4*Math.PI);
```

Listing 8.2 illustrates the applications of `SimpleUniverse` and the effects of controlling standard Java 3D views. This example displays a dodecahedron in a rotating view. The visual object in the content branch, a dodecahedron, is in a fixed position. However, the view is set to rotate about the *y*-axis, allowing the user to see the different sides of the dodecahedron (See Figure 8.8.)

Listing 8.2 `RotateView.java`

```
 1 package chapter8;
 2
 3 import javax.vecmath.*;
 4 import java.awt.*;
 5 import java.awt.event.*;
 6 import javax.media.j3d.*;
 7 import com.sun.j3d.utils.universe.*;
 8 import com.sun.j3d.utils.geometry.*;
 9 import chapter6.*;
10 import java.applet.*;
11 import com.sun.j3d.utils.applet.MainFrame;
12
13 public class RotateView extends Applet {
14   public static void main(String[] args) {
15     new MainFrame(new RotateView(), 640, 480);
16   }
17
18   public void init() {
19     // create canvas
```

```
20      GraphicsConfiguration gc =
21        SimpleUniverse.getPreferredConfiguration();
22      Canvas3D cv = new Canvas3D(gc);
23      setLayout(new BorderLayout());
24      add(cv, BorderLayout.CENTER);
25      SimpleUniverse su = new SimpleUniverse(cv, 2);
26      su.getViewingPlatform().setNominalViewingTransform();
27      BranchGroup bg = createSceneGraph(su.getViewingPlatform().
28        getMultiTransformGroup().getTransformGroup(0));
29      bg.compile();
30      su.addBranchGraph(bg);
31    }
32
33    private BranchGroup createSceneGraph(TransformGroup vtg) {
34      BranchGroup root = new BranchGroup();
35      // object
36      Appearance ap = new Appearance();
37      ap.setMaterial(new Material());
38      Shape3D shape = new Dodecahedron();
39      shape.setAppearance(ap);
40      Transform3D tr = new Transform3D();
41      tr.setScale(0.25);
42      TransformGroup tg = new TransformGroup(tr);
43      root.addChild(tg);
44      tg.addChild(shape);
45      // view rotator
46      Alpha alpha = new Alpha(-1, 4000);
47      RotationInterpolator rotator =
48      new RotationInterpolator(alpha, vtg);
49      BoundingSphere bounds = new BoundingSphere();
50      rotator.setSchedulingBounds(bounds);
51      root.addChild(rotator);
52      // lights
53      Background background = new Background(1.0f, 1.0f, 1.0f);
54      background.setApplicationBounds(bounds);
55      root.addChild(background);
56      AmbientLight light = new AmbientLight
57        (true, new Color3f(Color.red));
58      light.setInfluencingBounds(bounds);
59      root.addChild(light);
60      PointLight ptlight = new PointLight(new Color3f(Color.green),
61        new Point3f(3f,3f,3f), new Point3f(1f,0f,0f));
62      ptlight.setInfluencingBounds(bounds);
63      root.addChild(ptlight);
64      PointLight ptlight2 = new PointLight(new Color3f(Color.orange),
65        new Point3f(-2f,2f,2f), new Point3f(1f,0f,0f));
66      ptlight2.setInfluencingBounds(bounds);
67      root.addChild(ptlight2);
68      return root;
69    }
70  }
```

The scene graph is shown in Figure 8.9. This program is similar to Listing 6.3. However, in this case the rotation behavior is not applied to the visual object (a dodecahedron) but to the view (line 48). The object appears to be rotating in the opposite direction. But because the lights do not move, the lighting of the faces does not change as the view rotates. We can even see the unlit back faces.

The SimpleUniverse is created with two TransformGroup nodes (line 25). One transform node is used by the setNominalViewTransform method to move the view back. The other transform node is the target of the rotation.

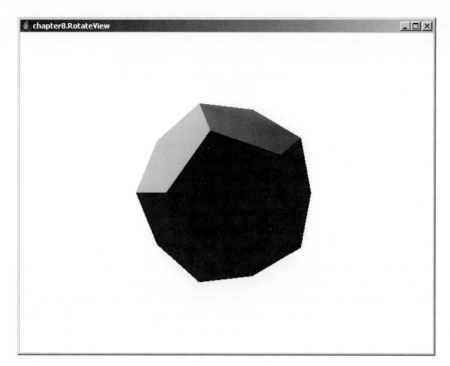

FIGURE 8.8
A rotating view lets you see the back sides of an object.

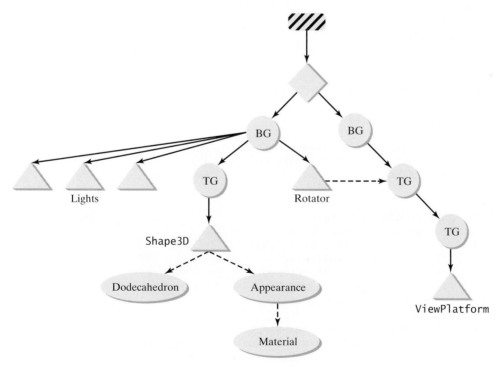

FIGURE 8.9   The scene graph of the view-rotation example.

8.4.4 Creating Your Own View

Even though SimpleUniverse provides a convenient way to construct the view branch for
many Java 3D applications, it may not be adequate in some cases. You can always construct
the view branch manually by setting up the appropriate view-related objects such as View,

create a view branch

ViewPlatform, PhysicalBody, PhysicalEnvironment, and so on. The following code illustrates the procedure to manually *create a view branch:*

```
View view = new View();
view.setProjectionPolicy(View.PARALLEL_PROJECTION);
ViewPlatform vp = new ViewPlatform();
view.addCanvas3D(cv);
view.attachViewPlatform(vp);
view.setPhysicalBody(new PhysicalBody());
view.setPhysicalEnvironment(new PhysicalEnvironment());
Transform3D trans = new Transform3D();
trans.lookAt(eye, center, vup);
trans.invert();
TransformGroup tg = new TransformGroup(trans);
tg.addChild(vp);
BranchGroup bgView = new BranchGroup();
bgView.addChild(tg);
```

A scene graph may contain more than one view. Multiple views on a single scene graph allow you to see the same virtual world from different perspectives.

Listing 8.3 shows an application with multiple views. The same object, a rotating 3D text, is rendered with four different views. One is a standard perspective view provided by the SimpleUniverse. The other three have parallel projections in the *x*-, *y*-, and *z*-directions. (See Figure 8.10.)

Listing 8.3 `MultipleViews.java`

```
 1 package chapter8;
 2
 3 import javax.vecmath.*;
 4 import java.awt.*;
 5 import java.awt.event.*;
 6 import javax.media.j3d.*;
 7 import com.sun.j3d.utils.universe.*;
 8 import com.sun.j3d.utils.geometry.*;
 9 import java.applet.*;
10 import com.sun.j3d.utils.applet.MainFrame;
11
12 public class MultipleViews extends Applet {
13   public static void main(String[] args) {
14     new MainFrame(new MultipleViews(), 640, 480);
15   }
16
17   public void init() {
18     // create 4 Canvas3D objects
19     this.setLayout(new GridLayout(2,2));
20     GraphicsConfiguration gc =
21     SimpleUniverse.getPreferredConfiguration();
22     // first view: standard
23     Canvas3D cv = new Canvas3D(gc);
24     add(cv);
25     SimpleUniverse su = new SimpleUniverse(cv);
26     su.getViewingPlatform().setNominalViewingTransform();
27     // second view: x direction
28     cv = new Canvas3D(gc);
29     add(cv);
30     BranchGroup bgView = createView(cv, new Point3d(2.7,0,0),
31       new Point3d(0,0,0), new Vector3d(0,1,0));
32     su.addBranchGraph(bgView);
33     // third view: z direction
```

```
34    cv = new Canvas3D(gc);
35    add(cv);
36    bgView = createView(cv, new Point3d(0, 0, 2.7),
37      new Point3d(0,0,0), new Vector3d(0,1,0));
38    su.addBranchGraph(bgView);
39    // fourth view: y direction
40    cv = new Canvas3D(gc);
41    add(cv);
42    bgView = createView(cv, new Point3d(0,2.7,0),
43      new Point3d(0,0,0), new Vector3d(0,0,1));
44    su.addBranchGraph(bgView);
45    // content branch
46    BranchGroup bg = createSceneGraph();
47    bg.compile();
48    su.addBranchGraph(bg);
49  }
50
51  private BranchGroup createView(Canvas3D cv, Point3d eye,
52    Point3d center, Vector3d vup) {
53    View view = new View();
54    view.setProjectionPolicy(View.PARALLEL_PROJECTION);
55    ViewPlatform vp = new ViewPlatform();
56    view.addCanvas3D(cv);
57    view.attachViewPlatform(vp);
58    view.setPhysicalBody(new PhysicalBody());
59    view.setPhysicalEnvironment(new PhysicalEnvironment());
60    Transform3D trans = new Transform3D();
61    trans.lookAt(eye, center, vup);
62    trans.invert();
63    TransformGroup tg = new TransformGroup(trans);
64    tg.addChild(vp);
65    BranchGroup bgView = new BranchGroup();
66    bgView.addChild(tg);
67    return bgView;
68  }
69
70  private BranchGroup createSceneGraph() {
71    BranchGroup root = new BranchGroup();
72    TransformGroup spin = new TransformGroup();
73    spin.setCapability(TransformGroup.ALLOW_TRANSFORM_WRITE);
74    root.addChild(spin);
75    // object
76    Font3D font = new Font3D(new Font("Serif", Font.PLAIN, 1),
77      new FontExtrusion());
78    Text3D text = new Text3D(font, "Java");
79    Appearance ap = new Appearance();
80    ap.setMaterial(new Material());
81    Shape3D shape = new Shape3D(text, ap);
82    Transform3D tr = new Transform3D();
83    tr.setTranslation(new Vector3f(-1f, -0.25f, 0f));
84    TransformGroup tg = new TransformGroup(tr);
85    spin.addChild(tg);
86    tg.addChild(shape);
87    // rotator
88    Alpha alpha = new Alpha(-1, 24000);
89    RotationInterpolator rotator = new RotationInterpolator
90      (alpha, spin);
91    BoundingSphere bounds = new BoundingSphere();
92    rotator.setSchedulingBounds(bounds);
93    spin.addChild(rotator);
```

```
94      // background and light
95      Background background = new Background(1.0f, 1.0f, 1.0f);
96      background.setApplicationBounds(bounds);
97      root.addChild(background);
98      AmbientLight light = new AmbientLight
99        (true, new Color3f(Color.red));
100     light.setInfluencingBounds(bounds);
101     root.addChild(light);
102     PointLight ptlight = new PointLight(new Color3f(Color.green),
103       new Point3f(3f,3f,3f), new Point3f(1f,0f,0f));
104     ptlight.setInfluencingBounds(bounds);
105     root.addChild(ptlight);
106     PointLight ptlight2 = new PointLight(new Color3f(Color.orange),
107       new Point3f(-2f,2f,2f), new Point3f(1f,0f,0f));
108     ptlight2.setInfluencingBounds(bounds);
109     root.addChild(ptlight2);
110     return root;
111   }
112 }
```

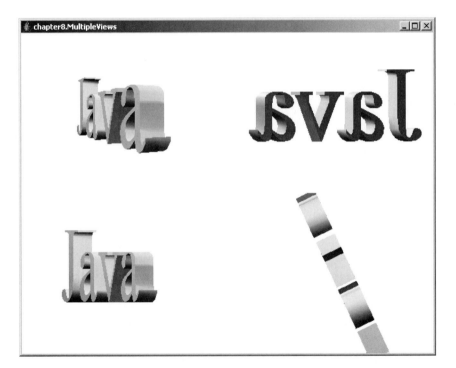

FIGURE 8.10   Four views of a scene.

This program creates four different views in the same scene graph. One view is the standard view in a SimpleUniverse with a perspective projection. The other three have parallel projections along the *x*-, *y*-, *z*-axes. Consequently, they are the front-elevation, top-elevation, and side-elevation projections found in engineering drawings.

The scene graph for the example is given in Figure 8.11. Four Canvas3D objects are placed in a grid. The createView method (line 51) creates the necessary objects for a parallel view. Each view has separate instances of BranchGroup, TransformGroup, ViewPlatform, View, PhysicalBody, PhysicalEnvironment. The type of projection is set with a method in View

```
view.setProjectionPolicy(View.PARALLEL_PROJECTION);
```

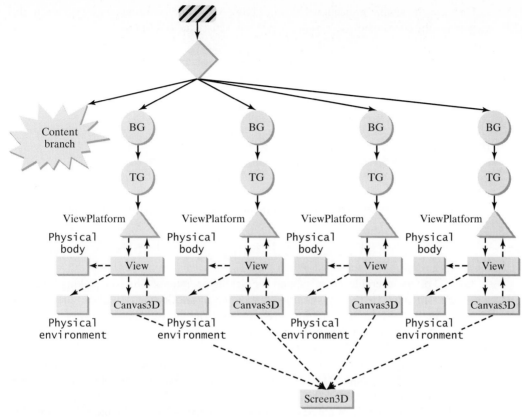

FIGURE 8.11 Scene graph of the multiple-view example.

The viewing matrix is set through the `TransformGroup`. The inverse of the matrix defined by the `lookAt` method is the appropriate matrix for the `TransformGroup`:

```
Transform3D trans = new Transform3D();
trans.lookAt(eye, center, vup);
trans.invert();
TransformGroup tg = new TransformGroup(trans);
```

Three calls to `createView` method are made to create three different views. Each view rooted at a `BranchGroup` is attached to the `Locale`. The three views are linked to three `Canvas3D` objects to display the rendered images.

The method `createSceneGraph` sets up the content branch of the scene graph. The scene contains a rotating 3D text "Java," a background, and lights.

8.5 Picking

It is sometimes necessary to consider the inverse process of the viewing. Given a point in the rendered view plate, one might want to determine the visual objects that project to the point. This is the process known as *picking*. A typical use of picking is to allow a user to select objects from the rendered image using a mouse.

Clearly a point in the 2D view plate does not correspond to a single point in the 3D virtual world under the projection. Instead, a ray of points will be projected to the point. If we treat the point more realistically as a disk of a positive radius, to allow a certain tolerance instead of an ideal point, then the pre-images of the point will be a cone (in perspective projections) or a cylinder (in parallel projections).

Consider the simple projection given in Figure 8.3. If the coordinates (x', y') are in the view plate, the coordinates (x, y, z) of the pick ray satisfy the equations

$$x = x'(1 - z/d)$$

$$y = y'(1 - z/d)$$

If one chooses the parameter $t = 1 - z/d$, then the line equation of the pick ray is

$$x = x't$$

$$y = y't$$

$$z = d(1 - t)$$

If the point is considered as a disk with radius r, then the pick cone has the equation

$$\left(\frac{x}{1 - z/d} - x' \right)^2 + \left(\frac{y}{1 - z/d} - y' \right)^2 = r^2$$

Java 3D offers several levels of support for picking operations. The core picking functionalities are supported by the `PickShape` classes, the `SceneGraphPath` class, and the pick methods in `BranchGroup` and `Locale` classes. The classes in the utility packages `com.sun.j3d.utils.picking` and `com.sun.j3d.utils.picking.behavior` provide high-level supports for picking operations.

A basic picking operation is performed by creating a `PickShape` object and calling a pick method in a `BranchGroup` or `Locale`. The results of the picking are returned as `SceneGraphPath` objects.

pick shapes

The `PickShape` family of classes defines various picking shapes. Figure 8.12. shows the hierarchy of pick shapes.

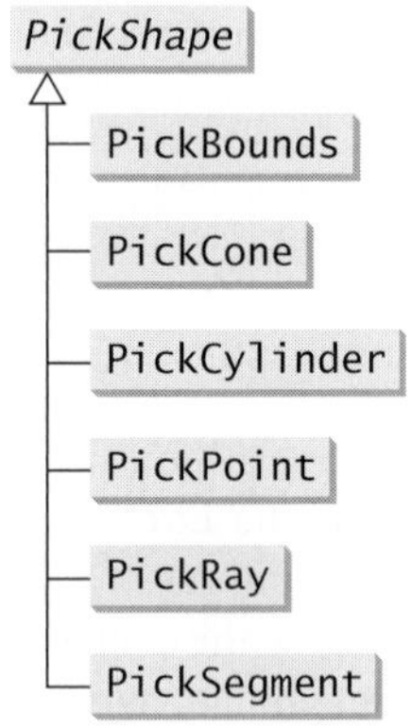

FIGURE 8.12 `PickShape` class hierarchy.

pick methods

The `BranchGroup` and `Locale` classes contain the following methods to perform picking:

```
SceneGraphPath[] pickAll(PickShape pickShape)
SceneGraphPath[] pickAllSorted(PickShape pickShape)
SceneGraphPath pickAny(PickShape pickShape)
SceneGraphPath pickClosest(PickShape pickShape)
```

A `SceneGraphPath` object represents a path from the `Locale` object to a terminal node in a scene graph. `SceneGraphPath` is useful for picking, because in the result of a picking operation it is often necessary to know the entire path rather than just the picked node.

The following code fragment outlines the procedure to perform a picking on a `BranchGroup`:

```
Point3d origin = new Point3d(0,0,0);
Vector3d direction = new Vector3d(0,1,-1);
PickShape pickShape = new PickRay(origin, direction);
SceneGraphPath[] paths = branchGroup.pickAll(pickShape);
for (int i = 0; i < paths.length; i++) {
    <operations on paths[i]...>
}
```

The most common application of picking is to allow users to select objects on a rendered image. To simplify this process, the utility package com.sun.j3d.utils.picking contains four classes for performing general picking operations on a branch of a scene graph (Figure 8.13).

The PickTool class provides a convenient way to set up a pick shape and perform picking on a branch of scene graph. It has the following pick methods:

FIGURE 8.13   Picking utility classes.

```
PickResult[] pickAll()
PickResult[] pickAllSorted()
PickResult pickAny()
PickResult pickClosest()
```

The PickCanvas subclass simplifies the pick shape setup by an association with a canvas. A mouse event can be used to automatically generate pick shape. The following constructor of PickCanvas establishes a connection with a Canvas3D object and a BranchGroup object. The picking operation will be performed on the branch, and the picking shape can be formed based on the mouse event on the canvas:

```
public PickCanvas(Canvas3D cv, BranchGroup bg)
```

A similar constructor exists for a Locale object:

```
public PickCanvas(Canvas3D cv, Locale lc)
```

The results of picking are returned in PickResult objects. PickResult contains information such as the picked node object, the SceneGraphPath, and the intersection. The PickIntersection class contains more detailed information about the intersection of the pick shape and the picked node.

Listing 8.4 illustrates a simple application of the picking utility classes. The scene in this example consists of six primitives: a sphere, a box, a cylinder, a cone, a tetrahedron, and a dodecahedron. They are rotating about the *y*-axis in a wireframe form. When the user clicks on one of the primitives, the object will take on an illuminated colored appearance. (See Figure 8.14.)

Listing 8.4 Picking.java

```
1 package chapter8;
2
3 import javax.vecmath.*;
```

```
 4 import java.awt.*;
 5 import java.awt.event.*;
 6 import javax.media.j3d.*;
 7 import com.sun.j3d.utils.universe.*;
 8 import com.sun.j3d.utils.geometry.*;
 9 import com.sun.j3d.utils.picking.*;
10 import chapter6.*;
11 import java.applet.*;
12 import com.sun.j3d.utils.applet.MainFrame;
13
14 public class Picking extends Applet implements MouseListener{
15   public static void main(String[] args) {
16     new MainFrame(new Picking(), 640, 480);
17   }
18
19   PickCanvas pc;
20   Appearance lit = new Appearance();
21
22   public void init() {
23     // create canvas
24     GraphicsConfiguration gc =
25     SimpleUniverse.getPreferredConfiguration();
26     Canvas3D cv = new Canvas3D(gc);
27     setLayout(new BorderLayout());
28     add(cv, BorderLayout.CENTER);
29     cv.addMouseListener(this);
30     BranchGroup bg = createSceneGraph();
31     bg.compile();
32     pc = new PickCanvas(cv, bg);
33     pc.setMode(PickTool.GEOMETRY);
34     SimpleUniverse su = new SimpleUniverse(cv);
35     su.getViewingPlatform().setNominalViewingTransform();
36     su.addBranchGraph(bg);
37   }
38
39   private BranchGroup createSceneGraph() {
40     BranchGroup root = new BranchGroup();
41     TransformGroup spin = new TransformGroup();
42     spin.setCapability(TransformGroup.ALLOW_TRANSFORM_WRITE);
43     root.addChild(spin);
44     // appearance
45     Appearance wireframe = new Appearance();
46     wireframe.setPolygonAttributes(new PolygonAttributes(
47       PolygonAttributes.POLYGON_LINE,
48         PolygonAttributes.CULL_BACK, 0f));
49     wireframe.setColoringAttributes(new ColoringAttributes(
50       0f, 0f, 0f, ColoringAttributes.SHADE_FLAT));
51     lit.setMaterial(new Material());
52     // objects
53     Box box =
54     new Box(1.2f, 0.3f, 0.8f, Primitive.ENABLE_GEOMETRY_PICKING |
55       Primitive.ENABLE_APPEARANCE_MODIFY |
56       Primitive.GENERATE_NORMALS, wireframe);
57     Sphere sphere = new Sphere
58       (1f, Primitive.ENABLE_GEOMETRY_PICKING |
59       Primitive.ENABLE_APPEARANCE_MODIFY |
60       Primitive.GENERATE_NORMALS, wireframe);
61     Cylinder cylinder = new Cylinder(1.0f, 2.0f,
62       Primitive.ENABLE_GEOMETRY_PICKING |
63       Primitive.ENABLE_APPEARANCE_MODIFY |
64       Primitive.GENERATE_NORMALS, wireframe);
```

```
65      Cone cone = new Cone
66        (1.0f, 2.0f, Primitive.ENABLE_GEOMETRY_PICKING |
67         Primitive.ENABLE_APPEARANCE_MODIFY |
68         Primitive.GENERATE_NORMALS, wireframe);
69      Transform3D tr = new Transform3D();
70      tr.setScale(0.2);
71      TransformGroup tg = new TransformGroup(tr);
72      spin.addChild(tg);
73      tg.addChild(box);
74      tr.setIdentity();
75      tr.setTranslation(new Vector3f(0f,1.5f,0f));
76      TransformGroup tgSphere = new TransformGroup(tr);
77      tg.addChild(tgSphere);
78      tgSphere.addChild(sphere);
79      tr.setTranslation(new Vector3f(-1f,-1.5f,0f));
80      TransformGroup tgCylinder = new TransformGroup(tr);
81      tg.addChild(tgCylinder);
82      tgCylinder.addChild(cylinder);
83      tr.setTranslation(new Vector3f(1f,-1.5f,0f));
84      TransformGroup tgCone = new TransformGroup(tr);
85      tg.addChild(tgCone);
86      tgCone.addChild(cone);
87      Shape3D tetra = new Shape3D(new Tetrahedron(), wireframe);
88      PickTool.setCapabilities(tetra, PickTool.INTERSECT_TEST);
89      tetra.setCapability(Shape3D.ALLOW_APPEARANCE_WRITE);
90      tr = new Transform3D();
91      tr.setScale(0.12);
92      tr.setTranslation(new Vector3f(0f, 0f, -0.4f));
93      tg = new TransformGroup(tr);
94      spin.addChild(tg);
95      tg.addChild(tetra);
96      Shape3D shape = new Dodecahedron();
97      shape.setAppearance(wireframe);
98      PickTool.setCapabilities(shape, PickTool.INTERSECT_TEST);
99      shape.setCapability(Shape3D.ALLOW_APPEARANCE_WRITE);
100     tr = new Transform3D();
101     tr.setScale(0.12);
102     tr.setTranslation(new Vector3f(0f, 0f, 0.4f));
103     tg = new TransformGroup(tr);
104     spin.addChild(tg);
105     tg.addChild(shape);
106     // rotation
107     Alpha alpha = new Alpha(-1, 4000);
108     RotationInterpolator rotator =
109     new RotationInterpolator(alpha, spin);
110     BoundingSphere bounds = new BoundingSphere();
111     rotator.setSchedulingBounds(bounds);
112     spin.addChild(rotator);
113     // background and light
114     Background background = new Background(1.0f, 1.0f, 1.0f);
115     background.setApplicationBounds(bounds);
116     root.addChild(background);
117     AmbientLight light =
118     new AmbientLight(true, new Color3f(Color.red));
119     light.setInfluencingBounds(bounds);
120     root.addChild(light);
121     PointLight ptlight = new PointLight(new Color3f(Color.green),
122       new Point3f(3f,3f,3f), new Point3f(1f,0f,0f));
123     ptlight.setInfluencingBounds(bounds);
124     root.addChild(ptlight);
125     PointLight ptlight2 = new PointLight(new Color3f(Color.orange),
```

```
126        new Point3f(-2f,2f,2f), new Point3f(1f,0f,0f));
127      ptlight2.setInfluencingBounds(bounds);
128      root.addChild(ptlight2);
129      return root;
130    }
131
132    public void mouseClicked(java.awt.event.MouseEvent mouseEvent) {
133      pc.setShapeLocation(mouseEvent);
134      PickResult[] results = pc.pickAll();
135      for (int i = 0; (results != null) &&
136        (i < results.length); i++) {
137        Node node = results[i].getObject();
138        if (node instanceof Shape3D) {
139          ((Shape3D)node).setAppearance(lit);
140          System.out.println(node.toString());
141        }
142      }
143    }
144
145    public void mouseEntered(java.awt.event.MouseEvent mouseEvent) {
146    }
147
148    public void mouseExited(java.awt.event.MouseEvent mouseEvent) {
149    }
150
151    public void mousePressed(java.awt.event.MouseEvent mouseEvent) {
152    }
153
154    public void mouseReleased(java.awt.event.MouseEvent mouseEvent) {
155    }
156 }
```

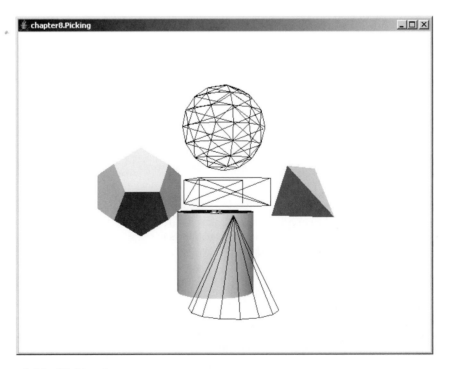

Figure 8.14   Picking demo.

Six visual objects—a sphere, a box, a cone, a cylinder, a tetrahedron, and a dodecahedron—are displayed in the wireframe form initially. When an object is clicked on with the mouse, it will change its appearance. It will become filled and illuminated by the lights.

The visual objects are created with a wireframe appearance. Permissions on each object are granted for picking and for appearance change.

A `PickCanvas` object is created (line 32) to perform the pick operation when a mouse click event is received on the `Canvas3D` object. The picked `Shape3D` object will change its appearance to enable lighting.

In the event handler `mouseClicked`, the picking shape is set according to the mouse location:

```
pc.setShapeLocation(mouseEvent);
```

The `pickAll()` method is called to retrieve all picked objects (line 134). For each of the picked `Shape3D` nodes, its appearance is changed.

Note that a primitive object may contain several `Shape3D` nodes, and a pick operation may not necessarily pick all the nodes associated with the primitive.

8.6 Head Tracking

The settings of a view depend on the location and orientation of the eyes. If the viewer's head position changes, the view needs to be adjusted accordingly. Dynamically recalculating the projection matrix and viewing matrix for a view can be a very tedious task for application programmers. It is therefore desirable for an API to offer the head-tracking feature.

Java 3D view model provides support for automatic head tracking through a set of classes including `View`, `Sensor`, `PhysicalBody`, and `PhysicalEnvironment`.

The head tracking is based on the input from certain *6DOF* (six-degrees-of-freedom) tracking devices. Java 3D provides the `InputDevice` interface to define input devices. An implementation of `InputDevice` for a specific device offers an array of `Sensor`. A `Sensor` object provides the input data from the device. The following methods of `InputDevice` initialize the device and retrieve a `Sensor` object:

6DOF

```
void initialize()
Sensor getSensor(int sensorIndex)
```

The `PhysicalEnvironment` object holds all registered input devices. To register an input device, you may use the following method of `PhysicalEnvironment`:

```
void addInputDevice(InputDevice device)
```

The `PhysicalEnvironment` object also maintains a list of associations between the 6DOF entities and sensors. For example, in a default `PhysicalEnvironment` object, the three predefined 6DOF entities—`UserHead`, `DominantHand`, and `NondominantHand`—have indices 0, 1, and 2, respectively. To assign a sensor to the `UserHead`, you may call the following method in `PhysicalEnvironment`:

```
setSensor(0, sensor);
```

The head tracking in a view is by default disabled. To *enable head tracking*, call the following method in `View`:

enable head tracking

```
view.setTrackingEnable(true);
```

There are two different mounting options for a display in a head-tracked view: room mounted and head mounted. To set this option, call the following method in `View`:

```
void setViewPolicy(int viewPolicy)
```

The following flags can be used to set room-mounted or head-mounted view policies:

```
SCREEN_VIEW
HMD_VIEW
```

In the head-mounted mode, it is also necessary to change the monoscopic view policy in the Canvas3D object from View.CYCLOPEAN_EYE_VIEW to View.LEFT_EYE_VIEW:

```
canvas.setMonoscopicViewPolicy(View.LEFT_EYE_VIEW);
```

The visual representation of the viewer itself in the scene is called the *avatar*. The Viewer object in a SimpleUniverse object provides an option to include a viewer avatar:

```
ViewerAvatar avatar = new ViewerAvatar();
su.getViewer().setAvatar(avatar);
```

The ViewerAvatar is a subclass of BranchGroup, so the shapes for the avatar can be added to it as child nodes. The location of the avatar defined here is associated with the view platform, and it may not be the actual head position. Listing 8.5 demonstrates the head-tracking feature of the Java 3D view model using a "virtual input device." The class in Listing 8.5 uses the LineAxes class in Listing 8.6. The scene contains a simple rotating color cube on a background image. The virtual input device in a separate window provides a 6DOF input to control the head position. An avatar consisting of three axis lines is also added to the scene. The avatar is visible when the head is moved behind it.

Listing 8.5 `HeadTracking.java`

```
 1 package chapter8;
 2
 3 import java.awt.*;
 4 import java.awt.event.*;
 5 import com.sun.j3d.utils.geometry.ColorCube;
 6 import com.sun.j3d.utils.universe.*;
 7 import javax.media.j3d.*;
 8 import javax.vecmath.*;
 9 import java.net.URL;
10 import java.awt.image.*;
11 import javax.imageio.*;
12 import java.applet.*;
13 import com.sun.j3d.utils.applet.MainFrame;
14
15 public class HeadTracking extends Applet {
16   public static void main(String[] args) {
17     new MainFrame(new HeadTracking(), 500, 500);
18   }
19
20   public void init() {
21     // create canvas
22     GraphicsConfiguration gc =
23     SimpleUniverse.getPreferredConfiguration();
24     Canvas3D cv = new Canvas3D(gc);
25     setLayout(new BorderLayout());
26     add(cv, BorderLayout.CENTER);
27     BranchGroup scene = createSceneGraph();
28     SimpleUniverse su = new SimpleUniverse(cv);
29     // add avatar
30     LineAxes axes = new LineAxes(0.2f);
31     Shape3D shape = new Shape3D(axes);
32     ViewerAvatar va = new ViewerAvatar();
33     va.addChild(shape);
34     su.getViewer().setAvatar(va);
```

```
35     // install the VirtualInputDevice
36     String[] args = new String[0];
37     InputDevice device = new VirtualInputDevice( args );
38     device.initialize();
39     PhysicalEnvironment pe = su.getViewer().getPhysicalEnvironment();
40     pe.addInputDevice(device);
41     pe.setSensor(0, device.getSensor(0));
42     // set up head tracking
43     su.getViewingPlatform().setNominalViewingTransform();
44     pe.setCoexistenceCenterInPworldPolicy(View.NOMINAL_HEAD);
45     View view = su.getViewer().getView();
46     view.setUserHeadToVworldEnable(true);
47     view.setCoexistenceCenteringEnable(false);
48     Screen3D screen = cv.getScreen3D();
49     Transform3D tr = new Transform3D();
50     tr.setTranslation(new Vector3d(0.1, 0.1, 0.0));
51     screen.setTrackerBaseToImagePlate(tr);
52     view.setTrackingEnable(true);
53     su.addBranchGraph(scene);
54   }
55
56   public BranchGroup createSceneGraph() {
57     BranchGroup objRoot = new BranchGroup();
58     TransformGroup objTrans = new TransformGroup();
59     objTrans.setCapability(TransformGroup.ALLOW_TRANSFORM_WRITE);
60     objRoot.addChild(objTrans);
61     objTrans.addChild(new ColorCube(0.2));
62     Transform3D yAxis = new Transform3D();
63     Alpha rotationAlpha = new Alpha(-1, Alpha.INCREASING_ENABLE,
64     0, 0,
65     4000, 0, 0,
66     0, 0, 0);
67     RotationInterpolator rotator =
68     new RotationInterpolator(rotationAlpha, objTrans, yAxis,
69     0.0f, (float) Math.PI*2.0f);
70     BoundingSphere bounds =
71     new BoundingSphere(new Point3d(0.0,0.0,0.0), 100.0);
72     rotator.setSchedulingBounds(bounds);
73     objTrans.addChild(rotator);
74     // background
75     URL url = getClass().getClassLoader().getResource
76       ("images/bg.jpg");
77     BufferedImage bi = null;
78     try {
79       bi = ImageIO.read(url);
80     } catch (Exception ex) {
81       ex.printStackTrace();
82     }
83     ImageComponent2D image =
84     new ImageComponent2D(ImageComponent2D.FORMAT_RGB, bi);
85     Background background = new Background(image);
86     background.setApplicationBounds(bounds);
87     objRoot.addChild(background);
88     return objRoot;
89   }
90 }
```

Listing 8.6 LineAxes.java

```
1 package chapter8;
2
```

```
3 import javax.media.j3d.*;
4 import javax.vecmath.*;
5
6 public class LineAxes extends LineArray{
7   public LineAxes(float len) {
8     super(6, LineArray.COORDINATES | LineArray.COLOR_3);
9     setCoordinate(0, new Point3f(-len,0f,0f));
10    setCoordinate(1, new Point3f(len,0,0f));
11    setCoordinate(2, new Point3f(0f,-len,0f));
12    setCoordinate(3, new Point3f(0f,len,0f));
13    setCoordinate(4, new Point3f(0f,0f,-len));
14    setCoordinate(5, new Point3f(0f,0f,len));
15    Color3f c0 = new Color3f(0f, 0f, 0f);
16    Color3f c1 = new Color3f(1f, 0f, 0f);
17    Color3f c2 = new Color3f(0f, 1f, 0f);
18    Color3f c3 = new Color3f(0f, 0f, 1f);
19    setColor(0, c0);
20    setColor(1, c1);
21    setColor(2, c0);
22    setColor(3, c2);
23    setColor(4, c0);
24    setColor(5, c3);
25  }
26 }
```

To demonstrate the view with head tracking, it is necessary to have a head-tracking device. A VirtualInputDevice class (which depends on three other classes: PositionControls, RotationControls, and WheelControls) is included in the demo programs of the Java 3D package. It is an implementation of the InputDevice interface that provides 6DOF input through a separate control window. The control window, as shown in Figure 8.15, allows movements in three directions and rotations about three axes. The VirtualInputDevice is used in this example to avoid dependency on special hardware devices (line 37).

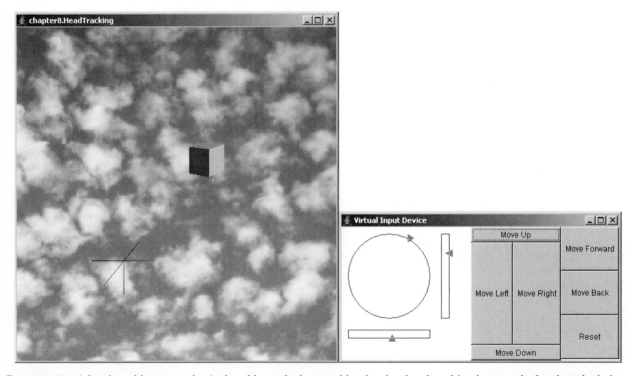

Figure 8.15 A head-tracking example. A virtual input device provides the simulated tracking input to the head-tracked view.

The scene graph is shown in Figure 8.16. The graphics content branch contains a rotating cube on an image-based background. The view branch is constructed with Simple-Universe. A ViewerAvatar is added to help visualize the effects of head tracking (lines 29–34). The avatar is a set of coordinate axes defined by the geometry class LineAxes. LineAxes is a subclass of LineArray and it defines three colored line segments.

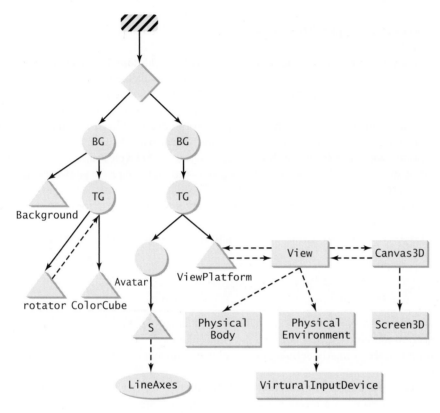

FIGURE 8.16   The scene graph for the head-tracking example.

An instance of VirtualInputDevice is added to the PhysicalEnvironment (line 40). The first Sensor object from the VirtualInputDevice is retrieved and assigned as the sensor for the UserHead entity in PhysicalEnvironment (line 41). The head tracking is enabled by calling the setTrackingEnable method in View (line 52).

When head tracking is enabled, the origin of the default screen coordinate system is located at the lower left corner of the physical display. This is usually inconvenient. To change the origin, a translation is performed by calling the method setTrackerBaseToImagePlate (Transform3D) in Screen3D (line 51).

KEY CLASSES AND METHODS

- **javax.media.j3d.View** A class encapsulating a 3D view.
- **javax.media.j3d.ViewPlatform** A leaf-node class representing the presence of a view in the virtual world.
- **javax.media.j3d.Canvas3D** An AWT component representing the drawing surface of Java 3D.
- **javax.media.j3d.Screen3D** A class encapsulating the physical display screen.
- **javax.media.j3d.PhysicalBody** A class encapsulating the body of the user.

- **javax.media.j3d.PhysicalEnvironment** A class encapsulating the physical environment, including the sensor input devices.
- **javax.media.j3d.InputDevice** An interface defining an input device for tracking.
- **javax.media.j3d.Sensor** A class encapsulating tracking-device input values.
- **com.sun.j3d.util.universe.ViewerAvatar** A BranchGroup class for avatar objects attached to a Viewer in SimpleUniverse.
- **javax.media.j3d.PickShape** The root class of a family of classes for the picking shapes.
- **javax.media.j3d.BranchGroup.pickAll(PickShape)** A method to pick all child objects that intersect the pick shape. It is also available in Locale.
- **javax.media.j3d.BranchGroup.pickAny(PickShape)** A method to pick any child object that intersects the pick shape. It is also available in Locale.
- **javax.media.j3d.BranchGroup.pickSorted(PickShape)** A method to pick all child objects that intersect the pick shape. It is also available in Locale.
- **javax.media.j3d.BranchGroup.pickClosest(PickShape)** A method to pick the closest child object that intersects the pick shape. It is also available in Locale.
- **com.sun.j3d.utils.picking.PickCanvas** A utility class for performing picking based on canvas coordinates.
- **javax.media.j3d.View.setTrackingEnable(boolean)** A method to enable head tracking.

KEY TERMS

view volume The portion of the virtual space that is visible in a view.

projection matrix A matrix defining the view volume.

viewing matrix A matrix defining the location and orientation of a view in the virtual space.

perspective projection A projection in which all projectors pass through a fixed point.

parallel projection A projection in which all projectors are parallel.

vrp View reference point, eye, or viewpoint. A point representing the eye position or center of projection.

view center A center location defining the direction in which the eye is looking.

view up direction A direction that is considered up from the viewer's perspective.

FOV Field of view. An angle for the visible portion of a view.

front clip plane The front plane of a view frustum.

back clip plane The back plane of a view frustum.

aspect ratio The ratio of height and width for an image.

compatibility mode A special Java 3D view mode that is highly compatible with traditional OpenGL view settings.

6DOF Six degrees of freedom. A device that provides 3D location and orientation information.

avatar A visual representation of the viewer itself in a 3D scene.

CHAPTER SUMMARY

- In this chapter, you learn the concepts of 3D views. A view defines the geometric aspects of rendering a virtual world scene to a 2D image. There are two sets of attributes for the definition of a view: those related to view projection and volume, and those related to the view positioning.

■ The projection matrix captures the projection and view-volume settings of a view. Two types of projections are commonly used in computer graphics: perspective projection and parallel projection. Both of them can be represented as matrices with homogenous coordinates and projective transformations. The projection matrix defines a projective transform that maps the specified view volume to a canonical volume such as a cube centered at the origin.

■ The viewing matrix represents the camera's position and orientation in the virtual world. It is typically specified with a point for the camera's location, a point at which the camera is looking, and an up direction for the camera. The viewing matrix defines a transform that maps the camera from the specified position to a canonical position.

■ Java 3D provides two different view modes: the compatibility mode and the standard noncompatibility mode. The compatibility mode offers a simple way to set up a static camera-based view similar to lower-level APIs such as OpenGL. The standard mode provides more powerful features such as supports for head-mount cameras and head tracking.

■ Picking is a partial inversion of the viewing process. Picking refers to the selection of virtual world objects based on the specifications of certain pick shapes. A typical application of picking is to allow the user to select objects in a rendered image.

■ Java 3D contains basic support for picking in scene graphs through the pick shape classes, pick methods in `Locale` and `BranchGroup`, and the `BranchGroupPath` class for pick results. Java 3D utility classes provide convenient classes to simplify common picking operations such as picking through mouse actions on a canvas.

■ Head tracking is integrated in the Java 3D view model. When enabled, the head-tracking feature automatically calculates the appropriate view matrices based on the head-position information from input devices.

REVIEW QUESTIONS

8.1 If a view frustum has a field of view $\pi/4$, and the two points $(-1, 0, 0)$ and $(1, 0, 0)$ are on the two horizontal boundaries of the frustum, find the viewpoint. (This is exactly the transform performed by `setNominalViewTransform()`).

8.2 Derive a matrix for the parallel projection along the direction $(1, 0, 1)$ to the xy-plane.

8.3 Derive a matrix for the perspective projection with vrp at the origin and the view plate perpendicular to z-axis centered at $(0, 0, 1)$.

8.4 Find the projection matrix for the view volume specified by the following method call:

```
frustum(-3,3,-2,2,1,10)
```

8.5 Find the projection matrix for the view volume specified by the following method call:

```
frustum(-2,2,-1,1,2,4)
```

8.6 Find the projection matrix for the view volume specified by the following method call:

```
perspective(Math.PI/3,1.5,1,10)
```

8.7 Find the projection matrix for the view volume specified by the following method call:

```
ortho(-3,3,-2,2,1,10)
```

8.8 Find the projection matrix for the view volume specified by the following method call:

```
ortho(-2,2,-1,1,2,4)
```

8.9 Find the viewing matrix for changing the view up direction to $(1, 1, 0)$.

8.10 Find the viewing matrix specified by the following method call:

```
Point3d eye = new Point3d(0,0,0);
Point3d look = new Point3d(0,0,1);
Vector3d up = new Vector3d(0,-1,0);
lookAt(eye, look, up);
```

8.11 Find the viewing matrix specified by the following method call:

```
Point3d eye = new Point3d(0,0,-1);
Point3d look = new Point3d(0,0,0);
Vector3d up = new Vector3d(1,0,0);
lookAt(eye, look, up);
```

8.12 Is it possible to set the front clip distance to 0?

PROGRAMMING EXERCISES

8.1 Write a Java 3D program to display a rotating `ColorCube` using a `SimpleUniverse` object. Modify the view platform transform to move the `ViewPlatform` to $(0, 0, 3)$.

8.2 Modify the program in Listing 8.1 to use a parallel projection in the view.

8.3 Use a `SimpleUniverse` object to set up a view and to display a sphere. Move the sphere close to the view until it is partially truncated by the front clipping plane.

8.4 Write a program to examine the matrix generated by the `lookAt` method of the `Transform3D` class. Allow users to enter the parameters for the method and print the resulting matrix.

8.5 Write a program to examine the matrix generated by the `perspective` method of the `Transform3D` class. Allow users to enter the parameters for the method and print the resulting matrix.

8.6 Write a program to examine the matrix generated by the `frustum` method of the `Transform3D` class. Allow users to enter the parameters for the method and print the resulting matrix.

8.7 Write a program to examine the matrix generated by the `ortho` method of the `Transform3D` class. Allow users to enter the parameters for the method and print the resulting matrix.

8.8 Write a Java 3D program with a compatibility-mode view. Use a perspective projection with a field of view $\pi/3$. Place the view at $(0, 0, 1)$ looking down the z-axis. Display an `Axes` object defined in Chapter 7.

8.9 Write a program with two different views. One view is positioned at $(0, 0, 2)$ looking along the negative z-axis with the y-axis as up direction. The other view is positioned at $(0, 0, -2)$ looking along the z-axis with the negative y-axis as up direction. Place a rotating 3D text near the origin.

8.10 Write a program with four views with different fields of view. All views are positioned at $(0, 0, 2)$ looking along the negative z-axis with the y-axis as up direction.

The fields of view are set to $\pi/8$, $\pi/4$, $\pi/2$, and $3\pi/4$. Place a 3D text and an `Axes` object (from Chapter 7) in the scene.

8.11 Construct a scene with a sphere and a cone, each attached to a `TransformGroup` node. Implement a picking operation with a `PickCanvas`. If an object is picked by a mouse click, it will rotate by $\pi/4$.

8.12 Construct a scene with two spheres. Implement a picking operation with `Pick Canvas`. If a sphere is picked by a mouse click, it changes to a cube. (*Hint:* You may use `Switch` nodes.)

8.13 Modify Listing 8.5 to create a head-mounted head-tracking view.

CHAPTER 9

LIGHTING AND TEXTURING

Objectives

- To understand lighting models.
- To identify point lights, directional lights, and spotlights.
- To identify material properties.
- To understand Java 3D coloring modes.
- To create lit scenes with lights, surface normals, and materials.
- To construct and apply fog nodes for atmospheric attenuation and depth cueing.
- To apply 2D texture mapping and texture cube mapping.
- To understand texture-coordinates generation.

9.1 Introduction

Geometry defines the shapes and metrics of visual objects. Colors, textures, and other appearance details constitute other important aspects of the rendering. Often the most computationally intensive tasks of graphics rendering are related to achieving high-quality, photorealistic appearance of the visual objects.

Various methods of defining appearance exist, with different levels of rendering quality and computational demand. Some of the simplest ways to render visual objects include:

- Draw the vertices of the objects only.

- Draw the outlines of the objects only (wireframe mode).

- Use a single color for all surfaces of an object.

- Use flat colors for faces of an object.

These simple coloring approaches are relatively easy to implement. However, they usually do not provide the quality that can match the real images seen by human eyes or captured by photography.

In order to create photorealistic 3D graphics renderings, more sophisticated lighting and shading models are needed. Illumination and texture models are computer graphics tools to enhance photorealism of the renderings.

A real image seen by an eye is formed by light energy emitted and reflected from the visual objects of a scene. The transmission and interaction of lights in an environment can be very complex. Light sources have different characteristics. Objects have different characteristics in reflection and refraction. Lights reflected off objects may travel complex paths in the scene.

To model such a complex system exactly in computers is usually not feasible. Different approximation methods are therefore necessary in order to implement a practical graphics system. A computer graphics system usually applies simplified illumination models to achieve a reasonably realistic rendering of the scene. The Phong illumination model is widely used. It incorporates light characteristics, geometry structures, and material properties to obtain effective and efficient lighting calculations.

Commonly used techniques for enhancing rendering quality also include atmospheric attenuation and texture mapping. An artificial fog is used to blend the distant objects in atmospheric attenuation and depth cueing. It creates a foggy appearance. The texture-mapping technique maps images to surfaces of visual objects. It has the advantage of creating a great deal of surface detail without complex modeling.

9.2 Lights

Lights provide the sources for illuminating the graphics objects in a virtual world. Lights have color attributes, positions, directions, and other characteristics depending on their specific types. There are typically four types of lights in graphics systems: ambient lights, directional lights, point lights, and spotlights.

ambient light

An *ambient light* is uniform in all directions and locations. It generally provides a simplified representation of the numerous and weak interobject reflections existing in the real-world scene (Figure 9.1).

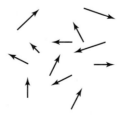

FIGURE 9.1   An ambient light represents weak random reflections.

A directional light has a fixed direction. All light rays travel along this direction. A *direc-* directional light
tional light does not have a specific location, although it can be conveniently regarded as being
located at infinity. It is a good model for a distant light source such as the sun (Figure 9.2).

FIGURE 9.2   A directional light emits parallel light rays.

A point light has a location in the virtual world. It emits in all directions (Figure 9.3). A point light
point light typically has an attenuation that describes the decrease of the intensity as the distance from the light increases. The attenuation is usually expressed as a coefficient (a function
of distance) from 0.0 to 1.0 multiplied on the original intensity of the light.

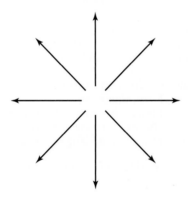

FIGURE 9.3   A point light has a specific location and emits light rays in all directions.

A *spotlight* is similar to a point light, but the directions of its emission are restricted. A spotlight
spotlight radiates light rays only in a focused, cone-shaped region (Figure 9.4). Besides the
attenuation associated with the distance to the light, as in a point light, a spotlight may also
define an attenuation as a light ray moves away from the central direction of the cone.

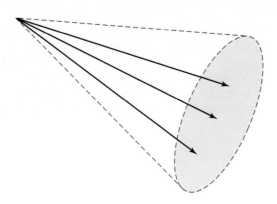

FIGURE 9.4   A spotlight emits light rays in a cone-shaped region.

Java 3D offers a family of `Light` classes for different types of lights described above. The `Light` class hierarchy is shown in Figure 9.5.

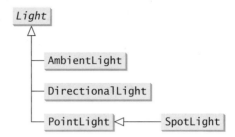

FIGURE 9.5 The `Light` classes.

Some of the constructors for `Light` classes are listed below:

```
AmbientLight()
AmbientLight(boolean lightOn, Color3f color)
AmbientLight(Color3f color)
DirectionalLight()
DirectionalLight(boolean lightOn, Color3f color, Vector3f direction)
DirectionalLight(Color3f color, Vector3f direction)
PointLight()
PointLight(boolean lightOn, Color3f color,
Point3f position, Point3f attenuation)
PointLight(Color3f color, Point3f position, Point3f attenuation)
SpotLight()
SpotLight(boolean lightOn, Color3f color,
Point3f position, Point3f attenuation,
    Vector3f direction, float spreadAngle, float concentration)
SpotLight(Color3f color, Point3f position, Point3f attenuation,
    Vector3f direction, float spreadAngle, float concentration)
```

A light can be turned on or off. Besides the flag in the constructors, the on/off state can be set by calling the following method:

void `setEnable(`**boolean** `state)`

attenuation The *attenuation* of `PointLight` and `SpotLight` due to the distance d to the light is defined with a quadratic model.

$$A(d) = 1/(a_0 + a_1 d + a_2 d^2)$$

The attenuation can be defined with constructors or set with the method:

void `setAttenuation(Point3f attenuation)`

The `Point3f` parameter specifies the coefficients (a_0, a_1, a_2) for the attenuation. For example, the coefficients $(1, 0, 0)$ represent no attenuation for the light, $A(d) = 1$. The coefficients $(1, 1, 0)$ represent the attenuation function $A(d) = 1/(1 + d)$, so at 1 meter away from the light the attenuation function has value 0.5 and at 4 meters away the attenuation is 0.2.

The attenuation due to the angle between a light ray and the central direction in a `SpotLight` is defined by an exponential function of the cosine value of the angle

$$A(\theta) = \cos^n \theta$$

The function has the value 1 when the angle is 0, so there is no attenuation at the central direction. The parameter n is the concentration exponent that takes a value from 0 to 128. It can be set by constructors or the method

void `setConcentration(`**float** `concentration)`

The value $A(\theta)$ decreases as the angle θ increases. If the concentration exponent is large, this decrease of $A(\theta)$ will be faster, resulting in a more concentrated spotlight. If $n = 0$, there will be no attenuation as the angle increases.

For the efficiency of rendering, a `Light` object has an associated influence bound. A visual object is affected by a `Light` object only if it is located within the influence bound of the light. For each light created, it is necessary to set an appropriate influence bound to avoid an unnecessarily lengthy rendering process. The following method sets the influence bound:

void setInfluencingBounds(Bound bounds)

The influence bound can also be specified with a bounding leaf node

void setInfluencingBoundingLeaf(BoundingLeaf bounds)

Listing 9.1 illustrates the effects of different types of lights. The program displays a sphere illuminated with different light sources (Figure 9.6). A list of checkboxes for the light types can be used to individually turn each type of lights on or off.

Listing 9.1 TestLights.java

```
 1 package chapter9;
 2
 3 import javax.vecmath.*;
 4 import java.awt.*;
 5 import java.awt.event.*;
 6 import javax.media.j3d.*;
 7 import com.sun.j3d.utils.universe.*;
 8 import com.sun.j3d.utils.geometry.*;
 9 import java.applet.*;
10 import com.sun.j3d.utils.applet.MainFrame;
11
12 public class TestLights extends Applet implements ItemListener {
13   public static void main(String[] args) {
14     new MainFrame(new TestLights(), 640, 480);
15   }
16
17   AmbientLight aLight;
18   DirectionalLight dLight;
19   PointLight pLight;
20   SpotLight sLight;
21   SpotLight sLight2;
22
23   public void init() {
24     // create canvas
25     GraphicsConfiguration gc =
26       SimpleUniverse.getPreferredConfiguration();
27     Canvas3D cv = new Canvas3D(gc);
28     setLayout(new BorderLayout());
29     add(cv, BorderLayout.CENTER);
30
31     Panel menu = new Panel();
32     menu.setLayout(new GridLayout(1,4));
33     add(menu, BorderLayout.SOUTH);
34     Checkbox mi = new Checkbox("Ambient", true);
35     menu.add(mi);
36     mi.addItemListener(this);
37     mi = new Checkbox("Directional", true);
38     menu.add(mi);
39     mi.addItemListener(this);
40     mi = new Checkbox("Point", true);
```

```
41      menu.add(mi);
42      mi.addItemListener(this);
43      mi = new Checkbox("Spot", true);
44      menu.add(mi);
45      mi.addItemListener(this);
46
47      SimpleUniverse su = new SimpleUniverse(cv, 2);
48      su.getViewingPlatform().setNominalViewingTransform();
49      BranchGroup bg = createSceneGraph(su.getViewingPlatform().
50        getMultiTransformGroup().getTransformGroup(0));
51      bg.compile();
52      su.addBranchGraph(bg);
53    }
54
55    Appearance ap;
56    private BranchGroup createSceneGraph(TransformGroup vtg) {
57      BranchGroup root = new BranchGroup();
58      // object
59      ap = new Appearance();
60      ap.setMaterial(new Material());
61      Sphere shape = new Sphere
62        (0.5f, Sphere.GENERATE_NORMALS, 150, ap);
63      root.addChild(shape);
64      // view rotator
65      Alpha alpha = new Alpha(-1, 4000);
66      RotationInterpolator rotator = new RotationInterpolator
67        (alpha, vtg);
68      BoundingSphere bounds = new BoundingSphere();
69      bounds.setRadius(2);
70      rotator.setSchedulingBounds(bounds);
71      root.addChild(rotator);
72      // background and lights
73      Background background = new Background(0.5f, 0.5f, 0.5f);
74      background.setApplicationBounds(bounds);
75      root.addChild(background);
76      aLight = new AmbientLight(true, new Color3f(Color.red));
77      aLight.setInfluencingBounds(bounds);
78      aLight.setCapability(Light.ALLOW_STATE_WRITE);
79      root.addChild(aLight);
80      dLight = new DirectionalLight(
81      new Color3f(Color.green), new Vector3f(0f,1f,0f));
82      dLight.setCapability(Light.ALLOW_STATE_WRITE);
83      dLight.setInfluencingBounds(bounds);
84      root.addChild(dLight);
85      pLight = new PointLight(
86      new Color3f(Color.white), new Point3f(-0.7f,0.7f,0f),
87        new Point3f(1f,0f,0f));
88      pLight.setCapability(Light.ALLOW_STATE_WRITE);
89      pLight.setInfluencingBounds(bounds);
90      root.addChild(pLight);
91      sLight = new SpotLight(
92      new Color3f(Color.blue), new Point3f(0.7f,0.7f,0.7f),
93        new Point3f(1f,0f,0f),
94        new Vector3f(-0.7f,-0.7f,-0.7f), (float)(Math.PI/6.0), 0f);
95      sLight.setCapability(Light.ALLOW_STATE_WRITE);
96      sLight.setInfluencingBounds(bounds);
97      root.addChild(sLight);
98      sLight2 = new SpotLight(
99      new Color3f(Color.orange), new Point3f(0.7f,0.7f,-0.7f),
100       new Point3f(1f,0f,0f),
```

```
101        new Vector3f(-0.7f,-0.7f,0.7f), (float)(Math.PI/12.0), 128f);
102      sLight2.setCapability(Light.ALLOW_STATE_WRITE);
103      sLight2.setInfluencingBounds(bounds);
104      root.addChild(sLight2);
105      return root;
106    }
107
108    public void itemStateChanged(ItemEvent itemEvent) {
109      Checkbox cmi = (Checkbox)itemEvent.getSource();
110      String label = cmi.getLabel();
111      boolean state = cmi.getState();
112      if("Ambient".equals(label)) {
113        aLight.setEnable(state);
114      } else if ("Directional".equals(label)) {
115        dLight.setEnable(state);
116      } else if ("Point".equals(label)) {
117        pLight.setEnable(state);
118      } else if ("Spot".equals(label)) {
119        sLight.setEnable(state);
120        sLight2.setEnable(state);
121      }
122      cmi.setState(state);
123    }
124 }
```

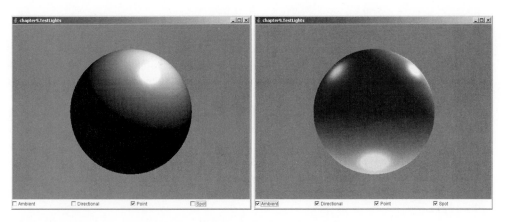

FIGURE 9.6   The effects of different types of lights. Left: a point light only.
Right: all four types of lights.

The scene graph of the program is shown in Figure 9.7. Four different types of lights (one
AmbientLight, one DirectionalLight, one PointLight, and two SpotLights) are
created to illuminate the scene (lines 76–104). The AmbientLight has a red color. The
DirectionalLight is green and has the direction (0, 1, 0), so its light rays are emitted
upward. The PointLight is white and is located at $(-0.7, 0.7, 0)$ with no attenuation. The
first SpotLight is blue and is located at $(0.7, 0.7, 0.7)$ with no attenuation related to the distance. It points at the direction $(-0.7, -0.7, -0.7)$ with a spread angle $\pi/6$. The concentration exponent is set to 0, so there is no attenuation related to the angle. The second
SpotLight is orange and is located at $(0.7, 0.7, -0.7)$ with no attenuation related to the distance. It points at the direction $(-0.7, -0.7, 0.7)$ with a spread angle $\pi/12$. The concentration exponent is set to 128, so the light is highly concentrated along its main axis. All the
lights use the same Bounds object for their influencing bound. The bounding sphere has a
radius of 2 to include all relevant objects. A gray background object is added using the same
bounding sphere.

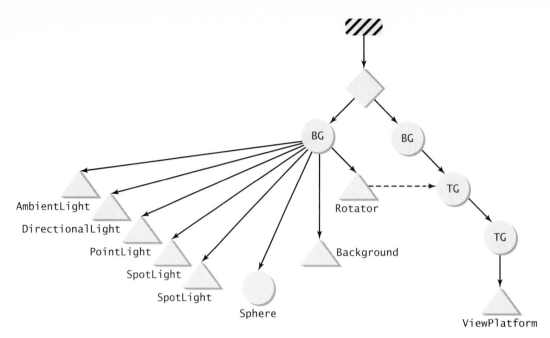

FIGURE 9.7 The scene graph for the example.

The visual object in the scene is a sphere of radius 0.5 (line 61). The number of divisions for the sphere is set to 150 to obtain a high-quality sphere. The sphere is centered at the origin. To support illumination the sphere has surface normals generated and includes, in its Appearance, a Material object.

At the bottom of the window, a list of four checkboxes of the class Checkbox is created: Ambient, Directional, Point, and Spot. The checkboxes turn the corresponding lights on or off. In order to switch the lights in the live scene graph, all the lights have their capability bit ALLOW_STATE_WRITE set. The class TestLights implements the ItemListener interface and listens to the item changes. When a menu item is selected, the state of the light is toggled and the check mark on the menu item reflects the state of the light (lines 109–122).

The view is rotated by an interpolator to show the illumination of the sphere by the lights from different angles. The directional light illuminates the bottom portion of the sphere. The point light and two spotlights cause three different reflection spots on the upper portion of the sphere.

9.3 Illumination Models

A truly accurate model of light reflection would be extremely complicated and impractical for computer graphics implementations. A common practice in graphics is to select computationally efficient models that provide a good approximation of visual realism. The classical Phong illumination model widely used in computer graphics is an example of such attempts to balance computational efficiency and rendering quality.

The illumination of a point on a surface is illustrated in Figure 9.8. The surface normal N at the point is a line perpendicular to the tangent plane at the point. L is the direction of the light source. The angle between L and N is θ. The direction R mirrors L and the angle between R and N is also θ. V is the view direction. The angle between V and R is denoted by α.

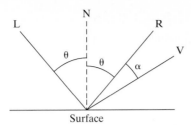

FIGURE 9.8 Geometry of light reflection.

Typically three types of reflection are considered: ambient, diffuse, and specular.

The *ambient reflection* is the response to ambient light sources. It is uniform in all direc-   ambient reflection
tions and is independent of the surface normal.

The *diffuse reflection* represents the large number of small reflections on a surface that is   diffused reflection
not perfectly reflective. Its intensity depends on the incidence angle θ, but does not depend on
the angle to the viewer. The intensity is the same when viewed from any direction. For most
visual objects, the diffuse reflection is a major portion of all reflections and is the one that
defines our usual notion of the object color.

The *specular reflection* represents the concentrated reflection around the direction R on a   specular reflection
shining surface. Its intensity depends on the angle α as well as θ. The reflection is maximal at
the direction R and decreases as the angle α increases.

In the *Phong model*, the intensity of the point is given by the following illumination equation: Phong model

$$I = I_a k_a + I_p k_d \cos \theta + I_p k_s \cos^n \alpha$$

In the equation, I_a and I_p denote the light intensities from ambient light and a pointlike light
source, respectively. The attenuation of light is already considered in I_p. The reflection coefficients k_a, k_d, and k_s correspond to the ambient reflection, diffuse reflection, and specular reflection, respectively. The coefficients are determined by the material properties of the
surface. The quantity n is the specular reflection exponent that is also determined by the
material. Larger exponents result in a more focused highlight.

The illumination equation above can be applied to each color wavelength. Therefore, the
coefficients k_a, k_d, k_s may vary depending on the color. Of course, calculating the illumination equation for a continuous spectrum of colors is not practical. The common practice is to
use a color model such as the RGB model. The illumination equation is applied to each component of the model (red, green, blue in the RGB model).

In the case of multiple light sources, the contributions from every light are summed to
obtain the total intensity.

The Phong illumination model is a local illumination model. It renders the visual objects
individually without considering the interactions among them. For example, reflections of
other objects and shadows are not generated. Advanced global models and techniques such as
radiosity and *ray tracing* can provide solutions to these questions, but these methods are also   radiosity
computationally much more expensive than the Phong model.   ray tracing

From the equation of the lighting model it is easy to see that the appearance of a visual
object depends on its material properties that define the reactions to lights as well as the
geometry of the object and light sources.

The material properties are primarily defined by the *reflection coefficients* k_a, k_d, k_s. These   reflection coefficients
coefficients are dependent upon the color wavelength. When using a color model, the coeffi-
cients are specified on each component of the color model. For example, in an RGB model, k_d
may be specified by three numbers (0.9, 0.2, 0.0). This indicates that in the diffused reflection
the material will reflect most of red, a little green, and no blue, so the visual object will appear
to be mostly red. The specular *shininess exponent* n is also a material property, but it is typi-   shininess exponent
cally specified as a fixed constant independent of the color.

9.4 Java 3D Lighting Models

Java 3D supports the Phong illumination model. A visual object is rendered according to this model when it is lit. Java 3D uses an RGB color model for rendering. The illumination equation is applied to each of the three color components.

The `Material` node-component class represents the material properties of the visual objects. The ambient, diffuse, and specular coefficients are represented in the class using an RGB color model. The specular reflection exponent n corresponds to the shininess in the `Material` class. The `Material` class also contains an emissive coefficient that defines the light emitted by the object itself instead of external light sources. The following is a partial list of methods for setting various parameters:

```
void setAmbientColor(Color3f color)
void setAmbientColor(float r, float g, float b)
void setDiffuseColor(Color3f color)
void setDiffuseColor(float r, float g, float b)
void setDiffuseColor(float r, float g, float b, float a)
void setSpecularColor(Color3f color)
void setSpecularColor(float r, float g, float b)
void setEmissiveColor(Color3f color)
void setEmissiveColor(float r, float g, float b)
```

There are three different coloring specifications for a visual object: the vertex color specification in its `Geometry`, the `ColoringAttributes` in `Appearance`, and the lighting model. The selection of the coloring method for a particular object is determined as follows:

coloring rules

1. If the vertex colors are specified in the geometry of the object, they are used to define the object coloring.

2. If a `Material` node component is defined for the object, the object is lit. The coloring of the object is defined by the lighting model.

3. If the `ColoringAttributes` is defined for the appearance of the object, its color is used for the coloring of the object.

4. Otherwise, the object is colored white.

The decision for the coloring mode is made individually for each object. It is allowed to have both lit and unlit objects in the same scene. For example, the following code fragment creates four objects with different coloring options:

```
// vertex color specified in geometry
TriangleArray geom = new TriangleArray(3,
  TriangleArray.COORDINATES|TriangleArray.COLOR_3);
Point3f[] coords = {new Point3f(1,0,0),
new Point3f(0,1,0), new Point3f(0,0,1)};
geom.setCoordinates(coords);
Color3f[] colors = {new Color3f(1,0,0),
new Color3f(0,1,0), new Color3f(0,0,1)};
geom.setColors(colors);
Shape3D shape1 = new Shape3D(geom);

// lit object
TriangleArray geom2 = new TriangleArray(3,
  TriangleArray.COORDINATES|TriangleArray.NORMAL);
geom2.setCoordinates(coords);
Appearance appear = new Appearance();
Material material = new Material();
appear.setMaterial(material);
Shape3D shape2 = new Shape3D(geom2, appear);

// coloring attributes in appearance
Appearance appear3 = new Appearance();
```

```
ColoringAttributes coloring = new ColoringAttributes(
  new Color3f(1f,0,0), ColoringAttributes.SHADE_FLAT);
appear3.setColoringAttributes(coloring);
Shape3D shape3 = new Shape3D(geom2, appear3);

// no coloring specification
Shape3D shape4 = new Shape3D(geom2);
```

The Shape3D object shape1 has a geometry that contains the vertex color definition. Therefore, the specified vertex colors will be used for rendering. The object shape2 has no vertex color definition in its geometry. Instead, normals are defined at the vertices. The appearance of shape2 contains a Material object. Consequently shape2 will be lit and its coloring will be derived from the lighting model. The object shape3 uses the same geometry as shape2 with no vertex colors, but it is not lit. Its appearance contains a ColoringAttributes object specifying a red color. Therefore, shape3 will be colored red. The object shape4 contains no vertex color definition, no Material object, and no ColoringAttributes object. It will be colored white.

To enable lighting for visual objects in a Java 3D program, therefore, we need to perform the following basic steps:

- Place lights in the scene graph.

- Provide surface normals for the geometry and do not set vertex colors.

- Set material for the appearance.

The following code segment illustrates these steps:

```
// add a light
Light light = new PointLight();
light.setInfluencingBounds(new BoundingSphere());
root.addChild(light);

// construct appearance with material
Appearance appearance = new Appearance();
Material material = new Material();
appearance.setMaterial(material);

// add a box with normals
Box box = new Box(1f, 1f, 1f, Box.GENERATE_NORMALS, appearance);
root.add(box);
```

Listing 9.2 shows the effects of different illumination parameter settings. It displays eight spheres with different material properties illuminated by a point light.

Listing 9.2 Lighting.java

```
 1 package chapter9;
 2
 3 import javax.vecmath.*;
 4 import java.awt.*;
 5 import java.awt.event.*;
 6 import javax.media.j3d.*;
 7 import com.sun.j3d.utils.universe.*;
 8 import com.sun.j3d.utils.geometry.*;
 9 import java.applet.*;
10 import com.sun.j3d.utils.applet.MainFrame;
11
12 public class Lighting extends Applet {
13   public static void main(String[] args) {
14     new MainFrame(new Lighting(), 640, 480);
15   }
16
```

```
17   public void init() {
18     // create canvas
19     GraphicsConfiguration gc =
20       SimpleUniverse.getPreferredConfiguration();
21     Canvas3D cv = new Canvas3D(gc);
22     setLayout(new BorderLayout());
23     add(cv, BorderLayout.CENTER);
24     BranchGroup bg = createSceneGraph();
25     bg.compile();
26     SimpleUniverse su = new SimpleUniverse(cv);
27     su.getViewingPlatform().setNominalViewingTransform();
28     su.addBranchGraph(bg);
29   }
30
31   private BranchGroup createSceneGraph() {
32     BranchGroup root = new BranchGroup();
33     // object
34     Vector3f pos = new Vector3f(0.5f,0f,0f);
35     Transform3D rotation = new Transform3D();
36     rotation.rotZ(Math.PI/4);
37     for (int i = 0; i < 8; i++) {
38       Node shape = createShape
39         (pos, 0.2f, .5f, (float)Math.pow(1.7,i));
40       root.addChild(shape);
41       rotation.transform(pos);
42     }
43     // lights
44     BoundingSphere bounds = new BoundingSphere();
45     PointLight pLight = new PointLight(new Color3f(Color.white),
46       new Point3f(0f,0f,1f/(float)Math.tan(Math.PI/8)),
47       new Point3f(1f,0f,0f));
48     pLight.setInfluencingBounds(bounds);
49     root.addChild(pLight);
50     return root;
51   }
52
53   private Node createShape(Vector3f pos,
54   float size, float spec, float shine) {
55     Material mat = new Material();
56     mat.setDiffuseColor(0.5f,0.5f,1f);
57     mat.setSpecularColor(spec, spec, spec);
58     mat.setShininess(shine);
59     Appearance ap = new Appearance();
60     ap.setMaterial(mat);
61     Sphere shape = new Sphere(size, Sphere.GENERATE_NORMALS, 50, ap);
62     Transform3D tr = new Transform3D();
63     tr.setTranslation(pos);
64     TransformGroup tg = new TransformGroup(tr);
65     tg.addChild(shape);
66     return tg;
67   }
68 }
```

The rendered scene of the program is shown in Figure 9.9 and the scene graph for the program in Figure 9.10. Eight spheres with different shininess exponents are placed circularly around the z-axis. The locations of the spheres are calculated with a successive rotation of $\pi/4$ about the z-axis. The position of the first sphere is (0.5, 0, 0). A `Transform3D` object is used to perform the rotations on the position vector.

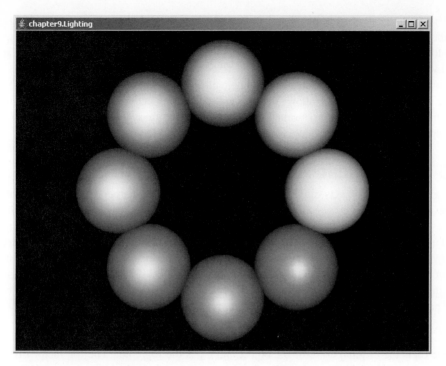

FIGURE 9.9   Material properties.

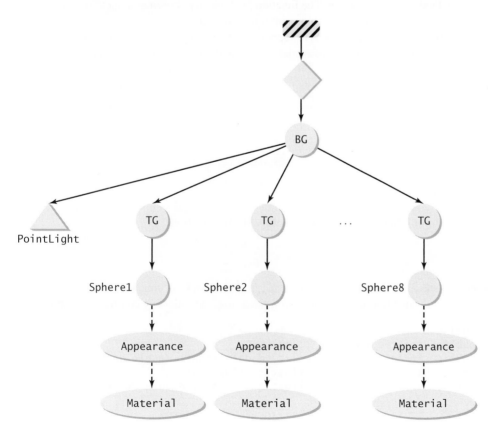

FIGURE 9.10   Scene graph.

The method `createShape` (line 53) creates a branch of the scene graph consisting of a `TransformGroup` and a sphere. The `TransformGroup` node moves the sphere to the specified location. The sphere appearance has a `Material` object with the shininess set to a specified value. The diffused reflection is set to a fixed value.

To provide equal illumination and viewing to all spheres, a point light is placed on the z-axis at the eye position. This also allows the focused specular reflection visible when the shininess exponent is large. The shininess values of the eight spheres are set to 1.7^i, $i = 0, 1, \ldots, 7$. The first sphere has the smallest value, 1, and the last sphere has the largest value, 41.

9.5 Atmospheric Attenuation and Depth Cueing

In real-life images, objects closer to the viewer appear to be sharper, clearer, and of higher intensity than objects far away. This is particularly apparent on a foggy day. The phenomenon is the result of atmospheric attenuation. This suggests a technique to improve realism. In computer graphics, the atmospheric attenuation effects can be simulated with a relatively efficient method known as *depth cueing*. Depth cueing blends the objects with the background color. The amount of background color used in the blending is an increasing function of the distance. More generally the fog color—the color used to blend the objects—can be arbitrarily specified.

depth cueing

The final color of a rendered point is given by

$$C = f \cdot C_o + (1 - f) \cdot C_f$$

where C_0 is the original color of the object and C_f is the fog color. The fog factor f is a decreasing function of the distance to the viewer. Consequently, as the object becomes more distant, more weight will be assigned to the fog color and less to the object color. The object will appear to fade away into the fog. The function f is typically chosen as a linear function, an exponential function, or a Gaussian function of the distance.

Java 3D provides `Fog` leaf nodes to support depth cueing. Two types of fogs with linear and exponential blending functions are available in Java 3D. Figure 9.11 shows the fog classes.

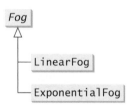

FIGURE 9.11 The Fog class hierarchy.

linear fog

The `LinearFog` class defines a fog with a linear f function.

$$f(z) = \frac{back - z}{back - front}$$

where z is the distance to the view point, and *front* and *back* are constants defining the bounds for f to vary from 1.0 to 0.0. To construct a linear fog, the following constructors can be used:

```
public LinearFog()
public LinearFog(Color3f color)
public LinearFog(Color3f color, double front, double back)
public LinearFog(float r, float g, float b)
public LinearFog(float r, float g, float b, double front, double back)
```

exponential fog

The `ExponentialFog` class uses an exponential f function

$$f(z) = e^{-density \cdot z}$$

The *density* parameter controls the speed of decrease of the function *f* and consequently the density of the fog. The following constructors are available for exponential fog:

```
public ExponentialFog()
public ExponentialFog(Color3f color)
public ExponentialFog(Color3f color, float density)
public ExponentialFog(float r, float g, float b)
public ExponentialFog(float r, float g, float b, float density)
```

Listing 9.3 illustrates the use of fog nodes. An array of dodecahedron objects is displayed in a gray background. A `LinearFog` node is placed in the scene. The fog has the same gray color as the background, creating an effect of a foggy environment with distant objects fading away to the background.

Listing 9.3 `TestFog.java`

```
1  package chapter9;
2
3  import javax.vecmath.*;
4  import java.awt.*;
5  import java.awt.event.*;
6  import javax.media.j3d.*;
7  import com.sun.j3d.utils.universe.*;
8  import com.sun.j3d.utils.geometry.*;
9  import chapter6.Dodecahedron;
10 import java.applet.*;
11 import com.sun.j3d.utils.applet.MainFrame;
12
13 public class TestFog extends Applet {
14    public static void main(String[] args) {
15       new MainFrame(new TestFog(), 640, 480);
16    }
17
18    public void init() {
19       // create canvas
20       GraphicsConfiguration gc =
21          SimpleUniverse.getPreferredConfiguration();
22       Canvas3D cv = new Canvas3D(gc);
23       setLayout(new BorderLayout());
24       add(cv, BorderLayout.CENTER);
25       BranchGroup bg = createSceneGraph();
26       bg.compile();
27       SimpleUniverse su = new SimpleUniverse(cv);
28       su.getViewingPlatform().setNominalViewingTransform();
29       su.addBranchGraph(bg);
30    }
31
32    private BranchGroup createSceneGraph() {
33       BranchGroup root = new BranchGroup();
34       // object
35       for (int i = 0; i < 5; i++) {
36          for (int j = 0; j < 5; j++) {
37             Vector3f pos = new Vector3f
38                (-0.8f+0.4f*i,-0.2f+0.2f*j,-0.4f*j);
39             Node shape = createShape(pos);
40             root.addChild(shape);
41          }
42       }
```

```
43      // lights
44      BoundingSphere bounds = new BoundingSphere
45        (new Point3d(), Double.MAX_VALUE);
46      Background background = new Background(.6f, .6f, .6f);
47      background.setApplicationBounds(bounds);
48      root.addChild(background);
49      DirectionalLight dLight = new DirectionalLight
50        (new Color3f(Color.white), new Vector3f(1f,0f,-1f));
51      dLight.setInfluencingBounds(bounds);
52      root.addChild(dLight);
53      // fog
54      LinearFog fog = new LinearFog(.6f, .6f, .6f, 2f, 4f);
55      fog.setInfluencingBounds(bounds);
56      root.addChild(fog);
57      return root;
58    }
59
60    private Node createShape(Vector3f pos) {
61      Material mat = new Material();
62      Appearance ap = new Appearance();
63      ap.setMaterial(mat);
64      Shape3D shape = new Dodecahedron();
65      shape.setAppearance(ap);
66      Transform3D tr = new Transform3D();
67      tr.setScale(0.1);
68      tr.setTranslation(pos);
69      TransformGroup tg = new TransformGroup(tr);
70      tg.addChild(shape);
71      return tg;
72    }
73 }
```

The result of the program is shown in Figure 9.12 and the scene graph in Figure 9.13.

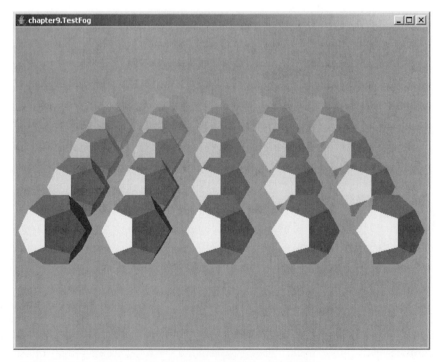

FIGURE 9.12 A foggy scene created with atmospheric attenuation.

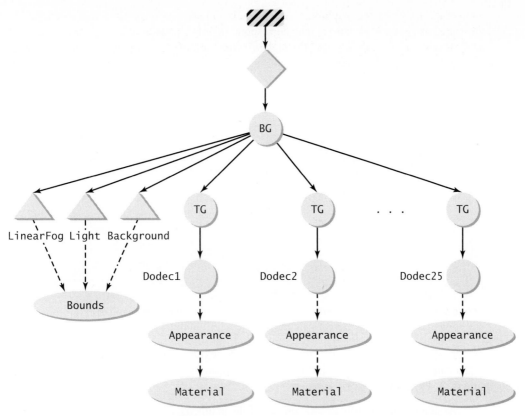

FIGURE 9.13 The scene graph for the fog example.

An array of twenty-five dodecahedra is placed in the scene graph in a 5×5 grid (lines 35–42). The method `createShape` creates a branch of the scene graph with a `TransformGroup` group node, a `Dodecahedron` object, and an `Appearance` object with `Material`. The transform node scales the dodecahedron and moves it to a specified location.

The scene is illuminated by a white directional light in the direction $(1, 0, -1)$. A gray background is used. A linear fog node with the same color as the background is added to the scene graph (line 54). The front of the linear fog is 2 and the back is 4. The distant objects show a clear fading into the background. A `Bounds` object is shared by the light, the background, and the fog.

9.6 Texture Mapping

Real-life objects often contain many small details. Modeling the entire set of details with the usual geometric structures can quickly exhaust the computing resources. Digital images, on the other hand, are relatively inexpensive in providing complex details. *Texture mapping* is a method that utilizes images in graphics rendering. It can provide a great deal of model details with efficiency.

9.6.1 Creating 2D Texture Mapping

The 2D texture-mapping method maps a 2D image to the surface of a 3D object. In the context of texture mapping a point in the texture image is called a *texel* and a point on the 3D surface a *pixel*. The texture image has its own coordinate system. A texture mapping is usually specified by assigning to each vertex of the surface the texture coordinate of the corresponding texel. Other pixels for the surface will be mapped to texture coordinates through

texel

pixel

interpolation. Clearly the mapping between pixels and texels is not one-to-one in general. As illustrated in Figure 9.14, a pixel may correspond to only a portion of a texel, or it may cover many texels. The former is called the *magnification* and the latter the *minification*. In either case, we need to establish certain rules to obtain the texture values. These rules are known as the *magnification filters* and *minification filters*. Commonly used filters include the selection of the closest texel and the linear interpolation (or combination) of neighboring texels.

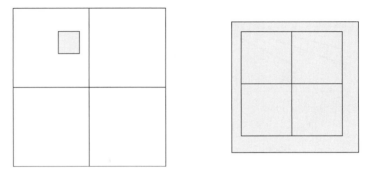

FIGURE 9.14 Magnification and minification. The grey square represents a pixel.

Java 3D supports texture mapping through the texture-coordinates settings in geometry objects and the texture objects in the associated appearance objects. Creating a texture mapping on a shape involves two steps:

1. Assign texture coordinates to vertices of the geometry.

2. Create a `Texture` object in the appearance bundle.

The `GeometryArray` class and its subclasses facilitate the per-vertex specification of texture coordinates. The texture coordinates define the positions of texels for the vertices. The `Texture2D` class defines the texture image used for texture mapping. It is a node component and can be referenced by an `Appearance` object.

In defining a `GeometryArray` object, texture coordinates for vertices of the geometry can be specified like other attributes, such as coordinates, colors, and normals. The constant flag for 2D texture coordinates is `TEXTURE_COORDINATE_2`.

A texture usually gets its content from an image. The class `Texture2D` is a subclass of `NodeComponent` representing the texture. The actual image for `Texture2D` is represented by the class `ImageComponent2D`. A `Texture2D` object is set to reference the `ImageComponent2D` object. The following method of `Texture2D` sets an image for the texture:

```
public void setImage(int index, ImageComponent2D)
```

An `ImageComponent2D` object may receive its image from a `BufferedImage` or more generally a `RenderedImage` object:

```
public void set(BufferedImage bi)
public void set(RenderedImage ri)
```

A `BufferedImage` can be created or loaded from a file using the methods described in Chapter 4. For example, the `ImageIO` class contains static methods for reading images. The following code fragment illustrates the procedure:

```
BufferedImage bi = ImageIO.read(file);
ImageComponent2D image =
new ImageComponent2D(ImageComponent2D.FORMAT_RGB, bi);
```

```
Texture2D texture = new Texture2D();
texture.setImage(0, image);
```

A utility class `TextureLoader` is also available to load a texture image from a file or a `BufferedImage`. The loaded image can be retrieved as an `ImageComponent2D` object or directly as a `Texture` object. The following code fragment shows the basic steps in loading a texture image with a `TextureLoader` object:

TextureLoader

```
TextureLoader loader = new TextureLoader(filename, this);
// retrieve the texture
Texture texture = loader.getTexture();
// or retrieve the image first
ImageComponent2D image = loader.getImage();
Texture2D texture2D = new Texture2D();
Texture2D.setImage(0, image);
```

The created `Texture2D` object can be added to an `Appearance` object using the `setTexture` method

```
Appearance appear = new Appearance();
appear.setTexture(texture);
```

After the texture coordinates are set in the geometry and the texture image is placed in the appearance, the texture mapping will be applied to the object.

Listing 9.4 illustrates 2D texture mapping. It shows a texture-mapped globe. The geometric object is a rotating sphere. An image of the earth is used as the texture and it is mapped to the surface of the sphere. This approach creates a realistic rendering of a 3D globe.

Listing 9.4 `TextureMapping.java`

```
1 package chapter9;
2
3 import javax.vecmath.*;
4 import java.awt.*;
5 import java.awt.event.*;
6 import java.net.*;
7 import javax.media.j3d.*;
8 import com.sun.j3d.utils.universe.*;
9 import com.sun.j3d.utils.geometry.*;
10 import com.sun.j3d.utils.image.*;
11 import java.applet.*;
12 import com.sun.j3d.utils.applet.MainFrame;
13
14 public class TextureMapping extends Applet {
15    public static void main(String[] args) {
16       new MainFrame(new TextureMapping(), 640, 480);
17    }
18
19    public void init() {
20       // create canvas
21       GraphicsConfiguration gc =
22          SimpleUniverse.getPreferredConfiguration();
23       Canvas3D cv = new Canvas3D(gc);
24       setLayout(new BorderLayout());
25       add(cv, BorderLayout.CENTER);
26       BranchGroup bg = createSceneGraph();
27       bg.compile();
28       SimpleUniverse su = new SimpleUniverse(cv);
29       su.getViewingPlatform().setNominalViewingTransform();
```

```
30      su.addBranchGraph(bg);
31    }
32
33    private BranchGroup createSceneGraph() {
34      BranchGroup root = new BranchGroup();
35      TransformGroup spin = new TransformGroup();
36      spin.setCapability(TransformGroup.ALLOW_TRANSFORM_WRITE);
37      root.addChild(spin);
38      // object
39      Appearance ap = createTextureAppearance();
40      Sphere shape =
41      new Sphere(0.7f, Primitive.GENERATE_TEXTURE_COORDS, 50, ap);
42      spin.addChild(shape);
43      // rotator
44      Alpha alpha = new Alpha(-1, 6000);
45      RotationInterpolator rotator =
46      new RotationInterpolator(alpha, spin);
47      BoundingSphere bounds = new BoundingSphere();
48      rotator.setSchedulingBounds(bounds);
49      spin.addChild(rotator);
50      // background
51      Background background = new Background(1.0f, 1.0f, 1.0f);
52      background.setApplicationBounds(bounds);
53      root.addChild(background);
54      return root;
55    }
56
57    Appearance createTextureAppearance(){
58      Appearance ap = new Appearance();
59      URL filename =
60        getClass().getClassLoader().getResource("images/earth.jpg");
61      TextureLoader loader = new TextureLoader(filename, this);
62      ImageComponent2D image = loader.getImage();
63      if(image == null) {
64        System.out.println("can't find texture file.");
65      }
66      Texture2D texture = new Texture2D
67        (Texture.BASE_LEVEL, Texture.RGBA,
68      image.getWidth(), image.getHeight());
69      texture.setImage(0, image);
70      texture.setEnable(true);
71      texture.setMagFilter(Texture.BASE_LEVEL_LINEAR);
72      texture.setMinFilter(Texture.BASE_LEVEL_LINEAR);
73      ap.setTexture(texture);
74      return ap;
75    }
76 }
```

The resulting screen capture of the program is shown in Figure 9.15. The scene graph of the program is given in Figure 9.16.

A sphere is created with texture coordinates. The format flag `Primitive.GENERATE_TEXTURE_COORDS` in the constructor of the sphere enables the generation of texture coordinates for the primitive (line 41). The sphere is rotated with a `RotationInterpolator` object.

The texture appearance is created with the method `createTextureAppearance` (line 57). An image of the earth is loaded from its disk file by the `TextureLoader` class. The loaded image is then assigned to an `ImageComponent2D` object, which is used to created a `Texture2D` object. The texture is mapped to the sphere through the associated `Appearance` object. Both magnification filter and minification filter are set to linear interpolation.

FIGURE 9.15 A rotating texture-mapped globe.

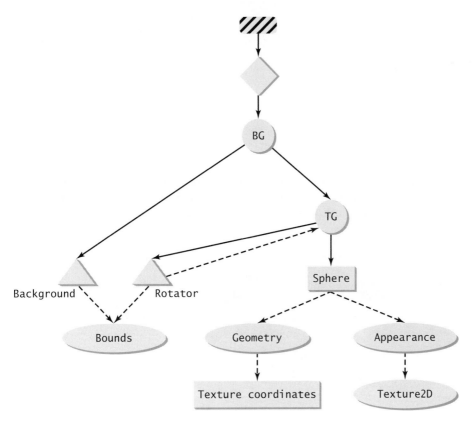

FIGURE 9.16 Scene graph for the texture-mapping example.

9.6.2 Texture Coordinates

Texture coordinates in a geometry control the mapping from the texture image to the surface. The methods for setting texture coordinates in the GeometryArray class include:

```
void setTextureCoordinate(int texSet, int index, float[] texCoord)
void setTextureCoordinate(int texSet, int index, TexCoord2f texCoord)
void setTextureCoordinates(int texSet, int index, float[] texCoords)
void setTextureCoordinates(int texSet, int index, TexCoord2f[]
  texCoords)
```

In the IndexedGeometryArray class and its subclasses, indices for texture coordinates can be applied using the methods:

```
void setTextureCoordinateIndex(int texSet, int index, int texCoordIdx)
void setTextureCoordinateIndices(int texSet, int index, int[]
  texCoordIdx)
```

The class TexCoord2f is defined in the package javax.vecmath to represent texture coordinates. Other similar classes include TexCoord3f and TexCoord4f for 3D and 4D texture coordinates. A set of texture coordinates can be defined for one object. A texture coordinate is a 2D vector (u, v) that specifies a location in a texture. Values for u and v range from 0.0 to 1.0. The four corners of the image have the texture coordinates shown in Figure 9.17.

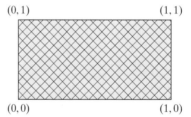

FIGURE 9.17 Texture coordinates define locations in an image.

Consider the problem of mapping the image shown in Figure 9.18 to a cube to create a die. The image can be divided into 6 squares, and there are 12 distinct texture coordinates to be assigned. To achieve the desired texture mapping, the vertices of a face of the cube should be assigned the texture coordinates of one square in the image.

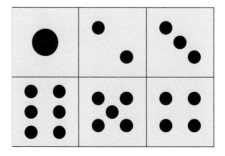

FIGURE 9.18 Mapping an image to the faces of a cube.

The following code fragment defines the geometry of the cube with the appropriate texture coordinates:

```
IndexedQuadArray qa = new IndexedQuadArray(12,
QuadArray.COORDINATES|QuadArray.TEXTURE_COORDINATE_2,24);

Point3f[] coords = {new Point3f(0,0,0),new Point3f(1,0,0),
new Point3f(1,1,0),new Point3f(0,1,0),
new Point3f(0,0,1),new Point3f(1,0,1),
new Point3f(1,1,1),new Point3f(0,1,1)};
int[] coordIndices =
{0,1,2,3, 0,1,5,4, 1,2,6,5, 2,3,7,6, 3,0,4,7, 4,5,6,7};
qa.setCoordinates(0, coords);
qa.setCoordinateIndices(0, coordIndices);

TexCoord2f[] tex = {new TexCoord2f(0, 1),new TexCoord2f(1f/3, 1),
new TexCoord2f(2f/3, 1),new TexCoord2f(1, 1),
new TexCoord2f(0, 0.5f),new TexCoord2f(1f/3, 0.5f),
new TexCoord2f(2f/3, 0.5f),new TexCoord2f(1, 0.5f),
new TexCoord2f(0, 0),new TexCoord2f(1f/3, 0),
new TexCoord2f(2f/3, 0),new TexCoord2f(1, 0)};
int[] texIndices =
{0,1,5,4, 1,2,6,5, 2,3,7,6, 5,6,10,9, 6,7,11,10, 4,5,9,8};
qa.setTextureCoordinates(0,0,tex);
qa.setTextureCoordinateIndices(0,0,texIndices);
```

9.6.3 Combining Texture Mapping and Lighting

It is also possible to combine texture mapping with other coloring models such as lighting. Java 3D includes the class `TextureAttributes` to control the options of texture mapping. For example, if we want to render an object with both texture mapping and lighting, we may create the configurations for both options and use a `TextureAttributes` object to combine the colors from the two sources. The geometry of the shape will have both normals and texture coordinates set. Lights will be placed in the scene graph, and a `Material` component will be used in the appearance bundle. We will also define a `Texture` component and select it in the appearance. The `TextureAttributes` class defines a variety of ways to combine texture mapping with the coloring options. The following code fragment shows a configuration to combine texture mapping with lighting:

`TextureAttributes`

```
TextureAttributes texatt = new TextureAttributes();
texatt.setTextureMode(TextureAttributes.COMBINE);
appearance.setTextureAttributes(texatt);
```

Listing 9.5 demonstrates the combination of texture mapping and lighting. It displays a texture-mapped cylinder that is also lit (Figure 9.19). It illustrates the procedures of setting texture coordinates in a geometry, creating a texture image in code, and combining texture mapping with lighting using the `TextureAttributes` class.

Listing 9.5 `Cup.java`

```
1 package chapter9;
2
3 import javax.vecmath.*;
4 import java.awt.*;
5 import java.awt.geom.*;
6 import java.awt.image.*;
7 import java.net.URL;
8 import java.util.*;
```

```
 9 import java.awt.event.*;
10 import javax.media.j3d.*;
11 import com.sun.j3d.utils.universe.*;
12 import com.sun.j3d.utils.geometry.*;
13 import com.sun.j3d.utils.image.*;
14 import java.applet.*;
15 import com.sun.j3d.utils.applet.MainFrame;
16 import com.sun.j3d.utils.behaviors.mouse.*;
17
18 public class Cup extends Applet {
19   public static void main(String[] args) {
20     new MainFrame(new Cup(), 640, 480);
21   }
22
23   public void init() {
24     // create canvas
25     GraphicsConfiguration gc =
26       SimpleUniverse.getPreferredConfiguration();
27     Canvas3D cv = new Canvas3D(gc);
28     setLayout(new BorderLayout());
29     add(cv, BorderLayout.CENTER);
30     BranchGroup bg = createSceneGraph();
31     bg.compile();
32     SimpleUniverse su = new SimpleUniverse(cv);
33     su.getViewingPlatform().setNominalViewingTransform();
34     su.addBranchGraph(bg);
35   }
36
37   private BranchGroup createSceneGraph() {
38     BranchGroup root = new BranchGroup();
39     TransformGroup spin = new TransformGroup();
40     spin.setCapability(TransformGroup.ALLOW_TRANSFORM_WRITE);
41     spin.setCapability(TransformGroup.ALLOW_TRANSFORM_READ);
42     root.addChild(spin);
43     // object transform
44     Transform3D tr = new Transform3D();
45     tr.setScale(0.3);
46     tr.setRotation(new AxisAngle4d(0, 0, 1, Math.PI/12));
47     TransformGroup tg = new TransformGroup(tr);
48     spin.addChild(tg);
49     // object
50     Geometry geom = createGeometry();
51     Appearance ap = createTextureAppearance();
52     PolygonAttributes pa =
53     new PolygonAttributes(PolygonAttributes.POLYGON_FILL,
54     PolygonAttributes.CULL_NONE,0);
55     ap.setPolygonAttributes(pa);
56     Shape3D shape = new Shape3D(geom, ap);
57     tg.addChild(shape);
58     // rotation
59     BoundingSphere bounds = new BoundingSphere();
60     Alpha alpha = new Alpha(-1, 10000);
61     RotationInterpolator rotator = new RotationInterpolator
62       (alpha, spin);
63     rotator.setSchedulingBounds(bounds);
64     spin.addChild(rotator);
65     // background and lights
66     Background background = new Background(1.0f, 1.0f, 1.0f);
67     background.setApplicationBounds(bounds);
68     root.addChild(background);
69     AmbientLight light = new AmbientLight(true,
```

```
70         new Color3f(Color.lightGray));
71     light.setInfluencingBounds(bounds);
72     root.addChild(light);
73     PointLight ptlight = new PointLight(new Color3f(Color.white),
74     new Point3f(3f,3f,3f), new Point3f(1f,0f,0f));
75     ptlight.setInfluencingBounds(bounds);
76     root.addChild(ptlight);
77     return root;
78  }
79
80  Geometry createGeometry() {
81    int m = 120;
82    int n = 2;
83    QuadArray qa = new QuadArray(4*m,
84    QuadArray.COORDINATES|QuadArray.NORMALS|
85    QuadArray.TEXTURE_COORDINATE_2);
86    // generate the cylinder
87    Transform3D trans = new Transform3D();
88    trans.rotY(2*Math.PI/m);
89    Point3f pt0 = new Point3f(1,1,0);
90    Point3f pt1 = new Point3f(1,-1,0);
91    Vector3f normal = new Vector3f(1,0,0);
92    for (int j = 0; j < m; j++) {
93      qa.setCoordinate(j*4, pt0);
94      qa.setCoordinate(j*4+1, pt1);
95      qa.setNormal(j*4, normal);
96      qa.setNormal(j*4+1, normal);
97      trans.transform(pt0);
98      trans.transform(pt1);
99      trans.transform(normal);
100     qa.setCoordinate(j*4+2, pt1);
101     qa.setCoordinate(j*4+3, pt0);
102     qa.setNormal(j*4+2, normal);
103     qa.setNormal(j*4+3, normal);
104     // set texture coordinates
105     TexCoord2f tex0 = new TexCoord2f(j*1f/m, 1f);
106     TexCoord2f tex1 = new TexCoord2f(j*1f/m, 0f);
107     qa.setTextureCoordinate(0,j*4,tex0);
108     qa.setTextureCoordinate(0,j*4+1,tex1);
109     tex0 = new TexCoord2f((j+1)*1f/m, 1f);
110     tex1 = new TexCoord2f((j+1)*1f/m, 0f);
111     qa.setTextureCoordinate(0,j*4+2,tex1);
112     qa.setTextureCoordinate(0,j*4+3,tex0);
113   }
114   return qa;
115 }
116
117 Appearance createTextureAppearance(){
118   Appearance ap = new Appearance();
119   BufferedImage bi = new BufferedImage(512,128,
120   BufferedImage.TYPE_INT_ARGB);
121   Graphics2D g2 = (Graphics2D)bi.getGraphics();
122   g2.setColor(Color.white);
123   g2.fillRect(0, 0, 512,128);
124   g2.setFont(new Font("Serif", Font.BOLD, 48));
125   g2.setColor(new Color(200,0,0));
126   g2.drawString("Java 3D",0,100);
127   ImageComponent2D image =
128     new ImageComponent2D(ImageComponent2D.FORMAT_RGBA, bi);
129   Texture2D texture = new Texture2D
130     (Texture.BASE_LEVEL, Texture.RGBA,
```

```
131      image.getWidth(), image.getHeight());
132      texture.setImage(0, image);
133      texture.setMagFilter(Texture.BASE_LEVEL_LINEAR);
134      ap.setTexture(texture);
135      // combine texture and lighting
136      TextureAttributes texatt = new TextureAttributes();
137      texatt.setTextureMode(TextureAttributes.COMBINE);
138      ap.setTextureAttributes(texatt);
139      ap.setMaterial(new Material());
140      return ap;
141   }
140 }
```

FIGURE 9.19 A texture-mapped and lit cylinder.

The createGeometry method (line 80) constructs the cylinder with a QuadArray. Both normals and texture coordinates are generated in the geometry.

The createTextureAppearance method constructs an appearance bundle that includes a Material component, a Texture2D component, and a TextureAttributes object. The image for texture mapping is created directly as a BufferedImage of size 512 by 128 (line 119). A Graphics2D object is retrieved to allow drawing on the image. The image is first cleared with the white color, and then the string "Java 3D" is drawn in red (lines 121–126). The BufferedImage is used to create a Texture2D object for the texture mapping.

The cylinder is lit with an ambient light and a point light. The TextureAttributes object in the appearance is set to the COMBINE mode to combine the effects of texture mapping and lighting (line 137).

9.6.4 Texture-Coordinates Generation

Texture coordinates can be specified directly in a geometry. It is also possible to generate the texture coordinates automatically using a model based on the object geometry and view configuration. The automatic generation of texture coordinates is achieved through a special node component in the appearance. The options of manual specification and automatic generation of texture coordinates are similar to the object coloring options: the colors may be specified directly in the object geometry or they can be generated with a lighting model.

In addition to the 2D texture coordinates, Java 3D also supports 3D and 4D texture coordinates. These texture coordinates are denoted by $(r,s),(r,s,t),(r,s,t,q)$, respectively. The constant flags for the three types of *texture coordinates* are defined as:

Texture-coordinate types

```
TEXTURE_COORDINATE_2
TEXTURE_COORDINATE_3
TEXTURE_COORDINATE_4
```

All three types of texture coordinates can be generated automatically. The node component class `TexCoordGeneration` facilitates texture-coordinates generation. Automatic texture-coordinates generation can be enabled by adding a `TexCoordGeneration` object to an appearance bundle. The `TexCoordGeneration` class defines five modes of texture-coordinates generation based on different criteria:

```
OBJECT_LINEAR
EYE_LINEAR
SPHERE_MAP
NORMAL_MAP
REFLECTION_MAP
```

The `OBJECT_LINEAR` and `EYE_LINEAR` modes compute the texture coordinates using the following matrix equation:

$$
\begin{bmatrix} r \\ s \\ t \\ q \end{bmatrix} = \begin{bmatrix} a_{11} & a_{12} & a_{13} & a_{14} \\ a_{21} & a_{22} & a_{22} & a_{24} \\ a_{31} & a_{32} & a_{33} & a_{34} \\ a_{41} & a_{42} & a_{43} & a_{44} \end{bmatrix} \begin{bmatrix} x \\ y \\ z \\ w \end{bmatrix}
$$

Therefore, the texture coordinates of an object are linearly dependent on the object's coordinates. In the `OBJECT_LINEAR` mode, the point (x,y,z,w) is given by object coordinates, so the texture is attached to the object and moves with the object. In `EYE_LINEAR` mode, the point is given by eye coordinates, so the texture is fixed relative to the eye. As the object moves, the texture does not move with it. As a result, the texture may appear to be a reflection on the object. The coefficients in the above matrix can be set with the following methods:

```
void setPlaneR(Vector4f coeff)
void setPlaneS(Vector4f coeff)
void setPlaneT(Vector4f coeff)
void setPlaneQ(Vector4f coeff)
```

Each of these methods sets one row of the matrix.

The `SPHERE_MAP` mode generates texture coordinates that can be used to simulate spherical reflections based on eye coordinates. The last two modes are available only for the special texture cube mapping. The ordinary `Texture2D` defines only a rectangular plane texture. The `TextureCubeMap` class defines a texture with six images configured as the six faces of a cube. The texture mapping will map each image to a specific side of the object. This type of texture mapping may be more convenient for certain 3D solids. In a `TextureCubeMap` object, the six images can be identified with the constants:

TextureCubeMap

```
NEGATIVE_X
NEGATIVE_Y
NEGATIVE_Z
POSITIVE_X
POSITIVE_Y
POSITIVE_Z
```

Listing 9.6 illustrates different modes of texture-coordinates generation using a Texture CubeMap. A rotating dodecahedron is displayed with a texture defined by a TextureCubeMap object. Three images are used for the six faces of the cube. Opposite faces receive the same image. (See Figure 9.20.) Texture coordinates for the dodecahedron are generated with a TexCoordGeneration object. Five buttons labeled with the texture-coordinates generation modes. When you click a button, the corresponding mode will be selected for the TexCoordGeneration to render the dodecahedron.

Listing 9.6 CubeTexture.java

```
1 package chapter9;
2
3 import javax.vecmath.*;
4 import java.awt.*;
5 import java.awt.event.*;
6 import java.net.*;
7 import javax.media.j3d.*;
8 import com.sun.j3d.utils.universe.*;
9 import com.sun.j3d.utils.geometry.*;
10 import com.sun.j3d.utils.image.*;
11 import chapter6.Dodecahedron;
12 import java.applet.*;
13 import com.sun.j3d.utils.applet.MainFrame;
14
15 public class CubeTexture extends Applet implements ActionListener{
16    public static void main(String[] args) {
17      new MainFrame(new CubeTexture(), 640, 480);
18    }
19
20    private Appearance ap = null;
21
22    public void init() {
23      setLayout(new BorderLayout());
24      Panel panel = new Panel();
25      panel.setLayout(new GridLayout(5,1));
26      add(panel, BorderLayout.EAST);
27      Button button = new Button("OBJECT_LINEAR");
28      button.addActionListener(this);
29      panel.add(button);
30      button = new Button("EYE_LINEAR");
31      button.addActionListener(this);
32      panel.add(button);
33      button = new Button("SPHERE_MAP");
34      button.addActionListener(this);
35      panel.add(button);
36      button = new Button("NORMAL_MAP");
37      button.addActionListener(this);
38      panel.add(button);
39      button = new Button("REFLECTION_MAP");
40      button.addActionListener(this);
41      panel.add(button);
42
43      GraphicsConfiguration gc =
44        SimpleUniverse.getPreferredConfiguration();
45      Canvas3D cv = new Canvas3D(gc);
46      add(cv, BorderLayout.CENTER);
47      BranchGroup bg = createSceneGraph();
48      bg.compile();
49      SimpleUniverse su = new SimpleUniverse(cv);
50      su.getViewingPlatform().setNominalViewingTransform();
```

```
51      su.addBranchGraph(bg);
52    }
53
54    private BranchGroup createSceneGraph() {
55      BranchGroup root = new BranchGroup();
56      TransformGroup spin = new TransformGroup();
57      spin.setCapability(TransformGroup.ALLOW_TRANSFORM_WRITE);
58      root.addChild(spin);
59      // object
60      ap = createTextureAppearance();
61      Shape3D shape = new Dodecahedron();
62      shape.setAppearance(ap);
63      Transform3D tr = new Transform3D();
64      tr.setScale(0.4);
65      TransformGroup tg = new TransformGroup(tr);
66      tg.addChild(shape);
67      spin.addChild(tg);
68      // rotator
69      Alpha alpha = new Alpha(-1, 18000);
70      RotationInterpolator rotator = new RotationInterpolator
71        (alpha, spin);
72      BoundingSphere bounds = new BoundingSphere();
73      rotator.setSchedulingBounds(bounds);
74      spin.addChild(rotator);
75      // background
76      Background background = new Background(1.0f, 1.0f, 1.0f);
77      background.setApplicationBounds(bounds);
78      root.addChild(background);
79      return root;
80    }
81
82    Appearance createTextureAppearance(){
83      Appearance ap = new Appearance();
84      URL filename =
85          getClass().getClassLoader().getResource("images/earth.jpg");
86      TextureLoader loader = new TextureLoader(filename, this);
87      ImageComponent2D image1 = loader.getImage();
88      filename = getClass().getClassLoader().getResource
89        ("images/stone.jpg");
90      loader = new TextureLoader(filename, this);
91      ImageComponent2D image2 = loader.getImage();
92      filename = getClass().getClassLoader().getResource
93        ("images/sky.jpg");
94      loader = new TextureLoader(filename, this);
95      ImageComponent2D image3 = loader.getImage();
96
97      TextureCubeMap texture =
98      new TextureCubeMap(Texture.BASE_LEVEL, Texture.RGBA,
99      image1.getWidth());
100     texture.setImage(0, TextureCubeMap.NEGATIVE_X, image3);
101     texture.setImage(0, TextureCubeMap.NEGATIVE_Y, image1);
102     texture.setImage(0, TextureCubeMap.NEGATIVE_Z, image2);
103     texture.setImage(0, TextureCubeMap.POSITIVE_X, image3);
104     texture.setImage(0, TextureCubeMap.POSITIVE_Y, image1);
105     texture.setImage(0, TextureCubeMap.POSITIVE_Z, image2);
106
107     texture.setEnable(true);
108     texture.setMagFilter(Texture.BASE_LEVEL_LINEAR);
109     texture.setMinFilter(Texture.BASE_LEVEL_LINEAR);
110     ap.setTexture(texture);
111
```

```
112      TexCoordGeneration tcg = new
113      TexCoordGeneration(TexCoordGeneration.OBJECT_LINEAR,
114      TexCoordGeneration.TEXTURE_COORDINATE_3);
115      tcg.setPlaneR(new Vector4f(2, 0, 0, 0));
116      tcg.setPlaneS(new Vector4f(0, 2, 0, 0));
117      tcg.setPlaneT(new Vector4f(0, 0, 2, 0));
118      ap.setTexCoordGeneration(tcg);
119      ap.setCapability(Appearance.ALLOW_TEXGEN_WRITE);
120      return ap;
121    }
122
123    public void actionPerformed(ActionEvent e) {
124      String cmd = e.getActionCommand();
125      TexCoordGeneration tcg = new TexCoordGeneration();
126      if ("OBJECT_LINEAR".equals(cmd)) {
127        tcg.setGenMode(TexCoordGeneration.OBJECT_LINEAR);
128      } else if ("EYE_LINEAR".equals(cmd)) {
129        tcg.setGenMode(TexCoordGeneration.EYE_LINEAR);
130      } else if ("SPHERE_MAP".equals(cmd)) {
131        tcg.setGenMode(TexCoordGeneration.SPHERE_MAP);
132      } else if ("NORMAL_MAP".equals(cmd)) {
133        tcg.setGenMode(TexCoordGeneration.NORMAL_MAP);
134      } else if ("REFLECTION_MAP".equals(cmd)) {
135        tcg.setGenMode(TexCoordGeneration.REFLECTION_MAP);
136      }
137      tcg.setFormat(TexCoordGeneration.TEXTURE_COORDINATE_3);
138      tcg.setPlaneR(new Vector4f(2, 0, 0, 0));
139      tcg.setPlaneS(new Vector4f(0, 2, 0, 0));
140      tcg.setPlaneT(new Vector4f(0, 0, 2, 0));
141      ap.setTexCoordGeneration(tcg);
142    }
143  }
```

FIGURE 9.20 Cube texture applied with different modes of texture-coordinates generation.

The scene graph is shown in Figure 9.21. A dodecahedron is attached to a series of two `TransformGroup` nodes: one for the rotation and the other to scale the size of the object down. The dodecahedron has an `Appearance` object that references a `TextureCubeMap` and a `TexCoordGeneration`. The capability bit `ALLOW_TEXGEN_WRITE` of the appearance is set to allow the change of the `TexCoordGeneration` in a live scene graph (line 119).

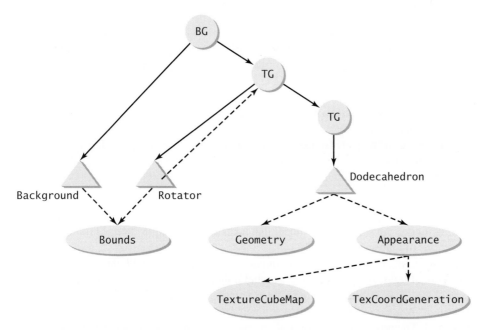

FIGURE 9.21 The scene graph for the example of texture-coordinates generation.

Three images of the same size are loaded from image files (lines 84–95). They are used for the six faces of the `TextureCubeMap` object. The opposite faces get the same images.

The 3D texture coordinates needed by the `TextureCubeMap` are generated automatically with the `TexCoordGeneration` object. Initially the generation mode is set to `OBJECT_LINEAR`.

The main program window uses a `BorderLayout` manager. The `Canvas3D` object is added to the "CENTER" region. Five buttons are created to represent the five modes of texture-coordinates generation: OBJECT_LINEAR, EYE_LINEAR, SPHERE_MAP, NORMAL_MAP, and REFLECTION_MAP. The buttons are added to a panel in the "EAST" region of the applet. The buttons register the applet object as their `ActionListener`. In the action handler `actionPerformed` (line 123), a new `TexCoordGeneration` object is created. The button label is retrieved, and the corresponding texture-coordinates generation mode is set with the method `setGenMode`. The appearance object's texture-coordinates generation is then changed to the new `TexCoordGeneration` object by calling the method `setTexCoordGeneration`.

KEY CLASSES AND METHODS

- **javax.vecmath.TexCoord2f** A class encapsulating a 2D texture coordinate.
- **javax.vecmath.TexCoord3f** A class encapsulating a 3D texture coordinate.
- **javax.vecmath.TexCoord4f** A class encapsulating a 4D texture coordinate.
- **javax.media.j3d.Light** A class encapsulating a light source.
- **javax.media.j3d.AmbientLight** A class encapsulating an ambient light.
- **javax.media.j3d.DirectionalLight** A class encapsulating a directional light.

- `javax.media.j3d.PointLight` A class encapsulating a point light.
- `javax.media.j3d.SpotLight` A class encapsulating a spotlight.
- `javax.media.j3d.Material` A class defining the material properties for illumination.
- `javax.media.j3d.Fog` A class encapsulating the blending effects.
- `javax.media.j3d.LinearFog` A fog with a linear blending coefficient function.
- `javax.media.j3d.ExponentialFog` A fog with an exponential blending coefficient function.
- `javax.media.j3d.Texture2D` A class encapsulating a 2D texture.
- `javax.media.j3d.ImageComponent2D` A class encapsulating an image.
- `javax.media.j3d.TextureLoader` A class for loading an image.
- `javax.media.j3d.TextureAttributes` An appearance component for controlling attributes of texture mapping.
- `javax.media.j3d.TextureCubeMap` A class defining a texture with six images on its cube faces.
- `javax.media.j3d.TexCoordGeneration` A class encapsulating texture coordinate generation.

KEY TERMS

Phong model An illumination model that takes into account the surface normals and directions of lights and the eye.

ambient light A model for uniform omnidirectional background light.

directional light A light that emits parallel light rays along a fixed direction.

point light A light radiating from a fixed point.

spotlight A point light with limited angle of radiation.

material The reflection properties of an object that affect the color calculations.

ambient reflection The reflection of ambient lights.

diffuse reflection The reflection of directional and point lights that are uniformly distributed in all directions.

specular reflection The reflection of directional and point lights that are concentrated on a fixed direction.

depth cueing A visual effect of blurring distant objects into the background.

texture mapping A rendering technique that maps an image to the surface of a 3D geometric object.

texel A basic element of a texture.

texture coordinate A coordinate used in a geometry to specify the location of the texel to be mapped.

CHAPTER SUMMARY

- In this chapter, you learn several methods to achieve realistic appearance in 3D rendering.

- Lighting provides a model for calculating colors based on the physical characteristics of the objects and the light sources. The Phong illumination model is a popular method for lighting. Java 3D supports the model through the light objects, surface normal definition in geometry, and material specification in appearance.

- There are usually four types of lights in computer graphics: ambient lights, directional lights, point lights, and spotlights.

- The material properties are defined in terms of coefficients for ambient reflection, diffuse reflection, and specular reflection. The coefficients are specified for each primary color. A shininess exponent independent of color spectrum is also used to define the concentration of specular reflection.

- The use of atmospheric attenuation and depth cueing is a method to enhance photorealism by blending distant objects. Java 3D provides the Fog class and subclasses LinearFog and ExponentialFog to support this effect.

- Texture mapping is another effective method that can dramatically improve the quality of rendered objects. Texture mapping uses images to provide details of rendered surfaces. To apply texture mapping in Java 3D, you need to define texture coordinates in the geometry of a visual object and include a texture image in its appearance. Texture coordinates may be specified directly in the geometry, or they can be generated automatically using a TexCoordGeneration object in the appearance.

REVIEW QUESTIONS

9.1 A point light has attenuation coefficients (1, 2, 1). At what distance is the attenuation 0.04?

9.2 Discuss the differences between a point light and a directional light in terms of their effects on the equation of the Phong illumination model.

9.3 How do you position the eye to maximize the specular reflection of a point light from a point on a surface?

9.4 The point (1, 0, 0) on an object has a surface normal in the direction (0, 1, 0). A directional light with intensity 1.0 is placed in the direction $(1, -1, 0)$. The eye is located at (5, 3, 0). If the RGB diffuse coefficients of the object are (0.3, 0.5, 0.2), find the RGB values of diffuse reflection at the point.

9.5 In the scene given in Question 9.4, if the RGB specular coefficients of the material are (1, 1, 0.5) and the shininess is 10, find the RGB values of specular reflection at the point.

9.6 The point (1, 0, 0) on an object has a surface normal in the direction (0, 1, 0). A point light with intensity 1.0 is placed at (0, 1, 0). The eye is located at (5, 3, 0). If the RGB diffuse coefficients of the object are (0.3, 0.5, 0.2), find the RGB values of diffuse reflection at the point.

9.7 In the scene given in Question 9.6, if the RGB specular coefficients of the material are (1, 1, 0.5) and the shininess is 10, find the RGB values of specular reflection at the point.

9.8 In the linear fog equation, find the distance at which the blending coefficient f is 0.5.

9.9 In the exponential fog equation, find the distance at which the blending coefficient f is 0.5.

9.10 What is the texture coordinate for the center of a texture image?

9.11 In a TexCoordGeneration object, how do you set the coefficient matrix so that the mirror image of the original texture image is mapped to an object?

PROGRAMMING EXERCISES

9.1 Write a program to show the four coloring modes of Java 3D. Create and place four squares in the scene. Each square uses one of the coloring options.

9.2 Modify the program in Listing 9.1 to display a 3D text string.

9.3 Write a program similar to Listing 9.2, but varying the specular reflection coefficients.

9.4 Display a long rectangle in a scene with a linear fog object. Observe the fading on the far side of the rectangle.

9.5 Modify Listing 9.3 to use an exponential fog. Add an option to allow the user to change the density parameter of the fog at runtime.

9.6 Write a Java 3D program to display a texture-mapped tetrahedron. Map the same texture to all four faces. Set the texture coordinates of the three vertices in a face to three corners of the texture. Rotate the tetrahedron in the scene.

9.7 Rewrite the program in Exercise 9.6 to use texture-coordinates generation with `OBJECT_LINEAR` mode.

9.8 Rewrite the program in Exercise 9.7 to use texture-coordinates generation with `EYE_LINEAR` mode.

9.9 Rewrite Listing 9.4 to light the texture-mapped globe with a red spotlight.

9.10 Write a Java 3D program to display a rotating die. Use a `TextureCubeMap` object with a cube geometry to construct the shape. Generate the six face images in the program by painting circles on `BufferedImage` objects. Set texture coordinates automatically with a `TexCoordGeneration` object in `OBJECT_LINEAR` mode.

CHAPTER 10

BEHAVIOR AND INTERACTION

Objectives

- To understand dynamic behaviors in graphics.

- To understand Java 3D `Behavior` and `WakeupCondition` classes.

- To apply `Behavior` nodes in scene graphs.

- To use mouse behaviors.

- To use key navigator behaviors.

- To use view platform behaviors.

- To combine picking and behaviors.

10.1 Introduction

Interaction
Animation

Modern computer graphics systems are not limited to rendering static scenes. Incorporating dynamic changes in a 3D scene is an important part of many graphics applications. Two types of dynamic changes are common in computer graphics: interaction and animation. *Interaction* changes the graphics scenes under the control of user input. *Animation* generates sequences of graphics renderings that vary with time, producing an effect of motion. Both mechanisms generate dynamic behaviors in graphics systems. The changes can occur in the virtual world of graphics objects or in the view that "sees" the world. The changes may involve the geometry, appearance, transformation, and other aspects of the visual system. In general the incorporation of dynamic behavior can be a complex process. It is usually necessary to allow the inclusion of general programming code to handle the dynamics. It is also desirable to include the dynamics logic as a part of the graphics programming paradigm in a systematic way.

Java 3D uses the notion of behavior to facilitate animations, interactions, and other dynamics in a scene graph. A `Behavior` object is a leaf node in a scene graph. It defines the actions to be performed when the behavior is activated (waked up). Special objects called wakeup conditions are used to trigger a behavior. If a wakeup condition is related to user actions such as moving a mouse, the behavior defines an interaction. If a behavior is triggered by a wakeup condition tied to time, it defines an animation.

In this chapter we will introduce the general concept of behavior and one common type of behavior: interaction. We will also discuss the application of picking in defining interaction. Animation, another important type of behavior, will be discussed in Chapter 11.

10.2 Behavior

Java 3D provides a general unified approach to implement both animation and interaction. It takes advantage of Java's OOP features and uses the `Behavior` class hierarchy and other related classes to incorporate animation and interaction logic into the scene graph. The class hierarchy of the `Behavior` classes is given in Figure 10.1.

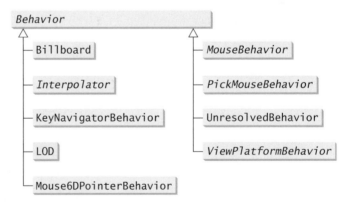

FIGURE 10.1 Behavior classes.

`Behavior` is an abstract class that extends the `Leaf` class. It defines the basic framework of a general behavior. The `Behavior` class has two abstract methods:

Behavior methods

```
void initialize()
void processStimulus(Enumeration wakeupCriteria)
```

The `initialize` method is invoked once when a `Behavior` object becomes live. The `processStimulus` method is invoked by Java 3D under certain wakeup conditions. Subclasses of `Behavior` override the two methods to fulfill specific behavior tasks.

A `Behavior` object works with `WakeupCondition` objects to complete its execution cycles. The `Behavior` class contains the following method to set a `WakeupCondition` that will trigger the behavior:

void wakeupOn(WakeupCondition wakeup)

The typical execution cycles of a `Behavior` object is illustrated in Figure 10.2.

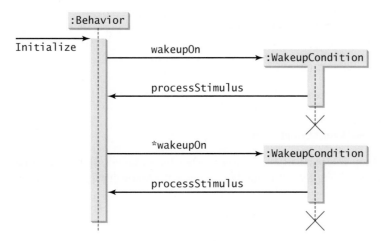

FIGURE 10.2   Interactions between `Behavior` and `WakeupCondition` objects.

During the initialization of the `Behavior` object, it sets a `WakeupCondition` object. When the specified wakeup condition occurs, the `WakeupCondition` object will awaken the `Behavior` object by calling its `processStimulus` method. The parameter `wakeupCriteria` of the `processStimulus` method is a list of `WakeupCriterion` objects that trigger the behavior. After executing the custom code in `processStimulus`, a wakeup condition can be set again by calling the `wakeupOn` method. The process will then repeat indefinitely.

Wakeup conditions are crucial parts of the behavior dynamics. They serve as the signals to   wakeup conditions
trigger different behaviors under different circumstances. Java 3D provides a large collection of wakeup criteria for various stimuli that can be used to trigger a behavior. It also provides the capability to combine the criteria in different ways using logical operators. The class hierarchy of `WakeupCondition` is shown in Figure 10.3.

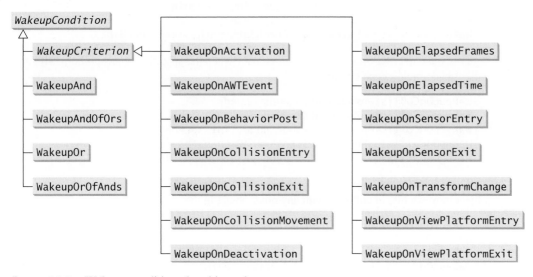

FIGURE 10.3   Wakeup condition class hierarchy.

WakeupCriterion

The subclasses of `WakeupCriterion` represent specific events and criteria that can trigger a `Behavior` object. For example, `WakeupOnElapsedTime` defines the wakeup condition triggered by the passage of a certain amount of time. `WakeupOnAWTEvent` allows the wakeup conditions related to the AWT events such as mouse movements and clicks. Constructors for common wakeup criterion classes are listed below:

```
WakeupOnElapsedTime(long ms)
```

This constructor is to create a wakeup criterion to trigger a behavior after the specified time in milliseconds:

```
WakeupOnElapsedFrames(int frames)
```

This constructs a wakeup criterion to trigger a behavior after the specified number of frames:

```
WakeupOnAWTEvent(int eventID)
WakeupOnAWTEvent(long eventMask)
```

This wakeup criterion triggers a behavior when the specified AWT events occur. An AWT event ID defines a single AWT event. For example, the following statement creates a criterion for the mouse-down event:

```
new WakeupOnAWTEvent(Event.MOUSE_DOWN);
```

If several AWT events are needed, the second constructor with event masks can be used. AWT event masks may be combined with logical OR operator. For example, the following wakeup criterion corresponds to mouse event and mouse-motion event:

```
new WakeupOnAWTEvent(AWTEvent.MOUSE_EVENT_MASK |
    AWTEvent.MOUSE_MOTION_EVENT_MASK);
```

Note that the class `Event` has been superseded by the `AWTEvent` class:

```
WakeupOnTransformChange(TransformGroup node)
```

This constructor is for a wakeup criterion to awaken a behavior when the transformation inside the specified `TransformGroup` node is changed:

```
WakeupOnCollisionEntry(Bounds bounds)
WakeupOnCollisionEntry(Node node)
WakeupOnCollisionEntry(Node node, int speedHint)
WakeupOnCollisionEntry(SceneGraphPath path)
WakeupOnCollisionEntry(SceneGraphPath path, int speedHint)
```

This wakeup criterion is to awaken a behavior when the specified object collides with any other object in the scene graph:

```
WakeupOnCollisionMovement(Bounds bounds)
WakeupOnCollisionMovement(Node node)
WakeupOnCollisionMovement(Node node, int speedHint)
WakeupOnCollisionMovement(SceneGraphPath path)
WakeupOnCollisionMovement(SceneGraphPath path, int speedHint)
```

These constructors are for a wakeup criterion to awaken a behavior when the specified object moves while in collision with any other object in the scene graph:

```
WakeupOnCollisionExit(Bounds bounds)
WakeupOnCollisionExit(Node node)
WakeupOnCollisionExit(Node node, int speedHint)
WakeupOnCollisionExit(SceneGraphPath path)
WakeupOnCollisionExit(SceneGraphPath path, int speedHint)
```

This is a wakeup criterion to awaken a behavior when the specified object exits the collision with any other object in the scene graph:

```
WakeupOnBehaviorPost(Behavior behavior, int postID)
```

This wakeup criterion activates when the specified behavior object posts the specified ID. A `Behavior` object can post an event with a `postID`. This wakeup criterion monitors the `postID` posted by `behavior`. If the parameter `behavior` is null, the post can come from any `Behavior` object. If the parameter `postID` is 0, any ID will satisfy this wakeup criterion.

Multiple wakeup conditions may be logically combined to form a new wakeup condition. The class `WakeupCondition` has four subclasses—`WakeupAnd`, `WakeupOr`, `WakeupOrOfAnds`, and `WakeupAndOfOrs`—that define *Boolean operators* to combine wakeup criteria. Each class has a constructor that takes an array of appropriate objects as the parameter:

Boolean operators

```
WakeupAnd(WakeupCriterion[] criteria)
WakeupOr(WakeupCriterion[] criteria)
WakeupOrOfAnds(WakeupAnd[] criteriaAnds)
WakeupAndOfOrs(WakeupOr[] criteriaOrs)
```

For example, the following code fragment defines a wakeup condition that either 10 seconds have passed or 5 frames are rendered and a collision has occurred:

```
WakeupCriterion[] criteria1 = {new WakeupOnElapsedTime(10000)};
WakeupCriterion[] criteria2 = {new WakeupOnElapsedFrames(5),
   new WakeupOnCollisionEntry(node)};
WakeupAnd[] ands = {new WakeupAnd(criteria1),
   new WakeupAnd(criteria2)};
WakeupOrOfAnds condition = new WakeupOrOfAnds(ands);
```

A `Behavior` object has a scheduling bound. It is active only if its scheduling bound intersects the view platform. You may use the following methods to set the scheduling bounds:

```
SetSchedulingBounds(Bounds bounds};
SetSchedulingBoundingLeaf(BoundingLeaf bounds};
```

The typical procedure for implementing a *custom behavior* is summarized below:

custom behavior

- Define a subclass of `Behavior` class and override the `initialize` and `processStimulus` methods.

- Set the appropriate wakeup condition in the initialize method. If necessary, set the wakeup condition again in `processStimulus`.

- Create an instance of the custom `Behavior` class and add it to the scene graph as a leaf.

- Set the influence bound for the behavior object.

Listing 10.1 shows an application using a custom `Behavior` class. The program displays a running analog clock showing the system time. The positions of the hands will constantly change. A custom behavior class (Listing 10.2) is implemented to update the clock based on the current time.

Listing 10.1 `Clock.java`

```
1 package chapter10;
2
3 import javax.vecmath.*;
4 import java.awt.*;
5 import java.awt.event.*;
6 import java.util.*;
7 import javax.media.j3d.*;
8 import com.sun.j3d.utils.universe.*;
```

```
 9 import com.sun.j3d.utils.geometry.*;
10 import java.applet.*;
11 import com.sun.j3d.utils.applet.MainFrame;
12
13 public class Clock extends Applet {
14   public static void main(String[] args) {
15     new MainFrame(new Clock(), 640, 480);
16   }
17
18   public void init() {
19     // create canvas
20     GraphicsConfiguration gc =
21       SimpleUniverse.getPreferredConfiguration();
22     Canvas3D cv = new Canvas3D(gc);
23     setLayout(new BorderLayout());
24     add(cv, BorderLayout.CENTER);
25     BranchGroup bg = createSceneGraph();
26     bg.compile();
27     SimpleUniverse su = new SimpleUniverse(cv);
28     su.getViewingPlatform().setNominalViewingTransform();
29     su.addBranchGraph(bg);
30   }
31
32   private BranchGroup createSceneGraph() {
33     BranchGroup root = new BranchGroup();
34     // clock face
35     Appearance apFace = new Appearance();
36     Material matFace = new Material();
37     matFace.setAmbientColor(new Color3f(0f,0f,0f));
38     matFace.setDiffuseColor(new Color3f(0.15f,0.15f,0.25f));
39     apFace.setMaterial(matFace);
40     Cylinder face = new Cylinder(0.6f, 0.01f,
41     Cylinder.GENERATE_NORMALS, 50, 2, apFace);
42     Transform3D tr = new Transform3D();
43     tr.rotX(Math.PI/2);
44     tr.setTranslation(new Vector3d(0,0,-0.01));
45     TransformGroup tg = new TransformGroup(tr);
46     tg.addChild(face);
47     root.addChild(tg);
48     // hour
49     Appearance ap = new Appearance();
50     ap.setMaterial(new Material());
51     Shape3D shapeHour =
52       new Shape3D(createGeometry(0.4, 0.02, 0.02), ap);
53     TransformGroup spinHour = new TransformGroup();
54     spinHour.addChild(shapeHour);
55     spinHour.setCapability(TransformGroup.ALLOW_TRANSFORM_WRITE);
56     root.addChild(spinHour);
57     // minute
58     Shape3D shapeMin =
59       new Shape3D(createGeometry(0.5, 0.02, 0.02), ap);
60     TransformGroup spinMin = new TransformGroup();
61     spinMin.addChild(shapeMin);
62     spinMin.setCapability(TransformGroup.ALLOW_TRANSFORM_WRITE);
63     root.addChild(spinMin);
64     // second
65     Shape3D shapeSec =
66       new Shape3D(createGeometry(0.5, 0.01, 0.01), ap);
67     TransformGroup spinSec = new TransformGroup();
68     spinSec.addChild(shapeSec);
69     spinSec.setCapability(TransformGroup.ALLOW_TRANSFORM_WRITE);
```

```
70       root.addChild(spinSec);
71       // Behavior node
72       ClockBehavior rotator =
73         new ClockBehavior(spinHour, spinMin, spinSec);
74       BoundingSphere bounds = new BoundingSphere();
75       rotator.setSchedulingBounds(bounds);
76       root.addChild(rotator);
77       // light
78       AmbientLight light =
79         new AmbientLight(true, new Color3f(Color.blue));
80       light.setInfluencingBounds(bounds);
81       root.addChild(light);
82       PointLight ptlight = new PointLight(new Color3f(Color.white),
83         new Point3f(0.7f,0.7f,2f), new Point3f(1f,0f,0f));
84       ptlight.setInfluencingBounds(bounds);
85       root.addChild(ptlight);
86       // background
87       Background background = new Background(0.7f, 0.7f, 0.7f);
88       background.setApplicationBounds(bounds);
89       root.addChild(background);
90       return root;
91    }
92
93    GeometryArray createGeometry(double l, double w, double h) {
94       GeometryInfo gi =
95         new GeometryInfo(GeometryInfo.TRIANGLE_ARRAY);
96       Point3d[] pts = new Point3d[4];
97       pts[0] = new Point3d(0, 0, h);
98       pts[1] = new Point3d(-w, 0, 0);
99       pts[2] = new Point3d(w, 0, 0);
100      pts[3] = new Point3d(0, l, 0);
101      gi.setCoordinates(pts);
102      int[] indices = {0,1,2,0,3,1,0,2,3,2,1,3};
103      gi.setCoordinateIndices(indices);
104      NormalGenerator ng = new NormalGenerator();
105      ng.generateNormals(gi);
106      return gi.getGeometryArray();
107   }
108 }
```

Listing 10.2 ClockBehavior.java

```
1 package chapter10;
2
3 import java.util.*;
4 import javax.media.j3d.*;
5
6 public class ClockBehavior extends Behavior {
7    TransformGroup tgH;
8    TransformGroup tgM;
9    TransformGroup tgS;
10
11   public ClockBehavior(TransformGroup transH,
12   TransformGroup transM, TransformGroup transS) {
13      tgH = transH;
14      tgM = transM;
15      tgS = transS;
16   }
17
18   public void initialize() {
```

```
19      wakeupOn(new WakeupOnElapsedTime(500));
20   }
21
22   public void processStimulus(java.util.Enumeration enumeration) {
23     int hour = Calendar.getInstance().get(Calendar.HOUR);
24     int min = Calendar.getInstance().get(Calendar.MINUTE);
25     int sec = Calendar.getInstance().get(Calendar.SECOND);
26     Transform3D tr = new Transform3D();
27     tr.rotZ(-Math.PI * (hour+min/60.0)/6.0);
28     tgH.setTransform(tr);
29     tr.rotZ(-Math.PI * min /30.0);
30     tgM.setTransform(tr);
31     tr.rotZ(-Math.PI * sec /30.0);
32     tgS.setTransform(tr);
33     wakeupOn(new WakeupOnElapsedTime(500));
34   }
35 }
```

The program produces a 3D clock as shown in Figure 10.4. The visual content branch of the scene graph is shown in Figure 10.5.

FIGURE 10.4   A clock driven by a `Behavior` object.

The program displays a real-time analog clock. The hour, minute, and second hands are created with the method `createGeometry` (line 93). `createGeometry` uses `GeometryInfo` to create a geometry with four vertices and four triangle faces. Surface normals are generated with a `NormalGenerator` object to facilitate lighting. A blue ambient light and a white point light are placed in the scene. The background is set to gray.

Each of three clock-hand objects is attached to a `TransformGroup` node. The transformations control the movements of the hands. In order to make the clock run, we need to update the transformations periodically. A behavior may be applied to drive the update.

The `ClockBehavior` class is a subclass of `Behavior` that acts on the `TransformGroup` objects controlling the hands of the clock. It is set to wake up after 0.5 second in the

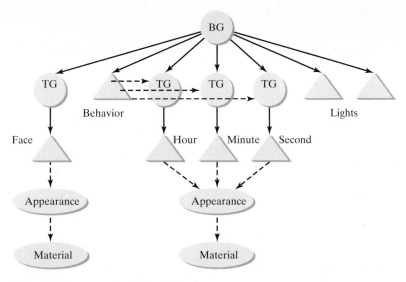

Figure 10.5 The scene graph of the clock.

initialize method (line 19) and also in the processStimulus method (line 33). The main task of the behavior is to update the clock-hands rotations based on the system time. The current time is obtained from the Calendar class. The rotations of the hands are calculated based on the time:

$$hourAngle = -\frac{2\pi}{12}\left(hour + \frac{minute}{60}\right)$$

$$minuteAngle = -\frac{2\pi}{60}minute$$

$$secondAngle = -\frac{2\pi}{60}second$$

10.3 Interaction

Interaction deals with the dynamic behavior triggered by user input. The general mechanisms for interaction and animation are similar under the behavior framework. The main difference is in the sources of wakeup conditions. In interaction the stimuli are from user input devices such as the mouse, keyboard, and 3D input devices.

Java 3D provides families of behavior subclasses for interaction. It is certainly possible to construct custom interaction behaviors using the basic Behavior class and wakeup conditions. However, the predefined utility classes are convenient for some commonly used interaction behaviors. Behavior classes related to interaction are shown in Figure 10.6.

10.3.1 Mouse Behaviors

The MouseBehavior classes define specific behaviors related to mouse motions. A behavior in this family operates on an associated TransformGroup object. Users can modify the target TransformGroup object with mouse movements. The types of mouse motions used in the behaviors are given below:

mouse behavior actions

- MouseRotate: drag the mouse with the left button down.

- MouseTranslate: drag the mouse with the right button down.

- MouseZoom: drag the mouse with the middle button down (or with left button down while holding the Alt key).

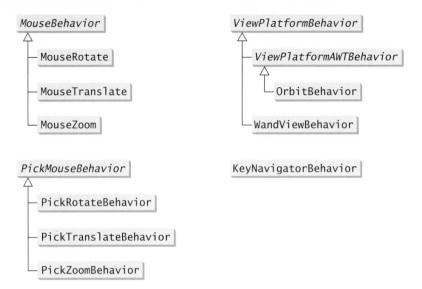

FIGURE 10.6 Interaction-related classes.

Usages of the three classes are similar. A `TransformGroup` object is selected as the target of the behavior object. The mouse behaviors can be linked to mouse events in two ways:

1. Use the `WakeupOnAWTEvent` to trigger the behavior. The target is controlled by the mouse events on the `Canvas3D` object.

2. Specify an AWT component to listen to the mouse events and use the `WakeupOn-BehaviorPost` to trigger the behavior. This mode is useful when you try to apply mouse controls from another AWT component.

Constructors of `MouseBehavior` classes include:

```
MouseRotate(TransformGroup tg)
MouseRotate(Component c)
MouseRotate(Component c, TransformGroup tg)
MouseTranslate(TransformGroup tg)
MouseTranslate(Component c)
MouseTranslate(Component c, TransformGroup tg)
MouseZoom(TransformGroup tg)
MouseZoom(Component c)
MouseZoom(Component c, TransformGroup tg)
```

The constructors with a `Component` parameter operate in the second mode that accepts a separate component for mouse actions.

Listing 10.3 shows an application of the various `MouseBehavior` classes. It displays a globe and a set of axes (Figure 10.7). A user may rotate, translate, and zoom the globe with the mouse. However, the axes are not affected by the mouse motions.

Listing 10.3 `MoveGlobe.java`

```
1 package chapter10;
2
3 import javax.vecmath.*;
4 import java.awt.*;
5 import java.awt.event.*;
6 import java.net.URL;
7 import javax.media.j3d.*;
8 import com.sun.j3d.utils.universe.*;
9 import com.sun.j3d.utils.geometry.*;
```

```
10 import com.sun.j3d.utils.image.*;
11 import com.sun.j3d.utils.behaviors.mouse.*;
12 import chapter7.Axes;
13 import java.applet.*;
14 import com.sun.j3d.utils.applet.MainFrame;
15
16 public class MoveGlobe extends Applet {
17   public static void main(String[] args) {
18     new MainFrame(new MoveGlobe(), 480, 480);
19   }
20
21   public void init() {
22     // create canvas
23     GraphicsConfiguration gc =
24       SimpleUniverse.getPreferredConfiguration();
25     Canvas3D cv = new Canvas3D(gc);
26     setLayout(new BorderLayout());
27     add(cv, BorderLayout.CENTER);
28     TextArea ta = new TextArea("",3,30,TextArea.SCROLLBARS_NONE);
29     ta.setText("Rotation: Drag with left button\n");
30     ta.append("Translation: Drag with right button\n");
31     ta.append("Zoom: Hold Alt key and drag with left button");
32     ta.setEditable(false);
33     add(ta, BorderLayout.SOUTH);
34     BranchGroup bg = createSceneGraph();
35     bg.compile();
36     SimpleUniverse su = new SimpleUniverse(cv);
37     su.getViewingPlatform().setNominalViewingTransform();
38     su.addBranchGraph(bg);
39   }
40
41   private BranchGroup createSceneGraph() {
42     BranchGroup root = new BranchGroup();
43     // axes
44     Transform3D tr = new Transform3D();
45     tr.setScale(0.5);
46     tr.setTranslation(new Vector3d(-0.8, -0.7, -0.5));
47     TransformGroup tg = new TransformGroup(tr);
48     root.addChild(tg);
49     Axes axes = new Axes();
50     tg.addChild(axes);
51     // transform
52     TransformGroup spin = new TransformGroup();
53     spin.setCapability(TransformGroup.ALLOW_TRANSFORM_WRITE);
54     spin.setCapability(TransformGroup.ALLOW_TRANSFORM_READ);
55     root.addChild(spin);
56     // texture mapped globe
57     Appearance ap = createAppearance();
58     spin.addChild(new Sphere(0.7f,
59     Primitive.GENERATE_TEXTURE_COORDS, 50, ap));
60     // rotation
61     MouseRotate rotator = new MouseRotate(spin);
62     BoundingSphere bounds = new BoundingSphere();
63     rotator.setSchedulingBounds(bounds);
64     spin.addChild(rotator);
65     // translation
66     MouseTranslate translator = new MouseTranslate(spin);
67     translator.setSchedulingBounds(bounds);
68     spin.addChild(translator);
69     // zoom
70     MouseZoom zoom = new MouseZoom(spin);
```

```
71      zoom.setSchedulingBounds(bounds);
72      spin.addChild(zoom);
73      // light
74      AmbientLight light =
75        new AmbientLight(true, new Color3f(Color.blue));
76      light.setInfluencingBounds(bounds);
77      root.addChild(light);
78      PointLight ptlight = new PointLight(new Color3f(Color.white),
79        new Point3f(0f,0f,2f), new Point3f(1f,0.3f,0f));
80      ptlight.setInfluencingBounds(bounds);
81      root.addChild(ptlight);
82      // background
83      Background background = new Background(1.0f, 1.0f, 1.0f);
84      background.setApplicationBounds(bounds);
85      root.addChild(background);
86      return root;
87    }
88
89    Appearance createAppearance(){
90      Appearance appear = new Appearance();
91      URL filename =
92        getClass().getClassLoader().getResource("images/earth.jpg");
93      TextureLoader loader = new TextureLoader(filename, this);
94      ImageComponent2D image = loader.getImage();
95      Texture2D texture = new Texture2D
96        (Texture.BASE_LEVEL, Texture.RGBA,
97      image.getWidth(), image.getHeight());
98      texture.setImage(0, image);
99      texture.setEnable(true);
100     texture.setMagFilter(Texture.BASE_LEVEL_LINEAR);
101     texture.setMinFilter(Texture.BASE_LEVEL_LINEAR);
102     appear.setTexture(texture);
103     return appear;
104   }
105 }
```

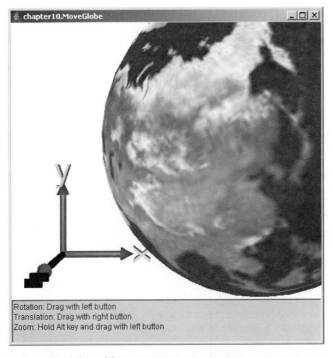

FIGURE 10.7   Moving the globe with a mouse.

A texture-mapped globe and a set of coordinate axes are displayed in the frame. The globe can be manipulated by mouse actions. A TextArea object placed under the 3D canvas displays instructions for mouse operations. When a user moves the mouse while holding down the left mouse button, the globe will rotate. Holding the right mouse button and dragging the mouse performs a translation. Holding the Alt key and dragging with the left mouse button down performs a scaling.

The scene graph of the program is shown in Figure 10.8. The Sphere object is attached to a TransformGroup object. A MouseRotate object, a MouseTranslate object, and a MouseZoom object are placed in the scene graph. They all operate on the same

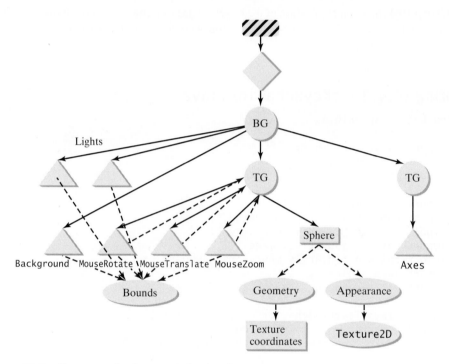

FIGURE 10.8   Scene graph of mouse behavior demo.

TransformGroup object above the sphere (lines 60–72). The three behaviors will modify different components of the transform. The behavior objects share the same bounds object for their scheduling bounds. A background node also references the bounds object.

The Axes object is on a separate branch of the scene graph with its own TransformGroup node. This transform is not controlled by the mouse behaviors. Consequently, the mouse motions will not affect the coordinate axes.

10.3.2 Key Behaviors

Similar to the mouse behaviors, the KeyNavigatorBehavior class operates on a TransformGroup object, but this behavior is controlled by key strokes. KeyNavigatorBehavior has the following constructors:

```
KeyNavigatorBehavior(TransformGroup tg)
KeyNavigatorBehavior(Component c, TransformGroup tg)
```

The built-in *key controls* of the KeyNavigatorBehavior class are defined as follows: key controls

- ■   ←, →: Rotate left/right

- ■   ↑, ↓: Translate forward/backward

- Alt- ← , Alt- → : Translate left/right

- PgUp, PgDn: Rotate up/down

- Alt-PgUp, Alt-PgDn: Translate up/down

- −: Reduce back clip distance

- +: Reset back clip distance

- =: Reset

Listing 10.4 shows an application of the KeyNavigatorBehavior class. It displays a texture-mapped globe and allows users to rotate, translate, and reset the scene through the keyboard (Figure 10.9).

Listing 10.4 TestKeyBehavior.java

```
 1 package chapter10;
 2
 3 import javax.vecmath.*;
 4 import java.awt.*;
 5 import java.awt.event.*;
 6 import java.net.URL;
 7 import javax.media.j3d.*;
 8 import com.sun.j3d.utils.universe.*;
 9 import com.sun.j3d.utils.geometry.*;
10 import com.sun.j3d.utils.image.*;
11 import com.sun.j3d.utils.behaviors.keyboard.*;
12 import java.applet.*;
13 import com.sun.j3d.utils.applet.MainFrame;
14
15 public class TestKeyBehavior extends Applet {
16    public static void main(String[] args) {
17      new MainFrame(new TestKeyBehavior(), 480, 480);
18    }
19
20    public void init() {
21      GraphicsConfiguration gc =
22        SimpleUniverse.getPreferredConfiguration();
23      Canvas3D cv = new Canvas3D(gc);
24      setLayout(new BorderLayout());
25      add(cv, BorderLayout.CENTER);
26      TextArea ta = new TextArea("",3,30,TextArea.SCROLLBARS_NONE);
27      ta.setText("Rotation: left, right, PgUp, PgDn\n");
28      ta.append("Translation: up, down,
29      Alt-left, Alt-right, Alt-PgUp, Alt-PgDn\n");
30      ta.append("Reset: =\n");
31      ta.setEditable(false);
32      add(ta, BorderLayout.SOUTH);
33      BranchGroup bg = createSceneGraph();
34      bg.compile();
35      SimpleUniverse su = new SimpleUniverse(cv);
36      su.getViewingPlatform().setNominalViewingTransform();
37      su.addBranchGraph(bg);
38    }
39
40    private BranchGroup createSceneGraph() {
41      BranchGroup root = new BranchGroup();
42      TransformGroup spin = new TransformGroup();
43      spin.setCapability(TransformGroup.ALLOW_TRANSFORM_WRITE);
```

```
44      spin.setCapability(TransformGroup.ALLOW_TRANSFORM_READ);
45      root.addChild(spin);
46      // texture mapped globe
47      Appearance ap = createAppearance();
48      spin.addChild(new Sphere(0.7f,
49      Primitive.GENERATE_TEXTURE_COORDS, 50, ap));
50      // key behavior
51      KeyNavigatorBehavior behavior = new KeyNavigatorBehavior(spin);
52      BoundingSphere bounds = new BoundingSphere();
53      behavior.setSchedulingBounds(bounds);
54      spin.addChild(behavior);
55      // background
56      Background background = new Background(1.0f, 1.0f, 1.0f);
57      background.setApplicationBounds(bounds);
58      root.addChild(background);
59      return root;
60    }
61
62    Appearance createAppearance(){
63      Appearance appear = new Appearance();
64      URL filename =
65        getClass().getClassLoader().getResource("images/earth.jpg");
66      TextureLoader loader = new TextureLoader(filename, this);
67      ImageComponent2D image = loader.getImage();
68      Texture2D texture =
69        new Texture2D(Texture.BASE_LEVEL, Texture.RGBA,
70      image.getWidth(), image.getHeight());
71      texture.setImage(0, image);
72      texture.setEnable(true);
73      texture.setMagFilter(Texture.BASE_LEVEL_LINEAR);
74      texture.setMinFilter(Texture.BASE_LEVEL_LINEAR);
75      appear.setTexture(texture);
76      return appear;
77    }
78 }
```

FIGURE 10.9   Controlling transformation through the keyboard.

This program allows the user to manipulate the visual object, a texture-mapped globe, through the keyboard. A text area at the bottom of the window displays the instructions to use the keyboard for navigating the scene.

The scene graph is shown in Figure 10.10. A texture-mapped sphere similar to the one in Listing 10.2 is created and attached to a `TransformGroup` object. A `KeyNavigator-Behavior` object is created to operate on the `TransformGroup` node (line 51). The behavior object will react to keyboard inputs by performing associated transformations. The `KeyNavigatorBehavior` object uses a `BoundingSphere` as its scheduling bounds. The bounds object is also referenced by a white background.

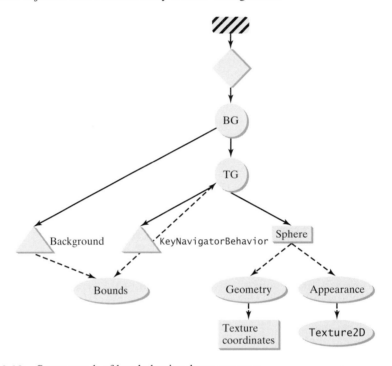

FIGURE 10.10 Scene graph of key behavior demo program.

10.3.3 View Platform Behaviors

The `ViewPlatformBehavior` classes support interaction with the view platform. The class `OrbitBehavior` allows changes in view platform through mouse-motion input. Unlike the `MouseBehavior` class that has three separate subclasses for different transformations, this single class `OrbitBehavior` supports three operations: rotation, translation, and zoom. The definitions for mouse operations are the same as the `MouseBehavior` classes. A `Canvas3D` object is used by `OrbitBehavior` `OrbitBehavior`. To create an `OrbitBehavior` object the following constructors can be used:

```
OrbitBehavior()
OrbitBehavior(Canvas3D cv)
OrbitBehavior(Canvas3D cv, int flags)
```

An `OrbitBehavior` object can be added to a scene graph by calling the method `setViewP-latformBehavior` in the class `ViewingPlatform` that is a part of `SimpleUniverse`.

Listing 10.5 illustrates the use of `OrbitBehavior` to manipulate the view platform. It displays a globe and allows users to rotate, translate, and zoom the entire view through mouse motions (See Figure 10.11.)

Listing 10.5 MoveView.java

```
1 package chapter10;
2
```

```
 3  import javax.vecmath.*;
 4  import java.awt.*;
 5  import java.awt.event.*;
 6  import java.net.URL;
 7  import javax.media.j3d.*;
 8  import com.sun.j3d.utils.universe.*;
 9  import com.sun.j3d.utils.geometry.*;
10  import com.sun.j3d.utils.image.*;
11  import com.sun.j3d.utils.behaviors.mouse.*;
12  import com.sun.j3d.utils.behaviors.vp.*;
13  import chapter7.Axes;
14  import java.applet.*;
15  import com.sun.j3d.utils.applet.MainFrame;
16
17  public class MoveView extends Applet {
18    public static void main(String[] args) {
19      new MainFrame(new MoveView(), 480, 480);
20    }
21
22    public void init() {
23      GraphicsConfiguration gc =
24        SimpleUniverse.getPreferredConfiguration();
25      Canvas3D cv = new Canvas3D(gc);
26      setLayout(new BorderLayout());
27      add(cv, BorderLayout.CENTER);
28      TextArea ta = new TextArea("",3,30,TextArea.SCROLLBARS_NONE);
29      ta.setText("Rotation: Drag with left button\n");
30      ta.append("Translation: Drag with right button\n");
31      ta.append("Zoom: Hold Alt key and drag with left button");
32      ta.setEditable(false);
33      add(ta, BorderLayout.SOUTH);
34      BranchGroup root = new BranchGroup();
35      // axes
36      Transform3D tr = new Transform3D();
37      tr.setScale(0.5);
38      tr.setTranslation(new Vector3d(-0.8, -0.7, -0.5));
39      TransformGroup tg = new TransformGroup(tr);
40      root.addChild(tg);
41      Axes axes = new Axes();
42      tg.addChild(axes);
43      // texture mapped globe
44      Appearance ap = createAppearance();
45      root.addChild(new Sphere(0.7f,
46      Primitive.GENERATE_TEXTURE_COORDS, 50, ap));
47      BoundingSphere bounds = new BoundingSphere();
48      // light
49      AmbientLight light = new AmbientLight(true,
50      new Color3f(Color.blue));
51      light.setInfluencingBounds(bounds);
52      root.addChild(light);
53      PointLight ptlight = new PointLight(new Color3f(Color.white),
54      new Point3f(0f,0f,2f), new Point3f(1f,0.3f,0f));
55      ptlight.setInfluencingBounds(bounds);
56      root.addChild(ptlight);
57      // background
58      Background background = createBackground();
59      background.setApplicationBounds(bounds);
60      root.addChild(background);
61      root.compile();
62      SimpleUniverse su = new SimpleUniverse(cv);
63      su.getViewingPlatform().setNominalViewingTransform();
64      // viewplatform motion
```

```
65     OrbitBehavior orbit = new OrbitBehavior(cv);
66     orbit.setSchedulingBounds(new BoundingSphere());
67     su.getViewingPlatform().setViewPlatformBehavior(orbit);
68
69     su.addBranchGraph(root);
70   }
71
72   Appearance createAppearance(){
73     Appearance appear = new Appearance();
74     URL filename =
75       getClass().getClassLoader().getResource("images/earth.jpg");
76     TextureLoader loader = new TextureLoader(filename, this);
77     Texture texture = loader.getTexture();
78     appear.setTexture(texture);
79     return appear;
80   }
81
82   Background createBackground(){
83     Background background = new Background();
84     BranchGroup bg = new BranchGroup();
85     Sphere sphere = new Sphere(1.0f, Sphere.GENERATE_NORMALS |
86     Sphere.GENERATE_NORMALS_INWARD |
87     Sphere.GENERATE_TEXTURE_COORDS, 60);
88     Appearance ap = sphere.getAppearance();
89     bg.addChild(sphere);
90     background.setGeometry(bg);
91
92     URL filename =
93       getClass().getClassLoader().getResource("images/stars.jpg");
94     TextureLoader loader = new TextureLoader(filename, this);
95     Texture texture = loader.getTexture();
96     ap.setTexture(texture);
97     return background;
98   }
99 }
```

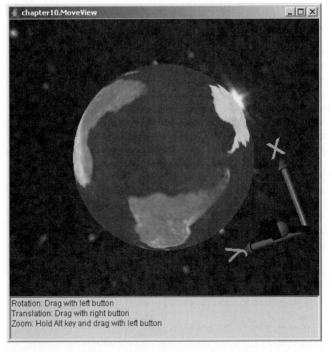

FIGURE 10.11 Manipulating the view. The view changes with the mouse motions.

This program appears to be similar to Listing 10.3. The user can rotate, translate, and zoom the scene with mouse motions. However, there are some differences. Because the behavior movement is applied to the view platform instead of to the objects, the directions of the motion will be the opposite of those in Listing 10.3. Another difference is that in this example the entire view of the scene changes as the mouse moves. In Listing 10.3 the movement applies only to the globe, and the axes do not move.

The scene graph is shown in Figure 10.12. The `OrbitBehavior` operates on the transform associated with the `ViewPlatform`. This configuration is established by the following statements (lines 65–67):

```
OrbitBehavior orbit = new OrbitBehavior(cv);
orbit.setSchedulingBounds(new BoundingSphere());
su.getViewingPlatform().setViewPlatformBehavior(orbit);
```

Because the behavior is in the view branch, the visual objects are not actually moved by the mouse motions. The behavior changes the positioning of the view platform. Therefore, the entire scene, including the globe and the axes, appears to move in the opposite directions of the mouse operations.

The method `createBackground` (line 82) creates a background using a texture-mapped sphere as its geometry. The background provides a better perception of the view motion.

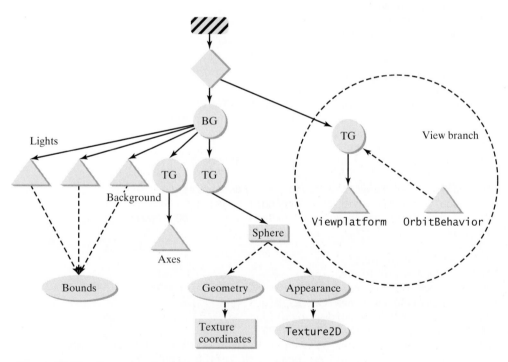

FIGURE 10.12   Scene graph of the View Behaviors example.

10.4 Behavior and Picking

Picking is often applied in conjunction with behaviors to perform interactions associated with specific visual objects. Picking provides a mechanism to dynamically select visual objects. The behavior structure offers a systematic way to incorporate operations on the scene.

10.4.1 Picking and Mouse Behaviors

The `PickMouseBehavior` classes, including `PickRotateBehavior`, `PickTranslate-Behavior`, and `PickZoomBehavior`, combine picking with mouse behaviors. The mouse-controlled rotation, translation, and zoom operations are the same as those defined in `MouseBehavior`, but they are applied only to the picked objects. Creating a `PickMouse-Behavior` node involves the `Canvas3D` object, the root of a branch of scene graph for picking, and the scheduling bounds. For example, the following code fragment sets up a `PickRotateBehavior` on the `root`:

```
PickRotateBehavior rotator = new PickRotateBehavior(cv, root, bounds);
root.addChild(rotator);
```

It is necessary to place a `TransformGroup` node over the object to be picked so that the behaviors can find a target to operate. It is also necessary to turn on the appropriate capability bits on the picked objects as well as the transformation nodes.

Listing 10.6 illustrates the application of `PickMouseBehavior` classes. The program displays a group of seagulls placed randomly in the scene (Figure 10.13). Users can individually rotate, translate, and zoom each of the seagulls through mouse motions.

Listing 10.6 `TestPickBehavior.java`

```
 1 package chapter10;
 2
 3 import javax.vecmath.*;
 4 import java.awt.*;
 5 import java.awt.event.*;
 6 import java.net.URL;
 7 import javax.media.j3d.*;
 8 import com.sun.j3d.utils.universe.*;
 9 import com.sun.j3d.utils.geometry.*;
10 import com.sun.j3d.utils.picking.PickTool;
11 import com.sun.j3d.utils.picking.behaviors.*;
12 import chapter7.Axes;
13 import java.applet.*;
14 import com.sun.j3d.utils.applet.MainFrame;
15
16 public class TestPickBehavior extends Applet {
17   public static void main(String[] args) {
18     new MainFrame(new TestPickBehavior(), 480, 480);
19   }
20
21   public void init() {
22     GraphicsConfiguration gc =
23       SimpleUniverse.getPreferredConfiguration();
24     Canvas3D cv = new Canvas3D(gc);
25     setLayout(new BorderLayout());
26     add(cv, BorderLayout.CENTER);
27     TextArea ta = new TextArea("",3,30,TextArea.SCROLLBARS_NONE);
28     ta.setText("Rotation: Drag with left button\n");
29     ta.append("Translation: Drag with right button\n");
30     ta.append("Zoom: Hold Alt key and drag with left button");
31     ta.setEditable(false);
32     add(ta, BorderLayout.SOUTH);
33     BranchGroup bg = createSceneGraph(cv);
34     bg.compile();
35     SimpleUniverse su = new SimpleUniverse(cv);
36     su.getViewingPlatform().setNominalViewingTransform();
```

```
37      su.addBranchGraph(bg);
38    }
39
40    private BranchGroup createSceneGraph(Canvas3D cv) {
41      BranchGroup root = new BranchGroup();
42      // add 8 seagulls
43      for (int i = 0; i < 8; i++)
44        root.addChild(createObject());
45
46      BoundingSphere bounds = new BoundingSphere();
47      // rotation
48      PickRotateBehavior rotator =
49        new PickRotateBehavior(root, cv, bounds,
50        PickTool.GEOMETRY);
51      root.addChild(rotator);
52      // translation
53      PickTranslateBehavior translator =
54        new PickTranslateBehavior(root, cv,
55        bounds, PickTool.GEOMETRY);
56      root.addChild(translator);
57      // zoom
58      PickZoomBehavior zoom = new PickZoomBehavior(root, cv, bounds,
59        PickTool.GEOMETRY);
60      root.addChild(zoom);
61      // light
62      AmbientLight light = new AmbientLight(true,
63      new Color3f(Color.blue));
64        light.setInfluencingBounds(bounds);
65      root.addChild(light);
66      PointLight ptlight = new PointLight(new Color3f(Color.white),
67        new Point3f(0f,0f,2f), new Point3f(1f,0.3f,0f));
68      ptlight.setInfluencingBounds(bounds);
69      root.addChild(ptlight);
70      // background
71      Background background = new Background(1.0f, 1.0f, 1.0f);
72      background.setApplicationBounds(bounds);
73      root.addChild(background);
74      return root;
75    }
76
77    private Node createObject() {
78      // transform
79      Transform3D trans = new Transform3D();
80      trans.setTranslation(new Vector3d(Math.random()-0.5,
81        Math.random()-0.5, Math.random()-0.5));
82      trans.setScale(0.3);
83      TransformGroup spin = new TransformGroup(trans);
84      spin.setCapability(TransformGroup.ALLOW_TRANSFORM_WRITE);
85      spin.setCapability(TransformGroup.ALLOW_TRANSFORM_READ);
86      spin.setCapability(TransformGroup.ENABLE_PICK_REPORTING);
87      // visual objects
88      Appearance ap = new Appearance();
89      ap.setMaterial(new Material());
90      Shape3D shape = new Shape3D(new GullCG(), ap);
91      PickTool.setCapabilities(shape, PickTool.INTERSECT_FULL);
92      spin.addChild(shape);
93      return spin;
94    }
95  }
```

FIGURE 10.13 `PickMouseBehavior` classes allow manipulations of individual objects.

The scene contains eight gulls located randomly. Each gull can be picked and manipulated with the mouse. Dragging with the left mouse button rotates the gull. Dragging with the right mouse button translates the gull. Dragging with the middle mouse button (or the left mouse button while holding the Alt key) zooms the gull.

The scene graph is shown in Figure 10.14. Three `PickMouseBehavior` objects: `Pick-RotateBehavior`, `PickTranslateBehavior`, and `PickZoomBehavior`, are created to act on the root `BranchGroup` node (lines 47–60). Eight gulls are created with identical structures. The `createObject` method builds a branch of the scene graph consisting of a `TransformGroup` object and a `Shape3D` object. The `GullCG` class defines the geometry for the `Shape3D`. An `Appearance` with a `Material` component is used for the shape. The dedicated `TransformGroup` node for each shape is necessary for the pick-mouse behaviors to operate individually on each gull. On the `TransformGroup` nodes the following *capability bits* are turned on (lines 85–87):

capability bits

```
TransformGroup.ALLOW_TRANSFORM_WRITE
TransformGroup.ALLOW_TRANSFORM_READ
TransformGroup.ENABLE_PICK_REPORTING
```

On the shapes, the following method is called to turn on all related capability bits (line 92):

```
PickTool.setCapabilities(shape, PickTool.INTERSECT_FULL);
```

Two lights are added to illuminate the gulls with material appearance. A white background is added. All the behavior nodes, the lights, and the background node share the same bounds object.

10.4.2 Data Visualization

The combination of picking and behaviors provides a powerful tool for interaction with a 3D scene. Picking allows for selections of specific scene-graph objects, and behaviors offer a way

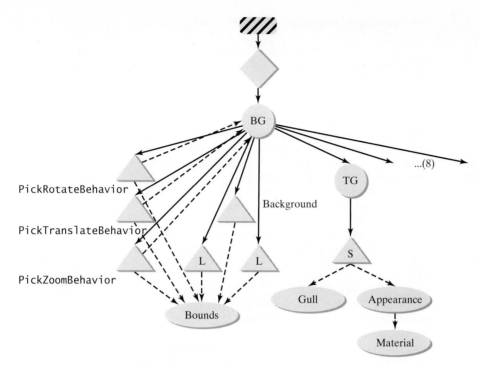

FIGURE 10.14   The scene graph.

to change the scene. In a data visualization application, for example, it will be a useful feature for the user to rotate, translate, and zoom a 3D plot with the mouse. The motions will significantly improve the perception of the 3D structure. It will also be useful to select specific data points with the mouse.

Listing 10.7 shows one approach to implementing such functions with picking and behaviors. The program displays a 3D scatter plot (Figure 10.15). 3D data points are plotted as colored dots. Users will be able to rotate, translate, and zoom the plot to view the data from different perspectives. The motions will help the user gain a better understanding of the 3D structure of the data from the 2D screen. Individual data points can also be selected on the plot with mouse clicking. A text field at the bottom of the window displays the index and coordinates of the selected point.

Listing 10.7 DataViewer.java

```
 1 package chapter10;
 2
 3 import javax.vecmath.*;
 4 import java.awt.*;
 5 import java.awt.event.*;
 6 import javax.media.j3d.*;
 7 import com.sun.j3d.utils.universe.*;
 8 import com.sun.j3d.utils.geometry.*;
 9 import com.sun.j3d.utils.picking.*;
10 import com.sun.j3d.utils.behaviors.mouse.*;
11 import chapter7.Axes;
12 import java.applet.*;
13 import com.sun.j3d.utils.applet.MainFrame;
14
15 public class DataViewer3D extends Applet {
16   public static void main(String[] args) {
```

```
17        new MainFrame(new DataViewer3D(), 640, 480);
18      }
19
20      PointArray geom;
21      PickCanvas pc;
22      TextField text;
23
24      public void init() {
25        setLayout(new BorderLayout());
26        GraphicsConfiguration gc =
27          SimpleUniverse.getPreferredConfiguration();
28        Canvas3D cv = new Canvas3D(gc);
29        add(cv, BorderLayout.CENTER);
30        cv.addMouseListener(new MouseAdapter() {
31          public void mouseClicked
32            (java.awt.event.MouseEvent mouseEvent) {
33            pick(mouseEvent);
34          }
35        });
36        text = new TextField();
37        add(text, BorderLayout.SOUTH);
38        BranchGroup bg = createSceneGraph(cv);
39        bg.compile();
40        SimpleUniverse su = new SimpleUniverse(cv);
41        su.getViewingPlatform().setNominalViewingTransform();
42        su.addBranchGraph(bg);
43      }
44
45      private BranchGroup createSceneGraph(Canvas3D cv) {
46        BranchGroup root = new BranchGroup();
47        TransformGroup spin = new TransformGroup();
48        spin.setCapability(TransformGroup.ALLOW_TRANSFORM_READ);
49        spin.setCapability(TransformGroup.ALLOW_TRANSFORM_WRITE);
50        root.addChild(spin);
51        // axes
52        Transform3D tr = new Transform3D();
53        tr.setScale(0.3);
54        TransformGroup tg = new TransformGroup(tr);
55        spin.addChild(tg);
56        Axes axes = new Axes();
57        tg.addChild(axes);
58        // appearance
59        Appearance ap = new Appearance();
60        ap.setPointAttributes(new PointAttributes(10f, true));
61        // objects
62        int n = 20;
63        geom = new PointArray(n,
64          PointArray.COORDINATES | PointArray.COLOR_4);
65        geom.setCapability(PointArray.ALLOW_COORDINATE_READ);
66        geom.setCapability(PointArray.ALLOW_FORMAT_READ);
67        geom.setCapability(PointArray.ALLOW_COLOR_READ);
68        geom.setCapability(PointArray.ALLOW_COLOR_WRITE);
69        geom.setCapability(PointArray.ALLOW_COUNT_READ);
70        Point3f[] coords = new Point3f[n];
71        Color4f[] colors = new Color4f[n];
72        for (int i = 0; i < n; i++) {
```

```
73     coords[i] = new Point3f((float)(Math.random()-0.5),
74       (float)(Math.random()-0.5),(float)(Math.random()-0.5));
75     colors[i] = new Color4f((float)(Math.random()),
76       (float)(Math.random()),(float)(Math.random()),1f);
77   }
78   geom.setCoordinates(0, coords);
79   geom.setColors(0, colors);
80   BranchGroup bg = new BranchGroup();
81   spin.addChild(bg);
82   pc = new PickCanvas(cv, bg);
83   pc.setTolerance(5);
84   pc.setMode(PickTool.GEOMETRY_INTERSECT_INFO);
85   Shape3D shape = new Shape3D(geom, ap);
86   bg.addChild(shape);
87   PickTool.setCapabilities(shape, PickTool.INTERSECT_TEST);
88   shape.setCapability(Shape3D.ALLOW_GEOMETRY_READ);
89   // rotation
90   MouseRotate rotator = new MouseRotate(spin);
91   BoundingSphere bounds = new BoundingSphere();
92   rotator.setSchedulingBounds(bounds);
93   spin.addChild(rotator);
94   // translation
95   MouseTranslate translator = new MouseTranslate(spin);
96   translator.setSchedulingBounds(bounds);
97   spin.addChild(translator);
98   // zoom
99   MouseZoom zoom = new MouseZoom(spin);
100  zoom.setSchedulingBounds(bounds);
101  spin.addChild(zoom);
102  // background and light
103  Background background = new Background(1.0f, 1.0f, 1.0f);
104  background.setApplicationBounds(bounds);
105  root.addChild(background);
106  AmbientLight light =
107    new AmbientLight(true, new Color3f(Color.red));
108  light.setInfluencingBounds(bounds);
109  root.addChild(light);
110  PointLight ptlight = new PointLight(new Color3f(Color.green),
111    new Point3f(3f,3f,3f), new Point3f(1f,0f,0f));
112  ptlight.setInfluencingBounds(bounds);
113  root.addChild(ptlight);
114  PointLight ptlight2 = new PointLight(new Color3f(Color.orange),
115    new Point3f(-2f,2f,2f), new Point3f(1f,0f,0f));
116  ptlight2.setInfluencingBounds(bounds);
117  root.addChild(ptlight2);
118  return root;
119  }
120
121  private void pick(MouseEvent mouseEvent) {
122    Color4f color = new Color4f();
123    pc.setShapeLocation(mouseEvent);
124    PickResult[] results = pc.pickAll();
125    for (int i = 0; (results != null) &&
126      (i < results.length); i++) {
127      PickIntersection inter = results[i].getIntersection(0);
128      Point3d pt = inter.getClosestVertexCoordinates();
```

```
129        int[] ind = inter.getPrimitiveCoordinateIndices();
130        text.setText("vertex " + ind[0] + ": (" + pt.x + ", "
131          + pt.y + ", " + pt.z + ")");
132        geom.getColor(ind[0], color);
133        color.x = 1f - color.x;
134        color.y = 1f - color.y;
135        color.z = 1f - color.z;
136        if (color.w > 0.8) color.w = 0.5f;
137        else color.w = 1f;
138        geom.setColor(ind[0], color);
139    }
140  }
141 }
```

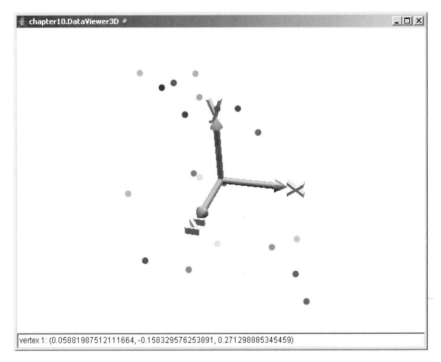

Figure 10.15   A 3D scatter plot featuring data-point selection and transformations under user control.

The scene graph of the program is shown in Figure 10.16. Three `MouseBehavior` objects: `MouseRotate`, `MouseTranslate`, and `MouseZoom` are set to operate on a `TransformGroup` node. The behaviors provide the capabilities to rotate, translate, and zoom the plot.

The data points to be plotted are generated randomly and represented with a `PointArray` geometry (lines 61–79). The colors of the points are randomly assigned with `Color4f` objects. An `Axes` object is used to provide a visual reference of the coordinate system. An extra `BranchGroup` node is placed on top of the data object. It is used for picking operation. Picking is not applied to the root `BranchGroup` node because the `Axes` object should be excluded from picking.

A mouse listener is placed on the `Canvas3D` object. It listens to mouse-click events and performs a picking on the branch for data points by calling the `pick` method (line 121). A

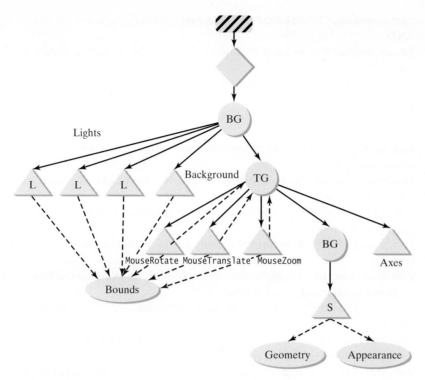

FIGURE 10.16 Scene graph.

`PickCanvas` object is used to perform picking based on the mouse location. Because all data points belong to one object as vertices, it is necessary to obtain the *intersections* of the pick-   intersection ing to determine the specific point (lines 127–128):

```
PickIntersection inter = results[i].getIntersection(0);
Point3d pt = inter.getClosestVertexCoordinates();
```

The index of the vertex in the geometry can also be obtained (line 129):

```
int[] ind = inter.getPrimitiveCoordinateIndices();
```

When the vertex in the intersection is retrieved, its index and coordinates are displayed in the text field at the bottom of the frame. The selected point will be shown in a different color. The new color is the complement of the original color, so if you select a point twice, it will return to its original color.

KEY CLASSES AND METHODS

- **javax.media.j3d.Behavior** A class encapsulating a dynamic behavior.
- **javax.media.j3d.WakeupCondition** A base class for wakeup conditions.
- **javax.media.j3d.WakeupCriterion** A base class encapsulating various specific wakeup conditions.
- **javax.media.j3d.WakeupOnElapsedTime** A wakeup criterion based on elapsed time.
- **javax.media.j3d.WakeupOnAWTEvent** A wakeup criterion based on AWT events.

- `javax.media.j3d.WakeupAnd` A class for combining wakeup criteria with logical AND.
- `javax.media.j3d.WakeupOr` A class for combining wakeup criteria with logical OR.
- `javax.media.j3d.WakeupAndOfOrs` A class for combining `WakeupOr` conditions with logical AND.
- `javax.media.j3d.WakeupOrOfAnds` A class for combining `WakeupAnd` conditions with logical OR.
- `com.sun.j3d.utils.behaviors.mouse.MouseBehavior` A base class for mouse-driven behaviors.
- `com.sun.j3d.utils.behaviors.mouse.MouseRotate` A mouse-controlled rotation behavior.
- `com.sun.j3d.utils.behaviors.mouse.MouseTranslate` A mouse-controlled translation behavior.
- `com.sun.j3d.utils.behaviors.mouse.MouseZoom` A mouse-controlled zoom behavior.
- `com.sun.j3d.utils.behaviors.keyboard.KeyNavigatorBehavior` A keyboard-based transformation behavior.
- `com.sun.j3d.utils.behaviors.vp.OrbitBehavior` A mouse-driven view-platform transformation behavior.
- `com.sun.j3d.utils.picking.behaviors.PickMouseBehavior` A base class for mouse-driven picking and transformation behaviors.
- `com.sun.j3d.utils.picking.behaviors.PickRotateBehavior` A mouse-controlled picking and rotation behavior.
- `com.sun.j3d.utils.picking.behaviors.PickTranslateBehavior` A mouse-controlled picking and translation behavior.
- `com.sun.j3d.utils.picking.behaviors.PickZoomBehavior` A mouse-controlled picking and zoom behavior.
- `javax.media.j3d.MouseBehavior.initialize()` An initialization method called once by the scheduler.
- `javax.media.j3d.MouseBehavior.processStimulus(Enumeration)` A method called when a wakeup condition occurs.
- `javax.media.j3d.MouseBehavior.wakeupOn(WakeupCondition)` A method to set a wakeup condition.

KEY TERMS

behavior A model for dynamics in a 3D scene.
interaction A dynamic behavior related to user input.
wakeup condition A condition to trigger a behavior.
picking behavior An interaction based on picking.

CHAPTER SUMMARY

- This chapter introduces the concept of behavior that represents dynamics of a 3D scene in a systematical way. Commonly used dynamic changes such as interactions and animations can be modeled as behaviors. The general behavior mechanism and the interaction behaviors are discussed in this chapter. Animation is covered in the next chapter.

■ Java 3D provides the classes in `Behavior` and `WakeupCondition` families to facilitate various behavior operations. A `Behavior` object establishes wakeup conditions and responds to stimuli from the wakeup conditions to fulfill their tasks. A large collection of specific wakeup conditions are supplied by Java 3D under the class hierarchy `WakeupCriterion`. The criteria can also be combined using certain logical operations to form composite wakeup conditions.

■ Interaction is typically accomplished through behaviors with wakeup conditions related to user input events such as mouse and keyboard actions. Java 3D contains several utility packages to support interaction.

■ The `MouseBehavior` family of classes provides behaviors for controlling `TransformGroup` nodes with mouse actions. The `KeyNavigatorBehavior` class uses the keyboard to control the transform. The `ViewPlatformBehavior` classes operate on view platforms.

■ Picking is often combined with behaviors to construct interactions. The utility classes in the `PickMouseBehavior` family provide convenient constructions of behaviors that link picking to affine transforms.

REVIEW QUESTIONS

10.1   Discuss the advantages of defining a behavior as a scene-graph node.

10.2   Describe the differences between interaction and animation.

10.3   Which `WakeupCriterion` classes are usually associated with interaction?

10.4   Describe the differences between `MouseBehavior` and `ViewPlatformAWT-Behavior` classes.

10.5   In Listing 10.6, what happens if all gulls are attached to the same `TransformGroup` node instead of their own transforms?

PROGRAMMING EXERCISES

10.1   Write a Java 3D program to display a real-time digital clock using 3D text.

10.2   Add a `MouseRotate` behavior to the program in Problem 10.1 to allow rotation of the clock by mouse dragging.

10.3   Add a `MouseTranslate` behavior to the program in Problem 10.2 to allow translation of the clock by mouse motion.

10.4   Add a `MouseZoom` behavior to the program in Problem 10.3 to allow zooming of the clock by mouse dragging.

10.5   Add a `KeyNavigationBehavior` to the program in Problem 10.4 to allow keyboard manipulation of the clock.

10.6 Modify the code in Listing 10.6 so that only one instance of the GullCG geometry is used.

10.7 Rewrite Listing 10.7 to use an OrbitBehavior for controlling the view with mouse actions.

10.8 Rewrite Listing 10.7 so it uses a Behavior instead of a mouse listener to handle the picking.

CHAPTER 11

ANIMATION

Objectives

- To understand the concept and methods of animation.
- To understand and create `Alpha` objects.
- To apply various interpolators to creating animations.
- To create morphing with `Morph` nodes and behaviors.
- To use LOD behaviors.
- To use billboard behaviors.

11.1 Introduction

Animation generates sequences of graphics renderings that vary with time, producing an effect of live motions. Both interaction and animation generate dynamic behaviors in graphics systems, but animation is usually time related, and producing the frames, the intermediate results of the changing process, is often the main objective of an animation.

Animation is a common dynamic effect in computer graphics. To produce the animated graphics effects, the rendered scene must change dynamically with time. The changes may involve different attributes of the scene such as geometry, transformation, position, color, and transparency.

interpolator

Java 3D provides extensive support for incorporation of animation into a scene graph through the Behavior class. A family of behavior classes known as the *interpolators* encapsulates the common animation actions. The Alpha class that represents a function of time serves as the driving force for the interpolators. It is easy to create an animation with an interpolator. You need only create an appropriate interpolator object with an alpha, and link the interpolator to its target object.

Other animation-related techniques include morphing, level of detail (LOD), and billboard behaviors. Morphing defines a smooth change of geometries. LOD provides a method to offer different levels of rendering details depending on the distance of the object from the eye. Billboard behavior provides a convenient method to automatically adjust the orientation of an object so that it will always face the viewer.

11.2 Alpha Objects

alpha

Animations tie the dynamic changes of a scene to time. An *alpha* object defines a (usually periodic) function of time that produces values between 0.0 and 1.0. It is usually more convenient to drive an animation with an alpha than with a real-time clock. Java 3D Alpha class is a subclass of NodeComponent. The Alpha objects provide inputs to the animation tool known as the Interpolator. The functional shape of an Alpha object is defined by several parameters. An example waveform of an Alpha object is shown in Figure 11.1.

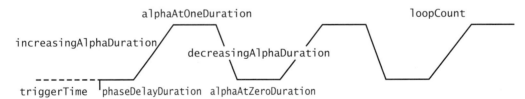

FIGURE 11.1 The waveform of an Alpha object.

Alpha parameters

A Java 3D Alpha object includes the following parameters:

■ LoopCount: The number of pulses or periods. The value −1 indicates an unlimited number of loops.

■ startTime: The absolute time for the initial reference point.

■ triggerTime: The time in milliseconds from the startTime for activating the Alpha object.

■ phaseDelayDuration: The time in milliseconds for the initial delay from the triggerTime.

■ alphaAtZeroDuration: The time in milliseconds for the alpha value to stay at 0.0.

■ alphaAtOneDuration: The time in milliseconds for the alpha value to stay at 1.0.

■ increasingAlphaDuration: The time in milliseconds for the alpha value to increase from 0.0 to 1.0.

- decreasingAlphaDuration: The time in milliseconds for the alpha value to decrease from 1.0 to 0.0.

- increasingAlphaRampDuration: The time in milliseconds for the alpha value to accelerate during the increasing phase.

- decreasingAlphaRampDuration: The time in milliseconds for the alpha value to accelerate during the decreasing phase.

The parameters increasingAlphaRampDuration and decreasingAlphaRamp-Duration define certain smoothing effects on the waveform. The value of increasing-AlphaRampDuration specifies an interval of acceleration at the beginning of the increasing phase and an interval of deceleration at the end of the increasing phase. Similarly the value of decreasingAlphaRampDuration specifies an interval of deceleration and acceleration for the decreasing phase.

The following constructors are available for Alpha objects:

```
public Alpha()
public Alpha(int loopCount, long increasingAlphaDuration)
public Alpha(int loopCount, long triggerTime,
  long phaseDelayDuration, long
  increasingAlphaDuration, long increasingAlphaRampDuration,
  long alphaAtOneDuration)
public Alpha(int loopCount, int mode, long triggerTime,
  long phaseDelayDuration, long
  increasingAlphaDuration, long increasingAlphaRampDuration,
  long alphaAtOneDuration, long
  decreaingAlphaDuration, long dereasingAlphaRampDuration,
  long alphaAtZeroDuration)
```

The alpha values of an Alpha object can be retrieved with the value methods:

```
public float value()
public float value(long atTime)
```

The first method gets the alpha value for the current time. The second method gets the value for the specified time.

Listing 11.1 plots the waveform of an alpha object (Figure 11.2). Parameters of the alpha can be changed at runtime to show the their effects on the waveform.

Listing 11.1 TestAlpha.java

```
1 package chapter11;
2
3 import java.awt.*;
4 import java.awt.event.*;
5 import javax.swing.*;
6 import javax.media.j3d.*;
7
8 public class TestAlpha extends JApplet {
9   public static void main(String s[]) {
10     JFrame frame = new JFrame();
11     frame.setTitle("Alpha");
12     frame.setDefaultCloseOperation(JFrame.EXIT_ON_CLOSE);
13     JApplet applet = new TestAlpha();
14     applet.init();
15     frame.getContentPane().add(applet);
16     frame.pack();
17     frame.setVisible(true);
18   }
19
```

```
20    Alpha alpha = new Alpha();
21    Plot plot;
22    JTextField tfLoopCount;
23    JTextField tfTriggerTime;
24    JTextField tfAlphaAtZeroDuration;
25    JTextField tfAlphaAtOneDuration;
26    JTextField tfIncreasingAlphaDuration;
27    JTextField tfDecreasingAlphaDuration;
28    JTextField tfIncreasingAlphaRampDuration;
29    JTextField tfDecreasingAlphaRampDuration;
30
31    public void init() {
32      Container cp = this.getContentPane();
33      cp.setLayout(new BorderLayout());
34      plot = new Plot();
35      cp.add(plot, BorderLayout.CENTER);
36      JPanel p = new JPanel();
37      p.setBorder(BorderFactory.createTitledBorder(
38        "Alpha parameters"));
39      cp.add(p, BorderLayout.SOUTH);
40      p.setLayout(new GridLayout(5, 4, 10, 5));
41      p.add(new JLabel("loopCount"));
42      tfLoopCount = new JTextField("-1");
43      p.add(tfLoopCount);
44      p.add(new JLabel("triggerTime"));
45      tfTriggerTime = new JTextField("0");
46      p.add(tfTriggerTime);
47      p.add(new JLabel("alphaAtZeroDuration"));
48      tfAlphaAtZeroDuration = new JTextField("0");
49      p.add(tfAlphaAtZeroDuration);
50      p.add(new JLabel("alphaAtOneDuration"));
51      tfAlphaAtOneDuration = new JTextField("0");
52      p.add(tfAlphaAtOneDuration);
53      p.add(new JLabel("increasingAlphaDuration"));
54      tfIncreasingAlphaDuration = new JTextField("1000");
55      p.add(tfIncreasingAlphaDuration);
56      p.add(new JLabel("decreasingAlphaDuration"));
57      tfDecreasingAlphaDuration = new JTextField("0");
58      p.add(tfDecreasingAlphaDuration);
59      p.add(new JLabel("increasingAlphaRampDuration"));
60      tfIncreasingAlphaRampDuration = new JTextField("0");
61      p.add(tfIncreasingAlphaRampDuration);
62      p.add(new JLabel("decreasingAlphaRampDuration"));
63      tfDecreasingAlphaRampDuration = new JTextField("0");
64      p.add(tfDecreasingAlphaRampDuration);
65      p.add(new JPanel());
66      JButton button = new JButton("Plot");
67      p.add(button);
68      button.addActionListener(new ActionListener() {
69        public void actionPerformed(ActionEvent ev) {
70          setAlpha();
71          repaint();
72        }
73      });
74      p.add(new JPanel());
75      button = new JButton("Reset");
76      p.add(button);
77      button.addActionListener(new ActionListener() {
78        public void actionPerformed(ActionEvent ev) {
```

```
 79          tfLoopCount.setText("-1");
 80          tfTriggerTime.setText("0");
 81          tfAlphaAtZeroDuration.setText("0");
 82          tfAlphaAtOneDuration.setText("0");
 83          tfIncreasingAlphaDuration.setText("1000");
 84          tfDecreasingAlphaDuration.setText("0");
 85          tfIncreasingAlphaRampDuration.setText("0");
 86          tfDecreasingAlphaRampDuration.setText("0");
 87          setAlpha();
 88          repaint();
 89        }
 90      });
 91    }
 92
 93    void setAlpha() {
 94      alpha.setMode
 95        (Alpha.INCREASING_ENABLE | Alpha.DECREASING_ENABLE);
 96      int n = Integer.parseInt(tfLoopCount.getText());
 97      alpha.setLoopCount(n);
 98      n = Integer.parseInt(tfTriggerTime.getText());
 99      alpha.setTriggerTime(n);
100      n = Integer.parseInt(tfAlphaAtZeroDuration.getText());
101      alpha.setAlphaAtZeroDuration(n);
102      n = Integer.parseInt(tfAlphaAtOneDuration.getText());
103      alpha.setAlphaAtOneDuration(n);
104      n = Integer.parseInt(tfIncreasingAlphaDuration.getText());
105      alpha.setIncreasingAlphaDuration(n);
106      n = Integer.parseInt(tfDecreasingAlphaDuration.getText());
107      alpha.setDecreasingAlphaDuration(n);
108      n = Integer.parseInt(tfIncreasingAlphaRampDuration.getText());
109      alpha.setIncreasingAlphaRampDuration(n);
110      n = Integer.parseInt(tfDecreasingAlphaRampDuration.getText());
111      alpha.setDecreasingAlphaRampDuration(n);
112    }
113
114    class Plot extends JPanel {
115      public Plot() {
116        this.setBackground(Color.white);
117        this.setBorder(BorderFactory.createLoweredBevelBorder());
118        this.setPreferredSize(new Dimension(800,200));
119      }
120
121      public void paintComponent(Graphics g) {
122        super.paintComponent(g);
123        long start = alpha.getStartTime();
124        int x1 = 0;
125        int y1 = 150;
126        int x2 = 0;
127        int y2 = 0;
128        for (int i = 1; i < 1000; i++) {
129          x2 = i;
130          y2 = 150-(int)(100*alpha.value(start+i*10));
131          g.drawLine(x1, y1,x2, y2);
132          x1 = x2;
133          y1 = y2;
134        }
135      }
136    }
137 }
```

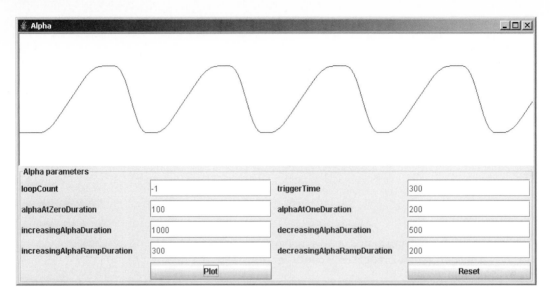

FIGURE 11.2   Plotting the waveform of an `Alpha` object.

The values of an `Alpha` object are plotted in a panel. Eight parameters for the alpha object can be set through the `JTextField` objects in the lower panel of the frame. Initially the default parameters are set for the `Alpha`. The Plot button will redraw the curve using the given parameters. The Reset button resets all parameters to the default.

The inner class `Plot` (line 114) extends `JPanel` and draws the waveform in its `paint Component` method (line 121). The points are plotted in 10-ms intervals. The method `value(long atTime)` of the `Alpha` object is used to obtain the alpha values (line 130).

11.3 Interpolators

The `Behavior` class includes a family of `Interpolator` subclasses that are predefined behaviors for animation. The `Interpolator` classes provide convenient ways to produce animation by setting two or more attribute points and interpolating the values between them. The concept of an interpolator is illustrated in Figure 11.3. Two endpoints of certain attribute are explicitly given. The interpolator will fill in the intermediate values to produce an animation. The targets of the interpolators may be colors, transformations, switches, and other attributes.

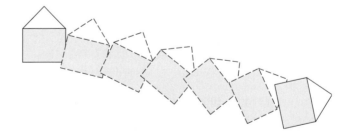

FIGURE 11.3   An interpolator interpolates the intermediate values.

An interpolator, like other animation tools, is driven by the time. To normalize the time input to an animation object, an `Alpha` object can be used. The `Alpha` objects provide a consistent interface for generating stimuli from time values. A Java 3D `Interpolator` is driven by an `Alpha` object. To create an animation using an interpolator, you may instantiate an appropriate `Interpolator` class, set its control points, and provide it with an `Alpha` object. Figure 11.4 shows the `Interpolator` class hierarchy in Java 3D.

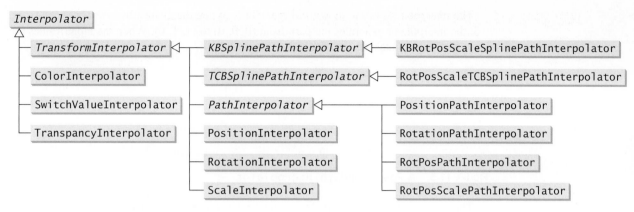

FIGURE 11.4   The interpolators.

The ColorInterpolator class interpolates between two color values for a Material   ColorInterpolator
object. The following code animates a color change from red to green:

```
Alpha alpha = new Alpha();
Material material = new Material();
Color3f red = new Color3f(1f, 0f, 0f);
Color3f green = new Color3f(1f, 0f, 0f);
ColorInterpolator ci = new ColorInterpolator
  (alpha, material, red, green);
ci.setSchedulingBounds(new BoundingSphere());
```

The TransparencyInterpolator class interpolates between two transparency values   TransparencyInter-
for a target TransparencyAttributes object. It has the following constructors: polator

```
TransparencyInterpolator(Alpha a, TransparencyAttributes target);
TransparencyInterpolator(Alpha a, TransparencyAttributes target,
  float t1, float t2);
```

The SwitchValueInterpolator class has a Switch node as its target. It interpolates   SwitchValueInter-
the indices of the Switch object's children.   polator

The TransformInterpolator class operates on a target TransformGroup object. It   TransformInterpolator
also maintains a Transform3D object to represent the axis of the operation. Rotation-
Interpolator interpolates between two angles. The default angles are from 0 to 2π. It
has already been used in many previous example programs to rotate objects. The
PositionInterpolator interpolates the translation component of the target along the
axis. The ScaleInterpolator performs an interpolation on the scaling of the target.

Sometimes just interpolating two endpoints may be inadequate for complex animations.   PathInterpolator
The PathInterpolator class and its subclasses are special TransformInterpolator
classes that allow a sequence of control points or key frames to be specified. The interpolator
will linearly interpolate the intermediate values between each pair of adjacent points. The tim-
ing of the interpolation related to the alpha values is controlled by a sequence of numbers
called *knots*. For example, the following statements set up a PositionPathInterpolator
that interpolates three positions:

```
Point3f[] positions = {new Point3f(0,0,0), new Point3f(1,1,0),
  new Point3f(2,0,0)};
float[] knots = {0f, 0.3f, 1f};
Alpha alpha = new Alpha();
TransformGroup target = new TransformGroup();
Transform3D axis = new Transform3D();
PositionPathInterpolator interpolator =
  new PositionPathInterpolator(alpha, target, axis, knots, positions);
```

The interpolated path is shown in Figure 11.5. When the alpha values are between 0 and 0.3, the interpolator generates the path from (0, 0, 0) to (1, 1, 0). When the alpha values are above 0.3, it generates the path from (1, 1, 0) to (2, 0, 0).

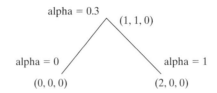

FIGURE 11.5 A `PositionPathInterpolator`.

The `RotationPathInterpolator` interpolates a sequence of rotations. The `RotPosPathInterpolator` interpolates a sequence of rotations and translations. The `RotPosScalePathInterpolator` interpolates a sequence of transforms with specified rotations, translations, and scales.

The `PathInterpolator` classes generate piecewise linear segments, and therefore the paths may not be smooth at the knots where different segments are joined. To produce smooth interpolations or to exercise more sophisticated controls over the interpolating curves, we may use the classes `KBSplinePathInterpolator` or `TCBSplinePathInterpolator`. They both have a concrete subclass that interpolates rotations, translations, and scales.

KBSplinePathInterpolator

TCBSplinePathInterpolator

Interpolators are behaviors and, consequently, they need to have appropriate scheduling bounds set.

Listing 11.2 shows an application of interpolators. Different types of interpolators are used in this example. The visual object is either a gull or a dodecahedron depending on a `Switch` value. Eight buttons labeled with the interpolator names are placed at the right side of the window. Clicking a button activates the corresponding interpolator. "Color" interpolates the colors of the object. "Transparency" changes the transparency. "SwitchValue" changes the shape from the gull to the dodecahedron. "Rotation," "Position," and "Scale" perform the transformations on the object. "RotPosPath" moves and rotates the object along a path. "RotPosScaleTCBSplinePath" interpolates smoothly along a path. (See Figure 11.6.)

Listing 11.2 `TestInterpolator.java`

```
 1 package chapter11;
 2
 3 import javax.vecmath.*;
 4 import java.awt.*;
 5 import java.awt.event.*;
 6 import java.net.*;
 7 import javax.media.j3d.*;
 8 import com.sun.j3d.utils.universe.*;
 9 import com.sun.j3d.utils.geometry.*;
10 import com.sun.j3d.utils.image.*;
11 import com.sun.j3d.utils.behaviors.interpolators.*;
12 import chapter6.Dodecahedron;
13 import chapter10.GullCG;
14 import java.applet.*;
15 import com.sun.j3d.utils.applet.MainFrame;
16
17 public class TestInterpolators extends Applet
18     implements ActionListener {
19   public static void main(String[] args) {
20     new MainFrame(new TestInterpolators(), 800, 600);
21   }
22
```

```
23    private ColorInterpolator color = null;
24    private TransparencyInterpolator transparency = null;
25    private SwitchValueInterpolator sw = null;
26    private RotationInterpolator rotator = null;
27    private PositionInterpolator translator = null;
28    private ScaleInterpolator zoom = null;
29    private RotPosPathInterpolator path = null;
30    private TCBSplinePathInterpolator spline = null;
31    private Interpolator current = null;
32
33    public void init() {
34      setLayout(new BorderLayout());
35      Panel panel = new Panel();
36      panel.setLayout(new GridLayout(8,1));
37      add(panel, BorderLayout.EAST);
38      Button button;
39      button = new Button("Color");
40      button.addActionListener(this);
41      panel.add(button);
42      button = new Button("Transparency");
43      button.addActionListener(this);
44      panel.add(button);
45      button = new Button("SwitchValue");
46      button.addActionListener(this);
47      panel.add(button);
48      button = new Button("Rotation");
49      button.addActionListener(this);
50      panel.add(button);
51      button = new Button("Position");
52      button.addActionListener(this);
53      panel.add(button);
54      button = new Button("Scale");
55      button.addActionListener(this);
56      panel.add(button);
57      button = new Button("RotPosPath");
58      button.addActionListener(this);
59      panel.add(button);
60      button = new Button("RotPosScaleTCBSplinePath");
61      button.addActionListener(this);
62      panel.add(button);
63
64      GraphicsConfiguration gc =
65          SimpleUniverse.getPreferredConfiguration();
66      Canvas3D cv = new Canvas3D(gc);
67      add(cv, BorderLayout.CENTER);
68      BranchGroup bg = createSceneGraph();
69      bg.compile();
70      SimpleUniverse su = new SimpleUniverse(cv);
71      su.getViewingPlatform().setNominalViewingTransform();
72      su.addBranchGraph(bg);
73    }
74
75    private BranchGroup createSceneGraph() {
76      BranchGroup root = new BranchGroup();
77      TransformGroup tg = new TransformGroup();
78      tg.setCapability(TransformGroup.ALLOW_TRANSFORM_WRITE);
79      tg.setCapability(TransformGroup.ALLOW_TRANSFORM_READ);
80      root.addChild(tg);
81      // switch node
82      Switch swNode = new Switch();
```

```
83      swNode.setCapability(Switch.ALLOW_SWITCH_WRITE);
84      tg.addChild(swNode);
85      // appearance
86      Appearance ap = new Appearance();
87      Material material = new Material();
88      material.setCapability(Material.ALLOW_COMPONENT_WRITE);
89      material.setColorTarget(Material.AMBIENT);
90      ap.setMaterial(material);
91      TransparencyAttributes transAttr = new TransparencyAttributes(
92      TransparencyAttributes.BLENDED,0.5f);
93      transAttr.setCapability
94        (TransparencyAttributes.ALLOW_VALUE_WRITE);
95      ap.setTransparencyAttributes(transAttr);
96      // gull
97      Shape3D shape = new Shape3D(new GullCG(), ap);
98      Transform3D trans = new Transform3D();
99      trans.setScale(0.5);
100     TransformGroup tgScale = new TransformGroup(trans);
101     swNode.addChild(tgScale);
102     tgScale.addChild(shape);
103     // dodecahedron
104     Dodecahedron dodec = new Dodecahedron();
105     dodec.setAppearance(ap);
106     trans.setScale(0.1);
107     tgScale = new TransformGroup(trans);
108     swNode.addChild(tgScale);
109     tgScale.addChild(dodec);
110     // interpolators
111     BoundingSphere bounds =
112       new BoundingSphere(new Point3d(0,0,0),100);
113     Alpha alpha = new Alpha(-1, 6000);
114     alpha.setMode
115       (Alpha.INCREASING_ENABLE | Alpha.DECREASING_ENABLE);
116     alpha.setDecreasingAlphaDuration(6000);
117     // color
118     color = new ColorInterpolator
119       (alpha, material, new Color3f(1,0,0), new Color3f(0,0,1));
120     color.setSchedulingBounds(bounds);
121     color.setEnable(true);
122     root.addChild(color);
123     // transparency
124     transparency = new TransparencyInterpolator(alpha, transAttr);
125     transparency.setSchedulingBounds(bounds);
126     transparency.setEnable(false);
127     root.addChild(transparency);
128     // switch
129     sw = new SwitchValueInterpolator(alpha, swNode);
130     sw.setSchedulingBounds(bounds);
131     transparency.setEnable(false);
132     root.addChild(sw);
133     // rotation
134     rotator = new RotationInterpolator(alpha, tg);
135     rotator.setSchedulingBounds(bounds);
136     rotator.setEnable(false);
137     root.addChild(rotator);
138     // translation
139     translator = new PositionInterpolator(alpha, tg);
140     translator.setSchedulingBounds(bounds);
141     translator.setEnable(false);
```

```
142      root.addChild(translator);
143      // zoom
144      zoom = new ScaleInterpolator(alpha, tg);
145      zoom.setSchedulingBounds(bounds);
146      zoom.setEnable(false);
147      root.addChild(zoom);
148      // path
149      Transform3D axis = new Transform3D();
150      float[] knots = {0,0.25f,0.5f,0.75f,1};
151      Quat4f[] rots = new Quat4f[5];
152      Point3f[] ps = new Point3f[5];
153      for (int i = 0; i < 5; i++) {
154        rots[i] = new Quat4f((float)Math.cos(0.5*Math.PI*i),0,0,
155          (float)Math.sin(0.5*Math.PI*i));
156        ps[i] = new Point3f(0.25f*(i-2),
157          (float)Math.sin(0.5*Math.PI*i), 0);
158      }
159      path = new RotPosPathInterpolator
160      (alpha, tg, axis, knots, rots, ps);
161      path.setSchedulingBounds(bounds);
162      path.setEnable(false);
163      root.addChild(path);
164      // spline
165      TCBKeyFrame[] frames = new TCBKeyFrame[5];
166      for (int i = 0; i < 5; i++) {
167        frames[i] = new TCBKeyFrame(0.25f*i, 0,
168        new Point3f(0.25f*(i-2),(float)Math.sin(0.5*Math.PI*i), 0),
169        new Quat4f((float)Math.cos(0.5*Math.PI*i),0,0,
170        (float)Math.sin(0.5*Math.PI*i)),
171        new Point3f(1,1,1),0,0,0);
172      }
173      spline = new RotPosScaleTCBSplinePathInterpolator
174        (alpha, tg, axis, frames);
175      spline.setSchedulingBounds(bounds);
176      spline.setEnable(true);
177      root.addChild(spline);
178      current = spline;
179      // light
180      AmbientLight light =
181      new AmbientLight(true, new Color3f(Color.blue));
182      light.setInfluencingBounds(bounds);
183      root.addChild(light);
184      PointLight ptlight = new PointLight(new Color3f(Color.white),
185        new Point3f(0f,0f,2f), new Point3f(1f,0.3f,0f));
186      ptlight.setInfluencingBounds(bounds);
187      root.addChild(ptlight);
188      // background
189      Background background = new Background(1.0f, 1.0f, 1.0f);
190      background.setApplicationBounds(bounds);
191      root.addChild(background);
192      return root;
193    }
194
195    public void actionPerformed(ActionEvent e) {
196      String cmd = e.getActionCommand();
197      if ("Rotation".equals(cmd)) {
198        current.setEnable(false);
199        current = rotator;
200        current.setEnable(true);
```

```
201     } else if ("Position".equals(cmd)) {
202       current.setEnable(false);
203       current = translator;
204       current.setEnable(true);
205     } else if ("Scale".equals(cmd)) {
206       current.setEnable(false);
207       current = zoom;
208       current.setEnable(true);
209     } else if ("RotPosPath".equals(cmd)) {
210       current.setEnable(false);
211       current = path;
212       current.setEnable(true);
213     } else if ("RotPosScaleTCBSplinePath".equals(cmd)) {
214       current.setEnable(false);
215       current = spline;
216       current.setEnable(true);
217     } else if ("Color".equals(cmd)) {
218       color.setEnable(!color.getEnable());
219     } else if ("Transparency".equals(cmd)) {
220       transparency.setEnable(!transparency.getEnable());
221     } else if ("SwitchValue".equals(cmd)) {
222       sw.setEnable(!sw.getEnable());
223     }
224   }
225 }
```

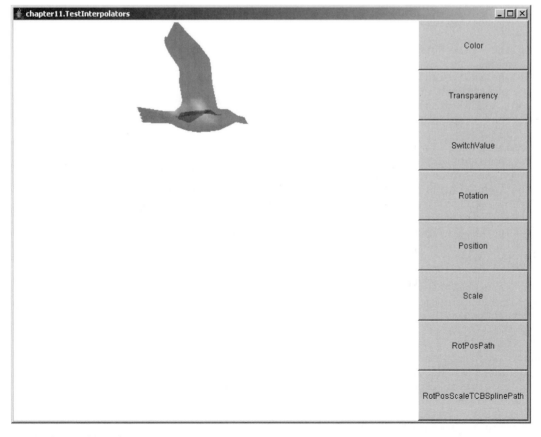

FIGURE 11.6 An interpolator showcase.

The scene graph is shown in Figure 11.7. Two lights, a white background, and a `Bound-ingSphere` object are not shown. A gull shape using a `GullCG` geometry and a `Dodecahedron` object are attached to a `Switch` node through some scaling. The appearance of the objects contains a `Material` object and a `TransparencyAttributes` object. There is a `Transform-Group` node on top of the `Switch`. The capability bits of the `TransformGroup`, `Switch`, `Material`, and `TransparencyAttributes` objects are set to allow writing.

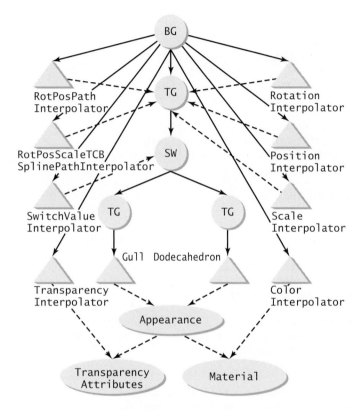

FIGURE 11.7 The partial scene graph with eight interpolators. For clarity, certain objects such as `Alpha`, `Bounds`, `Light`, `Background`, and view branch are not shown.

An `Alpha` object is constructed with both increase and decrease parameters enabled. It is applied to all the interpolators. Eight different interpolators are created: `ColorInterpolator`, `TransparencyInterpolator`, `SwitchValueInterpolator`, `RotationInterpolator`, `PositionInterpolator`, `ScaleInterpolator`, `RotPosPathInterpolator`, and `Rot-PosScaleTCBSplinePathInterpolator`. The `ColorInterpolator` operates on the `Material` object. The `TransparencyInterpolator` operates on the `Transparency-Attributes`. The `SwitchValueInterpolator` operates on the `Switch`. The other five transform interpolators all operate on the `TransformGroup` object.

Eight buttons corresponding to the eight interpolators are placed on the "EAST" side of the frame. The frame is the action listener for all the buttons. The first three buttons operate independently to enable or disable their associated interpolators. The other five interpolators act exclusively because they operate on the same target. The field `current` holds the currently enabled interpolator. Clicking one of the five buttons will first disable the current interpolator and then enable the interpolator corresponding to the button.

Listing 11.3 shows another application of the interpolators. It adds a swinging pendulum to the analog clock defined in the previous chapter by using a `RotationInterpolator` (Figure 11.8). An interpolator driven by an alpha object is used to swing the pendulum. The scene graph is shown in Figure 11.9.

Listing 11.3 `Pendulum.java`

```
1  package chapter11;
2
3  import javax.vecmath.*;
4  import java.awt.*;
5  import java.awt.event.*;
6  import java.util.*;
7  import javax.media.j3d.*;
8  import com.sun.j3d.utils.universe.*;
9  import com.sun.j3d.utils.geometry.*;
10 import chapter10.ClockBehavior;
11 import java.applet.*;
12 import com.sun.j3d.utils.applet.MainFrame;
13
14 public class Pendulum extends Applet {
15   public static void main(String[] args) {
16     new MainFrame(new Pendulum(), 480, 640);
17   }
18
19   public void init() {
20     // create canvas
21     GraphicsConfiguration gc =
22       SimpleUniverse.getPreferredConfiguration();
23     Canvas3D cv = new Canvas3D(gc);
24     setLayout(new BorderLayout());
25     add(cv, BorderLayout.CENTER);
26     BranchGroup bg = createSceneGraph();
27     bg.compile();
28     SimpleUniverse su = new SimpleUniverse(cv);
29     su.getViewingPlatform().setNominalViewingTransform();
30     su.addBranchGraph(bg);
31   }
32
33   private BranchGroup createSceneGraph() {
34     BranchGroup root = new BranchGroup();
35     // clock face
36     Appearance apFace = new Appearance();
37     Material matFace = new Material();
38     matFace.setAmbientColor(new Color3f(0f,0f,0f));
39     matFace.setDiffuseColor(new Color3f(0.15f,0.15f,0.25f));
40     apFace.setMaterial(matFace);
41     Cylinder face = new Cylinder(0.6f, 0.01f,
42     Cylinder.GENERATE_NORMALS, 50, 2, apFace);
43     Transform3D tr = new Transform3D();
44     tr.rotX(Math.PI/2);
45     tr.setTranslation(new Vector3d(0,0,-0.01));
46     TransformGroup tg = new TransformGroup(tr);
47     tg.addChild(face);
48     root.addChild(tg);
49     // hour
50     Appearance ap = new Appearance();
51     ap.setMaterial(new Material());
52     Shape3D shapeHour =
53     new Shape3D(createGeometry(0.4, 0.02, 0.02), ap);
54     TransformGroup spinHour = new TransformGroup();
55     spinHour.addChild(shapeHour);
56     spinHour.setCapability(TransformGroup.ALLOW_TRANSFORM_WRITE);
57     root.addChild(spinHour);
```

```
58      // minute
59      Shape3D shapeMin =
60        new Shape3D(createGeometry(0.5, 0.02, 0.02), ap);
61      TransformGroup spinMin = new TransformGroup();
62      spinMin.addChild(shapeMin);
63      spinMin.setCapability(TransformGroup.ALLOW_TRANSFORM_WRITE);
64      root.addChild(spinMin);
65      // second
66      Shape3D shapeSec =
67        new Shape3D(createGeometry(0.5, 0.01, 0.01), ap);
68      TransformGroup spinSec = new TransformGroup();
69      spinSec.addChild(shapeSec);
70      spinSec.setCapability(TransformGroup.ALLOW_TRANSFORM_WRITE);
71      root.addChild(spinSec);
72      // Behavior node
73      ClockBehavior rotator =
74        new ClockBehavior(spinHour, spinMin, spinSec);
75      BoundingSphere bounds = new BoundingSphere();
76      rotator.setSchedulingBounds(bounds);
77      root.addChild(rotator);
78      // pendulum
79      Cylinder rod =
80        new Cylinder(0.01f, 1f, Cylinder.GENERATE_NORMALS, apFace);
81      Transform3D trPend = new Transform3D();
82      trPend.setTranslation(new Vector3d(0,-0.5,-0.01));
83      TransformGroup tgPend = new TransformGroup(trPend);
84      Sphere mass = new Sphere(0.2f, Sphere.GENERATE_NORMALS, 30);
85      Transform3D trMass = new Transform3D();
86      trMass.setScale(new Vector3d(1,1,0.2));
87      trMass.setTranslation(new Vector3d(0,-0.5,0));
88      TransformGroup tgMass = new TransformGroup(trMass);
89      tgMass.addChild(mass);
90      tgPend.addChild(tgMass);
91      TransformGroup tgSwing = new TransformGroup();
92      tgSwing.setCapability(TransformGroup.ALLOW_TRANSFORM_WRITE);
93      tgPend.addChild(rod);
94      tgSwing.addChild(tgPend);
95      root.addChild(tgSwing);
96      Alpha alpha =
97        new Alpha(-1, Alpha.INCREASING_ENABLE|Alpha.DECREASING_ENABLE,
98        0,0, 500,0,0,500,0,0);
99      Transform3D trAxis = new Transform3D();
100     trAxis.rotX(Math.PI/2);
101     RotationInterpolator swing =
102     new RotationInterpolator(alpha, tgSwing, trAxis,
103       (float)(-Math.PI/6), (float)(Math.PI/6));
104     tgPend.addChild(swing);
105     swing.setSchedulingBounds(bounds);
106     // light
107     AmbientLight light =
108     new AmbientLight(true, new Color3f(Color.blue));
109     light.setInfluencingBounds(bounds);
110     root.addChild(light);
111     PointLight ptlight = new PointLight(new Color3f(Color.white),
112       new Point3f(0.7f,0.7f,2f), new Point3f(1f,0f,0f));
113     ptlight.setInfluencingBounds(bounds);
114     root.addChild(ptlight);
115     // background
116     Background background = new Background(0.7f, 0.7f, 0.7f);
```

```
117        background.setApplicationBounds(bounds);
118        root.addChild(background);
119        return root;
120    }
121
122    GeometryArray createGeometry(double l, double w, double h) {
123        GeometryInfo gi = new GeometryInfo(GeometryInfo.TRIANGLE_ARRAY);
124        Point3d[] pts = new Point3d[4];
125        pts[0] = new Point3d(0, 0, h);
126        pts[1] = new Point3d(-w, 0, 0);
127        pts[2] = new Point3d(w, 0, 0);
128        pts[3] = new Point3d(0, l, 0);
129        gi.setCoordinates(pts);
130        int[] indices = {0,1,2,0,3,1,0,2,3,2,1,3};
131        gi.setCoordinateIndices(indices);
132        NormalGenerator ng = new NormalGenerator();
133        ng.generateNormals(gi);
134        return gi.getGeometryArray();
135    }
136 }
```

FIGURE 11.8 A swinging pendulum.

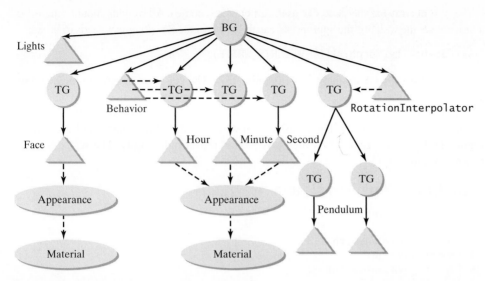

FIGURE 11.9 The scene graph shows additional structure for the pendulum and its driving interpolator.

This program adds a swinging pendulum to the analog clock example defined in Chapter 10. The pendulum consists of a rod and a mass. The rod is modeled with a cylinder and the mass with a sphere compressed in the *z*-direction.

A RotationInterpolator is used to swing the pendulum (line 102). The axis of rotation for the interpolator is the *y*-axis by default, since the pendulum is swinging about the *z*-axis. It is necessary to change the axis by supplying a Transform3D object. The Transform3D object defines a rotation of $\pi/2$ about the *x*-axis which maps the *y*-axis to the *z*-axis. The swing angle is limited to the range $[-\pi/3, \pi/3]$ by setting the two extreme values of the RotationInterpolator.

The Alpha object has both increasing and decreasing durations enabled. Both increasingAlphaDuration and decreasingAlphaDuration are set to 500 ms, and therefore the period of the alpha waveform is 1 second (line 97).

11.4 Morphing

Morphing is an animation technique that creates a visual effect of smoothly changing one object to another. Morphing is typically applied to a series of geometries. In terms of manipulating shapes, it is more flexible than interpolators on transformations, because the changes in morphing are not limited to affine transforms.

Java 3D provides a Morph leaf node class that, together with behavior objects, supports morphing. Morph contains one appearance bundle but it has an array of geometries. An associated array of weights is also defined for the object. The geometry of the Morph object at any given moment is defined by the weighted sum of the geometries in the array. Typically the weights are modified by a Behavior object to achieve the animation. To construct a Morph object, you may use the following constructors:

Morph

```
public Morph(GeometryArray[] geometryArrays)
public Morph(GeometryArray[] geometryArrays, Appearance appearance)
```

All GeometryArray objects in a Morph must have the same size and format. To set weights that combine the geometries you may call the method:

```
public void setWeights(double[] weights)
```

The weight array has the same size as the array of geometries. All weights should sum to 1.0. In order to set the weights, the appropriate capability bit of the `Morph` object needs to be set:

```
setCapability(Morph.ALLOW_WEIGHTS_WRITE);
```

Listing 11.4 shows a simple morphing animation. The class for describing the behavior of morphing is given in Listing 11.5. The example displays an object that changes its shape. Starting as a short cylinder, it smoothly increases its height. Then it will turn to left, forming a section of a torus. The torus section will extend to three-quarters of a full torus (Figure 11.10). This process will then reverse and repeat indefinitely. The scene graph is shown in Figure 11.11.

Listing 11.4 `Morphing.java`

```java
 1 package chapter11;
 2
 3 import javax.vecmath.*;
 4 import java.awt.*;
 5 import java.awt.event.*;
 6 import java.util.*;
 7 import javax.media.j3d.*;
 8 import com.sun.j3d.utils.universe.*;
 9 import com.sun.j3d.utils.geometry.*;
10 import java.applet.*;
11 import com.sun.j3d.utils.applet.MainFrame;
12
13 public class Morphing extends Applet {
14   public static void main(String[] args) {
15     new MainFrame(new Morphing(), 480, 480);
16   }
17
18   public void init() {
19     // create canvas
20     GraphicsConfiguration gc =
21       SimpleUniverse.getPreferredConfiguration();
22     Canvas3D cv = new Canvas3D(gc);
23     setLayout(new BorderLayout());
24     add(cv, BorderLayout.CENTER);
25     BranchGroup bg = createSceneGraph();
26     bg.compile();
27     SimpleUniverse su = new SimpleUniverse(cv);
28     su.getViewingPlatform().setNominalViewingTransform();
29     su.addBranchGraph(bg);
30   }
31
32   private BranchGroup createSceneGraph() {
33     BranchGroup root = new BranchGroup();
34     // geometry
35     GeometryArray[] geoms = new GeometryArray[4];
36     geoms[0] = createGeometry1(0.1);
37     geoms[1] = createGeometry1(0.7);
38     geoms[2] = createGeometry2(0.5);
39     geoms[3] = createGeometry2(0.8);
40     Appearance appear = new Appearance();
41     appear.setMaterial(new Material());
42     Morph morph = new Morph(geoms, appear);
43     morph.setCapability(Morph.ALLOW_WEIGHTS_READ);
44     morph.setCapability(Morph.ALLOW_WEIGHTS_WRITE);
45     Transform3D tr = new Transform3D();
46     tr.rotX(Math.PI/2);
```

```
47        TransformGroup tg = new TransformGroup(tr);
48        tg.addChild(morph);
49        root.addChild(tg);
50        // Behavior node
51        Alpha alpha = new Alpha(-1,
52        Alpha.INCREASING_ENABLE|Alpha.DECREASING_ENABLE,
53          0,0, 8000,0,0,8000,0,0);
54        MorphingBehavior mb = new MorphingBehavior(morph, alpha);
55        BoundingSphere bounds = new BoundingSphere();
56        mb.setSchedulingBounds(bounds);
57        root.addChild(mb);
58        // light
59        AmbientLight light =
60          new AmbientLight(true, new Color3f(Color.blue));
61        light.setInfluencingBounds(bounds);
62        root.addChild(light);
63        PointLight ptlight = new PointLight(new Color3f(Color.white),
64          new Point3f(0.7f,0.7f,2f), new Point3f(1f,0f,0f));
65        ptlight.setInfluencingBounds(bounds);
66        root.addChild(ptlight);
67        // background
68        Background background = new Background(0.7f, 0.7f, 0.7f);
69        background.setApplicationBounds(bounds);
70        root.addChild(background);
71        return root;
72      }
73
74      GeometryArray createGeometry1(double h) {
75        double r1 = 0.1;
76        double r2 = 0.5;
77        int m = 20;
78        int n = 40;
79        Point3d[] pts = new Point3d[m];
80        pts[0] = new Point3d(r1+r2, 0, 0);
81        double theta = 2.0 * Math.PI / m;
82        double c = Math.cos(theta);
83        double s = Math.sin(theta);
84        double[] mat = {c, -s, 0, r2*(1-c),
85                        s, c, 0, -r2*s,
86                        0, 0, 1, 0,
87                        0, 0, 0, 1};
88        Transform3D rot1 = new Transform3D(mat);
89        for (int i = 1; i < m; i++) {
90          pts[i] = new Point3d();
91          rot1.transform(pts[i-1], pts[i]);
92        }
93
94        Transform3D rot2 = new Transform3D();
95        rot2.set(new Vector3d(0,0,-h/n));
96        IndexedQuadArray qa =
97          new IndexedQuadArray(m*n, IndexedQuadArray.COORDINATES,
98          4*m*(n-1));
99        int quadIndex = 0;
100       for (int i = 0; i < n; i++) {
101         qa.setCoordinates(i*m, pts);
102         for (int j = 0; j < m; j++) {
103           rot2.transform(pts[j]);
104           int[] quadCoords = {i*m+j, ((i+1)%n)*m+j,
105           ((i+1)%n)*m+((j+1)%m), i*m+((j+1)%m)};
106           if (i < n-1)
```

```
107          qa.setCoordinateIndices(quadIndex, quadCoords);
108          quadIndex += 4;
109        }
110      }
111      GeometryInfo gi = new GeometryInfo(qa);
112      NormalGenerator ng = new NormalGenerator();
113      ng.generateNormals(gi);
114      return gi.getGeometryArray();
115    }
116
117    GeometryArray createGeometry2(double h) {
118      double r1 = 0.1;
119      double r2 = 0.5;
120      int m = 20;
121      int n = 40;
122      Point3d[] pts = new Point3d[m];
123      pts[0] = new Point3d(r1+r2, 0, 0);
124      double theta = 2.0 * Math.PI / m;
125      double c = Math.cos(theta);
126      double s = Math.sin(theta);
127      double[] mat = {c, -s, 0, r2*(1-c),
128                      s, c, 0, -r2*s,
129                      0, 0, 1, 0,
130                      0, 0, 0, 1};
131      Transform3D rot1 = new Transform3D(mat);
132      for (int i = 1; i < m; i++) {
133        pts[i] = new Point3d();
134        rot1.transform(pts[i-1], pts[i]);
135      }
136
137      Transform3D rot2 = new Transform3D();
138      rot2.rotY(h*2*Math.PI/n);
139      IndexedQuadArray qa =
140        new IndexedQuadArray(m*n, IndexedQuadArray.COORDINATES,
141        4*m*(n-1));
142      int quadIndex = 0;
143      for (int i = 0; i < n; i++) {
144        qa.setCoordinates(i*m, pts);
145        for (int j = 0; j < m; j++) {
146          rot2.transform(pts[j]);
147          int[] quadCoords = {i*m+j, ((i+1)%n)*m+j,
148            ((i+1)%n)*m+((j+1)%m),
149            i*m+((j+1)%m)};
150          if (i < n-1)
151          qa.setCoordinateIndices(quadIndex, quadCoords);
152          quadIndex += 4;
153        }
154      }
155      GeometryInfo gi = new GeometryInfo(qa);
156      NormalGenerator ng = new NormalGenerator();
157      ng.generateNormals(gi);
158      return gi.getGeometryArray();
159    }
160  }
```

Listing 11.5 `MorphingBehavior.java`

```
1 package chapter11;
2
```

```
 3 import javax.media.j3d.*;
 4
 5 public class MorphingBehavior extends Behavior {
 6   Morph morph;
 7   Alpha alpha;
 8
 9   public MorphingBehavior(Morph m, Alpha a) {
10     morph = m;
11     alpha = a;
12   }
13
14   public void initialize() {
15     wakeupOn(new WakeupOnElapsedFrames(10));
16   }
17
18   public void processStimulus(java.util.Enumeration enumeration) {
19     double[] w = new double[4];
20     double a = alpha.value();
21     w[0] = 0;
22     w[1] = 0;
23     w[2] = 0;
24     w[3] = 0;
25     int index = (int)(a*3);
26     if (index > 2) index = 2;
27     w[index+1] = (a-index/3.0)*3;
28     w[index] = 1.0-w[index+1];
29     morph.setWeights(w);
30     wakeupOn(new WakeupOnElapsedFrames(10));
31   }
32 }
```

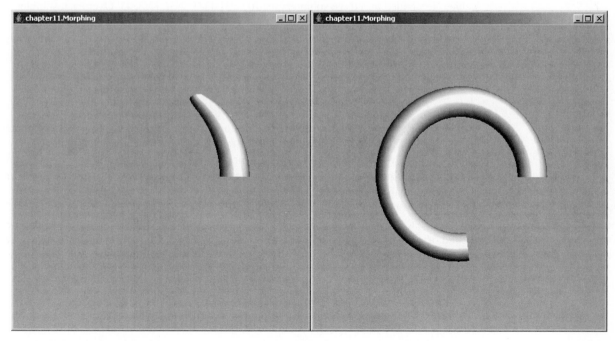

Figure 11.10   Morphing example.

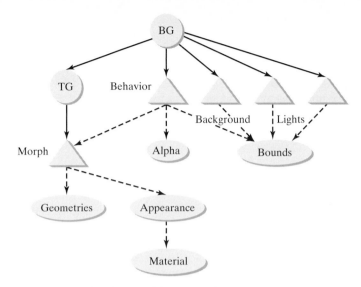

FIGURE 11.11   Scene graph for the morphing example.

Four `GeometryArray` objects are constructed to serve as the key frames in a `Morph` object. They are created by the methods `createGeometry1` and `createGeometry2`. `createGeometry1` (line 74) creates a vertical tube of a certain height. `createGeometry2` (line 117) creates a portion of a torus. The first and second geometries in the `Morph` object are tubes of different heights. The third and fourth geometries are torus sections of different lengths.

A custom `MorphingBehavior` class is defined to modify the weights in the `Morph` node. The weights are set based on `Alpha` values, similar to an interpolator (lines 21–29). The constructor takes a `Morph` object and an `Alpha` object as parameters. The wakeup condition is set to the elapse of 10 frames in the `initialize` and `processStimulus` methods. The alpha values are divided into three subintervals: [0, 1/3], [1/3, 2/3], [2/3, 1]. Over each subinterval, the weights are set to interpolate a pair of adjacent geometries. For example, if alpha is 0.6, it falls into the second subinterval. The second and the third geometries are interpolated through the weight setting: $w[0] = 0$, $w[1] = 0.2$, $w[2] = 0.8$, $w[3] = 0$.

11.5 LOD

The *level of detail* (*LOD*) is a technique useful for reducing the computational cost of rendering complex shapes. It takes advantage of the fact that in a perspective view, a visual object closer to the viewer will be larger and show more details than the same object viewed from a distance. Consequently, it may be possible to render a distant object with less resolution and detail without significantly affecting the quality.

Java 3D provides the abstract `LOD` class as a subclass of `Behavior` to support LOD. LOD has a concrete subclass `DistanceLOD`. An `LOD` object acts on a list of `Switch` nodes to select a child of a `Switch` as a particular level of detail. The `DistanceLOD` controls the selection based on the distances to the viewer. The `DistanceLOD` class has the following constructors:

DistanceLOD

```
public DistanceLOD()
public DistanceLOD(float[] distances)
public DistanceLOD(float[] distances, Point3f position)
```

The `distances` array defines the critical distances to switch to the next level. The default position to measure the distances to the viewer is the origin of the `DistanceLOD` object. The third constructor allows you to specify a different position.

The program in Listing 11.6 displays a texture mapped globe. A user can rotate and zoom the view with mouse actions. A `DistanceLOD` object is applied to a `Switch` node to select a sphere with a certain level of detail based on the distance to the viewer (Figure 11.12).

Listing 11.6 TestLOD.java

```
 1 package chapter11;
 2
 3 import java.awt.*;
 4 import java.awt.geom.*;
 5 import java.awt.event.*;
 6 import java.awt.image.*;
 7 import javax.imageio.*;
 8 import com.sun.j3d.utils.geometry.*;
 9 import com.sun.j3d.utils.behaviors.vp.*;
10 import com.sun.j3d.utils.universe.*;
11 import javax.media.j3d.*;
12 import javax.vecmath.*;
13 import java.io.*;
14 import java.net.*;
15 import com.sun.j3d.utils.image.*;
16 import java.applet.*;
17 import com.sun.j3d.utils.applet.MainFrame;
18
19 public class TestLOD extends Applet {
20   public static void main(String[] args) {
21     new MainFrame(new TestLOD(), 480, 480);
22   }
23
24   BufferedImage[] images = new BufferedImage[3];
25   public void init() {
26     // create canvas
27     GraphicsConfiguration gc =
28     SimpleUniverse.getPreferredConfiguration();
29     Canvas3D cv = new Canvas3D(gc);
30     setLayout(new BorderLayout());
31     add(cv, BorderLayout.CENTER);
32     BranchGroup bg = createSceneGraph();
33     bg.compile();
34     SimpleUniverse su = new SimpleUniverse(cv);
35     ViewingPlatform viewingPlatform = su.getViewingPlatform();
36     viewingPlatform.setNominalViewingTransform();
37     // orbit behavior to zoom and rotate the view
38     OrbitBehavior orbit = new OrbitBehavior(cv,
39       OrbitBehavior.REVERSE_ZOOM |
40       OrbitBehavior.REVERSE_ROTATE |
41       OrbitBehavior.DISABLE_TRANSLATE);
42     BoundingSphere bounds =
43       new BoundingSphere(new Point3d(0.0, 0.0, 0.0), 100.0);
44     orbit.setSchedulingBounds(bounds);
45     viewingPlatform.setViewPlatformBehavior(orbit);
46     su.addBranchGraph(bg);
47   }
48
49   public BranchGroup createSceneGraph() {
50     BranchGroup objRoot = new BranchGroup();
51     TransformGroup objTrans = new TransformGroup();
52     objTrans.setCapability(TransformGroup.ALLOW_TRANSFORM_WRITE);
53     objTrans.setCapability(TransformGroup.ALLOW_TRANSFORM_READ);
54     objRoot.addChild(objTrans);
```

```
55      // a switch to hold the different levels
56      Switch sw = new Switch(0);
57      sw.setCapability(javax.media.j3d.Switch.ALLOW_SWITCH_READ);
58      sw.setCapability(javax.media.j3d.Switch.ALLOW_SWITCH_WRITE);
59      objTrans.addChild(sw);
60      // 4 levels of globes
61      loadImages();
62      Appearance ap = createAppearance(0);
63      sw.addChild(new Sphere(0.4f,
64      Primitive.GENERATE_TEXTURE_COORDS, 40, ap));
65      ap = createAppearance(1);
66      sw.addChild(new Sphere(0.4f,
67      Primitive.GENERATE_TEXTURE_COORDS, 20, ap));
68      ap = createAppearance(2);
69      sw.addChild(new Sphere(0.4f,
70      Primitive.GENERATE_TEXTURE_COORDS, 10, ap));
71      ap = new Appearance();
72      ap.setColoringAttributes(new ColoringAttributes
73        (0f,0f,0.5f,ColoringAttributes.FASTEST));
74      sw.addChild(new Sphere(0.4f, Sphere.GENERATE_NORMALS, 5, ap));
75      // the DistanceLOD behavior
76      float[] distances = new float[3];
77      distances[0] = 5.0f;
78      distances[1] = 10.0f;
79      distances[2] = 25.0f;
80      DistanceLOD lod = new DistanceLOD(distances);
81      lod.addSwitch(sw);
82      BoundingSphere bounds =
83        new BoundingSphere(new Point3d(0.0,0.0,0.0), 10.0);
84      lod.setSchedulingBounds(bounds);
85      objTrans.addChild(lod);
86      // background
87      Background background = new Background(1.0f, 1.0f, 1.0f);
88      background.setApplicationBounds(bounds);
89      objRoot.addChild(background);
90      return objRoot;
91    }
92
93    void loadImages() {
94      URL filename =
95        getClass().getClassLoader().getResource("images/earth.jpg");
96      try {
97        images[0] = ImageIO.read(filename);
98        AffineTransform xform =
99        AffineTransform.getScaleInstance(0.5, 0.5);
100       AffineTransformOp scaleOp = new AffineTransformOp (xform, null);
101       for (int i = 1; i < 3; i++) {
102           images[i] = scaleOp.filter(images[i-1], null);
103       }
104     } catch (IOException ex) {
105         ex.printStackTrace();
106     }
107   }
108
109   Appearance createAppearance(int i){
110     Appearance appear = new Appearance();
111       ImageComponent2D image =
112         new ImageComponent2D(ImageComponent2D.FORMAT_RGB, images[i]);
```

```
113        Texture2D texture =
114          new Texture2D(Texture.BASE_LEVEL, Texture.RGBA,
115          image.getWidth(), image.getHeight());
116          texture.setImage(0, image);
117          texture.setEnable(true);
118          texture.setMagFilter(Texture.BASE_LEVEL_LINEAR);
119          texture.setMinFilter(Texture.BASE_LEVEL_LINEAR);
120          appear.setTexture(texture);
121      return appear;
122    }
123 }
```

FIGURE 11.12   LOD example.

As shown in the scene graph (Figure 11.13), a `Switch` node with four children is created to be the target of the `DistanceLOD` behavior (lines 55–81). All four children are spheres, but their appearances and quality are different. The first three use texture mapping with different image resolutions. The last sphere uses a flat color for its appearance.

The `loadImages` method (line 93) prepares three `BufferedImage` objects for the texture mapping. The first image is loaded from the file "earth.jpg." It has the size 512×512. The second image is obtained by scaling the first image down to 256×256 with an `AffineTransformOp` object. The third image is obtained similarly by scaling down further to 128×128.

The numbers of divisions of the spheres are also different. The first sphere has 40 divisions, resulting in a high-quality sphere. The other spheres have 20, 10, and 5, respectively.

When the sphere is close to the viewer, a high-quality version is used. As it moves away, other versions of the sphere with less quality will be selected by the LOD behavior.

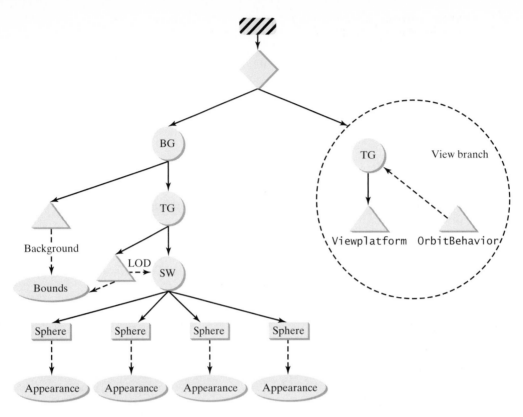

FIGURE 11.13   Scene graph of the LOD example.

11.6 Billboard

Billboard

A `Billboard` behavior operates on a target `TransformGroup` object so that the children of the target will always be aligned to face the viewer. The behavior sets an appropriate rotation on the target transform to achieve this alignment task, regardless of any other transforms on top of the target.

A billboard is useful for certain visual objects such as text labels. Another common application is to simulate a complex 3D scene with a 2D object, such as an image. A billboard behavior may help hide the 2D nature of the image if the user can never see the "depth" of the image. For example, to model a tree with 3D geometry will be expensive. It will be quite efficient to use a 2D image of the tree. Therefore, using an image with a billboard behavior may provide a good approximation. Of course, this method offers only a crude and "fake" model for the tree. The results may be satisfactory if the tree is roughly symmetric and is not close to the viewer.

Billboard modes

A `Billboard` object operates in one of two available modes:

```
ROTATE_ABOUT_POINT
ROTATE_ABOUT_AXIS
```

The first mode allows an arbitrary rotation to make a full alignment. The second mode allows only a rotation about an axis. The `Billboard` class has the following constructors:

Billboard constructors

```
public Billboard()
public Billboard(TransformGroup target)
```

```
public Billboard(TransformGroup target, int mode, Point3f point)
public Billboard(TransformGroup target, int mode, Vector3f axis)
```

Listing 11.7 is an example that displays a set of coordinate axes with *x, y, z* labels. Listing 11.8 gives a class that describes the axes with billboard behavior. The user may rotate, translate, and zoom the view with mouse operations. The 3D text labels attached to the axes will always face the viewer, regardless of the transformations. (See Figure 11.14.)

Listing 11.7 TestBillboard.java

```
 1 package chapter11;
 2
 3 import javax.vecmath.*;
 4 import java.awt.*;
 5 import java.awt.event.*;
 6 import java.net.URL;
 7 import javax.media.j3d.*;
 8 import com.sun.j3d.utils.universe.*;
 9 import com.sun.j3d.utils.geometry.*;
10 import com.sun.j3d.utils.image.*;
11 import com.sun.j3d.utils.behaviors.mouse.*;
12 import com.sun.j3d.utils.behaviors.vp.*;
13 import java.applet.*;
14 import com.sun.j3d.utils.applet.MainFrame;
15
16 public class TestBillboard extends Applet {
17   public static void main(String[] args) {
18     new MainFrame(new TestBillboard(), 480, 480);
19   }
20
21   public void init() {
22     // create canvas
23     GraphicsConfiguration gc =
24       SimpleUniverse.getPreferredConfiguration();
25     Canvas3D cv = new Canvas3D(gc);
26     setLayout(new BorderLayout());
27     add(cv, BorderLayout.CENTER);
28     TextArea ta = new TextArea("",3,30,TextArea.SCROLLBARS_NONE);
29     ta.setText("Rotation: Drag with left button\n");
30     ta.append("Translation: Drag with right button\n");
31     ta.append("Zoom: Hold Alt key and drag with left button");
32     ta.setEditable(false);
33     add(ta, BorderLayout.SOUTH);
34     BranchGroup root = new BranchGroup();
35     // axes
36     Transform3D tr = new Transform3D();
37     tr.setScale(0.5);
38     // tr.setTranslation(new Vector3d(-0.8, -0.7, -0.5));
39     TransformGroup tg = new TransformGroup(tr);
40     root.addChild(tg);
41     AxesBillboard axes = new AxesBillboard();
42     tg.addChild(axes);
43     BoundingSphere bounds = new BoundingSphere();
44     // light
45     AmbientLight light =
46     new AmbientLight(true, new Color3f(Color.blue));
47     light.setInfluencingBounds(bounds);
48     root.addChild(light);
49     PointLight ptlight = new PointLight(new Color3f(Color.white),
```

```
50            new Point3f(0f,0f,2f), new Point3f(1f,0f,0f));
51        ptlight.setInfluencingBounds(bounds);
52        root.addChild(ptlight);
53        // background
54        Background background = new Background(1.0f, 1.0f, 1.0f);
55        background.setApplicationBounds(bounds);
56        root.addChild(background);
57        root.compile();
58        SimpleUniverse su = new SimpleUniverse(cv);
59        su.getViewingPlatform().setNominalViewingTransform();
60        // viewplatform motion
61        OrbitBehavior orbit = new OrbitBehavior(cv);
62        orbit.setSchedulingBounds(new BoundingSphere());
63        su.getViewingPlatform().setViewPlatformBehavior(orbit);
64        su.addBranchGraph(root);
65    }
66 }
```

Listing 11.8 AxesBillboard.java

```
 1 package chapter11;
 2
 3 import javax.vecmath.*;
 4 import java.awt.*;
 5 import java.awt.event.*;
 6 import javax.media.j3d.*;
 7 import com.sun.j3d.utils.universe.*;
 8 import com.sun.j3d.utils.geometry.*;
 9
10 public class AxesBillboard extends Group {
11   public AxesBillboard() {
12     Appearance ap = new Appearance();
13     ap.setMaterial(new Material());
14     Font3D font = new Font3D(new Font("SanSerif", Font.PLAIN, 1),
15                             new FontExtrusion());
16     Text3D x = new Text3D(font, "x");
17     Shape3D xShape = new Shape3D(x, ap);
18     Text3D y = new Text3D(font, "y");
19     Shape3D yShape = new Shape3D(y, ap);
20     Text3D z = new Text3D(font, "z");
21     Shape3D zShape = new Shape3D(z, ap);
22     // transform for texts
23     Transform3D tTr = new Transform3D();
24     tTr.setTranslation(new Vector3d(-0.12, 0.6, -0.04));
25     tTr.setScale(0.5);
26     // transform for arrows
27     Transform3D aTr = new Transform3D();
28     aTr.setTranslation(new Vector3d(0, 0.5, 0));
29     // bounds
30     Bounds bounds = new BoundingSphere(new Point3d(0,0,0), 100);
31     // x axis
32     Cylinder xAxis = new Cylinder(0.05f, 1f);
33     Transform3D xTr = new Transform3D();
34     xTr.setRotation(new AxisAngle4d(0, 0, 1, -Math.PI/2));
35     xTr.setTranslation(new Vector3d(0.5, 0, 0));
36     TransformGroup xTg = new TransformGroup(xTr);
37     xTg.addChild(xAxis);
38     this.addChild(xTg);
```

```
39        TransformGroup xTextTg = new TransformGroup(tTr);
40        TransformGroup bbTg = new TransformGroup();
41        bbTg.setCapability(TransformGroup.ALLOW_TRANSFORM_WRITE);
42        xTextTg.addChild(bbTg);
43        bbTg.addChild(xShape);
44        Billboard bb = new Billboard(bbTg,
45        Billboard.ROTATE_ABOUT_POINT, new Point3f(0,0,0));
46        bb.setSchedulingBounds(bounds);
47        xTextTg.addChild(bb);
48        xTg.addChild(xTextTg);
49        Cone xArrow = new Cone(0.1f, 0.2f);
50        TransformGroup xArrowTg = new TransformGroup(aTr);
51        xArrowTg.addChild(xArrow);
52        xTg.addChild(xArrowTg);
53        // y axis
54        Cylinder yAxis = new Cylinder(0.05f, 1f);
55        Transform3D yTr = new Transform3D();
56        yTr.setTranslation(new Vector3d(0, 0.5, 0));
57        TransformGroup yTg = new TransformGroup(yTr);
58        yTg.addChild(yAxis);
59        this.addChild(yTg);
60        TransformGroup yTextTg = new TransformGroup(tTr);
61        bbTg = new TransformGroup();
62        bbTg.setCapability(TransformGroup.ALLOW_TRANSFORM_WRITE);
63        yTextTg.addChild(bbTg);
64        bbTg.addChild(yShape);
65        bb = new Billboard(bbTg,
66        Billboard.ROTATE_ABOUT_POINT, new Point3f(0,0,0));
67        bb.setSchedulingBounds(bounds);
68        yTextTg.addChild(bb);
69        yTg.addChild(yTextTg);
70        Cone yArrow = new Cone(0.1f, 0.2f);
71        TransformGroup yArrowTg = new TransformGroup(aTr);
72        yArrowTg.addChild(yArrow);
73        yTg.addChild(yArrowTg);
74        // z axis
75        Cylinder zAxis = new Cylinder(0.05f, 1f);
76        Transform3D zTr = new Transform3D();
77        zTr.setRotation(new AxisAngle4d(1, 0, 0, Math.PI/2));
78        zTr.setTranslation(new Vector3d(0, 0, 0.5));
79        TransformGroup zTg = new TransformGroup(zTr);
80        zTg.addChild(zAxis);
81        this.addChild(zTg);
82        TransformGroup zTextTg = new TransformGroup(tTr);
83        bbTg = new TransformGroup();
84        bbTg.setCapability(TransformGroup.ALLOW_TRANSFORM_WRITE);
85        zTextTg.addChild(bbTg);
86        bbTg.addChild(zShape);
87        bb = new Billboard(bbTg,
88        Billboard.ROTATE_ABOUT_POINT, new Point3f(0,0,0));
89        bb.setSchedulingBounds(bounds);
90        zTextTg.addChild(bb);
91        zTg.addChild(zTextTg);
92        Cone zArrow = new Cone(0.1f, 0.2f);
93        TransformGroup zArrowTg = new TransformGroup(aTr);
94        zArrowTg.addChild(zArrow);
95        zTg.addChild(zArrowTg);
96    }
97 }
```

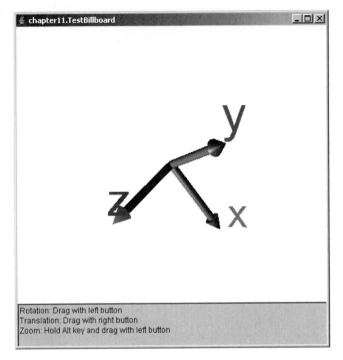

FIGURE 11.14 A `Billboard` behavior example.

The object displayed is a set of coordinate axes similar to the `Axes` class defined in Chapter 7. The difference is the addition of `Billboard` behavior nodes (lines 44, 65, 87) and extra `TransformGroup` nodes to the scene graph, as shown in Figure 11.15. The `Billboard` objects are created with the mode `ROTATE_ABOUT_POINT`.

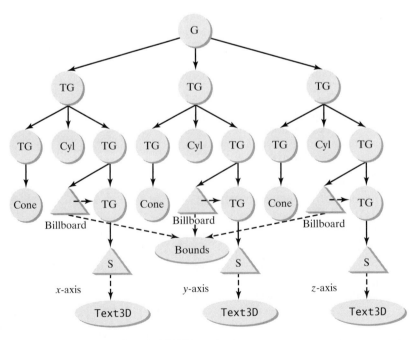

FIGURE 11.15 Scene graph of `AxesBillboard`.

The program displays an instance of the `AxesBillboard` with lighting. The view has an `OrbitBehavior` object attached to allow rotation, translation, and zooming with mouse operations. The "x," "y," and "z" labels will move with the axes under the transformations. However, because of the `Billboard` behaviors, the text labels will always be oriented to face the viewer.

Note that even though the `Billboard` object needs to change only the rotational component of the transform, it does clear the translation and scaling components. Therefore it is necessary to create an additional `TransformGroup` node for the `Billboard`.

KEY CLASSES AND METHODS

- `javax.media.j3d.Alpha` A class encapsulating an alpha function.
- `javax.media.j3d.Interpolator` A base class for the interpolator behaviors.
- `javax.media.j3d.ColorInterpolator` An interpolator operating on the colors in a `Material` object.
- `javax.media.j3d.TransparencyInterpolator` An interpolator operating on a `TransparencyAttributes` object.
- `javax.media.j3d.SwitchValueInterpolator` An interpolator operating on a `Switch` object.
- `javax.media.j3d.TransformInterpolator` A base class for transformation interpolators.
- `javax.media.j3d.RotationInterpolator` An interpolator for rotation.
- `javax.media.j3d.PositionInterpolator` An interpolator for translation.
- `javax.media.j3d.ScaleInterpolator` An interpolator for scale.
- `javax.media.j3d.PathInterpolator` A base class for transformation interpolators defined by a sequence of frames.
- `javax.media.j3d.RotationPathInterpolator` A path interpolator for rotation.
- `javax.media.j3d.PositionPathInterpolator` A path interpolator for translation.
- `javax.media.j3d.RotPosPathInterpolator` A path interpolator for rotation and translation.
- `javax.media.j3d.RotPosScalePathInterpolator` A path interpolator for rotation, translation, and scaling.
- `com.sun.j3d.utils.behaviors.interpolators.RotPosScaleTCBSplinePathInterpolator` A spline path interpolator for rotation, translation, and scaling.
- `com.sun.j3d.utils.behaviors.interpolators.KBRotPosScaleSplinePathInterpolator` A spline path interpolator for rotation, translation, and scaling.
- `javax.media.j3d.Morph` A leaf-node class for blending an array of geometries.
- `javax.media.j3d.LOD` A behavior class for LOD.
- `javax.media.j3d.DistanceLOD` An LOC class operating on a `Switch` node based on distances.
- `javax.media.j3d.Billboard` A behavior class to orient an object to face the viewer.

KEY TERMS

animation A process of rendering a sequence of frames of a dynamic scene.

alpha A function of time valued between 0 and 1. It is used to drive an interpolator.

interpolator A behavior driven by an alpha to produce animation.

path interpolator A transformation interpolator defined by a sequence of key frames.

spline path interpolator A transformation interpolator along a smooth path defined by a sequence of key frames.

morphing A dynamic change of an object's shape.

LOD (level of detail) A technique to change the level of detail rendered based on the circumstances of the view.

billboard behavior A behavior that automatically orients an object toward the viewer.

Chapter Summary

■ This chapter introduces commonly used animation techniques and the Java 3D animation support with behaviors.

■ The interpolators are easy-to-use animation tools. They are driven by alpha objects and they interpolate the intermediate values from the specified control points or key frames. Java 3D includes a large collection of interpolators that interpolate a variety of attributes from colors to spline curve paths.

■ A `Morph` node references a list of geometries and produces one object by combining the geometries with a list of weights. Typically the weights can be changed by a behavior object to produce a special animation of morphing from one object to another.

■ The LOD behaviors control `Switch` nodes to select a version of an object a with certain detail level. LOD provides a tool for automatically reducing the amount of detail rendered when the details are not essential. It is a useful method to improve the efficiency of rendering without significant loss in quality.

■ A `Billboard` behavior automatically rotates the target to maintain a direction facing the viewer. It is useful in setting text labels and in simulating 3D objects using 2D images.

Review Questions

11.1 Draw the waveform of an `Alpha` with the following parameters:

```
LoopCount = 5
TriggerTime = 0
PhaseDelayDuration = 100
AlphaAtZeroDuration = 0
AlphaAtOneDuration = 200
IncreasingAlphaDuration = 0
DecreasingAlphaDuration = 200
IncreasingAlphaRampDuration = 0
DecreasingAlphaRampDuration = 0
```

11.2 Draw the waveform of an `Alpha` with the following parameters:

```
LoopCount = -1
TriggerTime = 0
PhaseDelayDuration = 0
AlphaAtZeroDuration = 200
AlphaAtOneDuration = 200
IncreasingAlphaDuration = 400
DecreasingAlphaDuration = 200
IncreasingAlphaRampDuration = 100
DecreasingAlphaRampDuration = 0
```

11.3 Find the parameters for the `Alpha` with the waveform shown in Figure 11.16.

11.4 Listing 11.3 uses a `RotationInterpolator` to swing the pendulum. What other interpolators can be used for this task?

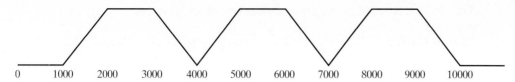

FIGURE 11.16 A1pha waveform.

11.5 Besides the distance-based LOD, can you think of other cases where the LOD technique might be appropriate?

11.6 Discuss the limitations of the ROTATE_ABOUT_AXIS mode in a Billboard object and the situations where this mode is adequate.

PROGRAMMING EXERCISES

11.1 In Listing 11.1, add two other parameters of the Alpha class—mode and phaseDelayDuration—to the panel of parameters.

11.2 Write a Java 3D program to display a tetrahedron that continuously moves left and right.

11.3 Write a Java 3D program to display a tetrahedron that continuously moves along a triangle path with vertices $(-0.5, 0, 0)$, $(0.5, -0.5, 0)$, and $(0, 0, 0.5)$.

11.4 Add the following transform interpolators to Listing 11.2:

```
RotationPathInterpolator
PositionPathInterpolator
RotPosScalePathInterpolator
KBRotPosScaleSplinePathInterpolator
```

11.5 Write a program that uses a Morph object and a Behavior object to display an object morphing between a cone and a cylinder.

11.6 Write a program that uses a DistanceLOD object to set up three levels of detail for displaying a 3D text object of the string "Java." The first level uses a Material object in the appearance to enable lighting. The second level uses a flat color. The third level uses only a filled rectangle to represent the text.

11.7 Write a Java 3D program that shows a texture-mapped rectangle with a Billboard behavior. Use an OrbitBehavior object to allow view manipulations through mouse operations.

CHAPTER 12

ADDITIONAL 3D TOPICS

Objectives

- To define and implement 3D curves.
- To define and implement 3D surfaces.
- To use sound in Java 3D scene graphs.
- To create simple shadows.
- To understand dynamic geometry change.
- To use off-screen rendering for capturing rendered images.
- To apply 3D texture mapping.
- To understand and implement synthetic textures.

12.1 Introduction

This chapter introduces several advanced techniques related to 3D graphics.

3D curves and surfaces are important building blocks of 3D geometries. Current versions of Java 3D do not have direct support for curves and surfaces. In this chapter, examples of constructing curves and curved surfaces are given. The deCasteljau algorithm for evaluations and subdivisions of Bézier curves is presented.

Sounds are used in conjunction with graphics in many applications. Java 3D offers support for direct incorporation of sounds into scene graphs. This approach allows easy association between graphics objects and sounds.

Shadows are complex objects to create in computer graphics. The local illumination models employed in Java 3D will not automatically generate shadows. A simplistic method for generating artificial shadows with polygon objects is introduced in this chapter.

In the animation and interaction examples introduced previously, geometry objects are usually not modified dynamically. It is possible to change geometry data in a live scene graph, but a special procedure is required. The `GeometryArray` object must be created in the `BY_REFERENCE` mode, and the change should be made only through a class implementing the `GeometryUpdater` interface. A dynamic shadow example is used to illustrate the procedure.

Capturing a rendered image from the `Canvas3D` object in a Java 3D scene is useful in some applications. The off-screen rendering capability of the `Canvas3D` class is introduced. It can be used to capture a frame to a `BufferedImage` object.

3D texture mapping applies a solid 3D image to an object. It creates a visual realism that is difficult to achieve in 2D texture mapping. Java 3D provides basic support for 3D texturing. One related topic is the generation of synthetic textures. The Perlin's noise is a random function that exhibits a certain smoothness. It may be used to generate textures that remarkably resemble natural textures such as marble, wood, and metal.

12.2 3D Curves

Bézier curve
control points

Definitions of Bézier and B-spline curves in 3D spaces are the same as for their 2D counterparts. The parametric equation of a general Bézier curve of degree n with *control points* $p_0, p_0, \ldots, p_n$ is given by

$$s(t) = \sum_{i=0}^{n} p_i B_{n,i}(t)$$

Bernstein basis

where $B_{n,i}(t)$ is known as the *Bernstein polynomial* or *Bernstein basis*

$$B_{n,i}(t) = \binom{n}{i} t^i (1 - t)^{n-i}$$

In particular, a cubic Bézier curve has degree $n = 3$ and is defined by four control points

$$s(t) = (1 - t)^3 p_0 + 3t(1 - t)^2 p_1 + 3t^2(1 - t)p_2 + t^3 p_3$$

deCasteljau algorithm

The *deCasteljau algorithm* provides a method to calculate a point on the curve from the control points using linear interpolations. The algorithm proceeds by constructing a triangular scheme of the points similar to a Pascal's triangle. For the cubic Bézier curve, the following triangular scheme is used:

$$p_0^0, p_1^0, p_2^0, p_3^0$$
$$p_0^1, p_1^1, p_2^1$$
$$p_0^2, p_1^2$$
$$p_0^3$$

The first row contains the original control points of the Bézier curve. The subsequent rows are calculated by the formula:

$$p_i^k = (1 - t)p_i^{k-1} + t p_{i+1}^{k-1}$$

The last entry gives the value of the point on the Bézier curve at t

$$s(t) = p_0^3$$

The process is illustrated in Figure 12.1. All the calculations are simple linear interpolations.

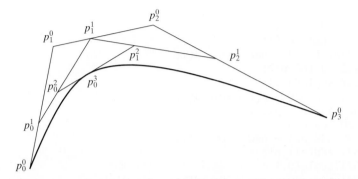

FIGURE 12.1 deCasteljau algorithm.

A Bézier curve can be subdivided into two Bézier curves. The deCasteljau algorithm also offers a method for the *subdivision*. In the cubic curve shown in Figure 12.1, the two subdivided Bézier curves have the control points p_0^0, p_0^1, p_0^2, p_0^3 and p_0^3, p_1^2, p_2^1, p_3^0, respectively.

subdivision

Current Java 3D API (version 1.3) does not include direct support for curves and curved surfaces. We will implement our own versions of Bézier curves and surfaces using the line and polygon arrays provided by Java 3D. Other spline curves and surfaces can be implemented as a series of Bézier curves or surfaces.

Listing 12.1 illustrates the rendering of cubic Bézier curves with recursive subdivisions. A test program that displays a Bézier curve is given in Listing 12.2. A `BezierCurve` class is implemented as a subclass of `LineStripArray`. A test program displays an instance of the curve class (See Figure 12.2.)

Listing 12.1 `BezierCurve.java`

```
 1 package chapter12;
 2
 3 import javax.vecmath.*;
 4 import java.awt.*;
 5 import java.awt.event.*;
 6 import javax.media.j3d.*;
 7 import com.sun.j3d.utils.universe.*;
 8 import com.sun.j3d.utils.geometry.*;
 9
10 public class BezierCurve extends LineStripArray {
11    static int level = 4;
12    static int[] vCnts = {(1<<level)+1};
13    int index = 0;
14
15    public BezierCurve(Point3d p0,Point3d p1,Point3d p2,Point3d p3) {
16      super(vCnts[0], GeometryArray.COORDINATES, vCnts);
17      setCoordinate(index, p0);
18      index++;
19      subdivide(0,p0,p1,p2,p3);
20    }
21
22    void subdivide(int lev, Point3d p0, Point3d p1,
23    Point3d p2, Point3d p3) {
24      if (lev >= level){
25        setCoordinate(index, p3);
```

```
26        index++;
27      }
28      else {
29        Point3d p10 = new Point3d();
30        p10.add(p0,p1);
31        p10.scale(0.5);
32        Point3d p11 = new Point3d();
33        p11.add(p1,p2);
34        p11.scale(0.5);
35        Point3d p12 = new Point3d();
36        p12.add(p2,p3);
37        p12.scale(0.5);
38        Point3d p20 = new Point3d();
39        p20.add(p10,p11);
40        p20.scale(0.5);
41        Point3d p21 = new Point3d();
42        p21.add(p11,p12);
43        p21.scale(0.5);
44        Point3d p30 = new Point3d();
45        p30.add(p20,p21);
46        p30.scale(0.5);
47        subdivide(lev+1,p0,p10,p20,p30);
48        subdivide(lev+1,p30,p21,p12,p3);
49      }
50    }
51 }
```

Listing 12.2 TestBezierCurve.java

```
 1 package chapter12;
 2
 3 import javax.vecmath.*;
 4 import java.awt.*;
 5 import java.awt.event.*;
 6 import javax.media.j3d.*;
 7 import com.sun.j3d.utils.universe.*;
 8 import com.sun.j3d.utils.geometry.*;
 9 import java.applet.*;
10 import com.sun.j3d.utils.applet.MainFrame;
11
12 public class TestBezierCurve extends Applet {
13    public static void main(String[] args) {
14      new MainFrame(new TestBezierCurve(), 640, 480);
15    }
16
17    public void init() {
18      // create canvas
19      GraphicsConfiguration gc =
20      SimpleUniverse.getPreferredConfiguration();
21      Canvas3D cv = new Canvas3D(gc);
22      setLayout(new BorderLayout());
23      add(cv, BorderLayout.CENTER);
24      BranchGroup bg = createSceneGraph();
25      bg.compile();
26      SimpleUniverse su = new SimpleUniverse(cv);
27      su.getViewingPlatform().setNominalViewingTransform();
28      su.addBranchGraph(bg);
29    }
30
31    private BranchGroup createSceneGraph() {
32      BranchGroup root = new BranchGroup();
```

```
33      TransformGroup spin = new TransformGroup();
34      spin.setCapability(TransformGroup.ALLOW_TRANSFORM_WRITE);
35      root.addChild(spin);
36      // object
37      Point3d p0 = new Point3d(-1,0,0.5);
38      Point3d p1 = new Point3d(-0.2,0.6,-0.2);
39      Point3d p2 = new Point3d(0.3,-0.8,0.3);
40      Point3d p3 = new Point3d(0.9,0.1,0.6);
41      Appearance ap = new Appearance();
42      ap.setColoringAttributes(new ColoringAttributes(0f, 0f, 0f,
43        ColoringAttributes.FASTEST));
44      Shape3D shape = new Shape3D(new
45      BezierCurve(p0,p1,p2,p3), ap);
46      spin.addChild(shape);
47      // rotation interpolator
48      Alpha alpha = new Alpha(-1, 10000);
49      RotationInterpolator rotator =
50      new RotationInterpolator(alpha, spin);
51      BoundingSphere bounds = new BoundingSphere();
52      rotator.setSchedulingBounds(bounds);
53      spin.addChild(rotator);
54      // background
55      Background background = new Background(1f, 1f, 1f);
56      background.setApplicationBounds(bounds);
57      root.addChild(background);
58      return root;
59    }
60 }
```

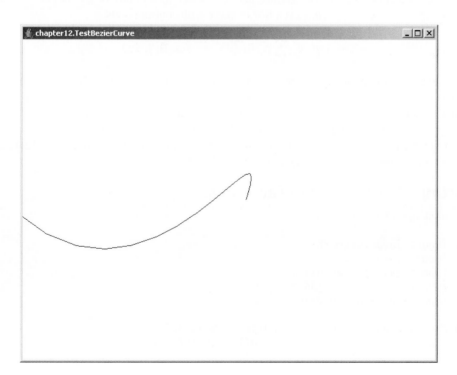

FIGURE 12.2   A cubic Bézier curve.

A Bézier curve is implemented in the class `BezierCurve` as a `LineStripArray`. The deCasteljau algorithm-based subdivision technique is applied recursively to break the curve into small segments. The final small Bézier curves are approximated by straight line segments. For simplicity a fixed level of recursion is used and no flatness test is applied to the segments.

If the depth of recursion is `level`, the number of line segments is 2^{level}, and the number of vertices in the `LineStripArray` is $2^{level} + 1$. The constructor of `BezierCurve` adds the first point to the array and calls the method `subdivide` (line 22) to start the subdivision.

The method `subdivide` is recursive. It divides a Bézier curve into two at $t = 0.5$ and calls itself for the two subdivided curves. When the recursion level reaches the specified value (4 in this example), the subdivision stops and the second endpoint is added to the array.

The test program `TestBezierCurve` displays an instance of the Bézier curve and rotates it with a rotation interpolator.

12.3 Surfaces

12.3.1 Bézier Surface

A Bézier surface is formed by extending a Bézier curve to a surface along another Bézier curve using a method called tensor product. The parametric equation of a general Bézier surface is given by

$$S(u, v) = \sum_{i=0}^{m} \sum_{j=0}^{n} p_{i,j} B_{m,i}(u) B_{n,j}(v)$$

The most commonly used type of Bézier surface is the bicubic surface with $m = n = 3$, which is defined by 16 control points.

evaluation

The *evaluation* of a point $S(u, v)$ on a Bézier surface can also be obtained from the deCasteljau algorithm. A Bézier surface may be viewed as a family of Bézier curves. For a fixed u, the curve $s(v) = S(u, v)$ is a Bézier curve with control points:

$$p_j = \sum_{i=0}^{3} p_{i,j} B_{3,i}(u), \qquad j = 0, 1, 2, 3$$

The four control points are themselves points on another Bézier curve. Consequently, these points can be calculated through four applications of the deCasteljau algorithm with $t = u$. After obtaining the four control points for the Bézier curve, we can calculate the point $s(v) = S(u, v)$ from another application of deCasteljau algorithm with $t = v$ on the curve.

A bicubic Bézier surface is implemented in Listing 12.3. A test program (Listing 12.4) displays a randomly generated Bézier surface. (See Figure 12.3.)

Listing 12.3 `BezierSurface.java`

```
1 package chapter12;
2
3 import javax.vecmath.*;
4 import java.awt.*;
5 import java.awt.event.*;
6 import javax.media.j3d.*;
7 import com.sun.j3d.utils.geometry.*;
8
9 public class BezierSurface extends Shape3D{
10   public BezierSurface(Point3d[][] ctrlPts) {
11     int m = 17;
12     int n = 17;
13     Point3d[] pts = new Point3d[m*n];
14     int idx = 0;
15     Point3d[] p = new Point3d[4];
16     double du = 1.0/(m-1);
```

```
17      double dv = 1.0/(n-1);
18      double u = 0;
19      double v = 0;
20      for (int i = 0; i < m; i++) {
21        for (int k = 0; k < 4; k++) {
22          p[k] = deCasteljau(u, ctrlPts[k]);
23        }
24        v = 0;
25        for (int j = 0; j < n; j++) {
26          pts[idx++] = deCasteljau(v, p);
27          v += dv;
28        }
29        u += du;
30      }
31
32      int[] coords = new int[2*n*(m-1)];
33      idx = 0;
34      for (int i = 1; i < m; i++) {
35        for (int j = 0; j < n; j++) {
36          coords[idx++] = i*n + j;
37          coords[idx++] = (i-1)*n + j;
38        }
39      }
40
41      int[] stripCounts = new int[m-1];
42      for (int i = 0; i < m-1; i++) stripCounts[i] = 2*n;
43
44      GeometryInfo gi =
45      new GeometryInfo(GeometryInfo.TRIANGLE_STRIP_ARRAY);
46      gi.setCoordinates(pts);
47      gi.setCoordinateIndices(coords);
48      gi.setStripCounts(stripCounts);
49
50      NormalGenerator ng = new NormalGenerator();
51      ng.generateNormals(gi);
52      this.setGeometry(gi.getGeometryArray());
53    }
54
55    Point3d deCasteljau(double t, Point3d[] p) {
56      Point3d[] pt = {new Point3d(p[0]),
57      new Point3d(p[1]),new Point3d(p[2]), new Point3d(p[3])};
58      for (int i = 0; i < 3; i++) {
59        for (int j = 0; j < 3-i; j++) {
60          pt[j].interpolate(pt[j+1], t);
61        }
62      }
63      return pt[0];
64    }
65 }
```

Listing 12.4 `TestBezierSurface.java`

```
1 package chapter12;
2
3 import javax.vecmath.*;
4 import java.awt.*;
5 import java.awt.event.*;
6 import javax.media.j3d.*;
7 import com.sun.j3d.utils.universe.*;
```

```
 8 import com.sun.j3d.utils.geometry.*;
 9 import java.applet.*;
10 import com.sun.j3d.utils.applet.MainFrame;
11
12 public class TestBezierSurface extends Applet {
13   public static void main(String[] args) {
14     new MainFrame(new TestBezierSurface(), 640, 480);
15   }
16
17   public void init() {
18     // create canvas
19     GraphicsConfiguration gc =
20       SimpleUniverse.getPreferredConfiguration();
21     Canvas3D cv = new Canvas3D(gc);
22     setLayout(new BorderLayout());
23     add(cv, BorderLayout.CENTER);
24     BranchGroup bg = createSceneGraph();
25     bg.compile();
26     SimpleUniverse su = new SimpleUniverse(cv);
27     su.getViewingPlatform().setNominalViewingTransform();
28     su.addBranchGraph(bg);
29   }
30
31   private BranchGroup createSceneGraph() {
32     BranchGroup root = new BranchGroup();
33     TransformGroup spin = new TransformGroup();
34     spin.setCapability(TransformGroup.ALLOW_TRANSFORM_WRITE);
35     root.addChild(spin);
36     // surface
37     Point3d[][] ctrlPts = new Point3d[4][4];
38     for (int i = 0; i < 4; i++) {
39       for (int j = 0; j < 4; j++) {
40         ctrlPts[i][j] = new Point3d(2-i, 3*(Math.random()-0.5), j-2);
41       }
42     }
43     Shape3D shape = new BezierSurface(ctrlPts);
44     Appearance ap = new Appearance();
45     ap.setMaterial(new Material());
46     shape.setAppearance(ap);
47     Transform3D tr = new Transform3D();
48     tr.setScale(0.25);
49     TransformGroup tg = new TransformGroup(tr);
50     spin.addChild(tg);
51     tg.addChild(shape);
52     // rotation interpolator
53     Alpha alpha = new Alpha(-1, 10000);
54     RotationInterpolator rotator =
55     new RotationInterpolator(alpha, spin);
56     BoundingSphere bounds = new BoundingSphere();
57     rotator.setSchedulingBounds(bounds);
58     spin.addChild(rotator);
59     // background and lights
60     Background background = new Background(1f, 1f, 1f);
61     background.setApplicationBounds(bounds);
62     root.addChild(background);
63     AmbientLight light = new AmbientLight(true,
64     new Color3f(Color.red));
65     light.setInfluencingBounds(bounds);
66     root.addChild(light);
67     PointLight ptlight = new PointLight
```

```
68        (new Color3f(Color.lightGray),
69         new Point3f(1f,1f,1f), new Point3f(1f,0f,0f));
70     ptlight.setInfluencingBounds(bounds);
71     root.addChild(ptlight);
72     return root;
73   }
74 }
```

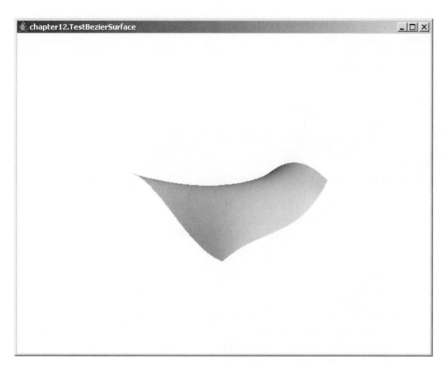

FIGURE 12.3 A bicubic Bézier surface.

The BezierSurface class encapsulates a bicubic Bézier surface. It is implemented by calculating $m \times n$ points on the surface and forming a polygon mesh. The calculations of the points on the surface are based on the deCasteljau approach. The 16 control points of the Bézier surface are given in the 2D array parameter ctrlPts. To calculate the point with parameter value (u, v), four Bézier curves defined by the four sets of control points ctrlPts[k], $k = 0, 1, 2, 3$, are evaluated at u. The resulting four points are stored in the array p. Then the four points are used as the control points to define a new Bézier curve which is evaluated at v. The resulting point of this evaluation is the point on the Bézier surface at (u, v).

The deCasteljau method (line 55) evaluates a point on a Bézier curve from the given parameter value and four control points. The linear interpolations required by the deCasteljau algorithm are carried out by simply calling the existing method interpolate in Point3d (line 60).

The calculated points on the surface are placed in a GeometryInfo object as vertices. The GeometryInfo object is created in the TRIANGLE_STRIP_ARRAY mode. The surface normals are generated automatically using a NormalGenerator object.

The test program in the class TestBezierSurface creates 16 control points based on randomly generated numbers. The BezierSurface class is used to generate the shape of the visual object. Lighting is enabled. Two lights are placed in the scene. A rotation interpolator is used to rotate the surface.

12.3.2 The Utah Teapot

One of the most famous objects in computer graphics is the "Utah teapot." It is defined by a set of Bézier surface patches. We may use the Bézier surface class to display the teapot, as illustrated in Listing 12.5. (See Figure 12.4.)

Listing 12.5 `Teapot.java`

```java
1 package chapter12;
2
3 import javax.vecmath.*;
4 import java.awt.*;
5 import java.awt.event.*;
6 import javax.media.j3d.*;
7 import com.sun.j3d.utils.universe.*;
8 import com.sun.j3d.utils.geometry.*;
9 import java.applet.*;
10 import com.sun.j3d.utils.applet.MainFrame;
11 import java.net.URL;
12 import java.io.*;
13 import java.util.StringTokenizer;
14
15 public class Teapot extends Applet {
16   public static void main(String[] args) {
17     new MainFrame(new Teapot(), 640, 480);
18   }
19
20   public void init() {
21     // create canvas
22     GraphicsConfiguration gc =
23       SimpleUniverse.getPreferredConfiguration();
24     Canvas3D cv = new Canvas3D(gc);
25     setLayout(new BorderLayout());
26     add(cv, BorderLayout.CENTER);
27     BranchGroup bg = createSceneGraph();
28     bg.compile();
29     SimpleUniverse su = new SimpleUniverse(cv);
30     su.getViewingPlatform().setNominalViewingTransform();
31     su.addBranchGraph(bg);
32   }
33
34   private BranchGroup createSceneGraph() {
35     BranchGroup root = new BranchGroup();
36     TransformGroup spin = new TransformGroup();
37     spin.setCapability(TransformGroup.ALLOW_TRANSFORM_WRITE);
38     root.addChild(spin);
39     // teapot data
40     int n = 0;
41     int[][] idx = null;
42     int np = 0;
43     Point3d[] pts = null;
44     URL url =
45       getClass().getClassLoader().getResource("images/teapot");
46     try {
47       BufferedReader br = new BufferedReader
48       (new InputStreamReader(url.openStream()));
49       String line = br.readLine();
50       n = Integer.parseInt(line);
51       idx = new int[n][16];
52       for (int i = 0; i < n; i++) {
```

```
53          line = br.readLine();
54          StringTokenizer st = new StringTokenizer(line, ", \n");
55          for (int j = 0; j < 16; j++) {
56              idx[i][j] = Integer.parseInt(st.nextToken());
57          }
58      }
59      line = br.readLine();
60      np = Integer.parseInt(line);
61      pts = new Point3d[np];
62      for (int i = 0; i < np; i++) {
63          line = br.readLine();
64          StringTokenizer st = new StringTokenizer(line, ", \n");
65          double x = Double.parseDouble(st.nextToken());
66          double y = Double.parseDouble(st.nextToken());
67          double z = Double.parseDouble(st.nextToken());
68          pts[i] = new Point3d(x, y, z);
69      }
70      br.close();
71  } catch (IOException ex) {
72      ex.printStackTrace();
73  }
74
75  // surface
76  Appearance ap = new Appearance();
77  ap.setMaterial(new Material());
78  Transform3D tr = new Transform3D();
79  tr.rotX(-Math.PI*0.5);
80  tr.setScale(0.25);
81  tr.setTranslation(new Vector3d(0,-0.5,0));
82  TransformGroup tg = new TransformGroup(tr);
83  spin.addChild(tg);
84  Point3d[][] ctrlPts = new Point3d[4][4];
85  for (int k = 0; k < n; k++) {
86    for (int i = 0; i < 4; i++) {
87      for (int j = 0; j < 4; j++) {
88        ctrlPts[i][j] = pts[idx[k][i+4*j]-1];
89      }
90    }
91    Shape3D shape = new BezierSurface(ctrlPts);
92    shape.setAppearance(ap);
93    tg.addChild(shape);
94  }
95  // rotation interpolator
96  Alpha alpha = new Alpha(-1, 10000);
97  RotationInterpolator rotator =
98  new RotationInterpolator(alpha, spin);
99  BoundingSphere bounds = new BoundingSphere();
100 bounds.setRadius(10);
101 rotator.setSchedulingBounds(bounds);
102 spin.addChild(rotator);
103 // background and lights
104 Background background = new Background(1f, 1f, 1f);
105 background.setApplicationBounds(bounds);
106 root.addChild(background);
107 AmbientLight light = new AmbientLight(true,
108 new Color3f(Color.white));
109 light.setInfluencingBounds(bounds);
110 root.addChild(light);
111 PointLight ptlight = new PointLight(new Color3f(Color.white),
112 new Point3f(0.7f,1.8f,1.8f), new Point3f(1f,0.2f,0f));
```

```
113      ptlight.setInfluencingBounds(bounds);
114      root.addChild(ptlight);
115      return root;
116  }
117 }
```

FIGURE 12.4   The Utah Teapot.

The teapot data, consisting of the coordinates and indices of the control points, is stored in a text file "teapot." The program reads the data and constructs the patches using the BezierSurface class.

12.4 Sound

Sound has become an important component of modern multimedia applications. Even though it is not graphical in nature, sound is often associated with graphics in applications such as games. Java 3D provides support for incorporating sound in scene graphs with the Sound class and its subclasses. The Sound classes are Leaf nodes. The class hierarchy of Sound is given in Figure 12.5.

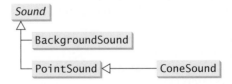

FIGURE 12.5   Sound classes.

The Sound classes are similar to Light classes. The BackgroundSound, like Ambient-Light, is distributed uniformly in the space. The PointSound has a specific location and may have attenuation, similar to the PointLight class. The ConeSound restricts the effects of the sound to a cone-shaped region, similar to a SpotLight.

To *add sound* to a Java 3D program, the following steps are usually required:

add sound

■ Create an AudioDevice. If a SimpleUniverse object is used for the scene graph, a convenient way to do this is to simply call the method **createAudioDevice()** in the Viewer:

```
su.getViewer().createAudioDevice();
```

■ Create a MediaContainer object to hold sound data. For example,

```
MediaContainer mc = new MediaContainer(url);
```

■ Create a Sound object with the sound data and add it to the scene graph. For example,

```
BackgroundSound sound = new BackgroundSound();
sound.setSoundData(mc);
sound.setSchedulingBounds(bounds);
root.addChild(sound);
```

A scheduling bound is required for a sound node, similar to other environmental nodes.

Listing 12.6 illustrates the application of sounds in Java 3D. This example shows a gull on a sky background (Figure 12.6). The gull can be rotated, translated, and zoomed by mouse operations. A sound of a bird originated from the location of the gull plays continuously. If the bird is moved to the left side, the sound also comes from the left. If the bird is moved farther away, the volume of the sound decreases.

Listing 12.6 Sound3D.java

```
 1 package chapter12;
 2
 3 import java.net.URL;
 4 import java.awt.*;
 5 import java.awt.event.*;
 6 import java.awt.image.*;
 7 import com.sun.j3d.utils.universe.*;
 8 import javax.media.j3d.*;
 9 import javax.vecmath.*;
10 import java.io.*;
11 import javax.imageio.*;
12 import com.sun.j3d.utils.behaviors.mouse.*;
13 import chapter10.GullCG;
14 import java.applet.*;
15 import com.sun.j3d.utils.applet.MainFrame;
16
17 public class Sound3D extends Applet {
18   public static void main(String[] args) {
19     new MainFrame(new Sound3D(), 640, 480);
20   }
21
22   public void init() {
23     // create canvas
24     GraphicsConfiguration gc =
25       SimpleUniverse.getPreferredConfiguration();
26     Canvas3D cv = new Canvas3D(gc);
```

```
27      setLayout(new BorderLayout());
28      add(cv, BorderLayout.CENTER);
29      SimpleUniverse su = new SimpleUniverse(cv);
30      AudioDevice audioDev = su.getViewer().createAudioDevice();
31      BranchGroup bg = createSceneGraph();
32      bg.compile();
33      su.getViewingPlatform().setNominalViewingTransform();
34      su.addBranchGraph(bg);
35    }
36
37    public BranchGroup createSceneGraph() {
38      // root
39      BranchGroup objRoot = new BranchGroup();
40      Transform3D trans = new Transform3D();
41      trans.setTranslation(new Vector3d(Math.random()-0.5,
42        Math.random()-0.5, Math.random()-0.5));
43        trans.setScale(0.3);
44      TransformGroup objTrans = new TransformGroup(trans);
45      objTrans.setCapability(TransformGroup.ALLOW_TRANSFORM_WRITE);
46      objTrans.setCapability(TransformGroup.ALLOW_TRANSFORM_READ);
47      objRoot.addChild(objTrans);
48      // visual object
49      Appearance ap = new Appearance();
50      ap.setMaterial(new Material());
51      Shape3D shape = new Shape3D(new GullCG(), ap);
52      objTrans.addChild(shape);
53      // behaviors
54      BoundingSphere bounds =
55        new BoundingSphere(new Point3d(0.0,0.0,0.0), 100.0);
56      // rotation
57      MouseRotate rotator = new MouseRotate(objTrans);
58      rotator.setSchedulingBounds(bounds);
59      objRoot.addChild(rotator);
60      // translation
61      MouseTranslate translator = new MouseTranslate(objTrans);
62      translator.setSchedulingBounds(bounds);
63      objTrans.addChild(translator);
64      // zoom
65      MouseZoom zoom = new MouseZoom(objTrans);
66      zoom.setSchedulingBounds(bounds);
67      objTrans.addChild(zoom);
68      // sound
69      PointSound sound = new PointSound();
70      URL url =
71        this.getClass().getClassLoader().getResource("images/bird.au");
72      MediaContainer mc = new MediaContainer(url);
73      sound.setSoundData(mc);
74      sound.setLoop(Sound.INFINITE_LOOPS);
75      sound.setInitialGain(1f);
76      sound.setEnable(true);
77      float[] distances = {1f, 20f};
78      float[] gains = {1f, 0.001f};
79      sound.setDistanceGain(distances, gains);
80      BoundingSphere soundBounds =
81      new BoundingSphere(new Point3d(0.0,0.0,0.0), 100.0);
82      sound.setSchedulingBounds(soundBounds);
83      objTrans.addChild(sound);
84      // light
85      AmbientLight light =
```

```
86          new AmbientLight(true, new Color3f(Color.blue));
87      light.setInfluencingBounds(bounds);
88      objRoot.addChild(light);
89      PointLight ptlight = new PointLight(new Color3f(Color.white),
90          new Point3f(0f,0f,2f), new Point3f(1f,0.3f,0f));
91      ptlight.setInfluencingBounds(bounds);
92      objRoot.addChild(ptlight);
93      // background
94      url = getClass().getClassLoader().getResource("images/bg.jpg");
95      BufferedImage bi = null;
96      try {
97          bi = ImageIO.read(url);
98      } catch (IOException ex) {
99          ex.printStackTrace();
100     }
101     ImageComponent2D image =
102         new ImageComponent2D(ImageComponent2D.FORMAT_RGB, bi);
103     Background background = new Background(image);
104     background.setApplicationBounds(bounds);
105     objRoot.addChild(background);
106     return objRoot;
107   }
108 }
```

Figure 12.6 A point sound associated with the bird.

The scene graph in Figure 12.7 shows the incorporation of a sound node. The sound node is under the same transform as the gull shape node. Three mouse behaviors operate on the transform. When the user moves the visual object through mouse operations, the sound node is also moved accordingly.

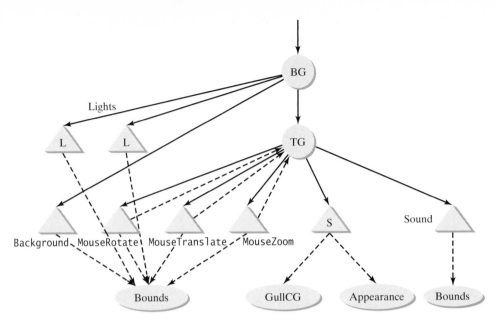

Figure 12.7 Scene graph for the sound example.

The sound node is an instance of `PointSound` with a distance attenuation (line 69). Two distance values with the corresponding gain values are specified. The gains will decrease from 1 to 0.001 as the distances increase from 1 to 20.

12.5 Shadows

As a real-time graphics API, Java 3D provides only local illumination options. Objects are rendered individually without considering the influences and interactions between them. For example, the light reflected off an object will not influence other objects. If one object is located between a light and another object, partially blocking the light, the effects will not be shown in the rendering. Consequently, shadows are not automatically generated with local illumination models.

Generating realistic shadows in a scene can be a very complex task. Multiple light sources, relations among different visual objects, and characteristics of lights and objects are all factors in this problem. A global illumination model may be applied to obtain good shadow effects, but the global techniques are computationally intensive and usually impractical for real-time rendering. In this section a method to create simple *artificial shadows* is introduced. It uses a polygon to approximate a shadow. The approach is quite efficient, but it has many limitations.

The shadow is assumed to be cast on a plane. Only a single point light is considered. The vertices of the polygon are calculated by projecting the vertices of the object to the plane from the position of the point light. Figure 12.8 illustrates the construction of the shadow polygon.

The transformation is a projection similar to the one in a view. The light position corresponds to the viewer. The only difference is that this projection indeed maps all points to the plane, and the depth information is not retained. When the projection is in a standard form that the light is located at the origin and the plane is $x = -d$, the transformation matrix for the projection is:

$$P = \begin{bmatrix} 1 & 0 & 0 & 0 \\ 0 & 1 & 0 & 0 \\ 0 & 0 & 1 & 0 \\ 0 & 0 & -1/d & 0 \end{bmatrix}$$

artificial shadows

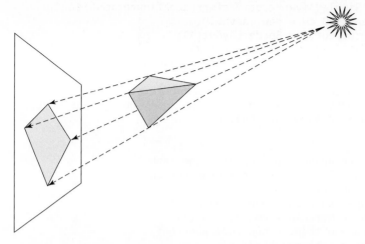

FIGURE 12.8 Generating a shadow by projection.

For a general configuration of the light position and the shadow plane, an affine transform U may be constructed to map the configuration to a standard form. The method `lookAt` in the class `Transform3D` generates such a transform. The final projection can be expressed as:

$$U^{-1}PU$$

Using the projection, the vertices of a geometric object are mapped to the projection plane and form the vertices of the shadow polygon.

Listing 12.7 implements the shadow generation. The scene contains a stone wall and a dodecahedron. A point light illuminates the dodecahedron casting a shadow on the wall. (Figure 12.9)

Listing 12.7 `Shadow.java`

```
1 package chapter12;
2
3 import javax.vecmath.*;
4 import java.awt.*;
5 import java.awt.event.*;
6 import java.awt.image.*;
7 import java.net.URL;
8 import java.io.*;
9 import javax.imageio.*;
10 import javax.swing.*;
11 import javax.media.j3d.*;
12 import com.sun.j3d.utils.universe.*;
13 import com.sun.j3d.utils.geometry.*;
14 import chapter6.Dodecahedron;
15 import java.applet.*;
16 import com.sun.j3d.utils.applet.MainFrame;
17
18 public class Shadow extends Applet {
19   public static void main(String[] args) {
20     new MainFrame(new Shadow(), 640, 480);
21   }
22
23   public void init() {
24     // create canvas
25     GraphicsConfiguration gc =
```

```
26        SimpleUniverse.getPreferredConfiguration();
27      Canvas3D cv = new Canvas3D(gc);
28      setLayout(new BorderLayout());
29      add(cv, BorderLayout.CENTER);
30      BranchGroup bg = createSceneGraph();
31      bg.compile();
32      SimpleUniverse su = new SimpleUniverse(cv);
33      su.getViewingPlatform().setNominalViewingTransform();
34      su.addBranchGraph(bg);
35    }
36
37    private BranchGroup createSceneGraph() {
38      BranchGroup root = new BranchGroup();
39      // object
40      Appearance ap = new Appearance();
41      ap.setMaterial(new Material());
42      Shape3D shape = new Dodecahedron();
43      shape.setAppearance(ap);
44      GeometryArray geom = (GeometryArray)shape.getGeometry();
45      // transform
46      Transform3D tr = new Transform3D();
47      tr.rotY(-0.2);
48      tr.setScale(0.2);
49      TransformGroup tg = new TransformGroup(tr);
50      root.addChild(tg);
51      tg.addChild(shape);
52      BoundingSphere bounds =
53      new BoundingSphere(new Point3d(0,0,0),100);
54      // light and background
55      Background background = new Background(1.0f, 1.0f, 1.0f);
56      background.setApplicationBounds(bounds);
57      root.addChild(background);
58      AmbientLight light =
59        new AmbientLight(true, new Color3f(Color.red));
60      light.setInfluencingBounds(bounds);
61      root.addChild(light);
62      Point3f lightPos = new Point3f(10f,3f,1f);
63      PointLight ptlight = new PointLight(new Color3f(Color.green),
64      lightPos, new Point3f(1f,0f,0f));
65      ptlight.setInfluencingBounds(bounds);
66      tg.addChild(ptlight);
67      // wall
68      Shape3D wall = createWall();
69      tg.addChild(wall);
70      // shadow
71      GeometryArray shadow = createShadow(geom,
72        lightPos, new Point3f(-2f, 3f, 1f));
73      ap = new Appearance();
74      ColoringAttributes colorAttr =
75        new ColoringAttributes(0.1f, 0.1f, 0.1f,
76        ColoringAttributes.FASTEST);
77      ap.setColoringAttributes(colorAttr);
78      TransparencyAttributes transAttr = new TransparencyAttributes(
79        TransparencyAttributes.BLENDED,0.35f);
80      ap.setTransparencyAttributes(transAttr);
81      PolygonAttributes polyAttr = new PolygonAttributes();
82      polyAttr.setCullFace(PolygonAttributes.CULL_NONE);
83      ap.setPolygonAttributes(polyAttr);
84      shape = new Shape3D(shadow, ap);
85      tg.addChild(shape);
```

```
86       return root;
87     }
88
89     private Shape3D createWall() {
90       URL url =
91         getClass().getClassLoader().getResource("images/stone.jpg");
92       BufferedImage bi = null;
93       try {
94         bi = ImageIO.read(url);
95       } catch (IOException ex) {
96         ex.printStackTrace();
97       }
98       ImageComponent2D image =
99         new ImageComponent2D(ImageComponent2D.FORMAT_RGB, bi);
100      Texture2D texture =
101        new Texture2D(Texture.BASE_LEVEL, Texture.RGBA,
102        image.getWidth(), image.getHeight());
103      texture.setImage(0, image);
104      texture.setEnable(true);
105      texture.setMagFilter(Texture.BASE_LEVEL_LINEAR);
106      texture.setMinFilter(Texture.BASE_LEVEL_LINEAR);
107      Appearance appear = new Appearance();
108      appear.setTexture(texture);
109      QuadArray rect = new QuadArray(4, QuadArray.COORDINATES |
110        QuadArray.TEXTURE_COORDINATE_2);
111      rect.setCoordinate(0, new Point3d(-2,3,2));
112      rect.setCoordinate(1, new Point3d(-2,-3,2));
113      rect.setCoordinate(2, new Point3d(-2,-3,-3));
114      rect.setCoordinate(3, new Point3d(-2,3,-3));
115      rect.setTextureCoordinate(0,0, new TexCoord2f(0f, 0f));
116      rect.setTextureCoordinate(0,1, new TexCoord2f(0f, 1f));
117      rect.setTextureCoordinate(0,2, new TexCoord2f(1f, 1f));
118      rect.setTextureCoordinate(0,3, new TexCoord2f(1f, 0f));
119      return new Shape3D(rect, appear);
120    }
121
122    private GeometryArray createShadow(GeometryArray ga, Point3f light,
123      Point3f plane) {
124      GeometryInfo gi = new GeometryInfo(ga);
125      gi.convertToIndexedTriangles();
126      IndexedTriangleArray ita =
127        (IndexedTriangleArray)gi.getIndexedGeometryArray();
128      Vector3f v = new Vector3f();
129      v.sub(plane, light);
130      double[] mat = new double[16];
131      for (int i = 0; i < 16; i++) {
132        mat[i] = 0;
133      }
134      mat[0] = 1;
135      mat[5] = 1;
136      mat[10] = 1-0.001;
137      mat[14] = -1/v.length();
138      Transform3D proj = new Transform3D();
139      proj.set(mat);
140      Transform3D u = new Transform3D();
141      u.lookAt(new Point3d(light),
142      new Point3d(plane), new Vector3d(0,1,0));
143      proj.mul(u);
144      Transform3D tr = new Transform3D();
145      u.invert();
```

```
146      tr.mul(u, proj);
147      int n = ita.getVertexCount();
148      int count = ita.getIndexCount();
149      IndexedTriangleArray shadow = new IndexedTriangleArray(n,
150        GeometryArray.COORDINATES, count);
151      for (int i = 0; i < n; i++) {
152        Point3d p = new Point3d();
153        ga.getCoordinate(i, p);
154        Vector4d v4 = new Vector4d(p);
155        v4.w = 1;
156        tr.transform(v4);
157        Point4d p4 = new Point4d(v4);
158        p.project(p4);
159        shadow.setCoordinate(i, p);
160      }
161      int[] indices = new int[count];
162      ita.getCoordinateIndices(0, indices);
163      shadow.setCoordinateIndices(0, indices);
164      return shadow;
165    }
166 }
```

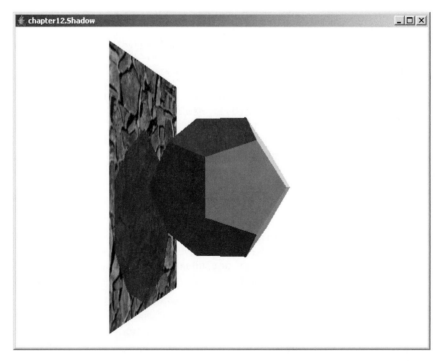

FIGURE 12.9 A shadow on the wall created with a polygon from the projection of the object.

The scene graph is shown in Figure 12.10. It contains a texture-mapped rectangle as the wall, a dodecahedron, and the shadow of the dodecahedron cast on the wall. An ambient light and a point light are used. The shadow calculation is related to the position of the point light.

The method createShadow (line 123) performs the necessary computations to create a shadow polygon from the projections of the vertices of the original object. The projection matrix is constructed by the matrix for the standard projection and the transform to the standard position. The transform to the standard position is formed using the method lookAt.

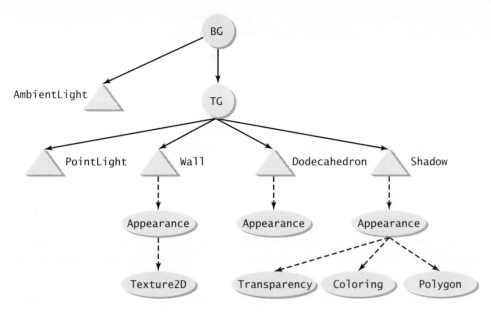

FIGURE 12.10   Scene graph for the shadow example.

The projection is actually done slightly above the plane in order to avoid interference between the shadow and the wall object.

   The shadow polygon has a gray color. It is set by a `ColoringAttributes` object. The polygon is also semitransparent to show some wall details under the shadow. The `Transparency-Attributes` object sets the transparency of the shadow polygon (lines 73–83).

12.6 Geometry Change

The animation and behavior objects introduced in Chapter 10 and Chapter 11 do not modify the geometry data in a live scene graph. The `Morph` object combines several geometry objects, but it modifies only the weights of the combination. In some circumstances, it is useful to able to modify the actual geometry data in a live scene graph. For example, the artificial shadow example introduced in the preceding section works only for static objects. If the dodecahedron moves relative to the wall or the light, the correct shadow polygon should change accordingly. This requires vertices of the polygon be recalculated. Simply placing the shadow polygon under the same transform group as the dodecahedron will not produce the correct result, because the polygon is formed through a projection.

   Java 3D provides a mechanism for modifying a live geometry through the `Geometry-Updater` interface and the `BY_REFERENCE` mode of `GeometryArray`. A `GeometryArray`   BY_REFERENCE
by default maintains a copy of the data, such as vertex coordinates. If a `GeometryArray` is created with the `BY_REFERENCE` flag set in the constructor, it will hold only the references to user-provided data. For example, the following code fragment creates a by-reference geometry for a triangle:

```
GeometryArray geom = new TriangleArray(3, GeometryArray.BY_REFERENCE
                                          | GeometryArray.COORDINATES);
float[] coords = {1,0,0,0,1,0,0,0,1};
geom.setCoordRefFloat(coords);
```

   The array `coords` contains the vertex coordinates for the geometry and is referenced by the `TriangleArray` object. Even though you supply the data buffer for the by-reference geometry, you still should not directly modify the contents in a live scene graph. The proper way to make a change is to implement the GeometryUpdater interface. The interface defines one method you need to implement to update the geometry:

```
public void updateData(Geometry geometry)
```

The parameter geometry provides a reference to the geometry that you may modify. This method is called by the system. You may call the method in the GeometryArray with the same name to invoke the update:

```
public void updateData(GeometryUpdater updater)
```

You need to pass an instance of your custom GeometryUpdater class as the parameter. In summary, to modify a geometry from a behavior, you may use the following procedure:

- Create the geometry with BY_REFERENCE.

- Write a class implementing the GeometryUpdater interface. Implement the method updateData(Geometry) in GeometryUpdater to perform the modifications on the geometry.

- Implement a Behavior class. At appropriate moments, call the method updateData-(GeometryUpdater) in GeometryArray to trigger the update.

Listing 12.8 shows an application of live geometry change. The program creates a scene similar to Listing 12.7. However, the dodecahedron is now rotating, and its shadow changes dynamically in accordance with the position of the dodecahedron.

Listing 12.8 MovingShadow.java

```
 1 package chapter12;
 2
 3 import javax.vecmath.*;
 4 import java.awt.*;
 5 import java.awt.event.*;
 6 import java.awt.image.*;
 7 import java.net.URL;
 8 import java.io.*;
 9 import javax.imageio.*;
10 import javax.swing.*;
11 import javax.media.j3d.*;
12 import com.sun.j3d.utils.universe.*;
13 import com.sun.j3d.utils.geometry.*;
14 import chapter6.Dodecahedron;
15 import java.applet.*;
16 import com.sun.j3d.utils.applet.MainFrame;
17
18 public class MovingShadow extends Applet {
19   public static void main(String[] args) {
20     new MainFrame(new MovingShadow(), 640, 480);
21   }
22
23   private TransformGroup spin = null;
24   private Transform3D shadowProj = null;
25   private GeometryArray geom = null;
26   private GeometryArray shadowGeom = null;
27   private ShadowUpdater updater = null;
28
29   public void init() {
30     // create canvas
```

```
31      GraphicsConfiguration gc =
32        SimpleUniverse.getPreferredConfiguration();
33      Canvas3D cv = new Canvas3D(gc);
34      setLayout(new BorderLayout());
35      add(cv, BorderLayout.CENTER);
36      updater = new MovingShadow.ShadowUpdater();
37      BranchGroup bg = createSceneGraph();
38      bg.compile();
39      SimpleUniverse su = new SimpleUniverse(cv);
40      su.getViewingPlatform().setNominalViewingTransform();
41      su.addBranchGraph(bg);
42    }
43
44    private BranchGroup createSceneGraph() {
45      BranchGroup root = new BranchGroup();
46      // object
47      Appearance ap = new Appearance();
48      ap.setMaterial(new Material());
49      Shape3D shape = new Dodecahedron();
50      shape.setAppearance(ap);
51      geom = (GeometryArray)shape.getGeometry();
52      geom.setCapability(GeometryArray.ALLOW_COORDINATE_READ);
53      // transform
54      Transform3D tr = new Transform3D();
55      tr.rotY(-0.2);
56      tr.setScale(0.2);
57      TransformGroup tg = new TransformGroup(tr);
58      root.addChild(tg);
59      spin = new TransformGroup();
60      spin.setCapability(TransformGroup.ALLOW_TRANSFORM_READ);
61      spin.setCapability(TransformGroup.ALLOW_TRANSFORM_WRITE);
62      tg.addChild(spin);
63      spin.addChild(shape);
64      // rotator
65      Alpha alpha = new Alpha(-1, 8000);
66      RotationInterpolator rotator =
67      new RotationInterpolator(alpha, spin);
68      BoundingSphere bounds = new BoundingSphere();
69      rotator.setSchedulingBounds(bounds);
70      spin.addChild(rotator);
71      // light and background
72      Background background = new Background(1.0f, 1.0f, 1.0f);
73      background.setApplicationBounds(bounds);
74      root.addChild(background);
75      AmbientLight light =
76      new AmbientLight(true, new Color3f(Color.red));
77      light.setInfluencingBounds(bounds);
78      root.addChild(light);
79      Point3f lightPos = new Point3f(10f,3f,1f);
80      PointLight ptlight = new PointLight(new Color3f(Color.green),
81      lightPos, new Point3f(1f,0f,0f));
82      ptlight.setInfluencingBounds(bounds);
83      tg.addChild(ptlight);
84      // wall
85      Shape3D wall = createWall();
86      tg.addChild(wall);
87      // shadow
88      shadowGeom =
89        createShadow(geom, lightPos, new Point3f(-2f, 3f, 1f));
90      ap = new Appearance();
```

```
91    ColoringAttributes colorAttr =
92    new ColoringAttributes(0.1f, 0.1f, 0.1f,
93      ColoringAttributes.FASTEST);
94    ap.setColoringAttributes(colorAttr);
95    TransparencyAttributes transAttr = new TransparencyAttributes(
96      TransparencyAttributes.BLENDED,0.35f);
97    ap.setTransparencyAttributes(transAttr);
98    PolygonAttributes polyAttr = new PolygonAttributes();
99    polyAttr.setCullFace(PolygonAttributes.CULL_NONE);
100   ap.setPolygonAttributes(polyAttr);
101   shape = new Shape3D(shadowGeom, ap);
102   tg.addChild(shape);
103   // shadow update
104   ShadowBehavior sb = new MovingShadow.ShadowBehavior();
105   sb.setSchedulingBounds(bounds);
106   tg.addChild(sb);
107   return root;
108 }
109
110 private Shape3D createWall() {
111   URL url =
112     getClass().getClassLoader().getResource("images/stone.jpg");
113   BufferedImage bi = null;
114   try {
115     bi = ImageIO.read(url);
116   } catch (IOException ex) {
117     ex.printStackTrace();
118   }
119   ImageComponent2D image =
120     new ImageComponent2D(ImageComponent2D.FORMAT_RGB, bi);
121   Texture2D texture =
122     new Texture2D(Texture.BASE_LEVEL, Texture.RGBA,
123     image.getWidth(), image.getHeight());
124   texture.setImage(0, image);
125   texture.setEnable(true);
126   texture.setMagFilter(Texture.BASE_LEVEL_LINEAR);
127   texture.setMinFilter(Texture.BASE_LEVEL_LINEAR);
128   Appearance appear = new Appearance();
129   appear.setTexture(texture);
130   QuadArray rect = new QuadArray
131     (4, QuadArray.COORDINATES|QuadArray.TEXTURE_COORDINATE_2);
132   rect.setCoordinate(0, new Point3d(-2,3,2));
133   rect.setCoordinate(1, new Point3d(-2,-3,2));
134   rect.setCoordinate(2, new Point3d(-2,-3,-3));
135   rect.setCoordinate(3, new Point3d(-2,3,-3));
136   rect.setTextureCoordinate(0,0, new TexCoord2f(0f, 0f));
137   rect.setTextureCoordinate(0,1, new TexCoord2f(0f, 1f));
138   rect.setTextureCoordinate(0,2, new TexCoord2f(1f, 1f));
139   rect.setTextureCoordinate(0,3, new TexCoord2f(1f, 0f));
140   return new Shape3D(rect, appear);
141 }
142
143 private GeometryArray createShadow
144     (GeometryArray ga, Point3f light, Point3f plane) {
145   GeometryInfo gi = new GeometryInfo(ga);
146   gi.convertToIndexedTriangles();
147   IndexedTriangleArray ita =
148     (IndexedTriangleArray)gi.getIndexedGeometryArray();
149   Vector3f v = new Vector3f();
150   v.sub(plane, light);
```

```
151    double[] mat = new double[16];
152    for (int i = 0; i < 16; i++) {
153      mat[i] = 0;
154    }
155    mat[0] = 1;
156    mat[5] = 1;
157    mat[10] = 1-0.001;
158    mat[14] = -1/v.length();
159    Transform3D proj = new Transform3D();
160    proj.set(mat);
161    Transform3D u = new Transform3D();
162    u.lookAt(new Point3d(light),
163    new Point3d(plane), new Vector3d(0,1,0));
164    proj.mul(u);
165    shadowProj = new Transform3D();
166    u.invert();
167    shadowProj.mul(u, proj);
168    int n = ita.getVertexCount();
169    int count = ita.getIndexCount();
170    IndexedTriangleArray shadow = new IndexedTriangleArray(n,
171    GeometryArray.COORDINATES | GeometryArray.BY_REFERENCE, count);
172    shadow.setCapability(GeometryArray.ALLOW_REF_DATA_READ);
173    shadow.setCapability(GeometryArray.ALLOW_REF_DATA_WRITE);
174    double[] vert = new double[3*n];
175    Point3d p = new Point3d();
176    for (int i = 0; i < n; i++) {
177      ga.getCoordinate(i, p);
178      Vector4d v4 = new Vector4d(p);
179      v4.w = 1;
180      shadowProj.transform(v4);
181      Point4d p4 = new Point4d(v4);
182      p.project(p4);
183      vert[3*i] = p.x;
184      vert[3*i+1] = p.y;
185      vert[3*i+2] = p.z;
186    }
187    shadow.setCoordRefDouble(vert);
188    int[] indices = new int[count];
189    ita.getCoordinateIndices(0, indices);
190    shadow.setCoordinateIndices(0, indices);
191    return shadow;
192  }
193
194  class ShadowUpdater implements GeometryUpdater {
195    public void updateData(Geometry geometry) {
196      double[] vert =
197        ((GeometryArray)geometry).getCoordRefDouble();
198      int n = vert.length/3;
199      Transform3D rot = new Transform3D();
200      spin.getTransform(rot);
201      Transform3D tr = new Transform3D(shadowProj);
202      tr.mul(rot);
203      Point3d p = new Point3d();
204      for (int i = 0; i < n; i++) {
205        geom.getCoordinate(i, p);
206        Vector4d v4 = new Vector4d(p);
207        v4.w = 1;
208        tr.transform(v4);
209        Point4d p4 = new Point4d(v4);
210        p.project(p4);
```

```
211            vert[3*i] = p.x;
212            vert[3*i+1] = p.y;
213            vert[3*i+2] = p.z;
214        }
215      }
216    }
217
218    class ShadowBehavior extends Behavior {
219      WakeupOnElapsedFrames wakeup = null;
220
221      public ShadowBehavior() {
222        wakeup = new WakeupOnElapsedFrames(0);
223      }
224
225      public void initialize() {
226        wakeupOn(wakeup);
227      }
228
229      public void processStimulus(java.util.Enumeration enumeration) {
230        shadowGeom.updateData(updater);
231        wakeupOn(wakeup);
232      }
233    }
234 }
```

The scene graph for the program is shown in Figure 12.11. Compared to Figure 12.10, the scene graph for Listing 12.4, several nodes are added. A TransformGroup and a RotationInterpolator are added on top of the dodecahedron to rotate it in the scene. A behavior node is added to modify the geometry of the shadow.

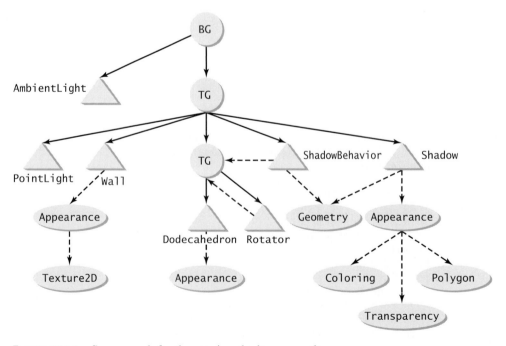

FIGURE 12.11   Scene graph for the moving shadow example.

The shadow polygon is created in the method createShadow (line 143) using the same projection as in Listing 12.4, but the IndexedTriangleArray is now created in the BY_REFERENCE mode (lines 170–171). The projection is saved in a field shadowProj. A float array vert is created to store the vertex coordinates of the polygon. The geometry of the shadow is saved in the variable shadowGeom, which is defined as a private field of the class.

An inner class ShadowUpdater (line 194) is defined to update the shadow polygon. It implements the GeometryUpdater interface. In the updateData method, the rotation from the transform on top of the dodecahedron is read and combined with shadowProj to form a new projection. This projection is applied to the vertices of the dodecahedron geometry to obtain the vertices of the shadow polygon. An instance of ShadowUpdater is created in the constructor and referenced as the field updater.

A custom Behavior class ShadowBehavior (line 218) is also defined as an inner class. It is set to wakeup at the end of the current frame. The processStimulus method invokes the geometry update by calling the method updateData in shadowGeom with the updater. An instance of ShadowBehavior class is added to the scene graph.

The behavior-driven geometry update makes the dynamic shadow possible. The display of the scene shows a rotating dodecahedron and its shadow on the wall. The shadow changes according to the dodecahedron positions.

12.7 Off-Screen Rendering

In Java 3D the outcome of rendering is sent to Canvas3D objects. Typically a Canvas3D object, as an AWT component, is displayed on a screen. In some cases, however, it may be desirable to perform off-screen rendering. For example, in order to save or print the image of a rendered scene, it will be convenient to render the scene to a memory-based image rather than the screen.

The Canvas3D class supports an off-screen rendering mode. To create an off-screen Canvas3D object, the following constructor may be used with the offScreen parameter set to true:

off-screen Canvas3D

```java
public Canvas3D(GraphicsConfiguration gc, boolean offScreen)
```

To render the scene to the off-screen canvas, you need to attach the canvas to the View object:

```java
view.addCanvas3D(canvas)
```

The following series of method calls of Canvas3D captures an image of the rendered scene:

```java
ImageComponent2D buffer =
    new ImageComponent2D(ImageComponent.FORMAT_RGB, bImage);
canvas.setOffScreenBuffer(buffer);
canvas.renderOffScreenBuffer();
canvas.waitForOffScreenRendering();
bImage = offScreenCanvas.getOffScreenBuffer().getImage();
```

Listing 12.9 illustrates off-screen rendering. A rotating dodecahedron is displayed on screen (Figure 12.12). A button labeled "save image" is placed at the bottom of the frame. Clicking the button captures one image and allows the user to save the image to a JPEG file.

Listing 12.9 `OffScreen.java`

```
 1 package chapter12;
 2
 3 import javax.vecmath.*;
 4 import java.awt.*;
 5 import java.awt.event.*;
 6 import java.awt.image.*;
 7 import java.net.URL;
 8 import java.io.*;
 9 import javax.imageio.*;
10 import javax.swing.*;
11 import javax.media.j3d.*;
12 import com.sun.j3d.utils.universe.*;
13 import com.sun.j3d.utils.geometry.*;
14 import chapter6.Dodecahedron;
15
16 public class OffScreen extends Frame{
17   public static void main(String[] args) {
18     Frame frame = new OffScreen();
19     frame.setTitle("Off Screen Rendering");
20     frame.setSize(640, 480);
21     frame.setVisible(true);
22   }
23
24   private Canvas3D cv;
25   private Canvas3D offScreenCanvas;
26   private View view;
27
28   public OffScreen() {
29     WindowListener l = new WindowAdapter() {
30       public void windowClosing(WindowEvent ev) {
31         System.exit(0);
32       }
33     };
34     this.addWindowListener(l);
35     GraphicsConfiguration gc =
36     SimpleUniverse.getPreferredConfiguration();
37     cv = new Canvas3D(gc);
38     setLayout(new BorderLayout());
39     add(cv, BorderLayout.CENTER);
40     BranchGroup bg = createSceneGraph();
41     bg.compile();
42     SimpleUniverse su = new SimpleUniverse(cv);
43     su.getViewingPlatform().setNominalViewingTransform();
44     su.addBranchGraph(bg);
45     // create off-screen canvas
46     view = su.getViewer().getView();
47     offScreenCanvas = new Canvas3D(gc, true);
48     Screen3D sOn = cv.getScreen3D();
49     Screen3D sOff = offScreenCanvas.getScreen3D();
50     Dimension dim = sOn.getSize();
51     sOff.setSize(dim);
52     sOff.setPhysicalScreenWidth(sOn.getPhysicalScreenWidth());
53     sOff.setPhysicalScreenHeight(sOn.getPhysicalScreenHeight());
54     Point loc = cv.getLocationOnScreen();
55     offScreenCanvas.setOffScreenLocation(loc);
56     // button
57     Button button = new Button("Save image");
58     add(button, BorderLayout.SOUTH);
```

```
59        button.addActionListener(new ActionListener() {
60          public void actionPerformed(ActionEvent ev) {
61            BufferedImage bi = capture();
62            save(bi);
63          }
64        });
65    }
66
67    private BranchGroup createSceneGraph() {
68      BranchGroup root = new BranchGroup();
69      TransformGroup spin = new TransformGroup();
70      spin.setCapability(TransformGroup.ALLOW_TRANSFORM_WRITE);
71      root.addChild(spin);
72      // object
73      Appearance ap = new Appearance();
74      ap.setMaterial(new Material());
75      Shape3D shape = new Dodecahedron();
76      shape.setAppearance(ap);
77      Transform3D tr = new Transform3D();
78      tr.setScale(0.25);
79      TransformGroup tg = new TransformGroup(tr);
80      spin.addChild(tg);
81      tg.addChild(shape);
82      Alpha alpha = new Alpha(-1, 10000);
83      RotationInterpolator rotator =
84        new RotationInterpolator(alpha, spin);
85      BoundingSphere bounds = new BoundingSphere();
86      rotator.setSchedulingBounds(bounds);
87      spin.addChild(rotator);
88      // background and light
89      URL url =
90        getClass().getClassLoader().getResource("images/bg.jpg");
91      BufferedImage bi = null;
92      try {
93        bi = ImageIO.read(url);
94      } catch (IOException ex) {
95        ex.printStackTrace();
96      }
97      ImageComponent2D image =
98        new ImageComponent2D(ImageComponent2D.FORMAT_RGB, bi);
99      Background background = new Background(image);
100     background.setApplicationBounds(bounds);
101     root.addChild(background);
102     AmbientLight light = new AmbientLight(true,
103       new Color3f(Color.red));
104     light.setInfluencingBounds(bounds);
105     root.addChild(light);
106     PointLight ptlight = new PointLight(new Color3f(Color.green),
107       new Point3f(3f,3f,3f), new Point3f(1f,0f,0f));
108     ptlight.setInfluencingBounds(bounds);
109     root.addChild(ptlight);
110     PointLight ptlight2 = new PointLight(new Color3f(Color.orange),
111       new Point3f(-2f,2f,2f), new Point3f(1f,0f,0f));
112     ptlight2.setInfluencingBounds(bounds);
113     root.addChild(ptlight2);
114     return root;
115   }
116
117   public BufferedImage capture() {
118     // render off-screen image
```

```
119    Dimension dim = cv.getSize();
120    view.stopView();
121    view.addCanvas3D(offScreenCanvas);
122    BufferedImage bImage =
123      new BufferedImage(dim.width, dim.height,
124      BufferedImage.TYPE_INT_RGB);
125    ImageComponent2D buffer =
126      new ImageComponent2D(ImageComponent.FORMAT_RGB, bImage);
127      offScreenCanvas.setOffScreenBuffer(buffer);
128    view.startView();
129    offScreenCanvas.renderOffScreenBuffer();
130    offScreenCanvas.waitForOffScreenRendering();
131    bImage = offScreenCanvas.getOffScreenBuffer().getImage();
132    view.removeCanvas3D(offScreenCanvas);
133    return bImage;
134  }
135
136  public void save(BufferedImage bImage) {
137    // save image to file
138    JFileChooser chooser = new JFileChooser();
139    chooser.setCurrentDirectory(new File("."));
140    if (chooser.showSaveDialog(null) ==
141    JFileChooser.APPROVE_OPTION) {
142      File oFile = chooser.getSelectedFile();
143      try {
144        ImageIO.write(bImage, "jpeg", oFile);
145      } catch (IOException ex) {
146        ex.printStackTrace();
147      }
148    }
149  }
150 }
```

FIGURE 12.12 Creating an image through off-screen rendering.

To capture an image from the rendered scene, an off-screen `Canvas3D` object is created. The off-screen canvas is not attached to the view until the capturing is performed.

The scene contains a dodecahedron illuminated with three lights. A sky image is used as the background. A rotation interpolator rotates the dodecahedron continuously.

The method `capture` (line 117) performs the actual capture of the image. First, the view is stopped by calling the method `stopView`. The off-screen canvas is attached to the view, and an `ImageComponent2D` object is set as the off-screen buffer for the canvas. Then the view is resumed by calling the method `startView`. The call to `renderOffScreenBuffer` method starts the off-screen rendering. The `waitForOffScreenRendering` method waits for the completion of the rendering. Finally the image is retrieved from the canvas and the off-screen canvas is detached from the view.

12.8 3D Textures

The technique of 2D texturing maps a 2D image to a surface of a 3D object. 3D texture mapping (or solid texture mapping) uses a 3D volumetric texture source. Certainly 3D texturing consumes more computing resources in terms of generation and storage of 3D texture data. However, it has the advantage that realistic texture features of true 3D characteristics can be rendered with relatively simple mapping functions.

Typically the solid textures used in 3D texturing are computer-generated synthetic textures. They are usually used to simulate the natural textures of materials such as marble and wood. This approach is also known as *procedural texturing*.   procedural texturing

In order to produce textures that resemble those in natural materials, certain randomness or noise in the pattern is necessary. On the other hand, totally random points will not produce useful textures. A certain amount of smoothness and coherence is also required.

Perlin's coherent noise function is a popular choice that produces amazing visual effects.   Perlin's coherent noise
The function `noise(x)` is a smooth and yet random function. At each grid point (a point with all integer coordinates) a random unit vector called the *gradient* is created. For an arbitrary   gradient
point x, the grid points surrounding x will influence the `noise(x)` value. The contribution from such a grid point g is the dot product of the vector from x-g and the random unit vector at g. The final value of `noise(x)` is an interpolation of these contributions.

Based on the noise function, a fractal sum can be defined:

$$perlinNoise(x) = \sum_{i=1}^{n} \frac{noise(\beta^i x)}{\alpha^i}$$

Another interesting function built from the noise function is the so-called *turbulence*   turbulence function
function:

$$turbulence(x) = \sum_{i=1}^{n} \frac{|noise(\beta^i x)|}{\alpha^i}$$

Remarkably realistic textures can be generated with the help of these noise functions. For example, the following color function produces a nice *marble texture*:   marble texture

$$\sin(x + turbulence(p))$$

Java 3D offers 3D texture-mapping support using an approach similar to 2D texture mapping. `GeometryArray` objects can include the `TEXTURE_COORDINATE_3` flag to allow the specification of 3D texture coordinates. An array of `BufferedImage` objects for the 3D texture image is used to create an `ImageComponent3D` object. The `ImageComponent3D` is referenced by a `Texture3D` object, and the `Texture3D` is a node component referenced by an `Appearance` object.

Listing 12.10 shows an application of the 3D texture mapping and Perlin's noise. It displays a tetrahedron with a 3D marble texture (Figure 12.13). This example displays a marble tetrahedron. The texture is 3D, and viewed from different sides of the tetrahedron the texture shows continuity in space. The 3D texture is synthesized from Perlin's noise function. Listing 12.11 gives the class for solid texture mapping.

Listing 12.10 `PerlinNoise.java`

```
 1 package chapter12;
 2
 3 import javax.vecmath.*;
 4
 5 public class PerlinNoise {
 6   final static int B = 0x100;
 7   int[] p = new int[2*B+2];
 8   Vector3d[] g3 = new Vector3d[2*B+2];
 9
10   public PerlinNoise() {
11     for (int i = 0; i < B; i++) {
12       p[i] = i;
13       double x = 2.0*Math.random() - 1.0;
14       double y = 2.0*Math.random() - 1.0;
15       double z = 2.0*Math.random() - 1.0;
16       g3[i] = new Vector3d(x, y, z);
17       g3[i].normalize();
18     }
19     for (int i = 0; i < B; i++) {
20       int k = p[i];
21       int j = (int)(Math.random()*B);
22       if (j >= B) j = B-1;
23       p[i] = p[j];
24       p[j] = k;
25     }
26     for (int i = 0; i < B+2; i++) {
27       p[B+i] = p[i];
28       g3[B+i] = g3[i];
29     }
30   }
31
32   public double noise(Point3d point) {
33     int bx0, bx1, by0, by1, bz0, bz1, b00, b10, b01, b11;
34     double rx0, rx1, ry0, ry1, rz0, rz1, sy, sz, a, b, c, d, t, u, v;
35     Vector3d q = null;
36     int i, j;
37
38     t = point.x + 0x1000;
39     bx0 = ((int)t) & 0xff;
40     bx1 = (bx0+1) & 0xff;
41     rx0 = t-(int)t;
42     rx1 = rx0-1;
43
44     t = point.y + 0x1000;
45     by0 = ((int)t) & 0xff;
46     by1 = (by0+1) & 0xff;
47     ry0 = t-(int)t;
48     ry1 = ry0-1;
49
50     t = point.z + 0x1000;
51     bz0 = ((int)t) & 0xff;
52     bz1 = (bz0+1) & 0xff;
53     rz0 = t-(int)t;
54     rz1 = rz0-1;
55
```

```
56      i = p[bx0];
57      j = p[bx1];
58
59      b00 = p[i+by0];
60      b10 = p[j+by0];
61      b01 = p[i+by1];
62      b11 = p[j+by1];
63
64      t = rx0*rx0*(3-2*rx0);
65      sy = ry0*ry0*(3-2*ry0);
66      sz = rz0*rz0*(3-2*rz0);
67
68      q = g3[b00+bz0]; u = rx0*q.x + ry0*q.y + rz0*q.z;
69      q = g3[b10+bz0]; v = rx1*q.x + ry0*q.y + rz0*q.z;
70      a = u + t*(v-u);
71
72      q = g3[b01+bz0]; u = rx0*q.x + ry1*q.y + rz0*q.z;
73      q = g3[b11+bz0]; v = rx1*q.x + ry1*q.y + rz0*q.z;
74      b = u + t*(v-u);
75
76      c = a + sy*(b-a);
77
78      q = g3[b00+bz1]; u = rx0*q.x + ry0*q.y + rz1*q.z;
79      q = g3[b10+bz1]; v = rx1*q.x + ry0*q.y + rz1*q.z;
80      a = u + t*(v-u);
81
82      q = g3[b01+bz1]; u = rx0*q.x + ry1*q.y + rz1*q.z;
83      q = g3[b11+bz1]; v = rx1*q.x + ry1*q.y + rz1*q.z;
84      b = u + t*(v-u);
85
86      d = a + sy*(b-a);
87
88      return c+sz*(d-c);
89    }
90
91    public double perlinNoise(Point3d pt,
92        double alpha, double beta, int n) {
93      double val;
94      double sum = 0;
95      double scale = 1;
96
97      for (int i = 0; i < n; i++) {
98        val = noise(pt);
99        sum += val / scale;
100       scale *= alpha;
101       pt.scale(beta);
102     }
103     return sum;
104   }
105
106   public double turbulence(Point3d pt, double alpha,
107       double beta, int n) {
108     double val;
109     double sum = 0;
110     double scale = 1;
111
112     for (int i = 0; i < n; i++) {
113       val = noise(pt);
114       sum += Math.abs(val) / scale;
115       scale *= alpha;
116       pt.scale(beta);
```

```
117      }
118    return sum;
119  }
120 }
```

FIGURE 12.13   Computer-generated 3D marble texture.

Listing 12.11 Marble.java

```
 1 package chapter12;
 2
 3 import javax.vecmath.*;
 4 import java.awt.*;
 5 import java.awt.event.*;
 6 import javax.media.j3d.*;
 7 import com.sun.j3d.utils.universe.*;
 8 import com.sun.j3d.utils.geometry.*;
 9 import com.sun.j3d.utils.image.*;
10 import javax.imageio.*;
11 import java.awt.image.*;
12 import java.io.*;
13 import java.applet.*;
14 import com.sun.j3d.utils.applet.MainFrame;
15
16 public class Marble extends Applet {
17   public static void main(String[] args) {
18     new MainFrame(new Marble(), 480, 480);
19   }
20
21   PerlinNoise pnoise = new PerlinNoise();
22
23   public void init() {
24     // create canvas
```

```
25      GraphicsConfiguration gc =
26        SimpleUniverse.getPreferredConfiguration();
27      Canvas3D cv = new Canvas3D(gc);
28      setLayout(new BorderLayout());
29      add(cv, BorderLayout.CENTER);
30      BranchGroup bg = createSceneGraph();
31      bg.compile();
32      SimpleUniverse su = new SimpleUniverse(cv);
33      su.getViewingPlatform().setNominalViewingTransform();
34      su.addBranchGraph(bg);
35    }
36
37    private BranchGroup createSceneGraph() {
38      BranchGroup root = new BranchGroup();
39      TransformGroup spin = new TransformGroup();
40      spin.setCapability(TransformGroup.ALLOW_TRANSFORM_WRITE);
41      root.addChild(spin);
42      //object
43      Appearance ap = createTextureAppearance();
44      Shape3D shape = new Shape3D(createGeometry(), ap);
45      spin.addChild(shape);
46      //rotator
47      Alpha alpha = new Alpha(-1, 8000);
48      RotationInterpolator rotator =
49      new RotationInterpolator(alpha, spin);
50      BoundingSphere bounds = new BoundingSphere();
51      rotator.setSchedulingBounds(bounds);
52      spin.addChild(rotator);
53      Background background = new Background(1.0f, 1.0f, 1.0f);
54      background.setApplicationBounds(bounds);
55      root.addChild(background);
56      return root;
57    }
58
59    GeometryArray createGeometry() {
60      IndexedTriangleArray ga = new IndexedTriangleArray(4,
61      TriangleArray.COORDINATES | TriangleArray.NORMALS |
62        TriangleArray.TEXTURE_COORDINATE_3, 12);
63      ga.setCoordinate(0, new Point3f(0.5f,0.5f,0.5f));
64      ga.setCoordinate(1, new Point3f(0.5f,-0.5f,-0.5f));
65      ga.setCoordinate(2, new Point3f(-0.5f,0.5f,-0.5f));
66      ga.setCoordinate(3, new Point3f(-0.5f,-0.5f,0.5f));
67      int[] coords = {0,1,2,0,3,1,1,3,2,2,3,0};
68      ga.setNormal(0, new Vector3f(1f,1f,-1f));
69      ga.setNormal(1, new Vector3f(1f,-1f,1f));
70      ga.setNormal(2, new Vector3f(-1f,-1f,-1f));
71      ga.setNormal(3, new Vector3f(-1f,1f,1f));
72      int[] norms = {0,0,0,1,1,1,2,2,2,3,3,3};
73      ga.setCoordinateIndices(0, coords);
74      ga.setNormalIndices(0, norms);
75      ga.setTextureCoordinate(0, 0, new TexCoord3f(1f,1f,1f));
76      ga.setTextureCoordinate(0, 1, new TexCoord3f(1f,0f,0f));
77      ga.setTextureCoordinate(0, 2, new TexCoord3f(0f,1f,0f));
78      ga.setTextureCoordinate(0, 3, new TexCoord3f(0f,0f,1f));
79      ga.setTextureCoordinateIndices(0,0,coords);
80      return ga;
81    }
82
83    Appearance createTextureAppearance() {
84      Appearance ap = new Appearance();
85      BufferedImage[] img = new BufferedImage[128];
```

```
86      for (int i = 0; i < 128; i++) {
87        img[i] = new BufferedImage(128,128,
88        BufferedImage.TYPE_INT_ARGB);
89        for (int r = 0; r < 128; r++) {
90          for (int c = 0; c < 128; c++) {
91            double v = pnoise.turbulence
92            (new Point3d(c/32.0, r/32.0, i/32.0),2,2,8);
93            int rgb = (int)((0.55+0.35*Math.sin(3*(c/32.0+v)))*256);
94            rgb = ((rgb << 16) | (rgb << 8) | rgb);
95            img[i].setRGB(c, r, rgb);
96          }
97        }
98      }
99      ImageComponent3D image =
100       new ImageComponent3D(ImageComponent3D.FORMAT_RGB, img);
101     Texture3D texture =
102       new Texture3D(Texture.BASE_LEVEL, Texture.RGBA,
103       image.getWidth(), image.getHeight(), image.getDepth());
104     texture.setImage(0, image);
105     texture.setEnable(true);
106     texture.setMagFilter(Texture.BASE_LEVEL_LINEAR);
107     texture.setMinFilter(Texture.BASE_LEVEL_LINEAR);
108     ap.setTexture(texture);
108     return ap;
110   }
111 }
```

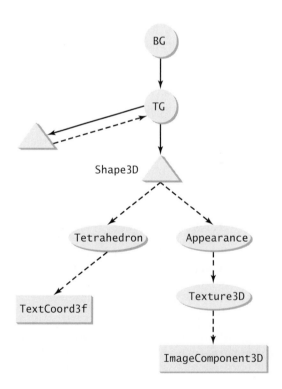

FIGURE 12.14 Scene-graph branch for the marble tetrahedron.

The PerlinNoise class implements the noise and turbulence functions based on Perlin's original methods. A grid of $256 \times 256 \times 256$ points is used for the initial random vectors. To reduce storage, only a 1D array of the random gradients g3 and a permutation p is created (lines 7–8). The gradient at a grid point (i, j, k) is obtained by $g(i, j, k) = g3(k + p(j + p(i)))$.

The value of the `noise` function (line 32) is interpolated from the contributions of the gradients.

The `perlinNoise` method (line 91) provides the fractal sum of the noise function. The `turbulence` method (line 106) calculates the turbulence function.

The `Marble` class displays a rotating tetrahedron with a solid marble texture. Its scene graph is shown in Figure 12.14.

The method `createGeometry` creates a tetrahedron with the TEXTURE_COORDINATE_3 flag to specify the 3D texture coordinates. The texture coordinates of the vertices are assigned based on their special coordinates with a translation to normalize the values to the range [0,1].

The method `createTextureAppearance` (line 83) creates an appearance for the tetrahedron. The `Appearance` is set to reference a `Texture3D` object. An array of 128 `BufferedImage` objects of size 128 × 128 is created and filled with the generated marble patterns based on the turbulence function (lines 85–96). This `BufferedImage` array forms a "texture cube" and is used to create an `ImageComponent3D` object. The `ImageComponent3D` object is passed to the `Texture3D` to serve as the source of the texture mapping.

KEY CLASSES AND METHODS

- **`javax.media.j3d.Point3d.interpolate(…)`** A method to perform a linear interpolation.
- **`javax.media.j3d.GeometryUpdater`** An interface for updating geometry data in a live scene.
- **`javax.media.j3d.GeometryArray.updateData(GeometryUpdater)`** A method to update the geometry data through the `GeometryUpdater`.
- **`javax.media.j3d.Sound`** A base class for sounds.
- **`javax.media.j3d.BackgroundSound`** A class encapsulating a background sound.
- **`javax.media.j3d.PointSound`** A class encapsulating a 3D point sound.
- **`javax.media.j3d.ConeSound`** A class encapsulating a 3D point sound with a limited angle.
- **`javax.media.j3d.MediaContainer`** A node-component class used as a container for sound data.
- **`com.sun.j3d.utils.universe.Viewer.createAudioDevice(…)`** A method to initialize the default audio device.
- **`javax.media.j3d.Canvas3D.setOffScreenBuffer(…)`** A method to set the off-screen rendering buffer.
- **`javax.media.j3d.Canvas3D.renderOffScreenBuffer(…)`** A method to start rendering an off-screen buffer.
- **`javax.media.j3d.Canvas3D.waitForOffScreenRendering(…)`** A method to wait for the completion of an off-screen rendering.
- **`javax.media.j3d.Canvas3D.getOffScreenBuffer(…)`** A method to retrieve an off-screen buffer.
- **`javax.media.j3d.Texture3D`** A node-component class for 3D textures.
- **`javax.vecmath.TexCoord3f`** A class for 3D texture coordinates.
- **`javax.media.j3d.ImageComponent3D`** A node-component class to define a 3D image component.

KEY TERMS

3D Bézier curve A polynomial parametric curve defined by a set of control points.
Bernstein polynomial (Bernstein basis) A special polynomial often used in approximation.
Bézier surface A polynomial parametric surface defined by a grid of control points.
deCasteljau algorithm A method to calculate a point on a Bézier curve through a series of linear interpolations.

off screen rendering A process to render a scene on a buffer other than the screen.

3D texture (solid texture) A texture defined as a 3D volume.

procedural texturing A method to create synthetic texture computationally.

Perlin's noise A coherent random function used to generate synthetic textures.

CHAPTER SUMMARY

■ In this chapter several miscellaneous topics related to 3D graphics are discussed.

■ Curves and surfaces are important modeling tools for geometries of visual objects. Implementations of Bézier curves and surfaces are discussed in this chapter. The fundamental tool is the deCasteljau algorithm that evaluates a point on the curve and subdivides a curve by linear interpolations.

■ Sound is supported in Java 3D through the Sound leaf node class and its subclasses. Adding sounds to a scene graph is similar to adding other nodes. An advantage of including sounds in the scene graph is to support a natural connection between audio and visual objects.

■ A method for generating simple shadows is discussed. A shadow is modeled as a plane polygon from the projections of the original object.

■ Dynamic data change for a geometry is possible through the BY_REFERENCE mode and the GeometryUpdater interface.

■ The Canvas3D class supports an off-screen rendering mode. It may be used to capture and save the rendered images.

■ 3D texture mapping maps a 3D volumetric image to a visual object. Java 3D provides support for 3D texturing mapping using the same framework as for 2D texture mapping. The 3D texture data are often synthesized with certain controlled randomness. Perlin's noise and turbulence functions can be used to generate patterns resembling marble, wood, and other natural textures.

REVIEW QUESTIONS

12.1 A cubic Bézier curve is defined by the following control points:

$$p_0 = (0, 0, 0), \; p_1 = (1, 0, 0), \; p_2 = (1, 1, 0), \; p_3 = (1, 1, 1)$$

Use the deCasteljau algorithm to evaluate the points on the curve at

a. $t = 1/2$

b. $t = 1/3$

c. $t = 2/3$

12.2 Subdivide the Bézier curve defined in Question 12.1 into two, using the deCasteljau algorithm at the points

a. $t = 1/2$

b. $t = 1/3$

c. $t = 2/3$

12.3 Derive a formula for the surface normal of a bicubic Bézier surface at a given point.

12.4 A point light is located at (0, 0, 1) and casts a shadow on the *xy*-plane. Derive a transformation matrix for projecting a vertex to its shadow on the plane.

PROGRAMMING EXERCISES

12.1 Implement a 3D B-spline curve by converting it to a series of Bézier curves, similar to the 2D curves defined in Chapter 4.

12.2 Write a 3D Bézier surface editor. Display the control points of the surface as square dots. Allow the user to select and move a control point with mouse operations and update the surface accordingly.

12.3 Write a Java 3D program to display a Bézier curve with its shadow on a plane.

12.4 Write a Java 3D program to display a sphere and its shadow on a wall, similar to Listing 12.7. Add an `OrbitBehavior` object to control view-platform changes with mouse actions.

12.5 Write a Java 3D program to display a `PointArray` object with 100 points. Use a behavior to move the points in the geometry randomly and independently.

12.6 Write a Java 3D program displaying a rotating cone. Create a `ConeSound` object associated with the cone so that the direction of the `ConeSound` coincides with the visual cone.

12.7 Write a Java 3D program showing two panels and a button. The first panel displays a scene of a rotating 3D text string. When the button is clicked, the image of the 3D scene is captured and the still image is displayed in the second panel.

12.8 Write a program to plot the *x*-components of a Perlin's noise.

12.9 A wood grain texture may be defined as

$$g(p) = turbulence(p) * 20$$
$$grain(p) = g(p) - \lfloor g(p) \rfloor$$

Write a Java 3D program to display a rotating cube mapped with a solid wood texture.

Mathematical Background for Computer Graphics

A.1 Introduction

This appendix provides a brief review of several mathematical topics that are closely related to computer graphics. Computer graphics depends heavily upon mathematical tools to accurately model, transform, and process graphics objects and systems.

Geometry, especially analytic geometry, offers an effective tool to model graphics objects. The coordinate systems in analytic geometry facilitate numerical representations of geometric models. This modeling scheme is fundamental in a computer graphics system, because geometric entities, properties, and transformations are directly related to the central problems in computer graphics.

Complex numbers and quaternions are highly structured algebraic systems. They have direct geometric interpretations, which make them valuable tools for solving certain problems in geometry and graphics.

Linear algebra is an algebraic subject that further extends the systems of real numbers, complex numbers, and quaternions to arbitrary dimensional vector spaces and systematically studies the properties and relationships on vectors. Matrices provide concrete representations for linear transformations and vectors. They can be directly implemented in computers to represent geometric transforms relevant to computer graphics.

Calculus may be applied to solve problems such as tangent lines and surface normals. These topics are related to certain modeling and rendering problems in graphics.

Graph theory studies a discrete structure called a *graph* that has a wide range of applications in computer science and graphics.

A comprehensive coverage of these mathematical topics cannot possibly fit into a single chapter or appendix. We introduce here the most fundamental concepts and results related to computer graphics. This material may serve as a quick reference for relevant mathematical problems throughout the book.

A.2 Analytic Geometry

A.2.1 Coordinate Systems

A geometric object is represented algebraically in a coordinate system. A point in a plane is represented by the *x*-coordinate and the *y*-coordinate in a *2D Cartesian coordinate system*, as shown in Figure A.1.

2D Cartesian coordinate system

Similarly, a point in a 3D space can be represented by a tuple of three real numbers (x, y, z) using a *3D Cartesian coordinate system*, as shown in Figure A.2.

3D Cartesian coordinate system

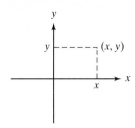

FIGURE A.1   The 2D coordinate system has the x-axis and y-axis.

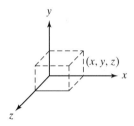

FIGURE A.2   The 3D coordinate system has the x-axis, y-axis, and z-axis.

With the established one-to-one correspondence between the points and their coordinates, geometric properties can be translated into algebraic quantities. For example, the distance between two points (x_1, y_1) and (x_2, y_2) in a plain is given by the *distance formula*:

2D distance formula

$$d = \sqrt{(x_2 - x_1)^2 + (y_2 - y_1)^2}$$

3D distance formula

The distance between (x_1, y_1, z_1) and (x_2, y_2, z_2) in a 3D space is given by the *distance formula*:

$$d = \sqrt{(x_2 - x_1)^2 + (y_2 - y_1)^2 + (z_2 - z_1)^2}$$

A.2.2 2D Equations

Geometric objects can often be represented by algebraic equations. The points on a geometric object are characterized by the fact that their coordinates satisfy the corresponding equation. In a 2D space, an equation $F(x, y) = 0$ or an explicit function $y = f(x)$ defines a curve.

A line is characterized by the general linear equation:

$$Ax + By + C = 0$$

A more convenient form of linear equation is the point-slope form, as illustrated in Figure A.3. Given two points $(x_0, y_0), (x_1, y_1)$ on the line, the differences in the x- and y-directions are defined as $\Delta x = x_1 - x_0, \Delta y = y_1 - y_0$. The slope of a line is the ratio $k = \Delta y/\Delta x$, which is a constant for any given line. Given a point (x_0, y_0) on the line and the slope k, the equation of the line can be written in the following *point-slope form*:

point-slope form

$$y - y_0 = k(x - x_0)$$

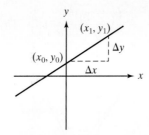

FIGURE A.3   A line can be represented by a linear equation.

A *circle* centered at (x_0, y_0) with radius R is represented by the equation: circle

$$(x - x_0)^2 + (y - y_0)^2 = R^2$$

A general quadratic equation represents a family of curves known as *conic sections*. conic section

$$Ax^2 + Bxy + Cy^2 + Dx + Ey + F = 0$$

Conic sections can be classified into three main categories: ellipses, parabolas, and hyper-bolas. Their standard equations are given below. (See Figures A.4, A.5, A.6.)

$$\frac{(x - x_0)^2}{a^2} + \frac{(y - y_0)^2}{b^2} = 1 \qquad (\textit{ellipses})$$

ellipses

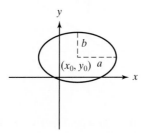

FIGURE A.4   An ellipse can be represented by a quadratic equation.

$$(x - x_0)^2 = 4p(y - y_0) \qquad (\textit{parabolas})$$

parabolas

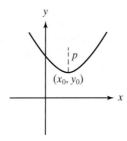

FIGURE A.5   A parabola can be represented by a quadratic equation.

hyperbolas

$$\frac{(x - x_0)^2}{a^2} - \frac{(y - y_0)^2}{b^2} = 1 \qquad (hyperbolas)$$

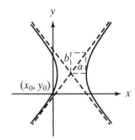

FIGURE A.6 A hyperbola can be represented by a quadratic equation.

A.2.3 Parametric Equations

line

A parametric equation of a curve uses a third variable t as the independent variable and defines x- and y-coordinates as functions of t. For example, a *line* through the point (x_0, y_0) with the direction (a, b), as shown in Figure A.7, has a parametric equation:

$$x = x_0 + at$$
$$y = y_0 + bt$$

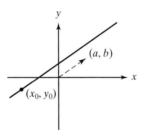

FIGURE A.7 A line can be represented by a parametric equation.

ellipse

An *ellipse* can be expressed as a parametric equation, as shown in Figure A.8:

$$x = x_0 + a \cos t$$
$$y = y_0 + b \sin t$$

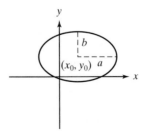

FIGURE A.8 An ellipse can be represented by a parametric equation.

A.2.4 3D Equations

In a 3D space, an equation $F(x, y, z) = 0$ or an explicit function $z = f(x, y)$ represents a surface in the space.

A general linear equation represents a plane

$$Ax + By + Cz + D = 0$$

The normal of a plane is a direction perpendicular to the plane. If the normal of a plane is given by (a, b, c) and a fixed point on the plane is (x_0, y_0, z_0), then an equation of the plane can be written as

> plane equation
> point and normal

$$a(x - x_0) + b(y - y_0) + c(z - z_0) = 0$$

A *sphere* centered at (x_0, y_0, z_0) of radius R has the following standard equation:

> sphere

$$(x - x_0)^2 + (y - y_0)^2 + (z - z_0)^2 = R^2$$

A line in a 3D space can be expressed as the intersection of two planes, or as a parametric equation.

$$x = x_0 + at$$

$$y = y_0 + bt$$

$$z = z_0 + ct$$

A parametric equation for a surface involves two variables.

$$x = f(u, v)$$

$$y = g(u, v)$$

$$z = h(u, v)$$

For example, a plane through three points (x_0, y_0, z_0), (x_1, y_1, z_1), and (x_2, y_2, z_2) has a parametric equation:

$$x = x_0 + (x_1 - x_0)u + (x_2 - x_0)v$$

$$y = y_0 + (y_1 - y_0)u + (y_2 - y_0)v$$

$$z = z_0 + (z_1 - z_0)u + (z_2 - z_0)v$$

A.3 Complex Numbers and Quaternions

A.3.1 Complex Numbers

Complex numbers can be used to represent 2D geometric objects and transforms. The set of complex numbers is an extension of the real number system. A complex number can be written as

$$a + bi$$

where a, b are real numbers and $i^2 = -1$. Addition and multiplication can be defined on the complex numbers. Let $z = a + bi$ and $w = c + di$ be two complex numbers. Then the operations are defined as

$$z + w = (a + c) + (b + d)i$$

$$z \cdot w = (ac - bd) + (ad + bc)i$$

The multiplication can be obtained symbolically by the distributive law and the fact that $i^2 = -1$. For example,

$$(2 - i) + (3 + 4i) = 5 + 3i$$

$$(2 - i) \cdot (3 + 4i) = 6 + 8i - 3i - 4i^2 = 10 + 5i$$

The set of complex numbers with the two operations has properties similar to those of real numbers. Both operations are associative and commutative. The multiplication is distributive over the addition. They have identity elements (0 and 1) and inverses. The inverse operation of addition is subtraction and the inverse of multiplication is division. Consequently, the set of complex numbers with the two operations forms an algebraic structure called a *field*, as in the real number system. Like addition, the subtraction of two complex numbers is performed on real and imaginary parts separately. For example,

field

$$(2 - i) - (3 + 4i) = -1 - 5i$$

complex conjugate

The division operation is more complicated, and several new terms are needed to introduce it. The *complex conjugate* and the absolute value of $z = a + bi$ are defined as

$$\bar{z} = a - bi$$

$$|z| = \sqrt{a^2 + b^2}$$

absolute value

The *absolute value* of a complex number is a nonnegative real number. It is easy to verify that $z\bar{z} = |z|^2$. The division of two complex numbers w and z can be calculated by multiplying the conjugate of the denominator on both the denominator and the numerator by—that is,

$$\frac{w}{z} = \frac{w\bar{z}}{z\bar{z}} = \frac{w\bar{z}}{|z|^2}$$

For example,

$$\frac{2 - i}{3 + 4i} = \frac{(2 - i)(3 - 4i)}{(3 + 4i)(3 - 4i)} = \frac{2 - 11i}{25} = (2/25) - (11/25)i$$

polar form

The standard rectangular form of complex numbers introduced above may not be the most convenient representation in some cases. A complex number can be written in the *polar form*

$$z = r(\cos \theta + i \sin \theta) = re^{i\theta}$$

where $r = |z|$ and θ is a real number known as the argument. The equation $e^{i\theta} = \cos \theta + i \sin \theta$ is the famous Euler's identity that establishes a relationship between trigonometric functions and exponential functions. It is much easier to calculate the multiplication, division, power, and roots of complex numbers in polar form.

Complex numbers have a geometric interpretation as points on a plane. A complex number $z = a + bi$ is associated with the 2D point (a, b) or the vector from the origin to the point (see Figure A.9). The absolute value r corresponds to the distance of the point to the origin or the length of the vector. The angle θ corresponds to the angle between the vector and the

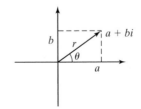

FIGURE A.9 Complex numbers can be used to represent geometric objects.

x-axis. The addition of two complex numbers corresponds to the addition of vectors. The geometric interpretation of multiplication of two complex numbers can be seen from its polar form:

$$z_1 z_2 = r_1 e^{i\theta_1} r_2 e^{i\theta_2} = (r_1 r_2) e^{i(\theta_1 + \theta_2)}$$

Therefore, the length of the resultant vector is the product of the lengths of the two vectors, and the angle of the resultant vector is the sum of the angles of the two vectors.

A Java class implementing the complex numbers is shown in Listing A.1.

Listing A.1 `Complex.java`

```
1 public class Complex {
2    public static void main(String[] args) {
3       Complex z = new Complex(1, -2);
4       Complex w = new Complex(3, 4);
5       System.out.println("z = " + z);
6       System.out.println("w = " + w);
7       System.out.println("|z| = " + z.abs());
8       System.out.println("|w| = " + w.abs());
9       System.out.println("arg z = " + z.arg());
10      System.out.println("arg w = " + w.arg());
11      System.out.println("conj z = " + z.conj());
12      System.out.println("conj w = " + w.conj());
13      System.out.println("z + w = " + z.add(w));
14      System.out.println("z - w = " + z.sub(w));
15      System.out.println("z * w = " + z.mul(w));
16      System.out.println("z / w = " + z.div(w));
17   }
18
19   private double x = 0.0;
20   private double y = 0.0;
21
22   public Complex() {
23   }
24
25   public Complex(double x, double y) {
26      this.x = x;
27      this.y = y;
28   }
29
30   public double getX() {
31      return x;
32   }
33
34   public double getY() {
35      return y;
36   }
37
38   public void setX(double x) {
39      this.x = x;
40   }
41
42   public void setY(double y) {
43      this.y = y;
44   }
45
46   public double abs() {
47      return Math.sqrt(x*x + y*y);
48   }
49
```

```
50    public double arg() {
51       return Math.atan2(y, x);
52    }
53
54    public Complex conj() {
55       return new Complex(x, -y);
56    }
57
58    public Complex add(Complex other) {
59       double a = x + other.getX();
60       double b = y + other.getY();
61       return new Complex(a, b);
62    }
63
64    public Complex sub(Complex other) {
65       double a = x - other.getX();
66       double b = y - other.getY();
67       return new Complex(a, b);
68    }
69
70    public Complex mul(Complex other) {
71       double a = x * other.getX() - y * other.getY();
72       double b = x * other.getY() + y * other.getX();
73       return new Complex(a, b);
74    }
75
76    public Complex div(Complex other) {
77       double a = x * other.getX() + y * other.getY();
78       double b = -x * other.getY() + y * other.getX();
79       double d = other.abs();
80       d = d * d;
81       return new Complex(a/d, b/d);
82    }
83
84    public String toString() {
85       if (y >= 0)
86          return "" + x + "+" + y + "i";
87       else
88          return "" + x + "" + y + "i";
89    }
90 }
```

The class `Complex` encapsulates the concept of complex numbers. It contains two fields x and y to represent the real and imaginary parts of a complex number (lines 19–20). The fields can be accessed individually with the getters and setters.

The default constructor creates the complex number 0. The other constructor creates a complex number with the specified real and imaginary parts (lines 25–28).

The absolute value and the argument of the complex number can be obtained with the methods `abs` and `arg`. The `conj` method returns a new `Complex` object that is the complex conjugate of the current object. The complex operations of addition, subtraction, multiplication, and division are performed by the methods `add`, `sub`, `mul`, and `div`. Each method takes a `Complex` parameter as the second operand and returns a new `Complex` object as the result of the operation.

The method `toString` (line 84) is overridden to provide a conventional string representation of the complex number in the form such as "$3 - 4i$."

A main method is implemented to test the `Complex` class. Two complex numbers are created. They are printed using the `toString` method implicitly. The results of all operations performed on the two numbers are also printed. The output of the program is shown below.

```
z = 1.0-2.0i
w = 3.0+4.0i
|z| = 2.23606797749979
|w| = 5.0
arg z = -1.1071487177940904
arg w = 0.9272952180016122
conj z = 1.0+2.0i
conj w = 3.0-4.0i
z + w = 4.0+2.0i
z - w = -2.0-6.0i
z * w = 11.0-2.0i
z / w = -0.2-0.4i
```

A.3.2 Quaternions

The quaternion system is an extension of the complex number system. A quaternion is expressed as:

$$q = a + bi + cj + dk$$

where a, b, c, d are real numbers. The i, j, k are elements satisfying the rules:

$$i^2 = j^2 = k^2 = ijk = -1$$

With the assumption of associativity in multiplication, it can also be shown that

$$ij = k = -ji, \qquad jk = i = -kj, \qquad ki = j = -ik$$

The addition and subtraction of quaternions are defined as componentwise operations similar to those of complex numbers. The multiplication of quaternions is also similar to that of complex numbers defined with the distributive law over addition and with the relationships among i, j, k given above.

The addition of two quaternions $q = a + bi + cj + dk$ and $p = e + fi + gj + hk$ is defined by:

$$q + p = (a + e) + (b + f)i + (c + g)j + (d + h)k$$

The multiplication of the quaternions is defined with distributive law and the properties on i, j, k:

$$q \cdot p = (ae - bf - cg - dh) + (af + be + ch - dg)i \\ + (ag - bh + ce + df)j + (ah + bg - cf + de)k$$

For example,

$$(1 - i + j - 2k) \cdot (2 + i - k)$$

$$= 1 \cdot 2 + 1 \cdot i - 1 \cdot k - 2 \cdot i - i \cdot i + i \cdot k + 2 \cdot j + j \cdot i - j \cdot k - 4 \cdot k - 2k \cdot i + 2k \cdot k$$

$$= 2 + i - k - 2i + 1 - j + 2j - k + i - 4k - 2j - 2$$

$$= 1 - j - 6k$$

Quaternion multiplication is not commutative, so in general $p \cdot q$ is not the same as $q \cdot p$. However, all other algebraic properties such as the associative laws, the distributive laws, and the existence of identity and inverse elements are valid, similar to real and complex number systems. The quaternion system is known as a *skew field*, or a *noncommutative field*. A skew field has all the properties of a field except that the multiplication is not necessarily commutative.

conjugate

absolute value

The *conjugate* and *absolute value* of a quaternion $q = a + bi + cj + dk$ are defined as

$$\overline{q} = a - bi - cj - dk$$

$$|q| = \sqrt{a^2 + b^2 + c^2 + d^2}$$

It can be shown that $\overline{q \cdot p} = \overline{q} \cdot \overline{p}$ and $q \cdot \overline{q} = \overline{q} \cdot q = |q|^2$. The last identity can be used to perform quaternion divisions in the same way as complex number divisions. For example,

$$\frac{-k}{1 + 2i - j} = \frac{-k(1 - 2i + j)}{(1 + 2i - j)(1 - 2i + j)} = \frac{-k + 2j + i}{6} = (1/6)i + (1/3)j - (1/6)k$$

One way to provide a geometric interpretation to quaternions is to associate a point (x, y, z) in 3D space with a pure quaternion—a quaternion with real part 0 (for example, $xi + yj + zk$).

Quaternions are especially useful in representing 3D rotations. The details will be introduced in Section A.5, "Geometric Transformations."

A.4 Linear Algebra

A.4.1 Vector Spaces

axioms of vector spaces

A general vector space over a field F (such as the field of real numbers or the field of complex numbers) is a set V with an addition, $+: V \times V \rightarrow V$, and a scalar multiplication, $\cdot: F \times V \rightarrow V$, satisfying the following conditions.

For all $u, v, w \in V$ and $k, l \in F$,

$$u + v = v + u$$

$$(u + v) + w = u + (v + w)$$

there exists a vector 0 such that $u + 0 = u$.

For every vector u there exists an inverse $-u$ such that $u + (-u) = 0$:

$$k(u + v) = ku + kv$$

$$(k + l)u = ku + lu$$

$$(kl)u = k(lu)$$

$$1u = u$$

As a concrete example, a typical n-dimensional vector is simply an ordered tuple of n real numbers. For example, $(3, 4), (1, 0, -2), (4, 5, -3, 1)$ are vectors of dimensions 2, 3, and 4, respectively.

The collection of all such vectors of dimension n forms a vector space of dimension n over the field of real numbers with two operations defined as componentwise operations. The addition of two vectors is defined as

$$(a_1, a_2, \ldots, a_n) + (b_1, b_2, \ldots, b_n) = (a_1 + b_1, a_2 + b_2, \ldots, a_n + b_n)$$

The scalar multiplication is defined as

$$k(a_1, a_2, \ldots, a_n) = (ka_1, ka_2, \ldots, ka_n)$$

This particular real vector space of dimension n is denoted by R^n.

The set of complex numbers can be regarded as a two-dimensional vector space over the real numbers. The quaternions form a four-dimensional vector space over the real numbers, or a two-dimensional space over the complex numbers.

The *inner product* (also known as the dot product or scalar product) is defined on R^n as

$$(a_1, a_2, \ldots, a_n) \cdot (b_1, b_2, \ldots, b_n) = a_1b_1 + a_2b_2 + \cdots + a_nb_n$$

The *norm* of a vector v is defined as $\|v\| = \sqrt{v \cdot v}$.

A point in a 2D geometric plane can be associated with a vector of dimension 2 using a rectangular coordinate system. This association establishes a one-to-one correspondence between the geometric plane and the algebraic vector space. Similarly a one-to-one correspondence can be established between a 3D geometric space and a vector space of dimension 3. This association is the exactly the same as the concept applied in the analytic geometry.

Geometrically, the norm of a vector is the length of the vector. The inner product of two vectors can be expressed as

$$v \cdot u = \|v\| \|u\| \cos \theta$$

where θ is the angle between the two vectors. Figure A.10 illustrates the inner product. If u is a unit vector, $\|u\| = 1$, then the inner product can be interpreted as the projection of v along the direction u.

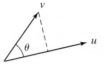

FIGURE A.10   Geometric interpretation of inner product.

If the angle between two vectors is 90 degrees or $\pi/2$ radians, the two vectors are said to be *orthogonal* or *perpendicular*. From the properties of the inner product, it is clear that two vectors v and u are orthogonal when $v \cdot u = 0$.

A.4.2 Linear Transformations and Matrices

Mathematically, a transformation (or a transform) T from a space V to a space W is a mapping (a function) from V to W:

$$T: V \rightarrow W$$

For each point v in V, there is a corresponding point $T(v)$ in W. If the mapping T is one-to-one and onto, then it has an inverse:

$$T^{-1}: W \rightarrow V$$

In computer graphics, the spaces V and W are usually the two-dimensional vector space R^2 or the three-dimensional vector space R^3. The general family of transformations is huge and complex. In graphics usually only certain special families of transformations are considered.

A transformation T is linear if, for any vectors u, v and scalars a, b,

$$T(au + bv) = aT(u) + bT(v)$$

Linear transformations are convenient for algebraic manipulation and computer representation and processing. A general linear transformation from an n-dimensional vector space

matrix

R^n to an m-dimensional vector space R^m can be represented by an $m \times n$ matrix. A *matrix* is a rectangular array of numbers. An $m \times n$ matrix has the following form:

$$A = \begin{bmatrix} a_{1,1} & a_{1,2} & \cdots & a_{1,n} \\ a_{2,1} & a_{2,2} & \cdots & a_{2,n} \\ \vdots & \vdots & \ddots & \vdots \\ a_{m,1} & a_{m,2} & \cdots & a_{m,n} \end{bmatrix}$$

For example, the following is a 2×3 matrix:

$$\begin{bmatrix} 3 & -1 & 2 \\ 1 & 0 & -3 \end{bmatrix}$$

Matrix addition is defined on two matrices with identical sizes by entrywise addition. For example,

$$\begin{bmatrix} 3 & -1 & 2 \\ 1 & 0 & -3 \end{bmatrix} + \begin{bmatrix} 1 & 0 & -3 \\ -1 & 2 & 5 \end{bmatrix} = \begin{bmatrix} 3+1 & -1+0 & 2-3 \\ 1-1 & 0+2 & -3+5 \end{bmatrix}$$

$$= \begin{bmatrix} 4 & -1 & -1 \\ 0 & 2 & 2 \end{bmatrix}$$

matrix multiplication

Matrix multiplication AB is defined only if the number of columns of A is the same as the number of rows of B. An entry in the product AB is obtained from a row of A and column of B by multiplying corresponding entries and taking the sum. For example,

$$\begin{bmatrix} 3 & -1 & 2 \\ 1 & 0 & -3 \end{bmatrix} \begin{bmatrix} 1 & -1 \\ 0 & 2 \\ -3 & 5 \end{bmatrix}$$

$$= \begin{bmatrix} 3 \times 1 + (-1) \times 0 + 2 \times (-3) & 3 \times (-1) + (-1) \times 2 + 2 \times 5 \\ 1 \times 1 + 0 \times 0 + (-3) \times (-3) & 1 \times (-1) + 0 \times 2 + (-3) \times 5 \end{bmatrix}$$

$$= \begin{bmatrix} -3 & 5 \\ 10 & -16 \end{bmatrix}$$

Matrices may also represent vectors. A vector of dimension m can be represented as an $m \times 1$ column matrix. For example, the following matrix represents a three-dimensional vector:

$$\begin{bmatrix} -1 \\ 4 \\ 0 \end{bmatrix}$$

A linear transformation may be constructed using a matrix. Let A be an $m \times n$ matrix and v an $n \times 1$ column matrix representing a vector. A linear transformation from R^n to R^m is defined by the matrix multiplication:

$$u = Av$$

For example, the following matrix equation defines a linear transformation from R^3 to R^2:

$$\begin{bmatrix} x' \\ y' \end{bmatrix} = \begin{bmatrix} 3 & -1 & 2 \\ 1 & 0 & -3 \end{bmatrix} \begin{bmatrix} x \\ y \\ z \end{bmatrix}$$

Conversely, any linear transformation from R^n to R^m admits a matrix representation with an appropriate $m \times n$ matrix.

Given an $m \times n$ matrix A, the transpose A^T is defined as the $n \times m$ matrix

$$A^T = \begin{bmatrix} a_{1,1} & a_{2,1} & \cdots & a_{n,1} \\ a_{1,2} & a_{2,2} & \cdots & a_{n,2} \\ \vdots & \vdots & \ddots & \vdots \\ a_{1,n} & a_{2,n} & \cdots & a_{m,n} \end{bmatrix}$$

For example,

$$\begin{bmatrix} 3 & -1 & 2 \\ 1 & 0 & -3 \end{bmatrix}^T = \begin{bmatrix} 3 & 1 \\ -1 & 0 \\ 2 & -3 \end{bmatrix}$$

An $n \times n$ matrix is called a square matrix. A square matrix represents a linear transformation from a vector space R^n to R^n. An *identity matrix* I is a square matrix of the form: identity matrix

$$I = \begin{bmatrix} 1 & 0 & \cdots & 0 \\ 0 & 1 & \cdots & 0 \\ \vdots & \vdots & \ddots & \vdots \\ 0 & 0 & \cdots & 1 \end{bmatrix}$$

The *inverse matrix* A^{-1} of a square matrix A satisfies the condition: inverse matrix

$$A^{-1}A = AA^{-1} = I$$

The inverse matrix A^{-1} represents the inverse of the linear transformation represented by the matrix A.

The *determinant* is a scalar-valued function on square matrices. The determinant of matrix A determinant
is denoted by $\det(A)$ or $|A|$. The formula for computing the determinant can be defined recursively as follows:

$$|a_{1,1}| = a_{1,1}$$

$$\begin{vmatrix} a_{1,1} & a_{1,2} \\ a_{2,1} & a_{2,2} \end{vmatrix} = a_{1,1}a_{2,2} - a_{2,1}a_{1,2}$$

$$\begin{vmatrix} a_{1,1} & a_{1,2} & a_{1,3} \\ a_{2,1} & a_{2,2} & a_{2,3} \\ a_{3,1} & a_{3,2} & a_{3,3} \end{vmatrix} = a_{1,1}\begin{vmatrix} a_{2,2} & a_{2,3} \\ a_{3,2} & a_{3,3} \end{vmatrix} - a_{1,2}\begin{vmatrix} a_{2,1} & a_{2,3} \\ a_{3,1} & a_{3,3} \end{vmatrix} + a_{1,3}\begin{vmatrix} a_{2,1} & a_{2,2} \\ a_{3,1} & a_{3,2} \end{vmatrix}$$

For example,

$$\begin{vmatrix} 2 & 1 & -3 \\ 0 & -1 & 5 \\ 4 & -2 & 3 \end{vmatrix} = 2\begin{vmatrix} -1 & 5 \\ -2 & 3 \end{vmatrix} - 1\begin{vmatrix} 0 & 5 \\ 4 & 3 \end{vmatrix} + (-3)\begin{vmatrix} 0 & -1 \\ 4 & -2 \end{vmatrix}$$

$$= 2(-3 + 10) - (0 - 20) - 3(0 + 4) = 22$$

The expansion method used in the 3×3 matrix can be extended to define the determinant of a general matrix recursively.

It can be proven that $\det(A^T) = \det(A)$ and $\det(AB) = \det(A)\det(B)$ if A and B are square matrices.

cross product

The *cross product* $v \times u$ (also known as the *outer product* or *vector product*) of two vectors $v = (x_1, y_1, z_1)$, $u = (x_2, y_2, z_2)$ is an operation defined on R^3. Using determinants, the cross product can be defined symbolically as

$$v \times u = \begin{vmatrix} i & j & k \\ x_1 & y_1 & z_1 \\ x_2 & y_2 & z_2 \end{vmatrix} = (y_1 z_2 - y_2 z_1)i - (x_1 z_2 - x_2 z_1)j + (x_1 y_2 - x_2 y_1)k$$

Geometrically, $v \times u$ is a vector perpendicular to both v and u with the length

$$\|v \times u\| = \|v\|\|u\| \sin \theta$$

This length is equal to the area of the parallelogram spanned by the vectors v and u. Figure A.11 shows the geometry of the cross product.

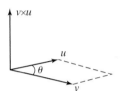

FIGURE A.11 Geometric interpretation of cross product.

The cross product is a useful tool to construct a vector perpendicular to some other vectors. For example, the cross product of the two vectors $(0, 1, 2)$ and $(3, 4, 5)$ is

$$\begin{vmatrix} i & j & k \\ 0 & 1 & 2 \\ 3 & 4 & 5 \end{vmatrix} = -3i + 6j - 3k = (-3, 6, -3)$$

It is easy to verify by inner products that $(-3, 6, -3)$ is orthogonal to $(0, 1, 2)$ and $(3, 4, 5)$:

$$(-3, 6, -3) \cdot (0, 1, 2) = 0 + 6 - 6 = 0$$

$$(-3, 6, -3) \cdot (3, 4, 5) = -9 + 24 - 15 = 0$$

Let A be a square matrix. If v is a nonzero vector and for some scalar λ,

$$Av = \lambda v$$

eigenvalue
eigenvector

then v is said to be an *eigenvector* of A, and λ an *eigenvalue* of A.
A real matrix A is symmetric if $A^T = A$. A real matrix U is said to be orthogonal if

$$U^T U = U U^T = I$$

The spectral theorem states that a symmetric matrix A can be decomposed into a matrix product:

$$A = U \Lambda U^T$$

where U is an orthogonal matrix and Λ is a diagonal matrix of eigenvalues of A.
More generally, any real matrix A can be decomposed into

$$A = U \Lambda V^T$$

where U and V are orthogonal matrices and Λ is a diagonal matrix. This decomposition is

SVD

known as the *singular value decomposition* (*SVD*).

A.5 Geometric Transformations

A.5.1 Homogeneous Coordinates

Transformations on R^2 and R^3 are directly related to 2D and 3D graphics. A linear transformation on R^3 can be represented by a 3×3 matrix:

$$\begin{bmatrix} x' \\ y' \\ z' \end{bmatrix} = T \begin{bmatrix} x \\ y \\ z \end{bmatrix} = \begin{bmatrix} a_{11} & a_{12} & a_{13} \\ a_{21} & a_{22} & a_{23} \\ a_{31} & a_{32} & a_{33} \end{bmatrix} \begin{bmatrix} x \\ y \\ z \end{bmatrix}$$

Families of transformations that are of special interest to computer graphics are often defined in terms of their properties in preserving certain geometric relationships. A *projective transformation* preserves lines—that is, it maps a line to a line. An *affine transformation* preserves lines and parallelism—that is, it is a projective transformation that maps parallel lines to parallel lines. All linear transformations defined above are affine, but not all affine transformations are linear. All affine transformations are projective, but not all projective transformations are affine.

Because affine transformations and projective transformations are in general not linear, they do not necessarily have the matrix representation shown above. However, if the coordinate system representing the points is modified by increasing its dimension, it will be possible to obtain a linear representation for any projective transformation. This coordinate system is known as the *homogeneous coordinates*.

The homogeneous coordinates add one dimension to the standard coordinates. For example, a 2D point is represented by homogeneous coordinates with three components (x, y, w) and a 3D point is represented by homogeneous coordinates with four components (x, y, z, w). Furthermore, homogeneous coordinates that differ by a nonzero factor represent the same point. Therefore, the relationship between the points in the space and the homogeneous coordinates is not one-to-one.

In a 2D space, instead of using two coordinates to represent a point, the homogeneous coordinate system uses three coordinates to represent a point: (x, y, w).

When w is not 0, the regular 2D coordinates (X, Y) of the same point are given by

$$X = x/w$$

$$Y = y/w$$

Similarly in a 3D space, instead of using three coordinates to represent a point, the homogeneous coordinate system uses four coordinates to represent a point: (x, y, z, w), or in the column form:

$$\begin{bmatrix} x \\ y \\ z \\ w \end{bmatrix}$$

When w is not 0, the regular 3D coordinates (X, Y, Z) of the point are given by

$$X = x/w$$

$$Y = y/w$$

$$Z = z/w$$

In the homogeneous coordinate system, 4D vectors are used to represent 3D points. It follows from the definition that the homogeneous coordinates for a point are not unique. Any nonzero multiple of a 4D homogeneous vector will still represent the same 3D point.

projective transformation
affine transformation

homogeneous coorinate

For example, the homogeneous coordinates $(1, -2, 4, 1)$, $(2, -4, 8, 2)$, and $(-3, 6, -12, -3)$, all represent the same point $(1, -2, 4)$ in a 3D space.

When w is 0, there is no regular 3D point associated with the homogeneous coordinates. In this case, the homogeneous coordinates may be regarded as a representation of *points at "infinity."* They may be viewed as directions. For example, $(1, 1, 0)$ in a 2D space represents a point at infinity along the 45-degree direction.

points at infinity

One advantage of a homogeneous coordinate system is that it will make all affine transformations and projective transformations linear and provide a uniform matrix representation. In a 3D space, the transformation can be expressed as a matrix equation:

$$\begin{bmatrix} x' \\ y' \\ z' \\ w' \end{bmatrix} = \begin{bmatrix} a_{1,1} & a_{1,2} & a_{1,3} & a_{1,4} \\ a_{2,1} & a_{2,2} & a_{2,3} & a_{2,4} \\ a_{3,1} & a_{3,2} & a_{3,3} & a_{3,4} \\ a_{4,1} & a_{4,2} & a_{4,3} & a_{4,4} \end{bmatrix} \begin{bmatrix} x \\ y \\ z \\ w \end{bmatrix}$$

A.5.2 Classification of Transformations

Transformations that preserve certain geometric properties have special significance in geometry and graphics.

projective transformation

A *projective transformation* preserves collinearity—that is, it maps a line to a line. A projective transformation is not necessarily linear. For example, a linear transformation always maps the vector 0 to 0. This is not true for projective transformations. However, as shown in the previous section, by using *homogeneous coordinates* you can obtain a linear representation for a projective transformation.

With the homogeneous coordinate system, a projective transformation can be represented as a linear transformation:

$$\begin{bmatrix} x' \\ y' \\ z' \\ w' \end{bmatrix} = \begin{bmatrix} a_{1,1} & a_{1,2} & a_{1,3} & a_{1,4} \\ a_{2,1} & a_{2,2} & a_{2,3} & a_{2,4} \\ a_{3,1} & a_{3,2} & a_{3,3} & a_{3,4} \\ a_{4,1} & a_{4,2} & a_{4,3} & a_{4,4} \end{bmatrix} \begin{bmatrix} x \\ y \\ z \\ w \end{bmatrix}$$

affine transformation

Affine transformations are projective transformations that preserve parallelism. For example, an affine transformation maps a parallelogram to a parallelogram. Affine transformations are the most common transformations employed in graphics applications. The transformation matrix has the following form:

$$\begin{bmatrix} a_{1,1} & a_{1,2} & a_{1,3} & a_{1,4} \\ a_{2,1} & a_{2,2} & a_{2,3} & a_{2,4} \\ a_{3,1} & a_{3,2} & a_{3,3} & a_{3,4} \\ 0 & 0 & 0 & 1 \end{bmatrix}$$

Examples of affine transformations include rotations, translations, scaling, reflections, and shearing.

rigid motion

A subset of affine transformations that also preserve distances is known as *rigid motions*, *Euclidean motions*, or *isometries*. Translations, rotations, and reflections are examples of rigid motions. The determinant of a rigid motion is either 1 or -1. The reflections have determinant -1.

A classification of common geometric transformations is illustrated in Figure A.12.

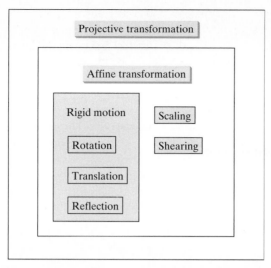

FIGURE A.12   Geometric transformations can be classified into translation, rotation, reflection, scaling, shearing, and so on.

A *translation* moves all points of a space by a fixed amount. It does not change the size and direction of any object. Figure A.13 shows an example of a 2D translation by an amount of $(2, -1)$ in the *x*- and *y*-directions.

translation

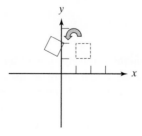

FIGURE A.13   A translation moves the shape.

A *rotation* rotates the object. A 2D rotation is around a point and a 3D rotation is around a line. A rotation does not change the size, but it changes the direction of the shape. Figure A.14 shows a 2D rotation about the origin.

rotation

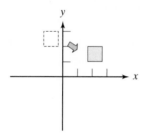

FIGURE A.14   A rotation rotates the shape.

A *reflection* maps the object to its mirror image. A 2D reflection is about a line and a 3D reflection is about a plane. A reflection preserves distance, but it changes the orientation of an angle. Figure A.15 shows a 2D reflection.

reflection

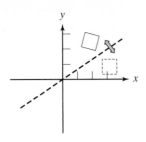

FIGURE A.15   A reflection mirrors the shape.

scaling

A *scaling* resizes the object by multiplying certain fixed factors in different directions. Figure A.16 shows a 2D scaling.

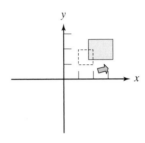

FIGURE A.16   A scaling resizes the shape.

shearing

A *shearing* shifts an object in certain directions. A 2D shear is along a line and a 3D shear shifts along a plane. The amount of shift is proportional to the signed distance to the fixed line or plane. Figure A.17 shows a 2D shear.

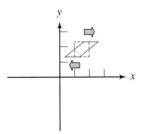

FIGURE A.17   A shearing shifts the shape.

Complex numbers and quaternions offer convenient analytic forms of transformations, especially for rotations. In a 2D space, a point may be associated with a complex number. A 2D rotation about the origin can be conveniently represented by the multiplication of a complex number $e^{i\theta}$.

In a 3D space, a point may be identified with a pure quaternion, $p = xi + yj + zk$. A 3D rotation about the origin can be expressed in the form

$$T_q(p) = qp\bar{q}$$

where q is a unit quaternion and can be written as

$$q = \cos\frac{\theta}{2} + u\sin\frac{\theta}{2}, \qquad u = ai + bj + ck$$

The pure unit quaternion u *defines* the axis of rotation, and θ is the angle of rotation.

For example, if you need to define a rotation of $\pi/3$ about the axis through the origin and $(1, 1, 1)$, you can use the following quaternion representation:

$$q = \cos\frac{\pi}{6} + \frac{1}{\sqrt{3}}(i + j + k)\sin\frac{\pi}{6} = \frac{\sqrt{3}}{2} + \frac{\sqrt{3}}{6}i + \frac{\sqrt{3}}{6}j + \frac{\sqrt{3}}{6}k$$

Clearly the quaternion representation offers a convenient way to specify a 3D rotation with explicit axis and angle. Consider another example. The set of 3D rotations is closed under the transformation composition—that is, the result of combining two rotations is still a rotation. However, the axis and angle of the composite rotation are not easily seen. If we have a rotation of $\pi/2$ about the y-axis followed by a rotation of $\pi/2$ about the x-axis, what are the axis and angle of the resulting rotation? The quaternion representation provides an easy solution. The composite transform of two rotations T_{q_1} and T_{q_2} is given by

$$T_{q_1}(T_{q_2}(p)) = q_1q_2 p \bar{q}_2 \bar{q}_1 = q_1q_2 p \overline{q_1q_2} = T_{q_1q_2}(p)$$

Therefore, the product of two quaternions represents the composite transform of the two rotations. The quaternions for the rotation of $\pi/2$ about x-axis and the rotation of $\pi/2$ about y-axis are

$$q_1 = \frac{\sqrt{2}}{2} + \frac{\sqrt{2}}{2}i$$

$$q_2 = \frac{\sqrt{2}}{2} + \frac{\sqrt{2}}{2}j$$

The composite rotation will have the quaternion

$$q_3 = q_1q_2 = \left(\frac{\sqrt{2}}{2} + \frac{\sqrt{2}}{2}i\right)\left(\frac{\sqrt{2}}{2} + \frac{\sqrt{2}}{2}j\right) = \frac{1}{2}(1 + i + j + ij)$$

$$= \frac{1}{2} + \left(\frac{i + j + k}{\sqrt{3}}\right)\frac{\sqrt{3}}{2}$$

$$= \cos\frac{\pi}{3} + \left(\frac{i + j + k}{\sqrt{3}}\right)\sin\frac{\pi}{3}$$

Therefore the resulting transform is a rotation of $2\pi/3$ about the axis through $(0, 0, 0)$ and $(1, 1, 1)$.

A.6 Calculus

Given a curve represented by the function $y = f(x)$, the slope of the tangent line to the curve at a point is the derivative of the function $dy/dx = f'(x)$. To find the equation of the *tangent line* at (x_0, y_0), we can use the point-slope form,

tangent line

$$y - f(x_0) = f'(x_0)(x - x_0)$$

In a 3D space, a curve may be represented as a parametric equation:

$$x = f(t)$$

$$y = g(t)$$

$$z = h(t)$$

At the point (x_0, y_0, z_0) defined by $t = t_0$, the direction of the tangent line is given by the vector:

$$(f'(t_0), g'(t_0), h'(t_0))$$

tangent line

The equation of the tangent line is:

$$x = x_0 + f'(t_0)(t - t_0)$$

$$y = y_0 + g'(t_0)(t - t_0)$$

$$z = z_0 + h'(t_0)(t - t_0)$$

surface normal

A smooth surface has a tangent plane at a given point. The normal of the tangent plane is called the *surface normal* at the given point of the surface. Given the parametric equation of a surface,

$$x = f(u, v)$$

$$y = g(u, v)$$

$$z = h(u, v)$$

we can find the surface normals by the partial derivatives. Consider the two vectors formed by the derivatives:

$$Du = (\partial x/\partial u, \partial y/\partial u, \partial z/\partial u) = (f_u, g_u, h_u)$$

$$Dv = (\partial x/\partial v, \partial y/\partial v, \partial z/\partial v) = (f_v, g_v, h_v)$$

The surface normal can be found by taking a cross product:

$$n = Du \times Dv$$

For example, a surface is defined by the following parametric equation:

$$x = 2uv - 1$$

$$y = v^2$$

$$z = u^2 - v^3$$

The partial derivatives are

$$Du = (2v, 0, 2u)$$

$$Dv = (2u, 2v, -3v^2)$$

The surface normals are defined by

$$(2v, 0, 2u) \times (2u, 2v, -3v^2) = (-4uv, 4u^2 + 6v^3, 4v^2)$$

At the point $(1, 1, 0)$ defined by the parameter values $u = 1, v = 1$, the surface normal is $(-4, 10, 4)$.

gradient

For a surface given by an implicit equation $F(x, y, z) = 0$, its surface normal may be found by the *gradient*:

$$\nabla F(x, y, z) = (\partial F/\partial x, \partial F/\partial y, \partial F/\partial z)$$

For instance, a hyperbolic paraboloid has the equation $z = xy$ or $xy - z = 0$. The gradient is

$$\nabla F(x, y, z) = (\partial F/\partial x, \partial F/\partial y, \partial F/\partial z) = (y, x, -1)$$

Therefore, the surface normal at the point $(-1, 2, -2)$ is in the direction $(2, -1, -1)$.

A.7 Graph Theory

A graph is a mathematical structure that describes a relationship on a set of objects called *vertices* (also known as *nodes* or *points*). *Edges* (also known as *arcs* or *lines*) are used to define the relationship. An edge links two vertices and it may be either undirected or directed. A graph with directed edges is called a *directed graph*, or a *digraph*. Figure A.18 shows a digraph and an undirected graph.

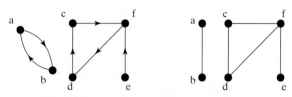

FIGURE A.18   A digraph (left) and an undirected graph (right).

Formally, an undirected graph is defined as $G = (V, E)$, where V is the set of vertices and E the set of edges. An edge uv that joins the vertices u and v is said to be incident with the vertices u and v. Two vertices are said to be *adjacent* if they are incident with the same edge. A *path* is an alternating sequence of distinct vertices and edges: $v_0 e_1 v_1 e_2 v_2 \cdots e_m v_m$, where e_i is incident with v_{i-1} and v_i. We can usually omit the edge specification in the sequence and simply define a path as $v_0 v_1 v_2 \cdots v_m$. A *cycle* is similar to a path except that the initial and final vertices coincide: $v_0 = v_m$. For example, in the undirected graph shown in Figure A.18, *cdfe* is a path and *cdfc* is cycle. path cycle

A graph is *connected* if any two vertices in the graph can be linked with a path. A graph is called *acyclic* if it contains no cycle. A graph is called a *tree* if it is both connected and acyclic. A tree is a minimally connected graph with many special properties. For example, the number of edges and the number of vertices of a tree are related by $|E| = |V| - 1$.

The terms related to digraphs can be defined similarly. For example, in the digraph shown in Figure A.18, *dcfe* is a directed path and *cfdc* is a directed cycle.

A *DAG* (*directed acyclic graph*) is a digraph without any directed cycles. However, if the directions on the edges of a DAG are ignored, the resulting undirected graph may contain undirected cycles. Figure A.19 shows an example. DAG

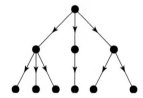

FIGURE A.19   A DAG (left) and a rooted tree (right).

A *rooted tree* is a tree with directed edges oriented away from a root, as shown in Figure A.19. A rooted tree is a DAG, but a DAG is not necessarily a rooted tree. From the root of the tree to any vertex, there exists a unique path. If uv is a directed edge from u to v, we call v a *child* of u and u the *parent* of v. A vertex without children is called a *leaf*. rooted tree

Key Terms

coordinate system A method to associate geometric points with algebraic quantities of ordered tuples of numbers.

parametric equation A set of equations that express coordinate variables as functions of parameters.

conic section A family of curves including ellipses, parabolas, and hyperbolas.

complex numbers A number system that is an extension of the real number field.

quaternion A number system that is an extension of the complex number field.

vector space An algebraic system with two operations: addition and scalar multiplication.

inner product A scalar function of two vectors.

linear transformation A mapping of vector spaces that preserves linear combinations.

matrix A rectangular array of numbers, often used to represent a linear transformation.

determinant A scalar function of a square matrix.

cross product A vector-valued function of two vectors defined in an 3D space.

eigenvalue, eigenvector A special value λ and vector v that satisfy $Av = \lambda v$ for a square matrix.

spectral theorem A symmetric matrix can be decomposed as $A = U\Lambda U^T$.

SVD (singular value decomposition). A matrix can be decomposed as $A = U\Lambda V^T$.

homogeneous coordinates A system to represent a point with an extra dimension so that all projective transformations can be represented linearly.

projective transformation A geometric transformation that preserves collinearity.

affine transformation A geometric transformation that preserves parallelism.

rigid motion A geometric transformation that preserves distances.

tangent line A line through a point on a curve. The slope of the line is the same as the rate of change of the curve at the point.

surface normal A vector perpendicular to the tangent plane of a surface at a point.

graph A mathematical structure consisting of a set of vertices and a set of edges.

digraph A graph with directed edges.

DAG Directed acyclic graph.

tree A connected acyclic graph.

Review Problems

A.1 Plot the following points in a 2D coordinate system:

$$(1, 3), (-2, 1.5), (0, -2), (0, 0)$$

A.2 Find the coordinates of the vertices of the triangle in Figure A.20.

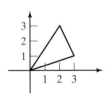

Figure A.20 A triangle for Problem A.2.

A.3 Find the distance between the two 3D points $(2, 1, 3)$ and $(0, -2, 5)$.

A.4 Find the inner product of the two 3D vectors $(2, 1, 3)$ and $(0, -2, 5)$.

A.5 Find the angle between the two 3D vectors $(2, 1, 3)$ and $(0, -2, 5)$.

A.6   Find the cross product of the two 3D vectors $(2, 1, 3)$ and $(0, -2, 5)$.

A.7   Find an equation of the line through the point $(0, 2)$ with slope -2.

A.8   Find the slope of the line $-2x + 3y = 4$.

A.9   Find an equation of the circle centered at the origin with radius 5.

A.10   Find the equation of the ellipse centered at $(-1, 3)$ and through the points $(1, 3)$ and $(-1, 4)$.

A.11   Find a parametric equation of the line through the points $(1, 3)$ and $(-1, 4)$.

A.12   Calculate the sum, difference, product, and quotient of the two complex numbers $-2 - 5i, 1 - 3i$.

A.13   Find the complex conjugate and the absolute value of the complex number $-2 - 5i$.

A.14   Find the product of two quaternions $-1 - 5i + k, 1 - 3i - j + 2k$.

A.15   Describe the rotation defined by the quaternion $1/2 - 1/2i + 1/2j + 1/2k$.

A.16   Construct a quaternion representing the 3D rotation of $2\pi/3$ about the axis $(1, -2, 2)$.

A.17   Find the sum and product of the following matrices:

$$\begin{bmatrix} 1 & 4 & -2 \\ 2 & 1 & 0 \\ -1 & -1 & -3 \end{bmatrix}, \quad \begin{bmatrix} 2 & -1 & 3 \\ 0 & 7 & -2 \\ 1 & 5 & 4 \end{bmatrix}$$

A.18   Find the determinant of the following matrix:

$$\begin{bmatrix} -3 & 5 \\ 10 & -6 \end{bmatrix}$$

A.19   Find the determinant of the following matrix:

$$\begin{bmatrix} 1 & 4 & -2 \\ 2 & 1 & 0 \\ -1 & -1 & -3 \end{bmatrix}$$

A.20   Find $\det(I)$.

A.21   Prove that $\det(A^{-1}) = 1/\det(A)$.

A.22   Show that the following matrix is orthogonal:

$$\begin{bmatrix} \cos\theta & -\sin\theta \\ \sin\theta & \cos\theta \end{bmatrix}$$

A.23   If A is orthogonal, show that $\det(A) = \pm 1$.

A.24   Using homogeneous coordinates in a 2D space, a line can be represented by an equation:

$$ax + by + cw = 0$$

If two lines are parallel, derive a relationship on their coefficients in the above equation.

A.25   Consider the line equations for homogeneous coordinates in Problem A.24. If two lines are parallel, can you find a point of intersection by solving a simultaneous equation?

A.26   Find an equation of the tangent line of the curve $y = x^3 + x - 1$ at the point $(1, 1)$.

A.27 Find an equation of the tangent line of the following 3D curve at the point $(1, -1, 0)$:

$$x = t + 1$$
$$y = t^2 - 1$$
$$z = t^3$$

A.28 Find the surface normals for the following surface:

$$x = 2 \cos u \cos v$$
$$y = 3 \sin u \cos v$$
$$z = 4 \sin v$$

A.29 A tree has 1000 vertices. How many edges does it have?

A.30 If a rooted tree has 1000 leaves and each nonleaf node has exactly two children, how many edges does it have?

GUI Programming with AWT and Swing

B.1 Introduction

There exist two sets of GUI programming interfaces for the Java platform: AWT and Swing. Swing is the newer and currently recommended system. However, because Java 3D depends on an AWT component Canvas3D for its rendering, a Java 3D program must include at least some elements of AWT. The readers are assumed to already have knowledge of Swing programming. This appendix will give a brief introduction to the AWT framework and its relationship to Swing.

A *graphical user interface* (*GUI*) is an indispensable part of modern computer systems. Virtually all operating systems provide some form of GUI support. However, the different GUI systems are usually not compatible with each other. Even though the basic elements of GUI programming, such as window systems and event-driven programming, are very similar in all platforms, GUI programming is usually platform dependent because of its heavy reliance on the specific facilities provided by the native system.

Java, on the other hand, provides a platform-independent GUI programming environment. From the very beginning of Java, GUI programming has been an integral part of standard Java APIs. Like other components of Java, Java's GUI support is fully object oriented and platform independent.

In the early Java versions, the GUI functions are achieved through an API package known as the *Abstract Window Toolkit* (*AWT*). AWT defines the basic mechanism of event-driven programming and a set of visual components. The AWT components are relatively simple, having features common to most GUI systems. They are implemented through direct mappings to similar components in a native system. | AWT

Swing is a new set of APIs for GUI programming. It differs from AWT mainly in a set of newly defined components. Most Swing components are not repackaged host-system components. They are built from the ground up within Java as "lightweight" components, independent of any native GUI system. As a result, Swing components are rich in features, and their appearance is independent of the host platform. Of course, Swing is not a complete replacement for AWT. It replaces only the AWT components. Swing programs still use other functions of AWT, such as layout managers and event handling. | Swing

B.2 AWT Components

AWT components are "*heavyweight*." They are always opaque and do not allow events such as mouse clicks to pass through. They are implemented using the components of the host platform. Consequently, only a limited set of features, common to all platforms, is available in AWT components. The class hierarchy of the major AWT components is shown in Figure B.1. | heavyweight

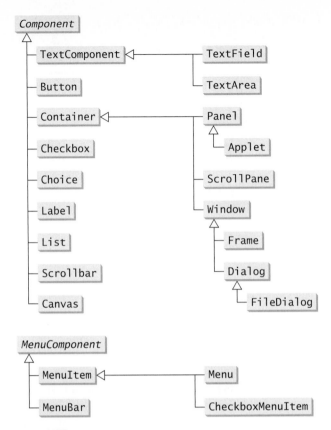

FIGURE B.1 Major AWT components.

Because AWT components are heavyweight, an AWT program will appear different when run under different platforms. Figure B.2 shows some screen shots of an AWT program under different operating systems. Of course, despite the differences, it is remarkable that the same GUI program can be executed in different systems without any change.

Many AWT components have approximate equivalents in Swing. Figure B.3 lists possible Swing replacements for AWT components. The Swing version usually has a name with the "J" prefix. For example, Swing components JTextField, JFrame, and JPanel correspond to the AWT components TextField, Frame, and Panel.

Of course, this is not an exact one-to-one correspondence. The Swing collection is more extensive than the set of AWT components, and sometimes there are also differences in their designs.

B.3 AWT Programming

A GUI program with all AWT components has the same basic structure as a Swing program. Constructing UI, event handling, and painting in AWT are almost identical to the procedures used in Swing. Because Swing provides more extensive functionality than AWT, using a pure AWT program to duplicate exactly the features of a Swing program can be difficult. Nevertheless, it is usually possible to convert a Swing program to a similar AWT version. The following guidelines may be useful if you need to perform such a conversion, or if you want to write an AWT program based on your knowledge of Swing:

1. Replace each Swing component by its closest AWT version. You may use Figure B.3 to find a matching component.

2. Unlike JFrame and JApplet, the top-level AWT containers, Frame and Applet, do not have content panes. The content is added directly to a Frame or Applet object.

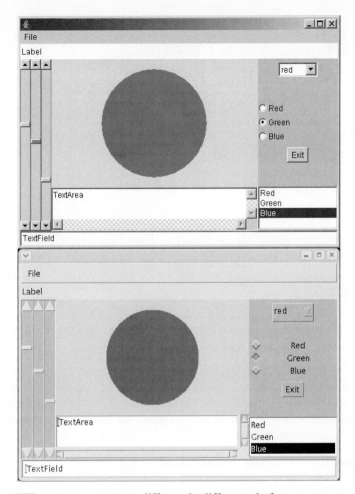

FIGURE B.2 AWT components appear different in different platforms.
Top: Windows 2000. Bottom: Linux.

AWT Component	Swing Component
Frame	JFrame
Applet	JApplet
Button	JButton
Label	JLabel
TextField	JTextField
TextArea	JTextArea
Panel	JPanel
List	JList
Checkbox	JCheckBox, JRadioButton
Choice	JComboBox
Canvas	JPanel, JLabel
MenuBar	JMenuBar
Menu	JMenu
MenuItem	JMenuItem
CheckboxMenuItem	JCheckBoxMenuItem
Scrollbar	JSlider, JProgressBar
ScrollPane	JScrollPane
Dialog	JDialog, JOptionPane
FileDialog	JFileChooser

FIGURE B.3 AWT components and their Swing equivalents.

3. The `Frame` class does not have the `setDefaultCloseOperation` method. You need to add a window event listener to get the effect. For example, the following code snippet terminates the program when the window is closed:

```java
public static void main(String[] args) {
  Frame frame = new Frame();
  // exit when the frame is closed
  frame.addWindowListener(new WindowAdapter() {
    public void windowClosing(WindowEvent ev){
      System.exit(0);
    }
  });
  frame.setVisible(true);
}
```

4. The `Applet` class, unlike `JApplet`, does not have a menu bar. Of course, it is not common for an applet to have its own menu.

5. AWT components do not have the `paintComponent(Graphics)` method. Use the `paint(Graphics)` method instead.

6. The AWT component `Canvas` is usually the base class for deriving a custom component class. Swing does not have a directly corresponding class. In Swing, `JPanel` is usually the blank base class for the same purpose.

7. There is no AWT radio-button class corresponding to the Swing class `JRadioButton`. You may use `Checkbox` and `CheckboxGroup` objects to achieve the effects of radio buttons. Note, however, that the usage is different from that of the `JRadioButton` and `ButtonGroup` objects in Swing. For example, the following code snippet creates a group of radio buttons in Swing:

```java
JRadioButton red = new JRadioButton("Red", true);
JRadioButton yellow = new JRadioButton("Yellow", false);
JRadioButton green = new JRadioButton("Green", false);
ButtonGroup group = new ButtonGroup();
group.add(red);
group.add(yellow);
group.add(green);
```

A similar AWT version is given below:

```java
CheckboxGroup group = new CheckboxGroup();
Checkbox red = new Checkbox("Red", group, true);
Checkbox yellow = new Checkbox("Yellow", group, false);
Checkbox green = new Checkbox("Green", group, false);
```

8. The AWT component `Scrollbar` is often used as an approximation for `JSlider`. One difference between the two components is that the `Scrollbar` fires the `AdjustmentEvent` and the `JSlider` generates the `ChangeEvent`.

Listings B.1 and B.2 illustrate the procedure of rewriting a Swing program in AWT. Listing B.1 is a typical Swing program and Listing B.2 is an approximately equivalent AWT version. (See Figure B.4.)

Listing B.1 `SwingProg.java`

```java
1 /*** Swing program ***/
2
3 package appendixB;
```

```
 4
 5  import javax.swing.*;
 6  import java.awt.*;
 7  import java.awt.event.*;
 8  import javax.swing.event.*;
 9
10  public class SwingProg extends Jframe
11    implements ActionListener, ChangeListener {
12
13    public static void main(String[] args) {
14      JFrame frame = new SwingProg();
15      frame.setVisible(true);
16    }
17
18    CirclePanel circle;
19    JSlider scrollR;
20    JSlider scrollG;
21    JSlider scrollB;
22
23    public SwingProg() {
24      setSize(500,350);
25      JMenuBar menuBar = new JMenuBar();
26      setJMenuBar(menuBar);
27      JMenu fileMenu = new JMenu("File");
28      menuBar.add(fileMenu);
29      JMenuItem exitItem = new JMenuItem("Exit");
30      exitItem.addActionListener(this);
31      fileMenu.add(exitItem);
32      // exit when the frame is closed
33      setDefaultCloseOperation(JFrame.EXIT_ON_CLOSE);
34
35      Container cp = this.getContentPane();
36      cp.setLayout(new BorderLayout());
37      // center
38      JPanel panel = new JPanel();
39      panel.setLayout(new BorderLayout());
40      cp.add(panel, BorderLayout.CENTER);
41      circle = new CirclePanel();
42      panel.add(circle, BorderLayout.CENTER);
43      JTextArea textArea = new JTextArea(3,10);
44      textArea.setText("TextArea");
45      panel.add(textArea, BorderLayout.SOUTH);
46      // north
47      JLabel label = new JLabel("Label");
48      cp.add(label, BorderLayout.NORTH);
49      // south
50      JTextField textField = new JTextField("TextField");
51      cp.add(textField, BorderLayout.SOUTH);
52      // west
53      panel = new JPanel();
54      panel.setLayout(new GridLayout(1,3));
55      cp.add(panel, BorderLayout.WEST);
56      scrollR = new JSlider(JSlider.VERTICAL, 0, 255, 0);
57      scrollR.addChangeListener(this);
58      panel.add(scrollR);
59      scrollG = new JSlider(JSlider.VERTICAL, 0, 255, 0);
60      scrollG.addChangeListener(this);
61      panel.add(scrollG);
62      scrollB = new JSlider(JSlider.VERTICAL, 0, 255, 0);
63      scrollB.addChangeListener(this);
64      panel.add(scrollB);
65      // east
```

```
 66       panel = new JPanel();
 67       panel.setBackground(Color.lightGray);
 68       panel.setLayout(new GridLayout(4,1));
 69       cp.add(panel, BorderLayout.EAST);
 70       JPanel chPanel = new JPanel();
 71       panel.add(chPanel);
 72       JComboBox choice = new JComboBox();
 73       choice.addItem("red");
 74       choice.addItem("green");
 75       choice.addItem("blue");
 76       chPanel.add(choice);
 77       JPanel cbPanel = new JPanel();
 78       cbPanel.setLayout(new GridLayout(3,1));
 79       panel.add(cbPanel);
 80       ButtonGroup group = new ButtonGroup();
 81       JRadioButton cbR = new JRadioButton("Red", true);
 82       group.add(cbR);
 83       cbPanel.add(cbR);
 84       JRadioButton cbG = new JRadioButton("Green", false);
 85       group.add(cbG);
 86       cbPanel.add(cbG);
 87       JRadioButton cbB = new JRadioButton("Blue", false);
 88       group.add(cbB);
 89       cbPanel.add(cbB);
 90       JPanel btPanel = new JPanel();
 91       panel.add(btPanel);
 92       JButton button = new JButton("Exit");
 93       button.addActionListener(this);
 94       btPanel.add(button);
 95       String[] listItems = {"Red", "Green", "Blue"};
 96       JList list = new JList(listItems);
 97       panel.add(list);
 98     }
 99
100     public void actionPerformed(ActionEvent ev) {
101       String cmd = ev.getActionCommand();
102       if ("Exit".equals(cmd))
103         System.exit(0);
104     }
105
106     public void stateChanged(ChangeEvent ev) {
107       int r = scrollR.getValue();
108       int g = scrollG.getValue();
109       int b = scrollB.getValue();
110       circle.setColor(new Color(r, g, b));
111     }
112
113 }
114
115 class CirclePanel extends JPanel {
116   private Color color = Color.black;
117
118   public CirclePanel() {
119     setBackground(new Color(220,220,220));
120   }
121
122   public void paintComponent(Graphics g) {
123     super.paintComponent(g);
124     g.setColor(color);
125     int w = getWidth();
126     int h = getHeight();
127     int d = (w > h)? h : w;
```

```
128      d -= 30;
129      g.fillOval((w-d)/2,(h-d)/2, d, d);
130    }
131
132    public void setColor(Color c) {
133      color = c;
134      repaint();
135    }
136 }
```

Listing B.2 AWTProg.java

```
 1 /*** AWT program ***/
 2
 3 package appendixB;
 4
 5 import java.awt.*;
 6 import java.awt.event.*;
 7
 8 public class AWTProg extends Frame
 9    implements ActionListener, AdjustmentListener {
10
11   public static void main(String[] args) {
12     Frame frame = new AWTProg();
13     frame.setVisible(true);
14   }
15
16   CircleCanvas circle;
17   Scrollbar scrollR;
18   Scrollbar scrollG;
19   Scrollbar scrollB;
20
21   public AWTProg() {
22     setSize(500,350);
23     MenuBar menuBar = new MenuBar();
24     setMenuBar(menuBar);
25     Menu fileMenu = new Menu("File");
26     menuBar.add(fileMenu);
27     MenuItem exitItem = new MenuItem("Exit");
28     exitItem.addActionListener(this);
29     fileMenu.add(exitItem);
30     // exit when the frame is closed
31     addWindowListener(new WindowAdapter() {
32       public void windowClosing(WindowEvent ev){
33         System.exit(0);
34       }
35     });
36     setLayout(new BorderLayout());
37     // center
38     Panel panel = new Panel();
39     panel.setLayout(new BorderLayout());
40     add(panel, BorderLayout.CENTER);
41     circle = new CircleCanvas();
42     panel.add(circle, BorderLayout.CENTER);
43     TextArea textArea = new TextArea(3,10);
44     textArea.setText("TextArea");
45     panel.add(textArea, BorderLayout.SOUTH);
46     // north
47     Label label = new Label("Label");
48     add(label, BorderLayout.NORTH);
49     // south
```

```
 50        TextField textField = new TextField("TextField");
 51        add(textField, BorderLayout.SOUTH);
 52        // west
 53        panel = new Panel();
 54        panel.setLayout(new GridLayout(1,3));
 55        add(panel, BorderLayout.WEST);
 56        scrollR = new Scrollbar(Scrollbar.VERTICAL,0,1,0,255);
 57        scrollR.addAdjustmentListener(this);
 58        panel.add(scrollR);
 59        scrollG = new Scrollbar(Scrollbar.VERTICAL,0,1,0,255);
 60        scrollG.addAdjustmentListener(this);
 61        panel.add(scrollG);
 62        scrollB = new Scrollbar(Scrollbar.VERTICAL,0,1,0,255);
 63        scrollB.addAdjustmentListener(this);
 64        panel.add(scrollB);
 65        // east
 66        panel = new Panel();
 67        panel.setBackground(Color.lightGray);
 68        panel.setLayout(new GridLayout(4,1));
 69        add(panel, BorderLayout.EAST);
 70        Panel chPanel = new Panel();
 71        panel.add(chPanel);
 72        Choice choice = new Choice();
 73        choice.add("red");
 74        choice.add("green");
 75        choice.add("blue");
 76        chPanel.add(choice);
 77        Panel cbPanel = new Panel();
 78        cbPanel.setLayout(new GridLayout(3,1));
 79        panel.add(cbPanel);
 80        CheckboxGroup group = new CheckboxGroup();
 81        Checkbox cbR = new Checkbox("Red", group, true);
 82        cbPanel.add(cbR);
 83        Checkbox cbG = new Checkbox("Green", group, false);
 84        cbPanel.add(cbG);
 85        Checkbox cbB = new Checkbox("Blue", group, false);
 86        cbPanel.add(cbB);
 87        Panel btPanel = new Panel();
 88        panel.add(btPanel);
 89        Button button = new Button("Exit");
 90        button.addActionListener(this);
 91        btPanel.add(button);
 92        List list = new List(3);
 93        list.add("Red");
 94        list.add("Green");
 95        list.add("Blue");
 96        panel.add(list);
 97    }
 98
 99  public void actionPerformed(ActionEvent ev) {
100      String cmd = ev.getActionCommand();
101      if ("Exit".equals(cmd))
102        System.exit(0);
103    }
104
105  public void adjustmentValueChanged(AdjustmentEvent ev) {
106      int r = scrollR.getValue();
107      int g = scrollG.getValue();
108      int b = scrollB.getValue();
109      circle.setColor(new Color(r, g, b));
110    }
111 }
```

```
112
113 class CircleCanvas extends Canvas {
114   private Color color = Color.black;
115
116   public CircleCanvas() {
117     setBackground(new Color(220,220,220));
118   }
119
120   public void paint(Graphics g) {
121     super.paint(g);
122     g.setColor(color);
123     int w = getWidth();
124     int h = getHeight();
125     int d = (w > h)? h : w;
126     d -= 30;
127     g.fillOval((w-d)/2,(h-d)/2, d, d);
128   }
129
130   public void setColor(Color c) {
131     color = c;
132     repaint();
133   }
134 }
```

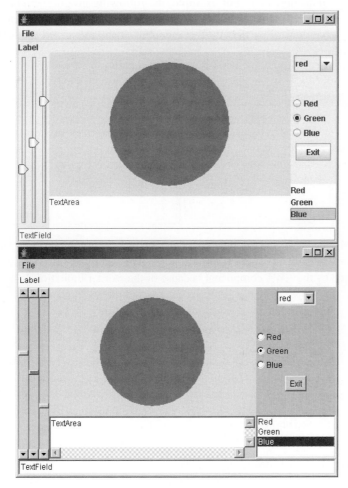

FIGURE B.4 A Swing program and its AWT clone.

The Swing version uses the components JFrame, JPanel, JButton, JLabel, JTextField, JTextArea, JList, JComboBox, JRadioButton, JSlider, JMenuBar, JMenu, and JMenuItem. They are replaced in the AWT version by the components: Frame, Panel (and Canvas), Button, Label, TextField, TextArea, List, Choice, Checkbox, Scrollbar, MenuBar, Menu, and MenuItem.

Changes are also necessary in using some of the components in AWT. Instead of using the content pane, the AWT program uses the Frame object as a container to directly add other components. The AWTProg class is an AdjustmentListener to handle the scrollbar events. The Swing version defines a ChangeListener for the same task with JSlider. The radio buttons in the two versions are also created differently.

B.4 Mixing AWT and Swing Components

It is possible to use a combination of AWT and Swing components in the same program. Mixing the two types of components will not cause any syntax errors, but it may lead to some undesirable visual effects in the resulting user interface.

z-order

The main problem with mixing components is related to the *z*-order of the components. The *z-order* determines which component will be shown on top when several components overlap. The heavyweight AWT components are opaque, and their *z*-orders are obtained from the host system. The Swing components can have transparent pixels, and their *z*-orders are implemented natively. When an AWT component and a Swing component overlap, the AWT component will block the Swing component, which may result in an incorrect visual arrangement. For example, the following program contains one AWT component, a TextArea object, in the right half of a JSplitPane. When the menu is selected, it may be blocked by the AWT component, if the menu and the text area overlap (Figure B.5).

FIGURE B.5 Mixing AWT and Swing components may cause problems. Left: The menu displays properly when it does not overlap with the AWT component. Right: The menu is partially blocked by the AWT component because of the *z*-order limitation.

Listing B.3 SwingAWT.java

```
1 package appendixB;
2
3 import javax.swing.*;
4 import java.awt.*;
5
6 public class SwingAWT extends JFrame {
7   public static void main(String[] args) {
8     JFrame frame = new SwingAWT();
9     frame.setSize(300, 200);
10    frame.setDefaultCloseOperation(JFrame.EXIT_ON_CLOSE);
```

```
11      frame.setVisible(true);
12   }
13
14   public SwingAWT() {
15      // set up menu
16      JMenuBar mb = new JMenuBar();
17      setJMenuBar(mb);
18      JMenu menu = new JMenu("File");
19      mb.add(menu);
20      menu.add(new JMenuItem("Open"));
21      menu.add(new JMenuItem("Save"));
22      menu.addSeparator();
23      menu.add(new JMenuItem("Exit"));
24      // add content
25      Container cp = this.getContentPane();
26      cp.setLayout(new BorderLayout());
27      JSplitPane sp = new JSplitPane(JSplitPane.HORIZONTAL_SPLIT);
28      JPanel panel = new JPanel();
29      sp.add(panel);
30      cp.add(sp);
31      sp.add(new TextArea("AWT TextArea",10,10));
32   }
33 }
```

If mixing the AWT and Swing components is necessary in a program, care should be taken to avoid the *z*-order problem. Besides the JMenuBar class, the Swing components JPopupMenu, JComboBox, JScrollPane, JInternalFrame often exhibit similar problems. For JPopupMenu and JComboBox objects, you have the option to turn off the lightweight popup by calling the method:

```
setLightWeightPopupEnabled(false)
```

INDEX